Automotive Undercar: Suspension, Steering, and Electronic Systems

West's Automotive Series
    — by Kalton C. Lahue

Automotive Undercar: Suspension, Steering, and Electronic Systems ©1996
    — combined classroom manual and shop manual

Automotive Chassis: Suspension, Steering, and Brakes ©1995
    — separate classroom manual and shop manual

Automotive Brakes and Antilock Braking Systems ©1995
    — combined classroom manual and shop manual

Automotive Undercar:
Suspension, Steering, and Electronic Systems

Kalton C. Lahue

WEST PUBLISHING COMPANY

Minneapolis/St. Paul • New York • Los Angeles • San Fransisco

NVIRONMENT

began recycling materials left over from the production
efficient and responsible use of resources. Today, up to
0 percent of our college and school texts are printed on
ly 22 million pounds of scrap paper annually — the
equivalent of some 182 thousand trees. Since the 1960's, West has devised ways to capture
and recycle wastes into inks, solvents, oils, and vapors created in the printing process. West
also recycles plastics of all kinds, wood, glass, corrugated cardboard, and batteries, and has
eliminated the use of Styrofoam book packaging. We at West are proud of the longevity and
the scope of our commitment to the environment.

 Printed on 10% Post-Consumer Recycled Paper

PRODUCTION CREDITS

Editing (Technical/Text/Graphics), Design, Layout, Appendixes, and Indexing	Electronic Publishing Division, PRAD, Inc.
Art Direction	Radhika Upadrashta, PRAD, Inc.
Front Cover Design	Stephen Slater, Slater Publishing
Accuracy Review	Miles Schofield, Consultant
Production, Prepress, Printing, and Binding	West Publishing Company

Printed in the United States of America
03 02 01 00 99 98 97 96   8 7 6 5 4 3 2 1 0

BRITISH LIBRARY CATALOGUING-IN-PUBLICATION DATA
A catalogue record for this book is available from the British Library.

LIBRARY OF CONGRESS CATALOGING-IN-PUBLICATION DATA
Lahue, Kalton C.
   Automotive undercar : suspension, steering, and electronic systems
/ Kalton C. Lahue
      p. cm. -- (West's automotive series)
   Includes index.
   ISBN 0-314-04550-3 (soft)
   1. Automobiles--Springs and suspension--Maintenance and repair. I. Title. II. Series
TL257.L34   1995   94-
43216
629.24'3'0288--dc20

To Kevin and Kory Lahue

Contents

SHOP MANUAL

CHAPTER EIGHT

ACKNOWLEDGMENTS

West Publishing Company acknowledges **Chrysler Corporation**, **Ford Motor Company**, and **General Motors Corporation**, and the **following organizations** for permissions to adapt/reproduce information/illustrations from their copyrighted materials.

American Honda Motor Company — Figures 11-34, 13-16 to 13-19 (Classroom); 4-21, 4-24, 6-36, 6-39, 6-43, 6-53, 6-54, 6-56, 7-39, 8-43 to 8-45 (Shop)

Bilstein Corporation of America — Figure 6-7 (Classroom)

Council of the Institution of Mechanical Engineers, England — Figures 11-35 and 11-36 (Classroom) (from IMechE Conference 1988-9, 'Advanced Suspensions', paper #C428/88)

Dana Corporation — Figures 2-9, 5-8, 6-17, 7-17 to 7-19, 9-11, and 9-24 (Classroom); 4-1, 4-2, 4-14, 6-27, 7-6, 7-7, and 7-10 (Shop)

Hennessy Industries, Inc. — Figures 2-10, 2-11, 5-2 and 5-3 (Classroom); 1-19 and 6-26 (Shop)

Institute of Electrical and Electronic Engineers, Inc. — Figure 11-2 (Classroom) (from IEEE publn #84CH1988-5, paper by Shinzo, pIII-37)

Mitsubishi Motor Sales America, Inc. — Figures 11-32 and 11-33 (Classroom)

Moog Automotive, Inc. — Figures 2-12, 2-14, 2-17, 3-1, 5-1, 5-7, 5-9, 5-10, 6-9, 6-13 to 6-15, 6-18, 6-19, 8-41, and 8-42 (Classroom); 4-15(A), 4-17, 4-18, 5-2, 5-3, 5-8 to 5-10, 5-12, 5-21, 6-37, 6-41, 6-44, 6-49, and 7-19 (Shop)

National Institute for Automotive Service Excellence — Information (from the Official ASE Prepn Guide to ASE Automobile Technician Tests) and ASE insignia in Appendix E (Classroom)

Nissan Motor Corporation USA — Figures 11-26 and 12-37 (Classroom)

Prentice-Hall, Inc., Upper Saddle River, NJ — Figure 11-49 (Classroom) (from Weathers/Hunter, Automotive Computers and Control Systems, ©1984, p90)

Robert Bosch Corporation — Figures 11-21 and S11-16 (Classroom)

Society of Automotive Engineers, Inc. — Figures 11-22, 11-23, and 11-25 (from paper #901123); 11-24 (from paper #910274); 11-34 (from paper #910014); and 11-45 and 11-46 (from paper #910273); information from TSB 003, J656, J670e, J1213, and J1930 (Classroom)

Toyota Motor Sales USA, Inc. — Figures 1-1, 1-7, 9-30, 11-28 to 11-30, and 13-4 (Classroom); 5-7, 5-18, 5-19, and 8-35 (Shop)

Preface

The area of suspension and steering systems service offers increasing opportunities for those interested in employment within the automotive field. If you have the desire and the ability to become a front-end technician, education and on-the-job training can help you acquire the necessary skills.

Of the many systems that make up a modern automobile, the suspension and steering system are at the top of the list in importance. An engine that will not start is frustrating; a heating system that delivers only cold air on a winter day is uncomfortable. Failures of this nature affect the driver's convenience and comfort, but can be easily corrected at the expense of time and money. A steering system failure, however, can result in possible damage to property, and serious injury or even possible death for the driver, passengers, and bystanders. Time and money cannot always correct the consequences of such a failure. Therefore, the quality of any service performed on an automobile must always be measured in terms of safety.

It takes more than the ability to remove and install parts to be a good front-end technician in today's world. True, a technician must possess certain hand skills, but more importantly, must know when and where to use them. You must be able to determine which part to replace or adjust. You must be able to locate the cause of the original failure to prevent it from occurring again. Adding power steering fluid to a system that is leaking will not solve the problem for long. You must have a working knowledge of other automotive systems and their interrelationship with each other. For example, the introduction of electronically controlled suspension and steering systems now requires that you have a basic knowledge of electrical and electronic systems.

This text in two manuals — Classroom and Shop — is job-oriented, and designed for those who want to work in the field of automotive suspension and steering. The Classroom Manual provides you with a solid foundation in the theory behind the front-end systems — both basic and computer-controlled. The Shop Manual helps you learn service the front-end systems on North American and import vehicles. The procedures covered are those specified by the carmakers and include the use of specific tools recommended to assure safety.

After thoroughly studying this text, you should have acquired enough knowledge, diagnostic skills, and repair skills which help you service the various automotive front-end systems to industry standards. Also, you should be ready for the Automotive Service Excellence (ASE) certification examination for suspension and steering technicians.

This Classroom Manual provides the theory as to how the suspension and steering systems work, and has the following features:

- Performance-based objectives open each chapter.
- Text is divided into sections within chapters, with three levels of heading; reviewing the headings allows for studying in outline form.
- Photographs and illustrations are provided by various manufacturers.
- Items of interest appear in each chapter under the title 'Spotlight'.
- 'Notes' are provided at intervals to call attention to particular points.
- Key terms are bold-faced and included in a glossary where appropriate.
- ASE-styled review questions test mastery at the end of each chapter.

The Shop Manual gives the actual procedures needed to install, repair or disassemble suspension and steering systems safely. It has several features in common with the Classroom Manual: •performance-based objectives; •text divided into sections; •photographs and illustrations; •key terms in a glossary; •ASE-styled review questions.

Additional features include:
- 'Tech Tips' that provide timely advice for ensuring smoother shop procedures
- 'Warnings' that call attention to important safety concerns.
- 'Cautions' that call attention to situations of vehicle damage.

In addition to the regular **glossary**, the classroom manual has several unique **appendixes** that should be of interest and reference value to a responsible technician:

- An explanation of the International System of Units (SI) and an elaborate table of conversion factors for units conversion from traditional to metric/SI -- especially important with the interchangeability of parts among US, Canada, Mexico, and Japan makes
- A listing of industrial standards developed by the Society of Automotive Engineers (SAE) and the American Society for Testing and Materials (ASTM) -- for various chassis components and related test procedures
- A synopsis of Federal Motor Vehicle Safety Standards (FMVSS) on steering, tires, and wheels, and also a note on the regulation by Occupational Safety and Health Administration (OSHA) concerning work place hazards
- J1930 -- SAE nomenclature on electrical/electronic systems in the automotive field (an attempt to provide one common set of lingo among several manufacturers); and J670e — SAE terminology on vehicle dynamics (helps understand mechanical terms)
- Information about the technician certification tests administered by the National Institute for Automotive Service Excellence (ASE)
- A listing of reference materials/sources -- which should be useful in identifying specific training videos as well as optical disks and print media that help the technician keep current in this rapidly changing automotive field.

Also an **instructor's manual** is available with answers to the ASE-styled review questions, and a set of transparency masters of selected text illustrations.

A NOTE OF APPRECIATION

The following individuals have contributed by either providing information or reviewing selected sections of the manuscript -- •John Holappa, •Don Mullin, and •Dan Sylvester (GM Training Center, Burbank, CA); •Ellen Smith (AC-Delco, Burbank, CA); •Jim Milum, •Ed Moreland, and •Robert Van Antwerp (Ford Motor Training Center, La Mirada, CA); •Armando Nogueiras and •Carlos Rodriguez (Firestone Auto, Downey, CA); •Dan Rupp and •Bill Takayama (Chrysler Training Center, Ontario, CA); •Miles Schofield (Tarzana, CA).

The following teachers have reviewed the manuscript and offered valuable suggestions -- •James Becker (Northwestern College, OH); •Ron Bell (Saddleback College, CA); •John Butcher (Advanced Technical Institute, VA); •Gary Dittmer (SUNY College of Technology, Farmingdale); •Roger Donavan (Illinois Central College); •Tim Huston (Southern Alberta Institute of Technology, Calgary, AB); •David Mayse (Kent State University, Trumbull, OH); •Donald Moody (Central Oregon Community College); •Michael Moore (Altamaha Technical Institute, GA); •Scott Scheife (Milwaukee Area Technical College, WI); •William Turner (Indiana State University); •Mitchell Walker (St. Louis Community College at Forest Park); •Marvin Williams (Oakland Technical Center Southeast Campus, MI).

Finally, the author places on record his deep sense of appreciation to Christopher Conty, Acquisitions Editor and John Lindley, Production Editor and Manager of College & General Publications at West, for their encouragement, suggestions, and help without which this automotive series could not have seen the light of day. The professionals with PRAD -- Pradyumna, Pradipta, and Kamesh Upadrashta, and others -- have well demonstrated their technical writing/editing and creative skills in turning a raw manuscript into an elegant text. Pradyumna has written a substantial portion of the chapter, 'Fundamentals of Electronic Control'. West, through over 100 years of publishing experience, has proved its expertise in producing a complex technical publication as this. The efforts of West's prepress, printing and binding departments, and of marketing department deserve special appreciation.

Symbols and Abbreviations

$\approx$	approximately equal to
'	feet; minute(s)
$>$	greater than
$\geq$	greater than or equal to
"	inch(es); second(s)
$<$	less than
$\leq$	less than or equal to
•	multiplied by
$\pm$	plus or minus
°C	degree(s) Celsius
ΔC	capacitance difference
°F	degree(s) Fahrenheit
4EAT	4-speed electronic automatic transaxle
4WAL	4-wheel antilock
4WD	4-wheel drive
µF	microfarad(s)
µm	micrometer(s)
Ω	ohm(s)
2WD	2-wheel drive
a	acceleration
A	ampere(s)
A/D	analog-to-digital
ABCM	antilock brake control module
ABS('s)	antilock brake system(s)
A/C	air conditioning
AC	alternating current
ACT	air charge temperature
ADS	adaptive damping system
AMC	American Motor Corporation
ANSI	American National Standards Institute
ARC	automatic ride control
ASARC	air suspension and automatic ride control
ASE	Automotive Service Excellence; *also* National Institute for Automotive Service Excellence
ASR	acceleration slip regulation
ASTM	American Society for Testing and Materials
ATC	automatic traction control

ATF	automatic transmission fluid
AWD	all wheel drive
BAC	bypass air control
BCM	body control module
BOF	body-over-frame
BP	barometric pressure
B+	battery (positive)
BPMV	brake pressure modulator valve
BTSI	brake/transmission shift inter lock
CAB	controller -- antilock brake
CAFE	corporate average fuel economy
CCDIC	climate control driver information center
CCM	central control module
CCR	computer command ride
CD-ROM	compact disk read-only memory
CES	clutch engages switch
CFI	central fuel injection
CHMSL	center high-mount stoplamp
CM	control module
CPA	connector position assurance
CPM, cpm	cycles per minute
CPS, cps	cycles per second
CPU	central processing unit
CRT	cathode ray tube
CSI	customer service index
CV joint	constant-velocity joint
DAT	digital audio tape
DC	direct current
DCV	direct current voltage
DIC	driver information center
DIP	dual inline package
DLC	data link connector; diagnostic link connector
DOT	Department of Transportation
DRA	digital ratio adapter
DRAB	digital ratio adapter buffer
DRAC	digital ratio adapter calibrator
DRB	diagnostic readout box
DRL	daytime running lights
DTC	diagnostic trouble code

DVOM	digital volt-ohm meter
E	elecromotive force (voltage)
EBCM	electronic brake control module
EBFD	electronic brake force distribution
ECA	electronic control assembly
ECM	engine control module
ECT	engine coolant temperature
ECU	electronic control unit
EEC	electronic engine control
EEPROM	electrically erasable programmable read only memory
EGR	exhaust gas recirculation
EHC	electronic height control
EHCU	electro-hydraulic control unit
E_k	kinetic energy
ELC	electronic level control
ELU	electrical load unit
EMB	electromagnetic brake
EMI	electromagnetic interference
EPA	Environmental Protection Agency
ESB	expansion spring brake
ESD	electrostatic discharge
EVO	electronic variable orifice
EVP	EGR valve position
fc	foot-candle(s)
F	farad(s); force; front
FET	field effect transistor
fF	femtofarad(s)
FLI	fluid level indicator
FMVSS	Federal Motor Vehicle Safety Standards
ft	foot, feet
FWD	front wheel drive
g	gravitational acceleration
g_c	gravitational constant
GM	General Motors
GND	Ground
h	hour(s)
HCU	hydraulic control unit
Hg	mercury
HPA	high pressure accumulator
Hz	hertz
I	current flow
IC	integrated circuit
IGFET	insulated gate field effect transistor
in	inch(es)
in. Hg	inches mercury
in^2	square inch(es)
IPC	instrument panel cluster

IRS	independent rear suspension
ISC	idle speed control
ISO	International Standards Organization
ISO valve	isolated solenoid operated valve
JFET	junction field effect transistor
KAM	keep-alive memory
KAMS	keep alive memory system
k	constant
k	kilo-
kg	kilogram(s)
km	kilometer(s)
km/h	kilometer(s) per hour
L	liter
lb	pound(s)mass
lb_f	pound(s)force
$lb_f \bullet ft$	pound(s)force-foot, unit for torque or energy
$lb_f \bullet in$	pound(s)force-inch, unit for torque or energy
LCD	liquid crystal display
LED	light emitting diode
LF	left front
LH	left hand
LHG	left hardshell grommet
LPA	low pressure accumulator
LPF	low-pass filter
LR	left rear
LS	left side
LVDT	linear variable differential transducer
LVIT	linear variable inductance transducer
LWG	left wheelwell grommet
m	mass
m	meter(s)
MAP	manifold pressure sensor
MIG (welder)	metal inert gas (welder)
mm	millimeter(s)
MOSFET	metal oxide semiconductor field effect transistor
mph	miles per hour
MPV	multipurpose passenger vehicle
MSC	mass storage cartridge
mV	millivolt(s)
NAND	combined NOT and AND gates
NC (solenoid)	normally closed (solenoid)
NGS	new generation STAR
NHSA	National Highway Safety Administration
N•m	Newton-meter
NO (solenoid)	normally open (solenoid)
NOR	combined NOT and OR gates

NPN	negative-positive-negative; not pointing in	RS	right side
NTC	negative temperature coefficient	RWAL	rear wheel antilock
NVH	noise, vibration, and harshness	RWD	rear wheel drive
OD	outside diameter	RWG	right wheelwell grommet
ODC	open dump circuit	s	second(s)
OEM	original equipment manufacturer(s)	SAE	Society of Automotive Engineers
OSHA	Occupational Safety and Health Administration	SAI	steering axis inclination
OVP	over voltage protection	SDC	shock damping control
oz	ounce(s)	SDL	serial data link
PCM	power-train control module	SIR	supplemental inflatable restraint
PCS	pressure control switch	SLA	short-long arm (suspension)
pF	picofarad(s)	SSN	suspension/steering module
PIP	profile ignition pickup	STAR	self-test automatic readout
PMV	power/motor/valve; pressure modulator valve	TCC	transmission/transaxle converter clutch
PNP	positive-negative-positive; pointing in permanently	TCCM	transfer case control module
PPS	progressive power steering	TCS	traction control system
PRC	programmed ride control	TDC	top dead center
PROM	programmable read-only memory	TEMS	Toyota electronically modulated suspension
psi	pounds force per square inch	TP	throttle position
PWM	pulse-width modulated	TPC	tire performance criteria
QDM	quad driver module	TPS	throttle position sensor
R	resistance	T/R	transmitter/receiver
R1, ... , R4	resistances in Wheatstone bridge	TSB	technical service bulletin
RABS	rear antilock brake system	TV	throttle valve
RAM	random access memory	v	velocity
RBG	rear battery grommet	V	volt(s)
RBWL	red brake warning lamp	VAPS	variable-assist power steering
RF	right front	VCM	vehicle control module
RFI	radio frequency interference	VES	variable effort steering
RH	right hand	VOM	volt-ohm meter
RHG	right hardshell grommet	V_{ref}	reference voltage
ROM	read-only memory	VSS	vehicle speed sensor
RPM, rpm	revolutions per minute	WSS	wheel speed sensor
rps	revolutions per second	x	observed displacement
RR	right rear	XOR	exclusive OR gate
		ZPRWL	zero pressure rear wheel antilock

AUTOMOTIVE UNDERCAR: SUSPENSION, STEERING & ELECTRONIC SYSTEMS

CLASSROOM MANUAL

AUTOMOTIVE CHASSIS

"The world is a book and those who do not travel read only one page." — St. Augustine

---

 OBJECTIVES

After completion of this chapter, you should be able to:

- Describe the major difference between body-over-frame (BOF) and unitized body designs.

- Distinguish between a ladder and a perimeter frame design.

- Explain the relationship of a space frame to a unitized body design.

In the early days of the motor car, the **chassis** was little more than two parallel **open-channel rails** that ran the length of the vehicle. The suspension, powertrain, and body were bolted to the rails, or to the crossmembers installed between them. This design provided the strength necessary to carry both the mass of the mechanical components and of the passengers. Because it was simple and inexpensive to manufacture, the parallel open-channel rail design was used for many years.

During the '20s and '30s, styling and speed became major sales factors. In the '30s even low priced cars grew in size, year after year. The more expensive cars had bodies that were long and impressive. Engines were made much larger to produce more power. To support the increased mass, the size and mass of the vehicle **frame** increased until it became quite heavy. As the vehicle size continued to increase, even heavier frames were needed for proper support, leading to even larger engines to pull them around. Unfortunately, this trend continued until the open-channel section rails lost their torsional stiffness, resulting in a frame that tended to flex in use.

The introduction of **box-type frame construction** minimized the problem of flexing. A box frame was made by closing in the open-frame rails on each side of the car so that they were more like a tube. The box frame increased frame strength by about 500 times over that of open channel frames. After World War II, lighter and more durable alloys were introduced for frame members, but perhaps most important, the unitized body construction has virtually replaced the body-over-frame (BOF) design. Whether BOF or unit body construction, the modern chassis is stronger and safer than its predecessors, and can absorb torsional (twisting) stress in a controlled manner.

In this chapter, you will learn about the different types of automotive frames, and how the modern automotive chassis is constructed.

FRAME DESIGN AND CONSTRUCTION

Automobiles are constructed using either a **body-over-frame (BOF)** or **unitized body** design. BOF designs use an independent frame. The powertrain and other major components are mounted on the frame,

with the body installed over them and bolted to the frame (Figure 1-1). Although there are many variations, independent frames fall into one of two general categories — ladder or perimeter-type.

LADDER FRAMES

Ladder-type frames date from the early days of the automobile. They are still used today, mainly for truck and other commercial vehicle chassis. This type of frame takes its name from its resemblance to a ladder, and consists of two parallel rails connected by crossmembers (Figure 1-2). Because the frame rails could not intrude into the passenger compartment, early vehicles with a ladder-type frame required a high roof line to accommodate the occupants. With the early attempts at aerodynamic

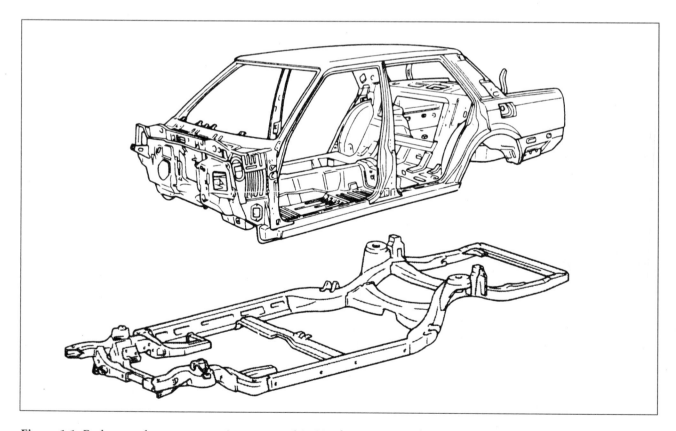

Figure 1-1 Body-over-frame construction was used in North American vehicles until the mid-1970s. Once the powertrain and suspension were installed on the perimeter frame, the body was lowered over the frame and bolted in place. (Toyota)

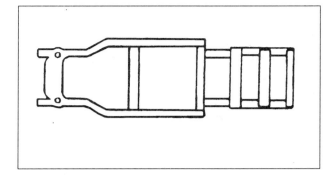

Figure 1-2 The ladder-type frame takes its name from the use of two side rails and crossmembers, and is still used today for pickups.

styling in the Thirties, some carmakers redesigned the automotive frame to:

- drop closer to the ground under the passenger compartment
- pinch in at the front to clear the front wheels
- raise up in the rear to pass over the rear axle.

PERIMETER FRAMES

This redesign of the ladder frame led to development of the perimeter frame, in which the front frame rails are curved inward to accept the engine mounts, hold the front suspension, and allow the front wheels to move as required (Figure 1-3). Several variations of the perimeter frame

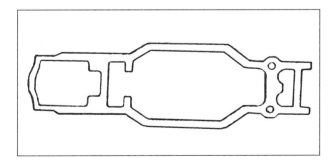

Figure 1-3 The perimeter frame was developed from the ladder frame, and enjoyed great popularity until FWD and the unitized body became a near-industry standard in the '80s.

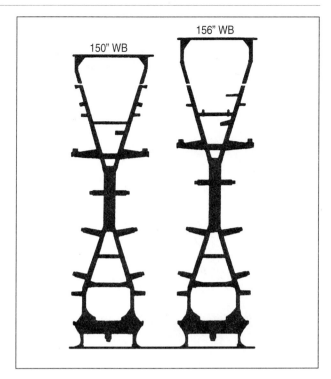

Figure 1-4 Cadillac's 'cruciform' frame design provided strength and could be used for different wheelbases simply by lengthening or shortening the center section.

have been used. In 1957, Cadillac introduced its 'cruciform' frame which was simply an X with a center section that could be lengthened as needed by wheelbase requirements (Figure 1-4). Since this design had NO side rails, the rear floor area could be lowered below the frame rails by the use of floorwells on either side of the cross point of the X.

Chevrolet engineers modified this design into the 'wasp-waist' frame used on 1958 Chevrolets (Figure 1-5). Both designs were extremely rigid, but did not afford much protection in case of a side impact. The most common modification of the perimeter frame was introduced by GM in 1964 and provides a perimeter of steel around the passenger area of the body, with torque boxes at all four corners and attached subframes at each end (Figure 1-6).

All North American carmakers used

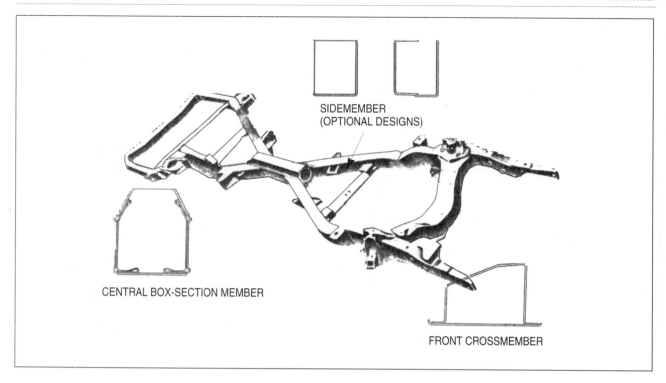

SIDEMEMBER
(OPTIONAL DESIGNS)

CENTRAL BOX-SECTION MEMBER

FRONT CROSSMEMBER

Figure 1-5 The 'wasp-waist' or X-type Chevrolet frame is extremely rigid, but does not provide much protection in a side collision. (General Motors)

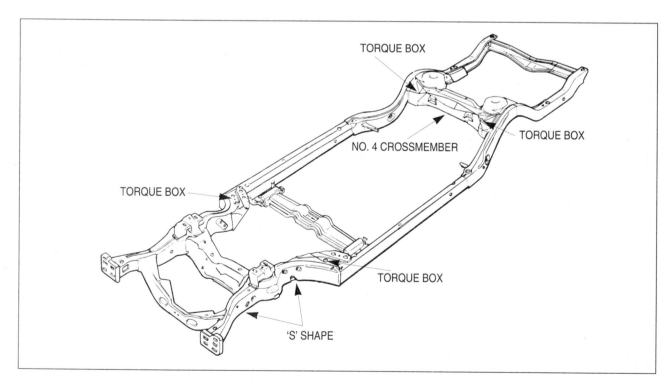

TORQUE BOX

TORQUE BOX

NO. 4 CROSSMEMBER

TORQUE BOX

TORQUE BOX

'S' SHAPE

Figure 1-6 The separate subframe and torque box concept was rigid, strong, and provided a perimeter of steel around the passenger area of the body. (Ford Motor)

some variation of this frame design until the mid-1970s. In general, cars were built on a perimeter frame, manufactured of 18 gauge mild steel, and the entire car weighed an average of 4,500 lb. Toward the end of the decade, oil shortages, combined with government legislation concerning fuel economy and emission controls, led to vehicle downsizing and acceptance of the unitized body design favored by European carmakers.

UNITIZED BODIES

Unit body designs use an integral body and frame (Figure 1-7). Some of the virtues of this type of construction are:

- reduced vehicle weight from use of thinner gauge metal
- fewer rattles and squeaks
- faster and easier manufacturing by automated machinery.

Unit body designs are most practical for vehicles with a wheelbase of approximately 115 inches or less. They must be built to close tolerances, and require correct steering and suspension alignment for proper body alignment. Although there are numerous variations in unit body construc-

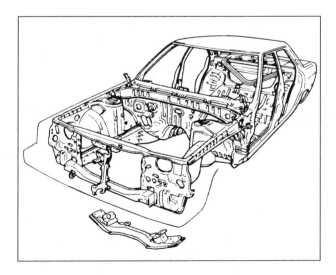

Figure 1-7 A typical example of a unit body design. (Toyota)

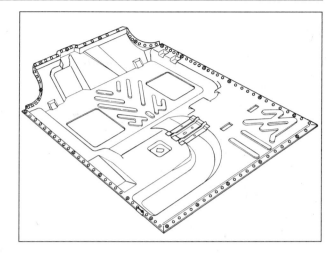

Figure 1-8 Unit body construction uses a stamped floorpan to add to the overall body/frame strength. (General Motors)

tion, the most common method is to form the body by welding a series of stamped metal panels to a platform-type floorpan of stamped metal.

This floorpan contains a series of ribs that run from the rear of the vehicle to the firewall (Figure 1-8). These ribs increase total structural rigidity, breaking up any resonant frequencies that would amplify vibrations. The instrument panel and firewall section includes parts of the front wheel wells to provide torsional stiffness to the platform. As other panels are welded to the assembly, local weaknesses are eliminated and the overall rigidity is increased.

In the most recent unitized designs, the engine, transaxle, front suspension control arms, and rack-and-pinion steering are supported by a cradle, or subframe, consisting of side rails and a front crossmember (Figure 1-9). This cradle bolts to the body and platform at the firewall with rubber insulators at fixed points. In a sense, modern unit bodies combine the older perimeter frame design with unitized construction. The insulators are designed to provide the proper amount of structural strength with maximum road noise

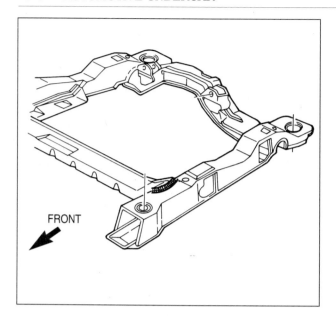

Figure 1-9 A subframe or cradle supports the power-train of most FWD unitized bodies. (General Motors)

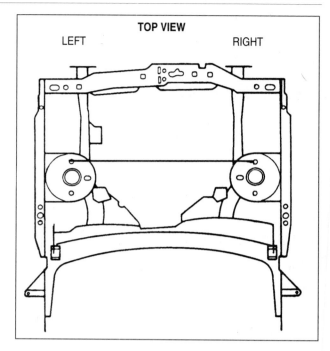

Figure 1-10 To maintain correct suspension geometry, the strut towers of a unitized body must be dimensionally correct, relative to the vehicle underbody. (General Motors)

isolation. Suspension system mounting also is shared by the strut towers at the front of the body and platform assembly. The rear suspension often is installed on a similar cradle attached to a crossbar at the rear of the body and platform assembly. Strut towers at the front and rear of the body and platform assembly perform the same function in suspension mounting. Strut towers can be seen on each side of the engine compartment in many vehicles. They provide the upper mounting points for the struts that are part of the suspension. (Figure 1-10).

Since the platform itself is fabricated from relatively lightweight materials (22 to 24 gauge high-strength steel), it is prone to twisting. The use of front and rear cradles helps to control this problem, but the strength required of the completed unit body comes from welding the various sections to the platform. Think of a unit body design as a bridge — the cradles and floorpan act as the basic structure, with the body panels welded together to form a superstructure. Each panel does a specific

job while working with adjacent panels to create a rigid, twist-free structure.

A unitized body has several inherent disadvantages over a BOF design, including:

- Styling changes — any changes in overall dimensions require major changes to the basic structure.
- Model interchangeability — separate tooling is required to produce both two- and four-door versions of the same model. With BOF designs, the center section of the separate frame can be lengthened or shortened as required.
- Corrosion protection — satisfactory underbody corrosion protection for the thin sheet metal requires additional dipping of the panels and body in protective chemicals, or the use of two-sided galvanized steel in certain applications.

- Sound deadening — the lightweight materials used in unit body construction require the use of increased sound deadening materials to isolate the vehicle from road noises. Early unit body designs required as much as 350 lb of insulating materials per vehicle.

The first two disadvantages remain essentially valid today, despite much progress in design from the early unit bodies. Advances in metallurgy and sound deadening materials have led to considerable progress in neutralizing the last two disadvantages.

Space Frames

A space frame is a specific type of unit body design that first appeared on European race cars. It consisted of many small diameter tubes welded together so that it looked very much like a birdcage. Individually, each tube was weak, but when they were all welded together with only a few inches separating the tubes, the strength was impressive. An adaptation of the space frame appeared in the 1984 Corvette and Pontiac Fiero. The two designs are hardly recognizable as space frames or birdcages, but that is where the ideas came from. The Corvette application of this concept used an integral perimeter frame-birdcage unitized structure (Figure 1-11). GM has since refined and extended use of the space frame to the multipurpose passenger vehicle (MPV) van (Figure 1-12) and Saturn vehicles, as well as the 1993 Camaro and Firebird. In the MPV cage-type design, the roof and

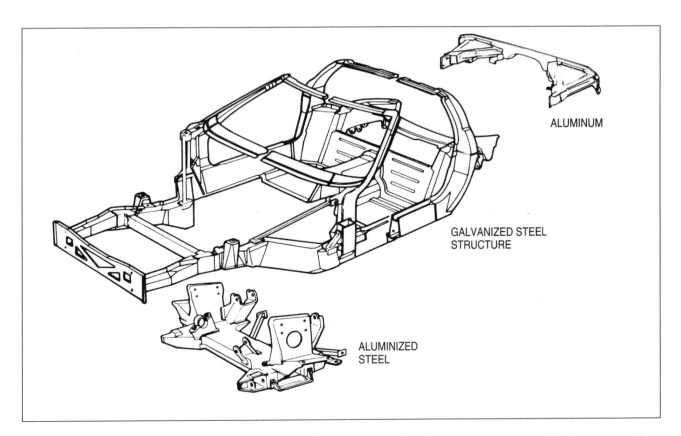

Figure 1-11 The 1984 Corvette frame-birdcage was the forerunner of today's space frame unit body construction. Except for the rear quarter and roof component, which is bonded to the unitized structure, all other exterior panels were bolted in place. (Chevrolet Division, General Motors)

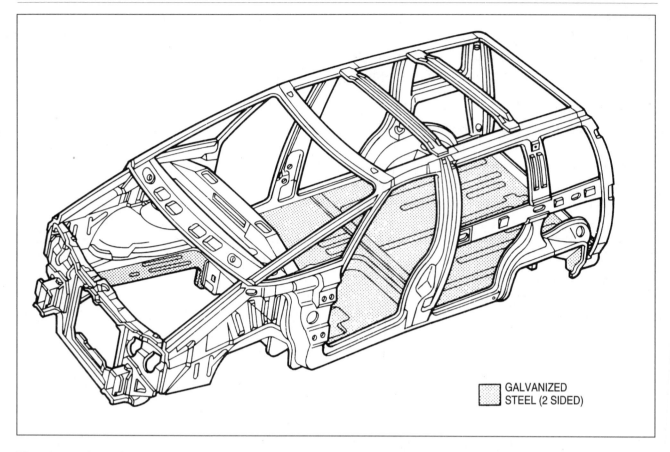

Figure 1-12 Space frame designs differ with vehicle application. The original birdcage concept of the Corvette evolved into this space frame used with the GM U-body van. (Oldsmobile Division, General Motors)

quarter panels are not welded to the structure, as is the case with conventional unit bodies. Instead, composite plastic body panels are bonded to the space frame with a special adhesive. This adhesive acts both as a seal against moisture and contributes to the overall structural integrity. **Mill-and-drill pads** (Figure 1-13) on the space frame are used to control exterior body dimensions and hold the panels in place until the adhesive has cured completely (Figure 1-14). One major advantage of the space frame design is its ability to meet crash standards without the exterior body panels attached. This means that the body panels do not have to contribute to the strength, and therefore may be made from plastic or fiberglass.

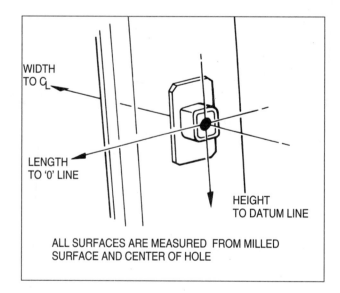

Figure 1-13 Mill-and-drill pads welded to the space frame at strategic points mechanically fasten the body panels in place. (Oldsmobile Division, General Motors)

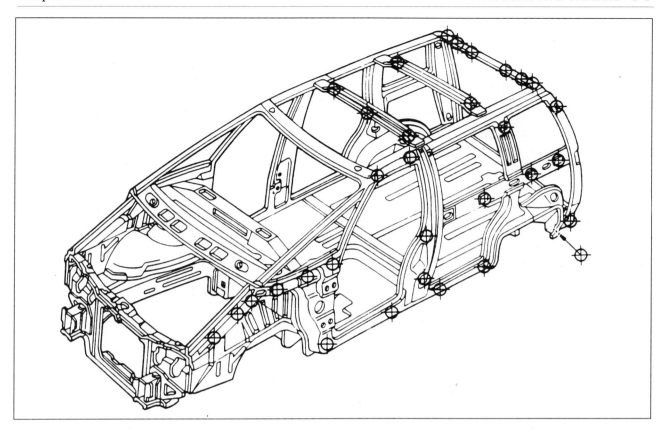

Figure 1-14 Typical location of mill-and-drill pads on one side of a U-body van. In cases of collision repair, the pads can be removed and new ones installed to maintain proper panel alignment. (Oldsmobile Division, General Motors)

VIBRATION DIAGNOSIS AND CORRECTION

Often called noise, vibration, and harshness (NVH) by engineers, the subject of vibration correction has become a large part of the Customer Service Index (CSI) programs of all carmakers during the past decade. The forces that control vehicle design and engineering have changed drastically, especially those mandated by legislation. These forces include:

- increased costs of fuel
- Corporate Average Fuel Economy (CAFE) requirements
- clean air legislation
- competition from imported vehicles
- safety and crashworthiness.

The heavier and smoother running V8 engines have been replaced by smaller and lighter four-cylinder and V6 engines, while options that increase engine load, such as power steering and air conditioning, have become increasingly popular. Smaller engines and more options combine to generate undesired noise and vibration. The change in vehicle design from a full-frame chassis with multiple isolating body mounts, to the lightweight unit body construction used for most current passenger cars, has made it much more difficult to keep noise, vibration, and harshness out of the passenger compartment. In addition, expansion of the light-duty truck and sport utility market during the past decade has changed the customer's perception of these vehicles. Because they are more likely to be used for going shopping than for an off-road experience, buyers expect the same ride qualities as passenger cars.

Of course, the brake and front end technician cannot be expected to solve all NVH problems; many result from engine operation, drive line boom, exhaust moan, and other areas outside that specialty. Since unwanted noise and vibrations detract from the customer's perception of quality, it is important to be able to quickly diagnose and correct NVH problems resulting from tire or wheel shake, incorrect wheel alignment, or suspension and steering systems. For this reason, the basics of NVH diagnosis are provided in this section to introduce you to the subject as it affects your automotive specialty.

VIBRATIONS

All vehicles have vibrations of some sort when the engine is running; when the vehicle is moving, other noises and vibrations are produced. Some noise and vibration is normal; some is not. Some noise and vibration problems can be corrected; others cannot. To solve an NVH problem, you must be able to recreate it during a road test.

Vibrations result from the repetitive motion, either up-and-down or back-and-forth. Automotive vibrations are caused by rotating components and/or firing impulses of the engine. Rotating components, such as wheels and tires, will vibrate as a result of excessive imbalance or runout. When diagnosing this type of vibration complaint, you should consider the allowable imbalance or runout as a 'tolerance', and NOT as a 'specification'. The less imbalance or runout of a wheel or tire, the better.

Vibrations have a tendency to be transmitted through the vehicle's body structure and consist of three elements (Figure 1-15):

- the source or cause
- the transfer path through the vehicle
- the responder or component through which the vibration is felt.

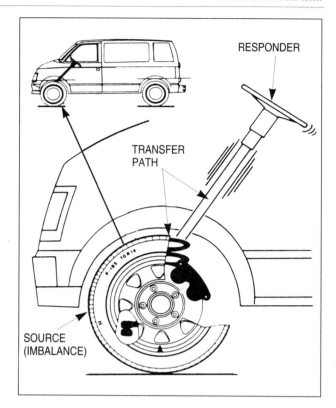

Figure 1-15 The three elements involved in transmission of a vibration. (General Motors)

Although vibrations may originate in different parts of the vehicle, the driver generally will feel them as repetitive motions from the floor, seat, or steering wheel. An NVH condition can be corrected by eliminating any one of the three elements above, although in the case shown in Figure 1-15, balancing the tire (the source) is a better solution than bracing the steering wheel (the responder).

Diagnosis

Diagnosis of vibration complaints involves:

- the physical properties of objects
- the conducting properties of mechanical energy.

We can demonstrate these properties by clamping a yardstick to the edge of a table with about 20 inches hanging off the edge (Figure 1-16), then pulling down and

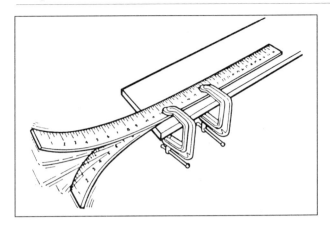

Figure 1-16 Example of a vibration. (General Motors)

releasing the edge of the stick while watching the results.

The motion of the stick that results occurs in repetitive **cycles** (Figure 1-17). The cycle starts at midpoint, continues to the lowest extreme of travel, back through the midpoint to the upper extreme of travel, and back to the midpoint where the cycle starts over again. These cycles repeat themselves at the same rate, or **frequency**. In our example, the frequency is about 6 complete cycles in one second of time, or 6 cps (Figure 1-18). By multiplying the cycle

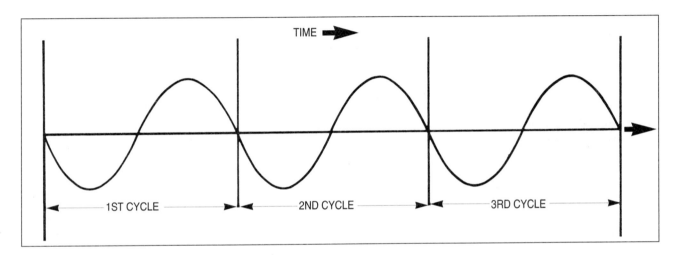

Figure 1-17 Vibration cycles. (General Motors)

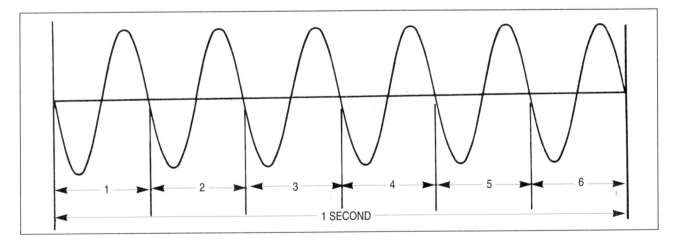

Figure 1-18 A visual representation of frequency. The frequency shown equals six cycles per second (cps). (General Motors)

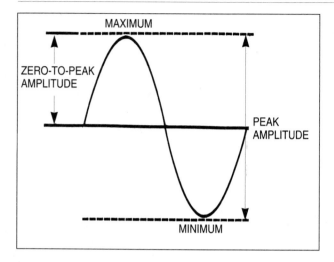

Figure 1-19 A visual representation of amplitude. (General Motors)

rate per second by the number of seconds in a minute, we can determine the number of cycles per minute (cpm). In this case, 60x6 equals a frequency of 360 cpm. The specific amount of motion, from the top to the bottom of the yardstick, is called the **amplitude** of the cycle (Figure 1-19). This motion, such as the oscillation of an automotive spring, can be brought under control by a damper, such as a shock absorber. Figure 1-20 shows the effects of high and low damping.

The first step in diagnosing a vibration

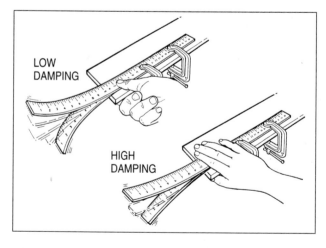

Figure 1-20 The effect of damping. (General Motors)

complaint is to identify the vibration, and drive the vehicle at any legal and safe speed where it occurs. If convenient, the vehicle should be road tested with the customer or even with the customer driving, to make certain that you understand exactly what the customer is complaining about. At this time, you should learn as much as possible about the problem by asking questions like:

- When was the vibration first noticed?
- Is it worse at one particular speed or speed range?
- Does engine or vehicle load affect the vibration?
- Does engine rpm or vehicle speed have any effect on the vibration?
- Does it occur in a particular gear range?

The answers to such questions can be helpful in identifying the cause of the noise or vibration. This is especially true if the problem only occurs under certain circumstances, such as when pulling a fully-loaded trailer, or if the vehicle suffered collision damage and the NVH was not noticed until after the repairs were made.

Some complaints may involve NVH problems that are inherent in current vehicle design, and must be explained to the customer as normal. One such example is the torque steer in an FWD vehicle. When attempts are made to correct conditions that are normal or inherent in design, the customer becomes convinced that the complaint is valid; why else would you attempt to solve the problem? At this point, it becomes very difficult to satisfy the customer with the explanation that the problem is a normal one which he or she must live with. Once you have made the diagnosis, it is best to explain the situation to the customer and if possible, demonstrate the same problem in another vehicle that is equipped in the same way.

After you have gained as much information as possible from the customer, the most important factor to determine during your road test is whether the NVH is related to vehicle speed or engine speed. Install an engine tachometer or scan tool before the road test (Figure 1-21), then record the engine rpm and vehicle mph (km/h) when the NVH condition is duplicated. A lot of vibration is caused by out of balance wheel/tire assemblies or by unevenly worn tires. But if you determine from the road test that the NVH condition is related only to engine speed, it can be caused by something in the engine, transmission, clutch, or driveline and may have nothing to do with the balance of the wheels and tires.

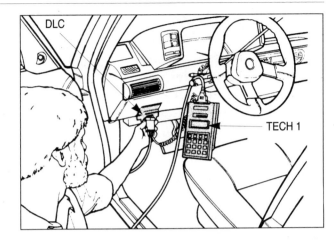

Figure 1-21 Use a tachometer or scan tool to determine engine rpm. (General Motors)

SUMMARY

Two types of automotive chassis designs are in use: body-over-frame (BOF) for most RWD vehicles, and unitized body construction for most FWD vehicles. In the BOF design, the body is bolted through insulators to a separate ladder or perimeter frame.

Unitized body construction incorporates a body platform with other body panels welded or otherwise attached to form a single body and frame assembly. The space frame is a specialized unit body design in which composite body panels are not welded to the cage-type structure, but are bonded with adhesive. One major advantage of the space frame design is that it can meet crash standards without the exterior body panels attached.

Vibration correction is an important concern to carmakers. Such problems result from the use of smaller unitized body vehicles with smaller engines and more accessories.

SPOTLIGHT

SPRUNG vs. UNSPRUNG MASS

A common misconception among many beginning students of automotive suspensions is that the spring's only purpose is to hold the chassis and body of a vehicle up. Actually, the springs push the wheels down because of body and chassis mass. If the wheels and tires were free to move without the push of the springs, they would leave the road surface whenever they passed over a bump in the road, returning only to bounce into the air again. The greater the restraint placed on the wheel/tire assembly, the better it will follow the road surface, bumps and all, without spending much time in the air. Ideally, the tire will not leave the road surface at all.

Suspension designers divide the total mass of a vehicle into sprung and unsprung.   Sprung mass is defined as all the mass carried by the springs (chassis, body, passengers, engine, transmission, etc.).   The mass not carried by the springs is called the unsprung mass and consists of the axles, steering linkage, wheel spindles, wheels, tires and even part of the spring itself. Put another way, all components that move with the movement of the wheels are unsprung. In general, the greater the amount of sprung mass relative to unsprung mass, the better the vehicle will ride and the better the springs will work.

Although adding sprung mass to a vehicle will make it ride better, this is NOT a good thing to do because it hurts gas mileage. Modern cars are made as small and lightweight as possible within each size class for best gas mileage. To improve the ride the designers have to work on reducing the sprung mass. Whenever possible, as many of the suspension and steering components as possible are mounted on the chassis, leaving less mass to bounce up and down with tire movement. With less unsprung mass to control, the tires grip the road better, which translates into better vehicle handling and control.

❓ REVIEW QUESTIONS

1. A BOF automotive chassis consists of the vehicle frame and:
   (A) a front suspension system
   (B) a rear suspension system
   (C) a steering system
   (D) all of the above

2. Most current passenger cars use a _____ type construction.
   (A) body-over-frame
   (B) space frame
   (C) unitized body
   (D) none of the above

3. Technician A says that unit body vehicles use an integral body and frame. Technician B says that unit body designs are most practical with a wheelbase under 100 inches. Who is right?
   (A) A only
   (B) B only
   (C) Both A and B

   (D) Neither A nor B

4. Technician A says that a unit body consists of a series of metal panels welded to a platform-type floorpan of stamped metal. Technician B says that ribs are used in the floorpan to increase structural rigidity. Who is right?
   (A) A only
   (B) B only
   (C) Both A and B
   (D) Neither A nor B

5. Technician A says that the running gear on current unit body designs is attached to a cradle bolted to the unit body and platform. Technician B says that the rear suspension of many unit body vehicles is attached to the body/ platform by a cradle. Who is right?
   (A) A only
   (B) B only
   (C) Both A and B
   (D) Neither A nor B

6. Technician A says that styling changes in a unit body design do NOT require major changes to the basic structure. Technician B says that separate tooling is needed to produce different unit body versions of the same model. Who is right?
   (A) A only
   (B) B only
   (C) Both A and B
   (D) Neither A nor B

7. Technician A says that noise, vibration, and harshness (NVH) problems have increased with the changeover to unit body construction. Technician B says NVH problems have decreased with the move to unit body construction. Who is right?
   (A) A only
   (B) B only
   (C) Both A and B
   (D) Neither A nor B

8. Technician A says that automotive vibrations are created by rotating com-
ponents or engine firing impulses. Technician B says that excessive imbalance or runout will cause wheel and tire vibration. Who is right?
   (A) A only
   (B) B only
   (C) Both A and B
   (D) Neither A nor B

9. Which of the following is NOT an element of a vibration?
   (A) source
   (B) transfer path
   (C) responder
   (D) pulsation

10. Technician A says that a road test should be used to determine whether an NVH problem is related to vehicle speed or engine speed. Technician B says that some NVH problems are normal and cannot be corrected. Who is right?
    (A) A only
    (B) B only
    (C) Both A and B
    (D) Neither A nor B

FRONT SUSPENSION SYSTEMS

"His motor car was poetry, tragedy, love,
and heroism." — Sinclair Lewis

 OBJECTIVES

After completion of this chapter, you should be able to:

- List the four functions of a front suspension system.

- Identify the components of a solid axle front suspension and briefly describe how they work together.

- List and briefly describe the four types of independent front suspensions.

The automotive front suspension is designed to perform a series of very complicated functions, including:

- connecting the wheels and tires to the frame, yet allowing them to pivot for steering control
- supporting the vehicle mass while keeping the wheels and axles aligned with the vehicle frame
- allowing the tires and wheels to move in a vertical direction relative to the frame
- absorbing road shock that otherwise would be transmitted to the steering system and passengers.

In order to perform these functions, the front suspension incorporates a method of attaching the wheel on an **axle** or **wheel spindle**, some method of absorbing road shock, and a way of mounting the suspension assembly to allow for adjustments in each of the planes in which the wheel must operate. Since front-end geometry involves the angular relationship between the front wheels, the suspension components, and the road surface, it is affected by operational factors such as vehicle load, speed, centrifugal force on curves, starting and stopping forces, as well as the alignment and condition of the suspension components.

FRONT SUSPENSION DESIGN

The suspension designs currently in use are classified either as nonindependent (rigid axle) suspensions, or independent suspensions. A vehicle may be equipped with a front suspension of one type and a rear suspension of the other, or front and rear suspensions of the same type. We will look at the several types of suspensions within each classification.

NON-INDEPENDENT FRONT SUSPENSIONS

A non-independent front suspension consists of a solid axle to which both wheels are attached. The solid axle also is called a rigid axle, or a beam axle. Historically, solid axle suspensions were developed in the early days of the automobile and were used on the front and rear of most passenger cars and trucks. Use of the solid axle on the front suspension of passenger cars gradually was abandoned in favor of an independent front suspension, but it continues to be used for the rear suspension on most rear wheel drive (RWD) vehicles.

A solid axle suspension consists of the axle with spindle assemblies attached on each end by **kingpins** or **ball joints** that allow the wheels to pivot. Either coil or leaf

springs may be used with solid axles. When a leaf spring is used, it is secured to each end of the axle by U-bolts (Figure 2-1). The leaf spring connects to the frame by a support bracket or hanger at one end of the springs, and by a spring **shackle** at the other end. The shackle acts as a hinge and a movable attaching point, allowing the spring to change its length as it absorbs road shock. Solid axle front suspensions on 4-wheel drive (4WD) vehicles may use **coil springs** to support the vehicle mass, radius arms to prevent fore and aft axle movement, and hydraulic shock absorbers to control coil spring oscillation (Figure 2-2). The large front drive axle housing acts the same as a beam axle, with swivel joints at each end to allow the wheels to be steered. Solid beam axle front suspensions (without front wheel drive) have certain inherent advantages. They are simple in design, relatively inexpensive to manufacture, and generally trouble-free in use. Because solid axles are strong and durable, they tend to

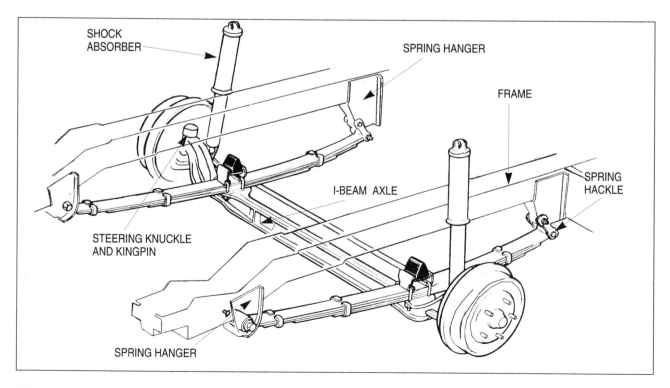

Figure 2-1 A typical solid axle leaf spring suspension. (Chevrolet Division, General Motors)

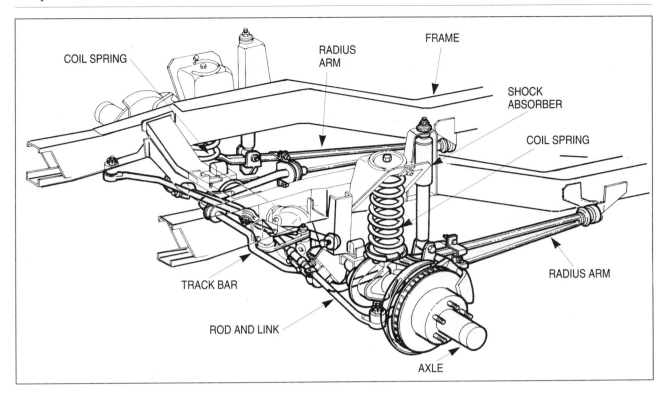

Figure 2-2 The mono-beam front suspension supplies the advantages of a coil-spring ride to the front axle of a 4WD vehicle. (Ford Motor)

resist both vertical and twisting forces, minimizing tire wear. At the same time, their inherent disadvantages tend to outweigh these advantages. Beam axles and front drive rigid axle housings are heavy. They increase the vehicle's **unsprung mass**, and require greater spring and shock absorber control to maintain tire contact with the road surface. When one tire on a solid axle goes over a bump on the road, the tire on the other side changes position, and may lose traction with the road, affecting handling. Solid axles have a harsher ride than that provided by an independent suspension. Any wear in the suspension or steering linkage also tends to affect directional control and vehicle stability.

INDEPENDENT FRONT SUSPENSIONS

Each of the wheels in an independent front suspension is mounted on a separate wheel spindle and **control arm** (Figure 2-3). This allows each wheel to move up or down independently of the other according to road conditions. Since an independent front suspension reduces unsprung vehicle weight, it offers the advantage of providing more control over wheel and tire movement. This results in a softer ride for vehicle occupants. The major disadvantage of an independent front suspension is its greater complexity in design. The wear created by the larger number of components, joints, and bushings required by this type of suspension can cause tire misalignment. And it is easily misaligned by striking curbs with the front wheels. There are four major types of independent front suspensions in use — short-long arm suspension, MacPherson strut suspension, swing axle suspension, and torsion bar suspension.

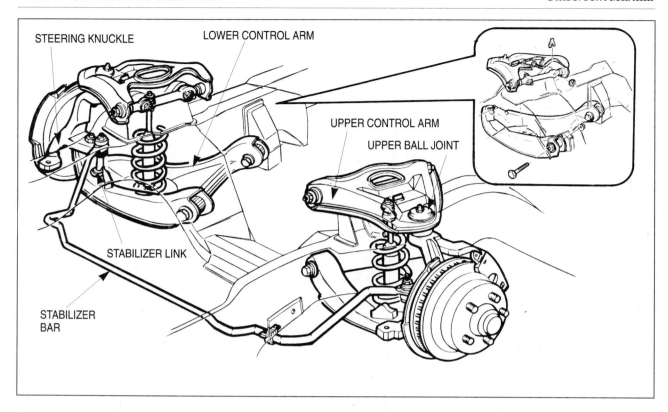

STEERING KNUCKLE

LOWER CONTROL ARM

UPPER CONTROL ARM

UPPER BALL JOINT

STABILIZER LINK

STABILIZER BAR

Figure 2-3 The components of the SLA independent suspension used for many years on North American RWD vehicles. (Chevrolet Division, General Motors)

Short-Long Arm (SLA) Suspension

Found on most North American RWD passenger cars, this design uses two triangular-shaped control arms (upper and lower) of unequal length. The triangle is one of the strongest structural shapes, because its outer pivot point (the ball joint) cannot move sideways once the legs are fastened to the vehicle. This results in a control arm that looks something like an 'A' or a wishbone (Figure 2-4). Because of the control arm shape, this type of front suspension sometimes is called an A-arm, or wishbone suspension. Since the control arms differ in length, with the longer arm used on the bottom, this design also is called an unequal arm suspension.

The inner end of each arm consists of two legs and is secured to the frame with a control arm shaft, a pivot bar, or pivot bolts and pivot bushings at each leg (Figure 2-5).

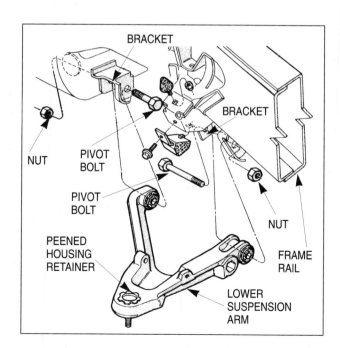

BRACKET

BRACKET

NUT

PIVOT BOLT

PIVOT BOLT

NUT

PEENED HOUSING RETAINER

FRAME RAIL

LOWER SUSPENSION ARM

Figure 2-4 Most control arms used with independent front suspensions are triangular in shape, and look like an 'A-arm' or 'wishbone'. (Chrysler)

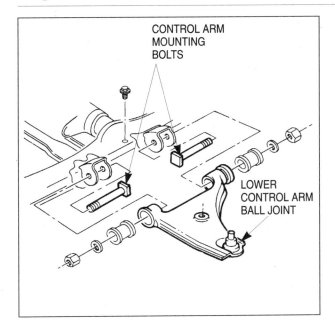

Figure 2-5 One type of control arm mounting uses pivot bolts to connect the inner legs, with a ball joint connecting the outer end to the knuckle. (Ford Motor)

The outer end of each arm, or end of the 'A', is fastened to the wheel spindle and **steering knuckle** with a ball joint (Figure 2-5). By mounting it in this manner, the control arm provides both vertical suspension motion and pivot points for steering control. Before there were ball joints, older cars with independent suspension used kingpins, a much heavier assembly of parts.

Up to a point, the greater the spread between the two control arm legs, the more stable and durable the front end. A stabilizer or sway bar is attached between the frame and lower control arm by stabilizer links (Figure 2-6). The twisting action of this spring steel bar reduces body roll when making a turn. It also makes the car ride better over potholes and bumps because the bar resists independent action by the wheels. The SLA suspension design normally uses coil springs, which can be positioned on the lower control arm (Figure 2-7) or on top of the upper control arm (Figure 2-8).

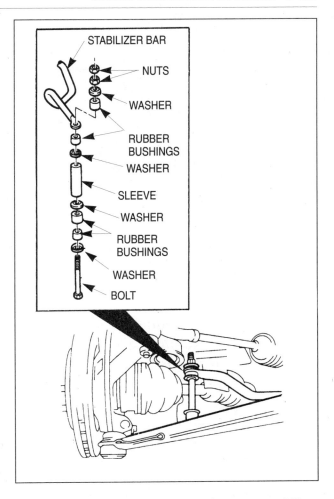

Figure 2-6 The link assemblies used to mount stabilizer or anti-roll bars to the control arm consist of bushings or insulators, washers or retainers, a sleeve or spacer, and an anchor bolt. (Ford Motor)

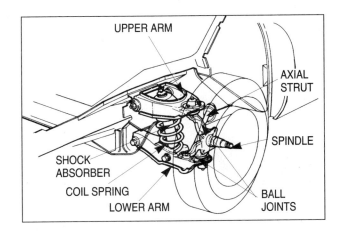

Figure 2-7 Coil spring on lower control arm. (Ford Motor)

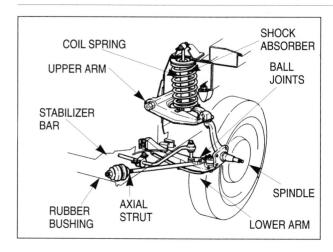

Figure 2-8 Coil spring on upper control arm. (Ford Motor)

A variation in SLA design uses a narrow lower control arm shaped more like an 'I', with only a single inner point mounting, or two bushings so close to each other that they have the effect of a single mounting point. The outer end of the control arm is attached to the steering knuckle with a ball joint. A strut rod is necessary to hold the control arm in alignment. This rod attaches to the control arm near the steering knuckle and runs forward to a point on the frame (Figure 2-9). Rubber

bushings at the frame mounting point allow the strut rod to 'give' when the wheel hits a bump on the road. With proper bushing tuning, less road shock will be transmitted to the vehicle frame.

Because the lower control arm is responsible for maintaining the distance between the two front tires, known as the tread or track, it is mounted as nearly horizontal as possible to lessen track changes as it swings up and down during vertical wheel travel. The job of the upper control arm is to control the camber angle of the tire. For this reason, it is mounted at a downward angle. The use of unequal length control arms mounted in a non-parallel position results in the tire leaning in or out as the tire moves up and down. This is not really desirable, but the use of equal length control arms would be even less desirable.

Parallel-mounted control arms of equal length would hold the tire perfectly vertical as it moves up and down, but the tire would move sideways as it goes over a bump, causing a change in the track (Figure 2-10). This **scrubbing** motion results in tire drag and wear.

The change in the lean of the tire resulting from the use of unequal length

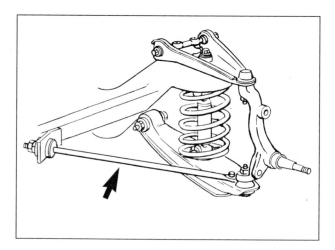

Figure 2-9 A strut rod installed on a narrow control arm keeps the arm in alignment. (McQuay-Norris)

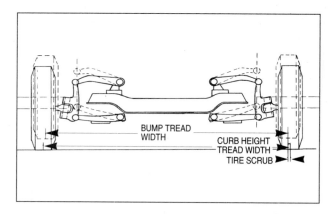

Figure 2-10 Tire wear caused by varying tread widths resulting from use of equal length control arms. (Ammco Tools / ©Hennessy Industries)

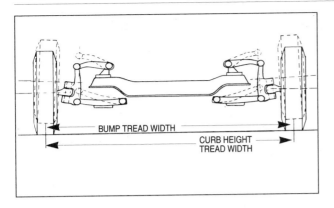

Figure 2-11 The use of unequal length control arms causes the wheel to lean in and out as the vehicle bounces. (Ammco Tools / ©Hennessy Industries)

control arms minimizes track changes as the vehicle passes over a bump (Figure 2-11). The portion of the tire tread that meets the road surface does suffer a small amount of scrubbing, but usually not enough to cause excessive tire wear. In other words, the leaning in or out of the tire during forward movement over a rough road is preferable

to track changes and scrubbing. Wheels that are not properly aligned also may cause tire scrubbing and abnormal wear.

MacPherson Strut Suspension

Used on front wheel drive (FWD) vehicles, the MacPherson strut suspension is another common independent suspension design (Figure 2-12). Originally named after the Ford engineer who devised it for use on British Fords during the early 1950s, it often is referred to now simply as a strut suspension. When used on the rear of a vehicle, it may be called a Chapman strut suspension.

The strut is a self-contained unit consisting of a large telescoping shock absorber surrounded by a coil spring. At its top, the strut is secured to the unitized body by a bearing assembly which transfers loads to the chassis. The bearing assembly is an integral part of a rubber mount and serves two purposes — it permits a slight

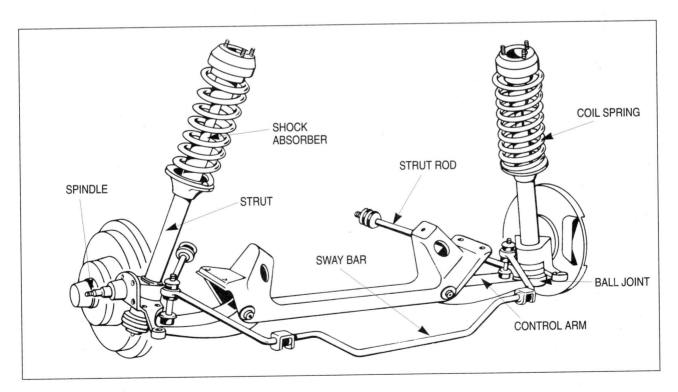

Figure 2-12 The MacPherson strut suspension. (Moog Automotive)

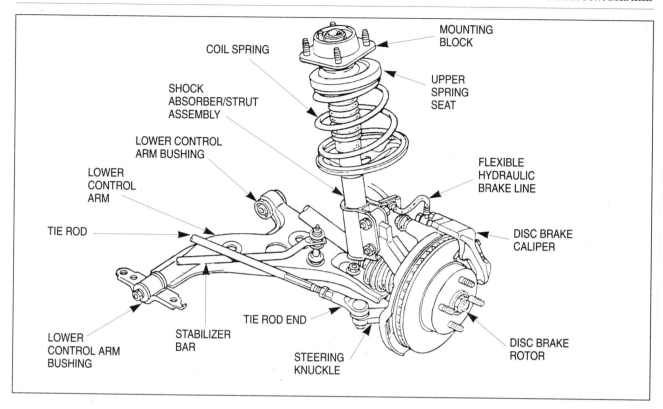

Figure 2-13 Components of a MacPherson strut suspension used by some Ford vehicles. Note that the bottom of the strut connects to the top of the steering knuckle, while the lower control arm connects to the bottom of the knuckle, keeping it in alignment. (Ford Motor)

change in the strut angle as the wheel moves up and down, and it allows the steering knuckle to pivot during turning maneuvers. In this respect, the strut performs the function of an upper control arm. The lower end of the strut connects to the steering knuckle (Figure 2-13). Some vehicles use a modified strut suspension, in which the coil spring is positioned between the lower control arm and frame crossmember (Figure 2-14). Since a strut suspension uses fewer parts, it is lighter in mass and less complicated than an SLA suspension. Strut designs are used with FWD vehicles because they allow more room in the engine compartment for engine and transaxle placement.

When front wheel drive is used with a strut suspension, the final drive is usually bolted to the vehicle frame and axles come out each side to drive the wheels. Each axle must have two universal joints (Figure 2-15), with a slip joint incorporated into one, so that the axle can lengthen or shorten as the wheel moves up and down. Having the final drive attached to the frame makes it unsprung weight, and greatly reduces the sprung mass in the suspension.

Swing Axle Suspension
The most basic type of independent suspension for drive axles is a swing axle suspension, which uses the driving axle and radius rods fore and aft to locate the wheel. The term swing axle comes from the up and down swinging action of the wheel as it moves through a large arc at the end of the axle. Because of the large swing, when the wheel drops down it leans out considerably, and when the vehicle is heavily loaded and

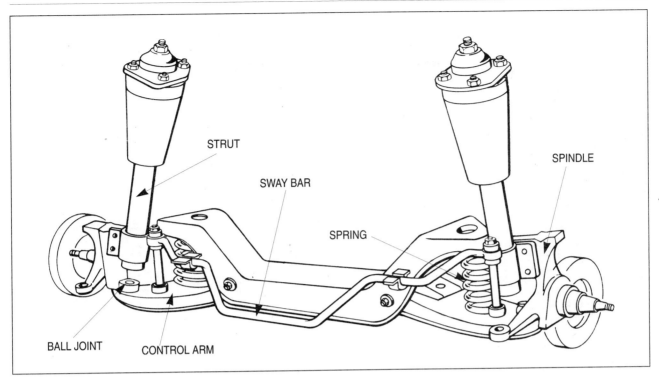

Figure 2-14 In a modified strut suspension, the coil spring is located between the frame and lower control arm. (Moog Automotive)

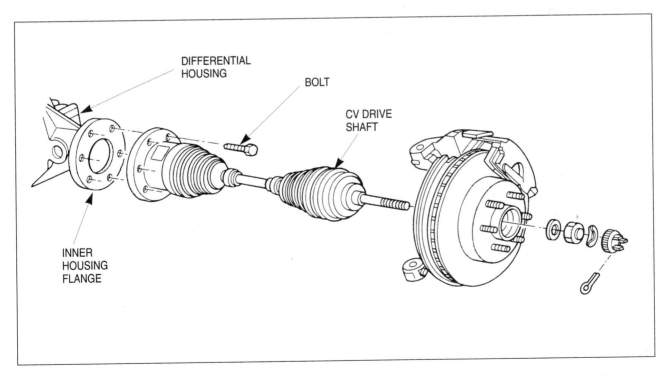

Figure 2-15 The most efficient independent suspensions have the final drive or differential housing bolted to the frame, and usually have two universal joints, with a slip joint built into the inner joint. (Chrysler)

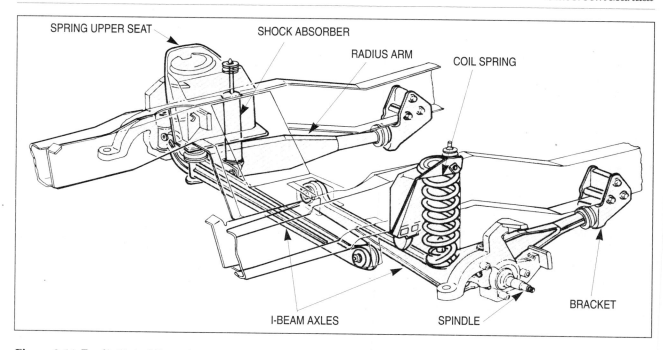

Figure 2-16 Ford's Twin I-Beam is one example of a swing axle suspension used at the front of a vehicle. (Ford Motor)

the wheel moves up, it leans in. Although the term swing axle was formerly used only for driving axles, such as found on the old Volkswagen Bug, the non-driving axles on the front of a Ford pickup are actually swing axles. Ford calls its swing axle design a 'Twin I-Beam' suspension, since it consists of two long solid axles shaped like an I-beam that pass under the nearest frame rail and pivot on the other side of the car (Figure 2-16).

When a rigid driving axle is used in the front to make a vehicle four wheel drive, Ford calls it the 'Mono Beam' because the axle housing consists of one (mono) rigid piece. The wheels pivot on large joints in each end of the housing. Radius arms attached to the housing prevent it from moving fore or aft; coil springs are installed between special frame pockets and the axle beams to support the vehicle mass and absorb road shock. The swing axle design causes both track and camber changes which can result in steering problems or tire wear.

Torsion Bar Suspension

Some Chrysler vehicles, as well as many import pickup trucks, use a **torsion bar** front suspension (Figure 2-17). GM also used a torsion bar design on the early Toronado and Eldorado FWD vehicles built in the late 1960s. Torsion bars are rods

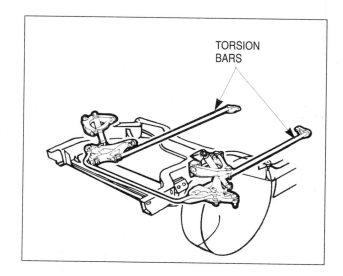

Figure 2-17 With a torsion bar suspension, the torsion bars replace the coil springs. (Moog Automotive)

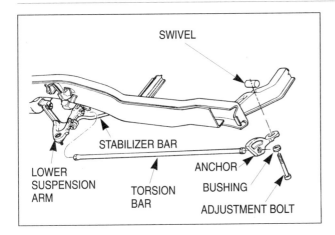

Figure 2-18 The front suspension ride height can be adjusted on a torsion bar design through use of the adjustment bolt. (Chrysler)

made from spring steel which replace the springs. Each torsion bar is attached between the lower control arm pivot point and the vehicle frame. When the vehicle wheel encounters irregularities in the road, such as bumps or potholes, vertical wheel

movement is transmitted through the lower control arm, causing the torsion bar to twist, then unwind to return the wheel to its normal position. Most such designs have an adjusting bolt that allows a limited amount of front curb height adjustment (Figure 2-18).

Chrysler and Volkswagen also have positioned the torsion bars on some models laterally between the control arms (Figure 2-19). Since strut rods are not required in this design, the resulting front suspension is highly compact.

SUMMARY

Front suspension designs are classified as non-independent (rigid axle) suspensions or independent suspensions. RWD vehicles generally use an independent front and non-independent rear suspension. FWD vehicles are most often equipped with both front and rear independent suspensions.

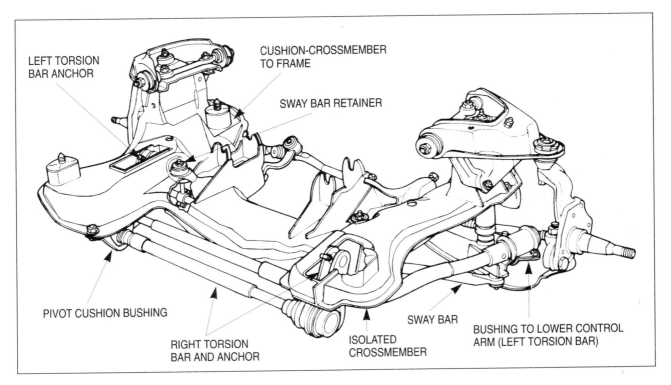

Figure 2-19 Volkswagen and Chrysler also have used transverse torsion bar suspensions. (Chrysler)

CROWNED ROADS AND THEIR EFFECT

How many times have you driven on a new stretch of highway, or one that has recently been resurfaced, and marveled about how nice and flat it is? Wrong! In many parts of the country, highways (not city streets) generally are crowned, or raised in the center, to allow water drainage. They may look perfectly flat to the human eye, especially at a distance, but they are not. If they were not crowned, highways would turn into miniature rivers and lakes during a heavy rainstorm, just as some city intersections do. Since this would make highway driving extremely dangerous during inclement weather, road engineers design a slight degree of center-to-edge curvature into new or resurfaced highways.

When driving on the right side of a crowned road, gravity tends to shift vehicle weight to its curb side. Under normal circumstances, this would cause the vehicle to pull to the right on most crowned roads. However, if the front end has been properly aligned, weight transfer to the right side of the vehicle will produce a slight negative camber at the right front wheel and a slight positive camber at the left front wheel. With the tendency of the front wheels to roll and steer in the same direction as they lean, the slight camber changes offset the weight transfer caused by gravity, allowing the vehicle to maintain a straight course on the crowned road surface.

Carmakers often specify a camber spread, or slightly more positive camber at the left wheel than at the right, to create a camber pull to the left. This is designed to offset the road crown pull and allow the vehicle to travel in a straight line on the crowned road surface. Since camber is a tire wear angle, there is a school of thought that says camber should be adjusted to the smallest tire wear angle and a caster spread used to compensate for road crown, as caster is a non-tire wear angle. When caster is set to a slightly more positive angle at the right wheel, and a slightly less positive angle at the left wheel, it will also offset the road crown effect by pulling to the left against the crown's pull to the right.

For many drivers, the effect of road crown is academic because they mainly drive on city streets. Those who do a considerable amount of high speed highway driving will be affected to a greater degree. As an alignment technician, you should try for a compromise setting that will give the best vehicle handling with the least tire wear.

The vehicle suspension must:

- connect the wheels and tires to the frame
- allow the wheels and tires to pivot for steering control
- support the vehicle weight
- keep the wheels and axles aligned with the vehicle frame
- allow the tires and wheels to move in a vertical direction relative to the frame
- reduce road shock transmission to the steering system and passengers.

A non-independent front suspension consists of a solid beam axle or housing to which both wheels are attached. Solid axle suspensions are heavy and require greater spring and shock absorber control to maintain tire contact with the road surface. When one tire on a solid axle goes over a bump on the road, the tire on the other side changes position, and may have an effect on handling.

The short-long arm (SLA) design found on the front of North American RWD passenger cars is one of the most common independent front suspensions. It uses two triangular-shaped control arms of unequal length on each side of the vehicle. This design is also called an 'unequal arm', 'A-arm', or 'wishbone' suspension.

Other common independent front suspensions are the MacPherson strut design used with FWD vehicles, the Twin I Beam or Mono Beam design used primarily on Ford pickup trucks and some 4WD vehicles, and the torsion bar design found on many Chrysler vehicles and imported pickup trucks.

Regardless of the type of suspension used, it must allow the tires to maintain contact with the road under various operating conditions. For example, it must travel smoothly on the roadway without transmitting bumps or vibration. It also must travel in a straight line unless the driver wishes to turn, and then respond quickly and easily during the turning maneuver. The tires must roll down the road with minimal drag and scrub to maintain tire life and fuel economy.

? REVIEW QUESTIONS

1. Which of the following is found in a non-independent suspension?
   (A) a solid axle
   (B) a swing axle
   (C) trailing arms
   (D) MacPherson strut

2. Technician A says that vertical wheel movement in an SLA suspension will cause a camber change. Technician B says that SLA suspensions use two equal length A-arms on each side of the vehicle. Who is right?
   (A) A only
   (B) B only
   (C) Both A and B
   (D) Neither A nor B

3. Technician A says that springs and shock absorbers permit upward tire travel by compressing whenever the tires pass over bumps. Technician B says that springs and shock absorbers permit downward tire travel by extending after the tires pass over bumps. Who is right?
   (A) A only
   (B) B only
   (C) Both A and B
   (D) Neither A nor B

4. Technician A says that normal non-air shock absorbers control the trim height of a vehicle. Technician B says that incorrect wheel alignment can cause tire scrub. Who is right?

(A) A only
(B) B only
(C) Both A and B
(D) Neither A nor B

5. Technician A says that a MacPherson front suspension uses trailing arms to control tire position. Technician B says that a modified strut suspension uses a coil spring between the upper control arm and frame. Who is right?
(A) A only
(B) B only
(C) Both A and B
(D) Neither A nor B

6. Technician A says that the lower control arm in an SLA suspension is mounted horizontally to control track width of the tires. Technician B says that the upper control arm is mounted at a downward angle to control the tire camber angle. Who is right?
(A) A only
(B) B only
(C) Both A and B
(D) Neither A nor B

7. Technician A says that a lower control arm may have either one or two inner mounting points. Technician B says that a lower control arm with a single inner mounting point requires the use of a strut rod to hold the arm aligned. Who is right?

(A) A only
(B) B only
(C) Both A and B
(D) Neither A nor B

8. In a torsion bar suspension, which components are replaced by the torsion bars?
(A) the control arms
(B) the stabilizer bars
(C) the strut rods
(D) the springs

9. Technician A says that the torsion bars must support the vehicle mass and control wheel position like a spring. Technician B says that torsion bars are not adjustable. Who is right?
(A) A only
(B) B only
(C) Both A and B
(D) Neither A nor B

10. Technician A says that the mount and bearing assembly used to attach the top of a strut to the unitized body allows the steering knuckle to pivot during steering maneuvers. Technician B says that it also allows the strut to change angle with wheel movement. Who is right?
(A) A only
(B) B only
(C) Both A and B
(D) Neither A nor B

REAR SUSPENSION SYSTEMS

"Expert: A mechanic away from home."
— Charles E. Wilson

 OBJECTIVES

After completion of this chapter, you should be able to:

- List the three functions of a rear suspension system.
- List and briefly describe the two types of non-independent rear suspensions.
- List and briefly describe the three types of independent rear suspensions.

The rear suspension of a vehicle has three major purposes. It must:

- support the vehicle mass
- keep the wheels and axles aligned with the vehicle frame to assure vehicle stability and directional control
- cushion any road shock that would otherwise be transmitted to the steering system and passengers.

Different designs of rear suspensions are used to accomplish the above purposes — non-independent (rigid axle or housing) and independent. In this chapter, we will look at both these classifications, including subclassifications within each.

NON-INDEPENDENT REAR SUSPENSIONS

The traditional arrangement with front engine/rear wheel drive uses a rigid rear axle housing containing the differential and axle shafts. At each outer end of the housing is a bearing which supports the axle and the wheel. The various arrangements of axle and wheel bearings and their terminology are covered in the chapter on wheel bearings, wheels and tires. The rear axle housing can be used with leaf springs, or coil springs and locating links, as shown in the combined illustration (Figure 3-1). When used with leaf springs, the springs hold the housing in position on each side of the housing. Coil springs require additional links to locate the housing, as shown in one half of Figure 3-1. While straightforward in design and requiring little maintenance, a rigid rear axle housing has the disadvantage of being very heavy. This hurts gas mileage, especially on a small car.

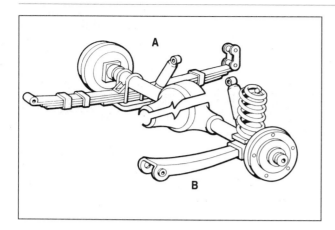

Figure 3-1 A non-independent rear suspension uses a solid drive axle. When used with leaf springs (A), the springs control the axle location. If coil springs are used (B), rear control or trailing arms are necessary, as the coil springs alone cannnot control axle position. (Moog Automotive)

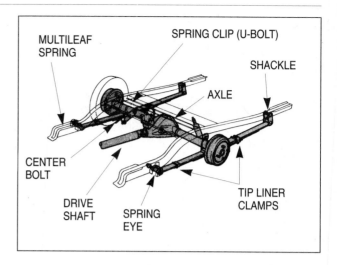

Figure 3-2 A typical leaf spring rear suspension. (Ford Motor)

LEAF SPRINGS

Although leaf spring suspensions are versatile and inexpensive, they have been replaced in all but a few cases by coil springs. Like the solid axle front suspension, the use of leaf springs dates back to the earliest automobiles. Leaf spring rear suspensions are rarely used today with passenger cars, but are still found on pickup trucks, vans, and sport utility vehicles (Figure 3-2).

The leaf spring assembly consists of several leaves of varying lengths. Each end of the longest leaf has been formed into an eye. A center bolt through the spring assembly keeps the leaves positioned relative to each other. The spring assembly is attached to the rear axle housing at or near its center with U-bolts. The front spring eye contains a bushing, which might be either rubber or metal. A heavy pin through the bushing is attached to a hanger on the frame. The hanger holds the spring assembly in place and the bushing and pin allows the spring eye to rotate as needed for spring action. The rear spring eye and hanger also have pins and

bushings, but in addition have a spring shackle connecting the spring eye to the hanger (Figure 3-3). The shackle acts as a hinge, allowing the spring assembly to change its length as it absorbs road shock. On some springs, tip liners are used to prevent metal to metal contact which can cause squeaks. Clips or clamps are used to align the spring leaves and prevent the rubber or plastic wear pads (tip liners) from falling out of position (Figure 3-4).

The use of long multiple **semi-elliptical** spring leaves controls lateral axle motion and absorbs driving and braking forces. The low **deflection rate** of the long upper leaves produces a smooth ride under light or no-load conditions; the higher deflection rate of the shorter lower leaves adds stiffness to the ride under increased loads.

In a few rear suspensions, such as those used by Corvettes and Yugos, single or multileaf springs also have been positioned transversely (Figure 3-5). Many other types and complicated arrangements of leaf springs have been used throughout the history of the automobile, but almost all of them have been abandoned for the simple leaf spring types described above.

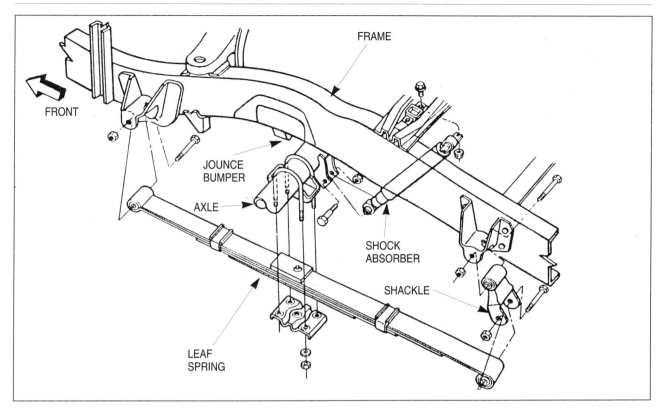

Figure 3-3 The components used to mount a leaf spring assembly. (Chrysler)

Coil Springs

The use of coil springs complicates rear suspension design. Rigid axle housings require lower control arms on each side of the vehicle pivoted to the frame at the front, and attached to the axle housing at the rear. Each lower control arm moves up-and-down around its single hinge point at the frame. In this way, the lower control arms maintain the fore-and-aft relationship of the axle to the vehicle chassis and frame. The solid rear axle maintains correct rear wheel and body alignment. To counteract axle wind-up during acceleration and braking, an upper control arm and track bar, or upper control arms on each side of the vehicle restrain sideways motion of the frame and body relative to the drive shaft and axle. The coil springs are installed between the axle housing or lower arms,

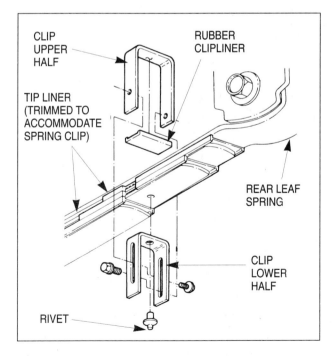

Figure 3-4 Spring tip liners are held in place by a clip or clamp arrangement. (Ford Motor)

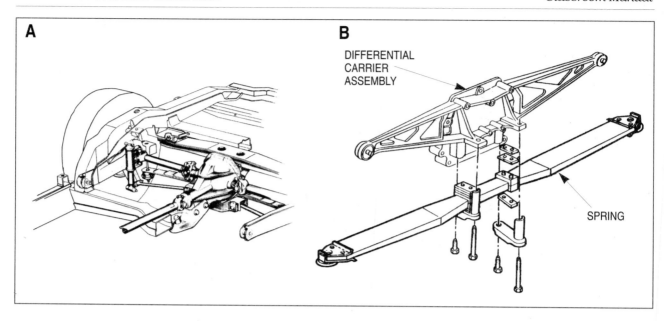

Figure 3-5   A transverse rear spring suspension is used on early Corvettes (A); current models use a single leaf fiberglass spring housed in an aluminum differential carrier cover (B). (Chevrolet Division, General Motors)

and the vehicle frame, and are retained by the vehicle mass, as well as the shock absorbers used to limit upward travel of the vehicle body. Since the shock absorbers are installed at an angle between the frame and axle housing, they reduce body sway as well as controlling ride (Figure 3-6 and Figure 3-7).

INDEPENDENT REAR SUSPENSIONS

Independent rear suspensions (IRS) offer a better ride and handling, but they are more complicated in design, as they use a variety of links to position the rear wheels. Such suspensions may use either a transverse multileaf spring, MacPherson struts, or trailing arms.

TRANSVERSE MULTILEAF SPRING SUSPENSION

On North American vehicles, this type of rear suspension is used primarily by Chevrolet on the Corvette. The spring is mounted on the frame-mounted final drive

differential housing, with a 3-link system used to locate each rear wheel (A, Figure 3-5). The 3 links consist of the rear axle drive shaft, the camber control strut rod, and the wheel spindle/support shaft. Short shafts connect the rear axle drive shafts to the differential with constant velocity (CV) joints or U-joints. Control arms running forward to the frame limit the fore-and-aft wheel movement.

The Corvette introduced in 1984 uses front and rear transverse fiberglass leaf springs, a refinement of the design originally pioneered at the rear of the 1981 model. The rear fiberglass leaf spring is mounted on an aluminum differential carrier cover (B, Figure 3-5). This carrier transmits vehicle mass to the spring. It also supports and locates the rear wheel suspension knuckles by connecting them to the frame with spindle support rods.

MACPHERSON STRUT SUSPENSION

Several different strut-type suspension configurations are used on the rear of FWD

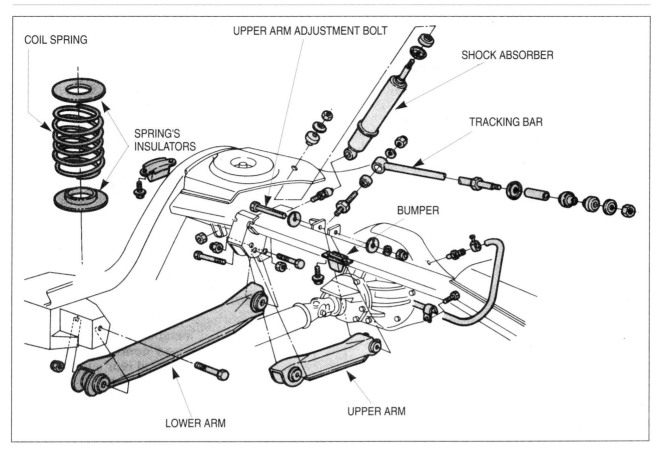

Figure 3-6   A typical coil spring rear suspension with one upper control arm. (Ford Motor)

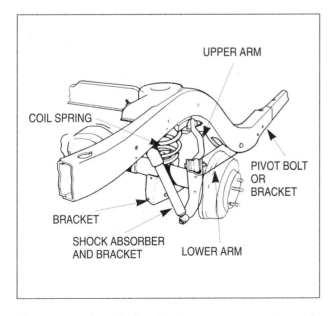

Figure 3-7   A typical coil spring rear suspension with two upper control arms. (Ford Motor)

vehicles. In one common design, two parallel control arms of stamped metal are fastened to the center of the underbody on each side. The outer ends of each pair of control arms are bolted to a cast spindle, and a strut rod secures the assembly to the frame rails on each side. The strut consists of a shock absorber inside a coil spring which is held in place by upper and lower spring seats. The lower end of the strut is bolted to the spindle; the upper end is attached by two studs and nuts to the inner body side panel (Figure 3-8). Note that in this design the arms that locate the wheels run from the center of the vehicle out toward the wheels. When these arms run forward and are attached to the frame in front of the wheels, they are known as trailing arms, because the arms point or

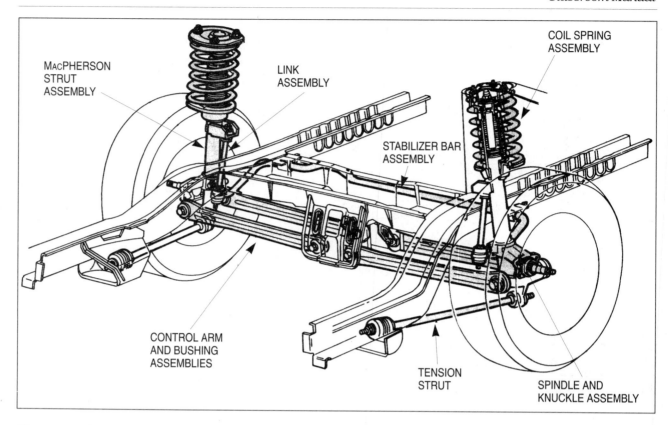

Figure 3-8 The control arms on Ford Tempo/Taurus and Mercury Topaz/Sable vehicles consist of two parallel stamped metal control arms secured between the wheel spindle and the center of the underbody. (Ford Motor)

trail toward the rear of the vehicle.

Another common rear suspension design is a cross between the strut and trailing arm suspensions. It uses a pair of lateral links instead of control arms on each side. The links are fastened between an open channel crossmember and the steering knuckle. A trailing link on each side bolts to the rear wheel spindle and vehicle frame, and performs the function of the strut rod. The strut itself mounts between the spindle and body as described earlier, and a stabilizer bar located inside the open channel crossmember is bolted between the trailing link and rear cross-member (Figure 3-9).

TRAILING ARM SUSPENSION

In this type of independent rear suspension, blade-type trailing arms are mounted

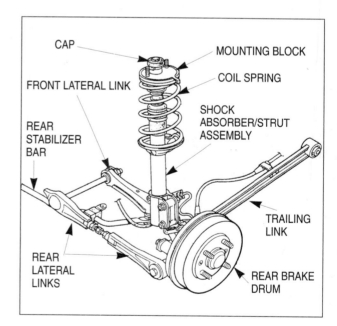

Figure 3-9 Lateral links replace the control arm on late-model Ford Escort and Mercury Tracer rear suspensions. (Ford Motor)

on an open channel section beam axle to which the spindle and wheel assemblies are bolted. Attached to body-mounted pivot points with bushings, the trailing arms provide fore-and-aft location of the suspension and pivot to permit suspension travel. Lateral location is provided by a track bar bolted between one end of the axle and a frame support bracket positioned by a diagonal brace. The channel beam axle maintains the tires parallel to each other and perpendicular to the road surface. A torque tube or rod located inside the axle channel is welded to the axle end plates on each side and provides body roll resistance. Camber change during suspension travel is controlled by positioning of the trailing arm bushings. Shock absorbers and coil springs are mounted between body and axle brackets (Figure 3-10). As with other types of independent suspensions, variations of this design are also used.

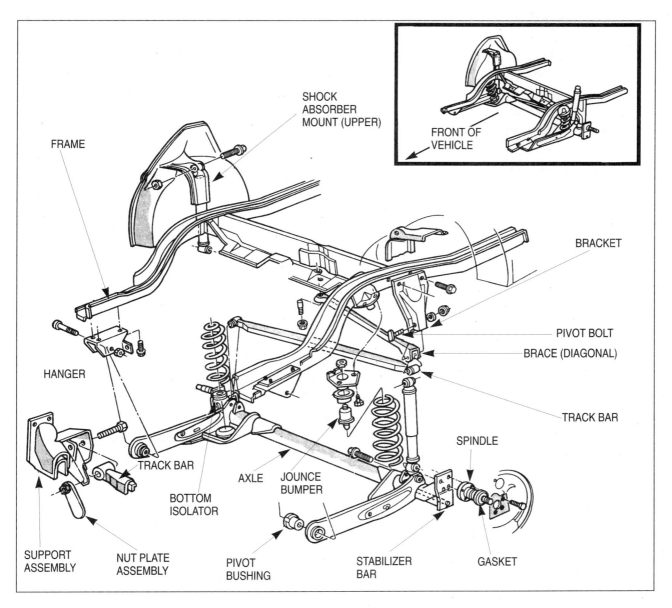

Figure 3-10 A typical blade-type trailing arm suspension. (Chrysler)

SPOTLIGHT

THE HYDROPNEUMATIC SUSPENSION

One of the strangest automotive suspension systems ever found on production vehicles used NO springs — NO leaves, coils, or torsion bars. It was a hydropneumatic (air/oil) system. The idea was so far removed from the conventional concepts of suspension used by carmakers that you might not believe that it worked. Yet, it was a hallmark of a strange looking French car called the Citroen for many years, and even found acceptance by bus and heavy truck manufacturers.

The basic component of the Citroen's air/oil suspension was a four-inch diameter steel sphere at each wheel. A rubber diaphragm inside each sphere divided it in half. The space on top of the diaphragm was filled with pressurized nitrogen; brake fluid filled the space under the diaphragm. A series of levers connected the wheel to a piston which acted on the brake fluid in the bottom of the sphere.

When the wheel hit a bump, the piston was driven into the brake fluid, which transmitted the force to the cushion of nitrogen. The brake fluid distributed the load evenly over the diaphragm surface. The nitrogen resisted this action just like a spring. The fluid end of the system connected to a pump operated by the engine. Pump output could be varied by the driver, varying the system pressure. In this way, the driver could adjust the car's ground clearance from a low of 6" to a high of 11".

A multifunction self-equalizing device kept the car level. A few seconds after passengers entered the rear of the vehicle, it would start to rise until the car was again level. During a cornering maneuver, the same device transferred system pressure to the outside wheels. This kept the outside wheels more stiffly suspended than those on the inside, and made the car very level in a turn.

The air-oil suspension was deceiving in appearance. With all its tiny tubes and switches, you might think it was a Rube Goldberg idea that wouldn't work with a full-size car. Yet, it worked so well that the Citroen was acclaimed as one of the world's best handling passenger sedans during the '60s. For its era, the Citroen was expensive and its styling as radical as its strange suspension. The company had little success in the United States. Low sales combined with increasingly stringent U.S. safety and emission requirements forced Citroen to gradually leave the American market, but former owners fondly recall the silky smooth ride hidden beneath the avant garde exterior.

SUMMARY

Like front suspensions, rear suspension designs are classified as nonindependent (rigid axle housing) suspensions or independent suspensions. RWD vehicles generally use an independent front and non-independent rear suspension. FWD vehicles are most often equipped with both front and rear independent suspensions.

The vehicle suspension must support the vehicle mass, keep the wheels and axles aligned with the vehicle frame, and prevent road shock transmission to the steering system and passengers.

Non-independent rear drive suspensions use a rigid tubular axle housing.

Axle shafts enclosed in the tubular housing are splined to the differential side gears and transmit driving torque to the rear wheels. A rigid rear axle housing may be used with either leaf or coil springs.

Several types of independent rear suspensions are used. The transverse multileaf spring suspension uses a spring mounted between the rear wheels. Strut suspensions are similar to those used for front suspensions, with several variations from the original MacPherson/Chapman design. The trailing arm suspension uses an open channel beam axle with blade-type trailing arms, a track bar, and a torque tube or rod.

? REVIEW QUESTIONS

1. Which of the following is NOT a usual function of the rear suspension?
   (A) allow the wheels to pivot for steering
   (B) support vehicle mass
   (C) maintain wheel/axle/frame alignment
   (D) reduce transmission of road shock

2. Technician A says that traditional non-independent rear suspensions are only used with RWD vehicles. Technician B says that a disadvantage of the rigid rear axle housing suspension is its relatively high unsprung weight. Who is right?
   (A) A only
   (B) B only
   (C) Both A and B
   (D) Neither A nor B

3. Technician A says that leaf spring rear suspensions are primarily used on passenger cars. Technician B says that semi-elliptical leaf springs control lateral axle motion. Who is right?
   (A) A only
   (B) B only
   (C) Both A and B
   (D) Neither A nor B

4. Technician A says that leaf springs are attached to the frame with a shackle to allow spring movement. Technician B says that leaf springs can be mounted across the vehicle centerline. Who is right?
   (A) A only
   (B) B only
   (C) Both A and B
   (D) Neither A nor B

5. Technician A says that rear suspension lower control arms maintain the fore-and-aft relationship of the axle to the chassis and frame. Technician B says that a rigid rear axle housing determines correct rear wheel alignment. Who is right?
   (A) A only
   (B) B only
   (C) Both A and B
   (D) Neither A nor B

6. Which of the following is NOT found in an independent rear suspension?

(A) transverse multileaf springs

(B) MacPherson struts

(C) trailing arms

(D) a rigid rear axle housing

7. Which of the following reduces RWD body sway during a cornering maneuver?

(A) stabilizer bar

(B) trailing arm

(C) radius arm

(D) torsion bar

8. In a trailing arm suspension, lateral location is provided by:

(A) a radius arm

(B) a track bar

(C) a sway bar

(D) a stabilizer bar

9. Technician A says that a track bar is used to maintain fore-and-aft suspension location in a trailing arm suspension design. Technician B says that the trailing arms locate the wheels fore and aft. Who is right?

(A) A only

(B) B only

(C) Both A and B

(D) Neither A nor B

10. Technician A says that some independent rear suspensions use rear axle drive shafts that connect to the differential with CV or U-joints. Technician B says that strut-type rear suspensions are common on both FWD and RWD vehicles. Who is right?

(A) A only

(B) B only

(C) Both A and B

(D) Neither A nor B

SUSPENSION DYNAMICS

"It is only when they go wrong that machines remind you how powerful they are." — Clive James

 OBJECTIVES

After completion of this chapter, you should be able to:

- Define the terms wheelbase and track.

- Explain the concepts of wheel setback, axle offset, and axle sideset.

- Discuss the five factors involved in vehicle handling and directional control, and explain their inter-relationship with suspension geometry.

- Explain the concept of wheel slip.

Numerous forces affect vehicle ride, handling, and control. All must be considered by engineers when they design a particular suspension. The traction force, or amount of adhesion between the tires and road surface, determines vehicle starting, acceleration, braking, cornering, and stopping. To produce a vehicle that is both safe and enjoyable to drive, the suspension design chosen must accommodate acceptable compromises. In this chapter, we will identify the more important forces, their relationship to each other, and how they affect the operation of an automobile.

WHEELBASE AND TRACK

When a vehicle is assembled at the factory, the suspension is attached to the frame according to two factors — wheelbase and track. **Track**, sometimes called tread, is the distance between the centerline of the wheels from one side of the car to the other. **Wheelbase** is a measurement of the distance between the centers of the front and rear wheel hubs (Figure 4-1). It should measure the same on both sides of the vehicle, except in extremely rare designs. The longer the wheelbase, the smoother the vehicle ride. The track, or distance between the wheels is usually the same in the front and in the rear (Figure 4-2). But there are some vehicles with different track dimensions between the front and the rear. Both, the wheelbase and the track, are correctly established when the vehicle leaves the factory, but can change as a

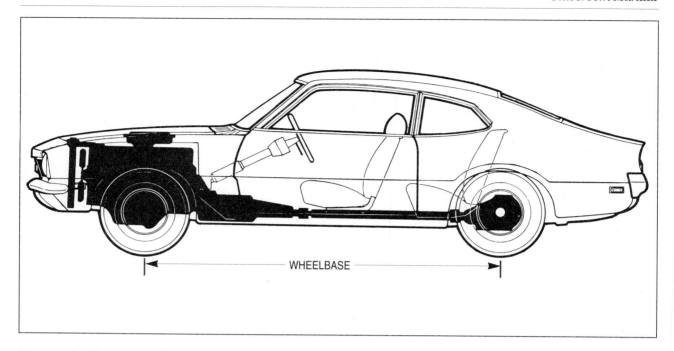

Figure 4-1   The vehicle wheelbase is determined by measuring the distance between the center of the front and rear axle spindles, or hubs.

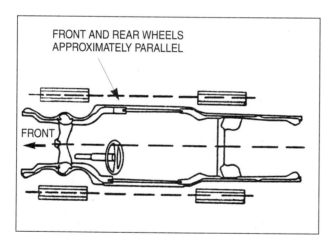

Figure 4-2   If a vehicle tracks correctly, its front and rear wheels will be parallel. The front and rear wheels on both sides are usually the same distance from the vehicle centerline.

result of suspension wear or damage, or as a result of a collision. Any change in the wheelbase will affect vehicle tracking and thus the directional control and **stability**.

Since directional control and vehicle stability are determined both by frame condition and suspension positioning/ alignment, the suspension system must keep the tires parallel with the vehicle's center line when it is moving forward in a straight line. In the event of a collision, frame-to-wheel dimensions can be used as a diagnostic measurement. By measuring from identical known good points on the frame or body structure, and comparing to specifications, the correct forward and rearward position of each wheel can be determined, as well as caster or axle positioning problems at each wheel.

Changes in frame or suspension positioning can affect vehicle tracking in three different ways — wheel setback, axle offset, or axle sideset.

WHEEL SETBACK

When one wheel spindle is positioned to the rear of the opposite spindle on the axle, an unequal wheelbase is created between the left and right sides of a vehicle (Figure 4-3). This condition is called 'wheel setback', and

NOTE On rare occasions, setback may be specifically designed in a suspension system. When this is the case, it can be identified by different Left and Right wheelbase specifications provided in a specification manual.

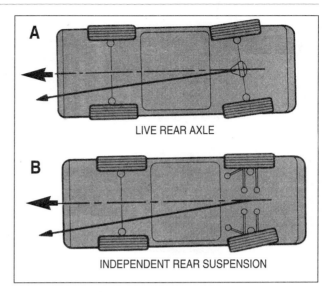

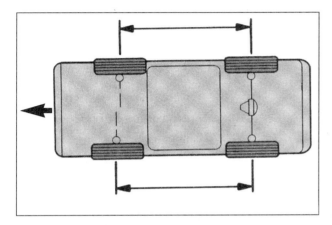

Figure 4-3 Wheel setback occurs when the two wheels on one axle do not share a common centerline or wheelbase. Setback generally results from collison damage and can be measured on an alignment machine. (Ford Motor)

Figure 4-4 The angle between the geometric centerline and the rear axle thrust is called the thrust angle. The thrust angle of RWD vehicles (A) can be affected by chassis damage; unequal rear toe adjustments on independent rear suspensions also can affect the thrust angle (B). (Ford Motor)

can occur to the front wheels of a solid axle suspension, or to any of the wheels in an independent suspension.

Setback generally results from an impact to a front wheel that changes the positioning of a lower control arm, engine cradle, or radius rod. When a vehicle with setback caused by an impact is driven down the road, it will have a tendency to pull to the side with the wheel that received the impact. To maintain the vehicle in a straight line, the driver must make steering corrections to the other side. The vehicle pull also is obvious during braking.

AXLE OFFSET

If the vehicle tracks properly, its rear wheels will follow the geometric center line of the vehicle when it is moving in a straight line (Figure 4-2). In this case, the geometric center line also acts as the rear axle thrust line. This line describes the direction in which the rear wheels will track (drive direction). Axle offset occurs when the rear axle position has changed so that the thrust line is no longer parallel with the vehicle center line (Figure 4-4). When there is a deviation between the geometric center line and the rear axle thrust line, it creates a **thrust angle**. If the thrust line deviates to the right of the vehicle (as seen from the top), the thrust angle is positive (A, Figure 4-5). A deviation to the left of the vehicle (B, Figure 4-5) is considered negative. To maintain vehicle movement in a straight line when offset is present, the steering wheel must be turned to the right (positive offset) or to the left (negative offset), causing the vehicle to 'dog track' with the rear of the vehicle obviously offset to one side when seen from behind while driving.

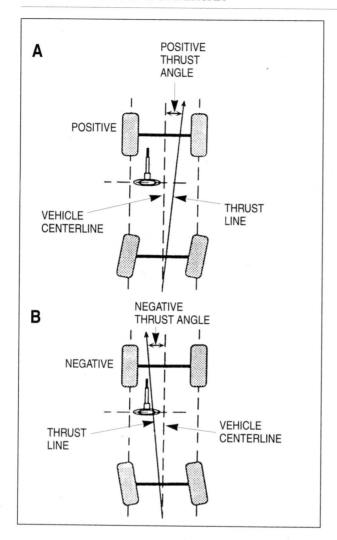

Figure 4-5   Either a positive (A) or negative (B) thrust angle will cause the vehicle to 'dog track'.

AXLE SIDESET

This condition occurs when the axle centers are not aligned with the vehicle center line, but all four wheels remain parallel to each other. If a rear axle is offset to one side, one wheel will be moved further into the wheelhouse and the other will be moved out (Figure 4-6). Although the thrust line remains parallel to the vehicle center line, the axle center lines do not follow each other when the vehicle is moving in a straight line. This condition also causes dog tracking.

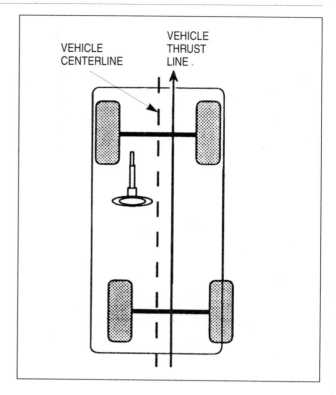

Figure 4-6   When an axle sideset condition exists, the thrust line will remain parallel to the vehicle centerline, but the axle centerlines do not follow each other when the vehicle is moving straight ahead.

DIRECTIONAL CONTROL AND STABILITY

How a vehicle reacts to its driver's demands and the feelings of controllability and predictability that are transmitted to the driver as a result form the basis of vehicle 'handling'. Good handling is not restricted to high cornering speeds. A vehicle that is easy to park, easy to back up, and needs only minimal steering corrections to travel in a straight line, is also said to have good handling. A vehicle not affected by crosswinds is said to handle better than the one that handles well with no wind, but wanders all over the road at the slightest breeze.

Ideally, the ultimate handling vehicle would be one with four equal size tires with each carrying 25% of the total vehicle mass. Its **center of gravity** would be at ground level and the relationship of all four wheels would remain constant. This ideal design concept eliminates the use of any kind of suspension, but keeps the wheels perpendicular to the roadway at all times. No engine or brakes could be used, since the **torque** transmitted to the **tire contact area** would reduce the cornering power. Note that all the features of this ideal vehicle center around one component — the tires. Tires have more influence on vehicle handling than any other factor. Whenever the vehicle moves, the tires are the contact points with the road surface. Where the tires go, so goes the vehicle.

TRACTION AND SLIP ANGLE

When a tire gets traction on the road surface, its tread is NOT moving relative to the pavement beneath it. This is how the tire gets traction to move the vehicle. If the tire moved on the pavement, it would be slipping, without any traction, and would NOT be able to move the vehicle. In addition, it would NOT be able to slow or stop the vehicle when the brakes were applied. To see this fact in operation, watch the movement of a bulldozer, tank, or other tracked vehicle. Although it appears to move steadily, that part of the track contacting the ground actually stops relative to the ground. Without this momentary stop to gain traction, there would be NO vehicle movement.

Since tires are inherently flexible, side loads such as those created when cornering cause the tires to deform and create what is called a **slip angle**. This angle is the difference between the direction in which the tires are pointing, and the direction in which the vehicle is actually traveling (Figure 4-7). The tires are not really

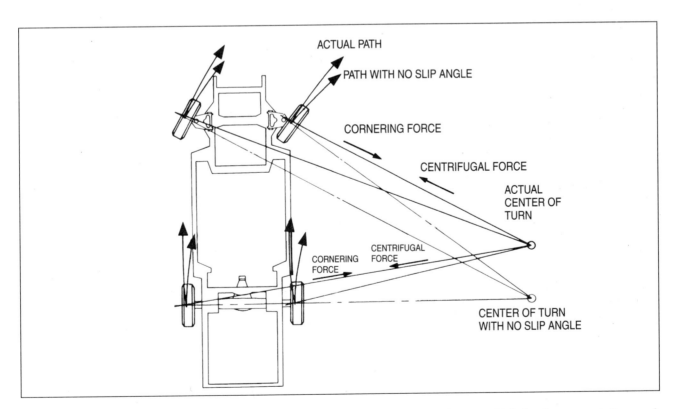

Figure 4-7 Tire slip or twist occurs when there is a difference between the direction in which the tires are pointing, and the direction in which the vehicle is actually traveling. (Ford Motor)

slipping, but rather are twisting at the point of contact. Slip angles exist at both the front and rear of the vehicle, with the front wheels generally having the larger angle because they are steerable.

Tires generally reach their maximum traction at a slight slippage to the road surface. The amount of slippage varies according to road surface condition and tire tread design. Under most conditions, maximum traction is reached with a tire-to-road slippage of 10-20%. If slippage exceeds 25%, the loss of traction can result in a skid.

CORNERING FORCE

The ability of a vehicle to negotiate a turning maneuver is called its cornering power or lateral acceleration, and involves centrifugal force. Although tire loading changes during a cornering maneuver, tire traction holds the vehicle to the road (Figure 4-8). When centrifugal force is less than the available tire traction, the vehicle will maintain its position on the road and go where it is pointed or steered. At the point where centrifugal force exceeds tire traction, the tires slip across the road

surface and the vehicle goes into a skid condition. During turning maneuvers, especially those involved in an S-curve, the load applied on the vehicle's tires and suspension constantly changes, affecting vehicle stability and handling.

UNDERSTEER AND OVERSTEER

The difference in slip angles between the front and rear of the vehicle creates the basic handling characteristics of the vehicle. If the front angle is greater, the vehicle is said to 'understeer'; if the rear angle is greater, it is termed 'oversteer' (Figure 4-9). When the angles are nearly identical, with the front and rear ends exhibiting the same characteristics, the vehicle is said to have 'neutral steer'. This characteristic, however, is seldom achieved in a 2WD vehicle. All three terms — understeer, oversteer, and neutral steer — refer

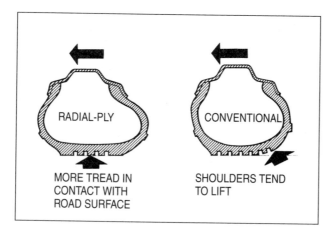

Figure 4-8 Tire tread experiences a sideways distortion during cornering due to a change in tire loading. A cornering load that is excessive can lift the edge of the tread from the road surface. (Ford Motor)

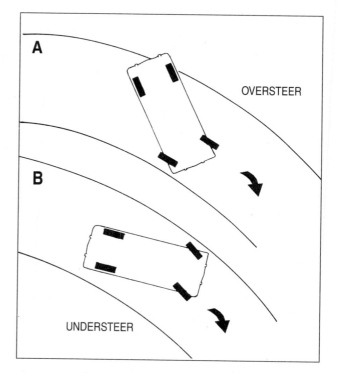

Figure 4-9 When a vehicle oversteers (A), it will turn sharper for a given amount of steering wheel motion than the one that understeers (B).

to the chassis and suspension reaction to cornering. Suspension engineers consider understeer as the safest condition for average drivers who have little experience in dealing with skids or spin outs.

A knowledgeable driver can control the vehicle's reaction by proper use of braking and acceleration. For example, if the vehicle has a bias toward a light understeer condition, a sharp or tight corner can be taken in three distinct stages. As the vehicle enters the corner, it is in the process of slowing down, and the weight bias is toward the front of the vehicle. This exaggerates the understeer characteristics, and generally requires that the wheels be turned sharper into the corner. As the vehicle approaches the middle of the corner and the driver starts to reapply power, the rear slip angles increase and bring the steering closer to a neutral condition. If too much power is applied too quickly or too soon, the steering will switch to a definite oversteer condition that requires steering corrections be made. As the vehicle exits from the corner under acceleration, the slight oversteer condition will be gradually reduced to zero because the front wheels are being straightened, and the weight transferred to the outside wheels during cornering will be decreased (Figure 4-10).

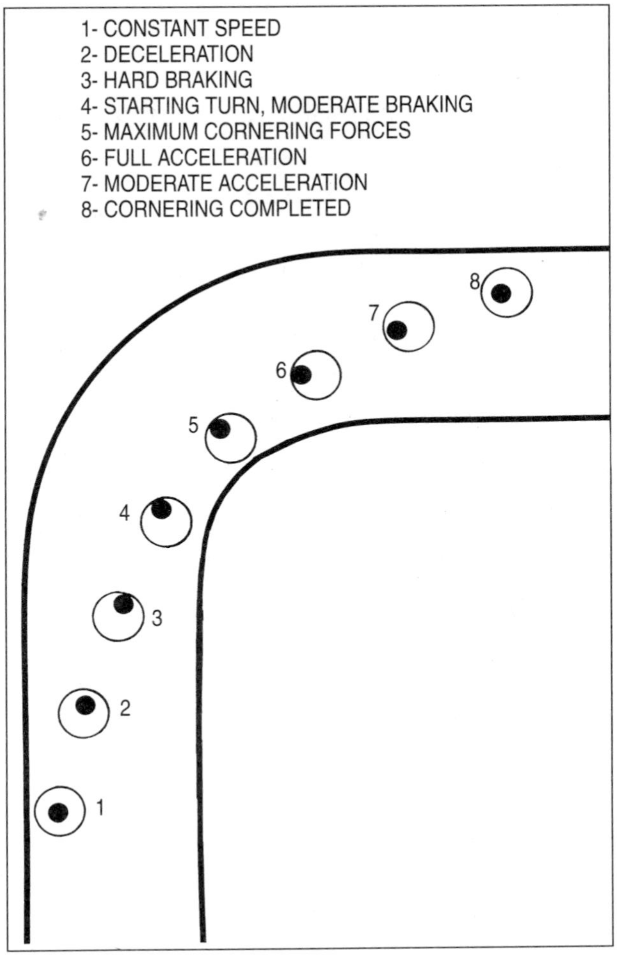

WEIGHT DISTRIBUTION AND TRANSFER

A constant weight distribution is almost impossible to achieve with modern vehicles. Vehicle weight is not distributed equally on all four wheels. Weight distribution varies according to the design of a specific vehicle, but in general, about 60-70% of the weight rests on the front wheels, with the remainder resting on the rear wheels (Figure 4-11). Why is the weight not distributed evenly? Mainly because the weight follows the engine. Rear engine vehicles have more weight on the rear wheels. More

1- CONSTANT SPEED
2- DECELERATION
3- HARD BRAKING
4- STARTING TURN, MODERATE BRAKING
5- MAXIMUM CORNERING FORCES
6- FULL ACCELERATION
7- MODERATE ACCELERATION
8- CORNERING COMPLETED

Figure 4-10 The various stages of cornering illustrate the changes in weight transfer and tire loading during a turn.

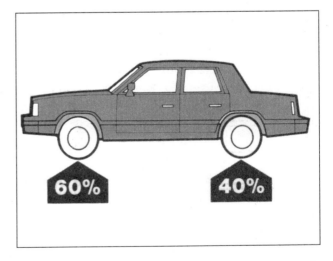

Figure 4-11 Typical vehicle weight distribution. (Chrysler)

weight on the front wheels is not a problem because handling and road holding ability are improved for ordinary drivers when more of the vehicle weight is positioned forward of its center.

When the brakes are applied, up to 70% of the vehicle weight is transferred to its front end. This weight transfer causes the front of the vehicle to sink or dip, allowing the rear to rise or lift up (Figure 4-12). To offset this weight transfer, the front brakes must be applied with more force than the rear brakes. If the front and rear brakes are applied equally under weight transfer conditions, the rear wheels can lock up and cause the vehicle to skid.

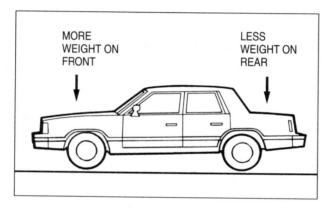

Figure 4-12 Applying the brakes suddenly causes a partial transfer of weight from the rear to the front, resulting in front end dip and rear end lift.

During cornering, centrifugal force transfers weight from the inside wheels to those on the outside. Such weight transfer loads the outside springs and tires, and unloads the inside springs and tires, with the result that traction is no longer equal on both sides of the vehicle. This does NOT change the total vehicle weight, but means that more weight is carried by the outer springs and tires. In some vehicles, weight transfer can create enough **body roll** to actually lift the inside wheels clear of the road surface.

CENTER OF GRAVITY AND THE ROLL CENTER

Vehicle mass is directly related to a theoretical point called the 'center of gravity'. Where the center of gravity is located determines the amount of weight transfer during cornering, and thus the amount of the total load that each tire must take. In theory, the center of gravity can be assumed to be located on the vehicle center line, but in real life, it may be located slightly to one side of the center line because the engine or other heavy components may be installed off-center. If the center of gravity could be located at ground level and exactly between the axles on the vehicle center line, there would be NO weight transfer at all. Realistically, however, the point must be clear of the road and located somewhere in the mass of the vehicle (Figure 4-13). The location will be influenced by vehicle load, just as the mass distribution is. If the load is uneven enough to move the center of gravity, cornering ability will increase in one direction, and decrease in the other.

As a vehicle negotiates a corner, mass transfers to the outside of the vehicle, and tries to roll it over. All vehicles have a roll center or theoretical point about which the

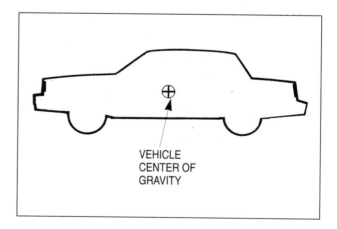

Figure 4-13 A vehicle's center of gravity is its balance point; and the exact center of the mass.

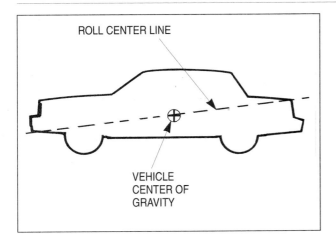

Figure 4-14 A vehicle's roll center is an imaginary line that traverses the center of the vehicle from front-to-rear at a declining angle.

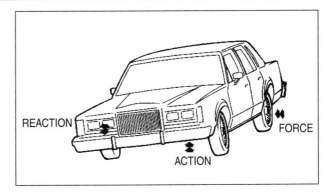

Figure 4-15 When a stabilizer or antiroll bar twists, the resistance of the bar tends to reduce body roll. (Ford Motor)

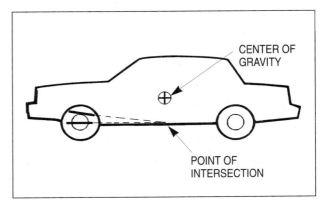

Figure 4-16 Front end dive can be minimized by changing the angle of the front control arm mounting points so that imaginary lines drawn from each control arm will meet at a point underneath the center of gravity.

vehicle mass rotates. Unlike the center of gravity, which is a single point somewhere near the center of the vehicle, the roll center is a line extending through the entire length of the vehicle. The rear of this line generally will be higher than the front, so a side view of the roll center would find it slanting downward toward the front (Figure 4-14).

Antiroll or **stabilizer bars** are used to create a firmer attachment between the wheels and the vehicle mass. They generally are used on front suspensions to reduce the amount of camber change (wheel lean) by offsetting the forces imposed on one wheel against the forces applied to the other (Figure 4-15). In this respect, they have a positive effect on tire loading during cornering. Unfortunately, the wheels are no longer truly independent, since the bar tries to make both wheels move together.

DIVE AND SQUAT CONTROL

During brake application, vehicle weight transfers from the rear to the front, causing the front of the vehicle to dip or dive, and the rear to lift up as shown in Figure 4-12.

This effect can be minimized by mounting the control arms at an angle, so that an imaginary line drawn through the inner control arm pivot points will meet or converge at a point under the center of gravity (Figure 4-16).

The opposite of dive is called 'squat' and occurs when the vehicle moves forward from a standing start under heavy acceleration. Squat involves a lifting of the front end while the rear end dives (Figure 4-17). It primarily affects RWD vehicles, since FWD vehicles apply power to the road through the front wheels. Squat is con-

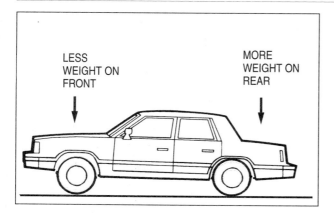

Figure 4-17 Power squat caused by heavy acceleration results in the rear of the vehicle diving, while the front lifts up.

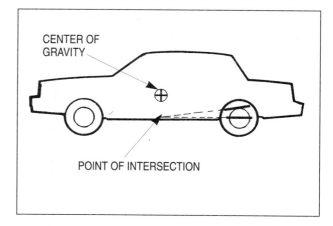

Figure 4-18 The problem of squat can be reduced by changing the angle of the rear control arm mounting points in the same way to lower the center of gravity when imaginary lines are drawn through the arms.

trolled in the same way as dive, except that the locating members for the rear axle housing are mounted at angles to provide a convergence of the imaginary lines under the center of gravity (Figure 4-18).

SUSPENSION GEOMETRY

The dictionary defines geometry as 'a branch of mathematics dealing with the measurement, properties, and relationships of points, lines, angles, surfaces and solids'. Applied to an automotive suspension, these related points, lines, and angles are primarily responsible for maintaining the tire contact patch in constant contact with the road surface with the least amount of tire wear and smoothest handling.

Since the wheel must be attached to the frame through pivot points of some kind, vertical movement of the wheel will take the path of an arc around those pivot points. This causes the wheel and tire to continually change attitude in relation to the road surface, except in the case of a rigid rear axle. In that design the wheels remain perpendicular to the roadway at all times, except for the effect that movement of one wheel has on the other. The front wheels on most vehicles are independently

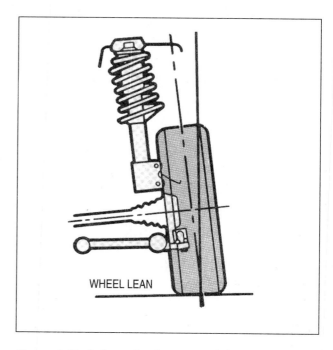

Figure 4-19 Independently mounted front wheels will lean, depending on how much the suspension is loaded. (Ford Motor)

suspended, causing the reaction known as 'camber change' or 'wheel lean' (Figure 4-19). While wheels attached to a solid axle essentially remain perpendicular to the road surface, independently suspended wheels will lean to the extent allowed by the geometry designed into the suspension, or allowed by wear or incorrect wheel alignment. You will learn more about camber and other aspects of suspension geometry in the chapter on suspension angles and wheel alignment.

SUMMARY

How a vehicle handles on the road depends on its wheelbase, track, and how well its suspension interacts with certain physical forces. Changes in wheelbase or track, such as wheel setback, axle offset, or axle sideset will affect the vehicle. Such changes generally result from collision damage, but also may be caused by worn or loose suspension components.

The key to directional control and vehicle stability is tire traction, or adhesion to the road surface. Tire adhesion is influenced by several factors, especially during cornering maneuvers. As long as the traction provided by the tires is greater than centrifugal force, the vehicle will go where it is steered. When centrifugal force exceeds tire traction, the tires will slip or skid across the road surface, and directional control will be lost. The load applied on a vehicle's tires and suspension changes constantly during steering maneuvers.

A vehicle designed with a slight amount of understeer is safest for average drivers, but a knowledgeable driver can control vehicle oversteer in a cornering situation by

ENGINEERING THE SUSPENSION

SPOTLIGHT

Tire design primarily determines how well a vehicle will grip the road. Suspension design has more to do with the way the vehicle feels as it enters and leaves a corner, how stable it is in a straight line, and how driveable and safe it is at or near the absolute limit in a turn. When you turn the steering wheel, you are changing the angle of the front wheels in an attempt to get them to go in the desired direction. At the same time, the wheels are doing a little steering of their own. Depending on how the vehicle is leaning or dipping on its springs, the suspension linkage is tilting and turning the wheels in subtle ways the engineers have pre-calculated, compensating for any faults or enhancing the virtues of the chassis.

Not too long ago, a suspension was engineered by trial-and-error. The basic design chosen was installed on a prototype vehicle and then 'tuned' with rubber isolation mounts and bushings. After the prototype was tested and evaluated, changes were made to the suspension components, mounts, and bushings that were likely to correct whatever faults the engineers found with their original design. Over the years, this gradually became one of the finest 'black arts' practiced by engineers — camber curves, stabilizer rates, compliance caused by linkage movement and bushing compression, sideview swing arm slope. These are only a few of the factors involved in the complex world of suspension geometry that are no longer calculated by seat-of-the-pants analysis.

What was once done by trial and error with graphs and slide rules is now the province of sophisticated computers and software. Engineers now feed a suspension design into the computer and are able to predict component performance almost instantly, without the extensive prototype work of the past. One such technique, finite element analysis, breaks the component design into its essential features and allows a computer-simulated analysis of its proposed operation. The entire suspension can be attached to a particular body design and test driven in the computer over a variety of simulated road conditions to test its response. Changes can be fed into the computer to see how they will alter the vehicle's handling characteristics. In this way, design modifications can be made while the vehicle is still on the drawing board.

proper use of braking and acceleration. Vehicle weight is distributed with a bias toward the front, but since this distribution changes under braking or cornering conditions, the suspension must be designed to function within specified parameters.

The center of gravity is a theoretical point located in the mass of a vehicle near the center line. The roll center is an imaginary line about which the vehicle mass revolves. The center of gravity will change according to vehicle load. Antiroll or stabilizer bars help to counteract the natural tendency of a vehicle to roll over during a sharp turn. Although it results from the use of a suspension, a certain amount of body roll is good, as it lets the driver know how hard the vehicle is cornering.

Vehicle dive is caused by braking; squat results from hard acceleration at a standing stop. Both conditions can be reduced by the angle at which the suspension control arms are mounted.

❓ REVIEW QUESTIONS

1. Technician A says that a vehicle's wheelbase is a measurement of the distance between the two wheels on one axle. Technician B says that a vehicle's track is the distance between the hubs of the front and rear wheels. Who is right?
   (A) A only
   (B) B only
   (C) Both A and B
   (D) Neither A nor B

2. Individual frame to wheel measurements can be used to determine:
   (A) if the rear axle is offset to the left or right.
   (B) the forward or rearward position of each wheel.
   (C) if the front wheels have a caster problem.
   (D) if the rear wheels have a camber problem.

3. Technician A says that an unequal wheelbase between the left and right sides of a vehicle is called wheel setback. Technician B says that it is called axle offset. Who is right?
   (A) A only
   (B) B only

(C) Both A and B
(D) Neither A nor B

4. Technician A says that the rear axle thrust line describes the direction in which the rear wheels will track. Technician B says that both axle offset and axle sideset will cause the vehicle to 'dog track'. Who is right?
   (A) A only
   (B) B only
   (C) Both A and B
   (D) Neither A nor B

5. A negative thrust angle results when the thrust line:
   (A) projects to the left of the geometric centerline.
   (B) projects to the right of the geometric centerline.
   (C) is the same as the geometric center line.
   (D) is aligned with the geometric center line.

6. When a tire revolves, the part of its tread that contacts the road surface is momentarily _____, relative to the road, regardless of vehicle speed.
   (A) going faster
   (B) stopped
   (C) going slower
   (D) none of the above

7. Technician A says that side loads transmitted to the tires cause them to deform, creating a slip angle. Technician B says that the tires do NOT really slip, but twist at the point of contact. Who is right?
   (A) A only
   (B) B only
   (C) Both A and B
   (D) Neither A nor B

8. Maximum tire traction is obtained when tire to road slippage is approximately:
   (A) 10-20%
   (B) 15-25%

(C) 20-25%
(D) 20-30%

9. Technician A says that vehicle oversteer is the most desirable condition. Technician B says that understeer is the safest condition for the average driver. Who is right?
   (A) A only
   (B) B only
   (C) Both A and B
   (D) Neither A nor B

10. Technician A says that vehicle weight generally is distributed with a bias toward the front. Technician B says that weight transfer during braking causes the front of the vehicle to dip and the rear to lift up. Who is right?
    (A) A only
    (B) B only
    (C) Both A and B
    (D) Neither A nor B

11. Technician A says that centrifugal force during cornering transfers weight from the outside wheels to those on the inside. Technician B says that a vehicle's center of gravity is located slightly to one side of of the centerline and near the center of the vehicle mass. Who is right?
    (A) A only
    (B) B only
    (C) Both A and B
    (D) Neither A nor B

12. The roll center of any vehicle is:
    (A) the distance between the center of the front and rear axle hubs.
    (B) the parallel alignment of the rear wheels to the front wheels and vehicle centerline.
    (C) a single point somewhere near the center of the vehicle.
    (D) a line extending the entire length of the vehicle.

13. Technician A says antiroll bars are used

to reduce wheel lean. Technician B says a vehicle's tendency to dip or dive at the front during braking can be controlled by the angle at which the control arms are mounted. Who is right?

(A) A only

(B) B only

(C) Both A and B

(D) Neither A nor B

14. Technician A says that squat occurs when a vehicle moves from a standing start under hard acceleration. Technician B says that squat primarily affects RWD vehicles. Who is right?

(A) A only

(B) B only

(C) Both A and B

(D) Neither A nor B

KINGPINS, BALL JOINTS, AND SPRINGS

"The cause of the problem is often prior solutions."
— Amory Lovins

 OBJECTIVES

After completion of this chapter, you should be able to:

- Explain the use of a kingpin and why it must be inclined.

- Describe the construction of a ball joint and tell why it is superior to a kingpin.

- Explain the difference between a compression-loaded ball joint and a tension-loaded ball joint.

- Explain steering axis inclination (SAI) and relate it to kingpin inclination.

- Compare leaf and coil springs, and discuss spring rate.

- Explain the function of torsion bars.

Various types of suspension systems are used to connect the wheels to the vehicle and minimize any jolting effect resulting from irregularities in the road. In addition to supporting the vehicle and cushioning the ride, front suspensions must be equipped with movable wheels for steering. The basic types of front and rear suspensions were discussed in two of the earlier chapters. In this chapter, you will learn about the design and operation of kingpins, ball joints, and the various types of springs used in automotive suspensions.

KINGPINS

As automotive suspensions evolved, it became clear that the answer both to steering the front wheels, and using brakes on all four wheels, was to keep the axle stationary and pivot each wheel on the axle end. The method used on early vehicles, and still found on some trucks today, was the use of kingpins as pivot points for the wheels. A kingpin is nothing more than a circular steel bar inserted through the steering knuckle yoke and the end of the axle (Figure 5-1). Initially, the yoke was a

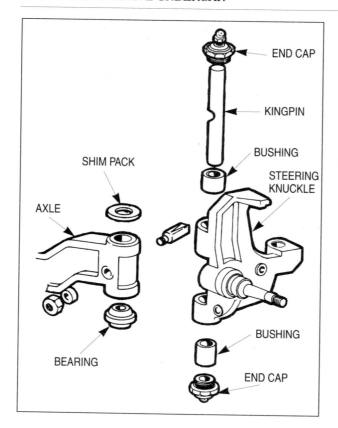

Figure 5-1 A typical kingpin front suspension. (Moog Automotive)

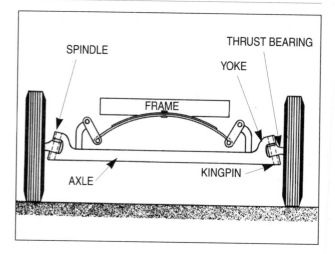

Figure 5-2 The most common suspension design used on early vehicles was the solid axle with an Elliott pivot. (Ammco Tools / ©Hennessy Industries)

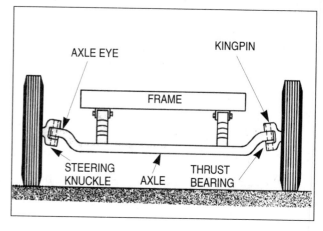

Figure 5-3 The solid axle with reversed Elliott pivot. (Ammco Tools / ©Hennessy Industries)

part of the axle, providing only a single pivot point. This design was called the Elliott kingpin (Figure 5-2). It was soon found to be wanting, and engineers moved the yoke to the steering knuckle. This provided two pivot points and became known as the 'reversed Elliott kingpin' (Figure 5-3). In all reversed Elliott designs, the kingpin is held in the axle by a clamp or tapered bolt, and the steering knuckle pivots on the kingpin.

Kingpin Inclination

In many early automotive designs, the kingpin was installed straight up and down. Steering a vehicle with a vertical kingpin is difficult because the steering pivot point is different from the road contact point of the tire. The distance between the steering pivot point and the tire center line is called the **scrub radius** (Figure 5-4). A large scrub radius makes it difficult to turn the wheels to either side. Since the pivot is inboard of the point of tire contact with the road, the tire does not pivot where it contacts the road, but has to move forward or backward as the steering wheel is turned. This has a direct and adverse effect on steering effort and the use of four-wheel brakes.

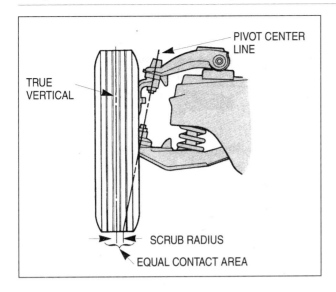

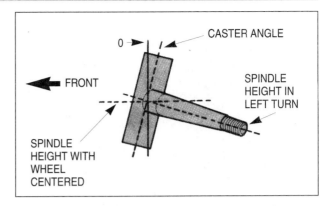

Figure 5-5 As the spindle swings, it either drops or raises, depending on which way it is turned. (Ford Motor)

Figure 5-4 The difference between the kingpin inclination line and where the tire/wheel center line intersect at the road is called the scrub radius. (Ford Motor)

To solve this problem, the kingpin must be inclined inward at the top and outward at the bottom, so that an imaginary line drawn through the kingpin will point exactly at the contact point of the tire with the road, reducing the scrub radius. By using an inclined kingpin, the wheel can simply pivot in place, and is not forced to move forward or backward during steering. Since only one point on the tire tread is the pivot center, the rest of the tire contact area scrubs or drags along, and the wider the tire, the greater the scrubbing action.

This tilting of the kingpin pivot center line also contributes to directional stability of the vehicle. Turning the front wheels to one side causes the spindle to revolve around the pivot. Due to the angle of the pivot, the spindle end on the inside of the turn swings down toward the road. Because the wheel and tire prevent the spindle end from getting closer to the road surface, the front of the vehicle on the inside of the turn is raised up whenever the wheels are turned from their straight-ahead position (Figure 5-5). The spindle on

the outside of the turn swings up, dropping the front of the vehicle on that side.

This inclination of the pivot lets the wheels resist turning initially, but also gives them a tendency to return to the straight-ahead position once the turn has been completed. This force is not sufficient to affect steering, and contributes to good directional stability. Kingpins ride on bushings or bearings, and must be kept properly lubricated.

BALL JOINTS

Ball joints appeared on the automotive scene during the 1950's and quickly replaced kingpins on passenger vehicles (some heavy-duty truck suspensions still use kingpins). By providing both a pivoting and a rotating motion, their use reduces the number of suspension pivot points and offers greater flexibility and mobility in the front suspension.

The ability to both pivot and rotate makes the ball joint ideal for use in connecting the top and bottom of the steering knuckle in an SLA suspension, the bottom of a strut suspension steering knuckle, and certain steering linkage connections. When a ball joint is used in a load-carrying position, vehicle mass prevents excessive play and clearance. If the ball joint is used

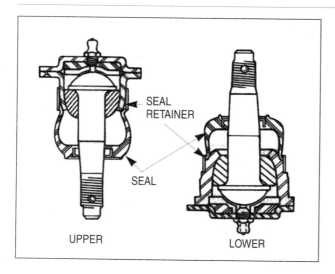

Figure 5-6 A cross section of a typical ball joint. Socket lubrication is retained by the seal. (Chevrolet Division, General Motors)

in an unloaded position that does not carry the mass of the vehicle, the joint is kept tight by friction inside the joint. Depending on design, this friction may be provided by a spring inside the ball joint.

The ball joint consists of a ball with a tapered stud and a cupped socket. The stud protrudes from the socket through a rubber seal that retains lubricating grease in the socket housing (Figure 5-6). Originally, ball joints used grease fittings for periodic lubrication, but many modern ball joints rotate in a prelubricated nylon bearing, and require no periodic service. They also have wear indicators that visually tell you when replacement is necessary (Figure 5-7). Other than wear, the major

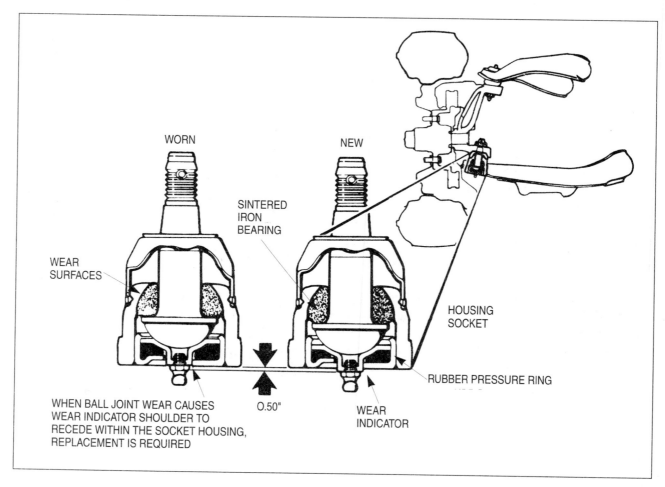

Figure 5-7 Operation of the wear indicator in a typical ball joint. (Moog Automotive)

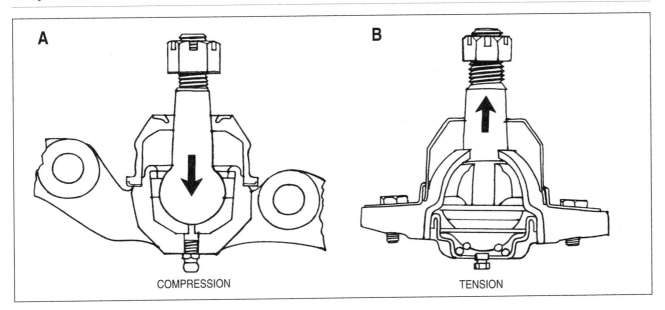

Figure 5-8 Compression- and tension-loaded ball joints. (McQuay-Norris)

problem with a ball joint involves damage to the rubber seal (Figure 5-6), which protects the lubricant in the ball socket from water, dirt, or sand contamination. Wear and seal damage are the only reasons for replacing a ball joint.

Depending on its use, a ball joint may support some part of the vehicle's mass. When it does, it is called either a tension- or a compression-loaded ball joint (Figure 5-8). The designs differ according to whether the force of the load tends to push the ball into the socket (compression) or pull it out of the socket (tension). Those ball joints that do NOT support the vehicle mass are called 'follower' or 'friction-loaded' ball joints. For example, if the coil springs in an SLA suspension are located between the control arms, the lower ball joints become the mass-carrying joints, with the upper ball joints acting as the follower joints (Figure 5-9). In an SLA suspension with the coil springs positioned on top of the upper control arms (Figure 5-10), the upper ball joints are the mass-carrying joints, with the lower ball joints serving as the follower joints.

In a strut suspension with the coil spring positioned at the top of the strut, the ball joint located at the bottom of the steering knuckle is a follower or friction-loaded joint (Figure 5-11). It allows the

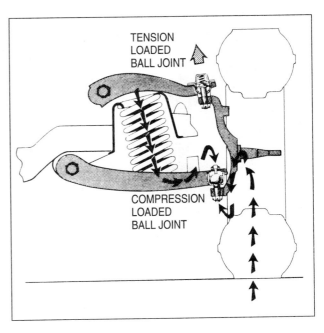

Figure 5-9 A coil spring suspension with a compression-loaded lower ball joint and tension-loaded upper ball joint. (Moog Automotive)

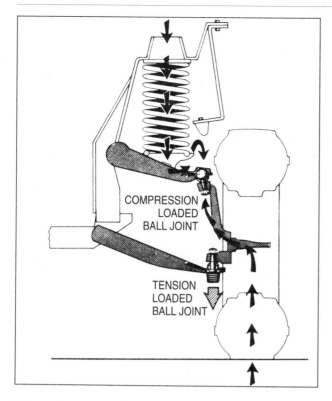

Figure 5-10 A coil spring suspension with a tension-loaded lower ball joint and compression-loaded upper ball joint. (Moog Automotive)

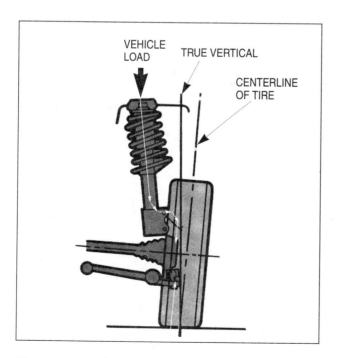

Figure 5-11 The ball joint used in a MacPherson strut suspension is tension-loaded. (Ford Motor)

strut and knuckle to pivot, but does NOT carry any mass. In a modified strut suspension, the ball joint becomes a mass-carrying joint because the coil spring is positioned between the frame crossmember and the lower control arm (Figure 5-12).

STEERING AXIS INCLINATION (SAI)

When ball joints are used instead of kingpins, they must have the same inclination angle as a kingpin. Before the development of strut suspensions, this inclination angle was called kingpin inclination or **ball joint inclination**, depending on the type of suspension used. The proper term now used is **steering axis inclination** (SAI), since strut suspensions have no kingpins or upper ball joints. SAI is the lean of an imaginary line drawn through the upper and lower pivot points (Figure 5-13). This line will intersect the road at the same point as the tire, just as a line drawn through the kingpin does. The number of degrees that this line will tilt inward from a true vertical line is called the **SAI angle**. Whether the suspension uses kingpins or ball joints, SAI provides both directional control and stability. It also helps return the wheels to a straight-ahead position after a turn and keep them there. You will learn more about SAI in the chapter on suspension angles and wheel alignment.

SPRINGS AND TORSION BARS

Springs provide the load-carrying connection between the frame and suspension components. When springs are compressed, they absorb energy by bending or twisting. The absorbed energy is retained by the spring momentarily, then released as the spring oscillates and gradually returns to its original shape. Three types of springs used in automotive suspensions: leaf springs, coil springs, and torsion bars (Figure 5-14).

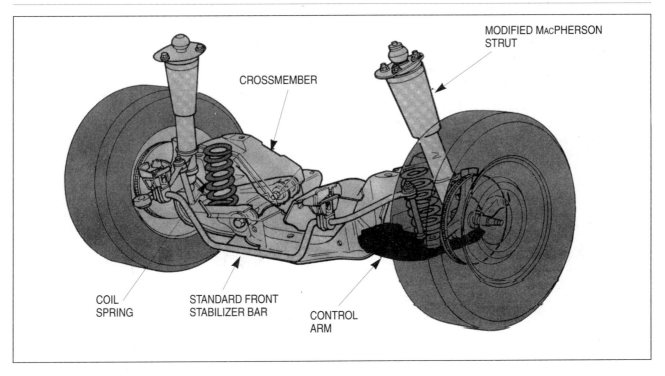

Figure 5-12 Positioning of the spring in a modified strut suspension turns the lower ball joint into one that carries mass. The MacPherson strut does NOT carry any mass, and acts as a shock absorber. (Ford Motor)

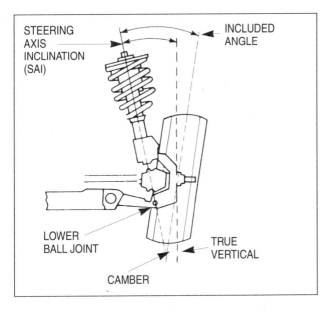

Figure 5-13 Like kingpin or ball joint suspensions, strut suspensions also create a scrub radius when an imaginary line between its pivot points does NOT intersect the road at the same point as a line drawn through the wheel/tire center line. This angle is referred to as the steering axis inclination, or SAI. (Oldsmobile Division, General Motors)

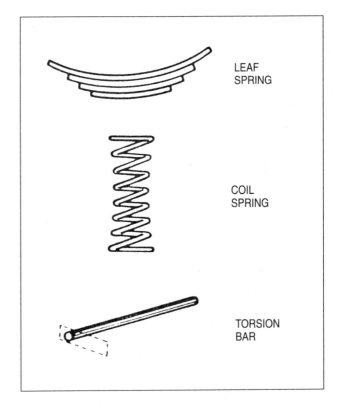

Figure 5-14 Types of automotive springs.

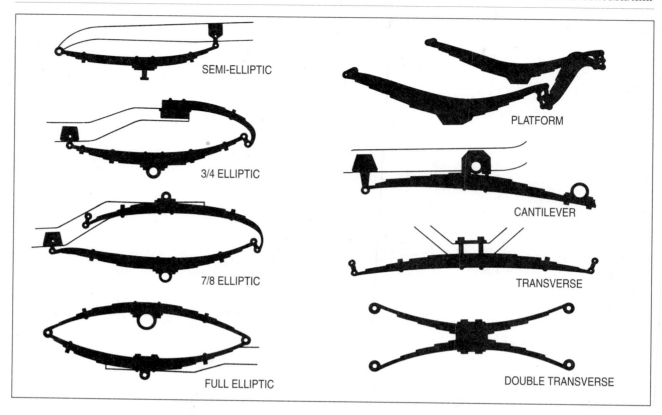

Figure 5-15 Leaf springs have been used in many different configurations, but the semi-elliptic design is the most popular.

LEAF SPRINGS

Leaf springs are the oldest, but not the most efficient type of energy absorber (Figure 5-15). They absorb **road shock** by flexing or bowing in the middle. Actually, leaf springs are the least efficient in terms of energy stored per pound of spring mass. While leaf springs typically store 300 in•lb_f of energy per pound of spring mass, a coil spring can store 700 in•lb_f, and a torsion bar will store 1,000 in•lb_f.

Early in their history, leaf springs were refined to a high degree. For example, the Chevrolet vehicles of the late 1920's incorporated the friction between the leaves as part of the damping system. In effect, this made the springs their own shock absorbers. While the ride was undeniably harsh, engineers learned that various substances, from asbestos to zinc, could be inserted between the leaves to reduce friction and transmitted road noise.

Although the energy-storing capability of a leaf spring is less than that of either a coil spring or torsion bar, it is possible to build a higher progressive spring rate into a leaf spring design. This means the further the spring is deflected, the greater the resistance it offers as more leaves are brought into play. With progressive springs, it is possible to provide a reasonably soft ride over minor road irregularities, with sufficient reserve action to prevent the suspension from bottoming when the vehicle encounters a severe bump.

Deflection Rate

Spring deflection rate is a term used to define how much force is required to bend a spring one inch. For example, if the spring has a rate of 300 lb, you must load it with 300 lb of either weight or impact force to bend it one inch. To bend it two inches, you need 600 lb, and so on until you reach the limit of the spring travel. Thus, a progressive rate spring might require 300 lb for the first inch, 600 lb for the second inch, and so forth.

Spring deflection rate can be varied in numerous ways; the most common methods used with leaf springs are to:

- increase the number of leaves
- increase the thickness of the leaves
- a combination of both.

Generally speaking, the heavier single leaf spring is used only on lightweight vehicles. As the vehicle mass increases, more leaves must be used to carry it. This results from the fact that as the thickness of a single leaf is increased, you encounter the limitation of elasticity. In this case, elasticity is defined not only as the ability to stretch, but also as the ability to return to its original shape after being deformed. When a flat spring leaf is bent, the molecules on the outside of the curve are stretched, while those on the inside are compressed (Figure 5-16). The thicker the

leaf, the more stretch is required to bend it a given amount. Thus, as you increase thickness, you soon reach a point called the **elastic limit** or 'limit of elasticity'. When the leaf is bent beyond this point, it will NOT return to its original shape and therefore is no longer a spring, but only a piece of permanently bent steel. Spring deflection rates vary considerably and you should make sure that any replacement springs you install have the same deflection rate as those being replaced. Coil springs and torsion bars have different deflection rate characteristics, and will be discussed individually.

Leaf Spring Designs

When leaf springs are used in a rear suspension, they may be symmetrical or asymmetrical.

- A spring is symmetrical when the rear axle is positioned in the center of the spring, or an equal distance from the two ends of the main leaf (Figure 5-17).
- The spring is asymmetrical when the rear axle is NOT positioned in the center of the spring (Figure 5-18).

Because of their short, stiff front section and longer flexible rear section, asymmetrical springs have a greater resistance to rear axle acceleration windup than those with a symmetrical design.

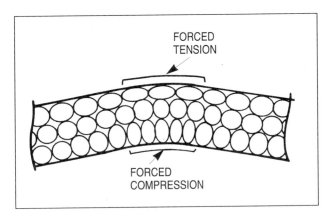

Figure 5-16 When a leaf spring moves, the molecules on one side stretch or elongate while those on the opposite side are compressed. If this stretch/compression process exceeds the elastic limit of the spring, it will be permanently bent. (General Motors)

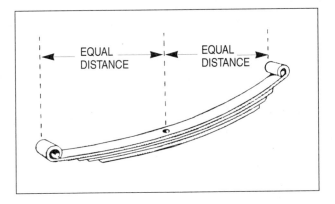

Figure 5-17 A symmetrical leaf spring. (Chrysler)

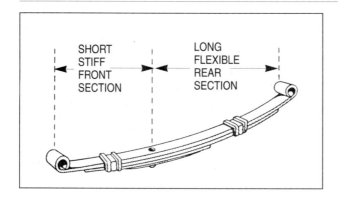

Figure 5-18 An asymmetrical leaf spring. (Chrysler)

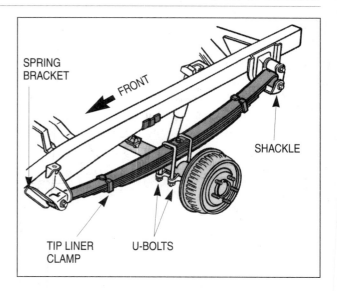

Figure 5-19 Leaf spring attachment. (General Motors)

The ability to mount leaf-type springs further apart and therefore closer to the rear wheels of a vehicle decreases body sway and increases lateral stability over the use of rear coil springs. Unfortunately, springs will eventually sag because of the mass they support. A sagging spring changes the trim height of the vehicle and decreases directional control and stability. All springs on the vehicle will not sag or fail at the same time. More likely, they will fail one at a time. For example, if the left rear spring fails, the left rear corner of the vehicle will sag and the right front corner of the vehicle will be raised up. When springs are replaced, they should be replaced in front or rear pairs, NOT individually, so that the vehicle will be the same height on both sides.

Leaf Spring Attachment

Shackles are the most common method of mounting leaf springs to the vehicle frame (Figure 5-19). These are connected to the main leaf of the spring at the shackle eye, which consists of a loop bent in the end of the leaf. A bolt inserted through the shackle and loop rests in a rubber bushing and is held with a nut. The spring assembly is positioned under or over the axle by a spring plate and two U-bolts. This type of mounting permits the shackle to swing as the spring flexes. Without this

movement, the entire spring assembly would be rigid, without any springing action. The shackle bushing also reduces transmission of spring vibration and road noise to the vehicle frame.

Coil Springs

Coil springs offer their own mixture of advantages and disadvantages, and have more in common with torsion bars than with leaf springs. Since coil springs absorb road shock primarily by twisting and flexing, there is only a slight amount of bending involved when a coil is compressed. The twisting of the spring wire is the same action that stores the energy in a torsion bar.

In spite of working to a lower stress point, the energy-storage capability of a coil spring is greater than that of a leaf-type spring, although less than that of torsion bars. Since it requires less material to make a coil of equal strength to a leaf, the unsprung mass also should be less, but the increased complexity of the suspension system required by the use of coil springs becomes a disadvantage.

Because of the smaller amount of space

they occupy, coil springs lend themselves to a wider range of design. An even more compact suspension package can be designed by positioning the **shock absorber** inside the coil. The use of coil springs requires a more sophisticated system of vibration damping and sway control. It was a lack of this technology in the early days of coil spring usage that led to the oversized swaying vehicles of the early 1950's.

The average coil spring used on a full-size North American passenger car requires approximately 10-12 ft of metal wound into a coil. The number and diameter of coils used in the spring are a function of a long and complicated set of formulas involving spring rate, pitch, and load, which in essence indicate that the heavier the vehicle, the more coils must be used and the thicker each coil must be. Like most suspension components, coil springs are at best a compromise. Their improved ride characteristic often is offset by the increased cost of the more elaborate suspension systems needed to accommodate them. As with all other types of springs, coils must be mounted on rubber. Metal-to-metal contact raises transmitted road noise inside the vehicle to an intolerable level. Rubber pads are located at the ends of the coil and should be checked for wear whenever the coil is replaced.

Like leaf spring assemblies, coil springs tend to eventually fail from supporting vehicle weight. When this happens, the trim height of the vehicle will change, causing reduced directional control and stability. A coil spring that has failed will affect the vehicle in the same manner as a failed leaf spring assembly, and like leaf springs, coils should be replaced in front or rear pairs, not individually.

TORSION BARS

Torsion bars have the greatest energy-absorbing ability of all automotive springs, and have been used since the mid-1950's, although their application has not been widespread. For the most part, their use has been restricted to Chrysler vehicles, some Volkswagen designs, and numerous small imported pickup trucks. Because this means of springing a vehicle takes the form of two long bars that hold vehicle mass in suspension by twisting, a torsion bar suspension can be used where coil springs would interfere with other components or require too much vertical room.

One reason why torsion bars have not been as popular as coil or leaf springs is that once a maximum load and stress has been decided, the bar must be a particular length with a specified cross-section. Unlike a coil spring, whose diameter and length can be varied to fit into the available space, the only practical way of varying a torsion bar is to change the size of its cross-section.

In most torsion bar installations, one end of the bar connects to a lower control arm, and is anchored to the frame at the other end (Figure 5-20). This allows the control arm freedom to pivot with the sus-

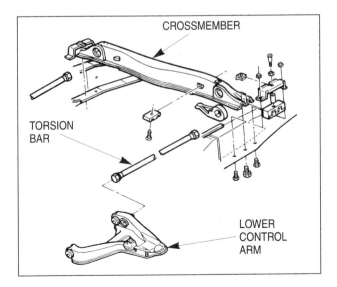

Figure 5-20 Typical torsion bar installation. (General Motors)

SPOTLIGHT

COMPOSITE LEAF SPRINGS

The time-honored multileaf spring, once commonly found on automobiles, seems to have found a new lease on life. Although independent suspensions and FWD vehicles have taken over much of the market once dominated by leaf springs, trucks and some specialty vehicles continue to use them. With recent advancements in technology, the leaf spring made of steel may be on its way out, to be replaced by computer-designed springs made of fiberglass strands and epoxy resin. While the 1981 Corvette generally is credited as the first production vehicle to use a composite rear leaf spring, the 1984 Corvette used them front and rear. Since then, other carmakers have taken a close look at the technology. One such is Chrysler, who introduced a fiberglass rear spring on some 2WD Dakota pickups in 1987.

There are several reasons why the automotive industry is interested in the use of composite rather than steel leaf springs. Composite springs reduce the mass of a vehicle by about 35 lb, yet they are just as durable. For example, if it fails, the composite spring delaminates. During this process, it loses load-carrying capacity gradually, just as a steel spring does when it starts to sag. Composite springs provide better ride control than steel springs, because they have a more consistent deflection rate and static load capability.

The composite spring is designed by computer to take into account the inherent qualities of the fiberglass and resin materials that provide the desired deflection rate and geometry. The design is then manufactured in a custom-design mold to produce a constant-width but variable-thickness single leaf. The thickness increases from the ends to the center, just as it would with a multileaf steel spring. This design improves the vehicle ride, since there is no inter-leaf friction when driving over small bumps. The damping quality of the composite material also reduces road noise transmitted to the inside of the vehicle. Equally important, the composite spring is more resistent to corrosion, chips, nicks, and damage from mechanical abuse.

There has been much research and talk over the years about the use of composite materials for automotive components, such as engines. Composite powertrains are still to come, but in the meantime, composites are gradually replacing metal in the form of body panels, gas tanks, and suspension parts.

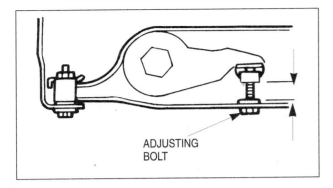

Figure 5-21 Torsion bar adjustment. (General Motors)

pension, twisting the torsion bar as the wheel moves up and down. An adjusting bolt on the end of the bar attached to the frame permits vehicle trim height adjustment (Figure 5-21), a feature not possible with leaf or coil spring suspensions. Because torsion bars are NOT interchangeable from one side of the vehicle to the other, they are marked to indicate the correct side of the vehicle on which they should be installed.

Torsion bars, like coil springs, also are prone to developing surface nicks or scratches that can create **stress raisers** and lead to cracks. Once this happens, the cracks will spread quickly through the spring steel of the bar and result in failure.

For this reason, torsion bars generally are coated with a protective coat of heavy paint and should be carefully inspected for defects whenever they are removed from the vehicle.

SUMMARY

The kingpins that connected early suspensions to the front wheels have been replaced by ball joints, which are more versatile. A kingpin permits only a circular rotation around its axis, but a ball joint can pivot and rotate freely. Ball joints may act as a load-carrying or non-load-carrying pivot point.

Both kingpins and ball joints have an inclination angle called steering axis inclination (SAI). This is the angle of lean of an imaginary line drawn through the upper and lower pivot points and intersects the road at the same point as the tire does. SAI provides directional control and stability.

Springs provide the load-carrying connection between the frame and suspension components. Carmakers use three types of springs: leaf, coil, and torsion bars. Springs absorb energy by bending or twisting. Torsion bars absorb the most energy; leaf springs absorb the least.

❓ REVIEW QUESTIONS

1. The first method developed for pivoting the front wheels of a vehicle was called:
   (A) an Elliott kingpin.
   (B) a reversed Elliott kingpin.
   (C) a compression-loaded ball joint.
   (D) a tension-loaded ball joint.

2. Technician A says that the use of a vertical kingpin increases steering effort during a turn. Technician B says that kingpin inclination reduces tire scrub radius. Who is right?

   (A) A only
   (B) B only
   (C) Both A and B
   (D) Neither A nor B

3. Technician A says that inclining a kingpin improves the directional stability of a vehicle. Technician B says that ball joints do NOT require the inclination angle necessary for kingpins.
   (A) A only
   (B) B only
   (C) Both A and B
   (D) Neither A nor B

4. Technician A says that kingpins tilt and swivel. Technician B says that ball joints permit only a circular rotation around their axis. Who is right?
   (A) A only
   (B) B only
   (C) Both A and B
   (D) Neither A nor B

5. Technician A says that the lower ball joint in an SLA suspension with the coil spring resting on the lower control arm is a load-carrying joint. Technician B says that a tension-loaded ball joint usually is a follower joint. Who is right?
   (A) A only
   (B) B only
   (C) Both A and B
   (D) Neither A nor B

6. When a coil spring rests on the upper control arm of an SLA suspension, which ball joint transmits the vehicle mass?
   (A) The lower
   (B) The upper
   (C) Both
   (D) Neither

7. Technician A says that a leaf spring absorbs emergy by bending. Technician B says that leaf springs are less efficient at storing energy than coil springs or torsion bars. Who is right?
   (A) A only
   (B) B only
   (C) Both A and B
   (D) Neither A nor B

8. Technician A says that as the spring leaf increases in thickness, its limit of elasticity decreases. Technician B says that bending a spring leaf beyond its elastic limit will only temporarily distort it. Who is right?
   (A) A only
   (B) B only
   (C) Both A and B
   (D) Neither A nor B

9. Technician A says that mounting a leaf spring close to the rear wheels of a vehicle increases body sway. Technician B says a leaf spring mounted close to the rear wheels provides better stability than coil springs. Who is right?
   (A) A only
   (B) B only
   (C) Both A and B
   (D) Neither A nor B

10. The weight or force necessary to deflect a leaf spring one inch is called:
   (A) spring rate
   (B) sprung mass
   (C) unsprung mass
   (D) spring rebound

11. Technician A says that a coil spring absorbs road shock by twisting and flexing. Technician B says that a torsion bar absorbs road shock by twisting. Who is right?
   (A) A only
   (B) B only
   (C) Both A and B
   (D) Neither A nor B

12. Technician A says that a coil spring will eventually sag and reduce the height of the vehicle. Technician B says that the only practical way to change the maximum load and stress carried by a torsion bar is to change its cross-section. Who is right?
   (A) A only
   (B) B only
   (C) Both A and B
   (D) Neither A nor B

SHOCK ABSORBERS, STRUTS, AND STABILIZER BARS

"He who seeks for methods without having a definite problem in mind seeks for the most part in vain." — David Hilbert

---

 OBJECTIVES

After completion of this chapter, you should be able to:

- Describe briefly the purposes and operation of hydraulic shock absorbers and struts.

- Explain why bushings and insulators are necessary, and list 3 reasons why they are made of rubber.

- Discuss the purposes of strut rods and stabilizer bars.

There is a common misconception that shock absorbers absorb road shock, as their name suggests. Actually, absorbing road shock is the job of the vehicle's springs; shock absorbers provide a damping action that controls spring action by preventing excessive spring oscillation.

When the vehicle wheel strikes an obstacle on the road surface, it moves upward. This causes the spring to deflect and absorb the upward motion, instead of allowing it to be transmitted to the frame. After passing over the bump on the road, the wheel is pushed by the spring back down to the road surface with considerable force. The shock of the tire hitting the road sends out shock waves that can actually break a spring. Early carmakers found out

very quickly that they needed shock absorbers not so much for ride control, but to keep the springs from breaking. Today, springs do not break as easily as they used to, and well designed shock absorbers contribute a lot to a good ride.

SHOCK ABSORBERS

When the spring releases the stored energy, it oscillates through a series of extensions and contractions until the energy is totally expended. How fast and how great these oscillations are, will depend on the design of the spring and the suspension, though most springs oscillate excessively. The stronger the spring, the faster the oscillations. If you stretch a rubber band between two fingers until it is taut, and then pull and release it, you are simulating the action of a spring. As the rubber band releases the energy, it will travel back and forth, or oscillate, until it finally returns to its original position.

To prevent spring oscillations from being transmitted through the vehicle to the driver or passengers, engineers found that shock absorbers (or dampers, as they are called in Europe) would change spring energy into heat that can be dissipated into the air. The heat created by shock absorber operation can have adverse effects on the fluid used inside the unit, and under certain conditions, can get so hot that touching the shock absorber will result in a serious burn. For this reason, race cars often duct cool air to the shocks, just as they do to the brakes.

Shock absorbers also have secondary functions. They help:

- keep the vehicle's wheels on the road
- control bounce and wheel **tramp** or **hop**
- reduce roll and side sway
- reduce shake and body pitch
- prevent the suspension from bottoming and topping.

HYDRAULIC OPERATION

Modern direct-action shock absorbers work on the principles of hydraulics, that is, fluid displacement through a series of valves. A shock absorber is a speed sensitive, hydraulic damping device — the faster its motion, the greater the internal resistance. Regardless of their manufacturer, nearly all hydraulic shock absorbers used on production vehicles are identical in design and appearance. They consist of a cylinder containing a fluid reservoir and a piston on the end of a rod. The rod extends from one end of the cylinder and generally is used as a mounting point. The other mounting point is attached to the closed end of the cylinder (Figure 6-1).

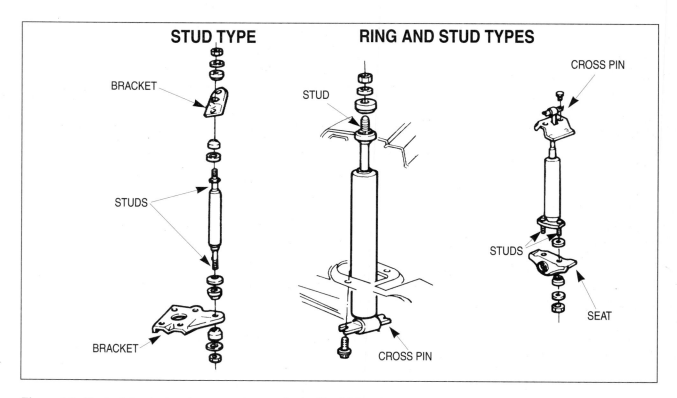

Figure 6-1 Typical shock absorber mounting methods. (Ford Motor)

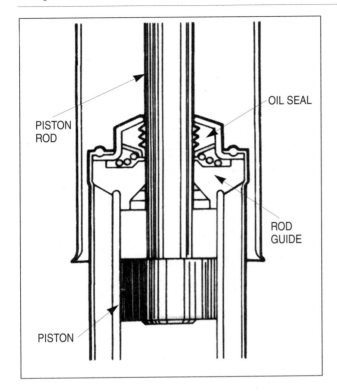

Figure 6-2 Piston operation in a typical shock absorber. (Chrysler)

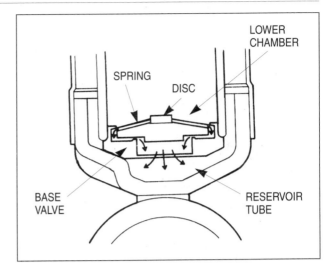

Figure 6-3 Shock absorber base valve operation. (Chrysler)

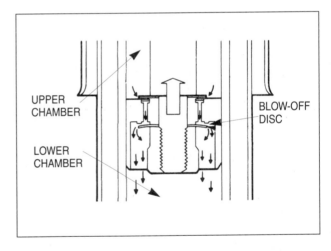

Figure 6-4 The blow-off valve disc deflects additional fluid flow. (Chrysler)

The up-and-down movement of the suspension pushes and pulls the actuating rod piston through the oil-filled cylinder (Figure 6-2). The piston contains metered orifices which allow the oil to pass from one side of the piston to the other at a specific rate. A second valve at the bottom of the oil reservoir controls the flow to provide a damping action in both directions of piston movement. When the suspension compresses, the piston moves downward and forces oil through the base valve at the bottom of the reservoir (Figure 6-3). The faster the piston speed, the greater the pressure that builds up below the piston and the greater the damping force. As the suspension rebounds, it pulls the piston up through the fluid above it. If the rebound speed becomes greater, the pressure build-up opens the blow-off disc (Figure 6-4). This permits the fluid to pass at a faster rate, preventing a harsh ride.

The larger the valves, the weaker the resistance, providing that a fluid of the proper consistency is used. As the piston moves within the cylinder, fluid flows from one side of the piston to the other, depending on the size of the valves. By changing valve and orifice sizes (Figure 6-5), engineers can provide a damping rate according to the requirements of any type of vehicle.

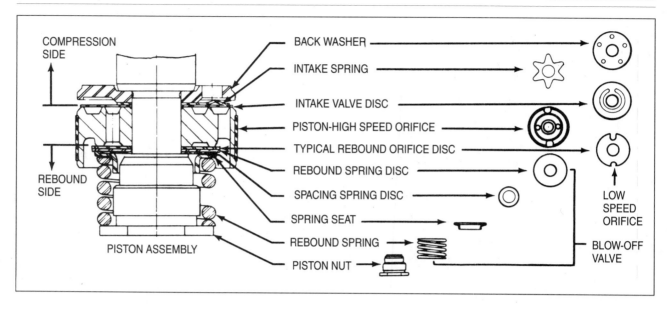

Figure 6-5 Redesigning the valves and orifices inside a shock absorber (called 'valving') will change the compression and rebound resistance levels according to piston speed. (Chevrolet Division, General Motors)

Compression Stroke

Downward movement of the actuating rod and piston lowers the pressure in the upper chamber A (Figure 6-6). As the volume of fluid in the lower chamber B is reduced, it flows up through the piston's outer passages, displacing the piston intake valve and filling chamber A. Since the piston rod takes up some of the volume in chamber A, an equivalent amount of fluid volume enters chamber C through the compression valve. Compression control results from the force required to move the fluid from chamber B to chamber A, and down through the three-stage compression valve to chamber C.

Rebound or Extension Stroke

Upward movement of the piston and rod applies pressure to chamber A (Figure 6-6). This forces the fluid down through the three-stage extension valve into chamber B. Now there is more volume in chamber B, but an insufficient amount of fluid remaining in chamber A to fill chamber B. Since the pressure in chamber C is greater, it forces the compression intake valve to unseat. Fluid now flows from chamber C into chamber B. The amount of force necessary to move the piston and transfer fluid through the 3-stage piston or rebound valve is known as 'extension control'.

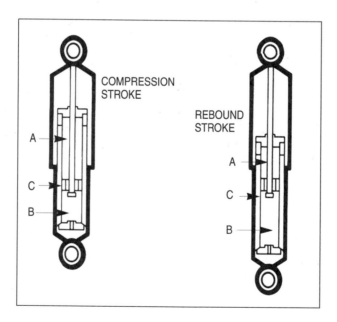

Figure 6-6 A shock absorber cycle consists of compression and rebound strokes. (Ford Motor)

VALVING AND FLOW VELOCITY

When fluid flows through an orifice, the pressure increases as the square of the speed or flow velocity. If an orifice is designed to provide restriction at high speeds (sharp blows), the same orifice will NOT create the necessary damping at low speed. For this reason, valves that open progressively as pressures increase are used. To further prevent the restriction from becoming excessive at high fluid speeds, progressive valves incorporate a relief valve that remains closed at low speeds.

Most shock absorbers have three or more operating stages during compression or extension. For example, during the compression cycle, oil flows through a small orifice at slow speed. As the flow velocity increases, it opens a spring operated valve, and under rapid flow velocity, the size of a valve pin orifice controls oil flow. During the extension cycle, the operation reverses: small orifices under the valve seat control oil flow at slow speed; oil flow works against a spring at higher speeds, and at very high speed, the size of the oil passages control oil flow.

Like any other hydraulic device, shock absorber fluid must be kept free of contamination by air. Since air can be compressed and will flow through an orifice or valving faster than a fluid, it will cause mushy operation. During conditions of heavy usage, the hydraulic fluid tends to foam or aerate, producing air bubbles. Generally, such air will pass through a drain passage into the reservoir, where an expansion space is provided above the fluid. If the air reaches the pressure cylinder, it will interfere with proper shock absorber operation and result in reduced efficiency. Many shock absorber designs contain a system of baffles that prevents air from working its way into the pressure cylinder.

OTHER TYPES OF SHOCK ABSORBERS

Although production vehicles generally are fitted with hydraulic shock absorbers that operate as described above, several other types are manufactured for automotive use. The most common are:

- Adjustable shock absorbers — this design contains an adjustable piston orifice. One approach is to rotate an adjuster nut to increase or decrease both compression and extension resistance. Another approach requires that the shock be compressed and the upper half rotated to align an arrow with a notch on the bottom half. Such shock absorbers usually provide three different settings — normal, firm, and extra firm. Their major disadvantage is that if the original setting selected is not suitable, the shock absorber must be removed from the vehicle, or at least detached at one end, to change the setting.

- Gas-charged shock absorbers — one type of gas-charged shock absorber contains a gas-filled plastic bag in the oil reservoir which compresses and expands during operation, or from heat expansion of the hydraulic fluid. Another type uses a pressurized reservoir. In both designs, the gas charge maintains a constant minimum pressure in the fluid chambers. Coupled with minor changes in valving, this results in an improved ride and damping. A major advantage of this design is that the oil in the chambers does NOT aerate (foam) or overheat during continuous operation on a rough road.

- Coil-over shock absorbers — this design generally is used to help the rear springs of a vehicle carry a heavier than normal load. They have

Figure 6-7 A coil-over shock absorber increases the load-carrying ability of the vehicle's springs. (Bilstein)

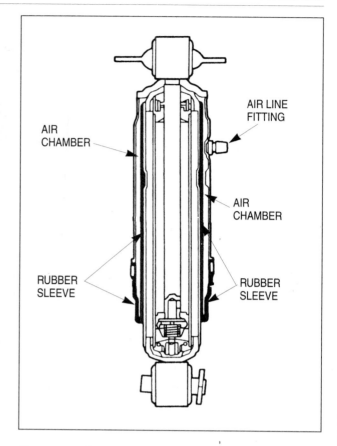

Figure 6-8 Cross-section of a typical air shock absorber. (General Motors)

a constant rate coil spring installed around the shock absorber body (Figure 6-7). The shock absorber mount contains the upper spring seat; the lower part of the body contains the lower seat.

- Air shock absorbers — are used as part of an automatic load leveling system on luxury passenger cars. A flexible membrane or neoprene bladder connects the piston rod dust shield to the shock absorber body, forming an air chamber (Figure 6-8). As the rear load increases, the air pressure in the shocks is automatically increased by a small compressor and air dryer assembly located in the engine compartment or under the rear crossmember; when the load

decreases, the shocks vent air pressure through the dryer as required. Aftermarket manufacturers also provide air shock absorbers, but they do NOT adjust automatically — their pressure must be adjusted manually, like that of a tire. The lift force provided by air shocks does NOT increase the load-carrying capacity of the vehicle; the axle and tires still have to carry the full load. Air shocks really act only as devices to maintain the vehicle at normal road height when carrying loads up to the vehicle's rated capacity.

- Steering dampers — some vehicles use a horizontally mounted shock absorber as a steering damper. This

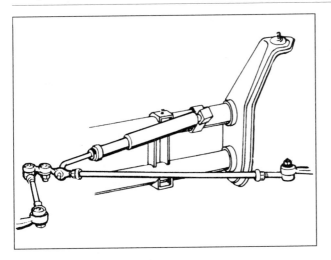

Figure 6-9 A type of shock absorber, the steering damper prevents the steering linkage from oscillating. (Moog Automotive)

SHOCK ABSORBER RATIOS

Shock absorbers used on production vehicles generally have more control over extension than compression. Shock absorber extension controls the sprung mass; shock absorber compression controls the unsprung parts of a chassis. The shock absorber ratio is designed according to suspension requirements, but is seldom published as a specification. The difference between, or the ratio of, extension and compression can be felt when you try to move a shock absorber in and out by hand. In most cases, it can be moved more easily in one direction than the other. The ratio can be anywhere in a range between 50/50 to 80/20; the first figure refers to extension and the second figure refers to compression.

MacPHERSON STRUTS

The switch to FWD cars has made the strut suspension popular. A strut generally is attached to the vehicle body at the top with an upper bearing plate (Figure 6-10), and

reduces road shock transmitted to the steering wheel and adds turning resistance to the steering. The damper body is connected to the frame or body, and the piston rod connects to the steering linkage (Figure 6-9).

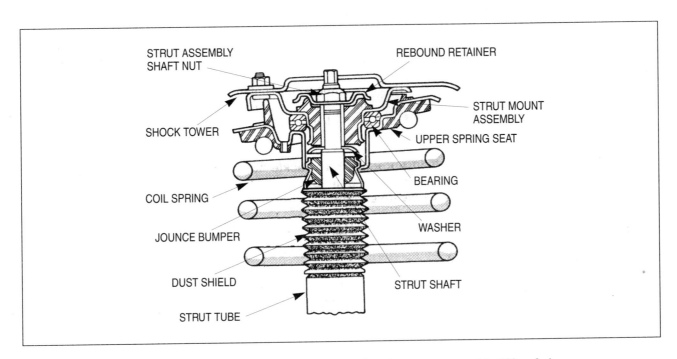

Figure 6-10 Struts are attached to the strut tower with an upper bearing mount assembly. (Chrysler)

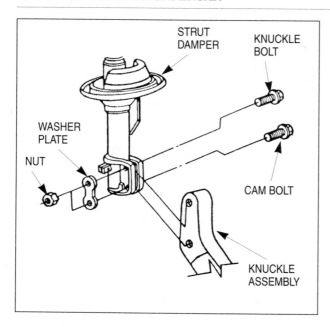

Figure 6-11 The lower end of a strut housing has an integral bracket that bolts to the steering knuckle. (Chrysler)

to the steering knuckle at the bottom by an integral mounting bracket on the strut housing (Figure 6-11). This method of mounting allows the strut to pivot with the steering action of the wheels.

Essentially an oversized shock absorber, the strut cartridge functions according to the same principles, controlling excessive spring movement and vehicle motion through the use of fluid under pressure. To prevent foaming of the fluid during its constant recirculation, many strut manufacturers pressurize the strut with a charge of nitrogen (like a gas-charged shock absorber) to reduce foaming and minimize fluid aeration.

CONVENTIONAL VS. MODIFIED STRUTS

Conventional struts have lower and upper spring seats built into the strut housing. A coil spring around the outside of the strut assembly supports the vehicle mass and maintains proper curb height. Modified strut designs do NOT incorporate the spring as part of the strut assembly, but

position it independently between the frame and lower control arm.

STRUT CARTRIDGE DESIGNS

The strut assembly used by some North American carmakers are sealed units and cannot be serviced separately. Although the coil spring can be replaced, a defective strut housing must be replaced with a new sealed unit. The strut assemblies used on many North American and most import vehicles contain a replaceable strut cartridge (Figure 6-12). This self-contained, factory-sealed unit consists of a pressure tube and piston rod that has been factory-calibrated. With this design, the strut assembly can be disassembled and a defective strut cartridge replaced.

SUSPENSION BUSHINGS AND INSULATORS

Carmakers use rubber bushings and insulators to prevent noise and vibration from frame, body, and suspension from reaching the passenger compartment. Most suspension designs incorporate rubber bumpers to limit the suspension travel caused by jounce and rebound (Figure 6-13). These bumpers are designed and located to prevent the suspension from hitting the frame or body as the vehicle travels over road irregularities. With the many different forces at work on a moving vehicle, bushings and insulators are important in preventing suspension movement that could affect directional control and stability.

For a number of reasons, rubber is the most efficient bushing and insulator material. It:

- has a high degree of compliance (the ability to allow for changes in position)
- does not require lubrication
- is silent and does not transfer minor vibrations.

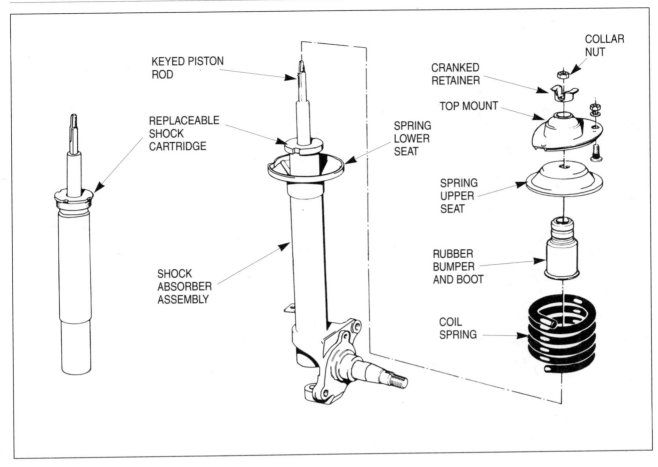

Figure 6-12 An exploded view of a strut with a replaceable shock cartridge. (Ford Motor)

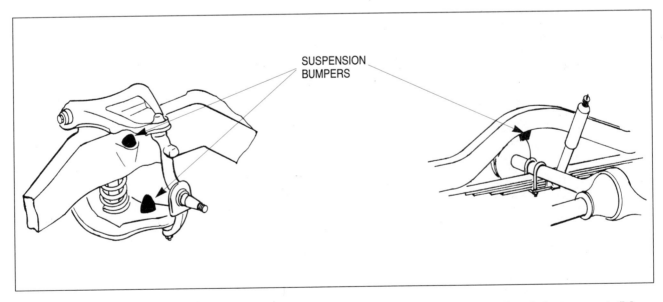

Figure 6-13 Rebound bumpers are strategically positioned to cushion the suspension when it bottoms out. (Moog Automotive)

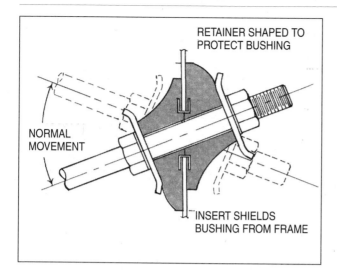

Figure 6-14 Bushing movement in a typical strut rod installation. (Moog Automotive)

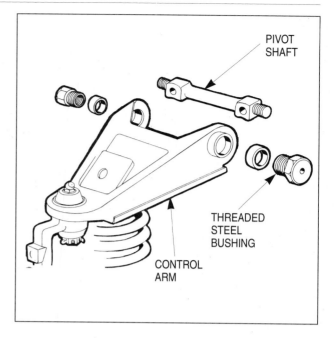

Figure 6-15 Pivot shaft and control arm bushings allow the control arm to move up and down, allowing the wheel/tire to move. (Moog Automotive)

Because of the torsilastic or elastic nature of rubber, bushings are highly efficient during a rotating, twisting, or swinging motion. They act in a manner similar to that of a torsion bar, which returns to its original position. This compliance or 'memory' feature helps components such as control arms to move without binding. When used at the ends of shock absorbers, strut rods, or in stabilizer bar links, they allow sufficient motion for suspension travel while absorbing road vibrations (Figure 6-14).

Control arms are attached to the vehicle frame at their pivot points by metal-clad rubber torsion bushings. Such bushings are susceptible to wear and deterioration, as they tend to develop cracks and checks. Some inner control arm pivots use a pivot shaft with metal screw-together bushings (Figure 6-15). The threaded ends of the pivot shaft mate with threaded nut-like bushings encased in metal and pressed into the ends of the control arm legs. The nut-like bushings allow control arm movement by rotating on the pivot shaft threads. This type of bushing tends to wear due to metal-to-metal contact.

Thick rubber insulators are used to mount the vehicle body to the frame of BOF designs. They are also used between the engine cradle and frame rail of a unitized body design (Figure 6-16). These insulators are specifically designed for each location to provide the greatest structural strength while minimizing road noise.

STRUT RODS

When the lower control arm pivot end is too narrow to control fore-and-aft movement, a bushing-mounted strut rod adds rigidity to the control arm (Figure 6-17). One end of the rod is bolted to the lower control arm; the other end attaches to a frame bracket with bushings (Figure 6-18). On many installations, the bushing end of the strut rod may be threaded to allow caster adjustment. If the bushing end or its frame mount become loose, it allows excessive lower control arm movement and changes the caster setting.

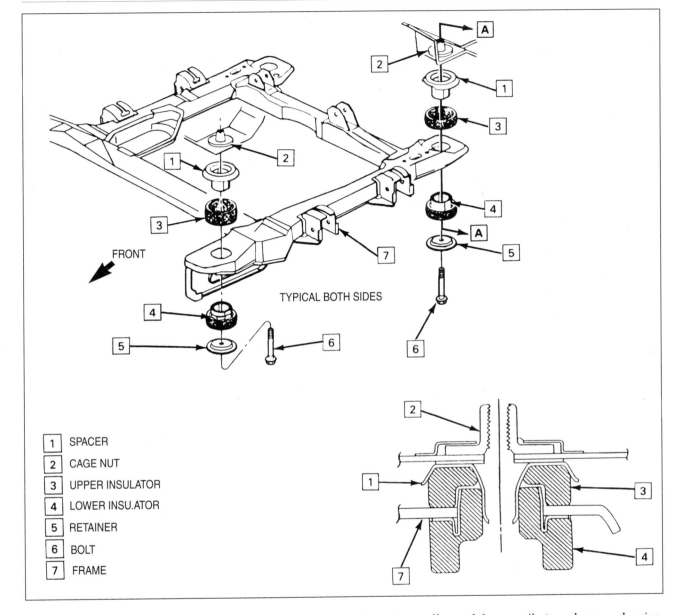

Figure 6-16 A typical example of insulators used with FWD engine cradles and frame rails to reduce road noise. (Oldsmobile Division, General Motors)

STABILIZER OR ANTI-ROLL BARS

Stabilizer or anti-roll bars (also called sway bars) connect both lower control arms (Figure 6-19) and transfer cornering forces from the outer to the inner wheel during a turn. This helps equalize wheel loads and counteracts the natural tendency for the body to lean or roll outward during cornering. When the vehicle is moving in a straight line, the bar helps to equalize spring action if one of the tires hits a bump or other irregularity in the road. In effect, the stabilizer bar acts as a miniature torsion bar connecting one side of the vehicle to the other. The bar is attached to the frame or a crossmember on each side of the vehicle with brackets containing

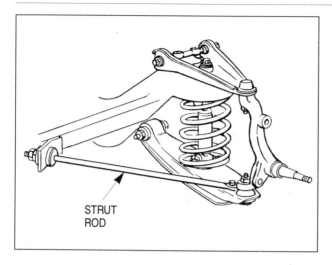

Figure 6-17 A strut rod and bushings is used with narrow control arms to add rigidity. (McQuay-Norris)

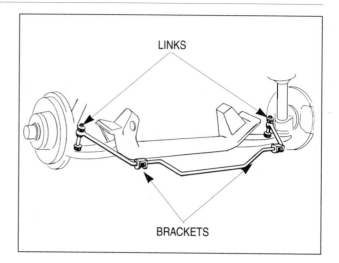

Figure 6-19 Stabilizer bars are bracket-mounted with bushings, and use a series of bushings in the links that connect the bar to the control arms. (Moog Automotive)

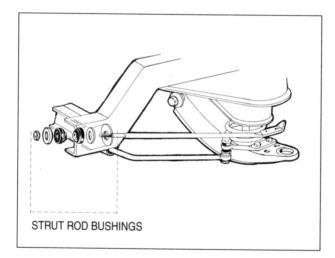

Figure 6-18 Strut rod bushings are used between the frame and strut rod to hold the control arm in the correct position. (Moog Automotive)

bushings, and at the control arm with a bolt, two sets of bushings, and steel washer to form a link.

SUMMARY

Shock absorbers and struts do not absorb road shock, as commonly thought, but instead provide a damping action to control excessive spring oscillations. Modern direct-action shocks and struts operate by displacing fluid through a series of valves, and orifices. The hydraulic fluid dampens spring movement by changing it into heat energy that is dissipated into the atmosphere. Shock absorbers and struts have two operational cycles — compression, and rebound or extension. Compression controls the unsprung parts of a chassis, while rebound or extension controls the sprung mass. Shock absorbers, and many struts, are factory-sealed units that must be discarded when defective, although some strut designs will accept a replacement shock absorber cartridge.

Rubber bushings and insulators are used to minimize frame, body, and suspension noise and vibration. Bushings prevent suspension movement that can affect directional control and stability. Strut rods are used to provide rigidity for narrow lower control arms. Stabilizer or anti-roll bars connect both lower control arms and transfer cornering forces from the outer to the inner wheel during a turn to equalize wheel loads.

SPOTLIGHT

FRICTION SHOCK ABSORBERS

In the early days of motoring, engineers found it necessary to devise some way of dampening spring action. Since the road conditions of that era left much to be desired, the wheel would inevitably hit another bump or series of bumps before the spring ever returned to its normal position. This resulted in a vehicle that had its wheels off the ground as much as they were in contact with it, and lots of broken springs, to say nothing about driver and passenger discomfort.

Early shock absorbers took the form of friction discs that were attached to the spring and frame with levers. Any vertical suspension movement caused the levers to rotate, generating friction by movement of the discs against each other that dampened suspension movement. A series of bolts located around the outside of the discs could be loosened or tightened to adjust the friction rate, and thus the rate at which spring energy was absorbed. If the discs were too tight, however, they would barely rotate, as this had the effect of virtually locking up the suspension. If the discs were too loose, they were ineffective in dampening the suspension. Their greatest disadvantage was the excessive disc wear caused by the constant friction. Mechanical friction dampers were very erratic in operation, and there was no efficient way at the time to calibrate their resistance-velocity curve to obtain the best ride-handling compromise on a given vehicle. They were a good idea, but their time came and went rather quickly, as hydraulic shock absorbers began to appear in the '20s.

? REVIEW QUESTIONS

1. Technician A says that the job of a shock absorber is to hold the vehicle up. Technician B says that the main function of stabilizer bar is to aid in braking control. Who is right?
   (A) A only
   (B) B only
   (C) Both A and B
   (D) Neither A nor B

2. Technician A says that a shock absorber dampens excessive spring oscillation. Technician B says that a shock absorber will get hot when driving on a rough road. Who is right?
   (A) A only
   (B) B only
   (C) Both A and B
   (D) Neither A nor B

3. Technician A says that the internal resistance of a shock absorber depends on the size of the fluid orifice and piston speed. Technician B says that fluid aeration in the reservoir causes mushy shock operation. Who is right?
   (A) A only
   (B) B only
   (C) Both A and B
   (D) Neither A nor B

4. Fluid aeration in a shock absorber can be reduced by:
   (A) driving slowly.
   (B) using a shock with a 70/30 ratio.
   (C) installing the shock upside down.
   (D) pressurizing the reservoir with a nitrogen gas charge.

5. Technician A says that the speed of shock absorber piston movement affects its resistance and damping ability. Technician B says that hydraulic shock absorbers control the vehicle's trim height. Who is right?
   (A) A only
   (B) B only
   (C) Both A and B
   (D) Neither A nor B

6. Which of the following is NOT used by a strut suspension to control tire position?
   (A) a lower control arm
   (B) a leaf spring
   (C) an oversized, telescoping shock absorber
   (D) an upper bearing plate in the top mount

7. Technician A says that the shock absorber cartridge used in some struts can be replaced. Technician B says that spring seats are built into the housing of conventional struts. Who is right?
   (A) A only
   (B) B only
   (C) Both A and B
   (D) Neither A nor B

8. Control arm bushings provide all of the following except:
   (A) damping of vibrations
   (B) suspension resistance
   (C) adjustment settings
   (D) compliance

9. Which of the following are installed on many vehicles to control body roll, provide cornering stability, and dampen wheel shock?
   (A) stabilizer bar
   (B) strut rod
   (C) adjustable ball joints
   (D) torsion bar

10. Technician A says that rubber bushings lack the compliance provided by neoprene bushings. Technician B says that metal screw-together control arm bushings wear out because of metal-to-metal contact. Who is right?
    (A) A only
    (B) B only
    (C) Both A and B
    (D) Neither A nor B

WHEEL BEARINGS, WHEELS, AND TIRES

"Experience: A dim lamp, which only lights the one who bears it." — Louis-Ferdinand Celine'

 OBJECTIVES

After completion of this chapter, you should be able to:

- Identify and explain the two major functions of wheel and axle bearings.

- Identify the components of a serviceable wheel bearing.

- Compare and contrast the serviceable wheel bearing with the non-serviceable cartridge and integral hub-bearing assemblies.

- Discuss the differences between semi- and full-floating rear axles, with emphasis on the axle bearings.

- Explain the four major functions of a tire.

- List the major components used to manufacture tires and describe their interrelationship.

- Explain the difference between bias ply, bias-belted, and radial tires.

- Demonstrate and explain static and dynamic wheel balance.

Passenger car and truck wheels must have enough resilience to:
- carry the vehicle mass
- transfer the driving braking torque to the tires
- withstand side thrusts over a wide range of road and speed conditions.

Machined, heat-treated, and ground to precision tolerances, wheel bearings are permanently assembled to provide correct running clearances. Wheel bearings are used to support the vehicle wheels, and allow the wheels to rotate smoothly, quietly, and with a minimum of friction. In this chapter, we will start with a discussion of wheel and axle bearings, and then move on to an understanding of how wheels and tires do their job.

WHEEL BEARINGS

Wheel bearings have two main purposes:

- To hold the hub, wheel, and tire in alignment with the steering knuckle or axle.
- To allow the hub, wheel, and tire to rotate freely and minimize rolling resistance while maintaining this alignment.

Three types of bearings are used: radial ball, roller, or tapered roller bearings. All are manufactured from hardened steel alloys, and their components ground to very precise tolerances.

BEARING CHARACTERISTICS

Each type of bearing does its job differently. Radial ball bearings control side thrust as well as load, but since there is only a small area of contact between the balls and their races, the amount of load they can support is limited. Non-tapered roller bearings have the opposite characteristics. The greater surface contact of the rollers spreads the load more evenly, but it does not control side thrust. Over the years, carmakers have found that the best way to control both load (as represented by vehicle mass) and side thrust (hub movement on the spindle) is the use of two tapered roller bearings in each hub. The tapers face each other to hold the hub in lateral alignment on the stationary spindle, and are retained by a hex nut and cotter pin with no preload.

Recent advancements in both bearing and suspension design have made the use of radial ball bearings popular on many FWD vehicles, since the new bearing designs require less space and do not need periodic adjustment.

SERVICEABLE VS. NON-SERVICEABLE WHEEL BEARINGS

The serviceable bearing design (Figure 7-1) is commonly used on the front wheels of

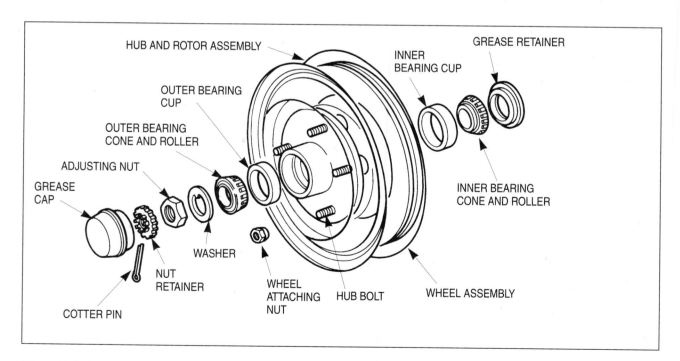

Figure 7-1 Serviceable bearings consist of two opposed tapered roller bearing assemblies, a grease seal and grease cap. The nut on the outer end of the spindle is used to adjust the bearing endplay. (Ford Motor)

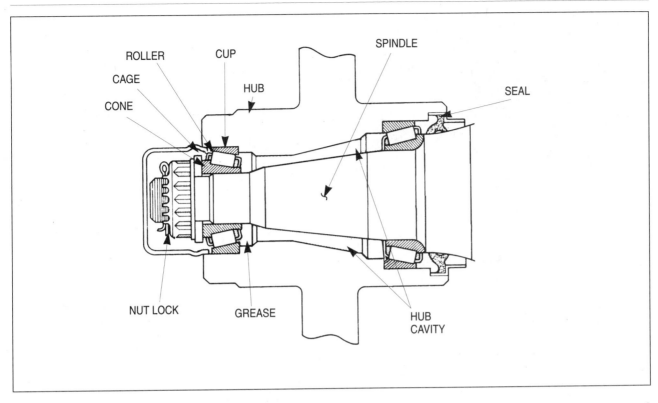

Figure 7-2 A cross-sectional view showing relative location of the inner and outer bearings. Some carmakers recommend filling the hub cavity with grease. Others say it should have only a coating of grease to prevent rust. (Chrysler)

RWD vehicles, and the rear wheels of many FWD vehicles. It consists of an inner and outer tapered roller bearing set, with separate outer cups or races pressed into the wheel hub. The two bearings are installed with their smaller diameters facing each other to control endplay (Figure 7-2). Since the larger or inner bearing is located near the center of the tire, it carries most of the vehicle mass. The smaller outer bearing acts mainly to prevent the drum or disc from wobbling. The inner bearing is protected by a grease seal or retainer, which retains the lubricant in the bearing, prevents contamination, and keeps grease away from the brakes. The outer bearing is protected in the same way by a grease cap on the end of the spindle (Figure 7-3).

To assure proper operation, serviceable bearings require periodic lubrication and

Figure 7-3 The grease cap keeps contamination away from adjustable wheel bearings.

Figure 7-4 The adjustment nut controls wheel bearing endplay.

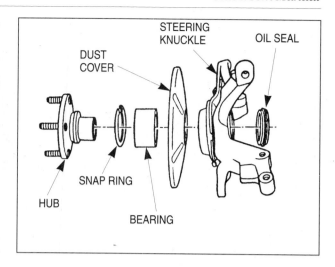

Figure 7-5 The cartridge bearing is pressed into the steering knuckle and retained by a snap ring. Cartridge bearings require no service and are discarded if defective. (Ford Motor)

adjustment (Figure 7-4). Proper adjustment is important, as it controls bearing endplay. Excessive endplay will allow the wheel to wobble and change alignment angles, affecting handling and causing unnecessary wear. Bearing endplay specified by the carmaker usually ranges between 0.001 and 0.005 inch, and allows for heat expansion during operation. Bearing lubrication is important, since it reduces friction, transfers heat, prevents bearing wear from abrasive contaminants, and protects the metal surfaces from corrosion.

Two different designs of non-serviceable wheel bearings are used — the cartridge-type and the integral hub-and-bearing assembly. The cartridge bearing (Figure 7-5) is used on the front wheels of some FWD vehicles — the integral assembly (Figure 7-6) is used mainly on the rear wheels of FWD vehicles, although some RWD pickups have them. Cartridge bearings are prelubricated, but the cartridge can be pressed

from the steering knuckle for replacement. The integral hub-and-bearing assembly contains a prelubricated and preadjusted double-row ball bearing, and is sealed at the factory. If the bearing is loose or defective, the entire assembly must be replaced.

REAR AXLE BEARINGS

Bearings used on the drive axle of RWD vehicles are called **axle bearings**. An axle bearing (also called a rear wheel bearing) is located at the outer end of the axle housing on each side (Figure 7-7). The wheel and tire is bolted to the axle shaft, which rotates in the bearing. Axle bearings perform the same functions as front wheel bearings.

SEMI-FLOATING AXLES

The most commonly used axle-and-bearing design is the semi-floating axle found on passenger cars. The word 'float' means that the axle does not support any vehicle load, but simply transmits the twisting force to turn the drive wheels. Since 'semi'

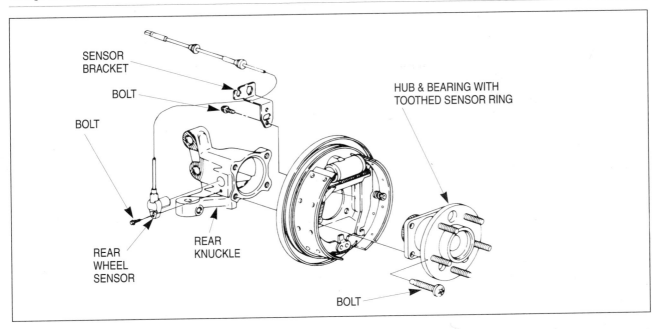

Figure 7-6 An integral hub and bearing assembly bolts to the steering knuckle. If the vehicle has an ABS, the hub and bearing unit also contains the sensor ring. The entire unit must be replaced if any part is defective. (General Motors)

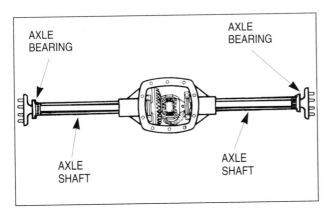

Figure 7-7 Rear axle outer (wheel) bearing location. (General Motors)

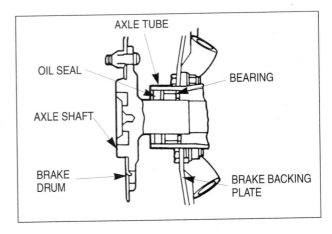

Figure 7-8 Outer bearing and seal location in a semi-floating axle design. (General Motors)

means 'half', a semi-floating axle is half floating. In the typical semi-floating design the inner end of the axle floats in the differential side gears, and does not support the mass of the gears. The gears are supported by their own bearings. The wheel end of the axle is not floating. The outer axle bearing is in the housing supporting the axle, and the full mass of the vehicle goes through the axle to the bearing (Figure 7-8).

When a semi-floating axle breaks at the outer end, the wheel falls off.

Bearing application on semi-floating axles is determined by how the axle is secured in place. In both cases, the axle shafts are machined with splines that mesh with splines in the inner bores of the differential side gears. In one design, C-type locking clips hold the axle shaft in place in

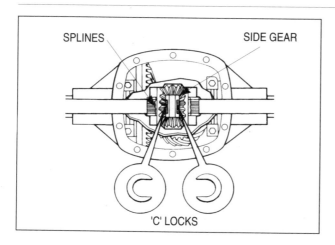

Figure 7-9 C-type lock clips are used to retain the axle shafts to the differential side gear in one type of semi-floating axle. (General Motors)

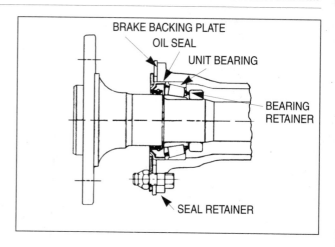

Figure 7-11 In this design, a seal retainer is bolted to the axle tube to hold the axle in place. (General Motors)

the differential (Figure 7-9). Support for the outer ends of C-type axle shafts comes from straight roller bearings, which use machined journal surfaces on the axle shaft as their inner races. The outer race is pressed into the axle tube bore, and lubricant is kept inside the tube by a grease seal.

In the other design, the axle shafts mesh with the differential side gears (Figure 7-10), but the shafts are retained in place by a seal retainer bolted to the outer

flange of the axle tube (Figure 7-11). Tapered roller bearings are held in place on the axle shaft by a ring-type retainer, with the seal retainer plate holding the axle in position.

FULL-FLOATING AXLES

Heavy-duty vehicles, such as 3/4 ton pickups and larger trucks, use full-floating axles. This means that the axle does not support any of the mass of the vehicle. If the axle breaks at the outer end, the wheel does not fall off because the wheel is supported by the bearing, NOT the axle. Full floating rear axles can usually be removed from the housing without taking the wheel off or even jacking up the vehicle. This axle design has tapered roller bearings like those used as front wheel bearings, but much larger in size (Figure 7-12). A full-floating axle uses the axle tube to transmit the vehicle mass directly to the wheels through a hub supported by bearings (Figure 7-13). You can usually identify a full-floating axle by the presence of shaft-to-hub bolts at the wheels.

The bearings in many late model vehicles with both semi- and full-floating axles are lubricated by gear oil from the

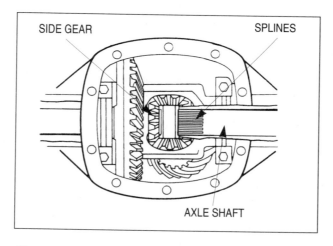

Figure 7-10 In another type of semi-floating axle, the axle shaft mates with the side gear splines without use of C-locks. (General Motors)

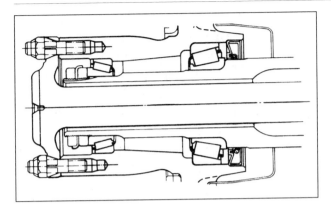

Figure 7-12 A full-floating axle uses opposed tapered roller bearings to support the mass of the vehicle. Note that the inside bearing is much larger than the outer one. (General Motors)

differential flowing in the axle tubes toward the outer ends. Older vehicles had an inner seal next to the bearing which prevented the axle gear oil from going into

the bearing. The seal prevented lubricant from going through the bearing and reaching the brake shoes, but it also prevented the bearing from getting any gear oil lubrication. Those bearings had to be removed and repacked with grease periodically. The axle bearings on some full-floating axles may also require grease for lubrication.

WHEELS

Wheel rims must hold the tires exactly centered radially and laterally under the varying loads created by such factors as vehicle mass, road surface, braking and acceleration, and cornering. Whether supplied by the carmaker (original equipment manufacturer, **OEM**) or purchased on the **aftermarket** as a replacement, virtually all wheels have two

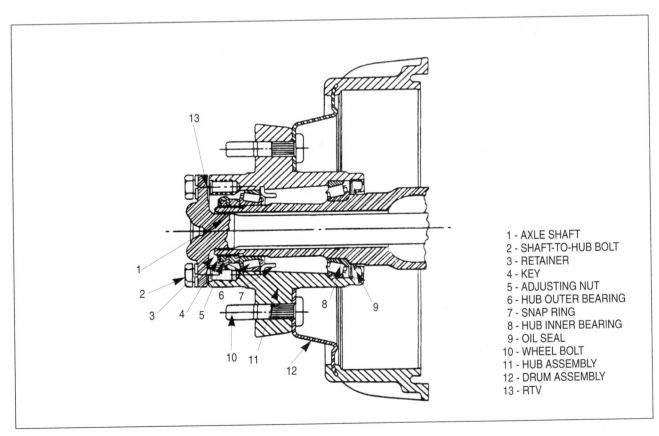

1 - AXLE SHAFT
2 - SHAFT-TO-HUB BOLT
3 - RETAINER
4 - KEY
5 - ADJUSTING NUT
6 - HUB OUTER BEARING
7 - SNAP RING
8 - HUB INNER BEARING
9 - OIL SEAL
10 - WHEEL BOLT
11 - HUB ASSEMBLY
12 - DRUM ASSEMBLY
13 - RTV

Figure 7-13 A cross sectional view of a full-floating axle shaft and bearings. (General Motors)

main parts — the disc, which is secured to the hub, and the rim, which holds the tire in place.

WHEEL DESIGN

The disc and rim may be made from steel, or cast, stamped, or spun aluminum or magnesium. These two pieces generally are welded together to form the wheel, but they also can be bolted, riveted, or connected with wire spokes. A spindle hole in the center of the disc is surrounded by the lug bolt holes, which can vary in size and number according to the vehicle and load capacity. Passenger cars generally use four or five lug bolts; light trucks and vans may have as many as eight lug bolts.

The rim is designed with two bead flanges against which the tire beads push. Air pressure in the tire forces the tire beads against the wheel flanges. Bead seats inside the flanges are placed at a slight angle. When a tire is mounted on the wheel, the bead seats keep the tire positioned vertically, while the wheel flanges control horizontal tire positioning. Wheels used on passenger cars and light trucks should have a raised safety lip just inside the bead seat (Figure 7-14), although some

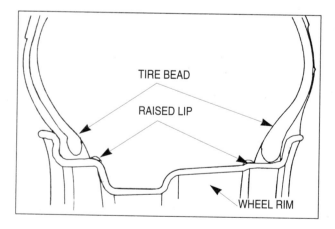

Figure 7-14 The ridges or raised lips between the rim flanges and rim well are a safety feature required on all passenger car wheels. (Chrysler)

aluminum wheels do not. Initial inflation forces the tire beads over the safety lips and against the rim flanges. If the tire fails, the safety lips help hold it in place on the rim until the vehicle can be safely stopped. Because they prevent a flat tire from working its way off the rim, safety lips are required under Department of Transportation (DOT) regulations. Wheel rims used on passenger cars are designed with a drop center, or well area, near the center. Since the well area provides the means for installing or removing the tire from the rim, it must be deep enough to hold one side of the tire bead while allowing the other side of the bead to be passed over the flange.

Wheels must be replaced if they are bent or dented, have excessive **runout** or **elongated** bolt holes, leak air through welds, or when the lug nuts will not stay tight. A replacement wheel or 'mag' wheel should be the equivalent of the OEM wheel, but many are NOT. An incorrect type or size wheel can affect wheel or bearing life, brake cooling, vehicle ground clearance, tire clearance to the body and chassis, scrub radius, and numerous other factors.

DIAMETER AND WIDTH

Wheel rims are designated primarily by their diameter and width. Wheel diameter is the distance across the center of the wheel from one bead seat to the other, and does NOT include the height of the flange (Figure 7-15). Common wheel diameters range from 13 to 16 inches, and the tire diameter selected must be the same as the wheel diameter.

Wheel width is the distance between the inside of the bead flanges across the rim. This measurement generally is somewhat smaller than the tire width. Common rim widths range from 4 to 10 inches, with those between 5 1/2 and 8 inches being the most popular. Tires should be selected

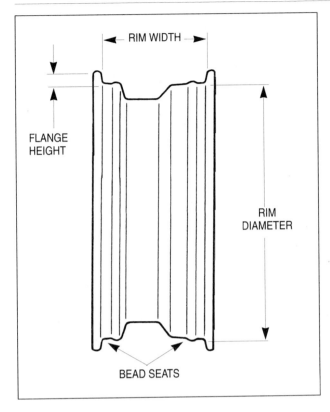

Figure 7-15 A cross section of a typical drop center wheel with dimensions.

according to the wheel width, and charts or tables are available showing the recommended rim width for each tire size, and conversely, the recommended tire width for each rim size. Narrow rims have a tendency toward greater sidewall flexing, possible sidewall damage, and deliver a softer ride. Sidewall flexing is reduced as rim width increases, resulting in increased steering response and a stiffer ride.

OFFSET

Wheel offset is another measurement of concern when replacing OEM wheels with ones of a different design. Offset refers to the placement of the wheel mounting flange relative to the center of the wheel. When the mounting flange is centered in the wheel, it is said to have zero offset (Figure 7-16). A wheel that sits in from its mounting flange has positive offset. If the wheel sits out from its mounting flange, the wheel has negative offset.

Offset in either direction affects vehicle

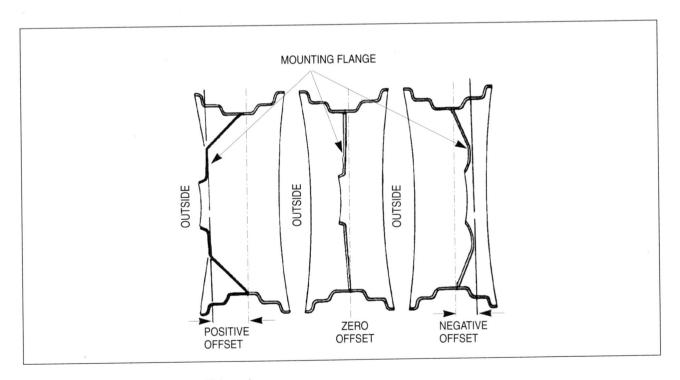

Figure 7-16 Wheel offset. (General Motors)

operation in several ways. Moving the tire center line outward (negative offset) increases the vehicle track and reduces lateral weight transfer. In return for these benefits, the tire-to-fender and tire-to-suspension clearance is reduced, the wheel bearing load is moved outward, and the scrub radius changes.

The use of a wheel and tire assembly that has a different offset than the one the vehicle was designed to use is NOT recommended by car manufacturers. It will affect the toe setting because of the change in the scrub radius, or difference between the steering axis and the center of the tire at the road surface. This change in scrub radius also can result in excessively hard steering. For this reason, replacement wheels should have the same degree of offset as the OEM wheels to avoid altering the scrub radius designed into the suspension.

WHEEL STUDS AND LUG NUTS

Most wheels are attached to a vehicle by a stud and nut system. The mounting holes in the wheel's nut bosses are tapered for easy installation and centering of the wheel on the mounting studs. The mounting studs have a head and serrated shank. When pressed through the rear of the brake drum or disc hub, the serrated shank prevents the stud from rotating, while the head prevents it from being pulled out of the drum or hub. The lug nuts used to hold the wheel on the studs have a tapered, conical face. When lug nuts are threaded in place on their studs, the conical faces enter the tapered wheel holes and center the wheel on the hub.

Once the lug nuts are properly tightened, friction between the stud and nut threads works with the friction between the face of the nut and the wheel to hold the wheel tightly against the hub or drum. If the nuts are NOT tightened enough, they can back off the stud. Nuts that are exces-

sively tightened can cause disc or drum warpage, and in extreme cases, break the studs. For this reason, wheels should be tightened to the carmakers' specification with a torque wrench. When using an air wrench, adjust the air pressure or the wrench so it does not overtighten the wheels, and check afterwards with a torque wrench.

TIRES

The tires installed on the vehicle's wheels are the all-important link to the road surface. They:

- hold the air that carries the vehicle's mass
- provide a cushion between the wheels and the road by flexing to absorb small road shocks
- provide the grip or traction necessary between the wheels and the road to transform engine power into motion.

TIRE DESIGN

All tires are a compromise of the rubber compounds used to construct the tire, the choice of ply materials and ply arrangement, tire tread pattern and depth, and other factors. By varying these factors, the manufacturer determines ride quality, tire life, and road adhesion. Some late-model vehicles use tires designed for specific conditions or purposes, such as directional tires that can be installed only on one side of the vehicle because they are designed to rotate in one direction only.

Bias Ply Tires

This is the oldest type of pneumatic tire construction, using plies that run with the rotation of the tire, but criss-cross each other at an angle of between 32° and 38° to the tread center line (Figure 7-17). This type of tire construction generally has a smoother and softer ride than belted tires.

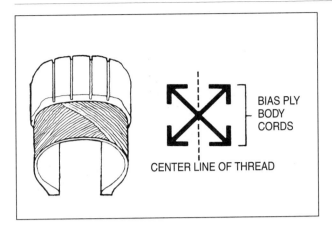

Figure 7-17 Bias ply tires use cords that run from bead-to-bead at an angle across the tread centerline; alternate plies cross at opposite angles. (McQuay-Norris)

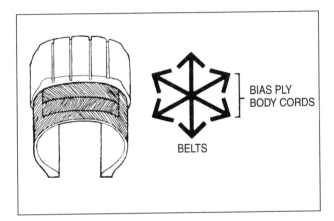

Figure 7-18 Belted bias ply tires add one or more belts to the bias ply design. (McQuay-Norris)

Bias Ply Belted Tires

In this variation of the bias ply design, several belts beneath the tread wrap around the plies to increase tread rigidity and sidewall flexibility (Figure 7-18). By restricting tread motion during contact with the road surface, tread life also is increased. Belts made of fabric produce a smoother ride than those made of steel.

Belted Radial Tires

In this design, the plies cross the tire at an angle of about 90° to the tread center line,

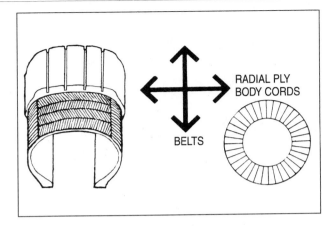

Figure 7-19 Radial ply tire design is similar to that of a belted bias tire, but the body cords cross the tread centerline at approximate right angles from bead-to-bead. Since the body cords radiate from the tire's centerpoint, the design is called a radial tire. (McQuay-Norris)

and are retained by several belts just under the tread that run with tire rotation at a 90° angle to the main radial plies (Figure 7-19). The handling characteristics of radial tires differ from those of bias or bias-belted tires, and they should never be intermixed with other tire types on the vehicle. When installing radial tires on an older vehicle originally equipped with bias or bias-belted tires, be aware that the handling and feel of the vehicle may change. Radial tires provide a very smooth ride at highway speeds above 40 mph, but a somewhat firm, harsh ride at lower speeds.

TIRE CONSTRUCTION

A tire is constructed of three basic parts (Figure 7-20):

1. the beads, which anchor the tire to the rim and help transmit starting and stopping force from the wheel to the tire
2. the carcass, or sidewalls, which contain the air under pressure and supports the vehicle mass
3. the tread, which contacts the road surface and develops traction.

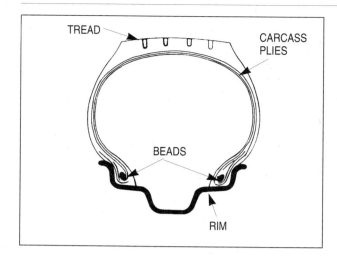

Figure 7-20 Major parts of a tire.

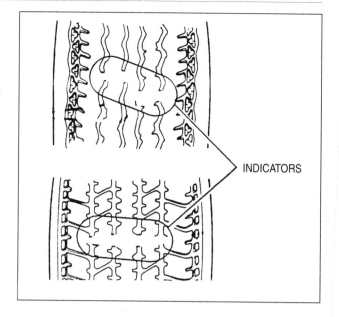

Figure 7-21 Tread wear indicators. (Oldsmobile Division, General Motors)

Starting at the inside diameter of a tire, let us look at how these parts are related as previously shown in Figures 7-17, 7-18, and 7-19. The sidewalls used to form the tire carcass consist of two or more strands of fabrics such as rayon, nylon, or polyester twisted or woven into cords. These cords are bonded together with thin layers of rubber. The bottom of the sidewall is looped over a series of steel wires to form the bead area of the tire, providing strength for the bead once the tire is mounted on the wheel. The plies incorporate a series of parallel cords, and are bonded to the sidewall with their ends wrapped around the tire beads. The belts are made of materials similar to that used in sidewalls, as well as stranded steel or fiberglass, and are bonded between the sidewalls and tread. An inner membrane, or liner, bonded to the inside of the carcass performs the same function as the tube used in older tires, and produces an airtight seal. This allows the air inside the tire to exert a uniform pressure against the entire interior. Properly designed, the sidewalls absorb minor road irregularities by flexing, and prevent damage to the cord plies. Sidewall rigidity is a result of the number of plies, the cord material stiffness, and the air pressure inside the tire. The tread area of the tire is formed from a rubber compound that resists abrasion and wear. The spacing in the tread pattern is designed to allow a degree of tire distortion on the road to reduce tread scrubbing. A wear indicator is molded in several places around the tread on OEM tires (Figure 7-21); when the indicator shows up, it alerts the driver or a highway inspection station to the need for new tires.

The number of plies used in a tire still causes consumer confusion. In the early days, as many as eight plies were required because the cotton plies used were relatively weak. Improvements in cord construction and fabric materials in the past few decades have made it possible for the same load to be carried by fewer plies. Tires have gone from eight plies of cheap cotton, to six plies of improved cotton, to four plies of rayon, to two plies of rayon and nylon. As the number of plies used in tire construction decreases, so does the amount of heat generated inside the tire.

Braking, acceleration, and road friction all contribute to the failure of a tire carcass, but a major cause of failure is the friction (heat) generated between the tire plies. As a tire rolls, the flexing of its tread and sidewalls causes the tire to distort and deform. This results in a rippling of the tire fabric, creating heat. When the number of plies increases, the sidewalls become stiffer and the ride gets harsher. The fewer the plies used, the greater the sidewall flexibility and the smoother the ride. The current 2-ply/4-ply rated tire uses only two plies, but can carry the same mass as a four-ply tire.

TIRE USAGE

All four wheels of a vehicle should be fitted with the same type of tire. Using tires of different types on a vehicle is NOT recommended, as it has a direct and adverse effect on directional control and 'roadability'. This is especially true when radial and bias ply tires are mixed. Remember, radial tire sidewalls are more flexible than those of bias, or bias-belted, tires. This allows them to maintain greater tread contact with the road and is important during cornering, as the more flexible sidewalls absorb side thrust without rolling the tread away from the road. The stiffer sidewalls of bias ply tires have a tendency to lift the shoulders off the road. This reduces traction, especially at high speeds.

Using one radial and one conventional tire on the front of a vehicle creates a side-to-side traction differential, causing the vehicle to pull to the side with the radial tire during normal driving and braking because of its greater traction. Using radial tires on the front and conventional tires at the rear creates a front-rear traction differential that can result in skidding or rear-end steering in turns because of the lower traction at the rear.

TIRE CODING AND SIDEWALL INFORMATION

Federal regulations require that all tires carry certain information. This information is molded into the tire sidewall and can be used to determine the following:

- tire size
- number of plies used and their material
- tire manufacturer and brand name
- a Department of Transportation (DOT) number
- maximum inflation pressure, load rating, and maximum load at maximum inflation
- tire grade designation

Tire Size

To replace a tire, you need to know the wheel size, tire width, and aspect ratio. Wheel size is indicated in inches by the last two digits of a tire size (i.e. 235/75 R 15). Passenger cars commonly use 13, 14, and 15 inch wheels. Wheel diameter is measured across the center of the wheel from one bead seat to the other, and does NOT include the height of the flange. Tires can only be installed on wheel rims of the same size and bead seat taper. Tire width is currently measured by the P-metric system (Figure 7-22), which has replaced the older alpha-numeric system. The order of information within the P-metric listing has changed over the years, so an older tire may not have the information in the same order as a later tire. The aspect ratio is the relationship of the tire's cross sectional height and width (Figure 7-23). For example, the height of a 60-16 series tire is 60% of the tire's width. Sidewall construction is designated by the letter between the aspect ratio and the wheel diameter.

Tire Plies

Every tire has markings to reveal the cord material and the number of plies in the sidewalls and in the belts, if it is a belted

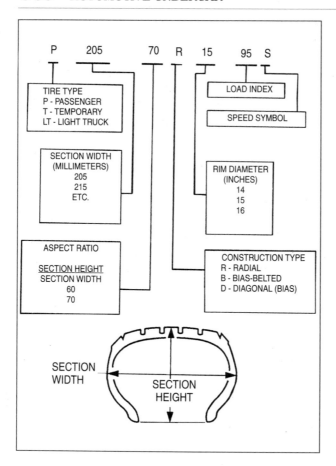

Figure 7-22 Interpretation of a typical P-metric tire designation. (Oldsmobile Division, General Motors)

tire. For example, one tire may have 4 tread plies, of which two are polyester and two are steel cord, with two sidewall plies of polyester cord. Another tire may use one rayon and two steel cord tread plies, with a single nylon sidewall ply.

DOT Number

This is a symbol and multi-digit serial number that denotes the tire meets or exceeds Federal requirements. The number is coded to indicate where and when the tire was manufactured, as well as to provide certain information regarding the tire construction. The DOT symbol and serial number appears only on the blackwall side of the tire.

Inflation Pressures and Load Range

The tire's maximum inflation pressure is calculated by the manufacturer to deliver a satisfactory ride, handling, and tread life within the recommended load carrying range. Tire load carrying capacity is dependent on inflation pressure; it can be increased by raising the inflation pressure. Thus, the maximum inflation pressure is controlled by the load range. The tire's load rating also indicates the strength of the tire's sidewall plies. It is neither safe nor legal to carry a load greater than the load rating of the tires. P-metric sized tires are available in two load ratings. Standard load tires are designed to hold a maximum of 35 psi; extra load tires can be inflated to 41 psi. Further tire inflation information is provided on a tire inflation label (Figure 7-24) generally located on the left front door or pillar.

Tire Grade Designation

A uniform tire grading system established by the National Highway Safety Administration (NHSA) set standards for treadwear, traction, and temperature resistance. Tire manufacturers must test and grade their tires according to these standards, and mold the results into the tire sidewall for consumer use in comparing various tires.

Tread wear is graded on a norm of 100 as the acceptable minimum tread life, which represents 30,000 miles. A tire that is graded as 150 has a rating of 1-1/2 times the minimum acceptable tread life or 45,000 miles. One graded at 200 will have a rating of twice the tread life, or 60,000 miles. While this number compares tread wear life against that of other tires, it does NOT state the exact life of the tread (i.e. how many miles it will deliver). Actually, tread life is dependent on how well the owner maintains the tires and other factors such as driving habits and road surface.

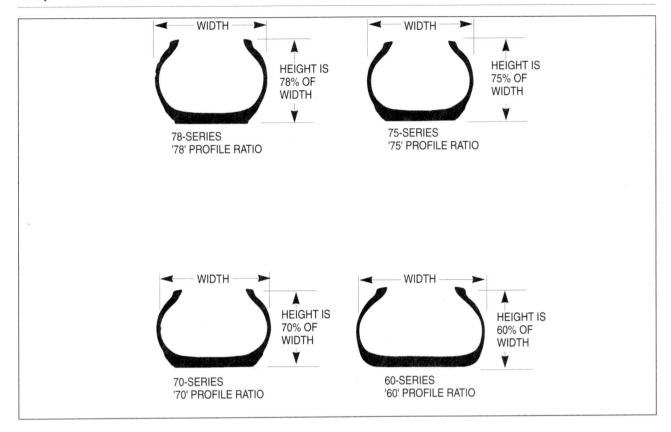

Figure 7-23 Common tire aspect ratios. (Chrysler)

Traction ratings are given as A, B, or C, with A being the highest and C the lowest. They are determined by the tire's ability to stop on wet pavement, but do NOT indicate the tire's cornering ability or its performance on a dry pavement.

Temperature resistance also is graded A, B, or C, and depends on how well the tire fares in a controlled laboratory test to determine its ability to withstand heat generated on a test wheel. Because heat is a natural enemy of tires, a tire must be able to resist cord and layer separation, as well as a natural tendency for the rubber to become harder and more brittle from the heat. The NHSA requires a minimum performance grade of C for the tire to be sold.

Other Information

The tire sidewall contains additional information. A safety warning informs the consumer that under- and overinflations can cause tire wear and damage. A tire

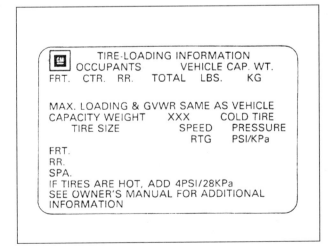

Figure 7-24 A typical tire inflation label. (Oldsmobile Division, General Motors)

performance criteria (TPC) specification is used on OEM tires fitted to GM cars to indicate that the tire meets the carmaker's own performance standards. Any combination of the letters M + S molded in the tire sidewall indicates the tire design meets the specifications for a mud and snow tire.

SPARE TIRES

A spare tire is a fifth tire carried in the vehicle to replace a flat or damaged tire while the vehicle is on the road. On older vehicles, the spare tire was a full-size wheel and tire that had all the qualities of the tires mounted on the vehicle. Today, new vehicles generally are sold with a temporary spare tire of bias ply design. Such tires have a useful life of about 3,000 miles (4,800 km), but should be used only at speeds under 50 mph (80 km/h). The major reason for the use of temporary spare tires is to provide more storage space in the vehicle and reduce weight.

The full-size temporary spare is a lightweight tire of the same size as the vehicle tires. The compact spare is a narrow, high pressure tire mounted on a narrow (usually a 4-inch wide) rim, but having a slightly larger wheel diameter than the road wheel. Always check the information molded into the sidewall to find out if the tire can be repaired. Many of them are NOT serviceable and must be thrown away, wheel included, if they will not hold air. Some vehicles may use a stowaway spare that folds up for storage. After installation on the axle, the stowaway spare is inflated with a pressurized canister or an air hose. When no longer needed, it can be deflated, refolded, and stored. This type of spare is NOT serviceable; the entire assembly is replaced if the tire is worn or damaged.

FREE AND ROLLING DIAMETERS

A tire has two different diameters (Figure 7-25). The free diameter is measured from the top to the bottom of a properly inflated tire when it is carrying no load. When a load is placed on the rolling tire, it flattens at the contact or patch area where it contacts the road. Because of the mass of the load, the rolling diameter, as measured from the top to the bottom of the tire, is somewhat smaller than the free diameter. The difference between these two diameters is called the tire's deflection. This differ-

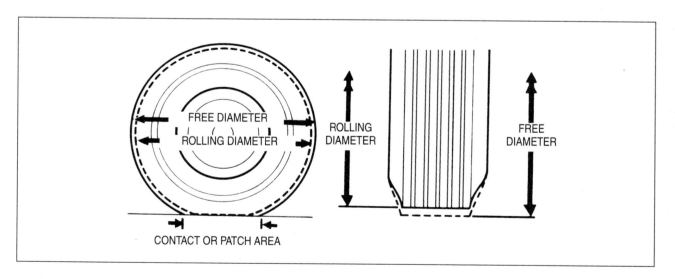

Figure 7-25 Free and rolling diameters. (Ford Motor)

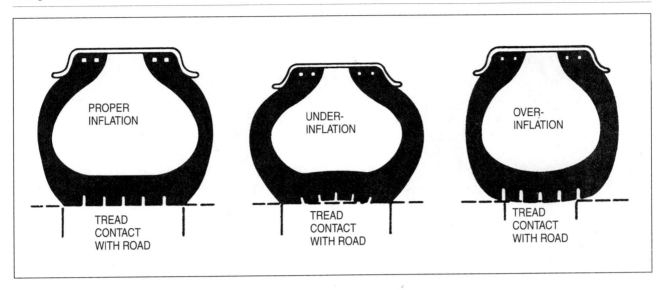

Figure 7-26 The effects of tire inflation. (Ford Motor)

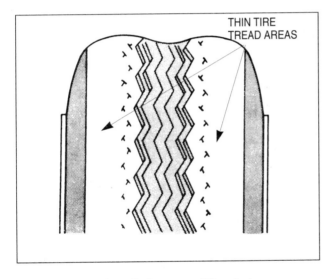

Figure 7-27 Underinflation wear. (Chrysler)

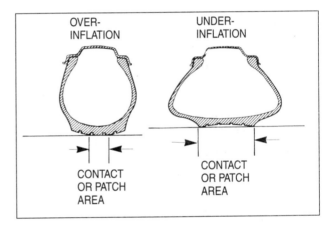

Figure 7-28 Tire contact area with the road surface decreases as tire pressure increases. (Ford Motor)

ence in diameter, or deflection, would cause scrubbing on the road, except that the tread grooves provide room for the excess rubber.

TIRE PRESSURE

Incorrect tire pressure is the most common cause of irregular or premature tire wear, followed by alignment problems. When a tire is underinflated, the rolling diameter decreases and the tire contact or patch area increases. An underinflated tire allows the sidewalls to flex excessively (Figure 7-26). This causes rapid shoulder wear (Figure 7-27) and eventual tire failure. An overinflated tire stiffens the sidewalls, increases the rolling diameter, and decreases the patch area (Figure 7-28). The result of overinflation is rapid center wear (Figure 7-29) and a loss of the tire's ability to cushion shocks. Incorrect inflation in either direction will affect

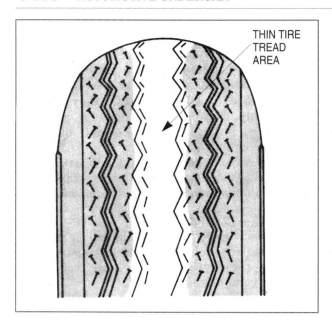

THIN TIRE
TREAD
AREA

Figure 7-29 Overinflation wear. (Chrysler)

vehicle stability and produce a sluggish response feeling or overresponse. When the tires on a vehicle are inflated unequally, its response to steering maneuvers may be erratic or unpredictable. The carmaker has determined the optimum inflation pressure range according to vehicle load and driving condition to provide for safe operation, proper stability, and a comfortable ride.

TIRE NOISE, VIBRATION, AND WEAR

When a tire travels over certain road surfaces, such as brick or poorly surfaced concrete, the resulting noise is sometimes misdiagnosed as a rear axle problem. Tire noise generally remains constant whether the vehicle is accelerating or decelerating, but will change according to road surface. Rear axle noise will NOT change on different roads, but does vary according to whether the vehicle is accelerating or decelerating. Tire defects, such as uneven tread surfaces, can produce noise or vibration that appear to be coming from any place in the vehicle except the tires.

A tire is not perfectly round when supporting the mass of a vehicle, but takes a slightly elliptical form. If the tire is not manufactured perfectly, placing mass on it will accentuate this elliptical shape and create an out-of-round condition called radial runout. As the tire rotates, it will cause tire thump or wheel hop. This will produce a noticeable up-and-down movement in the steering wheel at certain road speeds. A tire with this problem will NOT benefit from balancing; the problem can only be corrected by replacing the tire.

Radial tire waddle is the side-to-side movement of the front or rear of the vehicle (Figure 7-30). This problem can be caused by a radial tire whose steel belt inside the tire is crooked instead of straight, or it can result from excessive lateral runout of the wheel or tire. It is most noticeable at low speeds, but may also appear at cruising speeds as a roughness in the ride. To determine which end has the faulty tire, road test the vehicle. If the cause of the problem is at the front of the vehicle, the front sheet metal will appear to be moving from side-to-side. If the tire causing the problem is on the rear, it will feel as if someone is pushing on the side of the

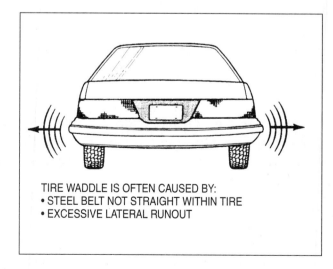

TIRE WADDLE IS OFTEN CAUSED BY:
• STEEL BELT NOT STRAIGHT WITHIN TIRE
• EXCESSIVE LATERAL RUNOUT

Figure 7-30 Causes of tire waddle. (Oldsmobile Division, General Motors)

vehicle. Once you have determined which tire is at fault, check the lateral runout to see whether the tire or the wheel is defective. An off-center belt in a radial tire also can cause the tire to develop a side force while moving straight down the road, and the tire will tend to roll like a cone.

When irregular tire wear is present, check for the following conditions and rotate the tires if any one is found:

- Front tire wear differs from rear tire wear
- Uneven wear across the tread of any tire
- Left and right front tire wear is unequal
- Left and right rear tire wear is unequal.

If the following conditions are noted, check the wheel alignment:

- Left and right front tire wear is unequal
- Uneven wear across the tread of either front tire
- A scuffed appearance on the front tire treads, with featheredging on one side of the tread ribs or blocks.

TIRE AND WHEEL BALANCE

Proper balance is an important factor throughout the vehicle, but it is crucial to proper operation of the wheel and tire assemblies. With a wheel and tire assembly rotating at an approximate speed of 800 rpm to 900 rpm, the tolerance is extremely exacting. So exacting, in fact, that an out of balance tire can exert sufficient influence, under centrifugal force at high speed, to turn the entire wheel assembly into an uncontrolled moving mass. When this happens, balance turns into severe imbalance and the wheel will hop up and down.

The wheel assembly revolves as a unit, giving firm support to the vehicle, and contributing to directional stability. The tire cushions the ride, absorbs the stresses of acceleration, braking, and the centrifugal force involved in turns, and develops traction. Since tire rotational speed results in considerable centrifugal force, a wheel assembly that is heavier at any one point will be out-of-balance and cause vibrations. Because the front wheels are connected to the suspension and steering systems, any condition causing the wheels to vibrate will have a serious and detrimental effect on both suspension and steering system components. Wheel balance falls into two general categories — **static balance** and **dynamic balance**.

NOTE Do NOT confuse wheel imbalance with out-of-round tires, or excessive wheel runout resulting from bent wheels or hubs.

STATIC BALANCE

When the mass of the wheel and tire assembly is equally distributed around the axis of wheel rotation, or spindle, while the wheel is NOT spinning, we say that the wheel is in static balance. When this condition exists, the wheel has NO tendency to rotate by itself, regardless of its position (Figure 7-31). If the wheel is NOT in static balance, it will NOT stay in any position, but will start to rotate until the heaviest spot is at the bottom. When a

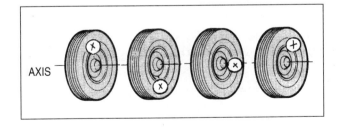

Figure 7-31 Static balance. If the wheel is mounted so it is free turning, the X marked on the tire will stay in any position without rotating to the bottom. (Ford Motor)

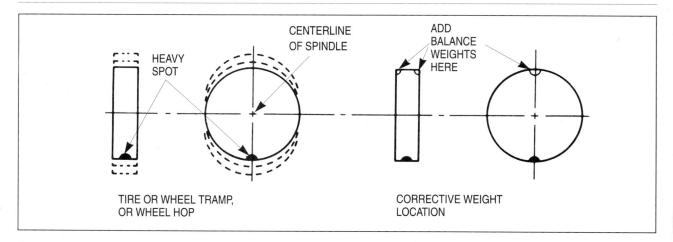

Figure 7-32 Static imbalance and added weights. Note that the weight is placed half inside and half outside to avoid upsetting the dynamic balance of the wheel. (Chrysler)

wheel is statically unbalanced, centrifugal force acting on the heavy spot causes it to tramp or hop as it rotates on the road (Figure 7-32). The vehicle speed at which this takes place depends on the degree the wheel is out-of-balance; the greater the imbalance, the lower the speed at which it occurs.

DYNAMIC BALANCE

Dynamic balance is defined as balance in more than one plane. When a wheel and tire assembly is in dynamic balance, it must also be in static balance, but a wheel and tire assembly in static balance is NOT necessarily in dynamic balance. To be in dynamic balance, the mass of a wheel and tire assembly must not only be equally distributed around the axis of rotation, but also with regard to the center line of the tire and wheel (Figure 7-33).

To demonstrate both the principle and the need for dynamic balance, attach a weight to a string and swing the weight around slowly (Figure 7-34). As the weight moves around the axis of rotation, centrifugal force will cause it to rise, creating a small angle with the axis of rotation. Increasing the speed of rotation causes the weight to rise until it is at right angles (90°)

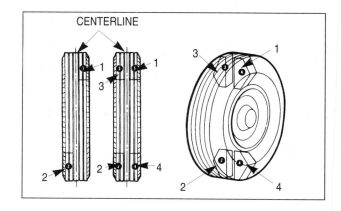

Figure 7-33 Dynamic balance. If weights are placed in zones 1 and 2, the tire will be in static balance but NOT dynamic balance. Weight must be added in zones 3 and 4 to get dynamic balance. (Chrysler)

to the axis of rotation. Now consider equal weights attached to the end of a stick, as shown in Figure 7-35. If we fit the stick on a pivot at a right angle (90°) and spin it around, the rotational path will remain at right angles to the stick. In this demonstration, the stick is in dynamic balance. Shifting the position of the weights, as shown in Figure 7-36, will NOT change the static balance, but will dramatically affect the dynamic balance. As weight movement and axis of rotation are now reversed with every 180° of rotation, the pivot will wobble

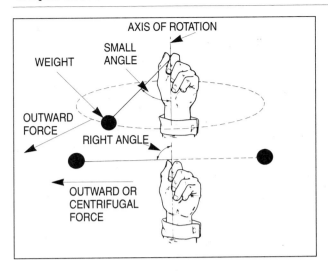

Figure 7-34 The effect of centrifugal force. (Ford Motor)

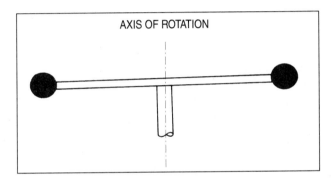

Figure 7-35 Equal weights in static and dynamic balance. (Ford Motor)

from side-to-side. This is dynamic imbalance, and when applied to the wheel and tire assembly, causes the wheel spindle to wobble (Figure 7-37).

When static balance is achieved by placing weights in segments 1 and 2, Figure 7-33, the wheel will tend to wobble when rotated at high speeds. This results from the attempt of the weights to reach a point exactly perpendicular to the center of rotation under centrifugal force. If the weights are on opposite sides of the center point, the wheel will wobble every half revolution, because the weights are trying to align with the rotational center. This is dynamic imbalance in action, and to compensate for it, other weights must be

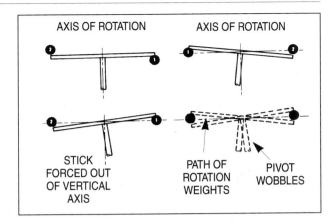

Figure 7-36 Dynamic imbalance occurs when one weight is above and the other below the axis of rotation. (Ford Motor)

installed in segments 3 and 4, Figure 7-33. If the weights are installed in this way, dynamic balance is obtained without affecting static balance.

A machine that balances by spinning the tire and wheel is NOT necessarily a dynamic balancer. If a machine tells the operator not only where to put the weights, but whether to put them on the outside or inside of the rim, then it is a true dynamic balancer. A balancer which only indicates the position of the weight and leaves it up to the operator to split the weight between the back and front of the wheel is NOT a dynamic balancer.

TREAD WEAR PATTERNS

If the front suspension is tight and mechanically sound, tire tread wear patterns are one of the best diagnostic tools available to help determine the cause of a problem. Since tire tread wear can be caused by incorrect inflation pressures, wheel and tire balance, and misalignment, we will discuss different wear patterns and what they indicate in the chapter covering wheel alignment.

SUMMARY

Wheel bearings keep the wheels aligned with the steering knuckle, allowing the

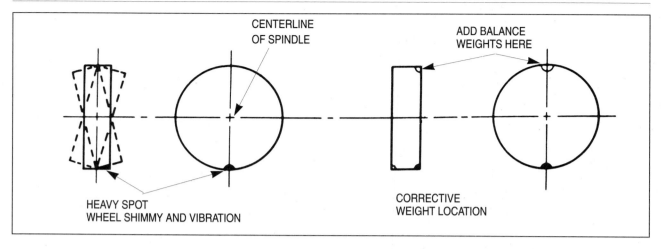

Figure 7-37 Dynamic imbalance and corrective measures. An off-the-car balancer indicates exactly where to put the weights. (Chrysler)

wheels and tires to rotate, while reducing the friction between the wheels and spindles and transmitting radial and thrust loads. Ball, roller, and tapered roller bearings may be used for this purpose, although the tapered bearings are the most common. Serviceable wheel bearings must be cleaned, inspected, repacked with grease, and adjusted at periodic intervals. If defective, they can be replaced with new bearings. Non-serviceable bearings are prelubricated and adjusted, and then sealed by the manufacturer. Two types of non-serviceable wheel bearings are used — a cartridge bearing or an integral bearing that is part of the hub assembly. Cartridge

WHEEL BEARING LUBRICANTS AND ADJUSTMENT

Not too many years ago, wheel bearings had to be cleaned, repacked with fresh grease, and adjusted at 5,000 mile intervals. Improvements in grease formulation have extended this service interval to 30,000 miles in the case of serviceable bearings, and eliminated it in the case of non-serviceable bearings. Although modern automotive greases resist heat, pressure, and moisture better than those used decades ago, care must be exercised when selecting and using wheel bearing lubricants.

Carmakers provide specifications for recommended wheel bearing lubricants. Grease manufacturers list those carmakers specs their product will meet, while continuing to improve it by reformulation. While no one lubricant meets the specs of ALL carmakers, one that meets as many specs as possible should be used. When repacking bearings, ALWAYS use the same type of grease. Do NOT mix the three popular types — moly-base (black grease), lithium-base (light yellow grease), or sodium-base (dark green grease) — because they are chemically incompatible.

By remembering **two simple rules**, you can adjust almost any automotive wheel bearing ever used:

1. Ball bearings should be set up with a slight preload.
2. Tapered roller bearings should be adjusted with slight endplay.

When serviceable ball bearings are used in wheel hubs, they are designed to take thrust. For this reason, they must have a slight preload to prevent the balls from running on the edge of the circular groove, instead of in it. Tapered roller bearings must be set up with slight endplay to prevent the rollers from taking end loads. When tapered rollers are slightly loose (up to 0.005" endplay), they simply move along the race slightly, which doesn't affect their load-carrying ability.

Wheel bearings can be adjusted either by feel or with a torque wrench. When necessary, an experienced technician can use the first method by bringing the nut up finger-tight and turning it a little at a time with a wrench while spinning the wheel until binding is felt. This is fine in emergency situations, but carmakers recommend seating the bearing first with a torque wrench, then backing the nut off and adjusting to the correct endplay.

bearings can be pressed out of the steering knuckle and replaced; a defective integral bearing is serviced by replacing the entire hub assembly.

Rear axle bearings perform the same functions as front wheel bearings, but those used with RWD vehicles differ in design and operation. Axle bearings are located at the outer end of the axle housing on each side of a vehicle, allowing the axle shaft to rotate in the bearing. Vehicle mass with a semi-floating rear axle design is transmitted to the wheels through the bearing and axle shaft. In a full-floating axle design, vehicle mass is transmitted directly to the wheels by the axle tube. In both semi- and full-floating axles, the bearings are lubricated by gear oil in the axle tubes, and a lip seal is used to prevent lubricant from leaking past the bearing into the brake assemblies.

Wheels hold the tires centered vertically and horizontally under loads created by varying factors. Diameter, width, and offset are important considerations when choosing replacement wheels. Tires must be selected to match the wheels with which they will be used. Tires have many items of information molded in their sidewalls, including tire size, maximum inflation pressure and load range, type of construction, and NHSA grade designations.

Wheels and tire assemblies must be properly balanced. If a wheel assembly is heavier at one point, it is out-of-balance. An out-of-balance condition creates and transmits vibrations to the suspension and steering systems. This affects directional stability and vehicle handling. Wheel balance takes two forms — static and dynamic. Static balance is the equal distribution of mass around the axis of wheel rotation. To be in dynamic balance, wheel and tire mass must also be equally distributed relative to the center line of the tire and wheel assembly.

❓ REVIEW QUESTIONS

1. Which of the following is NOT used in a front wheel bearing?
   (A) balls
   (B) needles
   (C) rollers
   (D) tapered rollers

2. Technician A says that a bearing cage is used to maintain proper ball or roller spacing and load distribution. Technician B says that cartridge bearings are adjustable and require lubrication. Who is right?
   (A) A only
   (B) B only
   (C) Both A and B
   (D) Neither A nor B

3. Technician A says that nonserviceable wheel bearings are used mainly with FWD vehicles. Technician B says that the inside wheel bearing used with adjustable bearings is larger than the outer one because it carries more of the vehicle mass. Who is right?
   (A) A only
   (B) B only
   (C) Both A and B
   (D) Neither A nor B

4. Technician A says that RWD vehicles usually have tapered roller wheel bearings on the front wheels. Technician B says that the inner race of a tapered roller bearing is called a cup. Who is right?
   (A) A only
   (B) B only
   (C) Both A and B
   (D) Neither A nor B

5. The endplay of adjustable tapered roller wheel bearings should be maintained between:
   (A) 0.010 to 0.015 in.
   (B) 0.007 to 0.010 in.
   (C) 0.005 to 0.007 in.
   (D) 0.001 to 0.005 in.

6. The rear axles of most RWD passenger cars are _____ type.
   (A) an elliptical
   (B) a symmetrical
   (C) a semi-floating
   (D) a full-floating

7. Technician A says that wheel diameter is measured to include the width of the flange. Technician B says that changing the wheel offset will not affect wheel bearing loading. Who is right?
   (A) A only
   (B) B only
   (C) Both A and B
   (D) Neither A nor B

8. Technician A says that wheel offset affects scrub radius. Technician B says that wheel width and tire tread width must be the same. Who is right?
   (A) A only
   (B) B only
   (C) Both A and B
   (D) Neither A nor B

9. Technician A says that a tire is designed to absorb road shock. Technician B says that the grip created between the tire and road is called traction. Who is right?
   (A) A only
   (B) B only
   (C) Both A and B
   (D) Neither A nor B

10. Technician A says that the bead wires of a tire help transmit starting and stopping force from the wheel to the tire. Technician B says that reinforced cotton is today commonly used for sidewall plies. Who is right?
    (A) A only
    (B) B only
    (C) Both A and B
    (D) Neither A nor B

11. Which part of a tubeless tire most nearly performs the function of the tube used in older tires?
    - (A) steel belts
    - (B) the liner
    - (C) sidewall plies
    - (D) none of the above

12. Technician A says that the tires support the vehicle. Technician B says that a tire with a tread wear grade of 100 will stop better under wet conditions. Who is right?
    - (A) A only
    - (B) B only
    - (C) Both A and B
    - (D) Neither A nor B

13. Technician A says that the more a tire's sidewall flexes, the more effective the tire is at dissipating heat. Technician B says that a major cause of heat is the friction between tire plies. Who is right?
    - (A) A only
    - (B) B only
    - (C) Both A and B
    - (D) Neither A nor B

14. Technician A says that wheel hop or tramp is caused by static wheel imbalance. Technician B says that this problem is may be caused by an out-of-round tire. Who is right?
    - (A) A only
    - (B) B only
    - (C) Both A and B
    - (D) Neither A nor B

15. Technician A says that when a wheel and tire are in static balance, the weight is distributed evenly around the axis of rotation. Technician B says that to be dynamically balanced, the weight must be distributed equally relative to the wheel and tire centerline. Who is right?
    - (A) A only
    - (B) B only
    - (C) Both A and B
    - (D) Neither A nor B

16. Technician A says that a wheel and tire assembly that is in static balance is also in dynamic balance. Technician B says that tire waddle can be caused by a crooked steel belt inside the tire. Who is right?
    - (A) A only
    - (B) B only
    - (C) Both A and B
    - (D) Neither A nor B

SUSPENSION ANGLES AND WHEEL ALIGNMENT

"Nothing is more terrible than to see ignorance in action."
— Johann Wolfgang von Goethe

OBJECTIVES

After completion of this chapter, you should be able to:

- List the five angles involved in wheel alignment, and identify which angles are adjustable.
- Define each of the alignment angles, and explain their relationship to each other.
- Explain the concept of scrub radius and its effect on tire tread wear.
- Explain the effect of caster on directional stability and steering effort.
- Define the terms 'at-rest' toe and 'running' toe.
- Explain the geometric principle behind turning radius.
- Explain trim height and describe its importance to front end geometry.
- Explain the concept of four-wheel alignment.

Proper front end **alignment** is important, if the vehicle is to follow a straight path on the highway with minimal steering effort on the driver's part. Front end alignment involves four factors: the suspension system, the steering system, the wheel and tire assemblies, and alignment angles.

The suspension system and the wheel/tire assemblies were discussed in earlier chapters. Only the angles of alignment and the steering system remain,

but both are vital factors in the proper operation of a vehicle on the road. In this chapter, you will learn the role alignment angles play in directional control, vehicle handling, and tire wear. Since the front wheels are connected to the steering and suspension systems, any condition that affects tire contact with the road will affect the life of the tires, suspension, and steering components.

A good alignment specialist can look at

a vehicle and determine exactly what has to be done to correct tire wear, difficult steering, and poor handling. Of course, it requires experience, but as knowledge must precede experience, we will learn in this chapter the basic factors involved in making such determinations.

WHEEL ALIGNMENT GEOMETRY

Front end geometry, as it is often called, is a term relating to the angular relationship between the front wheels, front suspension and steering components, and the road surface. There are five different angles involved in how the front wheels meet the road (Figure 8-1):

1. Camber
2. Caster
3. Toe
4. Steering Axis Inclination (SAI)
5. Turning radius.

The first three angles are adjustable; the other two are not. Alignment angles change as vehicle speed and load condition change, but should always return to their original setting when the vehicle is at rest and unloaded. Other factors, such as changes in road surface, and changes in

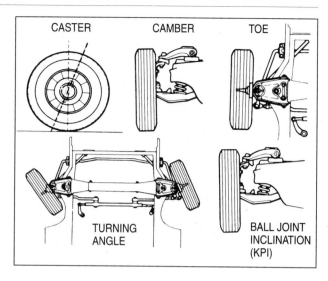

Figure 8-1 The five alignment angles involved in front-end geometry. (Ford Motor)

starting, cornering, and braking forces, also affect alignment angles.

CAMBER

Camber is defined as the inward or outward tilt of the wheels from a true vertical, as seen from the front of the vehicle. When a wheel tilts outward at the top, the camber is called 'positive', as shown in Figure 8-2. If the wheel tilts

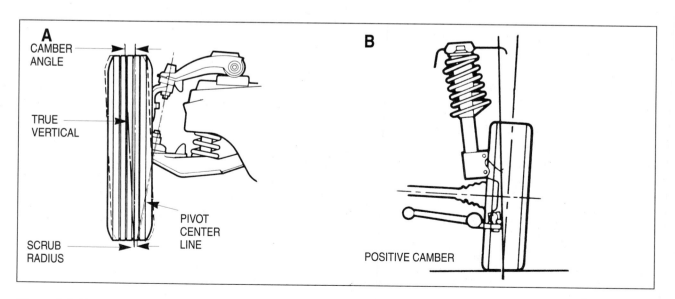

Figure 8-2 Positive camber with a ball joint suspension (A) or a strut suspension (B). (Ford Motor)

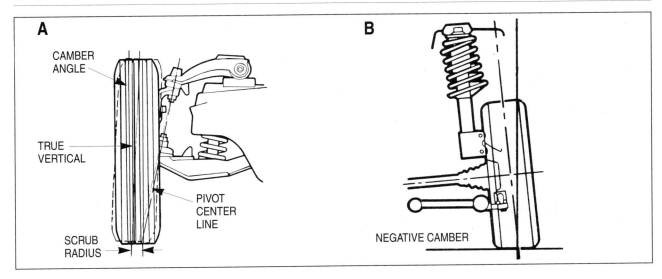

Figure 8-3   Negative camber with a ball joint suspension (A) or a strut suspension (B). (Ford Motor)

inward (Figure 8-3), the camber is 'negative'. The difference between the tilt of the wheel and true vertical is measured directly in degrees, and is called the **camber angle**.

When the center line of the wheel and tire assembly is the same as a true vertical line with the road surface, we say that the wheel has zero camber, which simply means that the wheel is straight up-and-down. In real world conditions, however, zero camber is seldom seen, since the camber angle of a vehicle in motion changes constantly according to the road surface and driving conditions (Figure 8-4).

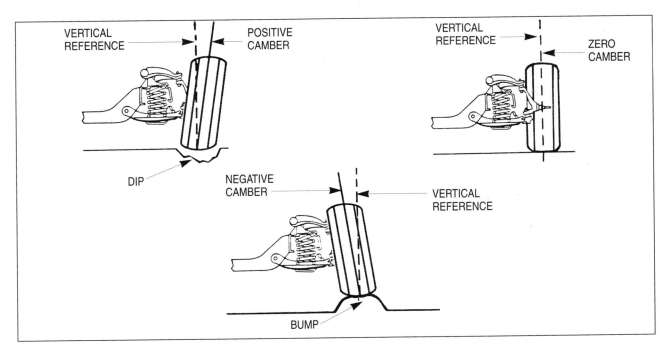

Figure 8-4   Camber changes from zero to positive or negative as the wheel passes over bumps and dips. (General Motors)

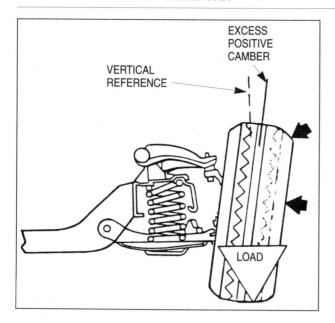

Figure 8-5 Excessive positive camber causes wear on the outside of the tire tread.

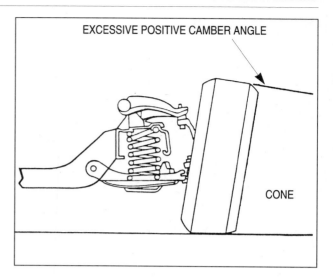

Figure 8-6 When a line is extended from the tread of a tire with positive camber, it results in a cone. This conical shape causes the tire to generate side force and roll toward the point of the cone. (General Motors)

The camber setting for a given vehicle is selected to take this fact into account.

The tread contact of the front tires with the road depends on the camber angle. When there is excessive positive camber, the outside of the tire is loaded (Figure 8-5). Excessive negative camber loads the inside of the tire instead. Because load distribution affects tire wear and steering control, the desired goal is to have maximum tread contact with the road under all conditions. If running camber can be maintained at or close to zero, load and wear will be evenly distributed over the full tread width, and steering will be much easier.

Incorrect camber will result in increased tire wear. It also can cause the vehicle to pull to one side. To demonstrate this, we will extend a line from the tread of a tire with excess positive camber. The result is a cone (Figure 8-6). When any conical object is rolled, it moves in a circle as it turns toward the smaller end of the cone. For this reason, when one tire has

more positive camber than the other tire, the vehicle will pull toward the tire with the most positive camber.

Scrub Radius

The distance between the center line of the steering axis, or pivot center line, and the center line of the tire to the road, is called

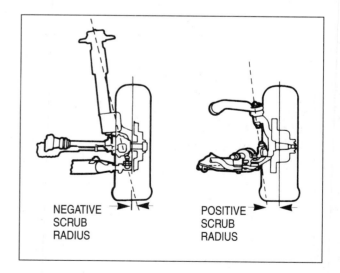

Figure 8-7 Examples of negative and positive scrub radius. (Chrysler)

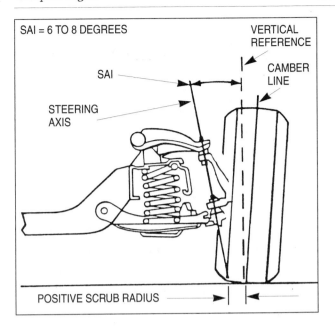

Figure 8-8 When the pivot point is inside the tire contact point, the scrub radius is positive. (General Motors)

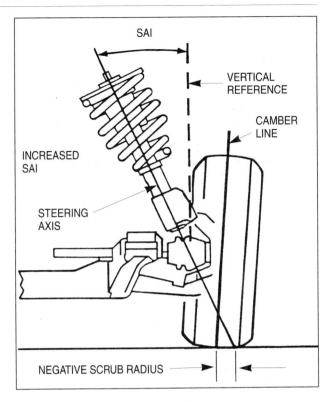

Figure 8-9 If the pivot point moves outside the tire contact point, the scrub radius becomes negative. (General Motors)

the 'scrub radius' (Figure 8-7). We encountered this imaginary line earlier during our discussion of various suspension designs. Scrub radius is NOT an alignment angle, and cannot be measured with conventional alignment equipment.

To see the effect of changes in scrub radius as camber angles change, refer to Figure 8-8 and Figure 8-9. Scrub radius is important because it affects steering control. Since the pivot point is inside the point of road contact, the tire does NOT pivot at its point of contact with the road, but has to move forward or backward as the steering wheel is turned. This makes it difficult to turn the wheels in either direction. The amount of scrub radius that is present directly affects steering ease, tire wear, the amount of road shock reaching the steering wheel, and braking effort.

The greater the amount of scrub radius present, the longer the lever arm acting against the steering wheel is, and the greater the front or rear movement of the wheels as they are turned from their straight-ahead position. Scrub radius can be controlled somewhat by tilting the top of the wheel outward enough to produce a slight degree of positive camber. This brings the tire's point of road contact closer to the pivot center line, reducing the scrub radius. This tends to reduce pivot binding, tire wear, road shock, and steering effort. With modern vehicles, however, steering axis inclination (SAI) has a greater effect on scrub radius.

Camber in Motion

When a front wheel strikes a bump on the road surface, its upward movement is called a 'jounce'. Because the upper control arm is shorter than the lower control arm, the two arms do not follow the same upward path, or arc. Upward wheel

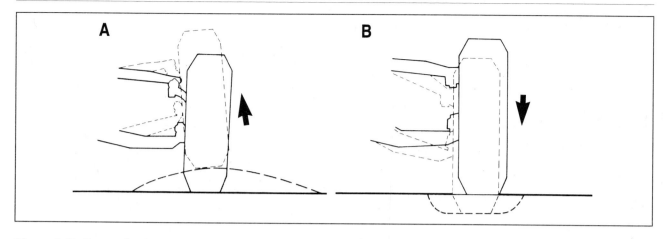

Figure 8-10 Front wheel jounce movements cause negative camber (A). Rebound movement of the wheel (B) produces zero or slightly positive camber. (Ford Motor)

movement, coupled with the shorter swing arc of the upper arm, causes the top of the wheel to tilt inward (A, Figure 8-10) and produces negative camber. Driving the vehicle into a smooth but fast turn causes the body and chassis to roll toward the outside of the curve. This creates a force, similar to that of a jounce condition, on the outside wheel. As the wheel is forced upward, its top leans inward and results in a negative camber condition relative to the vehicle body (Figure 8-11).

If the front wheel drops into a hole in the road surface, its downward movement

is called a 'rebound'. A rebound action (B, Figure 8-10) will produce either zero camber or a slight positive camber angle. Upward body movement, such as the roll effect of the body and chassis during a turn, lifts the mass from the inside wheel and causes the tire to lean outward at the top. This results in zero camber, or a slightly positive camber at the inside wheel (Figure 8-12).

The camber changes resulting from up-and-down movements of the tires offer some degree of directional stability. But the effect of camber changes on vehicle

Figure 8-11 Downward body movement during a turn produces negative camber. (Ford Motor)

Figure 8-12 Upward body movement during a turn produces zero or slightly positive camber. (Ford Motor)

Figure 8-13 How camber produces skid resistance during a turn. (Ford Motor)

handling and roadability is more evident in turns and on **crowned road** surfaces, since a mass shift to one side is present with the up-and-down movement. Centrifugal force, acting on the body during the turn, tries to push the vehicle sideways, but is resisted by tire traction.

During a turning maneuver, body lean produces negative camber at the outside wheel, with the amount of camber change becoming more pronounced as the vehicle speed increases. As a result, the inner part of the tire tread must brace itself against skidding sideways (Figure 8-13) to counter-act the centrifugal force trying to push the vehicle to the outer side of the turn. At the same time, the downward weight shift on the outer wheel increases traction to resist a skid. With the outer wheel tilting in a negative camber position, a bracing force against skidding is also applied by the zero or slight positive camber at the inside wheel. The outer wheel offers more resistance against skidding in this case because the load and traction placed on it is greater.

Cargo load or passenger position also affects camber angle. Camber specifications generally are set for a vehicle with only a driver, with slightly more positive

camber on the right wheel to compensate for the driver's weight on the left wheel. When the camber angle is not correct, or if the vehicle load is not distributed evenly, the vehicle may pull to one side. Uneven tire wear will result from incorrect running camber.

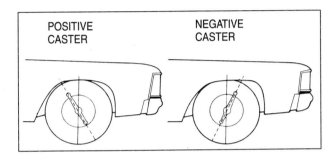

Figure 8-14 Positive and negative caster angles. (Ford Motor)

Caster

While camber relates to the lean of the wheel inward or outward from a true vertical as seen from the front of the wheel, **caster** is the forward or rearward tilt of the ball joint or kingpin from a true vertical, as seen from the side of the front wheel (Figure 8-14). When the tilt is toward the rear at the top of the wheel, the caster

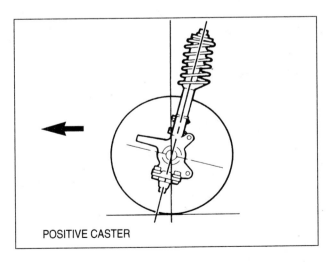

Figure 8-15 Positive caster in a strut suspension. (Ford Motor)

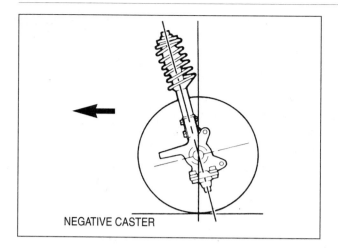

Figure 8-16 Negative caster in a strut suspension. (Ford Motor)

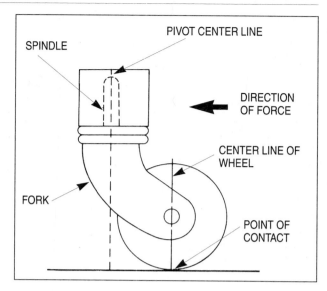

Figure 8-17 Operation of a typical tool chest wheel demonstrates the principles of caster. (Ford Motor)

angle is positive (Figure 8-15). When tilted forward, the caster angle is negative (Figure 8-16). Caster is measured in degrees of slant between the steering axis and true vertical. It cannot be measured directly, but must be calculated by an instrument attached to the front wheels.

The caster angle has only a minimal effect on tire wear. It is far more important because it:

- helps maintain directional stability by keeping the vehicle on a straight-ahead path
- helps to return the wheels to a straight-ahead position when completing a turn
- controls the steering effort required to turn the wheels from a straight-ahead position.

Directional Stability

To understand how caster affects a vehicle's wheels, let's look at a typical caster wheel used on your tool chest (Figure 8-17). In this example, the wheel follows the direction of the caster fork. Since the fork pivots freely on its vertical spindle, the caster wheel is always aligned with the direction of movement. The vertical center line of the caster wheel will

intersect the floor behind the vertical center line of the spindle, or pivot point.

The mass of the tool chest on the caster wheel causes a resistance to caster wheel movement. Any force placed on the pivot causes the caster wheel to align with the force applied to the pivot (Figure 8-18). Since the spindle is positioned vertically,

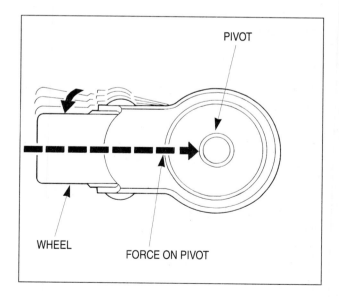

Figure 8-18 Shimmying action of a tool chest caster wheel. (Ford Motor)

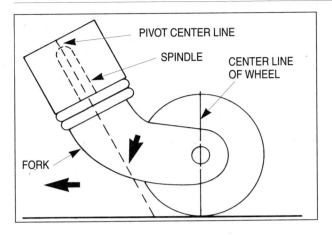

Figure 8-19 The spindle tilt loads the tool chest caster fork and reduces shimmy. (Ford Motor)

resistance to side movement is minimal, allowing the caster wheels to **shimmy** as they move. By tilting the spindle until its pivot center line contacts the surface at a point ahead of the caster wheel's center line (Figure 8-19), the wheel's directional effect can be controlled. When the spindle is tilted, any load applied to the caster fork will keep the wheel rolling in a straight line, minimizing the tendency of the wheel to shimmy. The tilt of the spindle also produces a downward force when the caster wheel is turned to one side or the other. The wheel attempts to move lower than the

floor, or road surface, which is not possible. Therefore, the rotating force lifts the caster wheel upward.

When applied to a vehicle in motion, this rotating force tries to lift the entire body and chassis upward. Since turning the wheels lifts the vehicle, the load on the spindle helps to return the wheels to their straight-ahead position. If the vehicle is equipped with power-assisted steering, the steering gear helps to hold the wheels in position both in a straight-ahead direction or on a curve. Because power steering resists any forces applied to the wheels, more directional force is required to automatically return them straight-ahead. This extra directional force is obtained through the use of positive caster. The increased turning effort required by positive caster is offset by the power steering. In contrast, negative caster may be used with non-power steering to place the ball joint center line behind the center of the tire tread contact patch. This makes it easier to steer the vehicle.

Zero Caster

Zero caster has no effect on directional stability (Figure 8-20). When the pivot

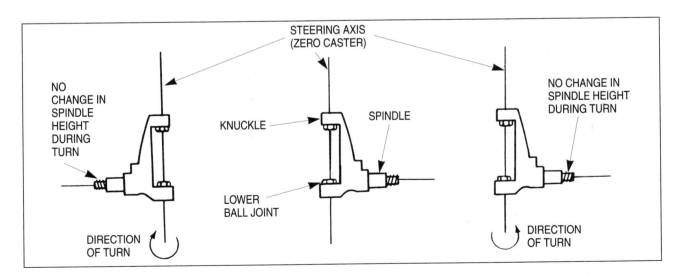

Figure 8-20 Steering axis and spindle angle at zero caster. (General Motors)

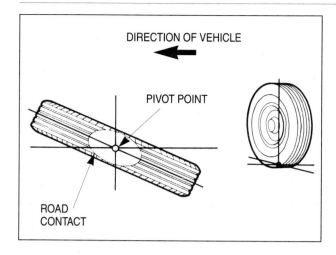

Figure 8-21 The directional stability of zero caster. (Ford Motor)

point center line is perpendicular to the road, it is aligned with the tire's pivot point (Figure 8-21). Since both points are the same, the wheel does not tend to move in either direction.

Positive Caster

When positive caster is present, the pivot point center line is forward of the tire contact point (Figure 8-22). The front part of the pivot point contact is off-center

relative to vehicle direction whenever the wheel is turned from the straight-ahead position. The friction or drag offered by the rear part of the pivot point contact causes a force that tends to hold or return the wheel to its straight-ahead position. When both front wheels have positive caster, the vehicle tends to lean outward, or roll outward, on turns.

Negative Caster

With negative caster, the pivot point forces are reversed, with the rear part of the pivot point contact providing the drag or friction (Figure 8-23). This location of the drag area tends to turn the wheel farther from the straight-ahead position. When both front wheels have negative caster, the vehicle tends to lean in, or bank, on turns.

Steering Effort

Since positive caster tends both to hold the wheels in a straight-ahead position, and return them to that position, the amount of steering effort required to change the position of the wheels and hold them there is greater. Remember, positive caster tends to raise the inside spindle and lower the

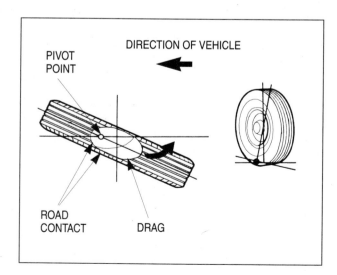

Figure 8-22 The effect of drag created by positive caster. (Ford Motor)

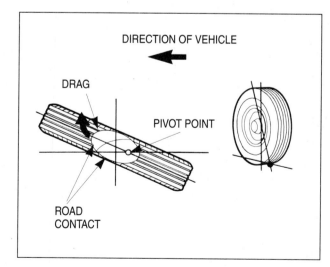

Figure 8-23 The effect of drag created by negative caster. (Ford Motor)

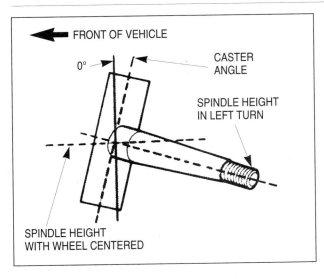

Figure 8-24 The effect of positive caster on spindle height in a turn. (Ford Motor)

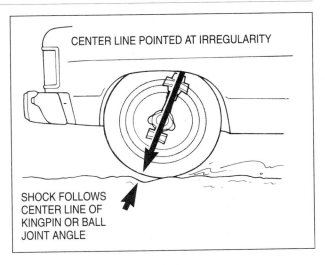

Figure 8-25 Road shock is created by the spindle pivot center line being pointed at road irregularities, preventing shock absorption by the suspension. (Ford Motor)

outside spindle on a turn (Figure 8-24).

Too much positive caster can result in a high steering effort, too rapid a wheel return, shimmy at low speed, and road shock. Road shock results when the spindle pivot center line is pointed at road irregularities, preventing the suspension from absorbing as much of the shock as it normally would (Figure 8-25).

Since the horizontal plane of the vehicle influences caster angle, positive caster will be decreased if the front springs sag. Rear spring sag, however, will increase positive caster (Figure 8-26). Large, heavy vehicles that use wide cross-section tires will have better directional stability with a smaller caster angle than smaller vehicles with narrow cross-section tires. In fact, because heavier vehicles do NOT require a positive caster angle (which increases steering effort) for stability, many such vehicles use negative caster. This reduces the steering effort required, as well as the tendency of the wheels to 'snap-back' or return on their own.

Changes in rear suspension height affect the front wheel caster angle. Installing new or stiffer rear springs will raise the rear of the vehicle, moving the caster angle in the negative direction. When one rear spring is higher than the other, the rear suspension height is uneven and so is the front wheel caster. This is the reason that rear springs always should be replaced in pairs, and why steering drift can result from a spring that sags.

TOE

Wheel toe is measured at the front and rear of the tires. If the wheels and tires are closer together at the front than at the rear, the wheels have toe-in (Figure 8-27). When they are farther apart at the front, the wheels have toe-out (Figure 8-28). Wheel toe, like camber, affects tire tread wear, but toe is the most important alignment angle involved in tire wear. Excessive toe-in or toe-out will cause a scrubbing effect as the tire revolves because the center line of its tread contact patch does not point straight ahead. In short, the vehicle and its front tire treads are not headed in the same direction. If the toe setting of a wheel is off as little as 0.125 inch, the result is tire wear equal to the tire being shoved

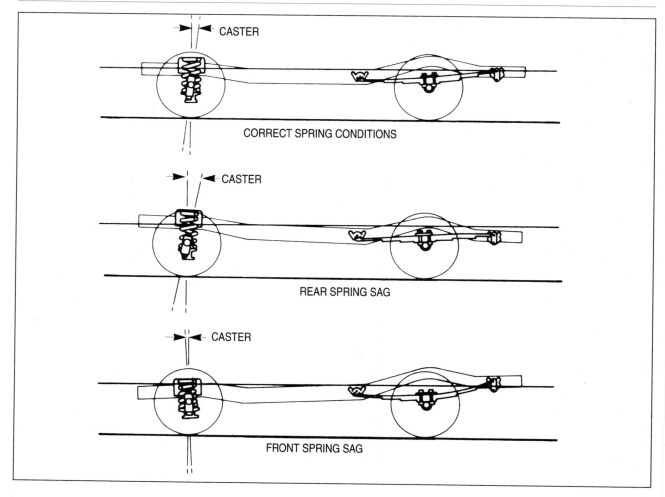

Figure 8-26 Caster changes resulting from spring sag. (Ford Motor)

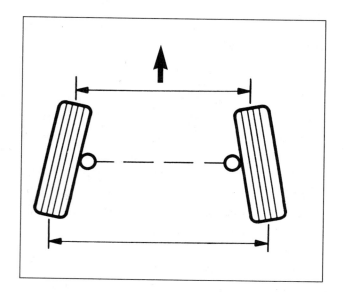

Figure 8-27 Toe-in. (Ford Motor)

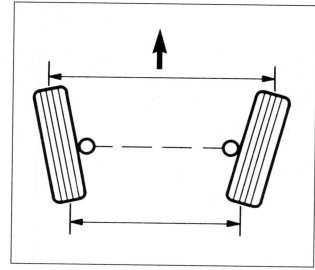

Figure 8-28 Toe-out. (Ford Motor)

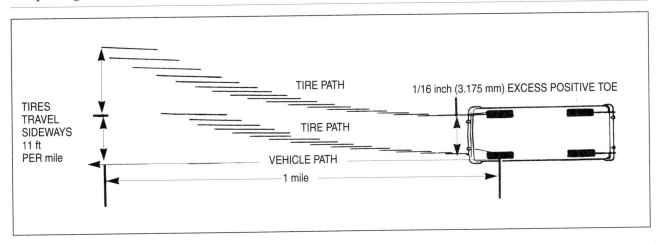

Figure 8-29 Tire wear caused by incorrect toe. (General Motors)

sideways 11 ft for each mile the vehicle is driven (Figure 8-29).

Proper toe alignment corrects changes in wheel alignment that result from driving and braking forces. The rolling resistance of the revolving tires and brake applications produce forces that tend to push the wheels outward. This compresses or pushes the tie rods behind the wheels inward, allowing the wheels and tires to move in the toe-out direction. Wear in

bushings, idler arms, and/or tie rod ends also have an effect on how much the tires will toe out while in motion.

With most RWD vehicles, the wheels are set to toe in with the vehicle stationary. This is called **at-rest toe**. Since the front wheels and tires on a RWD vehicle tend to toe outward when in motion, the **running toe** setting should be at or near zero when all normal steering clearances are taken into account (Figure 8-30). A slight

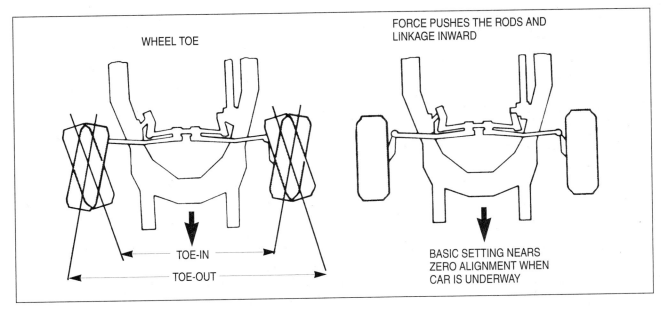

Figure 8-30 The at-rest toe setting changes to a running-toe setting when an RWD vehicle starts in motion. (Ford Motor)

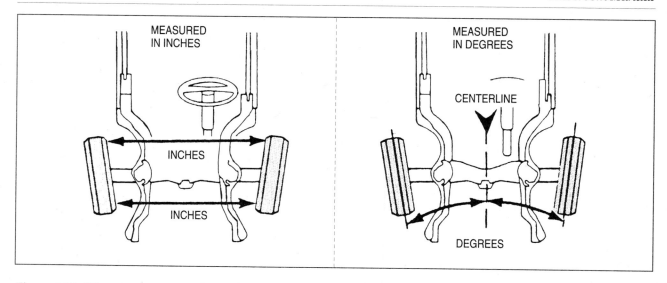

Figure 8-31 When toe is measured in inches or millimeters, the measurement is the difference in distance between the front and rear of the wheels. When measured in degrees, it is the angle between the wheel's plane of rotation and the vehicle centerline. (General Motors)

amount of running toe-in is acceptable under normal conditions, but a vehicle moving in a straight line with its wheels toed out can suffer from steering wander.

Since the front tires of FWD vehicles have a tendency to toe inward as they pull the vehicle down the road, they generally are set just the reverse of RWD vehicles. If the at-rest toe is set to a slight amount of toe-out, zero or near-zero toe will result when the vehicle is in motion. Excessive wheel toe in either direction will result in serious tire wear problems. Toe measurements may be expressed in inches, millimeters, or in degrees (Figure 8-31).

STEERING AXIS INCLINATION

Also known as kingpin or ball joint inclination, steering axis inclination (SAI) is the inward tilt of the top of the steering axis, when seen from the front of the vehicle. The lower control arm and its inner mount determine the position of the lower pivot point. On an SLA suspension, the upper ball joint determines the position of the upper pivot point (A, Figure 8-32). When a strut suspension is used, the position of the strut tower determines the location of the upper pivot point (B, Figure 8-32). The imaginary line drawn through the upper and lower pivot points is called the SAI; the number of degrees that this line tips inward from the true vertical is called the inclination angle, or the SAI angle. SAI cannot be measured directly, but must be calculated.

When the SAI angle and the camber angle are combined, the total is called the **included angle** (Figure 8-33). When the included angle is not given as such, it can be determined by adding positive or subtracting the negative camber reading from the specification for SAI. For example, if the SAI specification is 12°, and camber measures +2°, the included angle will be 14°. If the SAI specification is 12°, and camber measures -2°, the included angle will be 10°. If the measured included angle agrees with the specification book, the SAI must be correct.

SAI and included angles are used primarily as diagnostic angles. Measuring the SAI is more important with strut suspensions than with the older SLA suspen-

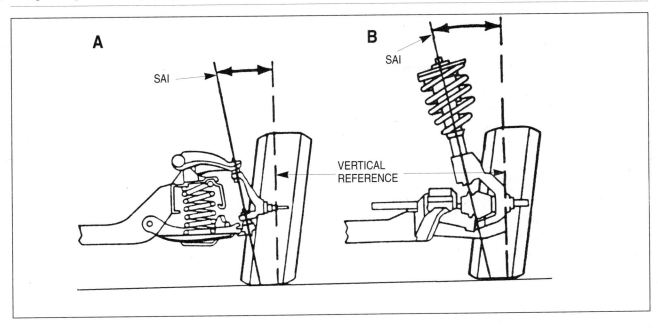

Figure 8-32 Steering axis inclination (SAI) works with camber to reduce the effect of road irregularities on vehicle steering. (General Motors)

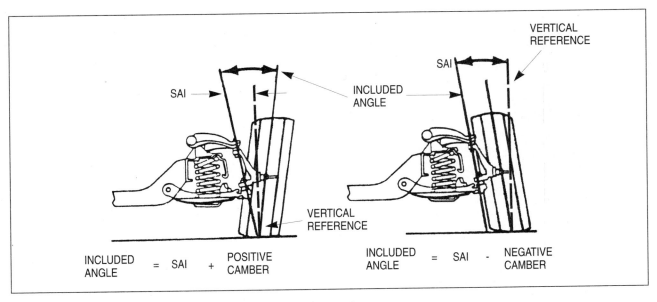

Figure 8-33 The included angles on each side of the vehicle should be within 0.5° of each other. (General Motors)

sions, because a strut suspension bends easier in a collision. After all other adjustable angles have been set at the proper specifications, both the SAI and the included angle should be checked. For example, if the camber has been set to specifications, and the SAI or included angle are not within specifications, the cause probably is a bent suspension component or a misaligned suspension attachment point. By measuring these angles and making side-to-side comparisons, it is possible to determine whether the damage is in the suspension or the body.

Both the caster angle and the SAI are related to the tilt of the steering axis. As we have seen, caster is the tilt of the steering axis to front or rear. SAI is the steering axis tilt to right or left. The effect of vehicle mass on the SAI and the caster is to help the vehicle remain on a straight course, and to return the wheels to a straight-ahead position when coming out of a turn. Because the SAI is greater than the caster angle, it has the greatest effect on directional stability.

SAI also has the greatest effect on steering effort. While the caster angle moves the turning axis center line away from the center of tread contact patch, the SAI places the ball joint or kingpin center line near the center of the tread contact patch. Without SAI, a greater effort is needed to steer the wheel because the full travel contact surface will turn sideways, or at an angle to the actual direction of travel (Figure 8-34). This sideways motion will cause the tire tread to scrub excessively on turns, resulting both in excessive turning effort and tire wear. With SAI, the axis

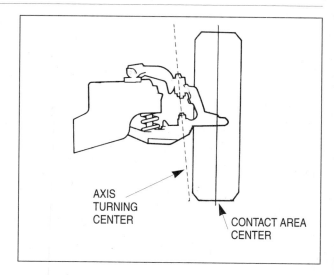

Figure 8-35 With SAI or ball joint inclination, tire scrubbing is reduced and steering is made easier. (Ford Motor)

turning center moves closer to the center of the tire tread contact patch (Figure 8-35). Because the tires rotate about this center, less scrubbing occurs when the wheels are turned, reducing both tire wear and steering effort.

TOE-OUT ON TURNS

Toe-out on turns is non-adjustable but must be checked. If it is incorrect, some part of the suspension may be bent. When rounding a corner, both front and rear wheels must turn around a common center with respect to the radius of the turn (Figure 8-36).

Because the inside wheel leads the outer wheel in a cornering maneuver, it must turn at a sharper angle if it is to remain perpendicular to the radius and avoid tire scrubbing. This means that in turns the wheels are toed out.

To see how this is accomplished, let us consider the geometric action of a lever that moves in a circle (Figure 8-37). If the lever is moved from point A to point B, it pivots around point O and moves the horizontal distance AB. Continuing to move the lever from point B to point C, it covers a much

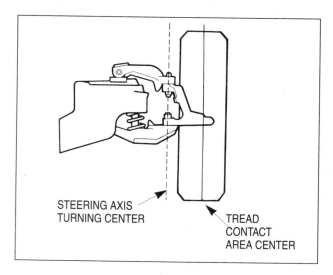

Figure 8-34 Without SAI, the full tire tread area would scrub the road surface, causing great difficulty in steering and turning. (Ford Motor)

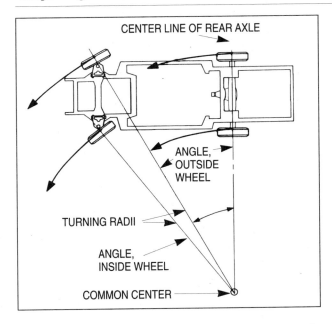

Figure 8-36 Turning radius or toe-out in turns controls front wheel tracking to minimize side slipping and tire wear. (Ford Motor)

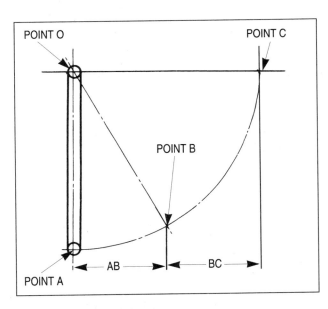

Figure 8-37 The geometric action of a lever moving in a circle. (Ford Motor)

greater distance, but the horizontal movement BC remains the same, despite the greater arc.

Applying this principle to the front end of a vehicle, we see that the inner wheel

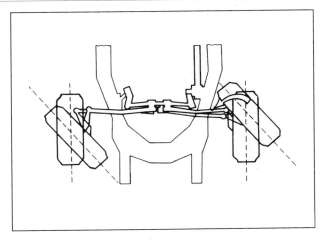

Figure 8-38 Steering arm travel varies with wheel direction. The inner wheel makes a smaller circle than the outer wheel. (Ford Motor)

must roll around a smaller circle than the outer wheel (Figure 8-38). To make this possible, the steering arms must be angled inward, away from the forward and rearward center lines of the front tires. Since the steering arms are not parallel to the wheels, but are angled inward, each arm moves through a different part of its arc during front wheel turning. This means that as the left arm moves away from the straight-ahead position during a left turn, a comparatively small amount of tire and steering arm travel results in a considerable amount of left wheel turning movement. While this is taking place, the right steering arm moves toward the straight-ahead position. In this part of its arc, the same amount of tie rod/steering arm travel results in less right wheel turning movement.

Since centrifugal force causes all the tires to slip somewhat, a slip angle condition is possible at almost any speed during a turn. For this reason, the actual turning center is considerably ahead of the theoretical center (Figure 8-39). Slip angles differ according to vehicle design; two vehicles with the same wheelbase may not necessarily have the same steering arm angles.

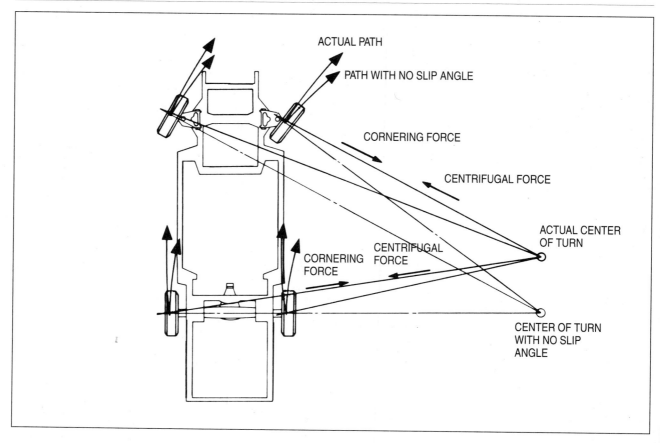

Figure 8-39 Slippage caused by centrifugal force moves the actual turning center ahead of the theoretical center. (Ford Motor)

TRIM HEIGHT

Trim height refers to the normal no-load height of a vehicle, and its measurement is a quick and easy way to check for possible weak or sagging springs that have changed the suspension system geometry. It also is called curb height or chassis height, since it is defined as the distance between the vehicle frame, or the bottom of the front and rear suspensions, and a level surface (Figure 8-40).

Some signs of trim height problems are:
- a harsh ride
- split or shiny rubber absorbers or jounce bumpers caused by excess suspension movement
- shiny areas on coil spring convolutions, indicating coil clash

- worn shock absorbers, ball joints, or tie rods caused by changes in steering geometry
- drive shaft rubbing on the undercarriage of RWD vehicles caused by the vehicle bottoming out.

Trim height serves as a primary engineering reference point on the vehicle, since control arm movement occurs within the specified vehicle height. If the springs are weak or sagged, the resulting change in suspension geometry (A, Figure 8-41) also will change the caster, camber, toe, and turning radius of the vehicle (B, Figure 8-41). For this reason, trim height must be within specifications before wheel alignment. Although there is no uniformity among carmakers in measuring locations

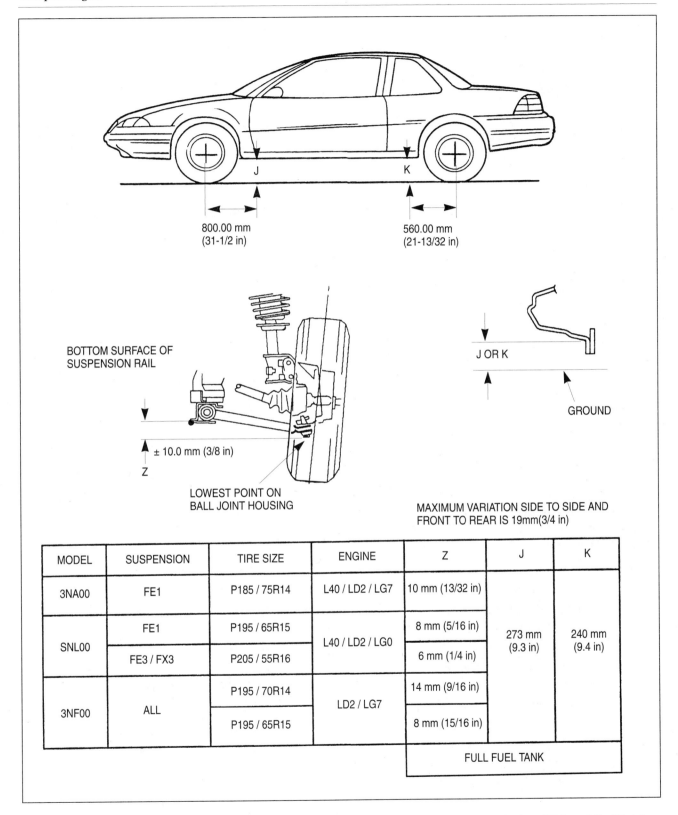

MODEL	SUSPENSION	TIRE SIZE	ENGINE	Z	J	K
3NA00	FE1	P185 / 75R14	L40 / LD2 / LG7	10 mm (13/32 in)		
SNL00	FE1	P195 / 65R15	L40 / LD2 / LG0	8 mm (5/16 in)	273 mm (9.3 in)	240 mm (9.4 in)
	FE3 / FX3	P205 / 55R16		6 mm (1/4 in)		
3NF00	ALL	P195 / 70R14	LD2 / LG7	14 mm (9/16 in)		
		P195 / 65R15		8 mm (15/16 in)		
				FULL FUEL TANK		

Figure 8-40 Typical trim height measuring points and specifications used with GM vehicles. (Oldsmobile Division, General Motors)

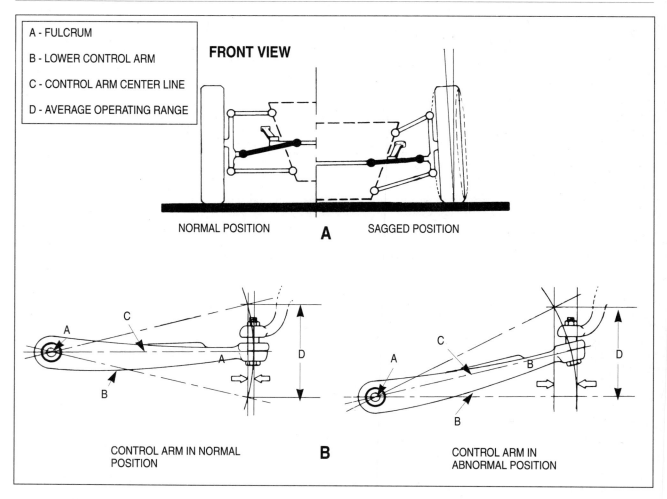

A - FULCRUM

B - LOWER CONTROL ARM

C - CONTROL ARM CENTER LINE

D - AVERAGE OPERATING RANGE

FRONT VIEW

NORMAL POSITION   **A**   SAGGED POSITION

CONTROL ARM IN NORMAL POSITION   **B**   CONTROL ARM IN ABNORMAL POSITION

Figure 8-41 Weak or sagged springs cause a change in steering link position, as well as control arm position (A). Sagged springs increase the lateral movement of the wheels (B). This causes the tires to move sideways across the road surface and results in tire wear (B). (Moog Automotive)

(Figure 8-42), trim height specifications are available from carmakers and aftermarket spring manufacturers. Trim height cannot be determined visually; the specified points must be measured to make any accurate assessment of the vehicle.

The front trim height of vehicles equipped with a torsion bar suspension is adjustable. Typically, this adjustment is made by turning an adjuster bolt on each torsion bar mount (Figure 8-43). In the case of the bolt shown in Figure 8-43, it changes the dimension between the lower control arm pivot bolt center line and the lower (inner) corner of the steering knuckle (Figure 8-44). The dimension changed by torsion bar adjustment will depend on the individual vehicle.

FOUR-WHEEL ALIGNMENT

Since the rear wheels are NOT involved in steering or turning, only the tire wear angles (camber and toe) are of concern. If the rear wheel camber or toe angles are NOT correct, the rear tires will wear in the same way as misaligned front tires.

The rear axle housing on RWD vehicles with a non-independent rear suspension

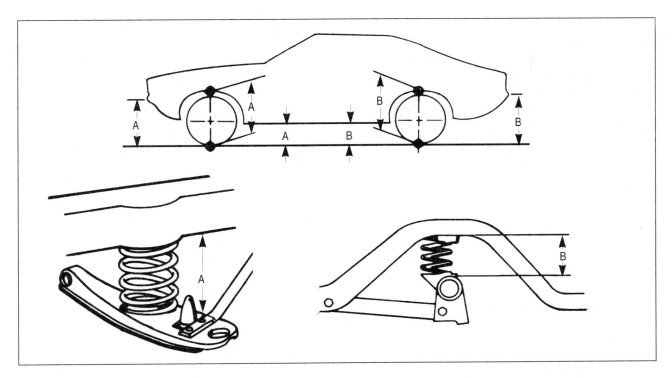

Figure 8-42 Carmakers use different points of measurement to determine trim height. (Moog Automotive)

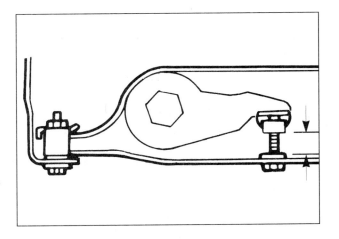

Figure 8-43 Typical torsion bar adjuster mechanism. (General Motors)

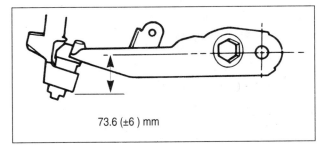

73.6 (±6) mm

Figure 8-44 One type of trim height specification for a torsion bar suspension. The measurement is from the centerline of the arm pivot to the bottom edge of the spindle arm. (General Motors)

maintains rear wheel alignment. If the rear wheel alignment is NOT correct, the housing is probably bent and must be replaced. When an independent rear suspension is used, camber and toe adjustments can usually be made. Most FWD vehicles have provisions for adjusting rear wheel camber or toe (Figure 8-45 and Figure 8-46).

Vehicle tracking and thrust angle, which were discussed in the chapter on suspension dynamics, are important in four-wheel alignment. The rear wheels should be parallel to each other, as well as parallel to the vehicle center line, in order

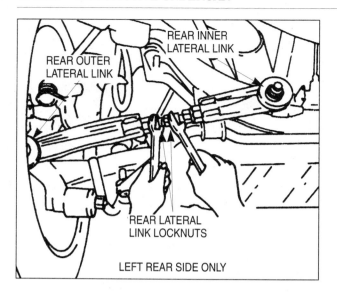

Figure 8-45 Rear wheel alignment is required on many FWD vehicles. One of the various methods used is an adjustable lateral link. (Ford Motor)

to track or directly follow the front wheels down the road. Rear wheels that are NOT parallel to the center line will cause the vehicle to move down the road with a slightly sideways motion, requiring constant steering corrections.

TIRE TREAD WEAR PATTERNS

The tire tread wear pattern (Figure 8-47) is one of the best diagnostic tools available to help pinpoint problems of excessive wear, providing that the front suspension is in good condition.

EXCESSIVE SHOULDER WEAR

Excessive wear on the outer shoulder of a tire generally is caused by too much positive camber, allowing the tire to tilt too far outward at the top (Figure 8-48). By placing too much of the vehicle's mass and load on the over-tilted outside shoulder of the tire, tread wear is greatly increased. Too much negative camber will tip the top of the tire too far inward (Figure 8-49), causing excessive wear on the inside shoulder of the tire.

Underinflation or high speed cornering can result in the presence of excessive wear on both shoulders. To distinguish between the two, check the center of the tread. If the edges of the center tread are reasonably

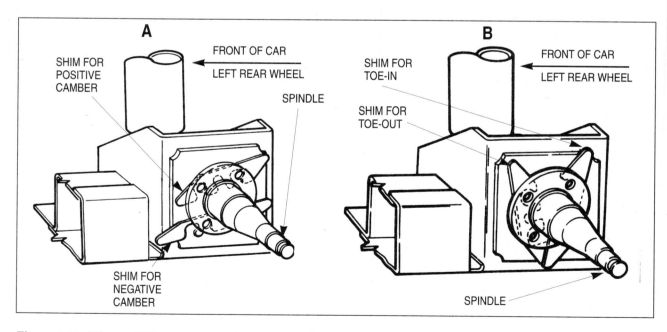

Figure 8-46 When a FWD rear suspension uses a stub axle, one method of adjusting camber and toe is to shim the spindle at the top or bottom to change camber (A), and at the sides to set toe (B). (Chrysler)

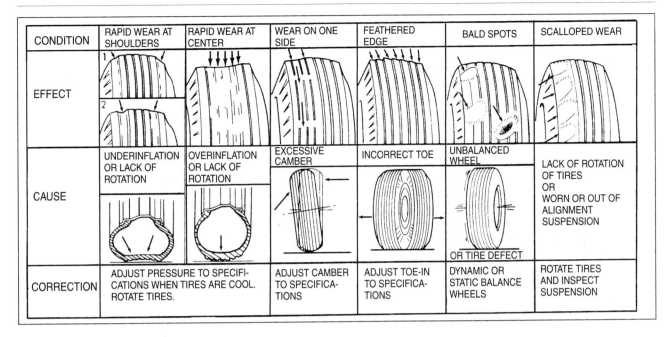

CONDITION	RAPID WEAR AT SHOULDERS	RAPID WEAR AT CENTER	WEAR ON ONE SIDE	FEATHERED EDGE	BALD SPOTS	SCALLOPED WEAR
EFFECT						
CAUSE	UNDERINFLATION OR LACK OF ROTATION	OVERINFLATION OR LACK OF ROTATION	EXCESSIVE CAMBER	INCORRECT TOE	UNBALANCED WHEEL OR TIRE DEFECT	LACK OF ROTATION OF TIRES OR WORN OR OUT OF ALIGNMENT SUSPENSION
CORRECTION	ADJUST PRESSURE TO SPECIFICATIONS WHEN TIRES ARE COOL. ROTATE TIRES.		ADJUST CAMBER TO SPECIFICATIONS	ADJUST TOE-IN TO SPECIFICATIONS	DYNAMIC OR STATIC BALANCE WHEELS	ROTATE TIRES AND INSPECT SUSPENSION

Figure 8-47 Tire wear patterns. (Chrysler)

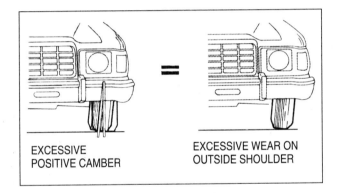

Figure 8-48 Effect of excessive positive camber on tire wear. (Ford Motor)

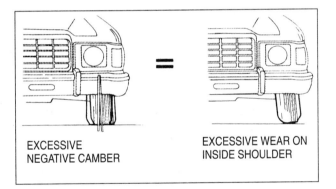

Figure 8-49 Effect of excessive negative camber on tire wear. (Ford Motor)

sharp, the cause is probably underinflation. When the tread rounds downward from the center to the edges smoothly, the wear probably results from high speed driving on curves. Such driving causes heavy side thrusts on the tire during turns, resulting in tread roll-under.

EXCESSIVE CENTER TREAD WEAR

If a tire is overinflated, the center of the tread will wear faster than the shoulders

because the tread does NOT lie flat on the road surface.

SAWTOOTHED OR FEATHERED WEAR

A sawtoothed or feathered wear pattern on the front tire tread usually indicates a problem in toe adjustment. To determine the exact cause, place the palm of your hand on the tread. Move your hand toward the center of the tire, then back to the edge, feeling the direction of the sawtooth or feather (Figure 8-50). One edge of the

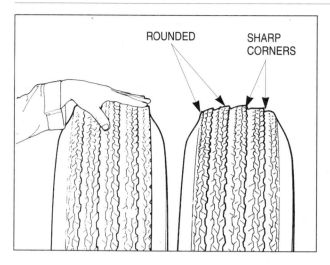

Figure 8-50 A sawtooth or feathered pattern can help determine whether toe is excessive in either direction. (Ford Motor)

tread may feel sharp, while the other edge feels rounded. If you feel the sharp edge as you move your hand toward the center of the tire, that is the sharp edge is pointing out, the wheel is toed-out too much. When the sharp edge is felt as your hand moves toward the outside of the tire, that is the sharp edge is pointing in, the wheel is toed-in too much. If there is no sharp edge in either direction, the toe setting is not causing a problem.

CUPPED OR DISHED WEAR

This type of wear may indicate a tire that is out of balance, or one with excessive radial runout. It also can result from a defect in tire manufacturing. If the cupping takes the form of a scalloped pattern, look for a worn suspension or alignment problem. Some tires do NOT wear evenly, especially on the front of FWD vehicles. If the cupping is severe, the only solution may be to replace the tire.

SUMMARY

Five different angles are involved in the relationship between the front wheels, front suspension and steering components, and

SPOTLIGHT

TORQUE STEER

Many FWD vehicles experience a problem called 'torque steer'. This causes a vehicle to lead or pull in one direction when accelerating from a standing start or during hard acceleration at lower speeds, and pull in the other direction when decelerating. This is caused by the use of unequal length drive axles, and the associated difference in drive axle angle at the CV joints. A vehicle with equal length drive axles, or an intermediate shaft to produce the equivalent of almost equal length axles, seldom suffers from this problem. When the axles are NOT equal in length, torque toe-in affects the wheel with the shorter axle (Figure S8-1).

This was a major steering problem with FWD vehicles in the early 1980's until intermediate shafts were introduced. Subsequent vehicle design corrected much of the problem by using equal length axles when possible. The condition still exists to some degree with any FWD vehicle, especially if the wheels are NOT pointing straight ahead when accelerating from a parked position. For example, if the wheels are turned slightly to one side, the vehicle will seem to 'jump' in that direction when power is applied.

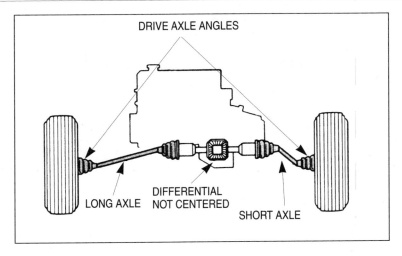

Figure S8-1 For unequal drive axle lengths, torque toe-in affects the wheel with the shorter axle.

Transaxles are designed so that the twisting force or drive torque that turns the drive wheels is equal at each wheel. A secondary twisting motion called 'steer torque' is created by the outer CV joint (A, Figure S8-2). As a result, the front wheels tend to turn in toward the vehicle center line when torque is applied.

With both axle angles equalized (B, Figure S8-2), the steer torque at one wheel cancels the steer torque at the other wheel. However, if the drive axle angle is greater on one side than the other (Figure S8-3), steer torque on that side increases. This causes a toe increase at that wheel and the vehicle steers to the opposite side.

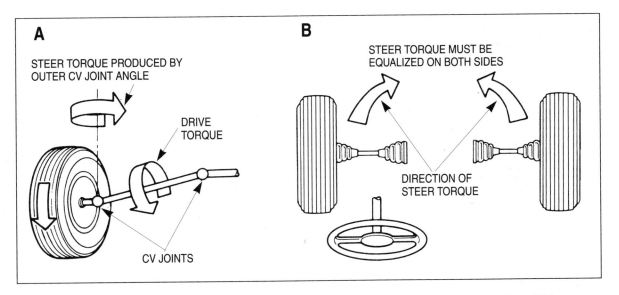

Figure S8-2 Steer torque due to outer CV joint causes the front wheels turn in toward the vehicle center line when torque is applied (A). With both axle angles equalized, the steer torque at one wheel cancels that at the other wheel (B).

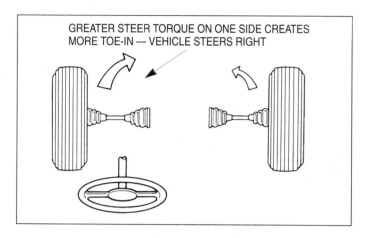

GREATER STEER TORQUE ON ONE SIDE CREATES
MORE TOE-IN — VEHICLE STEERS RIGHT

Figure S8-3 When the drive axle angle is greater on one side, steer torque on that side increases and a toe increase at that wheel causes the vehicle steer to the opposite side.

Although a normal condition, several other factors can cause excessive torque steer. If the tire on the longest axle is slightly smaller in diameter, it will increase the torque lead. A large difference in tire pressure also will accentuate the problem. Excessive play in tie rod assemblies, or steering gear mounting, can cause one front wheel to pull forward and toe-in under torque more than the other wheel. Drive axle differences resulting from a high front trim height, a binding or tight drive axle joint, or engine mounts that are loose or worn also can contribute to the problem.

Some other conditions will cause a steering problem that imitates torque steer in a vehicle that does not have it, or compound a torque steer problem in one that does. Incorrect front wheel alignment, or a rear wheel alignment problem, will cause the vehicle to track incorrectly. Suspension damage, such as a bent strut, will have an adverse affect.

When the vehicle completes a turn and wants to lead or pull in the direction of the turn, then makes a turn in the opposite direction and wants to lead or pull in that direction, it suffers from a rare condition called 'memory steer'. Memory steer can be caused by windup in the top of the strut mount (replace the mount), or by a top strut nut that is tight enough to cause binding (loosen the nut with the wheels in a straight-ahead position and retighten it to specifications).

The simplest way to determine excessive torque steer is to stick a small piece of tape at the top center of the steering wheel. Drive the vehicle, noting the degree of deflection necessary to steer the vehicle under heavy acceleration. Compare your findings to another vehicle of the same make and model to see if the one on which you are working has a greater than normal amount of torque steer.

the road. Camber and toe are tire position and wear angles. Zero camber positions the tire straight up-and-down; zero toe positions the center of the tire straight down the road. Either will cause tire wear if not correct, and have some effect on directional control.

Caster and steering axis inclination (SAI) are directional control angles. Caster positions the tire to the front (positive) or rear (negative) of the ball joint or kingpin. Zero caster has NO effect on directional stability. Caster is one plane of the steering axis; SAI is another plane. SAI is an imaginary line drawn through the kingpin or ball joints of an SLA suspension, or through the lower ball joint and steering pivot of a strut suspension.

Turning radius, turning angle, and toe-out on turns are the same, and relate to the angle of the tires during a turn. If this angle is NOT correct, tire wear will occur during turns.

Trim height, also called chassis height or curb ride height, is the normal no-load height of a vehicle and will change the caster, camber, toe, and turning radius of the vehicle if incorrect. RWD vehicles with IRS suspensions, and most FWD rear suspensions require rear wheel camber and toe adjustments. Tire tread wear patterns are a helpful diagnostic tool.

℗ REVIEW QUESTIONS

1. Which of the following is a non-adjustable alignment angle?
   (A) Camber
   (B) Caster
   (C) Toe
   (D) SAI

2. Technician A says that positive camber is the outward tilt of the tire as seen from the front of the vehicle. Technician B says that positive caster is the forward tilt of the tire as seen from the side of the vehicle. Who is right?
   (A) A only
   (B) B only
   (C) Both A and B
   (D) Neither A nor B

3. Technician A says that excessive positive camber loads the outside of the tire. Technician B says that too much negative camber loads the inside of the tire. Who is right?
   (A) A only
   (B) B only
   (C) Both A and B
   (D) Neither A nor B

4. Which of the following angles has the least effect on tire wear?
   (A) Camber
   (B) Caster
   (C) Toe
   (D) SAI

5. Which of the following angles has the most influence over scrub radius?
   (A) Camber
   (B) Caster
   (C) Toe
   (D) SAI

6. Technician A says that caster angle affects tire wear. Technician B says that caster helps maintain directional stability. Who is right?
   (A) A only
   (B) B only
   (C) Both A and B
   (D) Neither A nor B

7. Technician A says that too much positive caster increases steering effort. Technician B says that positive caster generally is used on vehicles with

manual steering. Who is right?
(A) A only
(B) B only
(C) Both A and B
(D) Neither A nor B

8. Technician A says that front spring sag will increase positive camber. Technician B says that rear spring sag will decrease positive camber. Who is right?
(A) A only
(B) B only
(C) Both A and B
(D) Neither A nor B

9. Which alignment angle may be specified in inches, millimeters, or degrees?
(A) Camber
(B) Caster
(C) Toe
(D) SAI

10. Technician A says that at-rest toe on FWD vehicles often is set with a small amount of toe-out. Technician B says that the front tires tend to toe-in as they pull an FWD vehicle down the road. Who is right?
(A) A only
(B) B only
(C) Both A and B
(D) Neither A nor B

11. Technician A says that running toe changes with vehicle movement over a rough road. Technician B says that some vehicles require a toe adjustment at the rear wheels. Who is right?
(A) A only
(B) B only
(C) Both A and B
(D) Neither A nor B

12. Technician A says that toe and SAI are both directional control angles. Technician B says that SAI was NOT

used until strut suspensions were developed. Who is right?
(A) A only
(B) B only
(C) Both A and B
(D) Neither A nor B

13. Technician A says that caster has a much greater effect on steering effort than SAI. Technician B says that the included angle is calculated by adding positive camber to, or subtracting negative camber from, SAI. Who is right?
(A) A only
(B) B only
(C) Both A and B
(D) Neither A nor B

14. Trim height should be checked and corrected:
(A) before installing new tires.
(B) never, as it cannot be changed.
(C) after the wheels are aligned.
(D) before the wheels are aligned.

15. Technician A says that a sagging rear suspension will affect front suspension alignment angles. Technician B says that trim height can be checked visually with a level and plumb line. Who is right?
(A) A only
(B) B only
(C) Both A and B
(D) Neither A nor B

16. Technician A says that the trim height of a torsion bar front suspension is adjustable. Technician B says that some vehicles require rear wheel alignment. Who is right?
(A) A only
(B) B only
(C) Both A and B
(D) Neither A nor B

MANUAL STEERING SYSTEMS

"We often discover what will do, by finding out what will not do; and probably he who never made a mistake never made a discovery." — Samuel Smiles

👁 OBJECTIVES

After completion of this chapter, you should be able to:

- Explain the relationship between the suspension and steering systems.
- Describe the evolution of conventional steering gearboxes, from worm-and-wheel to the recirculating ball design.
- Briefly explain the operating principles of a recirculating ball gearbox.
- Identify the components of a parallelogram steering linkage system and describe their interrelationship.
- Explain the operating principles of rack and pinion steering.
- Identify the safety features of the steering column.

Since the handlebar of a bicycle or motorcycle is connected directly to the front wheel, you can easily change direction while riding. Because these vehicles are relatively lightweight, their riders are physically strong enough to turn the front wheel without difficulty. It is considerably more difficult to turn the front wheels of an automobile because of its greater mass. To control the direction of an automobile's front wheels easily, the steering system must multiply the driver's effort. The **steering gearbox** provides the **mechanical advantage** or leverage required to change vehicle direction with only a small effort at the steering wheel.

The steering gearbox is the heart of any steering system, and one of the earliest mechanisms used consisted of a worm gear on the end of the steering column which drove another gear on the linkage. To reduce the friction between the two mating gears, ball bearings were added to this design in 1923. The **recirculating ball gearbox** still in use today can trace its ancestry back to this design. Although the **rack-and-pinion gearbox** was developed in Europe many years ago, it did not become popular in North American vehicles until the industry downsizing of its vehicles brought forth small FWD models in the late '70s.

In this chapter, we will look at the requirements of an automotive steering system, examine the components of a manual steering system, and see how they work together to provide the driver with directional control.

BASIC STEERING REQUIREMENTS

It is important that you understand the close relationship between the steering and suspension systems. Any condition that affects the position or operation of the suspension system also will affect both wheel alignment and steering. While only the front wheels are involved in steering, the rear suspension must keep the rear wheels parallel and straight behind the front wheels. Problems in the rear suspension, such as those caused by wear, or by modifying the springs, can dramatically affect both front suspension positioning and steering effort.

An automotive steering system must operate easily and precisely to fulfill the following requirements:

- the front wheels must have a built-in tendency to return to a straight-ahead position after a turn.
- it must isolate the driver from road shock resulting from road irregularities.
- it must provide feedback or response about the road surface to keep the driver informed of changing conditions.

To accomplish these goals, the automotive steering system consists of a steering wheel, column, and shaft that connects to the steering gear by one or more flexible couplings. The gearbox is connected to the wheels through the **steering linkage**. When the steering wheel is turned, the motion is transmitted through the column, shaft, and flexible coupling to the gearbox, where it is sent through the linkage and tie rods to the steering arms or knuckles, which pivot the wheels (Figure 9-1).

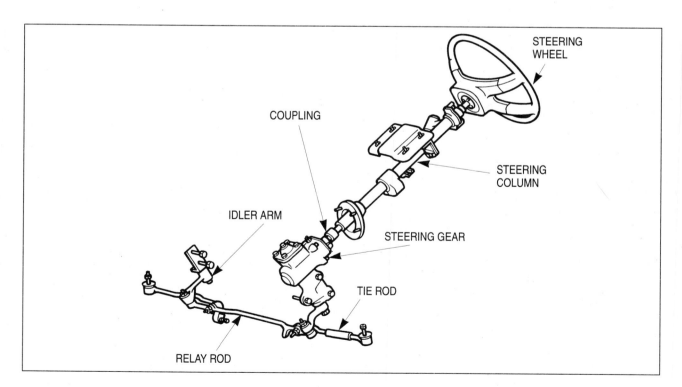

Figure 9-1 Components of a typical steering system. (Chrysler)

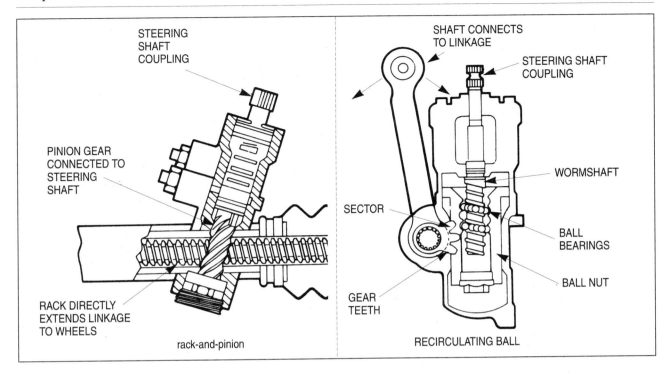

Figure 9-2 Both the rack-and-pinion and conventional steering gears do the same job, but the rack-and-pinion gear is more direct and responsive because it does not require a complex linkage arrangement to turn the wheels. (Chrysler)

GEARBOXES AND RATIOS

Modern automobiles use one of two different types of gearboxes — rack-and-pinion or conventional recirculating ball (Figure 9-2). Both types change the steering wheel's rotary motion into a straight-line motion at the tie rods (Figure 9-3). This results in a pivoting or turning motion of the wheels. Turning the front wheels from full left to full right (lock-to-lock) generally moves them through an arc of about 60-70°. This can involve three to six complete rotations of the steering wheel, depending on the design of the vehicle's front end and the **steering ratio** (mechanical advantage) of the gearbox.

The steering ratio indicates how many degrees the steering wheel must be turned to turn the wheels by one degree. For example, a 16:1 steering ratio means that for every 16 degrees the steering wheel is turned, the front wheels will move by one

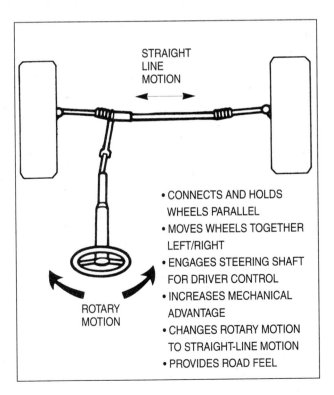

Figure 9-3 The functions of an automotive steering system. (Chrysler)

degree. Commonly used ratios range between 12:1 and 25:1. The exact ratio chosen by the carmaker depends on the vehicle's mass, and whether the steering is manual or power-assisted. In general, the faster ratios (like 12:1) are used to provide quicker steering with lighter vehicles or those with power-assisted steering. Slower ratios (like 25:1) are used to provide easier steering on heavier vehicles, especially those with manual steering. Some power-assisted conventional gearboxes are designed to produce a variable ratio. Some **variable ratio** gearboxes have a slightly faster than normal ratio (lower numerical value) in the center position so that the steering is precise and controllable. As the steering wheel is turned in either direction off of center, the ratio becomes slower (higher numerical value) to make it easier to turn the wheels during cornering or

parking. This is accomplished by changing the profile of the steering gear teeth (Figure 9-4). Other variable ratio power rack-and-pinion gearboxes, such has those used on 1980 and later Ford Thunderbird, Mustang, and others, have a slower ratio at the center position, so that the steering is not overly sensitive on the highway. When the wheel is off center the ratio is faster so the driver does not have to do so much wheel turning during parking. The faster ratio off center increases the driver's effort in turning the wheel only slightly because the power steering does almost all the work for the driver.

On vehicles using a conventional steering gearbox, the overall steering ratio is related to the length of the steering arms and **Pitman arm**. The longer the steering arm and shorter the Pitman arm, the slower the steering ratio. Conversely, the

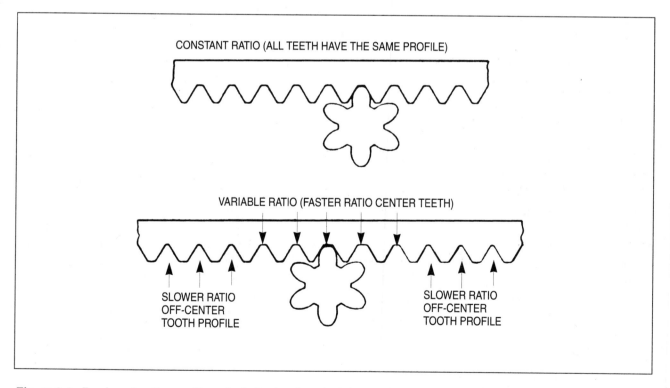

CONSTANT RATIO (ALL TEETH HAVE THE SAME PROFILE)

VARIABLE RATIO (FASTER RATIO CENTER TEETH)

SLOWER RATIO OFF-CENTER TOOTH PROFILE

SLOWER RATIO OFF-CENTER TOOTH PROFILE

Figure 9-4 By changing the profile and pitch of rack-and-pinion teeth (or sector shaft and ball nut teeth), the steering ratio can be varied to provide a faster ratio at the center for quicker highway steering and a slower ratio near the ends of the rack for ease in cornering and parking. (Ford Motor)

shorter the steering arm and longer the Pitman arm, the faster the steering ratio. The steering arms on some older vehicles were designed to connect with the tie rod ends at two different places. The connection nearest the steering axis provided the quickest steering and generally was used with power-assisted vehicles, or those equipped with lightweight engines. Installing the tie rod in the connection nearest the steering arm ends gave easier but slower steering response.

CONVENTIONAL STEERING GEARS

The function of a steering gear is to change rotary motion of the steering wheel and shaft into lateral motion that will cause the steering knuckles to pivot. In doing so, it must provide a gear ratio and work smoothly without excessive free play. The most common conventional steering gear used on RWD vehicles is the recirculating ball type, developed by the Saginaw Steering Division of General Motors, and introduced on the 1940 Cadillac. You also may encounter three other designs on some RWD vehicles — the worm-and-sector, the worm-and-roller, or the cam-and-lever. Let us examine their general operating principles, and then look at how they differ. This will give you an understanding of steering gear development.

OPERATING PRINCIPLES

Conventional gearboxes use a steering gear shaft with a worm gear on one end that connects to the steering wheel either directly or through some type of flexible joint). A worm gear was, and still is, almost universally used on the steering column shaft. A cross shaft positioned at right angles to the worm gear engages the worm either through wheel gear teeth, sector gear teeth, or a roller gear. In some

designs, a gear or notched arm on the cross shaft engages a ball nut that rides on the worm gear. Both ends of the worm gear are supported by adjustable ball or roller bearings to remove end or side play. The cross shaft is supported by bushings, needle bearings, or a combination of both. Adjustments are provided to control worm and cross shaft clearance. The gears and bearings are enclosed in a cast housing partially filled with lubricant and sealed to prevent dirt, water, or other contamination from entering, or lubricant from leaking out. The lubricant can be checked or replenished through a filler plug or one of the sector gear housing bolts. The steering gear housing is bolted to the frame for rigidity (Figure 9-5).

Worm-and-Sector Design

Most steering gears have drawn their inspiration from the original worm-and-wheel design used in the '20s. As its name

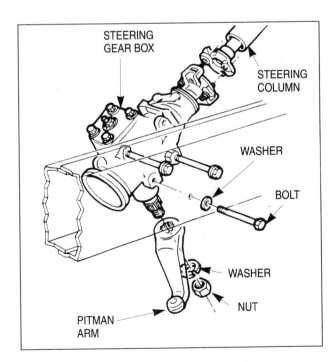

Figure 9-5 The large, heavy conventional steering gearbox gains rigidity when secured to a frame rail. (Ford Motor)

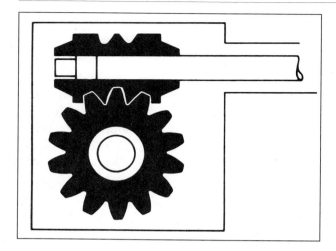

Figure 9-6 The worm and wheel was one of the first automotive steering gear designs. Only half or less of the teeth on the wheel were used, so it soon became obvious that a full circle wheel was unnecessary. (General Motors)

suggests, a toothed wheel connected to the Pitman arm by a cross shaft meshes with the teeth on the worm (Figure 9-6). Most of the wheel gear cannot be used because of the turning limits of the front wheels, so engineers replaced the wheel gear with a wedge-shaped sector gear (Figure 9-7) to produce the worm-and-sector gearbox. The major disadvantage of both designs is that much of the load is concentrated at the mesh points of the gears.

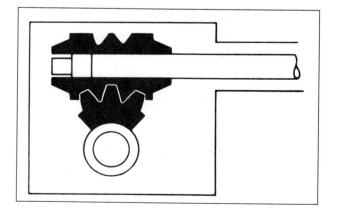

Figure 9-7 By using just a section of the wheel, the worm-and-sector gear resulted in a reduction in size and mass of the gearbox. (General Motors)

Worm-and-Roller Design

As vehicles became heavier and tires increased in size, friction and wear inside the gearbox also increased due to the greater loads. To combat this friction, Saginaw replaced the sector gear with a steel roller in 1926 and changed the shape of the worm to resemble that of an hourglass; thicker at the ends than in the middle. The roller is mounted on needle roller bearings, and may have one, two, or three teeth which mesh with the worm gear (Figure 9-8). Since the roller is free to turn, it eliminates much of the friction created by a wiping action of a wheel or sector gear. When the worm rotates, the roller teeth must follow, causing the cross shaft connected to the Pitman arm to rotate and carry the motion to the steering linkage as lateral motion. The worm-and-roller design is still used today on heavy-duty trucks.

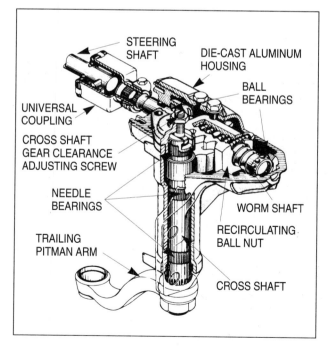

Figure 9-8 Excellent resistance to friction made the worm-and-roller gearbox a popular design for many years. (Chrysler)

Cam-and-Lever Design

Often known as the Ross steering gear, the cam-and-lever design introduced in 1923 features a long groove (the cam) that spirals around the end of the steering shaft. A peg on the Pitman shaft lever fits into the groove. Any turning motion of the steering wheel forces the peg to ride up or down the shaft groove, turning the Pitman shaft and arm. By varying the pitch of the groove, a variable steering ratio is possible. Steering ratio also depends on the pitch of the groove; if the spirals are wider apart at the middle, steering is faster with the wheels in the straight-ahead position. The ends of the spiral are closer together to make tight turns easier. More turns of the steering wheel are required when turning or parking, but the steering effort is reduced.

The Ross steering gear was one of the first to incorporate the concept of irreversibility, which is an important factor in any steering mechanism. With some older steering gear designs, road shocks and bumps were passed from the wheels back up through the steering wheel. This meant that the driver was constantly fighting the steering wheel to keep the road wheels straight ahead. Ross steering proved a good compromise, since it prevents most motion from being passed back to the steering wheel, but allows enough to be felt to give the driver a feel of the road. Like the worm-and-roller design, Ross cam-and-lever steering is still used today on commercial vehicles.

Recirculating Ball Design

The recirculating ball gearbox has been popular on RWD vehicles since the 1940's. Basically, this is a variation of the worm-and-sector steering gear. A sliding ball nut with an internal thread contains a spiral groove. The ball nut fits over the steering shaft, which also contains a spiral thread

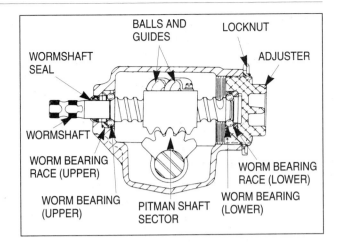

Figure 9-9 By using recirculating steel balls between the worm and ball nut, the modern conventional steering gear is virtually friction-free. The worm bearing preload is controlled by a locknut and adjuster plug at the lower end of the worm shaft. (Chrysler)

groove. A series of ball bearings ride between the two grooves, and act as the interconnecting threads. The teeth cut on one face of the sliding ball nut mate with the sector teeth, and as the steering wheel is rotated, the ball bearings force the ball nut to move up or down on the wormshaft (Figure 9-9). This converts the rotary motion of the wormshaft to the linear motion of the ball nut. Because the ball nut and sector are meshed, ball nut movement causes the sector shaft to rotate, converting the linear motion of the ball nut back to rotary motion. Since the sector shaft is connected to the steering linkage through the Pitman arm, the steering action is transmitted to the front wheels. Because the balls rotate and roll freely, the screw motion between the worm and ball nut provides a nearly friction-free rolling contact, rather than sliding contact.

The ball nut contains two complete circuits. Tubular ball guides are used to prevent the balls from running out of the end of either circuit. The guides deflect the balls away from their helical path at one end of their travel, guide them diagonally across the back of the nut, and return them to their helical path between the ball nut and worm at the other end of their travel. In this way, the balls are constantly recirculating.

Two steering gear adjustments are possible — worm bearing preload, and ball nut rack and sector gear mesh adjustment. The worm bearing preload is controlled by an adjuster plug at the lower end of the wormshaft (Figure 9-9) and must be correctly adjusted before adjusting the ball nut rack and sector gear. Since the ball nut is positioned at a slight angle, backlash between the nut and sector can be adjusted by shifting the sector shaft slightly along its own axis with a thrust screw called a lash adjuster screw (Figure 9-10).

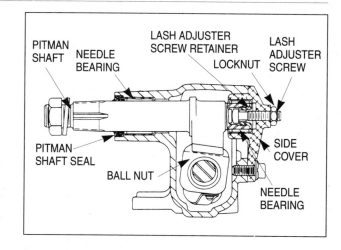

Figure 9-10 The lash adjuster screw located in the housing cover moves the sector shaft as required to maintain proper mesh load between the sector gear and ball nut teeth. (Chrysler)

STEERING LINKAGE

The conventional steering gear uses a rather complicated system of linkage to transmit the rotary output of its cross shaft or sector shaft and turn the front wheels during steering (Figure 9-11). All steering linkage parts are malleable and designed to bend, distort, or deflect rather than fracture under extreme shock loads, which would cause a total loss of control if any component were to break.

Early independent suspensions used a variety of different linkage designs, but the one most commonly found today on RWD vehicles with a conventional steering gear is called an **idler arm**, relay rod, or parallelogram linkage (Figure 9-11). The linkage takes its name from the fact that it actually forms a parallelogram with the center line of the wheel spindles. Parallelogram linkage has various designs with either long tie rods, as shown in Figure 9-11, or short tie rods (Figure 9-12).

Basically, a parallelogram linkage

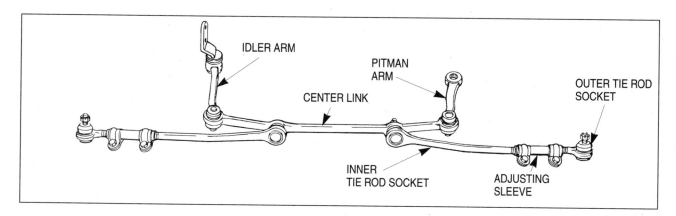

Figure 9-11 Use of a conventional steering gear requires an idler arm or parallelogram steering linkage. The idle arm and Pitman arm are in the end of the center link in this design. (McQuay-Norris)

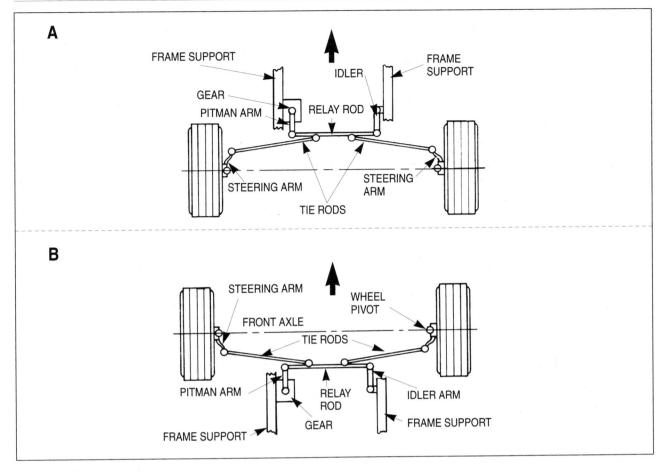

Figure 9-12 Parallelogram linkage can be located in front of the axle (A), or behind the axle (B). (Chevrolet Division, General Motors)

system consists of five major components (Figure 9-13): two adjustable tie rods, one center link or relay rod, one Pitman arm (also called a steering gear arm), and one idler arm.

Since the inner ends of the tie rods are in line with the lower control arm inner shaft, this type of linkage causes the least amount of toe change as the vehicle moves down the road. Before explaining how the components work together, let us define their function in the steering system:

• Tie rods — These connecting rods transmit movement of the center link or relay rod to the steering arms or steering knuckle. Tie rods generally

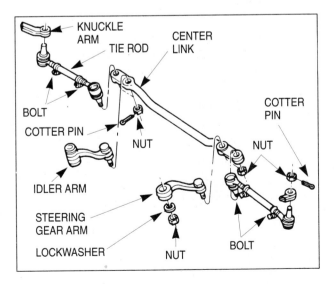

Figure 9-13 Another slightly different arrangement of parallelogram linkage. (Chrysler)

are equal in length, and are approximately the same length as the suspension lower control arms. Their outer ends are adjustable (by threaded sleeves locked by clamps) and have both left and right hand threads to allow for toe adjustment.

- Center link or relay rod — Depending on the linkage configuration, this also may be called a drag link, connecting arm, or steering arm rod. It transfers the rotary motion of the Pitman arm to a linear, or sideways, motion. Depending again on linkage configuration, it also can change the direction of the Pitman arm motion. The center link generally connects directly to the tie rods, although in some designs, it connects to an intermediate steering arm.

- Pitman arm — Sometimes called a sector shaft arm, the Pitman arm is splined on the steering gear sector shaft. As the sector shaft turns, the Pitman arm swings in an arc. The swinging end of this arm connects to the center link or relay rod.

- Idler arm — The same length as the Pitman arm, the idler arm pivots in a bushing and bracket attached to the frame or body on the opposite side of the vehicle. Since it is positioned parallel with the Pitman arm, it supports the other end of the center link or relay rod to assure that the link or rod moves straight across the vehicle.

- Steering arms — these are part of, or connected to, the steering knuckle or spindle assemblies. When the steering arms move, the spindle assemblies rotate on the suspension arm ball joints.

When these components are connected, rotation of the Pitman arm forces the center link or relay rod to one side. Since

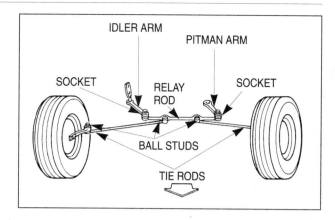

Figure 9-14 Movement of the Pitman arm is transferred to the wheels through the relay rod and tie rods of a parallelogram linkage. (Chevrolet Division, General Motors)

the center link or relay rod is connected to the tie rods, it moves the wheels, which pivot on the control arms (Figure 9-14). Ball sockets (often called ball studs) connect the center link or relay rod to the Pitman and idler arms, as well as the tie rod ends (Figure 9-15). These joints allow

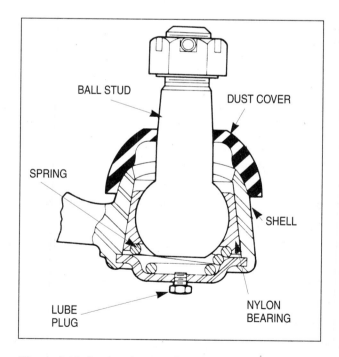

Figure 9-15 Sectional view of a tapered ball socket used to connect the tie rod end. If the ball socket requires lubrication, a lube fitting or plug is provided. (Chrysler)

the tie rods to follow the steering arms as the wheels are turned, and permit the control arms to move up and down with road shocks.

Parallelogram linkage is used primarily on passenger cars and light-duty trucks with an independent suspension. Heavy-duty vehicles with solid axles use a less complicated linkage system (A and B, Figure 9-16). In these designs, the steering gear is mounted with the Pitman arm pointing down on the left side of the frame. The drag link and steering arms may

change in design and positioning, according to the relative positioning of the steering wheel and front wheels.

RACK-AND-PINION STEERING GEARS

This type of steering gear (Figure 9-17) is used with FWD vehicles and offers several advantages. It is:

- less complicated and uses fewer parts
- lighter in mass and requires less vehicle space
- less expensive to manufacture.

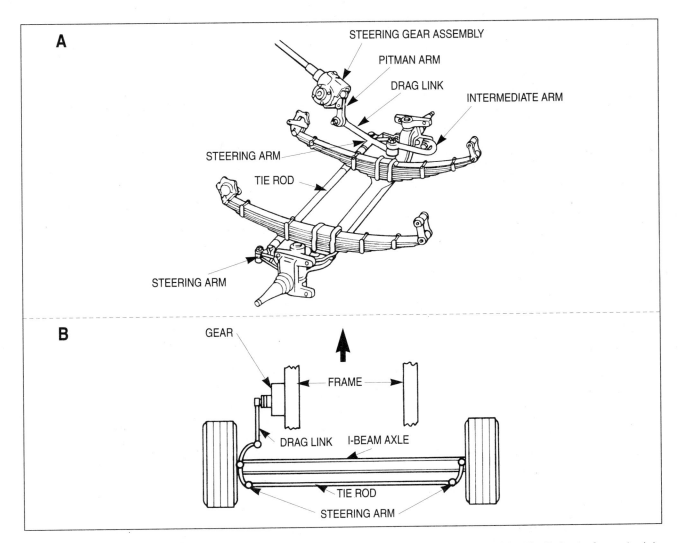

Figure 9-16 Solid axle steering linkage. The link from the Pitman arm is called the drag link. The linkage shown in A is typical of Ford vehicles; that shown in B is typical of GM vehicles. (Ford Motor and General Motors)

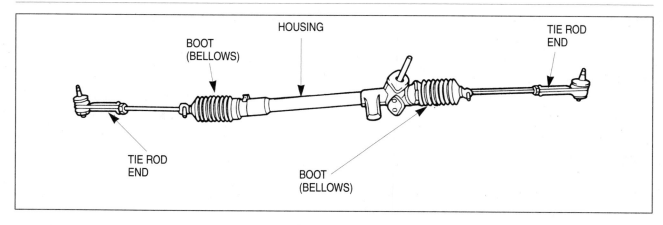

Figure 9-17 A typical manual rack-and-pinion steering gear. (Chrysler)

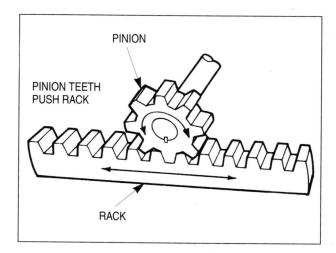

Figure 9-18 Steering wheel rotation of the pinion gear causes its teeth to push the rack in the desired direction. (Chrysler)

The rack-and-pinion housing contains a rack gear positioned between the wheels, with a mating pinion gear connected to the steering column and wheel (Figure 9-18). A bushing in one end of the housing is used to position and guide the rack; a spring-loaded support yoke or rack bearing at the other end keeps the rack engaged with the pinion (Figure 9-19). A ball socket housing threaded into each end of the rack is retained by a pin or jam nut, which also locks the inner tie rods in place. Each end of the rack-and-pinion housing is sealed by

flexible rubber dust boots or bellows to keep out contamination and prevent lubricant loss. Outer tie rod's ends on each inner tie rod connect to the steering knuckles with integral ball studs (Figure 9-20). These studs move from side-to-side with a rotary motion to transmit rack movement to the steering arms and knuckles. Most rack-and-pinion gear sets also have a yoke plug adjusting bolt and locknut to maintain rack engagement with the pinion under load. The assembly is lubricated during assembly, generally with gear oil or a semifluid grease. If the gear requires re-lubrication during its service life, it may have a filler plug, but many designs must be removed and disassembled to add or renew the lubricant.

The cast aluminum housing attaches to the front main crossmember with rubber insulators at two or more positions. A flexible coupling or universal joint connects the pinion shaft to the steering shaft, and generally is enclosed in a third flexible dust boot. The rubber insulators are used to minimize noise and dampen vibration, as this type of steering gear is prone to trans-mitting road shock to the steering wheel. Earlier rack-and-pinion installations often made use of a shock absorber-type damper on the linkage to reduce the problem of

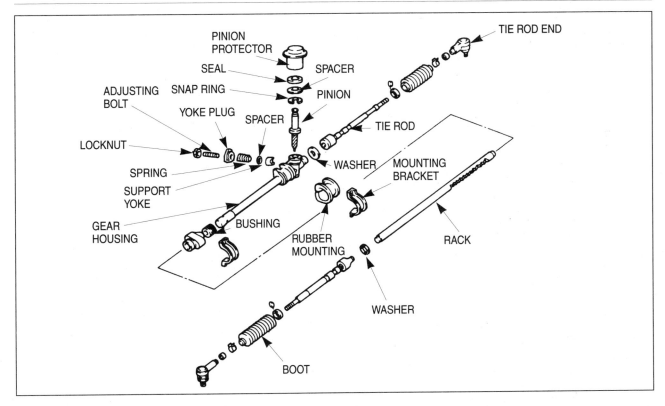

Figure 9-19 This exploded view of a typical manual rack-and-pinion gear used by Ford shows the location of the rack bushing and support yoke. (Ford Motor)

reversibility. Since the damper's action is proportional to the amount of force put on it, the small road shocks necessary for good road feel can be felt through the steering, but fast and hard bumps are dampened.

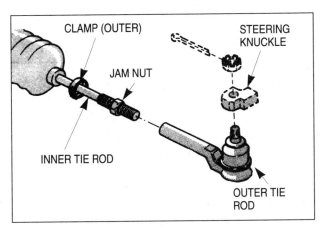

Figure 9-20 The outer tie rod connects the rack to the steering knuckle. (Chrysler)

Steering dampers still are used with rack-and-pinion gears on larger FWD vehicles (especially luxury models) to provide as smooth a steering feel as possible.

OPERATING PRINCIPLES

Turning the steering wheel rotates the pinion. Rotary movement of the pinion causes the rack to move from side to side (linear or transverse movement). Unlike the conventional steering gear, which changes rotary movement to linear and then back to rotary, a rack-and-pinion gear converts rotary motion directly to linear motion.

Like other gear sets, there is a ratio between the pinion (input) gear and the rack (output) gear; the rack moves a certain amount for each rotation of the pinion. This ratio, in combination with the lengths of the steering arms, will determine the overall ratio, or how far the driver has to turn the steering wheel to obtain the desired directional change. Generally, steering effort is easy and response is rapid. The ratio may be either fixed or variable, depending on tooth profile.

Fixed Gear Ratio

When a rack-and-pinion steering gear has a fixed ratio, the gear ratio remains the same throughout the motion of the rack and the pinion. As a result, turning the steering wheel a specific number of degrees will always cause the rack to move a certain amount, regardless of its location on the pinion.

Variable Gear Ratio

If a rack-and-pinion gear has a variable ratio, turning the steering wheel a specific number of degrees does NOT always cause the rack to move the same amount. The gear ratio will vary according to the location of the rack on the pinion. The variable ratio is obtained by varying the size or profile of the gear rack teeth, and the distance between them. The gear ratio at the center of the rack generally is higher, while the ratio at the ends of the rack is lower. This arrangement requires more effort but quicker response when the wheels are pointing straight ahead and the rack is centered. Less effort is required during turning or parking maneuvers.

STEERING LINKAGE

Compared to the parallelogram linkage used with conventional steering gears, the linkage used with a rack-and-pinion gear is simple, consisting only of two inner tie rods and tie rod ends. On most rack-and-pinion gears, the inner tie rods are attached to the ends of the rack by ball and socket joints. With older designs, the socket is a separate component which accepts the rounded inside end of the tie rod, and is secured to the rack by various methods, such as a jam nut, roll pin, set screw, or a staked end. This type of socket can be replaced, but requires an adjustment during the replacement procedure. Newer designs use an inner tie rod with an integral sealed socket that needs no adjustment. If either the socket or tie rod requires service, however, the entire assembly must be replaced.

On some rack-and-pinion gears used by General Motors, the inner tie rods connect directly to the center part of the rack (Figure 9-21) with replaceable rubber bushings and bolts. A large single flexible bellows protects the internal components in this design. The inner tie rods thread directly into the tie rod ends, but a threaded adjuster rod may be used between the inner tie rod and the outer tie rod, or tie rod end. The primary difference between these connecting methods is the way in which the toe is adjusted:

- the inner end of the tie rod is rotated and the adjustment locked in place with a jam nut (Figure 9-22).
- two clamps and an adjuster rod are used instead of a sleeve and clamps (Figure 9-23).

The outer tie rod ends connect to the steering arm or knuckle with a ball and socket joint similar to a conventional ball joint. They transmit steering motion to the wheel while maintaining the toe angle. To eliminate free play, two basic types of tie rod sockets are used. One uses a metal or rubber preload spring to maintain a slight friction load between the ball and socket and provide compressible vertical clearance (A, Figure 9-24); the other is preloaded with zero vertical clearance (B, Figure 9-24). To prevent any sideplay in the steering arm, the ball stud is a locking taper. Like conventional ball joints, a flexible rubber boot is used to keep lubricant in and contamination out of the joint. Damage or deteriora-

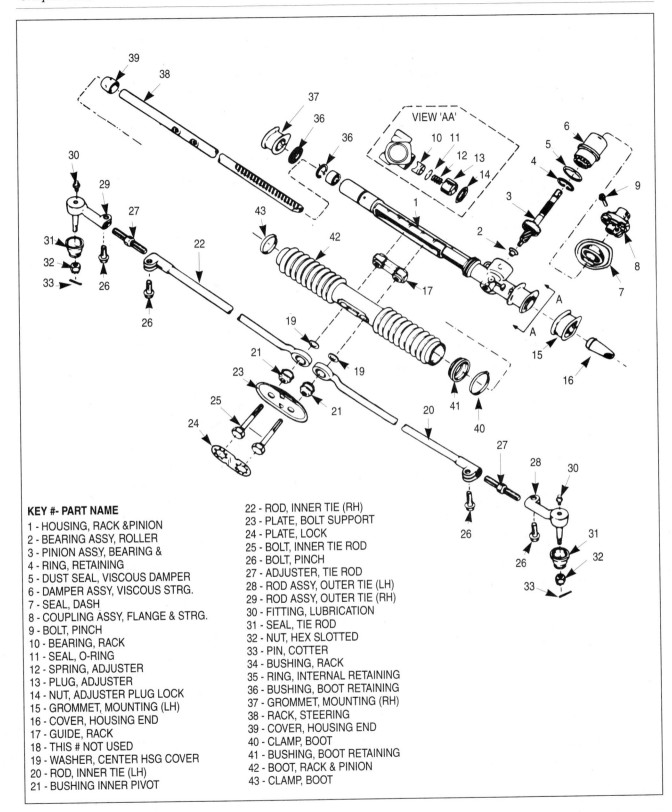

KEY #- PART NAME

1 - HOUSING, RACK &PINION
2 - BEARING ASSY, ROLLER
3 - PINION ASSY, BEARING &
4 - RING, RETAINING
5 - DUST SEAL, VISCOUS DAMPER
6 - DAMPER ASSY, VISCOUS STRG.
7 - SEAL, DASH
8 - COUPLING ASSY, FLANGE & STRG.
9 - BOLT, PINCH
10 - BEARING, RACK
11 - SEAL, O-RING
12 - SPRING, ADJUSTER
13 - PLUG, ADJUSTER
14 - NUT, ADJUSTER PLUG LOCK
15 - GROMMET, MOUNTING (LH)
16 - COVER, HOUSING END
17 - GUIDE, RACK
18 - THIS # NOT USED
19 - WASHER, CENTER HSG COVER
20 - ROD, INNER TIE (LH)
21 - BUSHING INNER PIVOT

22 - ROD, INNER TIE (RH)
23 - PLATE, BOLT SUPPORT
24 - PLATE, LOCK
25 - BOLT, INNER TIE ROD
26 - BOLT, PINCH
27 - ADJUSTER, TIE ROD
28 - ROD ASSY, OUTER TIE (LH)
29 - ROD ASSY, OUTER TIE (RH)
30 - FITTING, LUBRICATION
31 - SEAL, TIE ROD
32 - NUT, HEX SLOTTED
33 - PIN, COTTER
34 - BUSHING, RACK
35 - RING, INTERNAL RETAINING
36 - BUSHING, BOOT RETAINING
37 - GROMMET, MOUNTING (RH)
38 - RACK, STEERING
39 - COVER, HOUSING END
40 - CLAMP, BOOT
41 - BUSHING, BOOT RETAINING
42 - BOOT, RACK & PINION
43 - CLAMP, BOOT

Figure 9-21 An exploded view of the tie rod center take-off rack-and-pinion gear assembly used with some GM vehicles. (Oldsmobile Division, General Motors)

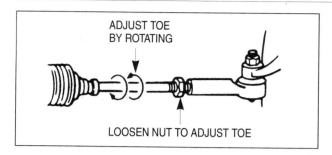

Figure 9-22 In this design, the outer tie rod threads onto the inner tie rod and adjustment is maintained by a jam nut. (Oldsmobile Division, General Motors)

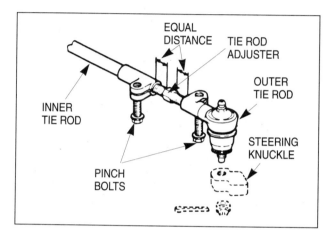

Figure 9-23 Another design uses a threaded adjuster rod between the inner and outer tie rods. Adjustment is maintained by the pinch bolts. (Chrysler)

tion of the boot will cause joint failure and require tie rod end replacement. Until the early 1980's, tie rod ends had a grease fitting (or a plug for installing a fitting) and required periodic joint lubrication. These have been replaced in recent years by prelubricated joints that are sealed during manufacture.

STEERING COLUMNS

To provide the driver with directional control, a steering shaft connected to the steering gear extends through the firewall and into the passenger compartment, where it is encased in a steering column and secured to the steering wheel. Bearings in the column are used to position

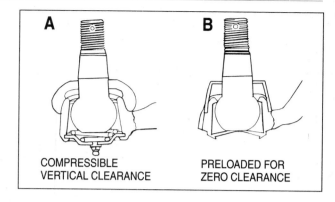

Figure 9-24 The two basic types of tie rod sockets. (McQuay-Norris)

the shaft, allowing it to rotate without side or endplay.

ENERGY-ABSORBING COLUMNS

Until the mid-1960's, vehicles were equipped with a rigid steering shaft enclosed in a mast jacket assembly. This assembly was unsafe during a collision, as it could easily be pushed into the driver's compartment by the force of impact. Under the pressure of federal safety regulations, the steering column was re-designed to absorb crash energy by collapsing during a collision (Figure 9-25). Early collapsible

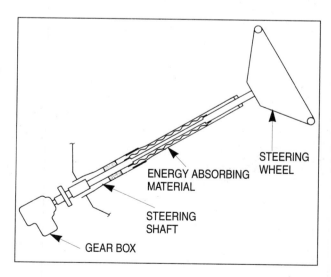

Figure 9-25 The basic design of a typical energy-absorbing steering column. (Chrysler)

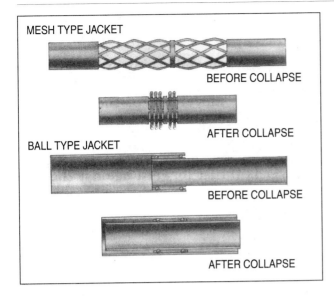

Figure 9-26 Operation of an energy-absorbing steering column. (Chevrolet Division, General Motors)

designs consisted of three main parts: a 2-piece outer jacket, a 3-piece shift tube, and a 2-piece steering shaft. During a collision, the outer jacket absorbed energy as it compressed, and the steering shaft tube telescoped into itself (Figure 9-26).

This basic design is still used, but there have been refinements. A majority of current applications have an expansion mandrel riveted to the center section of the column jacket (Figure 9-27). The force of a collision causes the rivets to shear and allows the jacket to collapse. The shift tube sections are held together by plastic injections that form interconnecting inserts and shear pins. Under impact, the knife-like edges of each tube section slice the plastic inserts, allowing the shift tube to

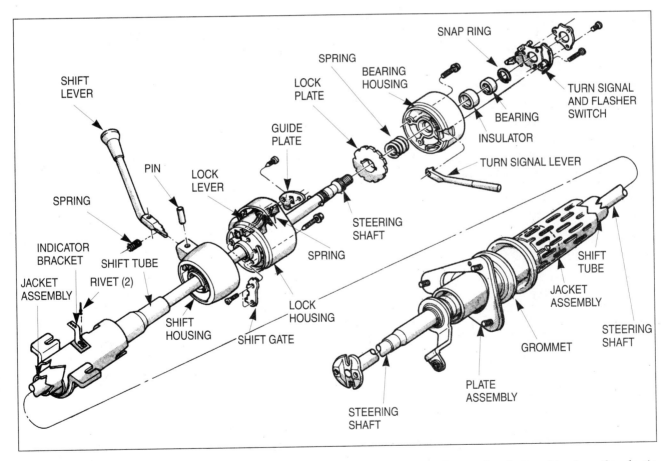

Figure 9-27 A typical energy-absorbing steering column using a perforated column jacket designed to shear the plastic expansion mandrel rivets and collapse in the event of a collision. (Chrysler)

telescope. The 2-piece shaft consists of a solid upper shaft and a hollow lower shaft formed to mate together with double-flatted ends. This allows continued steering, even when the shafts have completely telescoped. Plastic injected through holes in the hollow piece enters annular groove on the solid shaft and creates plastic shear pins in the holes. When impacted, the shear pins break off, allowing the shaft to gradually telescope against the resistance provided by the plastic collars in the annular grooves. Breakaway capsules are incorporated in the column mounting bracket, allowing the bracket to slip off its mounting points in the event of a severe side impact.

Connecting Joints

The steering shaft generally connects to the steering gear through a 2-piece flexible coupling. One piece of the coupling is secured to the steering gear input shaft; the other piece is secured to the steering shaft. The flexibility in this type of joint is provided by a circular piece of rubber, often reinforced with fabric, which allows for any angle difference between the shaft and gear (Figure 9-28). The rubber in the coupling also helps dampen road vibrations and noise from being transmitted to the steering wheel through the shaft.

Some steering columns use a short intermediate shaft between the main steering shaft and the steering gear (Figure 9-29). This shaft is attached with universal joints and pinch bolts (Figure 9-30), and makes possible greater differences in the angle between the main shaft and gear.

Other Features

Modern steering columns are much more than simply a housing for the steering shaft. Over the years, numerous functions and controls have been incorporated in the column, such as a steering rotation sensor, headlight dimmer, horn, wiper, washer, speed control and ignition switches, with the control levers performing multiple functions according to the direction they are moved. Some columns can be adjusted to change the position or angle of the steering wheel, or its fore-aft position. This allows a variety of drivers to adjust the steering wheel position to its most comfortable point. An increasing number of steering columns incorporate air bag modules for additional driver protection.

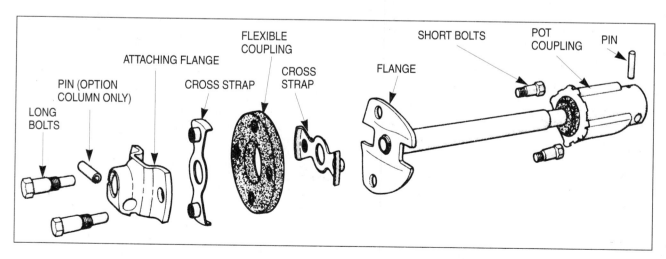

Figure 9-28 Flexible coupling components include a circular piece of fabric reinforced rubber that accommodates differences in angles between the shaft and gearbox. (Chrysler)

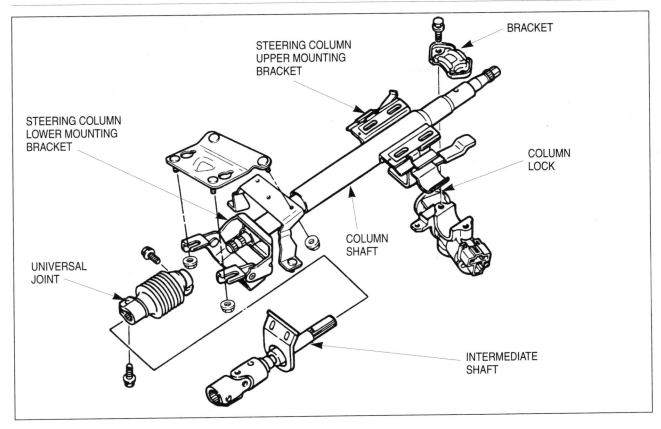

Figure 9-29 The use of an intermediate shaft increases the angle accommodation between steering gear and main steering shaft. (Ford Motor)

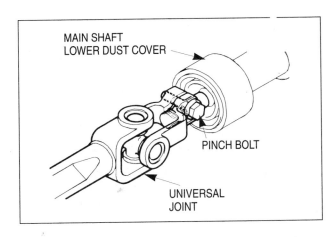

Figure 9-30 Intermediate shaft connections. (Toyota)

SUMMARY

An automotive steering system must provide directional control and easy maneuverability. It must also reduce the driver effort needed to turn the front wheels and give the driver sufficient feel of the road. RWD vehicles use a recirculating ball steering gear; FWD vehicles use a rack-and-pinion gear.

In the recirculating ball design, a ball nut rides up and down on a worm shaft on ball bearings that recirculate in grooves between the nut and worm. This steering gear requires a complex system of linkage called a parallelogram or idler arm linkage. This consists of the Pitman arm, an idler arm, the center link or relay rod, and two tie rods.

A rack-and-pinion gear contains a long toothed rack and circular pinion gear in an aluminum housing. Inner tie rods connected to the rack transmit its motion to the wheels through tie rod ends. Rack-

TUBES AND TUBELESS TIRES

The first air-filled or pneumatic tire was patented in 1845 by an Englishman named Robert William Thompson, but faced with competition the following year from the solid rubber tires manufactured by one Thomas Hancock, quickly disappeared from the scene. The concept of pneumatic tires remained in obscurity until the development of the automobile nearly a half-century later.

Originally, the pneumatic tire used an inner tube. This amounted to a rubber air bag installed between the wheel rim and the tire. When a tube-type tire is punctured, the air-holding body or inner tube deflates suddenly because the tube backs away from the object which caused the puncture and explodes inside the tire. When this occurs, the tube-type tire goes flat immediately, which presents a definite safety hazard for the driver.

Tubeless tires were developed after World War II. The term 'tubeless' is actually a misnomer because the tube was not really eliminated. Rather, it became a permanent part of the tire, taking the form of a lining of special soft rubber bonded to its inside. This inner liner is soft enough to seal around an object that punctures the tire. Since this made the wheel a part of the air-holding body, it had to be improved to prevent air leakage. When a tubeless tire does go flat, it releases the air slowly enough to stop the vehicle safely. In addition to this safety aspect of the tubeless tire, it also is lighter in mass, runs cooler, and the tube no longer chafes against the wheel rim or tire.

Punctures in tubeless tires are more difficult to repair than patching a tube. Only punctures in the tread area should be repaired; tires with punctures in the shoulders or sidewall should be replaced. If the tread is good, but the shoulder or sidewall was punctured, some customers will insist on having a tube installed inside their tubeless tire. This is NOT a safe practice, and should be avoided. Installing a tube inside a tubeless tire causes the tire to run hotter. At some point, the increased heat causes the tube to chafe against the soft inner lining of the tire, which eventually adheres to the tube. A continued increase in temperature can result in the tube exploding inside the tire, blowing a hole in the sidewall. This ruins the tire, causing an immediate safety hazard that can affect directional control and result in an accident. The use of talcum powder between the tube and tire is often suggested as a means of preventing the tube from sticking to the tire, but a better answer to the problem is to convince the customer that replacing the tire is the best approach.

and-pinion linkage is less complicated and more precise, since there are fewer joints to wear.

Commonly used steering ratios range between 12:1 and 25:1. The lower the numerical ratio, the quicker the vehicle wheels respond to the steering wheel. Quicker ratios provide faster steering and are used with lighter vehicles. Slower ratios make steering easier on heavier vehicles. Variable ratios have a faster ratio in the center position for more precise straight-ahead steering. As the steering wheel is turned, the ratio decreases and steering becomes easier during parking maneuvers.

The steering column contains the steering shaft, which connects to the steering gear through a flexible coupling or universal joint. As a safety measure, the column is designed to collapse during a collision. The column also houses a number of functional controls, such as washer, wiper, horn, headlight, and dimmer switches. Some columns can be adjusted to position the steering wheel more comfortably for various drivers. Many now contain an air bag module.

? REVIEW QUESTIONS

1. Technician A says that the Pitman arm connects to the sector gear shaft. Technician B says that the steering ratio indicates how many degrees the steering wheel must be turned to turn the wheels one degree. Who is right?
   (A) A only
   (B) B only
   (C) Both A and B
   (D) Neither A nor B

2. Technician A says that a fast steering ratio provides easier steering with heavy vehicles. Technician B says that a variable ratio produces a slow ratio in the center position. Who is right?
   (A) A only
   (B) B only
   (C) Both A and B
   (D) Neither A nor B

3. Which type of steering gear is used most often on RWD vehicles?
   (A) worm-and-roller.
   (B) recirculating ball.
   (C) cam-and-lever.
   (D) rack-and-pinion.

4. Technician A says that the conventional steering gear shaft to which the steering wheel attaches has a worm gear on one end. Technician B says that the worm engages the teeth of a sector gear positioned parallel with the worm gear. Who is right?
   (A) A only
   (B) B only
   (C) Both A and B
   (D) Neither A nor B

5. Technician A says that the worm gear meshes directly with the sector gear in a recirculating ball gearbox. Technician B says that ball nut moves up or down the worm shaft when the steering wheel is rotated. Who is right?
   (A) A only
   (B) B only
   (C) Both A and B
   (D) Neither A nor B

6. Technician A says that the balls in a recirculating ball steering gear roll in grooves in the worm shaft and ball nut when the steering wheel is turned. Technician B says that an adjuster plug at the bottom of the wormshaft controls worm bearing preload. Who is right?
   (A) A only

(B) B only

(C) Both A and B

(D) Neither A nor B

7. Technician A says that worm bearing preload must be properly adjusted before adjusting ball nut and sector gear backlash. Technician B says that parallelogram steering linkage is used with rack-and-pinion steering. Who is right?

(A) A only

(B) B only

(C) Both A and B

(D) Neither A nor B

8. Technician A says that paralleogram linkage is designed for use in front of the axle. Technician B says that it can be used behind the axle. Who is right?

(A) A only

(B) B only

(C) Both A and B

(D) Neither A nor B

9. Which of the following is NOT true regarding an idler arm?

(A) It supports one end of the relay rod.

(B) It is the same length as the Pitman arm.

(C) It is bracket-mounted to the vehicle frame.

(D) It is positioned at a right angle to the Pitman arm.

10. Technician A says that parallelogram linkage is used primarily with FWD vehicles. Technician B says that ball studs are used to connect the components of parallelogram linkage. Who is right?

(A) A only

(B) B only

(C) Both A and B

(D) Neither A nor B

11. Which of the following is NOT true about rack-and-pinion steering?

(A) It is lightweight and uses fewer parts than a conventional steering gear.

(B) It is used with FWD vehicles.

(C) The gear housing uses flexible dust boots at each end.

(D) The inner tie rods are attached with universal joints.

12. Technician A says that a conventional steering gear and associated linkage dampens road shock better than a rack-and-pinion gear. Technician B says that rack-and-pinion steering provides better road feel. Who is right?

(A) A only

(B) B only

(C) Both A and B

(D) Neither A nor B

13. Technician A says that the rack gear moves laterally a certain amount for each rotation of the pinion gear. Technician B says that a variable ratio is provided by varying the size of the pinion gear teeth and the distance between them. Who is right?

(A) A only

(B) B only

(C) Both A and B

(D) Neither A nor B

14. Technician A says that the inner tie rods of a rack-and-pinion gear may be connected either to the center or ends of the rack. Technician B says that rack-and-pinion linkage consists only of tie rods and tie rod ends. Who is right?

(A) A only

(B) B only

(C) Both A and B

(D) Neither A nor B

15. Technician A says that an energy-absorbing steering column collapses or telescopes under the impact of a collision. Technician B says that the flexible coupling allows for angle differences between the column shaft and steering shaft. Who is right?

(A) A only
(B) B only
(C) Both A and B
(D) Neither A nor B

16. Technician A says that the use of an intermediate shaft between the steering gear and steering shaft reduces the angle difference between the two.

Technician B says that universal joints used to connect the steering gear and shaft reduces road noise and dampens vibrations. Who is right?

(A) A only
(B) B only
(C) Both A and B
(D) Neither A nor B

POWER-ASSIST STEERING SYSTEMS

"Work expands so as to fill the time available for its completion." — Parkinson's First law

---

 OBJECTIVES

After completion of this chapter, you should be able to:

- Explain the principle of compression as it applies to air and liquids.

- Explain how a liquid can transmit motion and force.

- List the components of a power-assisted steering system and briefly describe their interrelationship.

- Identify the three types of power steering pumps and briefly explain the operation of each.

- Explain the difference in operation between rotary and sliding directional control valves.

- Describe the operation of a flow control valve and explain how it acts as a pressure relief valve.

A driver's physical effort, combined with the mechanical advantage provided by the steering gear, determines the amount of rotational motion sent to a manual steering gear. The application of hydraulic force to the steering system can assist the driver in turning the steering gear. Power-assisted steering requires less effort on the part of the driver, and delivers better response with less road shock. The addition of electronic controls, covered in the chapter on computer-controlled steering, allows steering to be fine-tuned to an even greater degree.

Although power-assisted steering is not a recent concept (it was used as early as 1903), serious efforts toward its development did not occur until the late 1940's. Hydraulic power-assisted steering first appeared as an option on 1951 Chrysler and DeSoto vehicles, and was introduced a year later on several Buick, Cadillac, and

Oldsmobile models. Since that time, many improvements have been made, and power-assisted steering is now standard equipment on many vehicles.

In this chapter, we will look at how hydraulic force is applied to the steering system, and how the various types of power-assisted steering systems currently in use operate.

HYDRAULIC PRINCIPLES

Hydraulics is the science of using a liquid under pressure to perform work, and transmit motion and force. The modern power-assisted steering system works on the principles of hydraulics first described by a 17th century French mathematician, Blaise Pascal. Pascal's Law contains three important physical factors that make hydraulic steering assist possible — compression, motion, and force.

COMPRESSION

Air can be compressed by forcing more and more of it into a container. As more air is put into the container, the pressure in the container goes up. Liquids cannot be compressed. Liquids can completely fill a container, but once it is full, no more liquid can be added because the liquid cannot be compressed to fill a smaller space. If the top of a liquid-filled container is fitted with a piston, and the piston is pushed into the container against the liquid, the pressure will rise everywhere in the container, but the piston will NOT move into the container and compress the liquid.

To prove this to yourself, place two bottles — one, a sealed bottle containing your favortie carbonated beverage and the second, a water-filled bottle — on a table. When you open up the carbonated bottle the CO_2 in solution and the excess CO_2 occupying the free space in compressed form gets released and starts rushing out

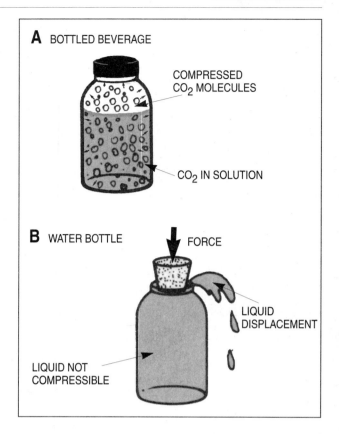

Figure 10-1 When a carbonated beverage is bottled, the carbon dioxide (CO_2) in solution gets released slowly when there is a free space above the liquid. As the gas cannot escape from the sealed bottle, its molecules are squeezed within the limited available space. The gas thus compressed rushes out with a hissing sound when the bottle is opened (A). Since liquids are incompressible, inserting a cork in a bottle filled with water displaces enough water from the bottle to accept the cork (B).

causing a hissing sound (A, Figure 10-1). Now try to cork the water-filled bottle; either the cork will not go in, or some water will squirt out from between the sides of the cork and the bottle neck. The molecules in water (a liquid) cannot be squeezed closer together (B, Figure 10-1). As this example demonstrates, compressing a liquid does not decrease its volume under normal circumstances. For the record, you could decrease the volume of one cubic inch of water by 10% — provided you apply

64,000 psi of pressure! Although any liquid could be used in a hydraulic system, a special one called power steering fluid is used for many power steering systems; others use automatic transmission fluid (ATF), which is similar.

MOTION

Because a liquid is NOT compressible, it can transmit motion. If you fill a length of tubing or hose with a liquid and insert a plunger at one end, the liquid will move through the tube or hose and spill out the other end. The plunger motion transmitted by the liquid forms the basis for a simple hydraulic system. If two pistons are enclosed in a cylinder with a liquid-filled area between them, one piston can be made to move the other (Figure 10-2). If pressure is applied to piston A in the cylinder, the liquid will transmit that pressure to piston B, moving it an equal distance, as long as the pistons are the same diameter. This example shows how a hydraulic link can be used to do a simple task. Suppose we put a piston in each of two different cylinders

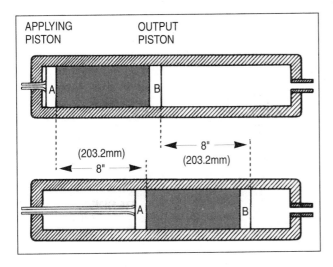

Figure 10-2 The non-compressibility of a liquid results in a hydraulic link between pistons A and B, since piston B will move the same distance as piston A when pressure is applied. (Chrysler)

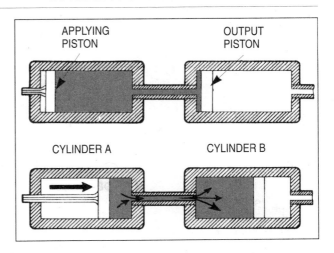

Figure 10-3 Fluid also can transmit motion between two cylinders. When both pistons are equal in size, the output piston will move the same distance as the input piston. (Chrysler)

and connect the two cylinders with a tube. Motion still can be transmitted between the two pistons (Figure 10-3). This makes the cylinder and piston arrangement far more versatile, and capable of doing more complex work. This concept of applying pressure to hydraulic fluid and using it to transmit force and motion is used in both the power steering and hydraulic brake systems.

FORCE

A predictable pressure/force relationship exists in the science of hydraulics. Applied pressure not only can cause a component to move, the pressure can be used to control applied force. This concept of fluid pressure is expressed as a simple equation — pressure multiplied by area equals force.

A simple hydraulic system shown in Figure 10-4 demonstrates this principle. When a force of 100 lb is applied to a pump piston with a cross-sectional area of one square inch, 100 lb_f per square inch (psi) of hydraulic pressure is created. The apply piston sends the same pressure to three other pistons. Now this system pressure can be multiplied into a higher force by

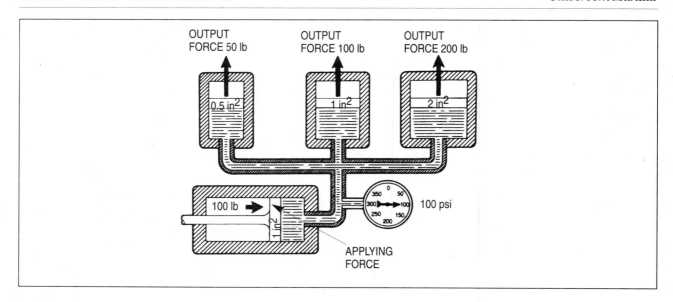

Figure 10-4   The output force is measured by the system pressure and the area of the output piston. (Chrysler)

varying the size of the output pistons. Because the system pressure is 100 lb$_f$ on every square inch, the output force of a piston depends on how many square inches its cross-sectional area is. In Figure 10-4 the central one of the three output pistons has a cross-sectional area of one square inch, the same as the applying piston. Therefore the output force of the central piston is equal to the input force. The piston to its left has only a one-half square inch cross-sectional area. When the 100 psi pressure is applied, its output is only half of the original force, or 50 lb$_f$. The piston on the right has a cross-sectional area of two square inches. With 100 psi input pressure, this piston's output is twice as great as the original force, or 200 lb$_f$. A power steering pump applies pressure to hydraulic fluid in a similar manner as the input piston. In a power steering system, the pump keeps the hydraulic pressure up so it can be used to make steering easier for the driver.

Hydraulic fluid under pressure acts as a flexible machine. Although it does not work like the simple lever in a mechanical system, it provides the same benefit by multiplying the amount of input effort to do more work than normal. For example, a mass of 10 lb requires 10 lb of lift effort when the pivot point, or fulcrum, is placed halfway between the lever ends (A, Figure 10-5). When the lever is divided into five equal lengths, and the pivot point is located at the end of the first length, the lever produces a 4:1 mechanical advantage. This means that lifting the 10 lb on the short end requires only 2 1/2 lb of effort at the long end (B, Figure 10-5).

Hydraulic fluid in a rack-and-pinion steering produces a mechanical advantage by pushing on the rack piston. We know that fluid under pressure in a chamber applies force against each square inch of area. If we assume that a power steering pump develops 750 psi maximum pressure, the fluid exerts 750 lb$_f$ on every square inch of the rack piston area. Since the rack pushes the steering arms, they offer the mechanical advantage of levers. In this way, the mechanical advantage of the hydraulic fluid pressure on the rack piston combines with the lever action of the

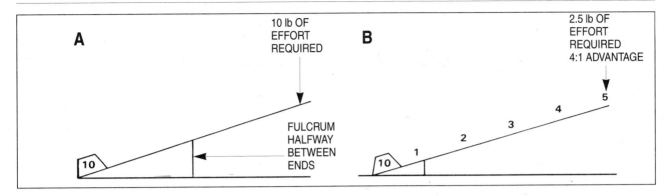

Figure 10-5   The mechanical advantage of a lever. (Chrysler)

steering arms to provide the power assistance.

Now that you have seen how hydraulic fluid can exert pressure and transmit motion equally in all directions, we will look at the basic components of modern power-assisted steering systems and how the various types of systems operate.

HYDRAULICS AND POWER STEERING

Modern power-assisted steering systems consist of a steering gear designed to work with hydraulic force (Figure 10-6). The additional components that must be added to a manual steering system for this purpose include the following:

- hydraulic pump to pressurize the fluid
- flow control valve to regulate the volume of fluid leaving the pump
- directional control valve that responds to the driver's steering effort
- hydraulic actuator, or piston and cylinder
- a pair of connecting hoses.

Two types of power steering systems have been used on passenger vehicles — the **non-integral** or linkage-type and the **integral**-type. Most systems in use today, whether conventional or rack-and-pinion, are of the integral type.

The piston that moves the steering is a modified recirculating ball nut or rack; the cylinder is a modified gear housing. A **rotary valve** or a **sliding valve** located in the gear housing interacts with the steering shaft to direct hydraulic flow to the piston. When the steering wheel is turned, the turning torque applied to the steering shaft moves this spool valve. The **spool valve** either rotates or slides to direct the pressurized hydraulic fluid supplied by the pump and **flow control valve** to the correct side of the piston, where the resulting pressure differential provides the hydraulic assist.

The power steering pump is bracket-mounted on the engine and driven by engine power through a V-belt. The pump draws hydraulic fluid from its reservoir, pressurizes the fluid, and delivers it to the directional valve in the linkage-type or the integral steering gear through a reinforced rubber hose. The fluid is returned to the pump through a second hose, and is constantly circulating whenever the engine is running. Fluid to the valve is transmitted through a high-pressure hose, and returned to the pump reservoir through a low-pressure hose.

If operating pressure is lost for any reason, a check valve in the system permits fluid to flow from one side of the piston to the other, eliminating all resistance. With the power assist missing, a few vehicles can

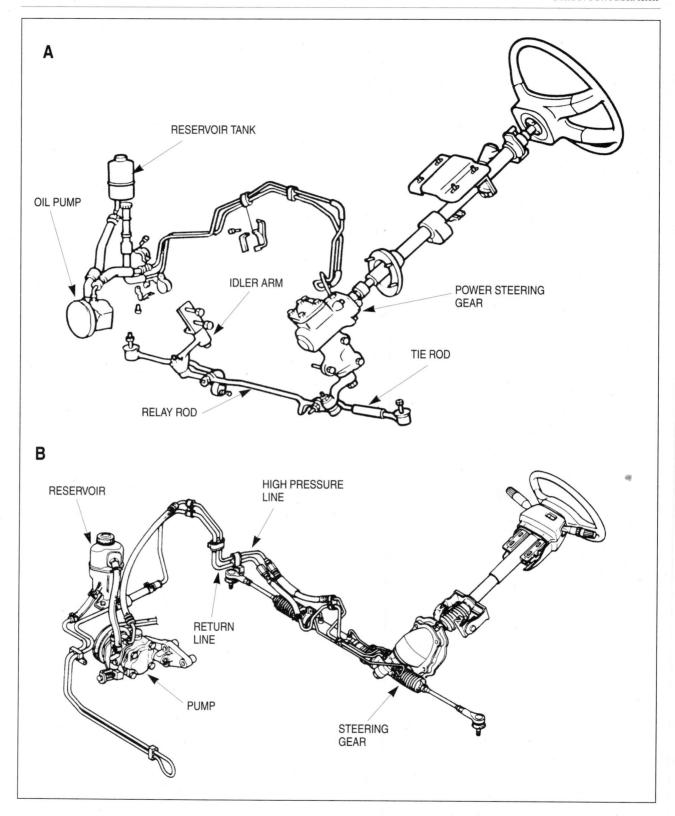

Figure 10-6 Components of a typical power-assisted recirculating ball steering system (A) and a typical power-assisted rack-and-pinion system (B). (Chrysler (A) and Ford Motor (B))

be steered, although with difficulty. On most vehicles, the loss of power to the steering means that the vehicle cannot be steered because it takes so much effort to turn the steering wheel.

DIRECTIONAL CONTROL

The direction of power assist in both conventional and rack-and-pinion steering systems is controlled by the pressure differential operating on the piston. Since a rack-and-pinion gear is less complicated, we will look first at how the pressure differential works with this type of steering. The rack piston is located in a hydraulic chamber sealed in the housing (Figure 10-7). If hydraulic pressure is the same (balanced) on each side of the piston, NO movement will occur and the wheels will remain in the straight-ahead position. When fluid pressure on one side of the piston exceeds that on the other side, the piston will move in the direction of the lower pressure (Figure 10-8).

In this type of steering gear, leakage of any of the three chamber seals shown in Figure 10-7 will affect pressure and piston movement. The piston and cover seals form the left chamber; the piston and bulkhead seals form the right chamber. If either the cover or bulkhead seals leak,

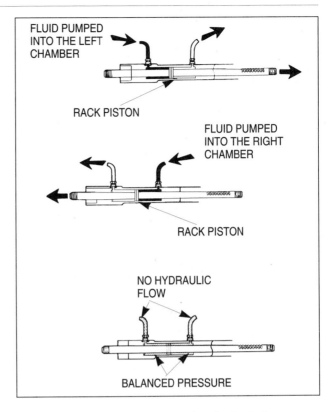

Figure 10-8 Pressure differential is the basis for power-assist steering. (Chrysler)

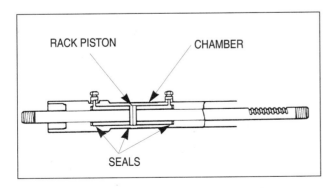

Figure 10-7 The hydraulic chamber in the rack-and-pinion housing is formed by seals on either side of the rack piston. (Chrysler)

pressure in the corresponding chamber will be lower and a loss of hydraulic assist in that chamber is likely. A leaking piston seal will allow fluid to enter both chambers, causing a reduction or total loss of assist in both directions.

In a conventional power-assist system, spool valve movement controls the system pressure differential (Figure 10-9). The spool valve is centered during straight-ahead driving. This allows fluid to circulate throughout the system and apply the same pressure on each side of the piston. As the steering wheel is turned, end thrust develops on the worm and steering shaft, causing the spool valve to move. Spool valve movement directs high-pressure fluid to one side of the piston, and opens the circuit between the other side of the piston and the reservoir. This creates a

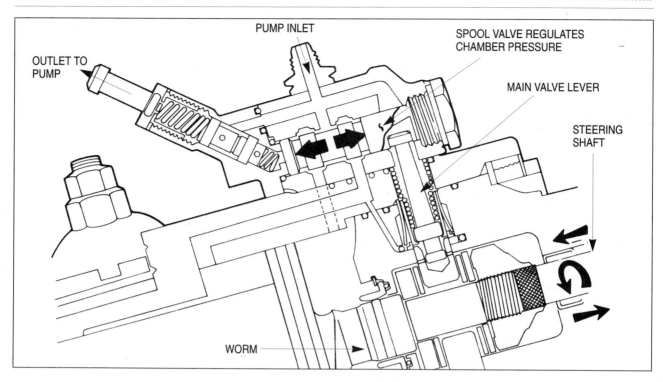

Figure 10-9 Movement of the spool valve creates the pressure differential in a conventional power-assisted steering gear. (Chrysler)

fluid pressure differential between the two sides of the piston, which provides the majority of the effort required to turn the front wheels. As the steering wheel is returned to the straight-ahead position, end thrust on the worm is relieved and the spool valve returns to its centered position. Since the spool valve reacts to the thrust on the worm, the turning force applied to the steering wheel results in a steering assist proportionate to spool valve movement.

This brief explanation of directional control provides a basis for understanding how hydraulic force is applied to produce a power assist for the steering system. We will discuss the concept in greater detail in the following sections.

CONVENTIONAL POWER-ASSIST SYSTEMS

A conventional power-assist steering system uses a recirculating ball steering gear and is found on RWD vehicles. Conventional power-assist systems may be either a non-integral or an integral type.

NON-INTEGRAL POWER STEERING

The non-integral or linkage-type power steering enjoyed its greatest popularity during the decade between 1954 and 1964. It consisted of a conventional steering gear, a hydraulic pump connected to a directional control valve assembly by two hoses, and a power cylinder (Figure 10-10). The directional valve and power cylinder were connected to the steering linkage, and acted on the tie rods to help in steering the vehicle. Since this type of power assist required no change in the steering gear, it was primarily an add-on or booster system and was inexpensive enough to be factory-installed on any vehicle equipped with manual steering.

In the typical linkage-type installation,

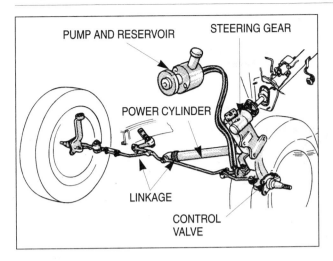

Figure 10-10 Linkage-type power steering. (Ford Motor)

the hydraulic pump was driven by a separate crankshaft-driven V-belt, or off the back of the generator. Early pumps with the extra capacity to perform at the low engine speeds required in parking situations were too large a pump for highway speeds. They pumped too much fluid on the highway and burned up the pump. To correct this, a pressure regulating or relief valve was incorporated in the pump body. If the pump output exceeded the system specifications, the relief valve released the fluid flow back into the return line to the pump. This prevented excessive pressure build-up and provided a steering boost only when needed.

A year after Ford's introduction of linkage-type power steering in 1954, GM's Saginaw division introduced a more refined unit. This incorporated a sliding directional control valve in the power cylinder, which was connected to the steering linkage. The control valve, which determined the direction that the cylinder pushed on the linkage, contained a spool valve and operated something like a miniature automatic transmission. The spring-loaded spool valve remained centered during straight-ahead driving. Pitman arm movement caused the valve spool to slide,

opening a series of ports that directed fluid pressure to one side or the other of the power cylinder.

For example, when the driver exerted a predetermined amount of effort on the steering gear during a left turn, the valve moved to the right against the pressure of its centering springs. This uncovered ports that allowed the fluid to be routed into the right side of the power cylinder. The power cylinder thus forced the steering likage to turn the wheels to the left.

Linkage-type power steering required a wheel rim effort of 4 to 7 lb on the part of the driver. While adequate for the vehicles on which it was used, it did NOT compare with modern power-assisted systems, which require about 3 lb. Nor did it give as good a sense of road feel, since the hydraulic cylinder functioned much like a shock absorber on the steering gear.

INTEGRAL POWER STEERING

The early integral Chrysler and GM power-assist systems were large, bulky, and expensive to manufacture. Several designs of integral power steering continued to be offered on the more expensive vehicles during the decade that linkage-type systems were popular, but by 1965, carmakers had refined the integral system into a smaller and far more efficient package.

Current steering gears owe much to the 1965 integral systems, which have continued virtually unchanged in basic design. The gear housing contains three main subassemblies (Figure 10-11):

- the power train consisting of the power piston and reaction assemblies, both mounted on the worm shaft
- the main valve assembly containing two valves with hydraulic passages and installed in a separate housing mounted on the main housing
- the sector shaft assembly.

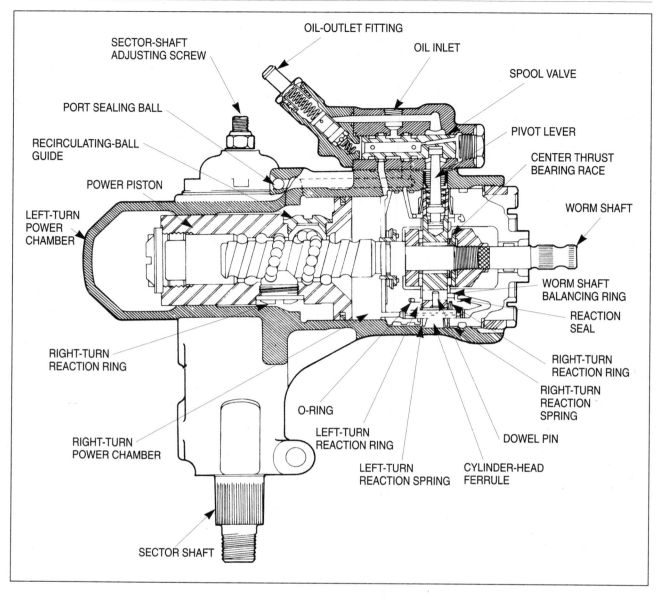

Figure 10-11 A sectional view of a typical recirculating ball gearbox. (Chrysler)

The worm shaft and steering shaft are linked by a short torsion bar. The lower end of the torsion bar connects to the worm shaft and also is pinned to the valve body, which is mounted in teflon ring seals inside the upper end of the steering gear housing. The other end of the torsion bar is pinned to the stub shaft. The strength of the torsion bar determines the amount of assist and steering feel.

Hydraulic flow to the piston is directed either by a rotary or sliding valve. While their mechanical action differs, both types of valves operate essentially the same in terms of fluid flow. Sliding valves are used with linkage-type power steering and the conventional power-assisted steering gears found on some older Chrysler and import vehicles. Rotary valves are used in most other North American, as well as newer

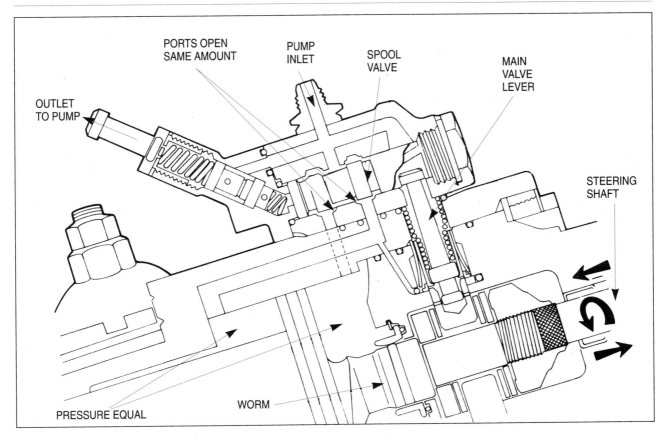

OUTLET
TO PUMP

PORTS OPEN
SAME AMOUNT

PUMP
INLET

SPOOL
VALVE

MAIN
VALVE
LEVER

STEERING
SHAFT

PRESSURE EQUAL

WORM

Figure 10-12 Spool valve positioning during straight-ahead driving. (Chrysler)

import steering gears. Since sliding valve operation was described during our discussion of the linkage-type system, we will discuss the operation of the rotary valve design below.

The rotary valve is centered when the wheels are in the straight-ahead position (Figure 10-12). Fluid from the pump enters the outer valve body from the housing ports. Since the valve spool is positioned with its ports open to both left- and right-turn passages, constant pressure is maintained on both sides of the piston and helps in absorbing road shock. With the valve spool ports and the fluid return circuit open, a constant flow occurs in the system.

Turning the steering wheel to the left twists the torsion bar. This causes the spool to change its position relative to the valve body. With its position changed, the

spool lands restrict fluid flow to the right-turn side of the piston and open the circuit to the return line (Figure 10-13). Since the movement restricts pump flow, pressure in the system rises. This creates a pressure differential on either side of the piston, forcing the piston to move in the direction of steering wheel rotation. The driver feels this movement as a reduction in turning effort.

When the steering wheel is released, the spool valve returns to its centered position and pressure equalizes on each side of the piston. The pressure equalization allows vehicle momentum and front-end geometry to force the piston back to its centered position. If the steering wheel is turned to the right, the process is reversed, and hydraulic force is applied to the right-turn side of the piston (Figure 10-14).

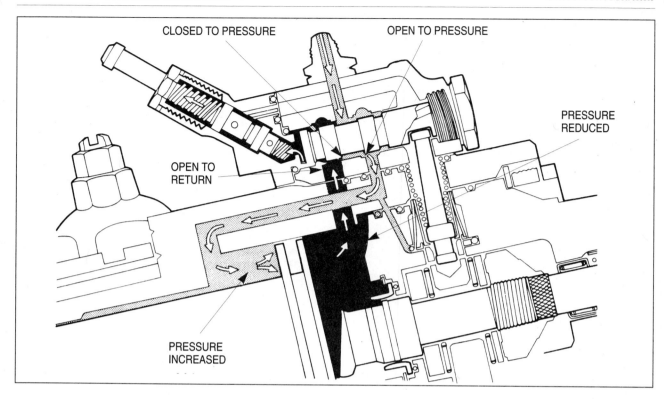

Figure 10-13 Spool valve positioning during a left turn. (Chrysler)

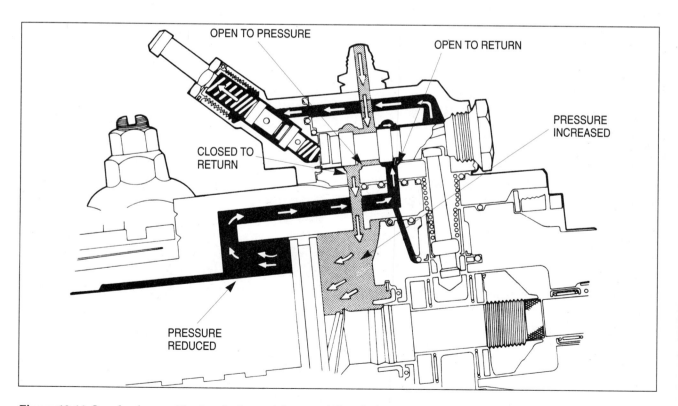

Figure 10-14 Spool valve positioning during a right turn. (Chrysler)

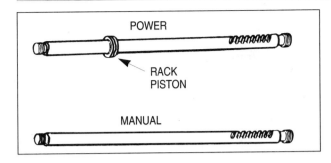

Figure 10-15 The rack piston is an integral part of the power-assisted rack. (Chrysler)

POWER RACK-AND-PINION STEERING

Power rack-and-pinion steering gears are used on FWD and RWD vehicles and operate in much the same way as the manual units. To make a power unit, the manual steering has been modified to accept a piston mounted on the rack inside the housing (Figure 10-15) and a rotary control valve integrated with the input stub shaft (Figure 10-16). The housing

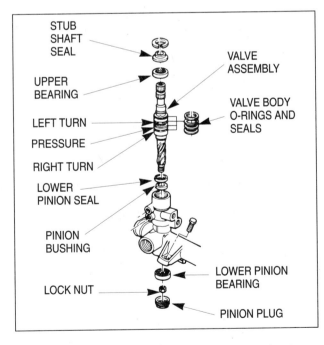

Figure 10-16 The rack-and-pinion rotary valve is an integral part of the stub shaft/pinion assembly. (Chrysler)

functions as the power cylinder and is sealed on each side of the rack piston, forming separate hydraulic chambers for the left and right turn circuits (Figure 10-17). Fluid flows between each end of the housing bore and the directional valve circuits through external steel tubes.

Hydraulic action inside the power rack housing is similar to that of the conventional power steering gear. With the wheels in the straight-ahead postion, there is NO hydraulic assist because equal pressure is exerted at each end of the piston bore (Figure 10-18). When the steering wheel is turned to one side, resistance of the wheels and the vehicle mass cause a torsion bar in the directional valve to deflect, changing the position of the valve spool and sleeve ports (Figure 10-17). This directs the pressurized fluid to the appropriate end of the power cylinder or housing and forces the fluid in the opposite end of the power cylinder to return to the pump reservoir. The pressure differential created on the piston causes the rack to move toward the area of lower pressure (Figure 10-18), reducing the effort required to turn the wheels. As soon as the driver stops applying steering effort, the torsion bar forces the rotary valve back to a centered position. This equalizes pressure on both sides of the piston, and the front wheels tend to return to their straight-ahead position.

During a turning maneuver with rack-and-pinion steering, one of the dust boots or bellows at the end of the housing extends while the other one contracts. With a manual steering rack, air moves through the center of the housing to make this possible, but the three separate seals in a power-assist rack-and-pinion gear make air movement through the housing impossible. To provide the necessary venting action, the two end boots or bellows are connected by a vent or breather tube (Figure 10-19).

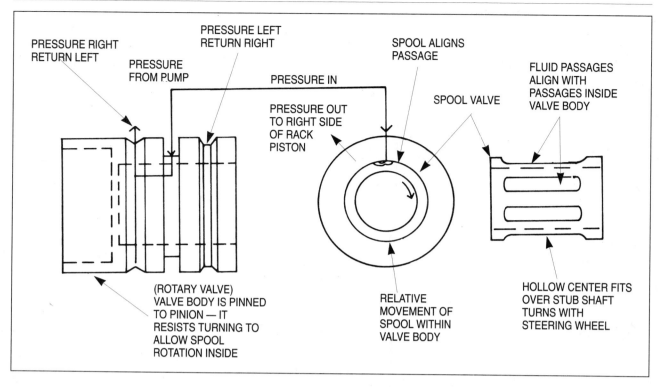

Figure 10-17 Operation of a typical rotary spool valve. (Chrysler)

When the steering wheel is turned fully to one side or the other, the pump produces maximum fluid pressure under load and causes a decrease in engine speed. To prevent this from affecting engine operation, a pressure switch is installed either at the pump or the steering gear. When the switch closes under heavy pressure conditions, the engine control computer speeds up the engine until pump pressure returns to normal, preventing the engine from stalling.

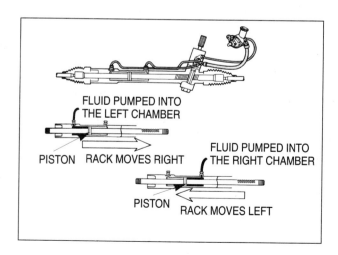

Figure 10-18 rack-and-pinion power-assist operation. (Ford Motor)

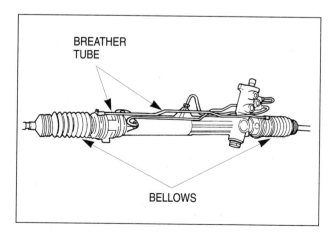

Figure 10-19 A breather tube vents air from the dust boots or bellows during turning maneuvers. (Ford Motor)

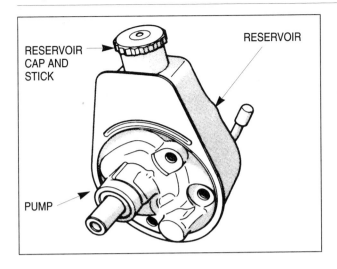

Figure 10-20 The most common power steering pump design in use, the Saginaw pump is housed inside the reservoir. (Chrysler)

POWER STEERING PUMPS

The power steering pump assembly (Figure 10-20) provides a steady flow of fluid for use by the steering system. The assembly consists of a belt-driven hydraulic pump, a flow control and pressure relief valve, and an integral reservoir (Figure 10-21). When engine compartment space is limited, the reservoir may be remotely mounted (Figure 10-22). All power steering pumps are a fixed or constant displacement design; the amount of hydraulic fluid delivered in one revolution of the rotor is the same, regardless of pump speed and outlet pressure.

Automotive power steering pumps are designed to pump a volume of fluid sufficient to accommodate the needs of the power steering gear when the engine is idling. Most such pumps will deliver about 1 to 1.5 gallons (3.8 to 5.7 liters) per minute at idle speed and low pressure. When the pump and its reservoir are an integral unit, the reservoir surrounds much of the pump body (Figure 10-20). The pump inlet is provided by passages in the pump body that are open to the reservoir; the pump outlet passage behind the flow

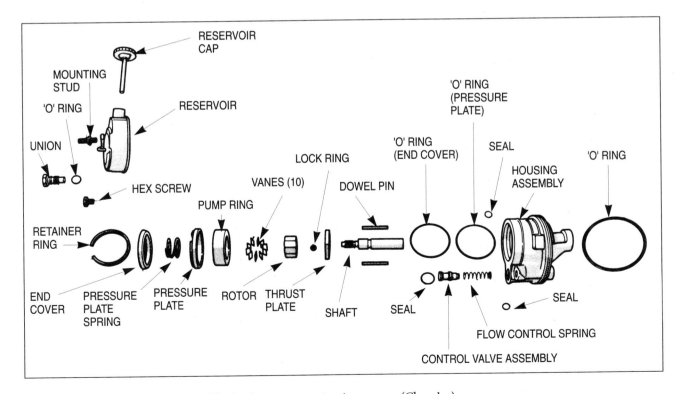

Figure 10-21 An exploded view of the Saginaw power steering pump. (Chrysler)

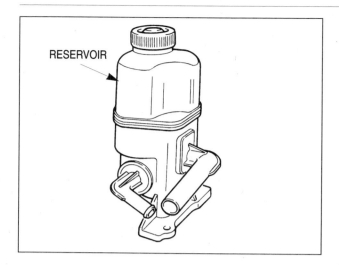

Figure 10-22 When engine compartment space is limited, the power steering pump may use a remote reservoir connected by hydraulic hoses. This approach is more common with import vehicles. (Ford Motor)

control valve connects directly to the high-pressure fitting. Integral reservoirs have a cap and dipstick to check fluid level. Remote reservoirs may use the cap and dipstick, or are made of translucent plastic to allow a visual fluid level check.

PUMP OPERATION

Three types of pumps are used — vane, slipper, and roller, but all use a rotor that spins inside the pump body, and operate essentially the same way.

Vane Pump

With the vane-type unit (Figure 10-23), the belt-driven pump shaft is splined at one end to a slotted rotor. The rotor is slotted to accept a number (usually 10) of blades or vanes (Figure 10-24). The vanes follow the inner cam-shaped surface of the cam ring, which encases the rotor and vanes, and the pressure and thrust plates. These two plates are set against the cam ring to form cavities between the rotor vanes. The cavities act as small pumping chambers that travel around the inside of the cam

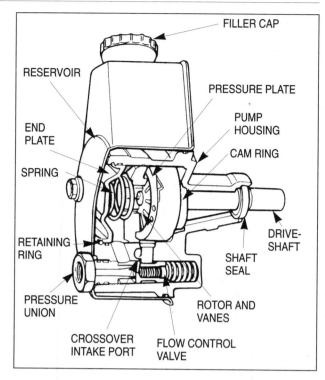

Figure 10-23 A cross-sectional view of the vane-type Saginaw pump. (Ford Motor)

ring with driveshaft rotation. The rotor slots are deep enough for the vanes to slide in or out of the slots. The oval shape of the inside of the pump body provides more room for the vanes to slide out when they pass the extended area around the rotor. Centrifugal force keeps the vanes in contact

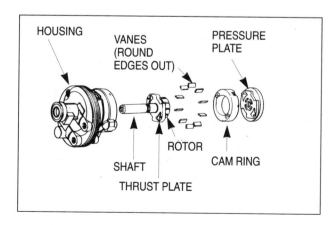

Figure 10-24 The rotating group of a vane-type pump. (Chrysler)

with the body walls at all time, even though they move in and out of their slots as the rotor turns. In one revolution of the rotor, there are two places where the vanes are loose enough to pick up fluid, and two places where they are forced in by the walls of the body, putting pressure on the fluid. Since the intake ports are opposite each other, as are the discharge ports, the pump is hydraulically balanced.

Slipper Pump

The rotor of this pump design has several wide slots cut into it. These slots are fitted with springs topped by scrubber-type 'slippers' (Figure 10-25). The springs keep the slippers in contact with the inner contour of the pump body. When the pump shaft rotates, the slippers follow the inside of the cam. As they near the inlet port, the chamber area between the slippers increases, causing a slight vacuum. Fluid flow into the chamber is trapped when the

second slipper passes the inlet port. Since the chamber area becomes smaller until it reaches the outlet port, the fluid is pressurized. Because the chamber pressure is higher than the pressure in the outlet port, the fluid flows out through the outlet port. As the pump has two inlet and two outlet ports located 180° apart, it is hydraulically balanced, reducing the load on the rotor shaft and bushing to a minimum.

Roller Pump

The third variation in power steering pump design is called a roller pump. The inside contour of this design is again oval-shaped, but the rotor has a set of wide V-grooves cut into it. Steel rollers ride in these grooves and, like the vanes or slippers, follow the inside contour of the pump body as centrifugal force pushes them out at the ends of the oval. The rollers trap fluid in the same way as the slippers or vanes, and pressurize the fluid when they pass the

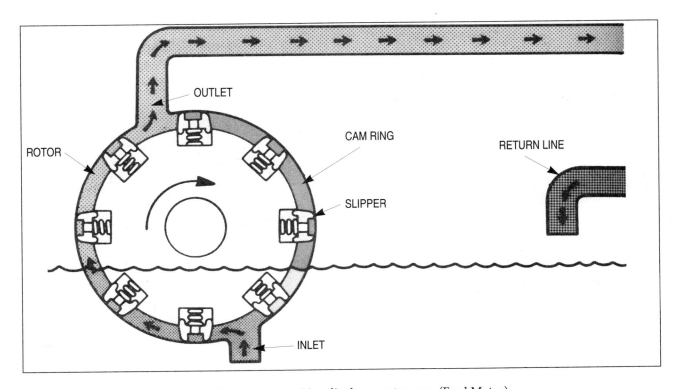

Figure 10-25 Operation of a typical slipper-type positive displacement pump. (Ford Motor)

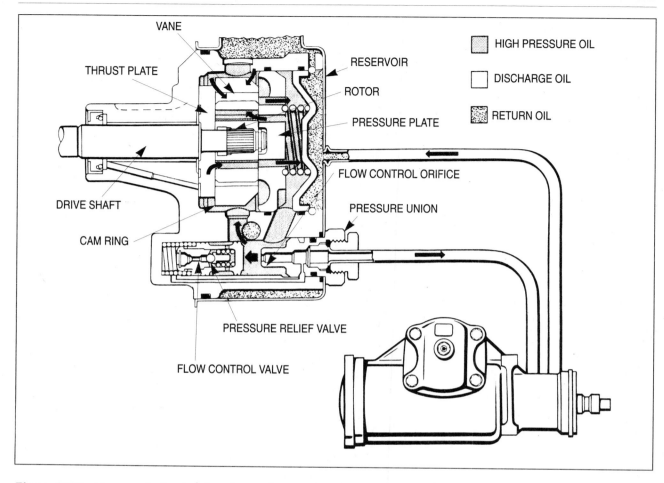

Figure 10-26 Flow control valve location and operation during a partial turning maneuver. (Chevrolet Division, General Motors)

narrow portions of the body, before forcing it out through the two outlets. Again, since there are two pickup and two compression areas in the housing, the pressure and side loads on the rotor shaft are equally distributed, or hydraulically balanced.

FLOW CONTROL VALVE

Since the power steering pump is a **positive displacement pump**, it continues to deliver flow at any outlet pressure, but NOT all of the flow is used by the steering gear. To supply the proper pressure and fluid flow, the flow control valve acts as the 'brain' of the system by regulating the pressure and flow rate. This allows the system pressure to rise and fall in proportion to the restriction encountered in the steering gear. In this way, the pump provides a variable pressure that relates the amount of power assist to the driver's effort.

The flow control valve is located in a chamber exposed to the pump outlet pressure at one end, and supply hose pressure at the other (Figure 10-26). A spring installed at the supply pressure end helps to maintain balance. Figure 10-27 shows the operation of a typical flow control valve during engine idle, flow control, and pressure relief. As fluid leaves the pump rotor, it passes the end of the

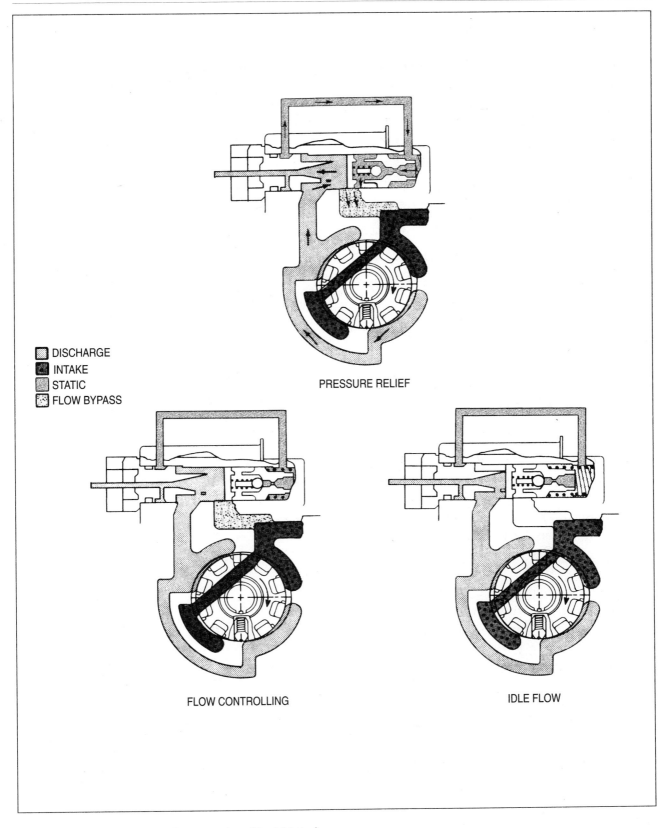

DISCHARGE
INTAKE
STATIC
FLOW BYPASS

PRESSURE RELIEF

FLOW CONTROLLING

IDLE FLOW

Figure 10-27 Flow control valve operation. (Ford Motor)

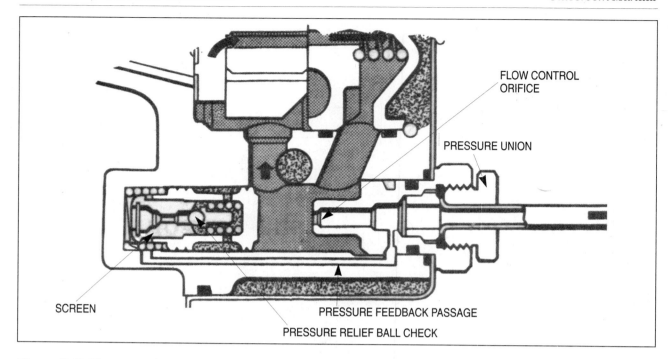

Figure 10-28 Flow control valve and pressure feedback passage. (Chevrolet Division, General Motors)

flow control valve where it is forced through an orifice, causing a slight drop in pressure. Assisted by the spring, the reduced pressure keeps the flow control valve in the closed position, allowing all pump flow to be sent to the steering gear.

As engine speed increases, the pump delivers more flow than necessary to operate the system. Because the outlet orifice restricts the amount of fluid leaving the pump, the pressure differential at the two ends of the valve increases until the pressure at the pump outlet overcomes the combined spring force and supply line pressure. This pushes the valve down against the spring, opening a passage that allows excess fluid to flow back to the inlet side of the pump.

Turning the steering wheel restricts the return fluid flow from the gear and increases pressure. The flow control valve is designed to allow the pump to produce more pressure through a pressure feedback passage (Figure 10-28) when pressure

increases in the gear due to the restriction. Any pressure increase in the gear is transmitted back into the flow control orifice pressure union and thus the flow control valve.

The flow control valve also contains a spring and check ball (Figure 10-29) that acts as a pressure relief valve. This

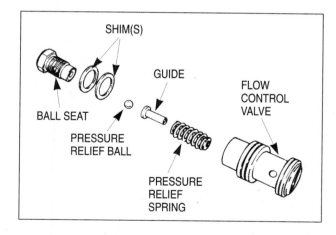

Figure 10-29 The pressure relief valve is an integral part of the flow control valve. (Chevrolet Division, General Motors)

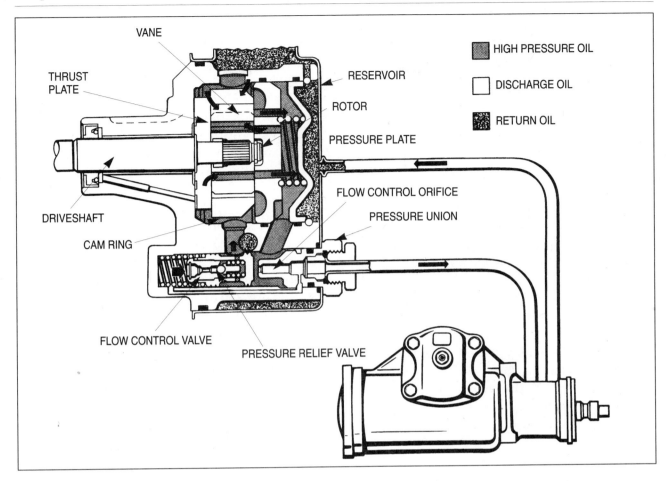

Figure 10-30 Pressure relief valve operation. (Chevrolet Division, General Motors)

protects the system from damage if the steering wheel is turned to one side as far as it will go and held there. When this happens, the resulting restriction in system flow causes pump outlet pressure to become excessive. Without some way to relieve this excess pressure, the pump will continue to build more pressure until it either destroys itself or ruptures a hose. Thus, when the pressure behind the flow control valve reaches a predetermined level, the pressure relief valve is forced off its seat against spring tension and releases fluid (Figure 10-30). The decrease in pressure allows the valve to open wider and relieves the pressure by allowing a greater volume of fluid to be recirculated. As the

pressure increases again, the ball again unseats. In this way, maximum pressure is held fairly constant at a safe level.

This pressure relief function of the flow control valve is noisy when it operates. The hissing or squealing noise heard during pressure relief often is accompanied by a screeching caused by the drive belt slipping. If the driver does NOT release the steering wheel slightly when this noise is present during a sharp turn, fluid temperature will rise and can cause damage to system components. As soon as the steering wheel is released slightly, the steering gear control valve will move back to its center position and allow fluid to return to the pump.

HOSES AND FLUID

The power steering pump is connected to the steering gear directional control valve by a pair of reinforced rubber hoses — one for the pressure line and the other for the return line.

Since the pressure hose must carry high pressure, it must be stronger and have pressure-tight connections. Like high-pressure air conditioning hoses, power steering pressure hoses are preformed, and are attached to steel end tubes by crimped metal connectors (Figure 10-31). Since the return hose carries only low pressure, it can be attached with the band or screw-type clamps used with cooling system hoses on some installations. The return hose in most late model systems also uses steel end tubes like the high-pressure hose. In this case, the major difference between the two hoses is in the material used in manufacturing; the return hose does NOT require as much reinforcement.

On a vehicle equipped with hydro-boost brakes, the brake and power steering systems are inter-related, with the power steering pump providing the power assist for brake application. Additional pressure and return hoses are required to connect the two systems. Heavy duty systems also may use a fluid cooler to prevent the hydraulic fluid from breaking down and oxidizing at high temperatures. This cooler can take the form of a small radiator, like those used for engine oil coolers, or simply be an additional loop of steel tubing in the line.

Either automatic transmission fluid (ATF) or power steering fluid may be used as the hydraulic fluid in most power steering systems. But some steering systems require ATF and the use of power steering fluid is prohibited. Other carmakers specify a special fluid that must conform to their specifications. ATF contains a red dye; power steering fluid contains a yellow or greenish dye. The dye color helps to identify the type of fluid used, as well as in locating system leaks. The hydraulic fluid dissipates heat and lubricates the steering gear. Because the viscosity of the two types of fluid differs, adding the wrong type to a power steering system can result in hose or seal damage, fluid leaks, and even cause damage to the pump. When adding or changing the fluid, always check the carmaker's specifications to determine the proper fluid type to be used.

FOUR-WHEEL STEERING SYSTEMS

Mechanical 4-wheel steering systems made a brief appearance on the scene in 1988 when Honda introduced the first mechanical system on some of its production models. The front and rear wheels are connected by a mechanical linkage. The degree and direction of steering is dependent on vehicle speed. At road speeds under approximately 22 mph, the front and rear wheels steer in opposite directions. This makes vehicle parking, U-turns, and other tight steering or turning

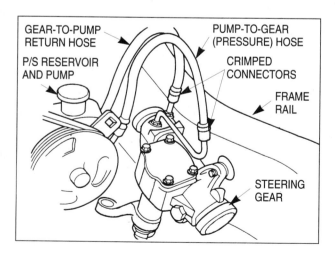

Figure 10-31 Crimped metal connectors are used to secure steel end tubes to the high-pressure hoses used in power steering systems.

maneuvers easier by reducing the turning radius of the car. At road speeds above approximately 22 mph, all four wheels steer in the same direction, improving directional control and cornering stability at cruising speeds, as well as making quick lane changes possible.

The mechanical 4-wheel steering quickly became a technological dead end, as Mazda and other carmakers introduced models the same year using an electrohydraulic steering mechanism with electronic controls. We will discuss 4-wheel steering further in the chapter covering computer-controlled steering.

SUMMARY

Power-assisted steering systems are based on the fact that hydraulic fluid can exert pressure and transmit motion equally in all directions. Hydraulic force is supplied by a belt-driven pump, regulated by a flow control valve, and applied to a piston in the steering gear. The piston moves the steering linkage to turn the wheels in the desired direction. The method of applying this force differs between the recirculating ball and the rack-and-pinion steering gear systems.

Non-integral or linkage-type systems are a booster system and can be used with any vehicle equipped with manual steering. Integral systems require a modified steering gear and have replaced the non-integral systems.

Power steering pumps are positive displacement designs using vanes, slippers, or rollers to pressurize the hydraulic fluid. A flow control valve in the pump regulates the volume of fluid leaving the pump according to system demand, and contains a pressure relief function to prevent excessive fluid pressure that could damage the system.

Power steering hoses carry the fluid from the pump to the steering gear and back. They are preformed hoses made of reinforced rubber and crimped to steel tube ends. The carmaker may specify the use of either automatic transmission fluid (ATF), ordinary power steering fluid, or a special fluid.

Four-wheel mechanical steering was used briefly by Honda, but proved to be a technological dead end, and has been replaced by electrohydraulic steering controlled by a computer module.

⑦ REVIEW QUESTIONS

1. Which of the following is NOT one of the physical factors that makes hydraulic power steering and brakes possible?
   (A) compression
   (B) depression
   (C) motion
   (D) force

2. Technician A says liquids cannot be compressed. Technician B says gases cannot be compressed. Who is right?
   (A) A only
   (B) B only
   (C) Both A and B
   (D) Neither A nor B

3. Technician A says that when a fluid is compressed, it can transmit motion. Technician B says that a fluid transmits motion because it cannot be compressed. Who is right?
   (A) A only
   (B) B only
   (C) Both A and B
   (D) Neither A nor B

4. Which of the following formulas express the pressure/force relationship in hydraulics?

(A) pressure + area = force

(B) pressure - area = force

(C) pressure x area = force

(D) pressure / area = force

5. Technician A says that hydraulic pressure is constant in a closed system. Technician B says that hydraulic pressure varies in a closed system. Who is right?

(A) A only

(B) B only

(C) Both A and B

(D) Neither A nor B

6. Technician A says that current power steering systems are an integral design. Technician B says that non-integral power steering systems are really an add-on or booster system. Who is right?

(A) A only

(B) B only

(C) Both A and B

(D) Neither A nor B

7. Technician A says that the pressure on each side of the rack piston is constant when the wheels are in a straight-ahead position. Technician B says that a directional control valve regulates fluid flow from the pump. Who is right?

(A) A only

(B) B only

(C) Both A and B

(D) Neither A nor B

8. Technician A says that the piston in a power rack-and-pinion gear is mounted on the outside of the housing. Technician B says that it is located on the ball nut. Who is right?

(A) A only

(B) B only

(C) Both A and B

(D) Neither A nor B

9. A rotary directional control valve uses:

(A) vanes.

(B) slippers.

(C) rollers.

(D) a torsion bar

10. Technician A says that the power steering pump is a piston-type, positive displacement hydraulic pump. Technician B says that it is a fixed-displacement, vane-type pump. Who is right?

(A) A only

(B) B only

(C) Both A and B

(D) Neither A nor B

11. The power steering pump provides:

(A) constant pressure with varying flow.

(B) constant flow with varying pressure.

(C) variable pressure according to gear restriction.

(D) its greatest pressure at idle.

12. The brains of the power steering pump is:

(A) the flow control valve.

(B) the pump rotor and cam ring.

(C) the flow control orifice pressure union.

(D) none of the above.

13. Technician A says that the hydraulic fluid used in a power steering system may be ATF. Technician B says that it may be power steering fluid. Who is right?

(A) A only

(B) B only

(C) Both A and B

(D) Neither A nor B

14. Which of the following is NOT a function of the hydraulic fluid in a power steering system?

(A) provide hydraulic force.

(B) lubricate the steering gear.

(C) dissipate heat build-up in the system.

(D) mix easily with other hydraulic fluids.

FUNDAMENTALS OF ELECTRONIC CONTROL

"The real danger is not that computers will begin to think like men, but that men will begin to think like computers." — S.J. Harris

 **OBJECTIVES**

After completion of this chapter, you should be able to:

- List the five major functions of a microcomputer and briefly explain their interrelationship.

- Explain the difference between analog and digital voltage signals.

- Define the binary code and explain how it is used by a microcomputer.

- Explain the two ways a sensor can provide an input signal to the microcomputer.

- Explain briefly the principles involved in the following sensors — potentiometers, switches, thermistors, piezoresistive and variable capacitance sensors, magnetic pickups, linear variable differential transformers, linear variable inductance transducers, Hall-effect sensors, photodiodes, and piezo-electric crystals.

- Describe the two types of signal conditioning.

- Describe briefly the three types of memory and explain what they are used for.

- Explain the six important logic gates used in digital integrated circuits.

- Explain how the microprocessor controls an actuator.

- Describe briefly the relationship between pulse-width modulation and duty cycle.

- Define a trouble or fault code and explain how and why they are used.

- Explain the three techniques of multiplexing.

- Explain the functioning of diodes and transistors.

- Define ESD and outline the precautions you take to avoid damage due to ESD.

Automotive electronics are evolving at an incredible rate. The electronic component content of the total value of a car has grown from 10% in 1988 to 15% in 1995, and is expected to exceed 20% by the year 2000. Industry experts estimate that as electronic control systems become more integrated and more complex, 20% of the electronics used in 1994 vehicles are obsoleted every six months and the pace continues to accelerate. Within 24 months after a vehicle is introduced, its electronic control system will be almost totally different in terms of components and functions. Already, some electronic systems have been discontinued in favor of less expensive and more efficient systems that provide the technician with more information for easier diagnosis.

With the automotive industry moving so rapidly in this direction, it is imperative that automotive technicians add electrical and electronic skills to their existing skills in hydraulic and mechanical systems. Each manufacturer offers one or more electronic systems, and taken as a whole, the many and varied systems in use can appear overwhelming to those not familiar with them. Fortunately, however, all systems operate on the same basic principles. If you understand these basic principles, you can troubleshoot and diagnose different electronic problems regardless of the manufacturer.

In this chapter, we will reduce an electronic control system to its major components and show you step-by-step how it works. Once you have mastered the fundamentals behind an electronic control system, you can apply what you have learned to any specific electronic suspension or steering regardless of who makes it, or what it is called. We will start with the heart of the electronic control system, the microcomputer, and for brevity, refer to it only as a computer.

AUTOMOTIVE COMPUTER FUNCTIONS

The automotive computer (Figure 11-1) is much like a small city. Its central processing unit (CPU), or **microprocessor**, acts like the city hall. It receives information from sensors in the field (policemen, firemen, and other employees) through semiconductor devices, such as transistors, **integrated circuits (IC)**, memory chips and other interfaces, which form miniature electrical circuits (streets). After considering the information, it makes and transmits decisions to **actuators** (other city employees) used to keep the system running properly. The computer receives information from vehicle sensors and other components, makes decisions based on the information, and takes action based on the decisions (Figures 11-2). The CPU is the 'brain' that performs calculations and makes decisions; the other semiconductor parts and actuators support the CPU.

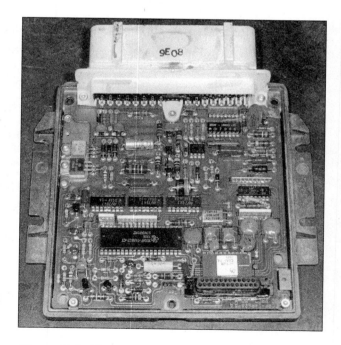

Figure 11-1 The automotive computer seems to be an electronic confusion, but is arranged logically and acts like a small city, with the CPU acting as the city hall.

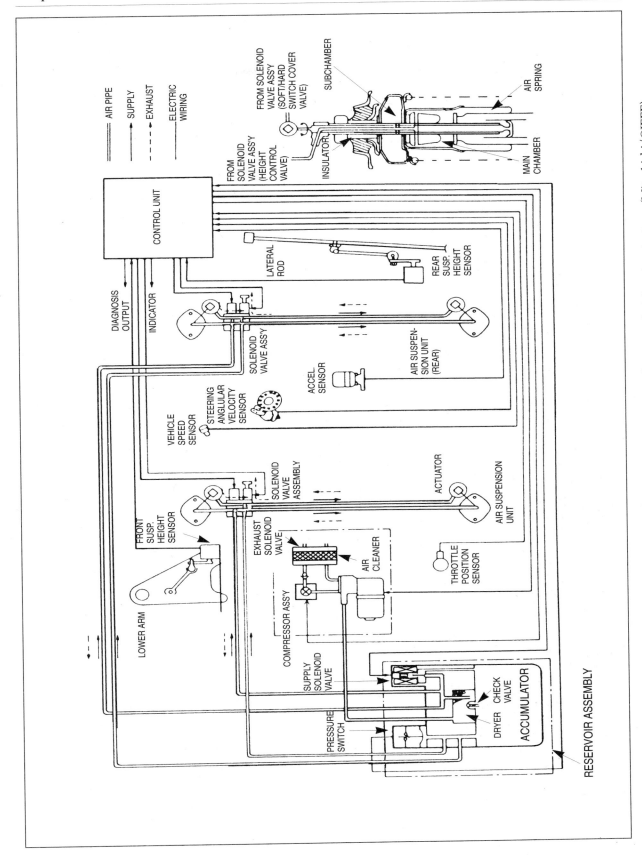

Figure 11-2 The computer receives inputs from various sensors and other components, and conveys decisions to actuators. (Mitsubishi/©IEEE)

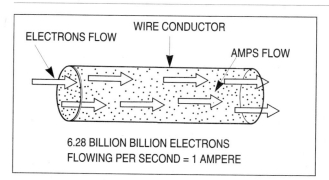

ELECTRONS FLOW   WIRE CONDUCTOR   AMPS FLOW

6.28 BILLION BILLION ELECTRONS
FLOWING PER SECOND = 1 AMPERE

Figure 11-3 Voltage, or electrical pressure, forces current through a circuit. Current is the flow rate of electrons in the circuit and is measured in amperes. (General Motors)

A computer communicates by electrical pressure, or voltage. Voltage does not flow through the circuits, but it does cause current to flow (Figure 11-3). In this way, tiny electrical voltages can be used as signals to transmit information. A voltage signal can transmit information in three ways, by changing:

- its level
- its waveform or shape
- the speed at which the signal switches its level.

A computer uses voltage signals to communicate with its various internal components. It also uses voltage signals to communicate externally with input and output devices. Voltage signals received by the computer from input devices (sensors) are processed and the results transmitted to output devices (actuators). The receipt, processing, and transmission of information — all happens with such speed and precision that no other device can match the computer's efficiency. It operates in milliseconds (a millisecond is one-thousandth of a second) with highly predictable and logical results. Even the earliest automotive computers receive, process, and send information much quicker than it takes to blink an eye.

Computers control an automotive system in much the same way a service technician solves a problem. After hearing the driver describe the problem, you visually inspect the vehicle, and then road test it or perform a few basic system tests. After collecting as much information, or data, as possible, you compare the information to your experience and the manufacturer's service manuals or other literature. This data helps you to make a decision about the possible cause or causes of the problem. With this as a basis, you make a decision about the problem and then repair, replace, or adjust the system components according to your diagnosis (Figure 11-4). This procedure can take several minutes or even several hours of your time. The computer does much the same thing in milliseconds.

All current electronic suspension or steering have a separate computer, or module, that controls the system without consulting with the engine management computer. As time passes, however, these control functions will be integrated in the engine management module.

COMPUTER'S JOB

The easiest way to understand how an automotive computer works is to divide its job into five steps. As we look at each step and its relationship with the other steps, the mystique of the 'black box' will give way to an understanding of how it controls the suspension, steering, or antilock brake operation. For the time being, we will take a brief look at each of the five sub-functions, then explore them in greater detail later in the chapter.

Input

Various sensors on the vehicle provide the computer with information about the vehicle's operation and performance (Figure 11-2). For example, a position sensor in a shock absorber (Figure 11-5) monitors the

YOU COLLECT INFORMATION (INPUT)

YOU ACT ON YOUR DECISION (OUTPUT) AND MAKE NECESSARY ADJUSTMENTS

YOU ANALYZE (PROCESS) INFORMATION, AND REFER TO TABLES AND DIAGNOSTIC CHARTS. YOU DECIDE HOW TO CORRECT A PROBLEM

Figure 11-4 Humans handle information in a similar way to computers, but are far less efficient and far less accurate. (Ford Motor)

size of a variable orifice so that the computer knows whether the orifice is set to give a firm ride or a soft ride. The sensors send the computer a voltage (input) signal on a signal line. Some sensors are grounded by the computer through a signal return line; others provide their own electrical ground. The type of input signal differs according to the type of sensor used and what it measures. For example, potentiometers, switches, and magnetic pickups signal the position or speed of a component; thermistors signal temperature (resistance decreases with an increase in temperature), and piezoelectric crystals respond to pressure (generating electrical voltage).

Conditioning

Computers can be designed to work with two types of signals — analog or digital. An analog signal is one that varies continuously and may be small, large, or some value in between at any given time (A, Figure 11-6). A **digital signal** has only two voltage values, high (on) or low (off) (B, Figure 11-6). Early computers used analog signals, but were much slower and inefficient compared to a digital computer. Modern computers are therefore designed to work only with digital signals. Upon receiving sensor input, the computer must condition it to a useful form (Figure 11-7). Computer circuitry and memory devoted to signal conditioning converts analog signals into digital signals. It also amplifies a weak voltage signal that otherwise is useless.

Processing

Once the sensor input is conditioned, the signals are sent to the computer's CPU or microprocessor, where they are used by the

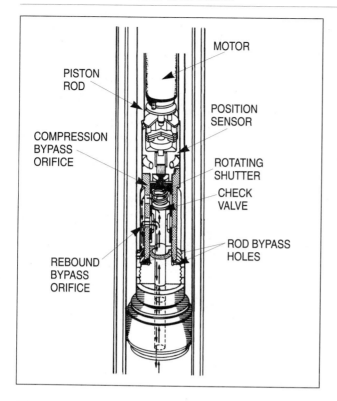

Figure 11-5 A position sensor in a shock absorber monitors the size of a variable orifice. (Chrysler)

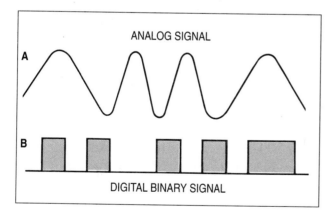

Figure 11-6 Analog and digital signal forms. (General Motors)

CPU to make calculations and logical decisions based on data stored in the computer memory (Figure 11-7). Just as you would check a diagnostic chart or a specification in a service manual, the CPU compares the input signal to data stored in

the computer's memory. It does this, by following a set of instructions called a **program** (Figure 11-8). The program tells the CPU what to do with the input signal.

Storage

The CPU's operating program and parameters are stored in permanent memory and remain intact when the engine is shut off, or when the battery is disconnected. The input data received from various sensors also is stored by the computer, but in temporary memory, or memory that disappears when power is disconnected. It may be stored for reference value, or constantly changed by new input signals. The operating program and parameters consist of all potential conditions that its designers can foresee, as well as a logical sequence of operations to be followed. This allows the computer to act in a predictable way every time it responds to a change in conditions.

OUTPUT

After the computer has received, conditioned, processed, and stored the input data, the CPU makes a decision and sends an output signal to the actuators (Figure 11-9). Electronic control systems generally use a variety of actuators — solenoid valves, stepper motors, magnetic reduction gear devices, etc. These actuators respond to the output signal by rotating control rods, opening or closing hydraulic or air vent solenoids, increasing or restricting hydraulic fluid flow to the wheels, etc. Remember, the output signal is sent to the actuator within a millisecond after the input signal is received.

This sequence of sensor input, signal conditioning, data processing, information storage, and actuator output, as well as the time interval required to complete the sequence, is called a **program loop**. A program loop takes an average of three milliseconds (0.003 second), with some

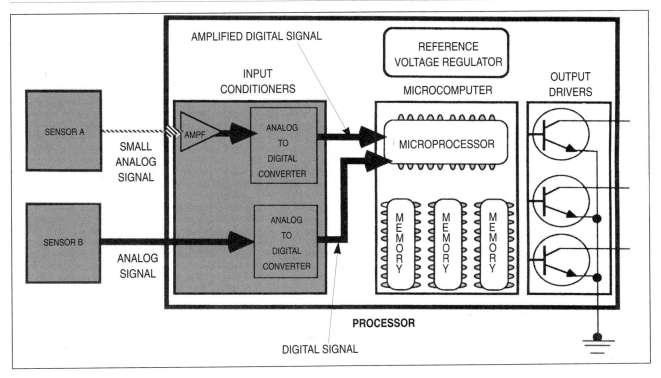

Figure 11-7 Input conditioning circuits in the computer amplify weak signals and changes analog signals to digital ones. (Ford Motor)

functions performed more or less often. On the average, the entire process is repeated 300 times or more every second. Some computers are slower, but others are faster.

When a program loop causes a change in the output signal to the actuator, the result of the change also changes the sensor inputs. This process of constantly changing the output according to the input is called 'feedback', because the computer can determine how effective its output signal has been. If the results are not as required, the computer makes additional changes to produce the desired results. Since the computer constantly reacts to its own decision, we call this 'closed-loop control'.

INPUT SENSORS

A sensor changes mechanical motion, temperature changes, or pressure changes into a voltage or frequency value. In an elec-

tronic shock dampening system, for example, voltage signals from the vehicle speed sensor keep the computer informed of vehicle speed by transmitting input signals to the computer's conditioning circuitry for comparison with other data to determine if the shock damping rate should be changed. Input sensor signals can take one of two forms. Some sensors control a reference voltage (V_{ref}) supplied by the computer; others generate their own voltage signal.

REFERENCE VOLTAGE SENSORS

A voltage regulator inside the computer (Figure 11-9) supplies this type of sensor with a constant voltage, usually 5-9 V. The sensor modifies the reference voltage signal according to what it is monitoring and sends the signal back to the computer input conditioners. The computer determines the ratio between the original signal

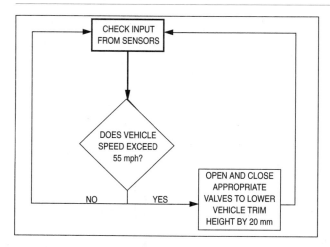

Figure 11-8 An example of a simplified trim height adjustment 'program'.

it sent and the signal returned to it by the sensor. This is called **ratiometric comparison**. By constantly monitoring both the reference voltage and the signal return lines, and comparing what it sees against the programmed ratio, the computer can

determine if the sensor is working correctly or not. Reference voltage sensors used in electronic control systems include — potentiometers, switches, thermistors, and certain strain gauges.

Potentiometers

A potentiometer converts mechanical motion to a voltage signal and consists of a resistive material with three connectors — a reference voltage (V_{ref}) connection, a signal return connection, and a signal voltage connection.

Reference voltage is supplied to the connector at one end of the resistive material. A connector at the other end of the resistive material acts as the signal return line to the computer. The remaining connector is secured to a movable contact called a wiper. As the tip of the wiper moves along the resistive material, the voltage sent back to the CPU is proportional

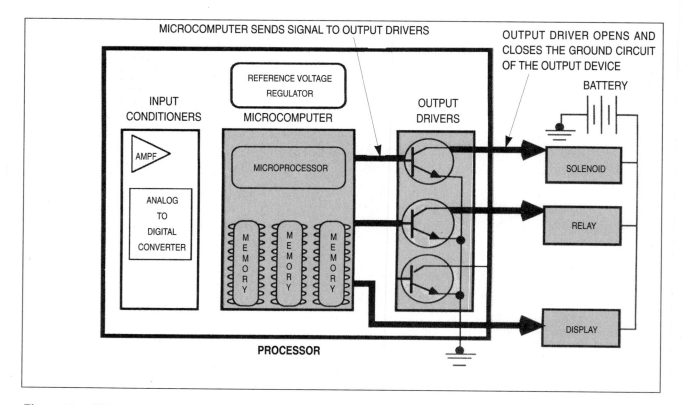

Figure 11-9 CPU control of actuators through the output drivers. (Ford Motor)

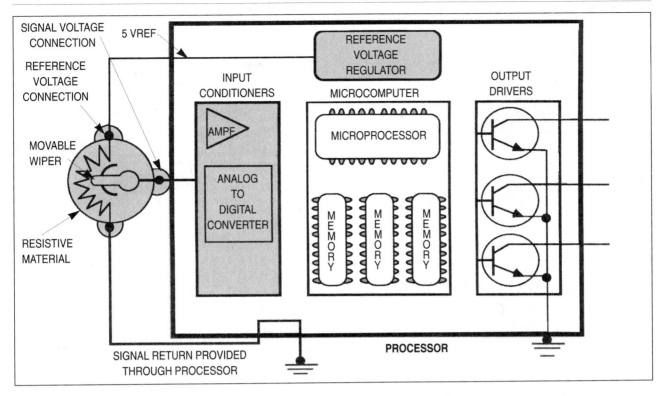

Figure 11-10 Schematic of a rotary potentiometer and its relation to the computer module. (Ford Motor)

to the distance the contact has moved. On some potentiometers, wiper movement is rotary (Figure 11-10); other potentiometers use a linear or straightline movement (Figure 11-11).

In a throttle position sensor (TPS) of the linear potentiometer type, the plunger in contact with a cam on the throttle shaft is pushed in as the throttle is opened (Figure 11-11, 11-12). The rotary type TPS (Figure 11-13) is similar to the linear type except that its resistor forms part of a circle instead of being straight, and the wiper pivots from the center of the circle. With the throttle plate fully open, the voltage signal to the input conditioners is about 5.1 V. The reference voltage drops to about 0.25-0.5 V at a closed throttle or idle position. With the throttle plate partially closed, a medium voltage is supplied to the input conditioners. These voltage signals are conditioned and then processed to

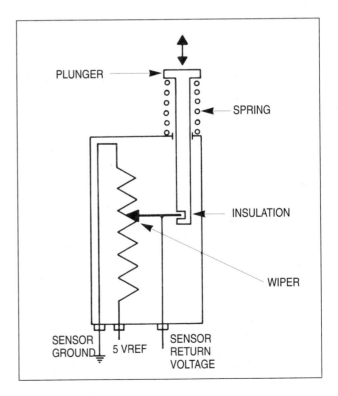

Figure 11-11 Schematic of a linear potentiometer.

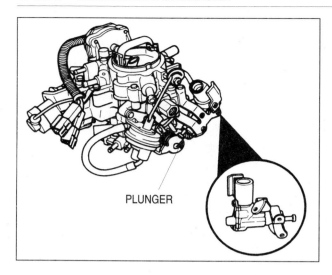

Figure 11-12 A linear potentiometer as a throttle position sensor. The plunger is pushed in as the throttle is opened. (Ford Motor)

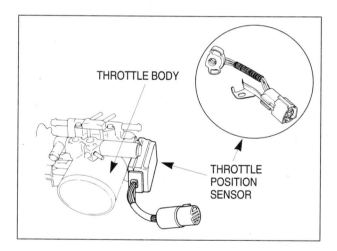

Figure 11-13 A rotary potentiometer as a throttle position sensor. (Ford Motor)

mance as well as suspension operation.

Position sensors, rotary and linear, are made of proprietary resistor materials on either ceramic or polyimide substrates. High-quality noble metal alloy contacts are used in order to allow at least 1 million full duty cycles and many millions of dither cycles (partially open and closed operation), which is a minimum of 100,000 miles of normal vehicle operation. Housings and other parts are made from high temperature thermoplastics or die castings to meet typical operating temperatures of from -40 °C to +150 °C.

Do NOT assume that every position sensor is a potentiometer. Some position sensors are only a simple **switch** which senses the position of a moving part at the end of its travel (Figure 11-14).

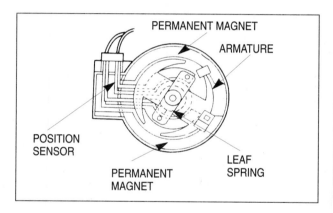

Figure 11-14 A magnetic actuator contains a 2-piece armature and dual magnets that create a magnetic field. The leaf spring switch provides a feedback signal to the module. (Ford Motor)

determine the exact position of the throttle plate. The linear potentiometer is adjustable; the rotary type is not adjustable and should be replaced if the voltage output from it is not within an acceptable range at a given throttle position.

Usually a TPS is part of the engine control system, and the engine control computer provides a throttle position signal to the suspension control unit. Any problem with this sensor would affect engine perfor-

Also, NOT ALL potentiometers are intended as position sensors. For example, the pressure sensor used by Ford in their electronic engine control (EEC-I/II) systems is a linear potentiometer, whose wiper is moved by an aneroid (Figure 11-15). The aneroid is an accordion type capsule that contains a gas (so it can be compressed and expanded) at atmospheric pressure. It

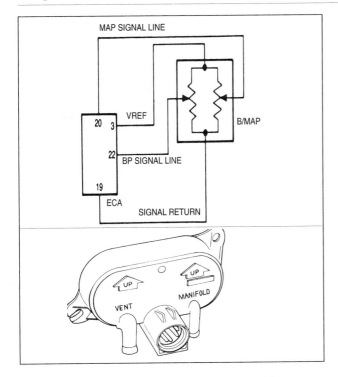

Figure 11-15 An aneroid-type linear potentiometer used as a pressure sensor. (Ford Motor)

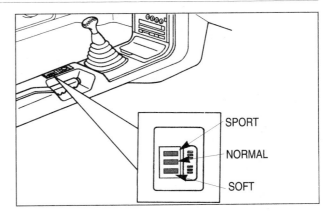

Figure 11-16 These three settings on the ride control switch allow choice of the optimal mode. (Ford Motor)

compresses or expands, depending on the increase or decrease of the outside pressure. The aneroid is placed in a housing connected to manifold vacuum. As manifold vacuum changes, the expansion or contraction of the aneroid moves the wiper of the potentiometer to provide a signal to the control module in proportion to the manifold pressure. The barometric pressure (BP) sensor works like the manifold pressure (MAP) sensor, except that it is open to atmospheric pressure instead of being connected to manifold vacuum.

Switches

A switch is a simple sensor, that sends either one constant signal or no signal. It has two positions, open and closed. When open, it does not allow current to flow through it, and when closed, it provides a path for current.

A suspension control switch allows the

driver to select a desired operating mode for the suspension (Figure 11-16).

Thermistors

A thermistor is a thermally sensitive resistor. It converts the temperature into a voltage signal through a semiconductor material (often, doped oxides of semi-metals as nickel, cobalt, manganese, iron, or copper) whose electrical resistance changes as the temperature changes. In a negative temperature coefficient (NTC) type thermistor (Figure 11-17), the resistance

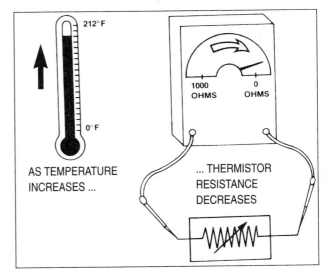

Figure 11-17 Thermistor resistance changes with temperature. (Ford Motor)

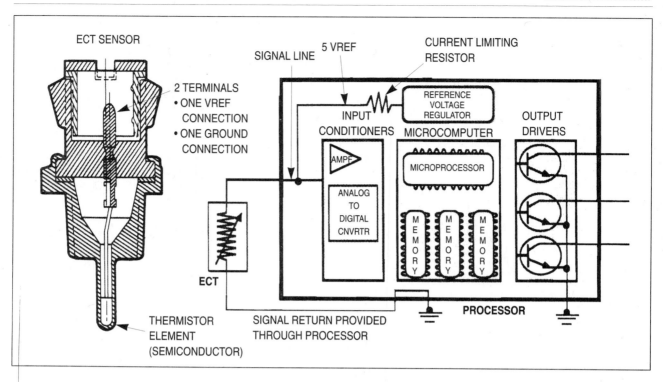

Figure 11-18 A cutaway of a thermistor sensor shown with the sensor circuit to the computer. (Ford Motor)

decreases (due to an increase in the number of charge carriers) with increase in temperature. A typical coolant sensor has a resistance of 100 kΩ at -40°C and 70 kΩ at 130°C. This decrease in resistance is exponential, not linear. By providing a reference voltage to the thermistor, the computer can determine temperature changes by looking at the voltage returned to it on the signal return line. To see how this works, consider an engine coolant temperature (ECT) sensor (Figure 11-18). When the engine is cold, the sensor resistance is high. This means that V_{ref} signal provided by the computer is returned to it almost unchanged. As the engine warms up, the sensor resistance decreases. Now the V_{ref} signal supplied to the sensor is returned as a low voltage signal. By comparing sensor input to its program, the computer can determine engine temperature at any given moment.

Piezoresistive Sensors

Widely known as the **straingage sensor**, the piezoresistive sensor works on the principle that the electrical resistance of a conductor or semiconductor varies when the material is subjected to mechanical stress. The change in resistivity as a result of a mechanical stress is called the **piezoresistive effect**. When a semiconductor is stressed, the piezoresistive effect dominates. There is a relationship between the change in the electric resistance of a material and the strain (fractional change in linear dimension) it experiences. If the relationship between that strain and the force causing it is known, from the measurement of resistive changes it is possible to infer the applied forces and the quantities that produce those forces in a sensor. A resistor arranged to sense a strain constitutes a strain gage.

Piezoresistive sensors are designed to overcome limitations as sensitivity to tem-

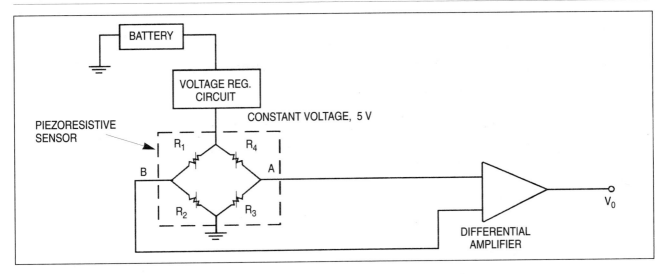

Figure 11-19 Piezoresistive sensor — Wheatstone bridge circuit. (General Motors)

perature variations, and are very popular because of their small size, high linearity, and low impedance. They are typically made of semiconductors as silicon and germanium, and also of different alloys as constantan and nichrome. The piezoresistive sensors can be either bonded or unbonded. If bonded, the straingage is chosen to have the same thermal expansion coefficient as the backing. Bonded metal straingages can be made with paper backing from parallel wire or from foil. Piezoresistive sensors can be applied to the measurement of any quantity that, by the use of an appropriate sensor, can be converted into a force capable of producing a deformation of 10 μm and even lower.

A typical piezoresistive sensor used in automotive applications consists of a small silicon diaphragm that flexes with application of stress. A set of resistors are placed around the edge of this diaphragm forming

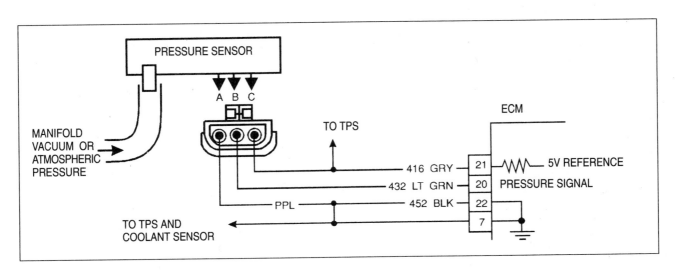

Figure 11-20 Piezoresistive pressure sensor circuit. (General Motors)

a circuit known as the **Wheatstone Bridge** (Figure 11-19). As the applied stress changes, it causes the diaphragm to flex. The deflection of the diaphragm causes the value of the resistors to change in proportion to the change in stress (Figure 11-24). This change in resistance, called piezoresistivity, is proportional to the change in the linear dimension of the diaphragm. The control module places a constant 5 V across the sensor. When there is no strain on the diaphragm, all four resistances are equal. As the diaphragm flexes, it causes the resistance to change in such a way that R1 and R3 increase, while R2 and R4 proportionately decrease. This results in a voltage difference at points 'A' and 'B'. The differential amplifier then outputs a proportionate voltage, for use by the control module to quantify the control needed.

Figure 11-20 illustrates the circuit for a **piezoresistive pressure sensor**. The sensor assembly is connected to the intake manifold vacuum or exposed to the atmospheric pressure depending on the application.

Figure 11-21 illustrates an **acceleration sensor** that can sense vehicle **deceler-**

ation characteristics. This sensor employs a simple weight suspended below a spring that employs four resistors in a bridge circuit. When a quick deceleration occurs, the mass of weight moving forward deflects the spring and causes a change in the resistance value of two of these four resistors. The voltage signal generated from these resistors is directly proportional to the rate of vehicle deceleration. This voltage signal is passed on into the trigger system. This type of sensor is used in an airbag inflating system. When a front end collision occurs, it can inform the trigger unit ahead of time, so that when impact does occur, the air bag will inflate within about 30 milliseconds in order to protect the driver from serious injury.

The **latest trend** in piezoresistive sensing is the use of a **micromachined silicon chip**. Figure 11-22 shows the similarities between a piezoresistive pressure sensor and a piezoresistive accelerometer. The accelerometer with beams and suspended mass is more complex than the simple diaphragm type pressure sensor. A three layer structure (Figure 11-23) is used to achieve over-range stops, bending beam, and air damping. The piezoresistive elements are ion implanted into the sus-

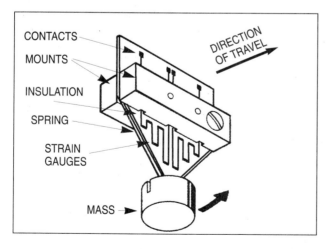

Figure 11-21 Piezoresistive acceleration sensor used in an airbag inflating system. When a vehicle collision occurs, a weight bends the straingages on the spring. This changes the resistance of the gages and the current flowing through them. (Robert Bosch)

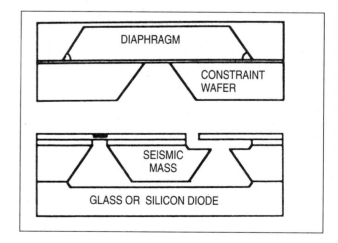

Figure 11-22 Micromachined piezoresistive pressure sensor and piezoresistive accelerometer. (Motorola/©SAE)

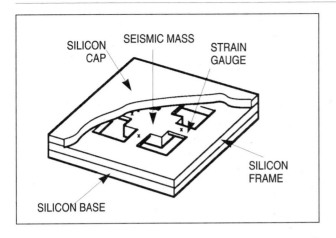

Figure 11-23 A piezoresistive accelerometer. (Motorola/ ©SAE)

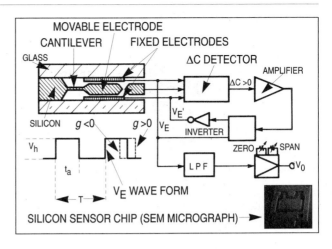

Figure 11-24 A capacitive-type semiconductor accelerometer with PWM electrostatic servo technique. (Hitachi/©SAE)

pension arm for maximum sensitivity. The resistive elements are temperature sensitive, and additional circuitry provides calibration, temperature compensation, and interface to external circuits.

Variable-Capacitance Sensors

If the space between two parallel plates is interposed by an insulating material or if the space between the two parallel plates is varied, then the capacitance existing between the plates will similarly vary. This principle can be used to detect motion.

A schematic of the **capacitive-type semiconductor accelerometer** developed by Hitachi, is shown in Figure 11-24. The sensor has a movable electrode, which is formed at the end of a cantilever, and acts as a weight. There are two fixed electrodes (parallel plates) one on each side of the movable electrode. The position of the movable electrode is determined by the difference of capacitances between it and the two fixed electrodes. The movable electrode reacts to g, the applied acceleration, and results in a change in the capacitance difference (ΔC).

Two pulse width modulated (PWM) signals, V_E (voltage V_h) and V_E', are applied across the movable and fixed elec-

trodes. By changing the pulse widths (t_a) of the PWM signals, the effective amounts of electrostatic forces to the movable electrode are controlled. Combination of capacitance difference detection and pulse width control enables the movable electrode to be kept exactly halfway between the fixed electrodes for any acceleration. With this technique, the pulse widths become proportional to the acceleration g.

A low-pass filter (LPF) converts the PWM signal V_E to an analog sensor output V_o (Figure 11-24). As the dimensions of the sensor may vary within a specified range, the output voltage needs to be adjusted to the specified value for an applied g. Only offset and sensitivity calibrations are needed. The measurement range of this sensor is 0 to $\pm 1g$ (=9.8 m/s^2), $\pm 2g$, and 0 to 50 Hz. Its power source and mass are 8 V and 0.05 kg.

Another design of capacitive-type semiconductor accelerometer is shown in Figure 11-25. Electroplated metal sense elements are fabricated partially on the top of a sacrificial layer. Selective chemical etching is used to produce two capacitors in asymmetrically shaped structures. Acceleration perpendicular to the substrate surface

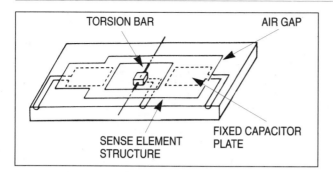

Figure 11-25 The components of a capacitive-type accelerometer. (Motorola/©SAE)

causes the sense elements to rotate around the torsion bars causing the capacitance of one side to increase and the capacitance of the other side to decrease. The output (in fF/g) is converted into a frequency that is proportional to acceleration and can be directly interfaced to the control module.

Sonar Road Surface Sensor

A sonar sensor (Figure 11-26) sends supersonic waves against the road surface ahead of the car and reads the signals that bounce back to sense bumps or dips before the car approaches them. A rear obstacle detection system (back sonar) also works on the same principle.

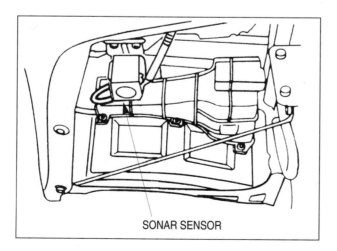

Figure 11-26 A sonar sensor is used to detect variations in upcoming road surface, so that the actuators may compensate for rough conditions. (Nissan)

Voltage Generators

This type of sensor does not require a reference voltage from the computer. It generates its own voltage signal and transmits the signal to the input conditioners. Of the various types of voltage generating sensors, mostly those that work on electromagnetic principles are used in the control systems for suspension, steering, or braking.

Magnetic Pickups

A magnetic pickup uses a wire coil wrapped around a permanent magnet core. The core creates a magnetic field in and around the coil. When a metal object disturbs (moves through) this magnetic field, an electrical voltage is generated in the wire coil (Figure 11-27). This voltage is sent to the input conditioners in the computer.

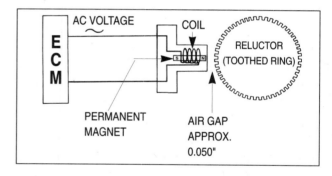

Figure 11-27 Operation of a magnetic wheel sensor. (General Motors)

The **vehicle speed sensor** used in an automatic ride control system is a good example of a magnetic pickup. This sensor is typically located on the transmission or transaxle output (Figure 11-28). The output of the sensor is linear with speed. The faster the sensor spins, the greater will be the voltage output. A higher speed is an indication to the module that a firmer suspension is required. The speed sensor is also used as an input for electronic

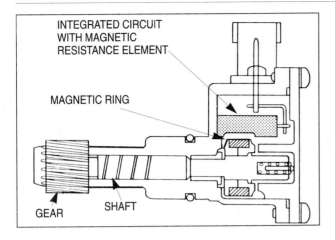

Figure 11-28 As the shaft in the speed gear rotates, the magnetic ring on it interacts with the magnetic resistance element, and creates a speed signal. (Toyota)

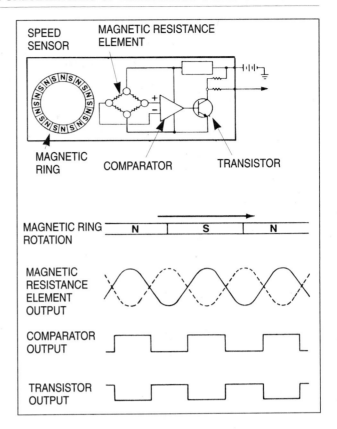

Figure 11-29 The magnetic resistance element generates an AC, the comparator changes it to a digital pulse, and the transistor inverts it and conveys the signal to the conversion circuit in the speedometer. (Toyota)

steering systems and in some cases the electronic engine control and speed control systems. Figure 11-28 shows a Toyota speed sensor in the Lexus 400 system. The sensor is located at the transmission output shaft, and uses a gear and shaft driven by the transmission shaft. The magnetic ring on the sensor shaft has 20 poles, alternating north and south (Figure 11-29). As the shaft and ring rotate, the magnetic resistance element inside the integrated circuit responds to the alternating poles by sending an AC to the integrated circuit. A comparator changes the current to a digital pulse, that enters a transistor and then a pulse conversion circuit in the dashboard speedometer. For each full rotation of the speed sensor shaft, the conversion circuit receives a 20-pulse signal, and changes it to a 4-pulse signal that operates the speedometer and signals vehicle speed to the suspension control unit and other speed-affected units.

In some cases, a backup unit that works with a **reed switch** (that transforms an analog signal to a pulse signal) is provided integral with the speedometer (Figure 11-30). In a reed switch, the magnetic flux embracing it is made to vary, usually by rotating a soft iron toothed disc between the source of flux and the reed. Rotation of the disc causes the reed to alternatively open and close and thus to pulse a current loop. The limiting frequency is about 600 Hz, and contact bounce starts to present a problem even at lower frequencies.

Linear magnetic sensors are installed between the body or frame rail and the suspension control arm to generate a signal indicating changes in vehicle trim height. A magnetic slide rides inside a housing containing two switches. As the slide moves upward with vehicle motion, it opens the above-trim switch; downward movement closes that switch and opens the below-trim switch. Changes in trim height are monitored by the control module through switch operation.

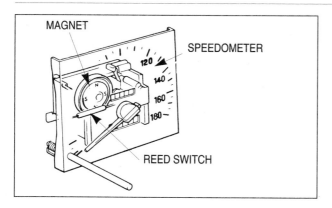

Figure 11-30 Vehicle speed sensor mounted in speedometer. (Toyota)

Variable-Inductance Sensors

Variable-inductance sensors generate an AC electrical output that varies in proportion to a mechanical displacement.

When the device is specifically designed to provide an inductively coupled AC output voltage that is linearly proportional to the input displacement, it is called a **linear variable differential transformer (LVDT).** The circuit diagram of a typical LVDT is given in Figure 11-31. The device

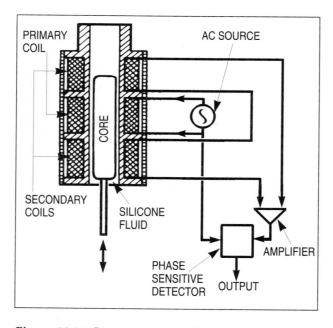

Figure 11-31 Linear variable differential transformer — as a g-force sensor.

consists basically of three fixed coils — one primary, and two secondary. The primary coil is energized by AC. The two secondary coils are connected to a phase-sensitive detector. As a core of ferromagnetic material moves in the coil axis, the output from the detector will be linearly proportional to the distance of the core from one end of the coils.

The LVDT is the most widely used sensor for displacement in the range of several microinches to a few inches. The advantages of LVDT as compared to other distance sensors, include — virtually zero friction, as the core need not be in contact with the coils, and so no wear; linear output; very high resolution, depending mainly on the detector; good electrical isolation between the core and the coils; a large output signal from the coils so that the phase-sensitive detector needs little or no amplification; no risk of damage if the core movement is excessive; strong construction and resistance to shock and vibration. Because of its advantages, the LVDT has superseded most other distance sensors. LVDTs can be used either with AC or DC supplies; the DC types use a miniature built-in oscillator inverted to provide the AC for the coils. A miniature LVDT with ±0.125" stroke, has body dimensions of 0.375" diameter x 1.4" length, not including the plunger arm. The longer stroke versions are larger, with a body diameter of 1" and body length (excluding arm) of 6" for a ±1" stroke.

The **lateral *g*-sensor** (Figure 11-32) is a good example of the LVDT. A *g*-force is the force of gravity that resists changes in the magnitude and the direction of velocity. When riding in a car, *g*-forces push us backward in our seats during acceleration, forward during braking, and to a side during cornering. Control systems typically derive their acceleration and braking force information from sensors which monitor

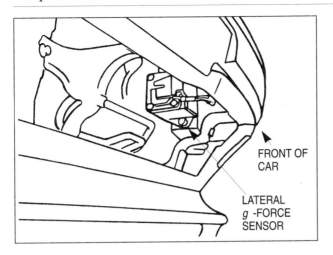

Figure 11-32 Lateral *g*-force sensor on the Mitsubishi A-ECS is mounted on to car frame at front and to a side. (Mitsubishi)

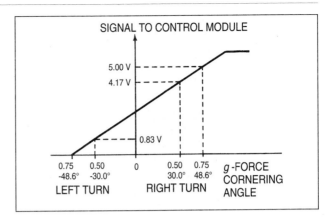

Figure 11-33 Based on the voltage signal from the *g*-force sensor, the computer determines the sharpness and direction of a vehicle's turn. (Mitsubishi)

throttle position or brake pedal position. More advanced systems use a special sensor that directly inputs sideways *g*-forces. Such a sensor reacts to the *g*-force exclusively, and NOT to the mechanical movement of any part of the car.

In the Mitsubishi's A-ECS, the movable core floats in silicone oil (Figure 11-31). The primary coil receives electrical power from the vehicle's battery and creates a magnetic field around the core. Depending on the position of the core, this magnetic field creates voltage in one or both of the secondary coils. The voltage from the secondary coils is the signal to the control unit. As the core floats in silicone fluid, *g*-forces can push it one side or the other, causing the secondary coil voltage to vary. Using this voltage value from the secondary coils, the computer determines the core position, and the magnitude and direction of the *g*-forces (Figure 11-33).

Another example of LVDT is the **steering torque sensor**, which senses the rotation torque of a steering wheel. A typical steering torque sensor (A, Figure 11-34) consists of an input shaft connected to the steering wheel, a pinion shaft with pinion

gear of the rack-and-pinion mechanism, a torsion bar connecting the input shaft and the pinion shaft, a slider with a movable iron core, a cam mechanism to convert relative torsional displacement between the input shaft and the pinion shaft to axial displacement of the slider, and an LVDT to convert the displacement of the slider to electric signal. The magnitude and the direction of the steering wheel torque are detected from displacement and direction of the slider. In Figure B, 11-34, S3 shows output signal of torque, and S1 and S2 show outputs for diagnosis use.

LVDTs are used to measure a variety of quantities that can be converted to a core movement. It is possible to apply the LVDT to acceleration and inclination measurements by means of mass-spring system. Pressure measurement can be made using a Bourdon tube, and also using diaphragm, bellows, or capsule.

There is also another sensor, the **linear variable inductance transducer (LVIT)**, that makes use of variation in inductance to sense displacement. The impedance of a coil with current flowing through it changes if a core (known as 'spoiler') is placed inside its magnetic field. This is due to the induction of magnetic currents in the

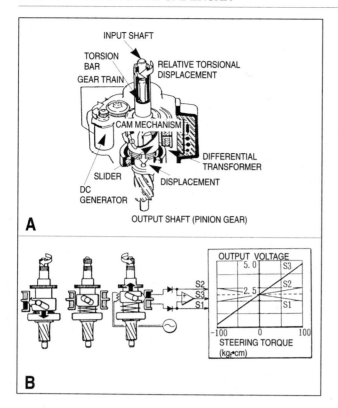

Figure 11-34 Steering sensor (A) and working diagram of torque sensor (B). (Honda/©SAE)

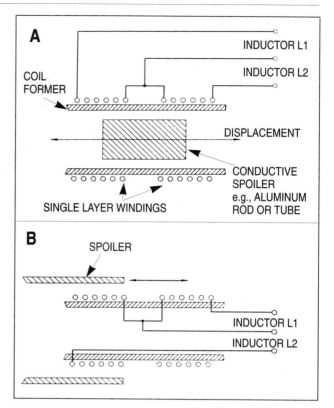

Figure 11-35 A schematic of the LVIT differential configurations — internal spoiler (A), and external spoiler (B). (Lucas Automotive /©IMechE-England)

spoiler that produce a magnetic field of their own, opposed to that of the coil. As the spoiler goes deeper into the coil, the impedance becomes larger. This principle is used in the LVIT, in sensing displacement.

A schematic of the LVIT arranged in differential configurations with options of both internal and external spoilers is given in Figure 11-35. In the sensor developed by Lucas Automotive, variation in inductance is produced by the introduction of a highly conductive spoiler into the electromagnetic field of the coil excited at frequencies of typically ≥100 kHz. The spoiler, made of copper or aluminum, takes the form of a movable tube or rod mounted coaxially with the sensor coil. Eddy currents induced in the spoiler lead to a reduction in coil inductance. Variations in the ratio of inductances L1 and L2 are translated into variations in the output signal which is

also ratiometric to supply voltage (5 V). The LVIT sensor can thus provide an output signal analogous to a potentiometric sensor. Lucas uses a resonant circuit method to determine variations in sensor inductance. The inductor is used as one component of a simple LC oscillator, shifts in inductance caused by movement of the sensor spoiler are converted to oscillator frequency variations.

Unlike the LVDT, no magnetic or ferrous materials are used in the LVIT. This enables the use of this sensor at relatively high temperatures. Also, the sensor design does not require the provision of the ferromagnetic flux return paths used in LVDTs, thus simplifying the overall design.

Although a differential configuration is attractive for high accuracies, in a suspension installation, it is not always conve-

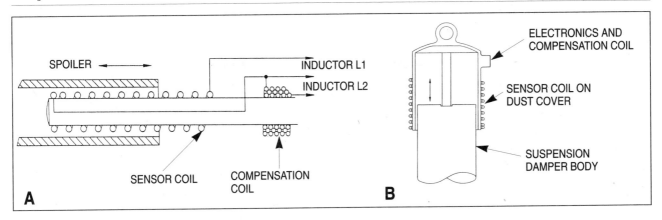

Figure 11-36 Single coil long stroke LVIT with compensation coil (A), and suspension damper position LVIT (B). (Lucas Automotive /©IMechE-England)

nient or possible to provide the space needed for the two coils. If necessary, one sensor coil may be separated from the active part of the sensor and used to provide a reference frequency for compensation purposes.

A basic sensor configuration used for suspension controls is shown in A, Figure 11-36. The sensor is installed within a suspension unit and can tolerate very high levels of fluid pressure. With a large length to diameter ratio, non-linear end effects are minimized. It is also possible to use the actual structure of the suspension unit as a spoiler. As an example of a sensor coil mounted on the dust cover of a damper unit, the steel body of the damper acting as a spoiler is shown in B, Figure 11-36. In this case, a proper arrangement for effective magnetic screening for the sensor coils is necessary to avoid any unwanted eddy current paths close to the coils.

Typical applications of this sensor are proximity detection and acceleration measurement based on spring-mass systems where the mass displacement is measured.

Hall-Effect Sensors

The Hall-effect sensor also generates a voltage signal. In an engine management system, it is generally used only in deter-mining engine speed and ignition timing. In some electronic suspension or steering control systems, it may be used in lateral acceleration sensors or rotary height sensors.

The sensor consists of a Hall-effect switch and a rotary vane cup. The Hall-effect switch contains a permanent magnet on one side and a Hall element on the other (Figure 11-37). A metal plate on each side of the switch concentrates the magnetic field. The switch has three electrical connections. One connection receives battery voltage; the second connection provides ground, and the third carries a signal to the input conditioners. The rotary vane cup has a set of protrusions, or vanes,

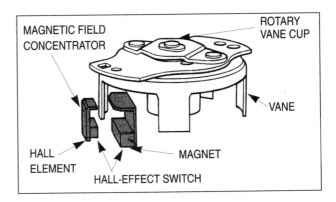

Figure 11-37 The components of a typical Hall-effect switch. (Ford Motor)

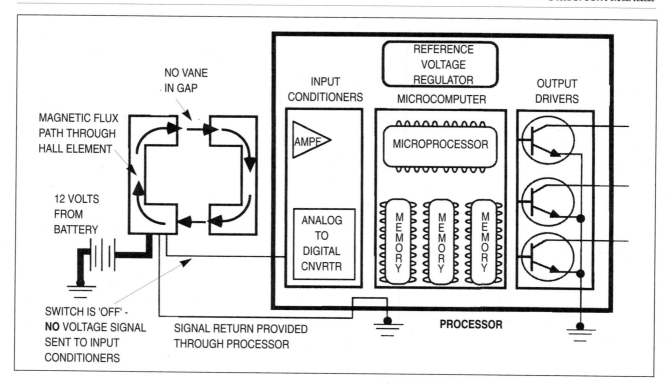

Figure 11-38 If the electromagnetic field is not broken, the Hall-effect switch is off and sends no signal to the computer. (Ford Motor)

around its circumference. One vane is used for each engine cylinder. The vanes on the rotary cup pass between the two magnetic field concentrators.

When the gap between the two magnetic field concentrators is empty, the magnetic flux path created between the magnet and Hall element remains unbroken (Figure 11-38). As long as the field is unbroken, no voltage signal is sent to the input conditioners. However, as the vane cup rotates, each vane that enters the gap shunts or moves the magnetic flux path away from the Hall element (Figure 11-39). This causes a voltage signal to be sent to the microprocessor input conditioners. The signal is used to determine how fast the engine is running.

The **lateral acceleration sensor** contains a permanent magnet attached to a flexible arm. A small weight on the end of the arm acts as a dampener. This arm,

magnet, and weight assembly is centered inside a Hall-effect switch similar to that just described (Figure 11-40). As the vehicle corners, its movement forces the arm and weight to one side of the centered position. When this happens, the permanent magnet moves away from the Hall-effect sensor and sends an analog signal to the control module. If lateral acceleration exceeds the computer's programmed limits, the microprocessor will change the shock damping rate during this time, returning the system to its original rate once lateral acceleration returns within its lower limit. The Hall-effect switch also can be used in rotary height sensors. The one shown in Figure 11-41 contains two Hall-switches with a magnetic rotor. One Hall switch provides the above-trim signal; the other Hall switch provides the below-trim signal.

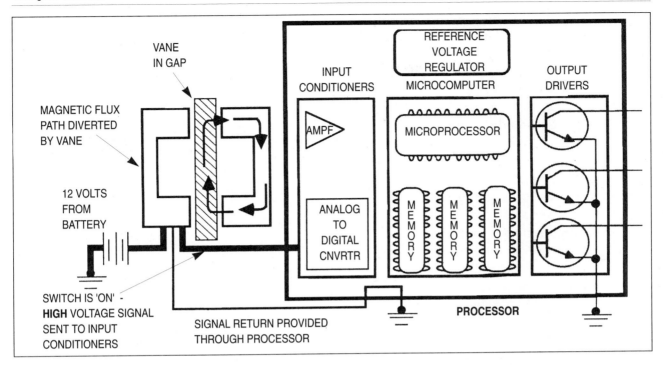

Figure 11-39 When a vane enters and breaks the electromagnetic field, the switch turns on and sends a high voltage signal to the computer. (Ford Motor)

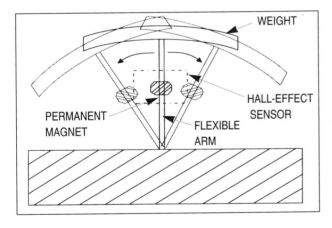

Figure 11-40 A lateral accelerometer uses a Hall-effect switch to measure cornering forces. (General Motors)

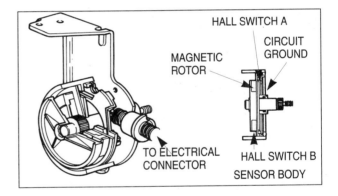

Figure 11-41 The rotary height sensor used with Ford air spring suspension systems contains two Hall-effect switches and a magnetic rotor. The Hall-effect switches provide the suspension module with above- and below-trim signals. (Ford Motor)

Optical Sensors

Photo optical sensors consist of a revolving disc or shutter and a **photodiode** (Figure 11-42). A photodiode is a type of photoresistor in which the incident light falls on a semiconductor junction, and the separation of electrons and holes caused by the action of light will allow the junction to conduct

even when it is reverse-biased. A photodiode is made like any other diode, using silicon, but without the opaque coating usually given to the signal and rectifier diodes. In the absence of such a coating, the material is sufficiently transparent to allow light to affect the junction conductivity and so alter the amount of reverse current that flows when the diode is reverse-biased.

This type of sensor can be used to determine **steering angle** or **road height**. As the slotted disc revolves, it makes and breaks the photodiode beam, and produces a voltage signal. A non-operational zone within the sensor will prevent system operation through a 3-5° (1 to 1-1/4") movement. Time delays are built into the logic of the sensor to prevent system operation due to normal vehicle movements.

In a progressive power steering system,

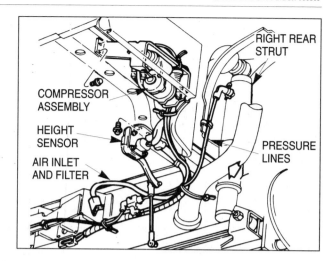

Figure 11-43 Height sensor determines the vehicle attitude. (Chrysler)

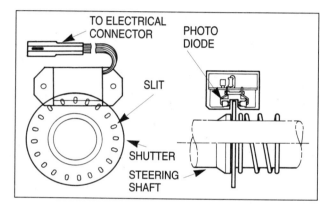

Figure 11-42 The steering angle sensor consists of a slotted shutter that revolves between photo diodes, creating a voltage signal that is sent to the control module. (Ford Motor)

the microprocessor uses the signal from the steering angle sensor (Figure 11-42) to determine the amount of power-assist required. In an electronic load leveling system, the signal from the height sensor (Figure 11-43) is used to operate the air compressor relay or the exhaust solenoid.

Piezoelectric Sensors

Some crystalline materials as quartz, Rochelle salt, and barium titanate contain charged particles (ions) which do not move uniformly when the crystal is stressed. This non-uniform movement of ions produces a

difference in charge between opposing faces of the crystal (Figure 11-44), and if these faces are metallised, a voltage can be measured. The voltage is proportional to the strain of the crystal.

This principle is utilized in the piezo-electric sensor. When the sensor is mounted on a vibrating surface, the piezo-electric crystal is alternately squeezed and stretched by the inertial mass, thus generating a small voltage, in proportion to the acceleration over a broad frequency range.

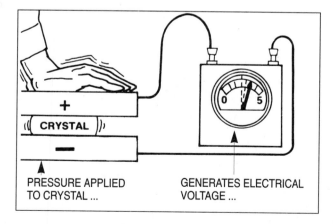

Figure 11-44 Pressure applied to the crystal produces a voltage in the wire causing the needle to jump. (Ford Motor)

The piezoelectric sensor has no moving parts and hardly needs any repair or replacement. Also, it is lightmass (≈2 grams).

The use of an inertial mass bonded to a piezoelectric crystal provides an accelerometer that requires no springs or special supports for the mass. It is even possible to obtain two-dimensional signals from one crystal, and the system will respond to a very wide range of accelerations. Piezoelectric transducers can cope with acceleration values from a very small fraction of g to several thousand g, a huge range compared to those that can be obtained using spring and displacement systems. A major limitation is that the piezoelectric crystal is, from the circuit point of view, a capacitor, and the signal is in the form of a charge. The connection of a resistance to the contacts on the faces of the crystal will therefore allow this capacitance to discharge with a time constant equal to capacitance times resistance between the crystal faces. If, for example, the capacitance is 1000 pF (=0.001 μF) and the resistance is 10000 MΩ (typical input of a FET DC amplifier), then the time constant is only 10 seconds. The piezoelectric sensor is therefore better suited for measuring changes of acceleration occurring over a short time, typically from a fraction of a second to a few seconds, than for measuring fairly constant values of acceleration over a long period.

The basic construction of a piezoelectric acceleration sensor developed at Matsushita (ref: SAE 910273) for **super low range frequencies** is illustrated in Figure 11-45. The theory of its operation is shown in Figure 11-46. Two piezo ceramic elements are bonded one on each side of a diaphragm to form the polarities shown. This design is said to enable cancellation of pyro charges (those generated with temperature variation) peculiar to piezo ceramics,

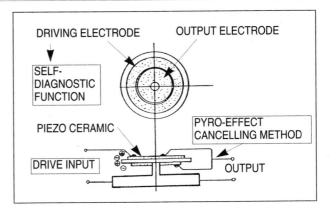

Figure 11-45 Basic construction of a piezoelectric acceleration sensor — disc center fixed type. (Matsushita/©SAE)

and thus prevent ill effects on output voltage. Piezo ceramic elements 1 and 2 have the same static capacity coefficient. Figure 11-46, B and C show cases where force F is applied. A positive potential difference (+) and a negative potential difference (-), are generated for use as output voltages due to electrode polarities on the

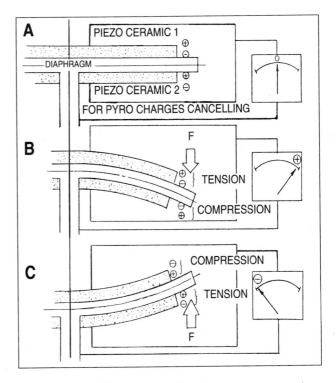

Figure 11-46 Theory of acceleration sensor operation. (Matsushita/©SAE)

tension side and compression side. As shown in Figure 11-45, the electrode of piezo-ceramic element 1 is divided into two parts to form a drive electrode and an output electrode to provide a self-diagnostic function, which constantly checks output voltages when the diaphragm is mechanically vibrated by applying an electrical drive input, and thus monitors the sensor for possible failure. The sensing range of the accelerometer is given as — 0.0002g-1g and 0.015 Hz-1 Hz. Such an accelerometer should find application in suspension control, antilock braking, antiskid control, 4-wheel steering control, and airbag control systems.

COMPUTING ACCELERATION AND RELATED PARAMETERS

Accelerations generated in a vehicle, are either linear or rotational. As linear accelerations, there are — lateral acceleration, horizontal direction acceleration (squat, dive), and vertical direction acceleration (bouncing). As rotation acceleration (angular rate), there are — yaw, pitch, and roll. The sensing ranges (acceleration and frequency) expected of an accelerometer in typical automotive applications are: right and left 0.02-0.8g at DC-10 Hz; back and front 0.03-1.1g at DC-10 Hz; up and down 0.03-2.0g at Max 30 Hz.

Accelerometers require the conversion of an acceleration into a force, causing a displacement, which is then turned into an electrical signal. This displacement is resisted by a restoration force (e.g., a calibrated spring) of some kind. Accelerometers determine acceleration 'a' from calibration (or spring) constant 'k', mass 'm', and observed displacement 'x', using the relationship: $a = k{\cdot}x/m$, in which the quantity $k{\cdot}x$ is the force.

When an accelerometer produces an electrical output, this output can be used for **computing other quantities**.

Acceleration is the time rate of change of velocity. **Velocity** is the time rate of change of distance or position. If the starting velocity of the car, its acceleration (assumed constant), and the time of acceleration are all known, then the final velocity can be calculated. The mathematical action needed to find change of velocity from acceleration and time is termed *integration*, and analog computers can perform this on a voltage signal from an accelerometer. The initial velocity is set in the form of a voltage applied from a position sensor, and the output of the analog computer is proportional to final velocity. A *second integration* of the output (the velocity output) produces a signal proportional to **distance**, so that this quantity also is determined using an analog computing action on the output of the accelerometer. If the starting point of the motion is rest (starting velocity of zero), then no constants need to be fed in. The analog computer can consist of little more than a pair of operational amplifiers if a simple one-directional motion is being sensed.

INPUT SIGNALS

Switches produce a digital voltage signal; sensors produce an analog voltage signal. Each type of signal has certain characteristics that make it appropriate for the job, but a computer cannot handle a voltage signal unless it meets certain requirements.

ANALOG SIGNALS

An analog signal is one that varies along a specified voltage range. The signal may be high, low, or some voltage value in between. A good example of an analog signal is that produced by a rheostat or variable resistance. When the rheostat is off, it opens the circuit, and no voltage signal is produced. As the rheostat is turned on and rotated, it allows a weak

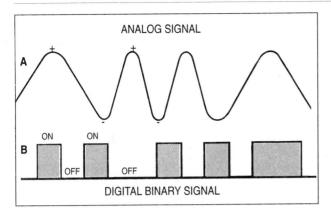

Figure 11-47 An analog signal consists of continuous peaks (positive) and valleys (negative) forming a sine wave (A). A digital signal takes the form of a square wave and is either on or off (B). (General Motors)

voltage signal that gradually increases in strength until it reaches a peak. Reversing the direction of the rheostat rotation decreases the strength of the voltage until it disappears as the rheostat reaches the off position. This action is graphically shown in A, Figure 11-47. The change in voltage from positive (+) to negative (-) and back to positive (+) is called an analog waveform.

Most automotive sensors produce an analog signal. The EGR sensor is a potentiometer which sends a varying voltage according to valve pintle position. The ECT sensor is a thermistor which varies its signal according to coolant temperature. A magnetic pickup, LVDT, Hall-effect switch, or a photodiode sensor varies its voltage signal according to component rotational speed or direction.

DIGITAL SIGNALS

Unlike the continually changing analog signal, a digital signal has only two values — 'on' or 'off'. A light switch is a good example:

- When the switch is off, the light is off.
- When the switch is turned on, the light comes on.
- Turning the switch off again turns the light off.

There are no mid-points — the light is either 'on' or it is 'off'. By rapidly turning the switch on and off, a digital or square waveform like that shown in B, Figure 11-47 is created. The computer's circuitry contains thousands of tiny switches. Since they can be cycled on/off thousands of times per second, the switches can transmit digital signals very rapidly.

BINARY CODE AND THE COMPUTER CLOCK

The computer communicates by converting analog voltage signals into a language called the binary code, which means the code has only two values. Since a digital signal is either on (high) or off (low), the computer can understand what the signal means by assigning a numeric value to it. A signal that is 'on' is represented by a '1' while a signal that is 'off' is represented by a '0'. This assignment of numeric values is called **binary coding**. By rapidly switching voltage on and off, data can be represented in binary code as a series of 1's and 0's (Figure 11-48). Each 0 or 1 is called a **bit**; eight bits together form a **byte** or **word**.

The following tabulation gives the first 13 numbers, their binary equivalents, and the binary coded decimals:

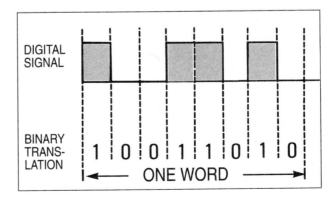

Figure 11-48 Computers communicate and store information by stringing thousands of bits together. To a computer, the binary word 10011010 will have a definite meaning. (General Motors)

Decimal	Binary	Binary Coded Decimal
0	0	0000 0000
1	1	0000 0001
2	10	0000 0010
3	11	0000 0011
4	100	0000 0100
5	101	0000 0101
6	110	0000 0110
7	111	0000 0111
8	1000	0000 1000
9	1001	0000 1001
10	1010	0001 0000
11	1011	0001 0001
12	1100	0001 0010

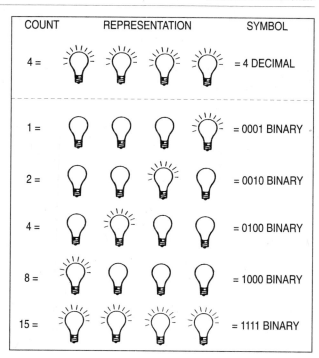

Figure 11-49 Using light bulbs to represent binary digits of '0' and '1'. (T. Weathers, Jr. and C. Hunter, *Automotive Computers and Control Systems*, p.90, ©1984, Prentice-Hall)

In the decimal (base 10) system, every time we run out of symbols (0, 1-9) in one column, we carry over to the next column (towards the left). That is how larger numbers are represented. The binary (base 2) system also works the same way. However, as it involves only two symbols (0 and 1) instead of 10, we have to carry over to the next column more often.

The value of the first position in a multi-digit binary number is 1 (2 to the power 0, or 2^0). The value of the second position is 2 (2^1), and that of the nth position is 2^{n-1}. To determine the value (in base 10) of the binary number 01010110, we multiply the value of the character times the value of its position, then add together the products: $(0 \times 2^0)+(1 \times 2^1)+(1 \times 2^2)+(0 \times 2^3)+(1 \times 2^4)+(0 \times 2^5)+(1 \times 2^6)+(0 \times 2^7)= 0+2+4+0+16+0+64+0 = 86$ total. Likewise, to determine the binary number for 69, we split the number as $2^6+2^2+2^0$. Equating each of the exponents to (n-1), the positions for 1's are 7, 3, and 1. The binary number is therefore 01000101.

Though the binary representation of data is too inconvenient for people to use, it is a very ideal way for computers to handle data. To illustrate this, let us represent numbers using four light bulbs connected by four switches to a power source. In the decimal system, we could represent only the numbers 0 through 4 — zero when all the bulbs are off, one when the first is on, two when the first and second are on, and so on. Using the binary system, we can represent 0 through 15 using only four light bulbs (Figure 11-49). Simply, each 'off' bulb equals 0 and each 'on' bulb equals 1.

The computer is programmed to recognize the long strings of ones and zeros that make up the data stream constantly pulsing through its circuits. However, it must have some way of determining when one pulse ends and another pulse begins, or it cannot tell the difference between a 01 and a 001 in a data stream that might read 01100101. The computer identifies bits and words by watching a clock generator, which provides constant pulses exactly the length of one bit. The microprocessor and

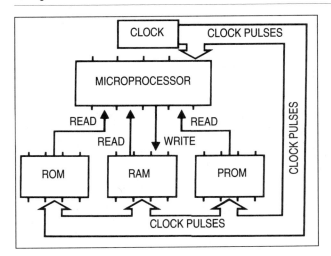

Figure 11-50 A clock generator (quartz crystal) provides timing pulses used by the microprocessor and memories to determine the exact length of a bit. (General Motors)

the computer memories both watch the clock pulses when reading or sending data (Figure 11-50). By comparing the clock pulses to the voltage pulses, the computer knows exactly how long each voltage pulse or bit is supposed to be.

Since it deals with the binary code, the computer can calculate very fast. This is why a computer cannot work with a raw analog signal (A, Figure 11-47). To convert the analog signal into a form the computer can use, it must be conditioned into a digital or binary signal (B, Figure 11-47).

INPUT CONDITIONING

Automotive sensors produce signals of varying strengths and ranges. The signals may be digital, although most are analog. To establish a uniformity with which the computer can handle, sensor input signals must be conditioned, or prepared by special circuits, before they can be processed by the CPU. Input conditioning takes two forms — amplification and analog-to-digital (A/D) conversion.

Amplification

Signals under 1 V are too weak to be used

by the CPU and must be strengthened. The input conditioning section of the computer contains a special amplification circuit through which weak signals are passed. The circuit then sends the strengthened signal to the CPU (Figure 11-51).

A/D Conversion

Most automotive sensors create an analog signal of varying voltage. This type of signal is incompatible with the computer's circuitry, which consists of thousands of tiny on/off (or digital) switches. For this reason, an analog signal must be converted from a continuous varying voltage to a digital (or on/off) signal before it can be used by the CPU. Signal conversion from analog to digital is the task of A/D circuitry in the computer's input conditioning segment (Figure 11-52).

During the process of conditioning an analog signal, the A/D converter checks voltage from the sensor at regular intervals, much like taking a series of pictures. Each time the converter checks the signal voltage, it assigns a specific numeric value to the signal, which the input conditioners change into binary code and send to the CPU as a digital signal. When the digital signal is received, the CPU can interpret exactly what the sensor is saying, and uses the digital signal for processing. Figure 11-53 illustrates this analog-to-digital conversion process.

PROCESSING

As the 'brain' or calculating part of the computer, the CPU receives the sensor data in the form of digital signals from the input conditioners. It then compares this data with other data stored in the memory. The data is processed using a predetermined set of commands called a program, which also is stored in the memory.

By following the program, the CPU can

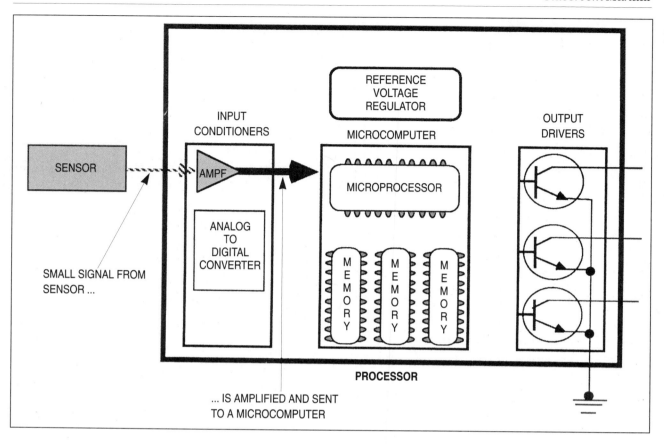

Figure 11-51 Signal amplification. (Ford Motor)

do simple math such as a comparison of two numbers to determine if they are equal to, less than, or greater than zero. It also can compare two numbers to determine if one is equal to, less than, or greater than the other. As a result of this comparison, the CPU can cause something else to happen. In this way, the CPU determines when and how to use the sensor input, as well as when and how to activate an output device, or actuator.

Information Storage and Retrieval

The program and data used by the CPU for its decision-making process is stored in memory. The stored data used with the program consists of vehicle calibration, wheel speed rotation schedules, and other information required to perform the necessary calculations. Before the CPU can read the data, or change it by writing new data into memory, it must have some way of finding it immediately. To expedite the search, computer memory is divided into a large number of individual locations, each with its own assigned number or address. You could compare this to a large postal sorting bin (Figure 11-54) in which each slot holds mail for a particular address. Each memory location holds one piece of information. Each memory location has an assigned address written in binary code and numbered in sequence starting with 0. These memory addresses are used by the CPU to find the particular memory segments it needs (Figure 11-55).

While the CPU is busy processing sensor input data, it also continues to

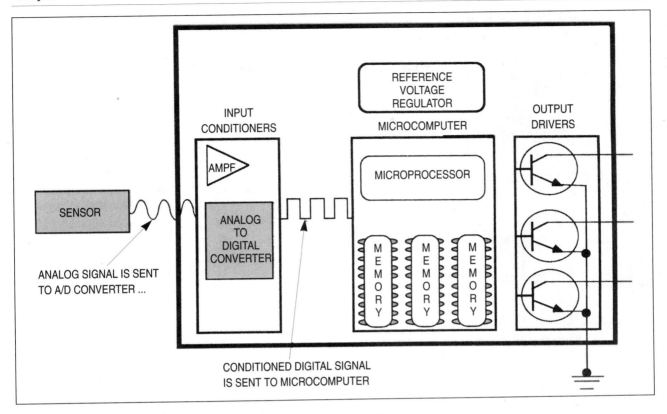

Figure 11-52 A schematic of the A/D converter circuit. (Ford Motor)

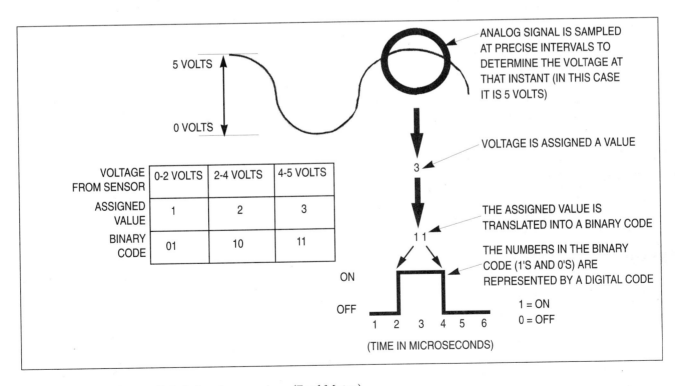

Figure 11-53 Analog-to-digital signal conversion. (Ford Motor)

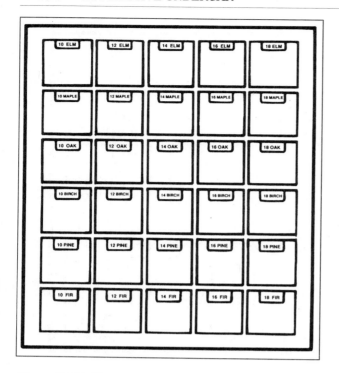

Figure 11-54 Computer memory is divided into unique addresses, much like post office pigeonholes used for sorting mail. (General Motors)

receive updated input. Since the additional input data cannot be used at the moment, it is written into the memory for temporary storage. The CPU assigns a memory address to the data and sends it there (Figure 11-52). Because it knows where the data is stored, the CPU can retrieve it whenever it is necessary. Once the CPU needs this data, it calls the specific memory location and asks for a copy of the stored information. This way, the original data is retained in memory for reuse as necessary.

To control air suspension system operation, for example, the CPU constantly refers to data stored in memory in the form of ideal and actual wheel rotation schedules for various vehicle operating conditions. The trim height sensors tell the CPU what the vehicle operating conditions are. The CPU reads the trim height tables stored in memory, and compares them to the sensor input. By using this compari-

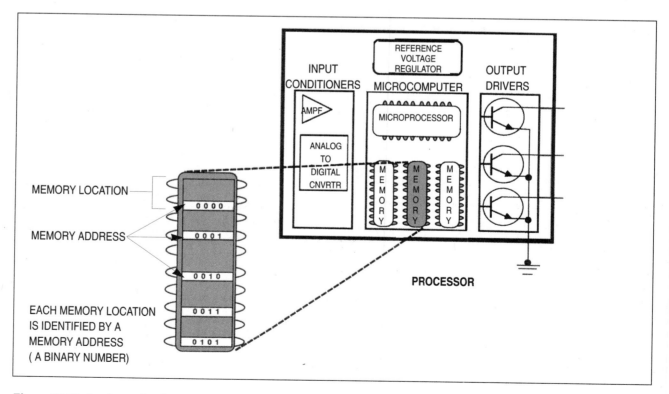

Figure 11-55 A schematic of computer memory construction. (Ford Motor)

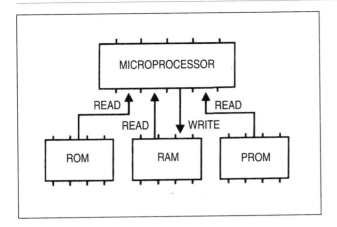

Figure 11-56 The CPU works with different types of memory. (General Motors)

son process, the CPU can make a decision regarding whether to maintain, decrease, or increase air compressor operation.

MEMORY

The different types of information required by a computer are stored in different types of memory (Figure 11-56). Computer memory consists of two basically different types — permanent and temporary. Permanent memory is called read-only memory (ROM) because the computer can only read the contents; it cannot change or erase the data stored in it. Permanent information such as the CPU operating program, and trim height tables and wheel rotation schedules is constantly used by the CPU. For this reason, the information is stored in ROM and will remain there even when battery power is disconnected.

In automotive computers, part of the ROM is a permanent part of the computer; the rest is contained within a replaceable IC chip called a programmable read-only memory, or PROM. The PROM acts as a calibration unit which tailors the computer for use with a specific vehicle/powertrain combination. The information in the PROM is programmed by the chipmaker and cannot be changed. To modify a PROM, it must be removed and replaced by another PROM which contains the revised data.

Temporary memory is called random-access memory (RAM) because the CPU can write or store new data into it, as well as read the data already in it (Figure 11-56). Information that is constantly changed, updated, or stored temporarily, such as sensor values, is stored in RAM. The computer writes these values to RAM while using them. RAM is sometimes called 'scratchpad' memory because the CPU uses it as we would use a note pad. In addition to reading, writing, and erasing information stored in RAM, the CPU can also retrieve it in any order required.

Two types of RAM are used in automotive computers — volatile and nonvolatile. Information stored in volatile RAM is lost whenever the ignition key is turned off. Once the key is turned back on, the CPU writes new information to volatile RAM. Some manufacturers use a type of volatile RAM called keep-alive memory (KAM) that is wired directly to battery power to prevent its data from being erased when the ignition is turned off. This type of memory is used to store adaptive strategies, or adaptive learning. Nonvolatile RAM retains its data even when battery power is disconnected. Nonvolatile RAM is used to store the odometer information in an electronic speedometer. If the speedometer must be replaced, the odometer memory chip containing the accumulated vehicle mileage can be removed and installed in the new speedometer.

Memory chips are installed in a black rectangular housing called a dual inline package or DIP (Figure 11-57). The DIP has a row of legs or pins on each side that connect the chip to the printed circuit board. Late-model computers may house the chips in a square housing called a quad pac (Figure 11-57). Quad pacs have a set of legs or pins on all four sides. There are also SIP (single inline package) and SIMM

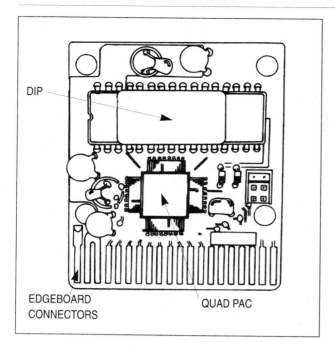

Figure 11-57 DIPs and quad pacs are two types of housings for memory chips. (General Motors)

(single inline memory module). When changing a memory chip, it must be replaced with the same type of chip. Each type has a different size or arrangement of pins so that they are not interchangeable. Memory chips are seldom removed and replaced today, but it won't be too long before this will become a routine job.

FAIL-SAFE OPERATION

Some control modules use a fail-safe system in which two CPUs in the module process the same input information.

Because both CPUs receive the same input and contain the same calibration program, the signals they produce should be identical. Since the CPUs constantly compare both input and output signals, the module cancels the control function if the signals do not match. Figure 11-58 is an internal schematic of a dual processor control module.

DIGITAL LOGIC

In the early days of computing, the eight-digit binary-coded decimals had to be entered for each number or letter by setting switches to either ON or OFF positions — a very tedious job. Today's digital integrated circuits still function on the same binary principle, irrespective of the level of complexity of these circuits. Digital integrated circuits are made up of tiny building blocks termed 'gates', which use diodes and transistors as electronic switches. In order to interpret and manipulate the binary signals, a set of rules, called the 'digital logic', are used, that allows the computer to perform complex calculations from simple inputs. Digital logic is based on a choice between only two conditions, typically — 'YES or NO', 'HIGH or LOW', or 'ON and OFF'. A signal based on this logic will then have only two voltage levels to be recognized — a high voltage (5 V) represented by 1, and a low voltage (0 V) represented by 0.

There are three important gates (A, B & C, Figure 11-59) — AND, OR, and NOT. The **AND gate** has at least two inputs and one output. The output is high (1) only when both the inputs are high (1). If one input is high (1) and the other low (0), then the output will be low (0). If both inputs are low (0), then the output is again low (0). The **OR gate** also requires at least two inputs and one output. If either of the inputs is high (1), then the output is high (1). If both the inputs are low (0), then the output is low (0). If both inputs are high (1), then the output is high (1). The third type of gate, the **NOT gate**, requires only a single input and a single output. Its basic function is to invert a digital signal. If the input is high (1), the output will be the opposite, or low (0). If the input is low (0), then the output is high (1). The various possible combinations of 0's and 1's can occur at any time, and it is an industry norm to display them as **truth tables**.

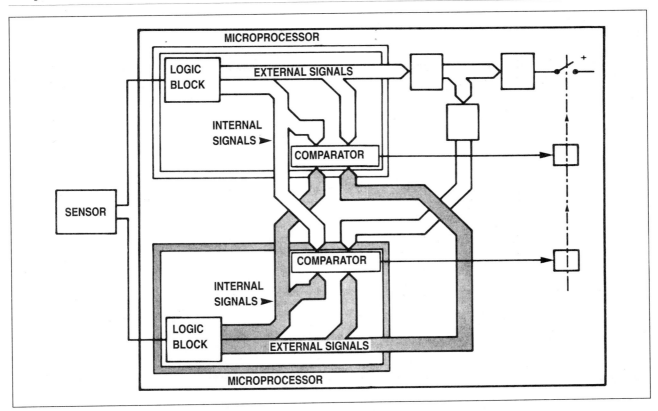

Figure 11-58 Operation of a dual processor module used to provide a fail-safe system. (Ford Motor)

The functions of the three primary gates are illustrated in Figure 11-59, using simple circuits involving a battery, two switches, and a light bulb. For an AND gate, the switches are normally open and the light is ON only when both the switches are ON. For an OR gate, the switches are again normally open and the light is ON if at least one switch is ON. For a NOT gate, only one switch is in the circuit and it is normally closed, so that the light is ON. Only when the switch is open, is the light OFF. Thus, the NOT gate inverts the usual action of a switch.

Other more complex logic functions can be generated using different combinations of the three gates just described. For example, the NAND and NOR gates (D&E, Figure 11-59) work by inverting (reversing) the outputs of the AND and OR gates respectively. So if the output of the AND gate was high (1) then the output of an NAND gate would be low (0). Another combination of gates performs the exclusive OR functions, abbreviated as XOR (F, Figure 11-59). The output is high (1) only when one input is high (1), but not when both are high (1). This gate is commonly used for comparison of two binary numbers because if both inputs are the same, the output is zero.

Also, there is a HALF-ADDER (A, Figure 11-60), that adds two one-bit numbers, to produce the sum and any carry. Since half-adder is not provided with an input to accept a carry from a previous place value, a circuit known as a FULL-ADDER (B, Figure 11-60) is used when needed. Combining a number of full-adders together in series allows the addition of binary numbers with as many digits as necessary to handle the information being

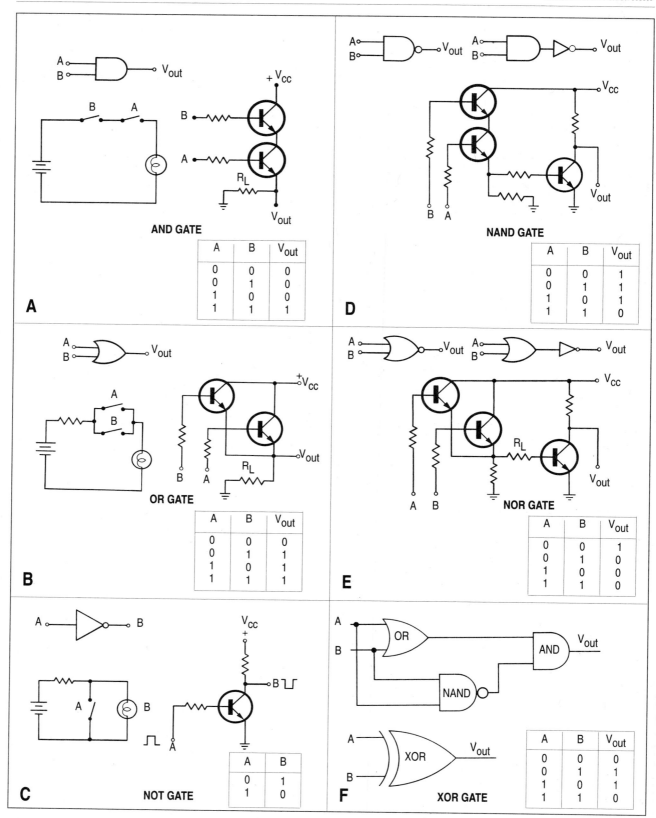

Figure 11-59 Six important logic gates, their truth tables, and electrical and transistor circuits.

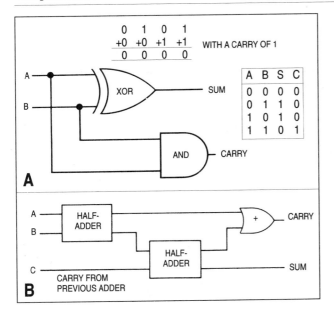

Figure 11-60 The half-adder circuit (A) and the full-adder circuit (B).

generated. For example, a typical hand-held calculator performs all of the arithmetic operations, together with several other logic circuits. Subtraction is changed to addition, multiplication becomes repeated addition, and division becomes repeated subtraction.

LOOK-UP TABLE

As indicated earlier, one of the functions of the computer is to compare binary numbers. For example, in Figure 11-61, numbers that represent vehicle speed are stored in a look-up table in the computer's memory (PROM). Voltage levels from the vehicle speed sensor are converted to binary numbers by the analog-to-digital converter and stored in a temporary register called the RAM. The computer then compares the number in the temporary register with the number in the look-up table; when it finds a match it knows the vehicle speed.

The number in the temporary register is connected to one input of the EXCLUSIVE OR gate, and a number from the look-up table is connected to the other input, bit by bit. The output of the 'XOR' is then loaded into the register #1, bit by bit. When all the bit positions in register #1 are '0', the computer knows it has a match. In this case, the number from the sensor matches the number in the table for 52 mph.

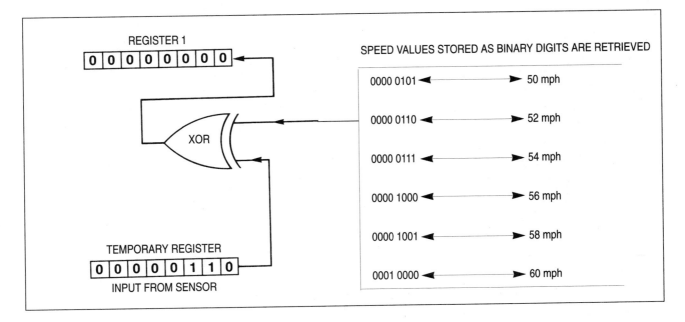

Figure 11-61 A look-up table for vehicle speed.

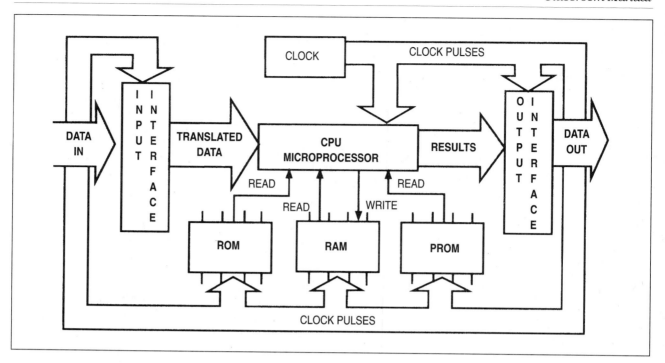

Figure 11-62 Data flow through a computer. (General Motors)

OUTPUT DEVICES

Once the CPU has processed the data, it sends a digital voltage signal to an output driver inside the computer. The output driver in turn controls an output device or actuator (Figure 11-62).

OUTPUT DRIVERS

An output driver acts as an electronic switch inside the computer. The actuator receives power either through the ignition switch or directly from the battery, but ground is provided through an output driver. A digital control signal from the CPU to the output driver causes it to open or close the ground circuit to an actuator. If the output driver is open, so is the actuator ground circuit, and NO current reaches the actuator. When the CPU closes the output driver, the actuator ground circuit is closed, allowing current flow to the actuator. Figure 11-63 shows output driver operation.

ACTUATORS

We have seen that a sensor converts mechanical motion into a voltage signal. The actuator changes a voltage signal back into mechanical motion. Most actuators work on the principle of electromagnetism. A wire coil surrounds a movable core made of a metal that is attracted by magnetic force. When electrical current passes through the coil, it produces a strong magnetic field that can be used to move valve pintles, or to open and close a switch.

Solenoids

Most actuators used in the control of steering, suspension, and braking systems are solenoids. A solenoid (Figure 11-64) consists of a movable core and return spring surrounded by a wire coil. Passing current through the wire coil generates a magnetic field, which causes the core to move and compress the return spring. As soon as current stops flowing through the

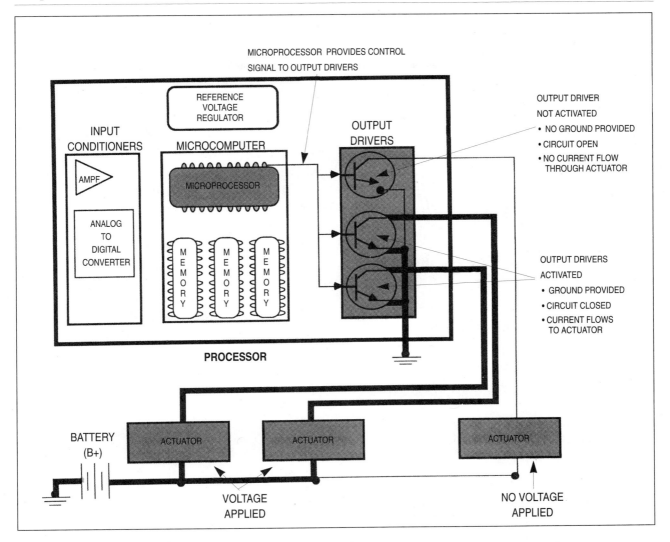

Figure 11-63 Output driver operation. (Ford Motor)

coil, the magnetic field collapses and the return spring forces the core back to its normal position. When current flow to the solenoid coil is turned on and off rapidly, the movement of the core will open and close (modulate) a valve to control vacuum, air, or hydraulic pressure.

Two types of solenoid valves are used — normally open (NO) or normally closed (NC). The NO solenoid is open when no current is present, and closes when current is applied. An NC solenoid works just the opposite. Electronic load leveling control systems use solenoids to control vehicle height by routing, blocking, or venting air pressure between the shocks or springs and the compressor.

Relays

A relay is a simple electrical device that uses one electrical current (control circuit) to control a second current (power circuit), as shown in Figure 11-65. If the control circuit is open, current cannot pass through the relay coil and so the switch remains open. When the control circuit closes, however, current flows through the coil to create a magnetic field which closes

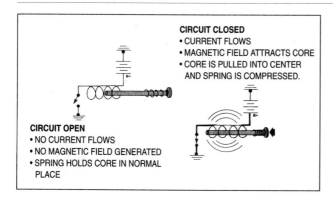

Figure 11-64 Principle of the solenoid. (Ford Motor)

the switch and sends current through the power circuit. Electronic control systems use relays to control the system power flow, and warning indicator lamps. In addition, the shock absorber operation in suspension systems is controlled by relays. A relay handles greater currents than a solenoid.

Stepper Motors

The stepper motor (Figure 11-66) is a small DC motor that acts as a digital actuator. It is powered by voltage pulses. It contains a permanent magnet armature and normally either two or four field coils. A voltage pulse applied to one coil or a pair of coils causes the motor turn a specific number of degrees or steps. The same voltage pulse applied to the other coil or pair of coils makes the motor turn an equal number of degrees or steps in the reverse direction. The armature shaft usually has a spiral on one end and this spiral connects to the object to be controlled. As the motor turns one way, the controlled device, typically a pintle valve, moves forward. As it turns the other way, the valve moves backward. The computer can apply a series of pulses to the motor's coil windings so as to move the controlled device to the location

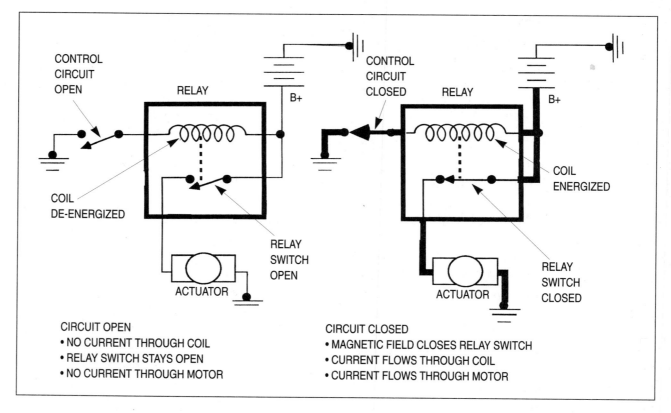

Figure 11-65 Operation of a relay. (Ford Motor)

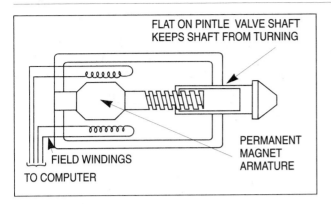

Figure 11-66 Stepper motor.

desired. The computer can also know the exact position of the valve keeping count of the pulses applied. The number of incremental steps for the shaft movement is typically 100 to 120, from de-energized (no voltage) to fully energized (full voltage) condition. Stepper motors are commonly used in progressive power steering systems to operate a hydraulic valve controlling fluid pressure to move the steering rack spool valve.

PULSE-WIDTH MODULATION (PWM)

As we have seen, the automotive computer is capable of making 300 or more decisions per second. To take advantage of this capability, an actuator must be able to respond just as quickly. Obviously, no solenoid can cycle 'on' and 'off' at that rate if it is operated by vacuum or controlled by pressure. However, the solenoid can easily operate it rapidly if run by electricity.

There are two methods of operating an electric solenoid and changing or modulating the amount of time that it is turned on. The method that turns on a solenoid at varying intervals for varying amounts of time is called **pulse width modulation** (PWM). The 'pulse' is the period of time that the solenoid is turned on, and it is only turned on when needed.

In the other method, called the **duty**

cycle modulation**, the solenoid is turned on at a set frequency or interval. In other words, the amount of time from one 'on' cycle to the next 'on' cycle is fixed by the computer at a certain number of milliseconds. The duty cycle is determined by how long the computer leaves the solenoid 'on' during the cycle. Duty cycles are usually measured in percent, varying from about 10% to 90%. In both methods, the computer is varying the length of the 'on' time of the solenoid. Because both methods have measurable 'on' and 'off' periods, the terms 'pulse width' and 'duty cycle' are sometimes applied interchangeably in either method (Figure 11-67).

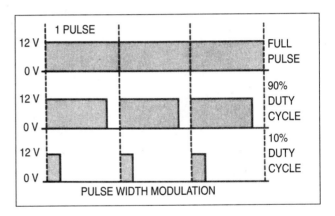

Figure 11-67 Pulse-width-modulation and duty cycle. (General Motors)

The duty cycle may be positive or negative (Figure 11-68). When the high or power side of the circuit is used to control solenoid operation, the duty cycle is called positive. When the low or ground side of the circuit controls solenoid operation, the duty cycle is called negative. PWM solenoids generally operate on a negative duty cycle, with the computer controlling the solenoid ground circuit.

SELF-DIAGNOSTICS

Automotive computers are programmed to locate problems in the circuits they monitor

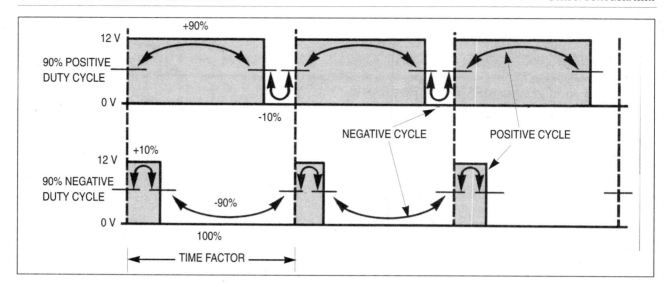

Figure 11-68 Positive and negative duty cycles in a pulse-width-modulated circuit. (General Motors)

and control. The self-diagnostics program can tell when a problem exists and indicate potential causes of the problem. When the ignition is turned on, power sent to the computer initializes or wakes it up. It then runs a start-up routine, or series of self-tests, that checks critical inputs and memory circuits before it initializes the entire system. It performs the following operations:

- checks RAM to make sure that the data storage areas are working properly
- checks ROM to ensure that the stored data is valid
- confirms the continuity of each output driver circuit
- verifies that all parts of the system are working properly
- sets a trouble code in memory if anything is found to be out of order
- powers up the system if no problems are found.

If any serious problems are discovered during the self-test routine, the CPU immediately cancels the control function and turns on a warning indicator lamp in the instrument cluster to alert the driver. It

also sets a 2- or 3-digit trouble or fault code in the memory. Disabling the control function will not affect vehicle operation under normal conditions, but it does prevent the control system from working until the problem has been corrected.

The computer program allows the CPU to determine when an input or output voltage signal from a sensor or actuator circuit is absent. This tells the CPU that the device has failed. It can also recognize when a voltage signal is NOT within the specified limits, or is otherwise highly unlikely. When necessary, it can check circuit continuity or a return voltage signal by sending a test voltage to a sensor or actuator. Under some circumstances, it can even substitute the input from one sensor for a missing or out-of-limits signal from another sensor. This backup system is a part of the program in many computers.

TROUBLE CODES

If the computer detects any problem in its own circuits, or in the circuits of sensors and actuators while the vehicle is in operation, it also sets a 2- or 3-digit trouble code in memory. In some cases, it can even detect a hydraulic or mechanical problem and set a trouble code. Each circuit or component monitored by the computer has its own individual trouble code. For example, some modules use four different codes for a wheel sensor problem, depending upon which wheel is involved. This trouble code only indicates which circuit is malfunctioning; it does not pinpoint a specific component as the cause of the problem.

Trouble codes are divided into two categories — hard or continuous, and soft or intermittent. A hard or continuous code is one that returns after it has been erased, indicating that the problem is present each time the computer checks the circuit. This means that the circuit or component failure is permanent and must be serviced to restore it to proper operating condition. A soft or intermittent code, however, is one that is set in memory but may not be present during testing, indicating a problem that appears and disappears. Soft codes generally are caused by wiring or connector problems.

Trouble codes stored by the control module may remain in memory until they are erased by the technician, or until they are displaced by more recent codes. Some modules, however, may erase the code when the ignition is switched off. The trend is toward providing more storage and making code retrieval easier. In the Shop Manual, you will learn how to retrieve trouble codes from memory and how to use them to diagnose system problems.

MULTIPLEXING

Multiplexing is sharing of one signal wire or channel by two or more electrical/electronic components. The primary advantage of multiplexing is that the size and number of wires required for a given circuit can be greatly reduced, thereby reducing the com-

plexity and size of wiring harnesses.

Two techniques of multiplexing are used — parallel data transmission and serial data transmission. In **parallel data multiplexing**, different voltage levels are used on a single input circuit. A typical example is the simple circuit for windshield wipe and wash operation. Transmitting data in the parallel form is very slow and gets tedious particularly when the signal is to be used by several different components or circuits simultaneously. A **serial data multiplexing** or time-division multiplexing is the most versatile type of multiplexing used for complex systems. A more recent development is the **optical datalink** that uses optical fibers for the peripheral serial bus instead of electrical wiring.

SERIAL DATA MULTIPLEXING

One example of a multiplexed system for digital signal transmission involving sensors is illustrated in Figure 11-69. A single wire with a ground return is connected between all of the sensors and the computer module. As all sensors access the same wire, it is called the **databus**. The CPU accesses a sensor by signalling it individually through a small transmitter/receiver (T/R) unit. The CPU sends out a code signal on the databus and through the connecting address bus to each T/R in the system. To avoid any confusion at the T/R units, each signal is assigned a coded address in binary form ('on'/'off' voltage pulses). Each T/R unit responds only to its own code, and to none else. When a specific T/R unit recognizes its code number or address, it activates an A/D converter. The sensor's analog voltage signal is then immediately converted to digital form to enable the CPU to understand its information. The digital sensor signal leaves the T/R unit and returns to the CPU along the *data line* (NOT the *address line)* and the common databus.

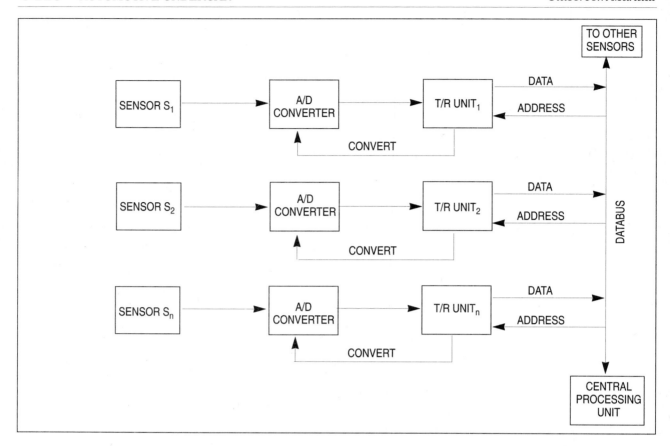

Figure 11-69 Simplified sensor multiplexing — single databus

The CPU reads and interprets the data from each specific sensor. The control module uses this information to control the operation of the monitored system — steering, suspension, braking, or whatever. The CPU then proceeds through a systematic analysis of the remaining sensors in a similar way. The sensor's sampling rate (i.e., the number of times it gathers information per second) can be adjusted for the type of control module being used.

Another multiplexing system in use involves a **two-bus setup** (Figure 11-70). One bus is for carrying the battery power, and the other for carrying the control signal from the particular accessory switch to be activated. The receiver module (RM) is controlled by the command signal received from the CPU, via the *signal bus* (NOT the bus that carries the battery power). When the operator activates a particular accessory switch (Sw), the CPU sends out a code binary address along the signal bus that can only be recognized by a certain receiver module. When the module recognizes its code, it activates its accessory switch to either an 'off' or 'on' mode, based on the CPU command signal.

OPTICAL DATALINK

Use of **optical fibers** for the signal bus (instead of the usual stranded 14 gauge copper wire) is a recent trend in automotive applications. The fiber is a very thin hollow capillary, typically of the thickness of human hair. Coded address signals (as binary pulses) from the computer are converted to light signals (instead of

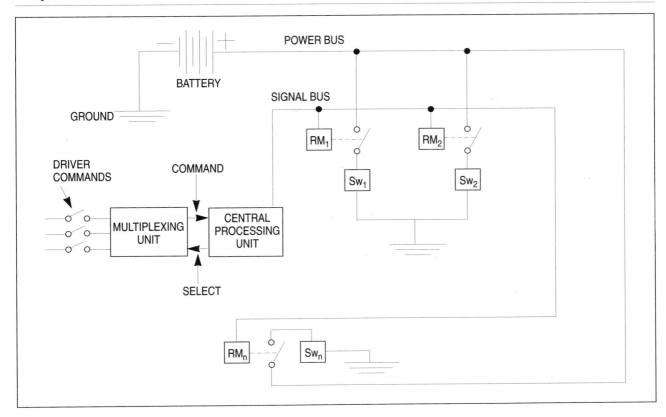

Figure 11-70 Control signal multiplexing — two-bus arrangement.

voltage), and continue to pass through the tube irrespective of bends until they reach their intended destination, usually a receiver module with an optical disc connected. The receiver module then switches a system 'on' or 'off'', as per the code from the computer. The major advantage of a fiber optic system is that it is not affected by external electrical noise, and the voltage signal remains intact. Various automotive systems as the active suspensions and ABS's require careful design considerations for electromagnetic interference protection. Fiber optics can provide this protection.

SUMMARY

The computer CPU provides the 'intelligence' behind an electronic control of suspension, steering, or braking system. The control modules for these are separate from the engine management computer. Computers have five basic functions in an operational cycle — input, conditioning, processing, storage, and output. Called a 'program loop', this cycle can occur as often as 300 times each second. The computer receives input from sensors in the form of voltage signals. These sensors — potentiometers, switches, piezoresistive and variable capacitance transducers, photodiodes, magnetic pickups, linear variable differential transformers, linear variable inductance transducers, and piezo-electric crystals — signal the position, speed or acceleration of a component. Thermistors measure temperature changes.

Input voltage signals are either analog and digital. An analog signal continuously varies from high to low. A digital signal is either high (on) or low (off). Computer circuits use digital signals. Analog signals must be converted to a digital form before they can be processed by the CPU. This signal conversion is called conditioning and is done by input conditioners in the computer. The analog signals are assigned 1's and 0's according to the binary code. The computer interprets them as 'on'/'off' signals to its thousands of tiny switches.

The conditioned signal is processed by the CPU following a program of instructions and procedures stored in memory. There are two types of memory, ROM (Read Only Memory) and RAM (Random Access Memory). ROM is permanent, but a part of it is contained within a replaceable IC chip, called a programmable read-only memory, or PROM. RAM is temporary, and is used to store data; it is lost when the ignition is turned 'off.

After the microcomputer has received, conditioned, processed, and stored the input data, it sends an output signal to the actuators through the output driver circuits. Some control modules use redundant CPUs which cross-check their output with each other and shut the module off if they do not agree. Most actuators are solenoids which control the passage of air or hydraulic fluid. Sensor input to the microcomputer changes when a program loop causes changes in output to the actuators. This feedback keeps the computer informed about vehicle operation and control requirements.

A solenoid can be pulse-width modulated by the computer's output drivers. It is pulsed 'on' and 'off' at a given frequency or number of cycles per second. The output driver varies the length of time the solenoid is energized during each 'on' cycle. This is the solenoid's 'duty cycle', and is (+) ve or (-) ve depending on whether the power side or the ground side of the circuit controls the solenoid operation.

Microcomputers have a self-diagnostic feature. They monitor the circuits they control and set a 2- or 3-digit trouble or fault code in memory if any problem is detected. This trouble code can be retrieved by the technician and tells him which circuit is causing the problem.

Multiplexing is sharing of one signal wire or channel by two or more electrical/electronic components. Serial data transmission, particularly that using optical datalinks is a recent trend.

SEMICONDUCTOR DEVICES

Diodes and **transistors** that constitute **integrated circuits** are the two basic building blocks for automotive electronics. These are made from solid materials called semiconductors, which are in a class between conductors and insulators. Common examples of semiconductor materials are silicon, germanium, gallium arsenide, selenium, and copper oxide. Of these, silicon is the most widely used, followed by germanium.

Silicon atoms have 4 valence (loose) electrons in their outer orbit. Two silicon atoms join together to form a crystal, sharing their valence electrons with each other. Thus, they will have 8 valence electrons in their outer orbit (A, Figure S11-1), making silicon a very stable, non-conducting (or insulator) material. To offset this stable balance of the silicon crystal to

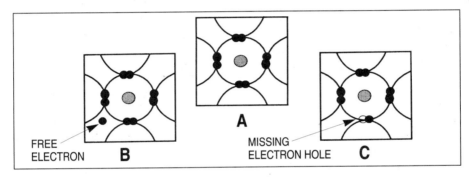

Figure S11-1 With eight electrons, silicon is a very stable, non-conducting material (A). Depending upon the 'dopant' used, either a P-type (B) or N-type (C) semiconductor silicon will result.

make it a semiconductor, minute quantities (typically, 1 part per 10 million parts of silicon crystal) of impurities from other elements are added to silicon; this process is called 'doping'. Depending on the element used to 'dope' silicon, either P-type or N-type silicon will result. If **arsenic** is added to silicon, the result is **N-type** (N = negative). Arsenic has 5 valence electrons, and if it is surrounded by silicon atoms, 4 of the valence electrons will be bound into the silicon atom's orbits. As there is no room left for the fifth arsenic valence electron, it becomes a free electron (B, Figure S11-1). Like arsenic, the elements phosphorus and antimony also have five valence electrons and their use as dopants will lead to an N-type silicon. When **boron** (or **indium**) is used as the dopant, the result is a **P-type** (P = positive) silicon. Boron (as also indium) offers only 3 valence electrons to its surrounding silicon atoms, one vacancy or **hole** remains (C, Figure S11-1). Holes travel through matter just as electrons do. The proportion of holes or free electrons determines the **resistance** of the P-type or the N-type semiconductor material. They can conduct electricity in any direction, and can also function as **resistors**.

DIODES

If a piece of N-type silicon is joined with that of a P-type silicon, the result is a **diode**, that conducts electricity in only one direction. As soon as the two pieces are combined, the free electrons in the N-type material and the positive ions in the P-type material attract each other and move together, creating a barrier of stable, neutral material — the PN-junction (Figure S11-2). When the barrier attains a certain strength that the remaining opposite charges cannot overcome, a potential difference develops at both ends of the diode.   Diode junctions can also be formed from P- and N- germanium. However, silicon and germanium are NEVER mixed to form a PN junction.

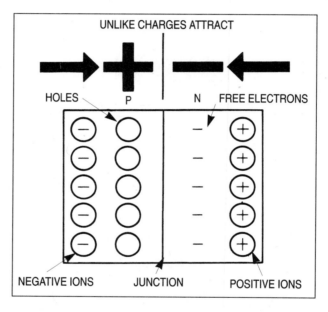

Figure S11-2 Electrons movement in a diode.

A diode is thus a **two-terminal** electronic device having two electrodes — the **anode** (P-type semiconductor) and the **cathode** (N-type semiconductor). The operation of a diode (Figure S11-3) is like a one-way valve for water flow. Also, the diode is like a 'smart' switch — when it detects the correct polarity, it turns ON; and when it detects a reverse polarity, it turns OFF. It also monitors the current pressure (voltage); if the voltage is not sufficiently high, the diode will not turn ON. There are some tiny positive and negative areas inside the diode. Both conduct current, but at the PN junction, they are separated by a thin boundary layer. When current flows in the forward (conducting) direction with a positive voltage on the anode, the diode has a low resistance (a few ohms). This condition

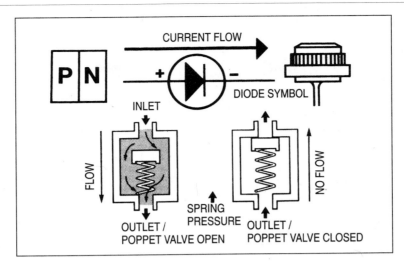

Figure S11-3 The diode is like a poppet valve. When the pressure of the inlet reaches a certain level, the poppet opens to let the fluid in, but it resists flow in the opposite direction. (General Motors)

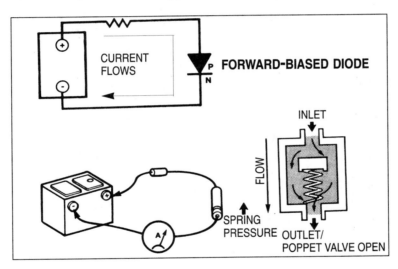

Figure S11-4 Like fluidflow in a poppet valve, a diode has a one-directional preference for current flow. (General Motors)

is called the **forward-bias** (Figure S11-4), and is necessary for current flow through a diode. To be conductive, a silicon diode needs a voltage of 0.6-0.7 V. A germanium diode needs 0.2-0.3 V. In the forward bias, the charge from the battery repels holes and electrons toward the junction. At a voltage greater than the minimum required, electrons cross the junction and join the holes, allowing the flow of current. When the current flows in the reverse (nonconducting) direction with a positive voltage on the cathode, a diode has a very high resistance (a few million ohms). This condition is called the **reverse-bias** (Figure S11-5). In the reverse bias, the charge from the battery attracts holes and electrons away from the PN junction, causing the diode to block current flow.

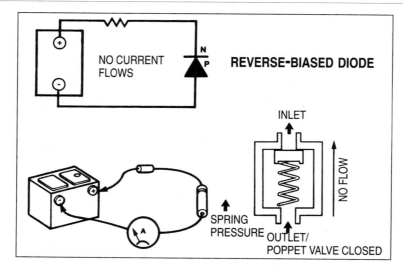

Figure S11-5 The reverse-biased condition resists the flow of current, similar to the action of a check ball in the poppet valve. (General Motors)

An important application of the diode is in **rectification**. In the **single wave** rectification (A, Figure S11-6), an undulating AC voltage is rectified into a single polarity (DC) voltage. Only the upper (positive) half of the pulse is allowed to pass through the diode. In the **full wave** rectification (B, Figure S11-6 shows a 4-diode bridge rectifier), both the positive and the negative halves of the AC voltage pulse are converted into DC.

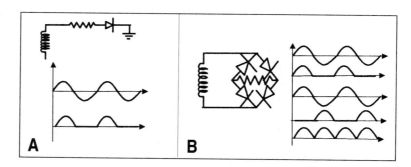

Figure S11-6 The outputs of single wave rectification (A) and full wave rectification (B). (General Motors)

In a typical battery-charging alternator, six diodes (3 positive and 3 negative) are used to handle the alternating current that is developed in the 3-phase stator windings, so that current can only flow to the battery in the direction to charge it. Any reversal of battery current is blocked by the diodes. In automotive applications, some diodes are designed for higher voltages than are others. Therefore, when replacing a faulty diode, the correct type is to be used. Excessive heat or mechanical stress can damage a diode.

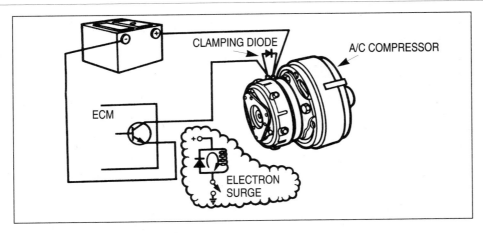

Figure S11-7 A clamping diode allows a voltage surge to dissipate by returning it to the coil. (General Motors)

A **clamping diode** (Figure S11-7) protects a circuit from surge currents that develop when the current flowing through an electromagnetic device is suddenly interrupted. Any coil — solenoid or relay — when energized, will create a magnetic field. Electrons passing through the coil do not tend to stop, so the coil tries to keep them moving even when the circuit is open. As the electrons pile up against the open in the circuit, they try to jump the open, resulting in a spark that may cause damage to related components. The clamping diode across the coil allows the electron pile-up to backup, bypassing the coil. This is like the pressure-relief valve in a pressure cooker.

A **Zener diode** is a voltage regulator, typically in the range of 2 -200 V. It is placed in a circuit 'backwards' from a regular diode (the symbol pointing the wrong way, Figure S11-8). When the Zener voltage is reached, the diode starts conducting, but maintains the voltage drop across itself, depending on the diode's rating. The Zener diode (also called the **avalanche diode**) acts like a regular diode when forward biased. Even if diode breakdown voltage is exceeded, NO permanent damage to the Zener can occur. Negatively mounted diodes used in CS

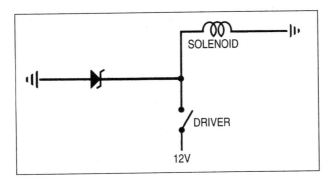

Figure S11-8 Zener diode operation. (General Motors)

charging systems and Bosch ABS module relay systems are Zener diodes. Also, Zener diodes are used in many computers and control circuits. Some circuits do not include clamping diodes or resistors to control voltage surges. A Zener diode placed parallel to the driver circuit protects it from surges occurring when a solenoid or relay is de-energized.

All diodes, when forward biased, emit some electromagnetic radiation. Diodes made from certain semiconductors as gallium arsenide phosphide, emit significantly higher radiation than silicon diodes, and are called **light emitting diodes (LED)**. Like signal diodes, LEDs function in the forward direction, and block a reverse bias voltage. Compared to standard light bulbs, LEDs (Figure S11-9) consume less power, operate at lower voltages (about 3 V), and have a longer life because of operation at a cooler temperature.

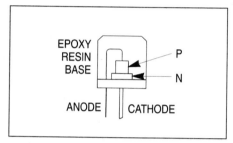
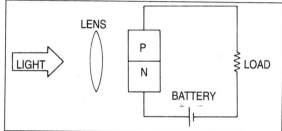

Figure S11-9 Schematic of an LED bulb.   **Figure S11-10**   Principle of a photodiode.

All diodes respond to some degree when illuminated by light, and those designed specifically to detect light are called **photodiodes** (Figure S11-10). Incoming light is absorbed, creating additional electron-hole pairs. Since additional charges are produced in the vicinity of the junction, they are separated by the electric field in this region and are swept across the junction. Because of the electric field direction, the charges move to their majority sides (electrons to N and holes to P). This charge flow constitutes additional current in the reverse direction. One of the primary applications of a photodiode is as a light detector. The photodiode will NOT conduct electricity in the reverse direction while the diode is in the dark. When exposed to light, it no longer blocks current flow. Therefore, the light triggers the diode and it operates as a switch.

Diodes are static circuit elements. They do not have gain (i.e., voltage is never greater than its input), and do not store energy. Small signal diodes are used to transform low current AC to DC, absorb voltage surges, regulate voltage, detect radio signals, perform logic, etc.

TRANSISTORS

A **transistor** is a three-terminal active circuit element that can **amplify** or **transform** a signal level. The transistor performs the functions of a switch without the need for a 'finger' (Figure S11-11). It enables a computer to turn ON and OFF many circuits, only with a small voltage signal.

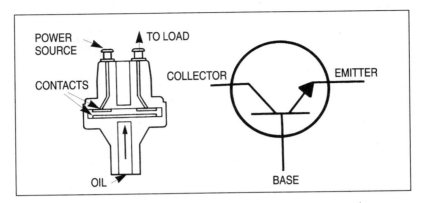

Figure S11-11 The operation of a transistor is analogous to a hydraulic switch. Current passes through collector/emitter circuit only when a small current is applied to the base. (General Motors)

The current flow through a transistor is like that of water in a faucet (Figure S11-12). The more the faucet is turned on (base path), the more water will flow out of the spigot (collector/emitter path). Thus, the transistor can also function as an **amplifier**.

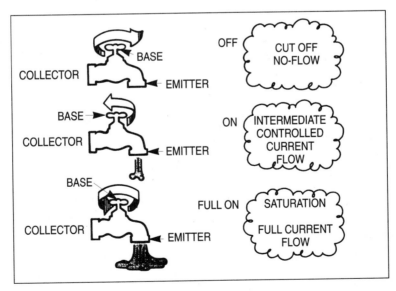

Figure S11-12 The amplifying action of a transistor is analogous to the functioning of a water faucet. (General Motors)

The most commonly used transistors are of **bipolar** type — the PNP and the NPN (Figure S11-13). For the PNP transistor, the arrow on the emitter is

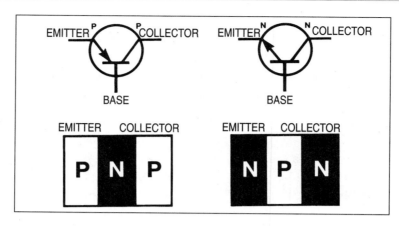

Figure S11-13 The two possible arrangements of the P- and N-type semiconductor in a transistor. (General Motors)

Pointing In Permanently (PNP). For the NPN transistor, the arrow on the emitter is **Not Pointing In (NPN)**. With an NPN transistor, the middle letter is a 'P', and a positive voltage must be applied to the base to turn the collector/emitter circuit ON. Similarly, with a PNP transistor, the middle letter is an 'N', and a negative voltage (ground path) must be completed from the base to turn the emitter/collector circuit ON.

Transistors offer several advantages over the relays and switches they replace. They are smaller, lighter, and faster, and are controllable with much lower current than typical relays. Further, transistors can be variable. The relay has a large current path of the controlled circuit (Figure S11-14). Also the path of the 'controlling' circuit is through the coil of the relay to the ground. A relay has a switch that can remotely control a larger (higher current) circuit. The switch can be placed on either the positive or the ground side of the relay's coil circuit. The two types of bipolar transistors (Figure S11-14) differ mainly in where the coil control circuit is switched — on the positive side or on the negative side.

Let us compare an NPN transistor circuit with a similar relay circuit. The relay circuit is turned ON and OFF by closing and opening the switch on the positive side of the coil circuit. This turns the lamp ON and OFF in the larger controlled circuit. The function of the transistor is similar. When the switch in the base circuit is opened and closed, the lamp turns ON and OFF just as it is being controlled by a relay.

The transistor works as a current amplifier in which the base current controls the collector current. The current amplification (or gain) of a transistor typically ranges from 10 to 300. For a transistor with 1 mA of current in the base, and a specified current amplification of 100, the collector current would be 100 mA.

Field Effect Transistors (FETs) are **unipolar**. Their function is the same as that of bipolar transistors, to turn ON or OFF the current to a load in

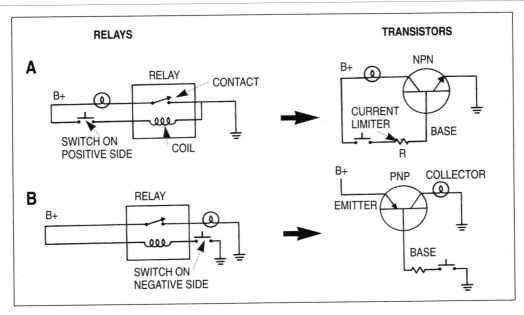

Figure S11-14 Electromagnetic relays are replaced with smaller, faster, and lighter transistors. (General Motors)

the circuit. Unlike a bipolar transistor that has current flowing through regions of both N and P polarity, the working current in an FET flows through only one type of semiconductor material, either N or P, as it flows from the drain to the source. Compared to bipolar transistors, FETs are much smaller and simpler to build, and are therefore less expensive. These are a basic part of Integrated Circuits (ICs).

The components of an FET function the same way as those of a bipolar transistor — the source acts as the emitter; the gate acts as the base; and the drain acts as the collector. In contrast to a bipolar transistor that uses a base current, an FET uses voltage to control current flow through the drain/source circuit. Applying a voltage to the gate creates an electric field, that causes attraction or repulsion of electrons, depending on the type of the transistor — P-channel or N-channel. That is why these are 'Field Effect' transistors.

There are two types of FETs (Figure S11-15) — the **Junction Field Effect Transistor** (JFET) and the **Metal Oxide Semiconductor Field Effect Transistor** (MOSFET). A **JFET** (A, Figure S11-15) is normally ON, and allows current to pass through without activating the gate circuit. Applying a positive voltage to the gate of a P-channel JFET repels and chokes off current. Applying a negative voltage to the gate of an N-channel JFET turns the JFET OFF. The gate voltage is negative with respect to the source voltage, as in the case of reverse biasing a diode. Free electrons are repelled and their flow is throttled. Zero volts turn the JFET ON.

A **MOSFET** (also known as **Insulated Gate FET** or **IGFET**) (B, Figure S11-15), is a special type of FET whose gate is insulated from the source/drain material by a film of silicon dioxide.   Like the JFET, it comes in two varieties — N-channel and P-channel.   The function of each is the same, only the polarity is different.   With zero volts at the gate, the channel is conductive and the MOSFET is ON.

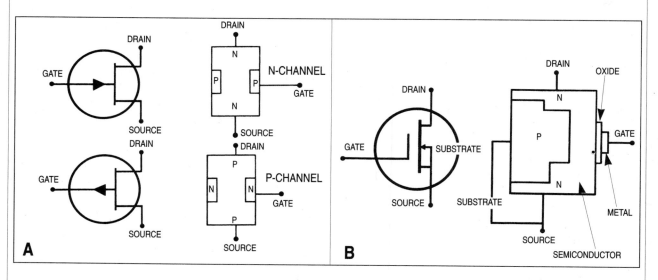

Figure S11-15 Circuit diagrams of unipolar transistors — JFETs (A) and N-Channel MOSFET (B). (General Motors)

INTEGRATED CIRCUITS

An **Integrated circuit** is primarily a single-crystal chip of silicon on which resistors, capacitors, diodes, and transistors are formed as needed to make a complete circuit with all the required interconnections.   The entire circuit is on a tiny chip.   Thousands of transistors and other devices are accommodated in areas of a square millimeter. Circuits with more than 100,000 transistors are conveniently fabricated by micromachining techniques involving chemical etching. The reliability of these chips is very high as all the components are fabricated simultaneously with NO solderings.   The chips are encased in insulated capsules. The two major IC categories are analog (or linear) and digital (or logic).   Analog ICs produce, amplify, or respond to variable voltages, and include various types of amplifiers, timers, oscillators, and voltage regulators.   Digital ICs respond to or generate signals having only two voltage levels, and include microprocessors, memories, microcomputers, and a variety of simple chips.   Modern automobiles use ICs in control modules for engine management, climate control, cruise control, suspension and steering, antilock braking systems, and others.   Figure S11-16 illustrates an IC chip (magnification 400) and its schematic for a passenger car hazard-warning and turn-signal flasher.   The numbers 1 through 10 indicate the number of terminals connected to the IC.

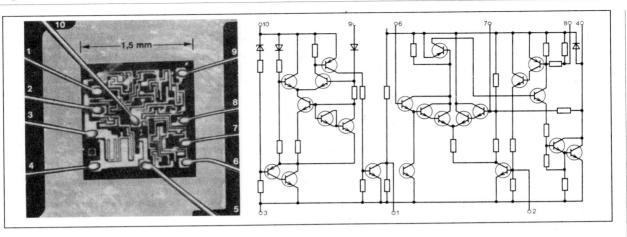

Figure S11-16 An IC chip and its schematic. (Robert Bosch)

BEWARE OF ESD

SPOTLIGHT

Electrostatic discharge, or ESD, is a condition that results when two dissimilar materials are rubbed together, or separated. The strength of the electrical charge that builds up under such conditions will depend on the types of materials, their closeness to each other, the speed with which they make or break contact, and the amount of humidity in the air.

Static electricity is one form of ESD that we all know about. After walking across a carpet when the humidity is low, touching a metal object will result in a 7,000 volt shock and perhaps even a tiny spark. Although smaller discharges that we do not feel or see often are present, under certain conditions, static discharges can reach 40-50,000 V. This is enough to give you a good sting.

Since solid state components are designed to operate on milli-volts, any electrical surge often can spell the end of a microchip or micro-circuit. One of two things will happen when a static discharge reaches the component — ESD can blow a hole in a microcircuit, causing a complete and immediate failure; or it can result in only minor damage to the circuit, allowing the component to continue working under gradually deteriorating circumstances, eventually leading to total failure of the component. Sliding across the vehicle's seat to unplug a computer and destroying it, is a hard and expensive way to learn a simple lesson — you can't be too careful about ESD when working with electronic components.

All solid state components are ESD-sensitive. Some carmakers use the symbol shown in Figure S11-17 on both wiring diagrams and service replacement components as a warning that the circuit and/or part is subject to ESD damage. This symbol serves as a reminder that static charges and discharges must be avoided when working on an ABS control system. Even if the symbol is not present, you should assume that any solid state component is ESD-sensitive.

Figure S11-17 ESD warning symbol.

A special wrist strap is available from some manufacturers. This strap plugs into a grounded mat for use when working on the vehicle. Although somewhat awkward to use at first, this combination lets you work on sensitive components without fear of expensive electrical damage. As long as you do not remove the strap, or step off the grounded mat, continuity is maintained and static charges cannot buildup or discharge.

There are other precautions you can take to avoid ESD damage:
- Do NOT remove electronic parts from their static-free packing materials until you are ready to install them. Ground the wrapping to a known good vehicle ground before removing the contents.
- Do NOT wear clothes made from synthetic materials, as they tend to create ESD buildups and discharges.
- Unless you wear a grounded wrist strap, ALWAYS touch a known good ground before handling ESD-prone components.
- Unless a specific diagnostic procedure calls for it, do NOT touch the electrical terminals of a solid state component.
- When using a DVOM to perform electrical checks, ALWAYS connect the DVOM's ground lead first.

❓ REVIEW QUESTIONS

1. An engine coolant temperature sensor is:
   - (A) a thermistor.
   - (B) a switch.
   - (C) a potentiometer.
   - (D) an output.

2. The throttle position sensor is:
   - (A) a thermistor.
   - (B) a voltage generator.
   - (C) a Hall-effect device.
   - (D) a potentiometer.

3. An analog signal is:
   - (A) high.
   - (B) low.
   - (C) in between high and low.
   - (D) continuously varying.

4. An analog waveform is:
   - (A) horizontal.
   - (B) vertical.
   - (C) bell-shaped.
   - (D) square.

5. The reference voltage supplied to a sensor by the microcomputer is:
   - (A) high.
   - (B) low.
   - (C) constant.
   - (D) varied.

6. A digital waveform is:
   - (A) horizontal.
   - (B) vertical.
   - (C) bell-shaped.
   - (D) square.

7. Technician A says that a potentiometer changes mechanical motion to a voltage signal. Technician B says that an actuator changes electrical signals to mechanical motion. Who is right?
   - (A) Technician A
   - (B) Technician B
   - (C) Both A and B
   - (D) Neither A nor B

8. Technician A says that a photo optical device is a voltage generating sensor. Technician B says that a Hall-effect switch is a voltage generating sensor. Who is right?
   - (A) Technician A
   - (B) Technician B
   - (C) Both A and B
   - (D) Neither A nor B

9. Technician A says that '1' and '0' represent 'on' and 'off' in binary code. Technician B says that '0' and '1' represent 'on' and 'off'. Who is right?
   - (A) Technician A
   - (B) Technician B
   - (C) Both A and B
   - (D) Neither A nor B

10. Technician A says that a digital signal must be conditioned before it can be processed by the microcomputer. Technician B says that this type of signal conditioning is called amplification. Who is right?
    - (A) Technician A
    - (B) Technician B
    - (C) Both A and B
    - (D) Neither A nor B

11. Technician A says that the microprocessor locates information stored in memory by its assigned address. Technician B says that the microcomputer uses four different types of basic memory. Who is right?
    - (A) Technician A
    - (B) Technician B
    - (C) Both A and B
    - (D) Neither A nor B

12. Permanent memory that CANNOT be changed by the microcomputer is called:
    - (A) RIM
    - (B) RAM
    - (C) ROM
    - (D) KAM

13. Memory that can be read and/or changed by the microcomputer is called:
    - (A) RIM
    - (B) RAM

(C) ROM

(D) KRAM

14. Which of the following are NOT control system actuators?

(A) Relays

(B) Solenoids

(C) Stepper motors

(D) Rheostats

15. Technician A says that a pulse-width modulated actuator is turned on and off at a given frequency. Technician B says that the length of time the actuator is energized during each 'on' cycle is called its 'duty' cycle. Who is right?

(A) Technician A

(B) Technician B

(C) Both A and B

(D) Neither A nor B

16. Technician A says that the microcomputer output drivers supply voltage to the actuators. Technician B says that they supply the actuator ground. Who is right?

(A) Technician A

(B) Technician B

(C) Both A and B

(D) Neither A nor B

17. Technician A says that the length of time required to process an input signal and send an output to an actuator is called a program loop. Technician B says that a program loop requires an average of 0.003 second to complete. Who is right?

(A) Technician A

(B) Technician B

(C) Both A and B

(D) Neither A nor B

18. Technician A says that each circuit monitored by the microcomputer has its own trouble code that can be set in memory. Technician B says the trouble code identifies the defective component. Who is right?

(A) Technician A

(B) Technician B

(C) Both A and B

(D) Neither A nor B

19. Which sensor works on the principle that electrical resistance of a semiconductor varies when the material is stressed?

(A) Piezoresistive accelerometer

(B) LVIT

(C) Steering torque sensor

(D) None of the above

20. LVDT is:

(A) an optical sensor.

(B) a straingage.

(C) a displacement sensor.

(D) none of the above.

21. Which of the following is a variable inductance sensor?

(A) Lateral *g*-force sensor

(B) Steering angle sensor

(C) Height sensor

(D) None of the above

22. Which of the following sensors is NOT voltage generating?

(A) Piezoresistive sensor

(B) Piezoelectric sensor

(C) LVDT

(D) LVIT

23. NOT gates can be added to AND gates and OR gates to create NAND and NOR gates — because they:

(A) are binary in nature.

(B) invert the signal.

(C) have two inputs and one output.

(D) reroute the signal.

24. Multiplexing is:

(A) a novel technique of data storage.

(B) using half-adder circuits to multiply.

(C) sharing of one signal channel by two or more electronic components.

(D) none of the above.

CHAPTER TWELVE

COMPUTER-CONTROLLED SUSPENSIONS

"Modern technology owes ecology an apology."
— Alan M. Eddison

 OBJECTIVES

After completion of this chapter, you should be able to:

- Explain the difference between an active and a passive suspension system.

- Explain the relationship between vehicle operation and electronic control of the suspension.

- List and describe the sensors and actuators used in each of the following systems — variable shock damping, electronic level control, and air spring suspension.

- Describe the basic operation of each of the following systems — variable shock damping, electronic level control, and air spring suspension.

As discussed in earlier chapters, all automotive suspension systems are a compromise designed to provide both a smooth ride and adequate steering. Steering and handling suffers when suspensions are engineered to provide a soft cushiony ride. If suspensions are designed to provide excellent steering and handling, the ride suffers. A suspension designed to do both ride and handling equally well, instead of being a compromise between the two, would be a giant step forward.

By adding electronics to monitor driving and road conditions, a computer called a 'suspension module' can change the suspension calibration according to vehicle needs and the driver's preferences. The simplest application of a suspension module can level the vehicle to compensate for extra luggage or weight. A module with more complex programming can recalibrate the entire suspension system to accommodate evasive or high speed maneuvers. Some highly refined experimental systems can even lift a wheel when the tire first contacts a bump in the road, so that the bump is not even felt in the vehicle. This points up the fact that all of the electronic suspensions are not the same, and they accomplish specific functions through the use of different components.

As we discuss the various computer-controlled suspension designs in this chapter, you will notice that the primary components to be electronically controlled are springs, shocks, and struts. Of course, these are just a few of the many components involved in a suspension, but at this time, there is no practical way to control components such as control arms and stabilizer bars with a computer module. The module uses a number of sensor inputs to make decisions that affect suspension operation. How a computer or module gathers the necessary information, and how it arrives at a decision, was discussed in the chapter on fundamentals of electronic control. Now let us take a look at the various electronically controlled suspension systems currently in use, and how they work to change the suspension from a passive to an active mode.

ACTIVE vs. PASSIVE SUSPENSIONS

Until the computer arrived on the scene, vehicle ride control relied on a **passive suspension** with fixed spring rates and shock absorber valving. Although luxury cars have been equipped for many years with pressurized air shock absorbers and a ride height sensor to act as a load-leveling system, it amounted to little more than a static form of road control. In such a system, ride height is dependent on the amount of mass in the rear of the car, and does not change until the vehicle load changes. These and other standard suspensions are considered to be passive because their reaction to road conditions is determined by factory settings.

Passive suspensions began to feel the challenge of electronics in the 1980's, as the first primitive computer-controlled suspensions appeared on Japanese vehicles.

Since the computer allows a suspension to adapt instantly to changing road conditions without driver input, such designs have been nicknamed "smart" suspensions. The earliest designs took the form of electronically controlled shock absorbers with variable damping rates, although many were little more than remotely controlled shock absorbers that allowed the driver to choose between a soft, medium, or firm ride. They opened the door for the development of an **active suspension**; one that integrates spring action, shock absorber damping, and ride height into a single system whose operation is determined by a module that senses road conditions. While many carmakers refer to their current systems as active suspensions, few truly deserve the term. When a vehicle with a standard suspension passes over a bump or uneven road surface, the wheels drop into dips and bounce back out. A truly active suspension not only pushes the wheel into the dip and keeps the vehicle level to reduce the first bounce, it should also release pressure as the wheel comes out of the dip to reduce the second bounce while keeping the vehicle level. Such systems are beginning to be used on luxury cars, but they are still only one-way active — they can push a wheel down, but cannot pull it back. Two-way, or truly active, suspensions are still under development.

Like many other technical advances in automotive engineering, the concept of active suspension came out of the competitive world of Grand Prix racing. Lotus International generally receives credit for developing the first computer-controlled suspension. During the early 1980's, the precise height control required by aerodynamic developments such as ground effects conflicted with the comparatively low suspension stiffness necessary for good grip and driver comfort. Lotus developed a system of high-pressure hydraulic actuators to carry the vehicle mass instead of conventional leaf, coil, or air springs. A series of sensors fitted to each actuator measured load, displacement, and vertical acceleration. By controlling and venting fluid pressure inside the actuators (similar to modulating fluid pressure in an antilock brake system), the actuators performed the combined functions of springs and shock absorbers.

As a wheel on the Lotus racing suspension crosses a rough road and meets a bump, sensors in an active suspension transmit the increased upward acceleration and vertical load to the suspension module. The module then calculates the required wheel velocity and displacement, sending a control signal to the actuator. The actuator then picks the wheel up or pushes it down, whatever is necessary to keep the tire in constant contact with the road surface. Since this sensing and movement of the wheel occurs hundreds of times a second, each wheel is accurately controlled to follow the contours of a bump or dip and cushion the body from any unwanted forces. Cornering forces and handling are thus improved by maintaining constant contact between the tire and road surface. Body-mounted sensors that measure longitudinal forces (braking and acceleration) and lateral direction (cornering) provide the suspension module with data that allows it to maintain a stable attitude at all times.

Ford has been in the forefront of North American carmakers in developing various computer-controlled suspensions. Its efforts began in 1984 with the air suspension system used on Mark VII and Continental models, evolved into the air suspension and automatic ride control (ASARC) system introduced on the 1988 Continental, and added speed-dependent height adjustment to its full-time, four-corner, automatic air spring system used on the 1993 Mark VIII. Other carmakers,

not to be outdone, have followed Ford's lead, and a variety of different computer-controlled suspension designs abound. To understand the various approaches to active suspensions used on production vehicles, let us look at typical examples.

VARIABLE SHOCK DAMPING SYSTEMS

Variable shock damping systems (Figure 12-1) first appeared on Japanese vehicles. These systems depend on the suspension module to vary the amount of resistance in the shock absorber or the strut. Each wheel is equipped with a gas-filled shock absorber fitted with a small actuator motor; the motor may be mounted either on top of, or inside the top of the shock. Each actuator motor is connected to a rotary valve inside its shock absorber by a control rod. In some designs, a control switch located in the driver's compartment can be set for a soft, medium, or firm ride. When the switch is activated, it sends a voltage signal to the suspension module, which then signals each actuator motor to rotate its control rod. As the control rod rotates, it repositions the rotary valve, changing the size of the metering orifice inside the shock absorber. A large orifice allows the hydraulic fluid inside the shock absorber to pass from chamber to chamber quickly and provides a soft ride setting. A small orifice does the opposite. The shock absorbers remain where they are set until the control switch is activated again. In other systems, the module is programmed to make the mode control decision according to vehicle speed, amount of braking, or degree of turning right or left. In those systems the driver has no control switch.

SENSORS

Variable shock damping systems all use speed, brake, and steering angle sensors.

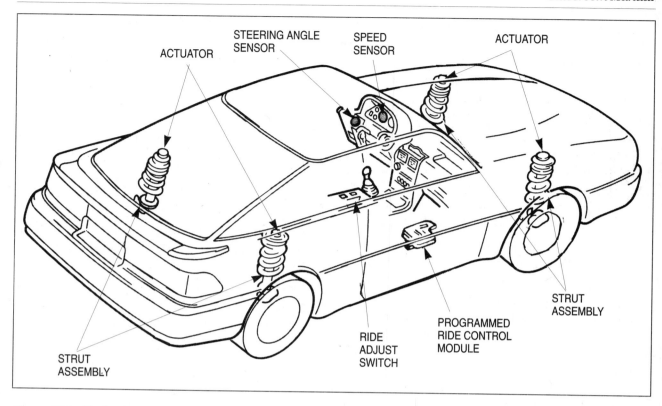

Figure 12-1 The basic components of a typical variable damping system. (Ford Motor)

A few systems may monitor signals from the throttle position sensor.

Speed Sensor

A speed sensor (Figure 12-2) provides signals used by the suspension module to determine how fast the vehicle is traveling. In many cases, the input from this sensor also is used to control an electronic speedometer, electronic steering, and/or cruise control. The speed sensor typically is mounted on the transmission or transaxle output shaft, although some systems incorporate it as part of the speedometer. Sensor voltage output is linear — the faster the sensor revolves, the greater the frequency and voltage it produces. As vehicle speed decreases, the sensor slows down and its voltage output also decreases. In most cases, the suspension module interprets high vehicle speed as a need for a firmer suspension.

Brake Sensor

The brake sensor signals the suspension module when heavy braking occurs. This allows the module to change the shock absorber damping rate to a firmer mode as

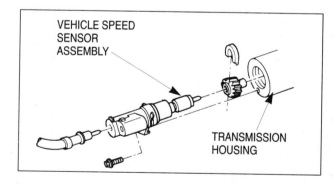

Figure 12-2 Most speed sensors are mounted on the transmission housing and driven by the output shaft. The low voltage signal generated by the sensor is monitored by the computer and used by the engine management, speed control, and other systems that require a vehicle speed input. (Ford Motor)

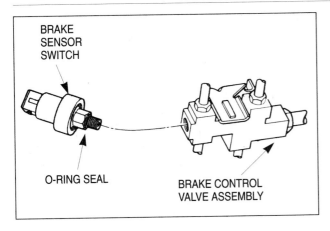

Figure 12-3   A pressure switch can be used as a brake sensor. Other systems may use an input from the stop lamp switch. (Ford Motor)

with data from the speed sensor to determine the amount of damping required.

Other systems use a pressure switch (Figure 12-3) as a brake sensor. The normally-open pressure switch threads into the brake system combination valve, and is operated by the front brake circuit hydraulic pressure. If pressure exceeds a predetermined limit, the switch closes and signals the suspension module to change the shock absorber damping. Most variable damping systems return to their previous rate a few seconds after the module stops receiving signals from the brake sensor.

Steering Sensor

This sensor is sometimes called a steering wheel rotation sensor, or a steering angle sensor. It consists of a revolving disc and a photocell, or photodiode (Figure 12-4). Mounted on the steering shaft, the disc

a way of minimizing front suspension squat or nose dive.   In some systems, the stop lamp switch acts as the brake sensor. When the module receives a stop lamp switch signal, it processes the information

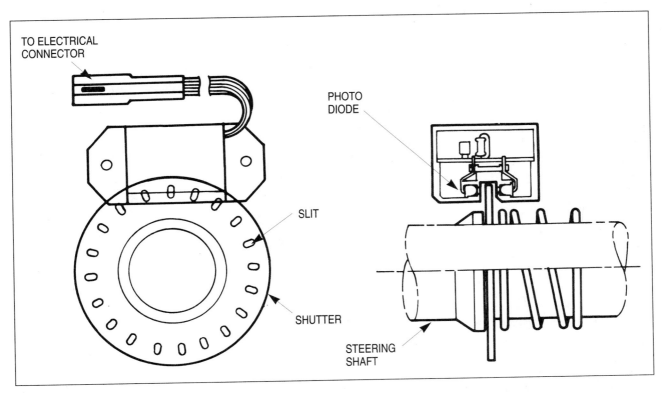

Figure 12-4   The steering angle sensor consists of a slotted shutter that revolves between photo diodes, creating a voltage signal that is sent to the control module. (Ford Motor)

makes and breaks the photocell beam as it rotates. This produces a series of voltage signals used by the suspension module to determine how fast the steering wheel is being rotated, or the turning angle of the vehicle. Generally, rapid steering wheel rotation, or a hard turn above a predetermined speed, will result in a change in shock damping rate that produces the firmer suspension required by an evasive maneuver. Once the need for the firmer suspension mode is no longer indicated by the steering sensor, the module returns the system to its previous damping rate.

Throttle Position (TP) Sensor

Some variable damping systems use an input from the TP sensor (Figure 12-5) to determine the rate of vehicle acceleration. If throttle opening is above a predetermined

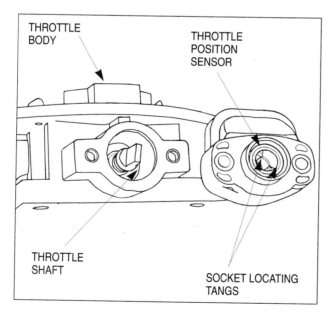

Figure 12-5 The throttle position (TP) sensor is a rotary potentiometer that fits over a tanged end on the throttle shaft on the air intake throttle body. As the throttle shaft moves, the potentiometer sends the engine management computer a voltage signal which tells the computer the degree of throttle opening. When its input also is used by a variable shock damping system, it is interpreted as rate of vehicle acceleration. (Chrysler)

angle, the suspension module will switch the shock absorbers to a firm mode to minimize any tendency toward rear end squat or dive, and front end rise during vehicle acceleration at lower speeds.

Other Sensor Inputs

Depending on the system, the suspension module also may receive an input from the ignition switch to turn the system on when the ignition is turned on. If the system uses a driver-operated ride control switch, it will receive an input from the switch to indicate the driver's preference.

Some systems use an input from an accelerometer to detect cornering speed. This sensor generally contains two normally closed (NC) mercury switches connected in series. One mercury switch opens during high-speed right turns; the other opens during high-speed left turns. If either switch opens, the suspension module modifies strut or shock valving.

SUSPENSION MODULES

The microprocessor used in a variable damping system suspension module has a diagnostic capability, and can determine when the system is not operating properly. Early modules may indicate system malfunctioning by flashing indicator lamps; later modules contain a self-diagnostic program and will set a diagnostic trouble code (DTC) if a malfunction occurs. The system may be designed to allow DTC retrieval through a flashing indicator lamp, an analog voltmeter, or through special test equipment.

ACTUATORS

In a variable shock damping system, each shock absorber or strut contains an actuator. The actuator is connected to a shaft or control rod that controls internal shock or strut valving. When signaled to

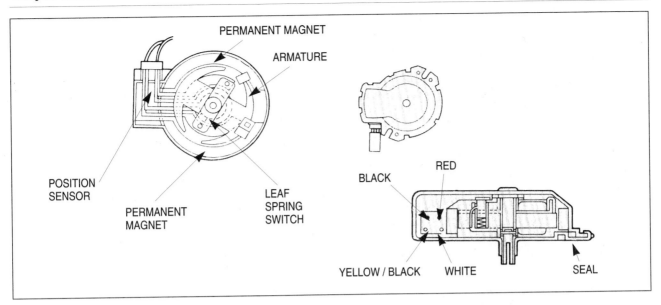

Figure 12-6. A magnetic actuator contains a 2-piece armature and dual magnets that create a magnetic field. The leaf spring switch provides a feedback signal to the module. (Ford Motor)

do so by the suspension module, the actuator rotates the shaft or rod in the appropriate direction. The actuator may be located on top of the shock or strut, installed on the side of the shock or strut at its top, or mounted internally.

A magnetic actuator (Figure 12-6) contains a small 2-piece armature, two permanent magnets, and a leaf spring position switch. The position switch sends a feedback signal to the suspension module. This allows the module to determine if the actuator is operating properly, and enables it to identify a malfunctioning actuator. Current to the armature is applied by the module through one of two relays, creating a magnetic field that causes the armature to rotate until it reaches an internal stop. The position switch opens or closes (according to rotational direction) and turns off the feedback signal to inform the module that the actuator has responded properly.

A reduction-gear actuator (Figure 12-7) uses a small DC motor to turn the reduction gear when signalled by the

module. This rotates a control rod and energizes a solenoid to engage the correct detent. The suspension module modulates the signal to the actuator to obtain the necessary damping mode appropriate to vehicle speed and road conditions.

When an internal actuator is used, it generally takes the form of a small DC

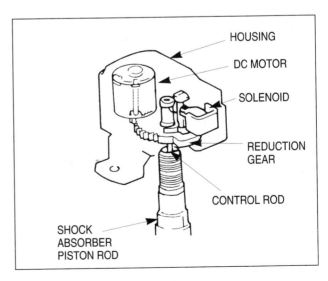

Figure 12-7 An example of a reduction-gear actuator used to position shock absorber valving.

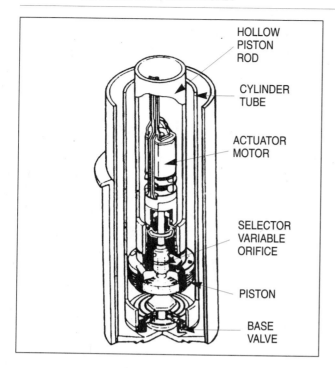

Figure 12-8 A small DC actuator motor inside the strut can drive the selector valve to change the damper settings. (Oldsmobile Division, General Motors)

motor which drives a selector valve inside the shock or strut (Figure 12-8).

SYSTEM EXAMPLES

To illustrate the basic approaches to computer-controlled variable shock damping systems, we will look at four different systems currently in use:

- Ford's Programmed Ride Control (PRC)
- Toyota's Electronically Modulated Suspension (TEMS)
- GM's Computer Command Ride (CCR)
- Mercedes-Benz's Adaptive Damping System (ADS)

Each of these systems is designed to minimize undesired suspension changes during heavy braking, rapid acceleration, and sharp cornering.

PROGRAMMED RIDE CONTROL (PRC)

Ford has three similar variable shock damping systems. The original PRC system was introduced on 1987-1988 Thunderbird Turbo Coupes. A modified version called automatic ride control (ARC) followed on the 1989 Thunderbird Super Coupe and Mercury XR7, and a second PRC system appeared on the 1989 Ford Probe. The Probe system was developed by Mazda and is used on some Mazda models. All three systems automatically change strut damping according to road conditions.

Original PRC System

The original Thunderbird PRC system (Figure 12-9) consists of:

- a suspension module
- a firm shock relay
- a soft shock relay
- a steering sensor
- a brake pressure sensor
- a speed sensor
- a strut actuator at each strut
- a ride control switch

Placing the ride control switch in the FIRM position turns off the soft ride relay and activates the firm ride relay. This locks the actuators in the firm ride mode and will NOT allow the module to adjust vehicle ride regardless of sensor input. When the ride control switch is in this position, an indicator lamp located in the lower right corner of the tachometer comes on and remains lighted until the driver selects the AUTO position.

Switching to the AUTO position turns off the firm ride relay and activates the soft ride relay. The suspension system now operates in the soft ride mode, unless the control module determines from its sensor inputs that a large change is occurring in vehicle speed or direction. In such cases, the module will automatically switch modes from soft to firm and turn on the firm ride indicator lamp. When the module switches back to the soft ride mode, it turns off the indicator lamp.

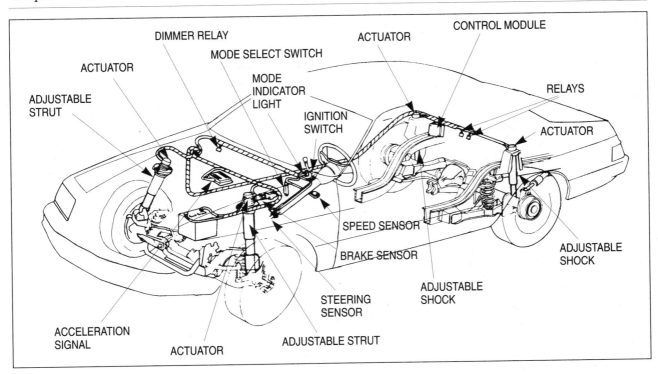

Figure 12-9 Components of the original Programmed Ride Control system installed on certain 1987-88 Thunderbirds. (Ford Motor)

The suspension module continuously monitors system operation. If it detects a system malfunction, it causes the indicator lamp to flash. When this happens, the driver should operate the ride control switch several times to clear any erroneous codes from memory. If the lamp continues to flash after the switch has been cycled, a problem exists that can be located by using the module's self-test capability.

With the ignition switch in the 'run' position, battery voltage flows to the suspension module and both relays through the No. 5 fuse. When the ride control switch is in the FIRM ride position, voltage from the energized firm ride relay rotates the actuators to their firm position. Placing the ride control switch in the AUTO position deenergizes the firm ride relay and energizes the soft ride relay. This applies battery voltage to the opposite input on the actuators, which rotate to their soft position.

Because the PRC module requires time to calculate the straight-ahead position of the vehicle when activated, the system will not respond to any changes in vehicle direction during its first 80 s of operation. This system delay can be even longer if the vehicle makes several tight turns immediately after activation but it will continue to respond to all other sensor inputs.

Automatic Ride Control (ARC)

There are four basic differences between the 1987 Thunderbird PRC system and the second generation ARC system (Figure 12-10). All other system components are the same as those used in the original PRC system, and operate in the same manner.

1. The ARC suspension module also controls the electronic variable orifice (EVO) power steering system (discussed in the chapter on Power-Asisst Steering Systems).

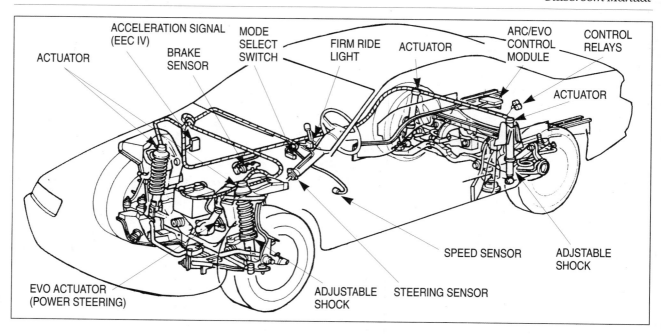

Figure 12-10 Components of the second-generation Ford PRC system renamed Automatic Ride Control. (Ford Motor)

2. Changes in the suspension module software require inputs concerning supercharger boost.
3. The ARC system can be diagnosed with a STAR or SUPER STAR II tester through a diagnostic connector in the wiring harness.
4. The actuators were modified to incorporate a continuous feedback signal to the suspension module.

Probe PRC System

This system is similar in design and operation to the original Thunderbird PRC and second generation ARC systems, but allows the driver to control three available ride modes — soft, normal, or sport. Three modes are possible because a 3-position actuator is used, instead of the 2-position actuator found in the other Ford systems. Although the driver must select the desired mode, the suspension module varies the combination of shock damping according to sensor input (Figure 12-11). For example, with the ride adjust switch set to 'normal' and the vehicle traveling under 50 mph on

a straight course, the front and rear actuators remain in the 'soft' mode. If road speed exceeds 50 mph, the front actuators will automatically switch to the 'hard' mode. Should hard cornering or braking occur above 50 mph, the suspension module also will switch the rear actuators to the 'hard' mode. As soon as the braking or cornering maneuver has been completed, the module will return the actuators to their previous setting.

TOYOTA ELECTRONICALLY MODULATED SUSPENSION (TEMS) SYSTEM

The TEMS system was introduced on some 1985 sport coupes and has since been used on other Toyota performance models. It consists of:

- a speed sensor
- a steering sensor
- the stop lamp switch
- a TP sensor input
- an actuator at each strut
- a mode control switch
- a TEMS computer (suspension module)

VEHICLE CONDITION	RIDE ADJUST SWITCH POSITION	SOFT		NORM		SPORT	
	ACTUATOR	FRONT	REAR	FRONT	REAR	FRONT	REAR
BELOW 50 mph (80 km/h) STRAIGHT AHEAD		SOFT	SOFT	SOFT	SOFT	HARD	HARD
ABOVE 50 mph (80 km/h) STRAIGHT AHEAD		SOFT	SOFT	HARD	SOFT	VERY HARD	HARD
HARD CORNERING		SOFT	SOFT	HARD	HARD	VERY HARD	VERY HARD
ABRUPT ACCELERATION (READ NOTE)		SOFT	SOFT	HARD	HARD	VERY HARD	VERY HARD
HARD BRAKING (READ NOTE)		SOFT	SOFT	HARD	HARD	VERY HARD	VERY HARD

NOTE: THE PRC SYSTEM CALCULATES THESE CRITERIA BY THE CHANGE IN VEHICLE SPEED AND STEERING ANGLE.

Figure 12-11 Probe PRC actuator positions. (Ford Motor)

The driver can select two operational modes using the switch; the suspension module can provide three damping modes. When the driver chooses the normal mode, the module will switch between the three damping modes according to vehicle speed and road conditions. If the driver chooses the 'sport' mode, the module will respond by providing only two damping modes.

COMPUTER COMMAND RIDE (CCR)

This GM variable strut damping system (Figure 12-12) was introduced on 1991 Cadillac and Oldsmobile luxury models. A variation called 'Road Sensing Suspension' (RSS) appeared on 1993 Cadillac models (Figure 12-13). The CCR system consists of:

- a suspension module
- a powertrain control module (PCM)
- a accelerometer (mercury switch)
- a speed sensor
- a strut actuator inside each strut
- a select switch

An anti-lift and anti-dive feature is provided through a signal from the power-

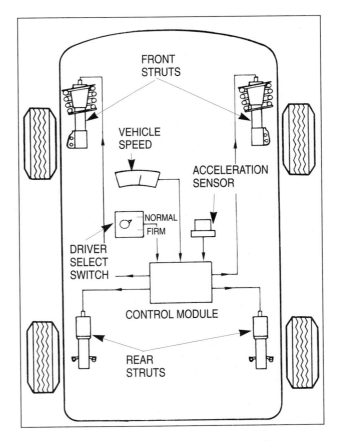

Figure 12-12 Components of the GM Computer Command Ride (CCR) system. (General Motors)

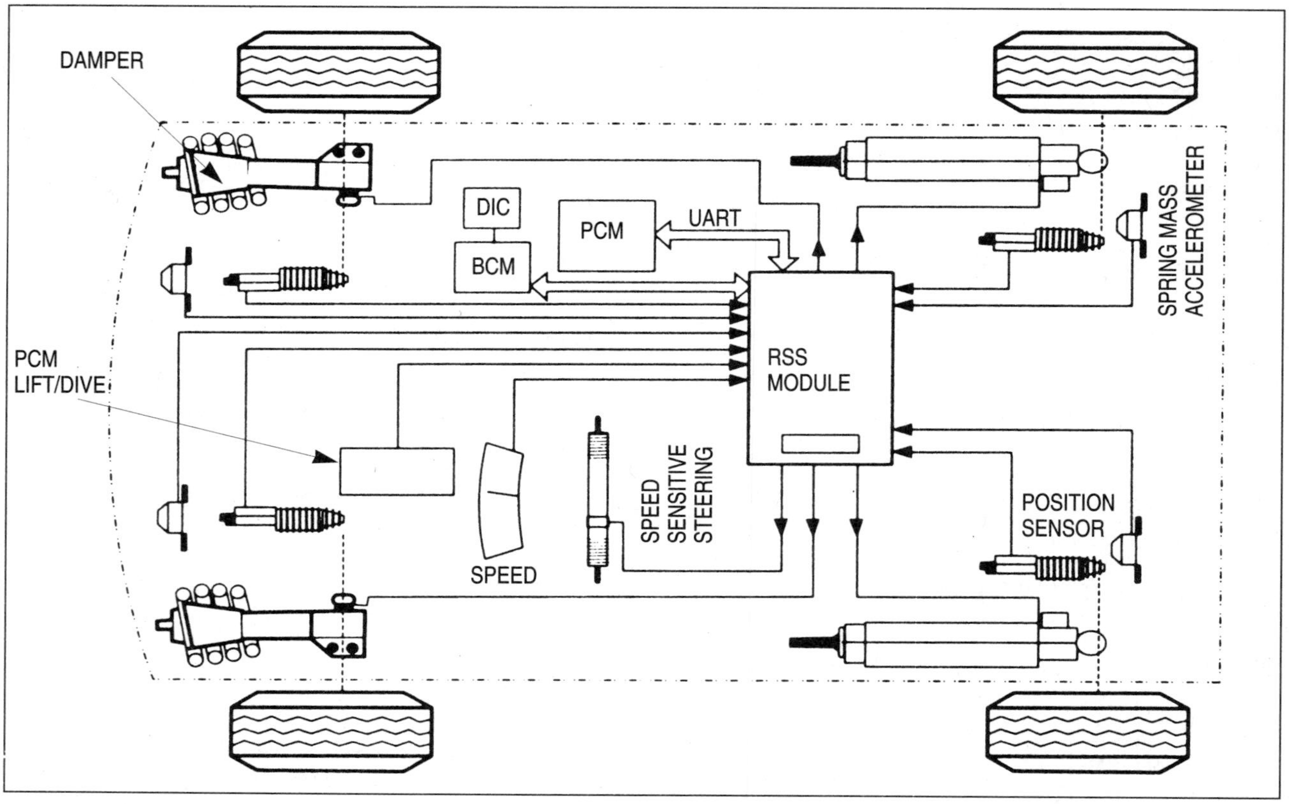

Figure 12-13 Components of the Cadillac Road Sensing Suspension (RSS) system. (General Motors)

train control module (PCM) on Allante, Eldorado, and Seville models with a powertrain interface. Other models sense acceleration through a fore-and-aft accelerometer. Except for the Allante, all models use a lateral (side-to-side) accelerometer to command the firmest damping mode when cornering conditions exceed a predetermined amount of lateral acceleration.

Operation of the CCR system is similar to that of other variable damping systems. CCR controls vehicle ride by operating a small DC actuator motor inside each strut to increase ride firmness as vehicle speed increases. The damping mode of the struts is selected by the suspension module according to vehicle speed, accelerometer input, and select switch position.

In addition to the normal fixed valve, each strut contains a selector valve connected to a DC actuator motor (Figure 12-14). The selector valve varies the size of its opening to control the amount of hydraulic fluid passing through the fixed main valve. The suspension module sets the selector valve opening to the 'comfort' or 'firm' positions (Figure 12-14); some applications have a third, or 'normal', position. The larger the opening, the more fluid passes through and the faster the piston stroke, producing a soft ride.

Under typical circumstances, the suspension module selects the light damping 'comfort' position at speeds up to about 40 mph (fluid flow wide open). If the system has a 'normal' setting, the module will select this at road speeds between 40 to about 60 mph (fluid flow slightly restricted). The module selects the 'firm' setting at road speeds above 60 mph, under heavy acceleration, or during hard braking conditions (fluid flow very restricted) to stiffen

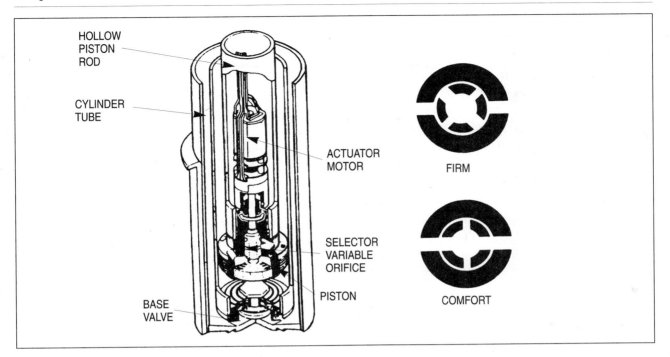

Figure 12-14 The DC motor used in CCR struts varies the selector orifice according to suspension module commands. Selector valve size regulates the amount of hydraulic fluid that passes through the fixed main valve, controlling shock damping. (Oldsmobile Division, General Motors)

the suspension. Changes in the damping rate take only about 1/10 second, and are made without input from the driver. During hard cornering maneuvers, the module will use accelerometer input to select the 'firm' setting regardless of speed, giving the driver maximum control of the vehicle.

Damping level determination depends on model application and does NOT always follow the description above. For example, if the 'normal' position is selected on a 1993 Oldsmobile 98, the system will start off in the 'firm' mode until road speed reaches about 8 mph, then switch to the 'comfort' mode (Figure 12-15). If the 'firm' position is chosen by the driver, the suspension will remain in that mode regardless of speed. To determine the exact system operation, you must refer to the carmaker's service manual for the year and model vehicle being serviced.

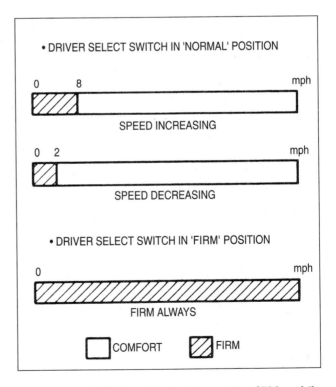

Figure 12-15 CCR damping level operation. (Oldsmobile Division, General Motors)

The suspension module also receives a feedback signal from each strut to determine proper system operation. If the module receives an incorrect feedback signal, or otherwise determines that the system is malfunctioning, it sets a diagnostic trouble code (DTC) and switches the system to the 'firm' mode. When the module sets a DTC, it illuminates a SERVICE CCR SYSTEM lamp in the Driver Information Center (DIC). On vehicles that are not equipped with a DIC, the two light-emitting diodes (LEDs) on the driver select switch glow to indicate a system problem. The exact method of DTC retrieval also differs according to model application.

The RSS system uses sensors to measure body velocity and wheel position during suspension travel. The control module can respond to changes in road irregularity in less than 15 milliseconds. Each RSS strut contains an integral two-position solenoid valve. The solenoids are 'on' for a soft ride and 'off' for a firm ride. Vertical velocity of the vehicle body is measured by four accelerometers; one on each front strut tower and one on each side of the rear crossmember. Four position sensors are installed between the control arms and body to measure wheel location relative to the body.

The RSS control module receives input data from the vehicle speed sensor, the accelerometers, and the position sensors. In addition, it also receives a calculated lift/dive signal from the powertrain control module (PCM). When the module detects a system malfunction, it illuminates a SERVICE RIDE CONTROL lamp in the DIC.

MERCEDES-BENZ ADAPTIVE DAMPING SYSTEM (ADS)

The ADS system was introduced as an option on 1991 Mercedes-Benz models. Like other variable shock damping systems, it also controls hydraulic fluid flow in the struts through electronically controlled valves, but uses a different approach. The ADS system consists of the following components:

- suspension module
- steering angle sensor
- body acceleration sensor
- suspension acceleration sensor
- a strut at each wheel
- a variable damping unit with pressure container at each strut
- ride control switch
- indicator lamp.

Variable damping units at each wheel connect the top of each strut with a pressure container. The pressure containers act much like an accumulator in an antilock brake system, and contain hydraulic fluid and compressed nitrogen gas separated by a diaphragm. The damping units contain two solenoid valves and two sets of damping pistons. By directing fluid through one or both sets of pistons, the solenoid valves change the balance of pressure between the strut and pressure container to automatically provide four different damping settings — 'comfort', 'soft', 'normal', or 'firm'.

Since the solenoid valves remain closed when the system is not operating, the hydraulic fluid flows through both sets of damping pistons to produce the firmest setting. The solenoids can change valve settings in as little as 1/20 second, allowing the ADS system to respond quickly to changes in driving conditions. Although a ride control switch allows the driver to choose between 'comfort' and 'sport' ranges, the driver has no control over which damping setting the suspension module selects. If the driver places the system in the 'sport' range, the module will switch to the 'firm' setting more often than the 'comfort' setting.

A steering angle sensor installed directly behind the steering wheel sends a position signal to the suspension module. The body acceleration sensor is located at the front of the left strut tower, while the suspension acceleration sensor is positioned on the right front steering knuckle. Both sensors respond to up-and-down motion by sending a voltage signal to the module. The module uses these signals to determine whether to close or open the solenoid valves in the variable damping units.

> **⚠ WARNING:** Variable shock damping systems like the Mercedes-Benz ADS that pressurize the hydraulic fluid must be depressurized before disconnecting any hydraulic line to any part of the suspension. This involves connecting hoses to the bleed valves and draining the system fluid. Be sure to check the carmaker's service manual for the correct procedures to be followed.

An indicator lamp in the instrument cluster glows when the engine is started, and then goes off. If this lamp does NOT go off, or if it glows while the engine is running, there is a system problem. If a problem exists, strut damping automatically switches to the 'firm' setting and the ADS system is disabled.

ELECTRONIC LEVEL CONTROL (ELC) SYSTEMS

Electronic level control systems, sometimes called automatic leveling or ride height control systems, are simply computer-controlled versions of the static load-leveling systems found on luxury vehicles for decades. As such, they are really assist systems that work with the vehicle's coil springs to maintain trim height, unlike the stand-alone air spring suspension systems to be discussed later in this chapter.

ELC systems generally control trim height only at the rear wheels. These systems rely on a single sensor to keep the suspension module informed of vehicle height at the rear. The module controls operation of an air compressor to control trim height by adding air to the air shocks, or venting it from them. We will examine the components used in ELC systems, and then look at how they operate in specific systems.

SENSORS

The only sensor required by an ELC system is one that will measure changes in trim or ride height. The design and operation of a height sensor is dependent on the leveling system design, but two basic types are used in an ELC system:

- rotary optical sensors
- linear magnetic sensors

Rotary Optical Sensors

This type of height sensor contains a slotted disc or shutter inside a housing with a photocell. As the disc or shutter rotates, it makes or breaks the **photoelectric** circuit. This signals the suspension module to either operate the air compressor or the exhaust solenoid. The sensor housing is attached to the frame rail, a crossmember, or some other non-moving vehicle component. The sensor actuator arm is connected by a short link to a moveable part of the suspension, such as the rear upper control arm or a track bar (Figure 12-16). The sensor may contain the system logic and circuitry to process its own signal, or it may send the signal to a suspension module for trim level determination. The system will contain a time delay feature to prevent it from operating under normal ride conditions.

Linear Magnetic Sensors

Linear sensors (also called magnetic switches) are installed between the body or

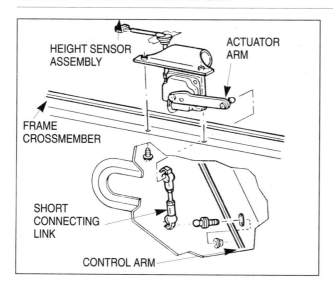

Figure 12-16 The actuator arm of a rotary height sensor connects to a moveable part of the suspension. (Ford Motor)

frame rail and the suspension control arm (Figure 12-17). The sensor end connected to the control arm contains sliding magnets which move with changes in vehicle height. Some magnetic switches are an integral part of a shock or strut assembly, and the entire shock/strut assembly must be replaced if the switch is defective (Figure 12-18).

Magnet movement generates a voltage signal that passes through two switches containing electronic circuits. The switches transmit the signal to the suspension module. If the vehicle is at its proper trim height, then both switches remain closed and the module does NOT receive any trim signal. Upward movement of the magnets will open one switch, which sends

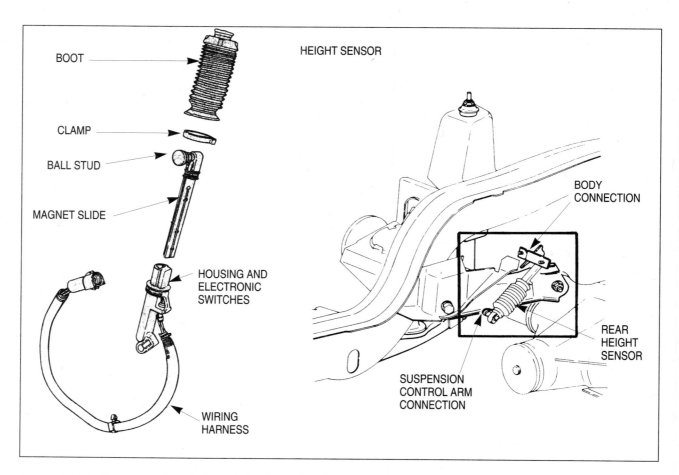

Figure 12-17 The magnetic switch end of a linear height sensor also connects to a movable suspension part. (Ford Motor)

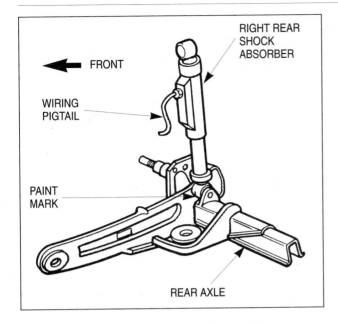

Figure 12-18 The magnetic switch of a linear sensor may be an integral part of a shock absorber or strut on some vehicles. (Chrysler)

an above-trim signal; downward movement reverses switch position and a below-trim signal is sent to the module. By monitoring the opening and closing of the switches, the module is able to determine changes in trim height.

SUSPENSION MODULES

With the exception of the combined sensor/module used in the Chrysler Electronic Height Control System and GM Electronic Level Control System, suspension modules used with ELC systems incorporate a diagnostic capability similar to that of the more sophisticated modules used with variable shock damping systems. In addition, they contain time delay circuitry that prevents the suspension from constantly reacting to momentary road irregularities and excessively cycling the air compressor. A separate timing circuit prevents continuous compressor operation in the case of a system leak or a vent/exhaust failure in the open mode.

Some modules may indicate system malfunctioning by flashing indicator lamps; others contain a self-diagnostic program and will set a diagnostic trouble code (DTC) if a malfunction occurs. The system may be designed to allow DTC retrieval through a flashing indicator lamp, an analog voltmeter, or with special test equipment.

ACTUATORS

An air compressor is the primary actuator in an ELC system; an air vent or exhaust solenoid valve is the secondary actuator (Figure 12-19). The compressor operates with battery voltage and supplies the air pressure necessary to operate the system. A self-regenerating dryer attached to the compressor manifold contains silica gel to remove moisture from air entering or leaving the system. Pressurized air is transmitted to the shocks through nylon

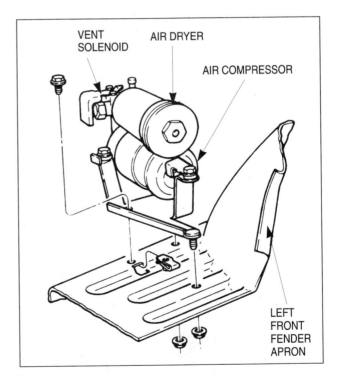

Figure 12-19 The air compressor, dryer, and vent solenoid generally take the form of an integral unit in load leveling or height control systems. (Ford Motor)

lines. The vent or exhaust solenoid provides the passage for air leaving the system. An internal valve maintains a residual pressure in the system to prevent pressure at the rear shock absorbers from falling below their minimum operating level.

SYSTEM EXAMPLES

To illustrate the basic approaches to ELC systems, we will look at three different systems currently in use:

- Chrysler Automatic Air Load Leveling System
- Ford Rear Load Leveling System
- GM Electronic Level Control (ELC) System

Each system operates only on the rear wheels, and adjusts vehicle trim height according to mass load.

CHRYSLER AUTOMATIC AIR LOAD LEVELING SYSTEM

This system began life in 1986 as the Electronic Height Control System, an optional rear suspension on some Chrysler FWD vehicles. The original system consisted of a combination height sensor/module, an air compressor with integral exhaust solenoid, air shocks, and the necessary connecting lines and wiring (Figure 12-20). The adjustable air shock absorbers are standard shock absorbers, but with a rubber sleeve connected between the dust boot and shock reservoir to form a flexible air chamber around the outside. The shock absorber extends when pressure is increased in the air chamber; reducing chamber pressure allows the vehicle mass to collapse the shock absorber.

Turning the ignition 'on' provides power to the height sensor and one side of the

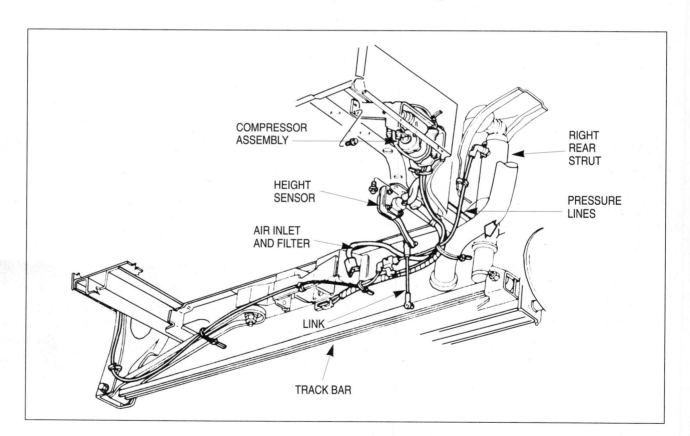

Figure 12-20 Components of the Chrysler Electronic Height Control (EHC) system. (Chrysler)

compressor relay coil. A 42 ±4 s delay sequence in the height sensor circuitry allows the module to determine vehicle load condition. If the vehicle load condition is found to be normal, a replenishment mode activates the compressor through the relay for 3 to 5 seconds to maintain the shock air pressure between 14 and 21 psi. If the vehicle load condition is NOT normal, the sensor circuitry operates the air compressor through the relay until a level vehicle condition is sensed.

When the change in vehicle trim height exceeds what the module logic will accept as normal during a key-on cycle, a 13 to 27 second delay sequence occurs before the compressor is activated to correct a low trim height or the exhaust solenoid is opened to correct a high trim height. If the ignition is turned off with the vehicle unloaded, the exhaust solenoid also operates to prevent a high trim height with an unloaded vehicle.

The position of the height sensor arm can be readjusted within a one-inch range when minor changes in trim height are necessary (Figure 12-21). If this adjustment fails to bring trim height with specifications, check for possible damage to the suspension components.

A second generation system appeared in 1990 on some Chrysler FWD vehicles. This system was renamed Automatic Air Load Leveling (Figure 12-22) and differs from the original one in the following respects:
- A magnetic switch sensor installed in the right rear air shock absorber monitors rear vehicle height.
- A separate suspension module controls the ground circuits for the compressor relay and exhaust valve solenoid.
- The module program contains a self-diagnostics feature NOT present in the initial system.
- Time delay sequences are changed.

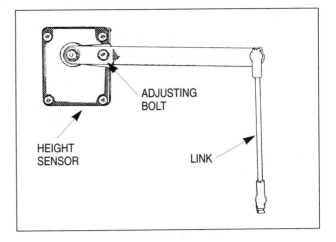

Figure 12-21 The Chrysler EHC height sensor can be adjusted within a specified range. (Chrysler)

The initial key-on delay of 13-27 s is extended to 22-28 s. All other time delays are 12-18 s.

FORD REAR LOAD LEVELING SUSPENSION

Also called the Automatic Leveling System by Ford, this system consists of air-adjustable rear shocks, an air compressor with an integral exhaust solenoid, a dryer unit with a minimum retention valve, a compressor relay, a rotary height sensor, a suspension module, and the connecting lines and wiring (Figure 12-23).

System operation is essentially the same as that of the Chrysler system described above, but with the following differences:
- The dryer assembly retention valve maintains a minimum 10 to 24 psi to the rear shock absorbers for proper operation at all times.
- The suspension module does NOT activate the system for 10 s after the ignition is turned on. It also delays air compressor or exhaust solenoid operation for 7 to 13 s between cycles. This prevents continuous compressor or solenoid operation during normal ride motions. The

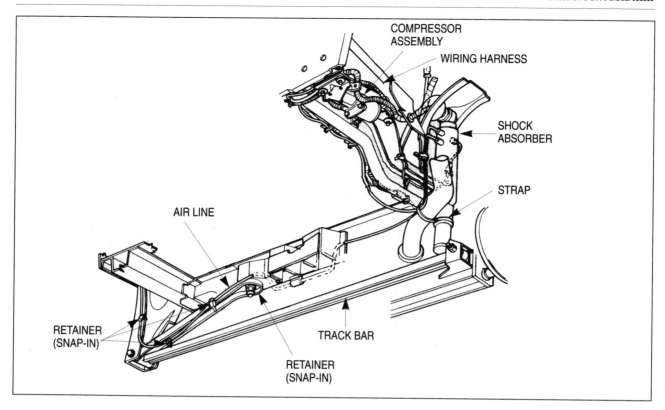

Figure 12-22 Components of the Chrysler Automatic Air Load Leveling system, a second-generation application of the original EHC system. (Chrysler)

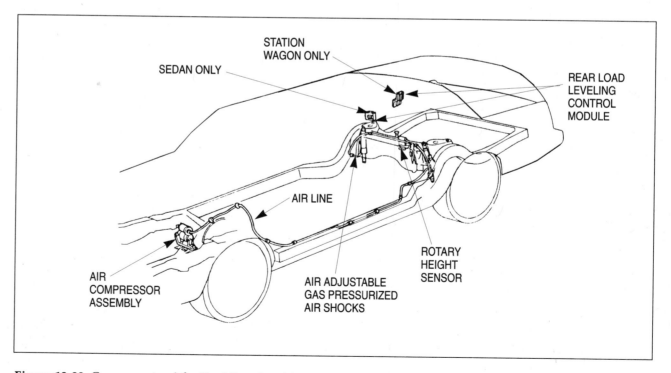

Figure 12-23 Components of the Ford Rear Load Leveling Suspension. (Ford Motor)

module also limits compressor operation to two minutes, and exhaust solenoid operation to a maximum of one minute. This prevents nonstop operation in case of a leak.

- The suspension module contains a self-diagnostic function using a test lamp and analog voltmeter.
- An indicator lamp in the instrument cluster glows when the ignition is turned on; then it goes out. The lamp flashes when the compressor is running, and remains on if a malfunction occurs in the system.

GM ELECTRONIC LEVEL CONTROL (ELC) SYSTEM

The ELC is very similar in design and operation to the original electronic height control system used by Chrysler. It consists of a combination height sensor/module, an air compressor with integral exhaust solenoid, compressor relay, pressure limiter valve, air struts, and the necessary connecting lines and wiring. The height sensor is installed on the underbody frame in the rear and its actuating arm link-connected to the right rear control arm. A 7 to 10 second delay built into the sensor circuitry prevents the compressor relay or exhaust solenoid circuits from energizing during normal ride motions. Voltage is applied at all times to the height sensor, relay, and exhaust solenoid, allowing the system to change vehicle height even when the ignition is off. Voltage is applied to the height sensor only when the ignition switch is in the 'run' position. When the ignition is turned to the 'run' position and vehicle load is sensed as normal, an internal timer circuit activates for 35 to 45 s. Once this circuit times out, the compressor comes on for 3 to 5 s to maintain the shock air pressure between 7 and 14 psi. A pressure limiter

valve in the compressor line restricts maximum strut pressure to 64-74 psi.

Adding a load to the vehicle moves its body downward, and the height sensor arm upward. The relay coil is energized after a 17 to 27 second delay, closing the relay contacts. This applies battery voltage to the compressor, which inflates the struts. As the body moves upward, the sensor arm moves downward until it returns to its original position (±1") and de-energizes the relay to shut the compressor off. Removing the load from the vehicle reverses body and sensor arm movement, exhausting air through the exhaust solenoid until the sensor arm returns to its original position (±1").

Like the Chrysler application, the height sensor arm can be readjusted within a one-inch range when minor changes in trim height are necessary. If this adjustment fails to bring trim height with specifications, check for a problem with the rear springs or suspension.

AIR SPRING SUSPENSION SYSTEMS

An air spring suspension system replaces the conventional coil spring suspension at all four wheels, providing automatic height control and low spring rates to improve a vehicle's suspension characteristics. The first computer-controlled air spring suspension appeared on the 1984 Lincoln Mark VII and Continental models. Since that time, Ford has combined the basic air spring system with the Thunderbird PRC system to produce the air suspension and automatic ride control (ASARC) suspension used on the 1988 Continental. Further improvements added a speed-dependent height adjustment feature introduced on the 1993 Mark VIII. Chrysler introduced a similar air spring suspension system on selected 1990 models.

Air spring suspensions are stand-alone systems, NOT an assist to the vehicle's coil springs. The four-wheel system forms three subsystems by using a height sensor at each front wheel and one for both rear wheels. To maintain proper trim height, the suspension module receives inputs from the three height sensors, ignition switch, brake switch, and door courtesy switches. Such systems are more sophisticated than the ones we have discussed to this point, combining variable shock damping and ride height control with variable spring height and rates. A reduced spring rate gives a smooth ride at cruising speed; increasing the spring rates stiffens the suspension to minimize body roll during acceleration, cornering, and braking. Varying the spring height changes the vehicle's ride height, increasing control over vehicle handling.

Sensors

All air spring suspension systems use ride height sensors. The more sophisticated systems that incorporate variable shock damping also use the same sensors discussed earlier in this chapter. We have already discussed the rotary optical and linear magnetic types of ride height sensors used with ELC systems; air spring suspensions use a third type — the rotary **Hall-effect sensor** (Figure 12-24). The sensor housing contains two Hall-effect switches to provide the above-trim and below-trim signals. By passing current through the Hall element (a semiconductor material) in one direction, and applying a magnetic field at a right angle to its surface, the Hall element can be made to generate a small voltage. Rotating a shutter between the Hall element and a magnetic rotor creates a magnetic shunt, changing the field strength through the Hall element. The signal voltage created by the Hall element (an IC chip) is sent to an output voltage generator,

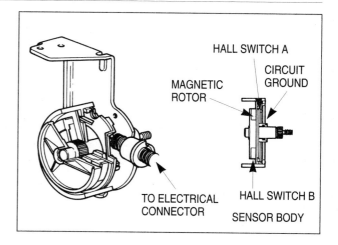

Figure 12-24 The rotary height sensor used with Ford air spring suspension systems contains two Hall-effect switches and a magnetic rotor. The Hall-effect switches provide the suspension module with above- and below-trim signals. (Ford Motor)

where it is converted to a square wave or digital pulse.

Suspension Modules

Air spring systems modules contain more sophisticated software than that used with ELC systems, especially if the system incorporates a variable damping function. In addition to their more complicated programming, such modules often are capable of expanded self-diagnostics to determine malfunctions. As a general rule, they also set a greater variety of diagnostic trouble codes (DTC).

Actuators

Just as in an ELC system, an air compressor is the primary actuator in an air spring system; an air vent or exhaust solenoid valve is the secondary actuator. In addition to these, some systems use an air spring solenoid valve. The primary and secondary actuators operate in the same way as in an ELC system, but the suspension module must also open and close the air spring solenoid valve as required.

SYSTEM EXAMPLES

Air suspension systems replace the coil springs of a conventional suspension with air springs at the front and rear to provide four-wheel ride height control. The more sophisticated systems found on late-model vehicles also incorporate variable shock damping and ride height control with air spring damping. To understand air suspension system development, we will look at the following systems:

- Ford Air Suspension System
- Ford Air Suspension and Automatic Ride Control (ASARC)
- Ford Speed-Dependent Air Suspension System
- Chrysler Automatic Air Suspension.

FORD AIR SUSPENSION SYSTEM

The Air Suspension System first appeared on 1984 Lincoln Mark VII and Continental models, and forms the basic system of all other Ford air spring suspensions. The system is air-operated and computer-con-

trolled to provide automatic front and rear load leveling. In this respect, it operates much like the two-wheel ELC systems described earlier, but the suspension module logic is more complicated, and the variable rate air spring design is unique. Figure 12-25 shows the system components.

Made of rubber and plastic, the air springs support the vehicle load. Front air springs are mounted in spring pockets between the crossmember and lower control arms, while the rear air springs are mounted ahead of the rear axle between the body subframe side members and the lower control arms (Figure 12-26). This mounting arrangement is similar to that used with a conventional coil spring suspension. The vehicle's mass rides on a cushion of compressed air contained within the air spring's rubber membrane. During vehicle operation, normal suspension actions like jounce and rebound are controlled by the flexible rubber membrane and the compressibility of the air in the spring. Air is added to, or removed from, the spring

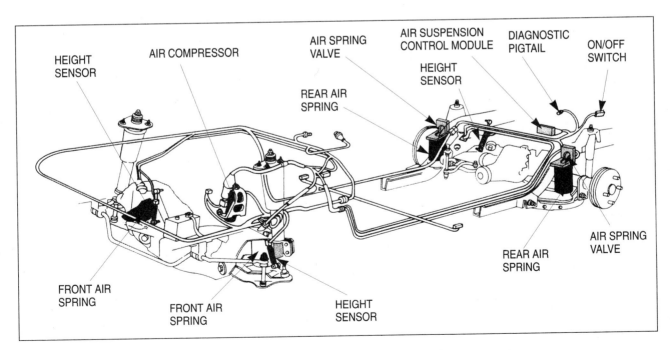

Figure 12-25 Components of the Ford Air Suspension System. (Ford Motor)

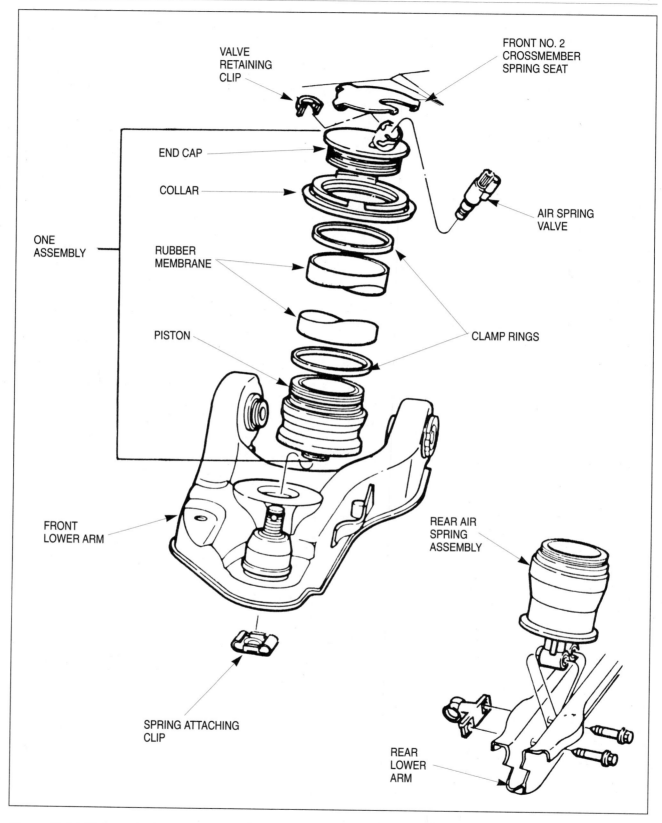

VALVE RETAINING CLIP

FRONT NO. 2 CROSSMEMBER SPRING SEAT

END CAP

COLLAR

AIR SPRING VALVE

ONE ASSEMBLY

RUBBER MEMBRANE

CLAMP RINGS

PISTON

FRONT LOWER ARM

REAR AIR SPRING ASSEMBLY

SPRING ATTACHING CLIP

REAR LOWER ARM

Figure 12-26 This exploded view shows air spring construction and mounting locations. (Ford Motor)

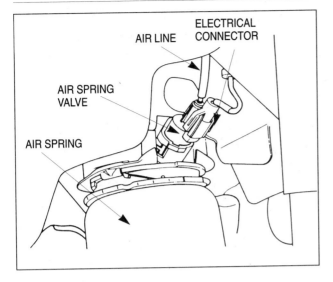

Figure 12-27 A cross section of the air spring solenoid valve used by Ford, and its location in the top of the air spring. (Ford Motor)

through a solenoid valve controlled by the suspension module (Figure 12-27), as in the previous systems described. Spring design and operation are shown in Figure 12-28.

When air is added to or released from the air springs, it is for the purpose of maintaining trim height, NOT to compensate for road surface irregularities. Air spring compression that results from road irregularities increases pressure inside the spring. As pressure increases, the air spring resists compression until pressure is great enough to stop further suspension compression. At this point, the air spring pushes back against the suspension, changing to rebound mode and returning the wheel to its original position. This compression and release of air produces a

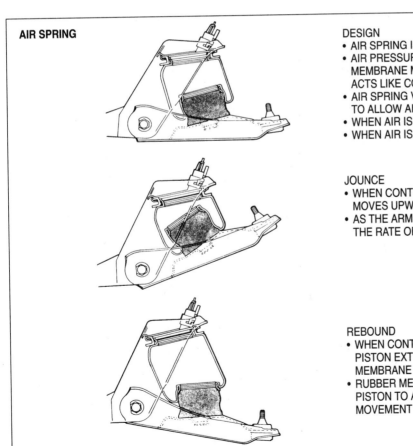

AIR SPRING

DESIGN
• AIR SPRING IS AT NORMAL TRIM HEIGHT
• AIR PRESSURE CONTAINED IN RUBBER MEMBRANE MAINTAINS VEHICLE HEIGHT AND ACTS LIKE COIL SPRING
• AIR SPRING VALVE MOUNTED IN END CAP OPENS TO ALLOW AIR TO ENTER AND EXIT SPRING
• WHEN AIR IS ADDED, VEHICLE WILL RISE
• WHEN AIR IS REMOVED VEHICLE WILL LOWER

JOUNCE
• WHEN CONTROL ARM MOVES UPWARD, PISTON MOVES UPWARD INTO RUBBER MEMBRANE
• AS THE ARM MOVES UPWARD TOWARD JOUNCE THE RATE OF THE AIR SPRING INCREASES

REBOUND
• WHEN CONTROL ARM MOVES DOWNWARD, PISTON EXTENDS OUTWARD FROM RUBBER MEMBRANE
• RUBBER MEMBRANE UNFOLDS FROM AROUND PISTON TO ALLOW DOWNWARD SUSPENSION MOVEMENT

Figure 12-28 Operation of the air spring used in Ford's air suspension system. (Ford Motor)

variable spring rate, since the air spring acts like a soft spring when traveling over small obstacles, and as a hard spring if the vehicle strikes large obstacles. It also operates at any rate between the minimum and maximum required by the suspension system. The ability to tailor air spring rate according to road conditions makes such a suspension far more flexible than one using standard steel coil springs. In the case of coil springs, the carmaker can design two different spring rates into the suspension by the manner in which the coil spring is wound, but this limitation affects ride quality. A standard coil spring system also is limited since it cannot adjust trim height without the use of another subsystem.

The suspension module receives input signals from the vehicle door and brake switches, as well as the three height sensors (Figure 12-25). These sensors keep the module informed of changes in load, and actions of the vehicle occupants such as opening or closing a door or applying the brakes. When the system is operational, the suspension module checks sensor inputs against a time delay before generating any output signals. This prevents any system action until the module is certain that the vehicle is out of trim and NOT just hitting road irregularities. If the module determines that a sensor's input signal is incorrect, or that a part of the system has malfunctioned, it will turn on an amber indicator lamp in the overhead console as an indication to the driver that system service is required. During diagnostic testing, the indicator lamp also blinks the test number being run during the test.

FORD AIR SUSPENSION AND AUTOMATIC RIDE CONTROL (ASARC)

This system was introduced on the 1988 Continental (Figure 12-29) and is basically a combination of the air suspension system just described and the second generation Thunderbird variable shock damping system or automatic ride control (ARC) system described earlier in this chapter. Figure 12-30 is a block diagram of the ASARC system.

Some ASARC system components were changed or are modified versions of those used in the original systems:

- Hall-effect rotary sensors (Figure 12-24) replace the linear magnetic sensors used with the air suspension system.
- MacPherson struts (Figure 12-31) containing an integral air spring and 2-stage shock absorber replace the individual shocks and air springs used in the original systems.
- Counterbalancing torsion springs on the rear suspension (Figure 12-32) produces an outward force on the rear struts to reduce strut side load and twisting induced by the rear wheels.
- Suspension module software integrates both air spring and ARC logic and adds new control features of its own, such as using steering angle sensor input to calculate steering wheel turning rate in addition to its position. This data allows the module to switch shock damping under a wider variety of conditions, such as accident avoidance maneuvers.
- Module diagnostic software can locate over 50 specific component or system failures, including intermittent conditions. A diagnostic trouble code (DTC) can be set in module memory for each failure, and retrieved with the STAR tester or any scan tool with this system test capability.

FORD SPEED-DEPENDENT AIR SUSPENSION SYSTEM

The combined air suspension and automatic ride control (ASARC) system

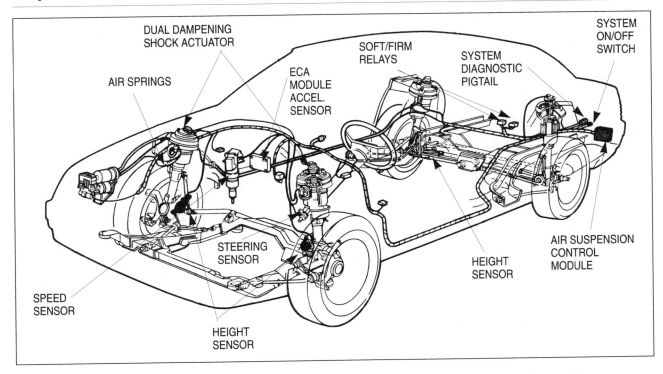

Figure 12-29 Components of the Ford ASARC system as introduced on the 1988 Continental. (Ford Motor)

used on the 1988 Continental was divided back into its individual systems for use with the 1993 Mark VIII (Figure 12-33 and Figure 12-34). The air suspension system now uses inputs from the vehicle speed sensor to determine the correct trim height of the vehicle according to its speed. Above approximately 55 mph, the suspension system automatically lowers the vehicle trim height by 0.8 inch. When vehicle speed drops below about 45 mph, the suspension raises the vehicle to a higher trim position. Ford calls this feature 'speed-leveling' and claims it provides better handling at higher speeds, as well as improved fuel economy. The control module is now called a suspension/steering module (SSN). Other than the software programming of the SSN module, the major difference in this air suspension system and its operation is a return to the linear magnetic height sensors used on the original air suspension system.

The Mark VIII variable shock damping system (Figure 12-34) uses a separate shock damping control (SDC) module to control rear and end lift during hard braking conditions. It operates only on the rear shock absorbers, and its only input signal is provided by the brake pressure switch. The rear shocks remain in the Soft mode when brake hydraulic pressure is below 750 psi; as pressure rises above this level, the SDC module switches the shocks to their Firm mode.

CHRYSLER AUTOMATIC AIR SUSPENSION

Chrysler's air suspension design (Figure 12-35) uses air struts at the front, and air springs at the rear. Each front air strut contains an integral magnetic height sensor and airflow solenoid. Rear air springs contain individual airflow solenoids, but the rear magnetic height sensor is an integral part of the right rear shock absorber (Figure 12-36). Basic system

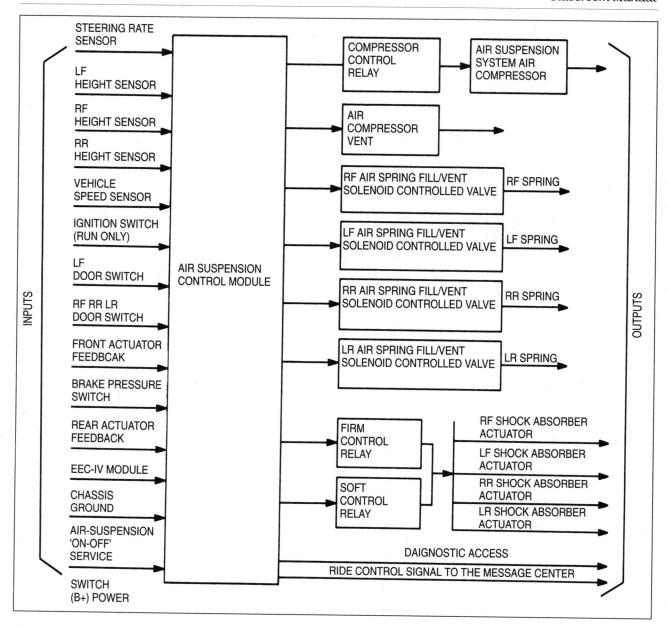

Figure 12-30 A block diagram of the ASARC system. (Ford Motor)

operation is similar to that of the original Ford air suspension, with the suspension module controlling the ground circuits of the compressor relay, exhaust solenoid valve, and the front/rear solenoid valves. The module logic contains a 14-16 s delay to prevent excessive compressor/exhaust solenoid cycling during normal ride conditions, and limits compressor on-time to 170-190 s to prevent compressor damage. It also receives a throttle position (TP) sensor input and will inhibit system operation whenever throttle angle exceeds 65%.

The system also is non-operational under the following conditions:

- the trunk lid is open
- one or more doors are open

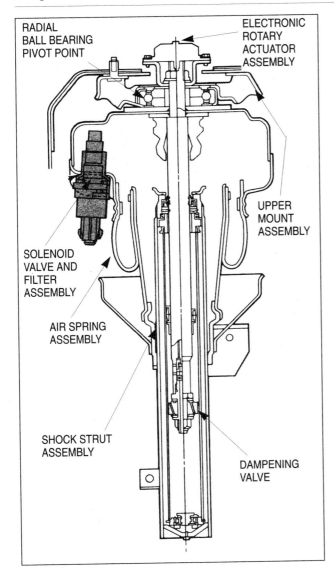

Figure 12-31 A cross section of the combined shock strut and air spring assembly as used with the Ford ASARC system. (Ford Motor)

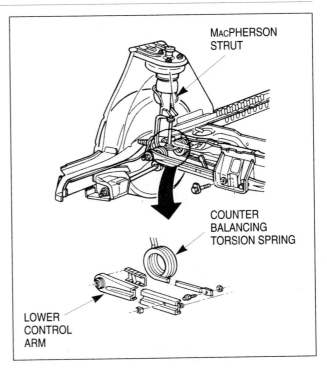

Figure 12-32 Counter-balancing torsion springs are used in the ASARC system to reduce strut side load. (Ford Motor)

- the service brake is applied
- charging system failure
- during high speed cornering maneuvers.

If the module determines that a part of the system has malfunctioned, it will turn on an amber indicator lamp in the overhead console as an indication to the driver that system service is required. Diagnostics require the use of Chrysler's DRB II tester and the appropriate Chassis (Air Suspension) software cartridge. Once the DRB II tester is connected to the system, it completely checks the system status and lists the steps required to diagnose the failure.

SONAR SUSPENSIONS

The electronic control modules discussed in this chapter are programmed to react to vehicle and road conditions. The suspension systems they control provide a ride that is noticeably superior to most conventional suspensions, especially under adverse driving conditions. But what if the control module could be programmed to anticipate up-coming road conditions, and make the necessary corrections ahead of time? This is the logic underlying **sonic road surface sensing**, developed by the Japanese.

The sonar sensor sends ultrasonic waves against the road surface ahead of the

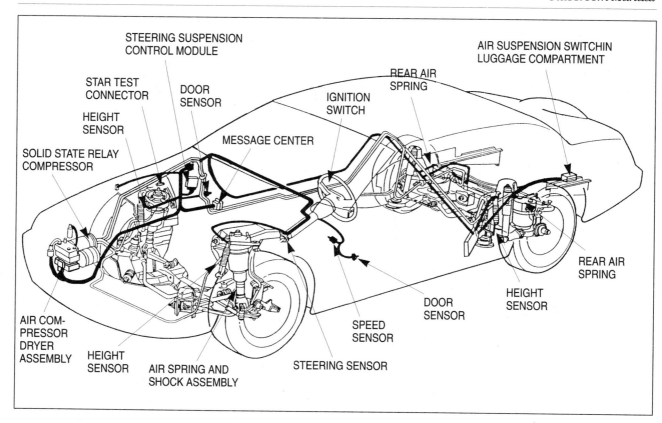

Figure 12-33 Components of the 1993 Mark VIII Speed-Leveling Air Suspension system. (Ford Motor)

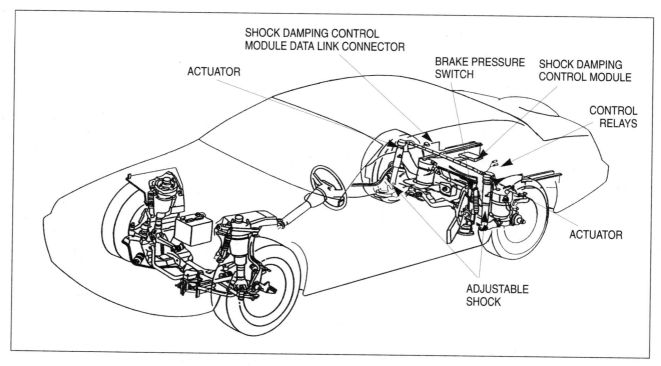

Figure 12-34 Components of the 1993 Mark VIII Shock Damping Control system. (Ford Motor)

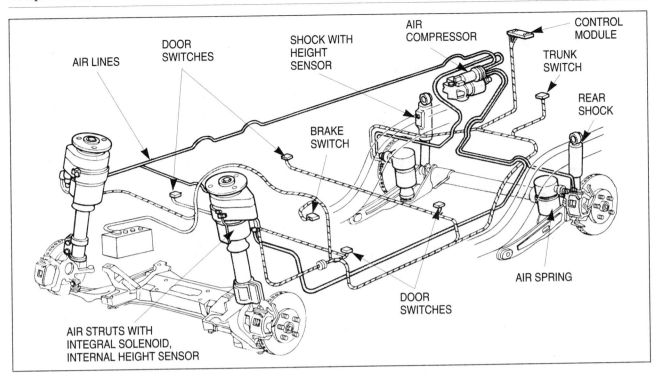

Figure 12-35 Components of the Chrysler Automatic Air Suspension system. (Chrysler)

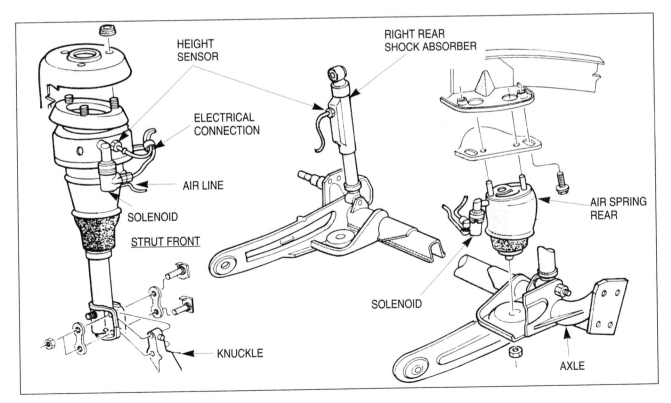

Figure 12-36 The height sensors are integral parts of the air struts and shock absorbers in Chrysler's air suspension system. (Chrysler)

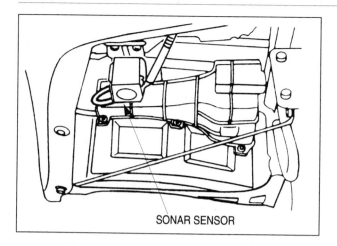

SONAR SENSOR

Figure 12-37 A sonar sensor detects upcoming road surface variations so that the actuators compensate for any rough conditions. (Nissan)

car and reads the signals that bounce back to sense bumps or dips before the car approaches them. Input signals to the control module come from various sensors:

- the speed sensor signal is used for determining the length of time between the sonar recognizing road irregularities and when the vehicle will reach them.
- the steering angle sensor data enables the control module to help it make the required calculations during turns.
- the throttle position and brake sensors inform the module about acceleration and deceleration, allowing it to change shock dampening as required to prevent front end dive or rear end squat.

Nissan has a sonar system on the Maxima and the Infiniti M30 (Figure 12-37).

SUMMARY

Until the computer arrived, suspension design was the science of combining a comfortable ride with acceptable road handling to obtain a satisfactory compromise. Non-computerized suspensions with fixed spring rates and shock absorber valving are called 'passive' suspensions. Suspensions that use a computer module to integrate spring dampening, shock absorber valving, and ride height into a single system that functions according to road conditions are called 'active' suspensions.

Shock absorbers controlled by a computer module first appeared in the mid-1980's on Japanese vehicles, and have since become the basis of the programmed ride control (PRC) systems found on many current vehicles. Such systems use input from a steering angle sensor to control actuators at each shock absorber that change the shock valving and vary the damping rate.

Automatic load leveling systems using a single height sensor have been available on luxury cars for several decades, but the application of the computer to such systems makes them far more versatile. An air spring suspension replaces the coil spring suspension on all four wheels, and uses separate height sensors at each front wheel. A third sensor controls the rear wheels as an axle set. Height sensors may be one of three designs — rotary optical, rotary Hall-effect, or linear magnetic switches. Electrical solenoids generally act as suspension actuators.

☏ REVIEW QUESTIONS

1. Technician A says a non-computerized load leveling system is a dynamic form of road control. Technician B says spring rates and shock absorber valving is fixed in a passive suspension. Who is right?
   (A) A only
   (B) B only
   (C) Both A and B
   (D) Neither A nor B

2. Technician A says automatic load leveling systems have been available for several decades on luxury cars. Technician B says an active suspension can respond to road conditions instantly. Who is right?
   (A) A only
   (B) B only
   (C) Both A and B
   (D) Neither A nor B

3. Technician A says the size of the shock absorber metering orifices are changed by an actuator to produce the desired damping in a programmed ride control (PRC) system. Technician B says variable shock damping systems first appeared on German luxury vehicles. Who is right?
   (A) A only
   (B) B only
   (C) Both A and B
   (D) Neither A nor B

4. Which of the following sensors is NOT used by a variable shock damping system?
   (A) brake sensor
   (B) speed sensor
   (C) steering angle sensor
   (D) height sensor

5. Technician A says the steering angle is measured by a linear magnetic sensor in the shock absorber. Technician B says it is a photo sensor mounted on the steering shaft that measures it. Who is right?

   (A) A only
   (B) B only
   (C) Both A and B
   (D) Neither A nor B

6. Technician A says a shock absorber actuator may be an integral part of the shock or an external device connected to an internal control rod. Technician B says some actuators use a reduction gear to rotate the control rod. Who is right?
   (A) A only
   (B) B only
   (C) Both A and B
   (D) Neither A nor B

7. Technician A says a pressure switch installed in the brake line can act as a brake sensor in a variable shock damping system. Technician B says input from the throttle position (TP) sensor tells the module when the brakes are applied. Who is right?
   (A) A only
   (B) B only
   (C) Both A and B
   (D) Neither A nor B

8. Technician A says a 2-wheel automatic leveling system uses a height sensor at each wheel. Technician B says a 4-wheel system uses three height sensors. Who is right?
   (A) A only
   (B) B only
   (C) Both A and B
   (D) Neither A nor B

9. Which of the following sensor types is NOT used in road height control systems or air spring suspension systems?
   (A) rotary Hall-effect
   (B) rotary optical
   (C) linear magnetic
   (D) linear Hall-effect

10. Technician A says the air compressor is the primary actuator in an electronic level

control (ELC). Technician B says a self-regenerating dryer removes moisture from the air used in an ELC. Who is right?

(A) A only
(B) B only
(C) Both A and B
(D) Neither A nor B

11. Technician A says an ELC system adds air to the shocks to increase trim height and exhausts air to decrease trim height. Technician B says the system exhausts air to increase trim height and adds air to decrease trim height. Who is right?

(A) A only
(B) B only
(C) Both A and B
(D) Neither A nor B

12. Technician A says separate sensors are required when two or more vehicle control systems require a speed input. Technician B says a signal from a single speed sensor can be shared by two or more systems. Who is right?

(A) A only
(B) B only
(C) Both A and B
(D) Neither A nor B

13. Technician A says a suspension module with a self-diagnostic program sets a diagnostic trouble code (DTC) when a malfunction occurs. Technician B says modules without self-diagnostics indicate a malfunction by flashing indicator lamps. Who is right?

(A) A only
(B) B only
(C) Both A and B
(D) Neither A nor B

14. Technician A says an air spring suspension is an assist system added to a coil spring suspension. Technician B says air spring suspensions are composed of four

individual subsystems. Who is right?

(A) A only
(B) B only
(C) Both A and B
(D) Neither A nor B

15. Technician A says suspension modules contain a time delay feature to prevent the system from operating under normal road conditions. Technician B says two-way active suspensions are currently in use. Who is right?

(A) A only
(B) B only
(C) Both A and B
(D) Neither A nor B

16. Proper trim height of the speed-dependent air suspension system used on the 1993 Lincoln Mark VIII is determined by:

(A) vehicle cornering.
(B) hydraulic pressure.
(C) shock damping.
(D) vehicle speed.

17. Technician A says an air suspension may use either air springs or struts. Technician B says adding air to or releasing air from air springs does not compensate for road irregularities, but only maintains trim height. Who is right?

(A) A only
(B) B only
(C) Both A and B
(D) Neither A nor B

18. Technician A says an air spring has a variable spring rate. Technician B says adding a load to a vehicle equipped with ELC moves its body-mounted height sensor upward. Who is right?

(A) A only
(B) B only
(C) Both A and B
(D) Neither A nor B

CHAPTER THIRTEEN

COMPUTER-CONTROLLED STEERING

"He was so learned that he could name a horse in nine languages; so
ignorant that he bought a cow to ride on." — Benjamin Franklin

---

 OBJECTIVES

After completion of this chapter, you should be able to:

- Explain the difference between conventional and electronically controlled steering systems.

- Explain the relationship between vehicle speed and electronic control of the steering system.

- List and describe the sensors and actuators used in each of the following — VAPS, EVO power steering, and 4-wheel steering systems.

- Describe the basic operation of each of the following systems — VAPS, EVO power steering, and 4-wheel steering systems.

Power-assisted steering systems were designed to give the driver help in turning the steering wheel. This assistance is very helpful during periods of low speed driving, such as parking, and during evasive maneuvers at any speed. The major disadvantage of conventional power-assisted steering is a reduction in the amount of road feel transmitted to the driver. This is especially true at medium to high speeds, when a feeling of increased control and performance is desirable. Conventional power-assisted steering systems generally are a compromise between power assist and road feel. If they provide good road feel, power assist is reduced; when power assist is high, road feel is reduced.

By adding electronic control to a power-assist steering system, a computer called the 'steering module' can control the rate of power assist provided to the driver. This eliminates the steering effort compromise common to all conventional systems. Steering effort and sensitivity are light at low speeds but increase progressively to higher levels as road speeds increase. The result is a higher degree of responsiveness and driving ease than any non-electronic steering system can offer.

This chapter will discuss the various electronically controlled steering designs currently in use, and how they operate.

ELECTRONIC VARIABLE-ASSIST POWER STEERING (VAPS)

Also called progressive power steering (PPS), electronic variable-assist power steering (VAPS) made its first appearance on Japanese cars during the mid-1980's. Nissan and Toyota PPS systems were early examples and typical of the applications now used by many Japanese carmakers on their high-line models. A similar system first appeared on North American models with the 1988 Continental.

The principle behind VAPS operation is similar to that of the variable shock damping or PRC systems discussed in the chapter covering computer controlled suspensions. In these systems, the suspension module changes shock damping by varying the size of the metering orifices inside the shocks. In a VAPS or PPS system, the module changes the amount of power assist by varying the hydraulic pressure applied to the power steering spool valve.

SENSORS

The primary input to the steering module in all VAPS/PPS systems is vehicle speed. Some systems also use a secondary input from a steering wheel rotation or steering angle sensor (Figure 13-1). The input from the speed sensor is shared with other electronically controlled systems, such as an electronic speedometer, suspension, and/or cruise control. The speed sensor generally is located at the transmission or transaxle, although some systems incorporate it as part of the speedometer. Sensor voltage output is linear — the faster the sensor revolves, the greater the voltage it

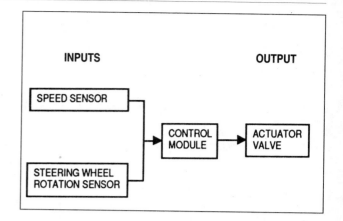

Figure 13-1 A basic schematic of an electronic steering system. Some use only the speed sensor input; others also use a steering wheel sensor. (Ford Motor)

produces. As vehicle speed decreases, the sensor slows down and its voltage output decreases at the same linear rate.

Those systems that monitor a steering wheel rotation or angle sensor use the signal to determine the turning angle of the vehicle. This same sensor is used by variable shock damping or programmed ride control systems and was described in the chapter covering computer controlled suspensions. Some steering angle sensors are designed as an integral assembly; others use a 2-piece design in which the sensor ring is separate from the photocell (Figure 13-2).

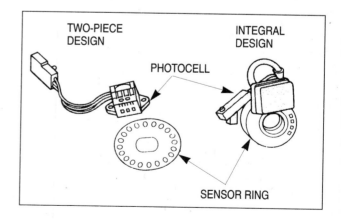

Figure 13-2 Two-piece and integral steering wheel rotation sensors. (Ford Motor)

CONTROL MODULES

VAPS/PPS systems generally use a separate control module, although some modules may contain the **software** to control another system using the same input signals, such as a variable shock damping system. When a vehicle uses more than one control system, the individual systems generally have their own diagnostic connectors. In some cases, multiple systems may share the same connector.

Some modules with a self-diagnostic feature do not set a diagnostic trouble code (DTC) if the system does not operate properly. When the module detects a malfunction, it disables the system to allow normal power steering. Since some systems have no indicator lamp to warn the driver of a malfunction, many drivers may not even be aware of a system failure. Because the solenoid valve is NOT energized at low speeds, the system will continue to function in its full-assist mode, even if the solenoid or module fails. The lack of progressively higher steering effort at higher road speeds also may go undetected by many drivers. If such a vehicle is brought in for service with a customer complaint that the steering is too sensitive at cruising speeds, it can be diagnosed through its self-test program with a voltmeter and the diagnostic connector.

With modules capable of setting a DTC, the code can be retrieved with the help of an analog volt-ohmmeter (Figure 13-3). As each generation of computer-controlled steering systems becomes smarter and increasingly integrated with other systems, module diagnostic capabilities will increase accordingly.

ACTUATORS

VAPS systems electronically control steering through an actuator mounted on the steering gear. The actuator may take the form of a solenoid valve (Toyota), a pressure-balanced variable orifice valve (Lincoln), or a rotary valve inside a housing

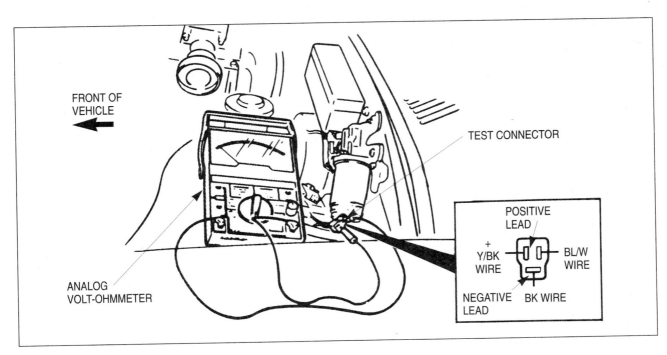

Figure 13-3 Retrieving Probe VAPS codes through an analog volt-ohmmeter. (Ford Motor)

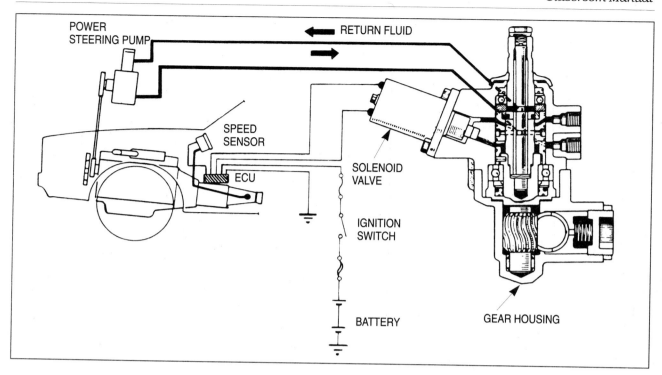

Figure 13-4A Components of the Toyota PPS system. (Toyota)

with reaction force chambers (Mazda/Probe). Since actuator operation depends on the system application, we will look at how the device works in each system example below.

SYSTEM EXAMPLES

VAPS/PPS systems are relatively simple in design and operation. To illustrate the basic approaches involved, we will examine the following typical systems representative of those currently in use:

- Toyota Progressive Power Steering (PPS)
- Continental Variable-Assist Power Steering (VAPS)
- Probe GT Variable-Assist Power Steering (VAPS)

TOYOTA PROGRESSIVE POWER STEERING (PPS)

The Toyota PPS system adds a solenoid valve to the standard power steering rack.

The valve is operated by a control module that receives an input from the speed sensor (Figure 13-4A). The system circuit diagram is shown in Figure 13-4B.

Turning the ignition switch 'on' sends battery voltage to the control module. Although the control module processes speed sensor signals at road speeds below approximately 25 mph, it ignores them. Since the module sends no power to the normally closed solenoid on the power steering rack, full power-assist is provided. Once road speed increases above 25 mph, the control module sends a pulse-width modulated (PWM) signal to the solenoid. The strength of this signal varies according to road speed. As vehicle speed increases, the signal sent to the solenoid becomes stronger (longer pulse width), opening the solenoid valve wider to reduce system pressure. Decreases in vehicle speed shorten the pulse width, which gradually closes the solenoid valve to increase system

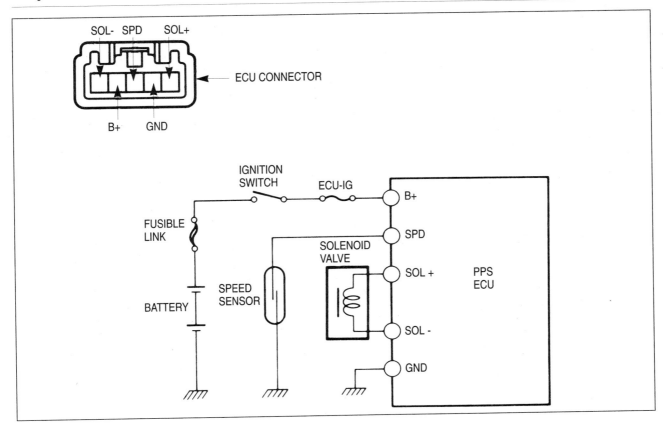

Figure 13-4B   The Toyota PPS system schematic and connector terminals. (Toyota)

pressure. If vehicle speed decreases below about 25 mph, the valve is fully closed and full power assist is available.

Major points to remember about the PPS system are:

- The actuating device is installed on the steering gear.
- Steering assist is based only on vehicle speed and is varied by pulse-width modulated operation of the solenoid.

CONTINENTAL VARIABLE-ASSIST POWER STEERING (VAPS)

The Continental VAPS system adds an actuator valve with **stepper motor** to the standard power steering rack (Figure 13-5). The actuator valve is a pressure-balanced variable orifice valve (Figure 13-6). The stepper motor is operated by a control

module that receives an input from the speed sensor. The steering gear contains a modified rotary valve with two independent hydraulic circuits (primary and secondary). The VAPS system schematic is shown in Figure 13-7.

During parking and other low speed (below 10 mph) maneuvers, the actuator valve routes power steering pump flow to the primary circuit, providing full power assist. As vehicle speed increases above 10 mph, the actuator valve stepper motor gradually varies the position of the rotary valve. This diverts fluid flow into the secondary circuit. As fluid flow increases in the secondary circuit, power assist decreases and driver steering effort increases. Changes in steering effort occur up to about 55 mph, after which the level of power assist remains steady at its lowest

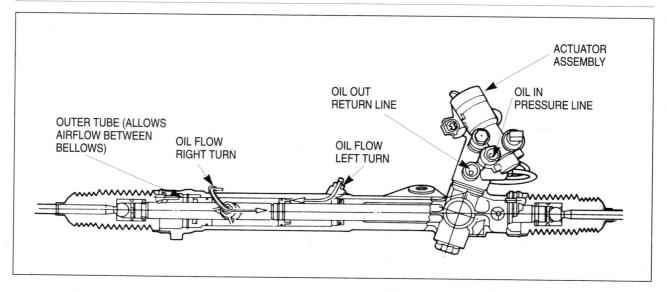

Figure 13-5 The Continental VAPS actuator valve mounted on the power steering rack controls fluid flow. (Ford Motor)

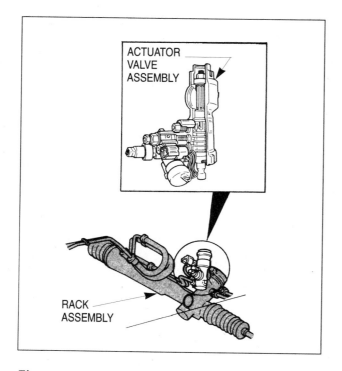

Figure 13-6 A cross section of the stepper motor-operated VAPS actuator assembly. (Ford Motor)

The actuator valve assembly acts as two valves in one — one valve for low speed operation and one for high speed operation.

The VAPS module is programmed to perform a self-diagnostic check every 16 milliseconds. If a malfunction is detected during this self-diagnostic check, the module shuts down and the system reverts back to normal power steering operation. Although the vehicle is equipped with a steering angle sensor for the suspension system, its input is NOT used by the VAPS module for steering control.

Major points to remember about the Continental VAPS system are:

- The actuating device is installed on the steering gear.
- Steering assist is based only on vehicle speed and is varied by routing fluid pressure to different hydraulic circuits in the steering gear.

PROBE GT VARIABLE-ASSIST POWER STEERING (VAPS)

This system performs the same function as the Continental VAPS, but the only similarity between the two is the location of the actuator on the steering gear. The system

level. As vehicle speed decreases, the actuator valve stepper motor changes the rotary valve position, diverting fluid back into the primary circuit. This increases power assist and decreases steering effort.

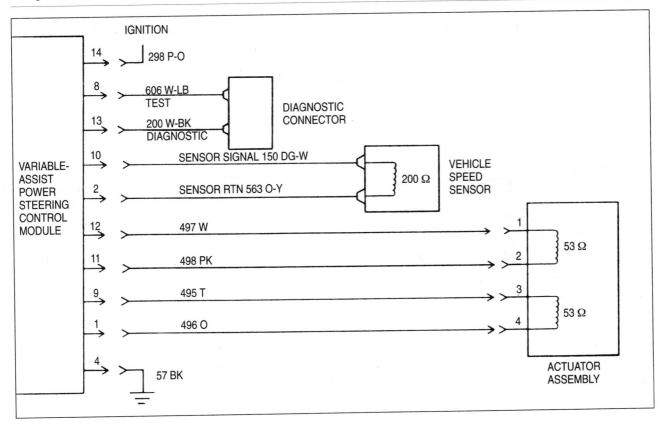

Figure 13-7 The VAPS system schematic. (Ford Motor)

consists of an actuator control valve, control module, speed and steering wheel angle sensors, solenoid valve, reserve tank, and power steering pump (Figure 13-8). The degree of steering effort required is controlled by the module, which uses vehicle speed and steering wheel turning angle signals to determine the amount of hydraulic fluid pressure to be applied to the actuator reaction force chambers.

Power steering fluid sent to the actuator reaction force chambers is fed into the solenoid valve through an orifice. Simultaneously, fluid also is fed into the reserve tank or power cylinder according to spool valve movement. The solenoid valve then controls fluid flow to the reserve tank. Pinion gear rotation causes a control valve lever to pivot, moving the horizontally mounted spool valve to overcome both

spring pressure and reaction force chamber pressure. The higher the reaction force chamber pressure, the lower the amount of power assist. When pressure in the chamber is reduced, the amount of power assist increases. In this design, the steering effort required of the driver is controlled by the amount of pressure within the reaction force chambers, NOT by the overall fluid pressure applied to the steering gear pinion.

When the module signals the solenoid with a high current, the solenoid overcomes internal spring pressure and increases the size of the passage between the force chamber and reserve tank. This causes fluid pressure to decrease, providing greater power assist because the spool valve can move more easily. A low current signal from the module causes spring

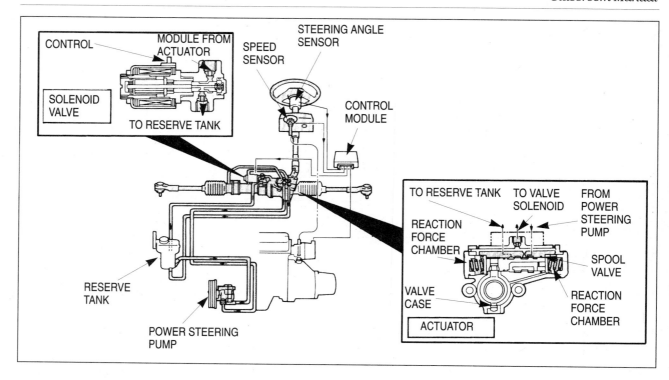

Figure 13-8 The Probe VAPS system. (Ford Motor)

pressure to overcome the solenoid and decreases the passageway to the reserve tank. This causes an increase in fluid pressure, reducing the power assist since spool valve movement is inhibited by the higher pressure. Figure 13-9 is an operational schematic of the system.

Like the Continental VAPS control module, the Probe control module is programmed to perform a self-diagnostic check at periodic intervals. If a malfunction is detected during this self-diagnostic check, the module shuts down and the system reverts back to normal power steering operation. A 3-position slide switch on the side of the module marked HNL can be set to increase (H) or decrease (L) steering effort by 10% from the normal production setting (N).

Major points to remember about the Probe VAPS system are:

- The actuating device is installed on the steering gear.

- Steering assist is based only on vehicle speed and is varied by bleeding fluid at differing rates from the actuator reaction chambers.
- Fluid pressure to the steering gear is NOT regulated by the actuator.

SPEED-SENSITIVE ELECTRONIC VARIABLE ORIFICE (EVO) STEERING

A more complex and sophisticated VAPS system balances the driver's need for road feel with the need for reduced steering effort by providing varying levels of power assist based on speed and steering wheel rotation. The result is an improved steering feel, compared to that of a VAPS system (which is an improvement over a conventional system). Such systems are called EVO systems because an electronic variable orifice is used to control power steering fluid flow. This EVO actuating device is located on the power steering

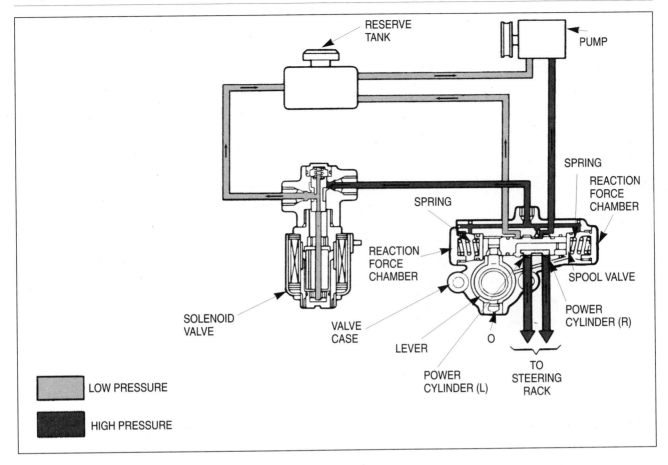

Figure 13-9 An operational schematic of the Probe VAPS system. (Ford Motor)

pump instead of being mounted on the steering gear, as in a VAPS system.

SENSORS

EVO systems use the same sensors as those in a VAPS system. Again, the speed sensor provides the primary input to the control module, but output current to the EVO actuator is a function of both vehicle speed and steering wheel rotation rate.

CONTROL MODULES

EVO control modules continuously analyze the inputs from the speed sensor and steering wheel rotation sensor to control the actuator valve. GM modules have NO self-diagnostic program; Ford modules contain a lamp driver circuit that flashes a

diagnostic indicator lamp. If the Ford module is combined with software for another system, such as automatic ride control (ARC), a STAR or SUPER STAR II tester is required for diagnostic testing.

ACTUATORS

An EVO actuator assembly (Figure 13-10) is located at the power steering pump outlet to regulate the hydraulic flow from the pump. It contains a solenoid-operated pintle valve operated by a differential pressure created by fluid flow and current input. At low vehicle speeds, the orifice in the actuator remains open and allows full pump flow for maximum power steering assist. As vehicle speed increases, the control module signals the pintle to move

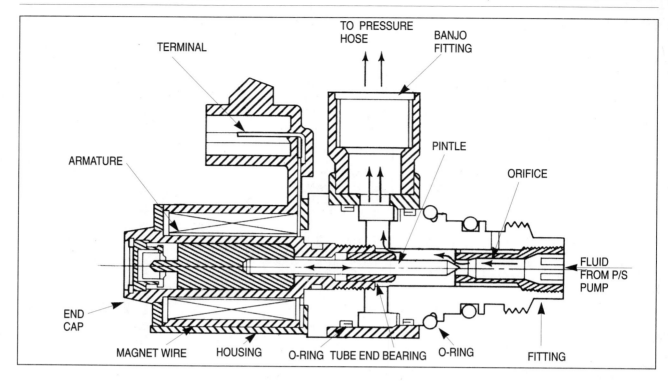

Figure 13-10 A cross section of the Ford EVO actuator assembly. (Ford Motor)

into the orifice. This reduces pump flow, which in turn reduces the amount of steering assist. The greater the vehicle speed, the smaller the orifice opening. When steering wheel rotation exceeds a predetermined rate, the module in some systems interprets this as evasive maneuvering at high speeds. Under this condition, the actuator pintle valve is backed out of the orifice to increase pump flow, increasing the amount of steering assist. Steering assist does NOT decrease with increased speed in a straight line, but at three different rates according to the amount of current flow to the EVO actuator. The higher the current, the less the assist (Figure 13-11).

System Examples

EVO power steering systems also are relatively simple in design and operation. The complexity in the system rests in the software programming of the control module. To illustrate the basic approaches

to EVO, we will examine the following systems representative of those currently in use:

- Speed Sensitive Electronic Variable Orifice (EVO) Power Steering
- Electronic Variable Orifice (EVO) or Variable Effort Steering (VES)

Speed Sensitive Electronic Variable Orifice (EVO) Power Steering

Variations of the basic EVO system have been used on several different Ford, Lincoln, and Mercury models since its 1989 introduction on Thunderbird and Cougar models (Figure 13-12). EVO system operation is designed to adjust steering effort for an optimum road feel, and is quite similar to that of a VAPS system. The major difference between the two types of systems is in the use of the EVO actuator installed on the power steering pump.

Full steering assist is provided during low speed operation and maneuvering, such as parking. As vehicle speed

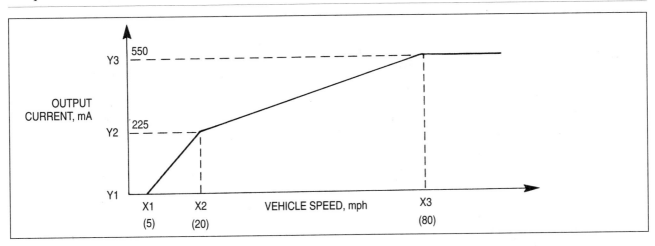

Figure 13-11 The actuator valve provides sharply decreasing pump flow as it receives increased current from the module, up to a predetermined vehicle speed, when it tapers off to a gradually increasing flow. At even higher speed, pump flow levels off and does not change. (Ford Motor)

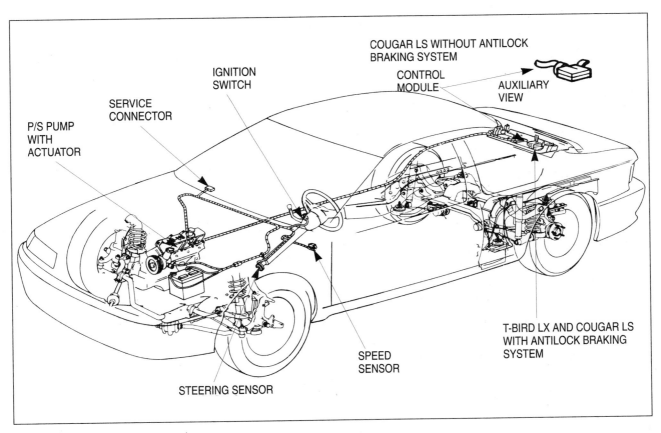

Figure 13-12 The Thunderbird and Cougar EVO system components. (Ford Motor)

increases, the control module starts moving the actuator pintle into the orifice. This gradually increases steering effort through-out the driving range until a predetermined speed is reached. Above that speed, the required steering effort remains constant.

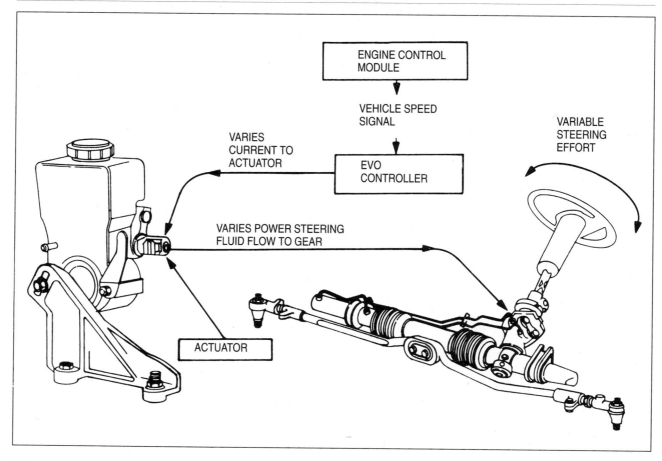

Figure 13-13 Components and operation of the original GM EVO power steering system, redesignated as EVO-1. (General Motors)

ELECTRONIC VARIABLE ORIFICE (EVO) OR VARIABLE EFFORT STEERING (VES)

General Motors introduced the EVO steering system on some 1991 models; it also is known as variable effort steering, or VES. The GM EVO application (Figure 13-13) differs from those used by Ford in the following ways:

- The EVO controller receives vehicle speed data from the engine control module (ECM) instead of directly from the speed sensor. After processing this input, it sends a pulse-width modulated control signal to the EVO actuator.
- An inline check valve in the power steering pressure hose reduces the amount of steering wheel kickback during operation at speeds with reduced flow rate and pressure while driving over irregularities in the road surface.
- The control module is capable of disabling the system if a malfunction occurs, but sets NO diagnostic trouble codes. System diagnosis relies on use of a Tech 1 or equivalent scan tool and a signal generator to monitor actuator duty cycle.

Starting with 1992 models, GM redesignated its 1991 system as EVO-1. GM expanded its use of EVO steering by adding a steering wheel rotation sensor (a potentiometer with 2 wipers positioned 90° out of

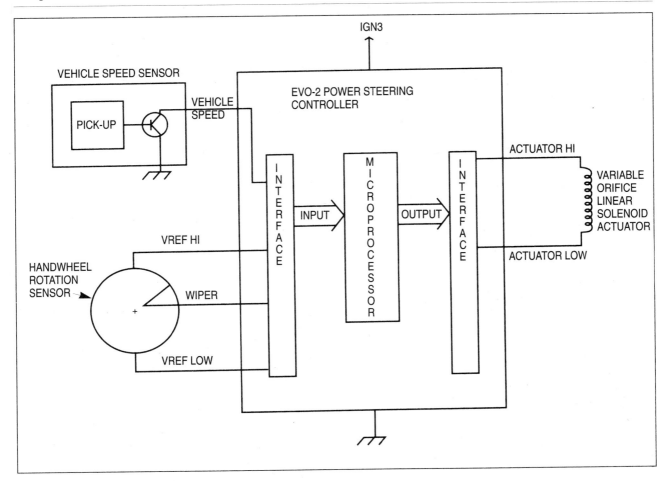

Figure 13-14 A schematic of the GM EVO-2 power steering system. (General Motors)

phase with each other), and calling the system EVO-2 (Figure 13-14).

EVO-3, also called Two-Flow Electronic (TFE) power steering, is a simplified system that provides full power assist at low road speeds, and a preset reduced level of assist at higher speeds. A two-position solenoid valve is controlled by on-off signals from the multifunction chime module, which receives speed-related input signals from the PCM. At vehicle speeds below approximately 20 mph, the solenoid is energized to provide maximum fluid flow through the system, resulting in less steering effort. Above that speed, the solenoid is de-energized to restrict fluid flow and provide direct steering feel at higher speeds.

Major points to remember about the Ford or GM EVO systems are:

- Steering assist is based on both vehicle speed and steering wheel rotation, and is varied by changing the orifice size within the EVO actuator.
- The actuating device is installed on the power steering pump.
- Full power assist is returned during evasive maneuvers at higher speeds.

ELECTRO-HYDRAULIC 4-WHEEL STEERING

Electronic 4-wheel steering first appeared on 1988 turbocharged Mazda 626 models, the same year that Honda brought forth its

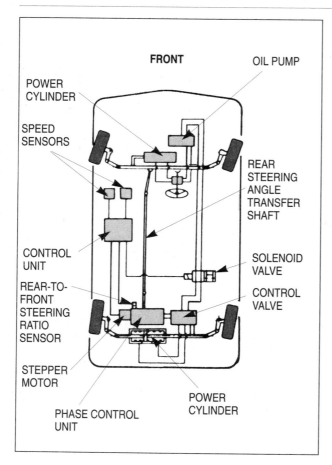

Figure 13-15 A representation of the Mazda 4-wheel steering system components.

mechanical 4-wheel steering system. The mechanical system quickly faded from the scene, and was replaced by Honda with a highly sophisticated electronic 4-wheel steering system on high-line models. Four-wheel steering improves directional stability and vehicle stability at higher speeds, making quick lane changes easier. We will examine the Mazda and Honda systems as typical examples of computer-controlled 4-wheel steering.

Mazda 4-Wheel Steering System

A steering angle transfer shaft connects a hydraulic phase control unit located on the rear steering gear to the front power rack and pinion gear (Figure 13-15). To transmit the front wheel steering angle, the shaft rotates a small bevel gear to turn a larger bevel gear in the phase control unit. The control module receives vehicle speed input from two speed sensors. One sensor is installed at the transaxle; the other is located in the speedometer unit. Input from both sensors is compared by the module. If the inputs do not agree with each other, or if they are outside the module's programmed parameters, the system is disabled and returned to normal 2-wheel steering. The module also receives input from a front-to-rear steering ratio sensor. After processing the input from all three sensors, the module activates a stepper motor in the phase control unit to change bevel gear phasing and yoke angle, if required. Hydraulic pressure to the rear steering gear is transmitted through a solenoid-operated control valve and moves the power cylinder output rod to steer the rear wheels.

A failure in the hydraulic system causes the power cylinder centering lock spring to lock the output rod in its neutral or straight-ahead position. An electrical malfunction in the system activates the solenoid valve to disengage the hydraulic boost. This also locks the output rod in a neutral position. A tandem or twin pump at the front of the vehicle provides the hydraulic pressure used by both front and rear steering gears. System malfunctions are detected by the control module's self-diagnostic program, which turns on an indicator lamp in the instrument cluster. The indicator lamp flashes a specific pattern for 60 s, indicating to the driver that the system needs service.

Honda Electronically Controlled Power-Assisted 4-Wheel Steering

Honda's application of electronic 4-wheel steering to its production vehicles consists of the front power steering gear, a rear

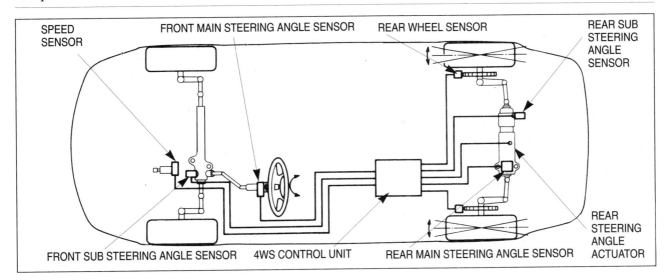

Figure 13-16 Components of the Honda 4-wheel steering system. (Honda)

wheel steering actuator, front and rear main steering angle sensors, front and rear sub steering angle sensor, two rear wheel sensors, a speed sensor, and the control module (Figure 13-16). The front steering gear and rear actuator are connected by a wiring harness. Because the system controls the rear steering angle electrically, the rear wheels can be set at any designated steering angle.

The control module receives input signals from the front steering angle and speed sensors. It uses these inputs to calculate vehicle speed, steering turning angle, steering speed, and steering direction. These calculations are then used to determine the appropriate angle for steering the rear wheels. A motor built into the rear steering actuator changes the angle of the rear wheels when activated by the control module power circuit. The rear steering angle sensors provide input signals to the module that allow it to determine the actual steering angle of the rear wheels. Using this data, the module adjusts the rear wheel steering angle according to the difference between the sensed angle and the desired angle. Figure 13-17 is a flow

chart of system operation.

When the vehicle is traveling at 18 mph or less, the rear wheels steer in an opposite direction from the front wheels proportionate to the rotation angle of the steering wheel. At speeds above 18 mph, the module increases rear wheel steering angle in the same direction as the front wheels, and varies the angle according to the speed of steering wheel rotation (Figure 13-18).

The front and rear main steering angle sensors use Hall-effect switches to sense the direction and angle of steering wheel rotation (front sensor) and the rear wheels (rear sensor). The front and rear sub steering angle sensors use spring-loaded plungers that ride in a sloped groove. As the wheels turn, the plungers ride up in their grooves and signal their position to the module, which uses the input to determine how far the wheels have turned. The speed sensor is a trochoid-rotor, hydraulic pump driven by the speedometer gear shaft and containing a relief valve and a one-way valve (Figure 13-19).

If the control module's self-diagnostic program detects a system malfunction, it switches to a fail-safe mode by powering the fail-safe and damper relays. The fail-safe relay shuts off power to the rear steering motor; the damper relay slows the motor's return to a neutral position. These actions allow the rear wheels to slowly return to the straight-ahead position where

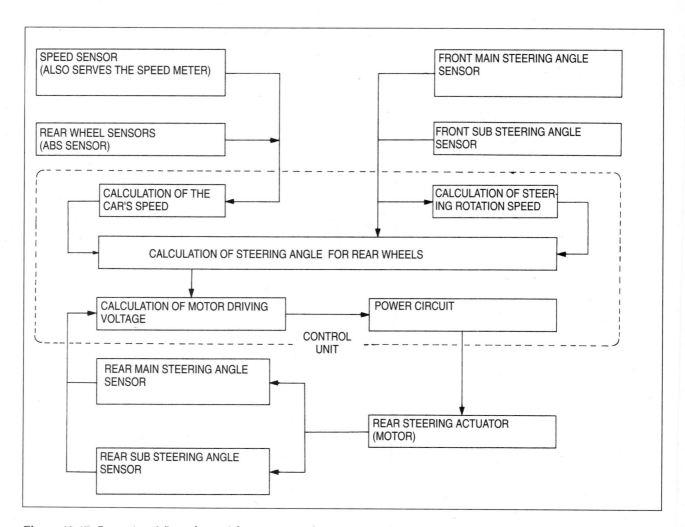

Figure 13-17 Operational flow chart of the Honda 4-wheel steering system. (Honda)

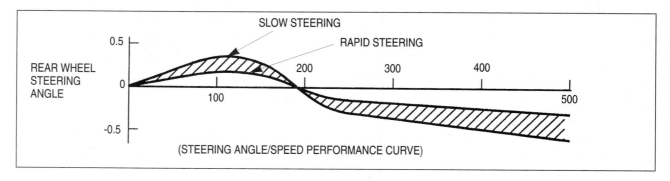

Figure 13-18 With the Honda 4-wheel steering system, the rear wheel steering angle varies with how fast the steering wheel is turned. (Honda)

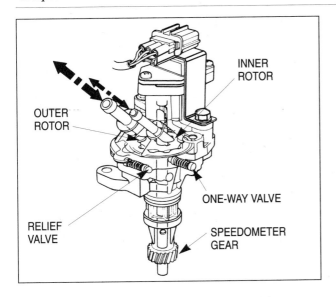

Figure 13-19 The Honda speed sensor. (Honda)

they remain, and the vehicle continues to drive with front wheel steering. The module also sets a diagnostic trouble code (DTC) and turns on an indicator lamp in the instrument cluster to tell the driver that the system needs service. The module can detect 48 different problems and retain up to 10 separate codes in memory. Codes can be retrieved by grounding the service check connector with a jumper wire and reading the series of long and short blinks of the indicator lamp.

SUMMARY

Input from the speed sensor is used by the module of computer-controlled power-assist steering systems to change the amount of power-assist in proportion to vehicle speed. Some systems also use

input from a steering angle or steering wheel rotation sensor. Electronic control eliminates the steering effort compromise usually found in power-assisted steering systems. Because the light steering effort provided during parking maneuvers and driving at low speeds increases progressively as vehicle speed increases, such systems are called variable-assist power steering (VAPS) systems or progressive power steering (PPS) systems.

VAPS or PPS systems use an actuator mounted on the steering gear; electronic variable orifice (EVO) systems have the actuator installed in the discharge fitting of the power steering pump. The operation of an EVO system is essentially the same as that of a VAPS or PPS system except for the EVO actuator, which contains a pintle that controls fluid flow from the pump.

Electronic 4-wheel steering systems have power steering gears at each end of the vehicle. The Mazda system uses a transfer shaft to transmit front wheel position to the rear gear and changes rear wheel position as directed by the control module. The Honda system transmits wheel position to the rear actuator electrically. The direction and degree of rear wheel steering is dependent on vehicle speed inputs from a series of speed and steering angle sensors. At slow speeds, the rear wheels steer in an opposite direction from the front wheels to reduce the turning radius of the vehicle. This makes parking, U-turns, and other sharp maneuvers easier. All four wheels steer in the same direction at higher speeds.

❓ REVIEW QUESTIONS

1. Technician A says that the amount of power assist in a progressive power steering system can be controlled by routing fluid pressure to different hydraulic circuits in the steering gear. Technician B says assist can be controlled by bleeding fluid at differing rates from the actuator reaction chambers. Who is right?
   (A) A only
   (B) B only
   (C) Both A and B
   (D) Neither A nor B

2. Technician A says that the control module of some progressive power steering systems may contain the software of another control system that uses the same input signals. Technician B says that two control systems may use separate modules, but share the same diagnostic connector. Who is right?
   (A) A only
   (B) B only
   (C) Both A and B
   (D) Neither A nor B

3. Technician A says that VAPS systems electronically control steering through an actuator mounted on the steering gear. Technician B says that it is mounted on the power steering pump. Who is right?
   (A) A only
   (B) B only
   (C) Both A and B
   (D) Neither A nor B

4. Which of the following systems use a pulse-width modulated (PWM) signal to control the actuator?
   (A) Continental VAPS
   (B) Toyota PPS
   (C) Probe GT VAPS
   (D) Ford EVO System

5. In which of the following systems is steering assist based ONLY on vehicle speed?
   (A) Ford EVO System
   (B) GM EVO System
   (C) GM VES System
   (D) Continental VAPS

6. Technician A says that the EVO actuator contains a solenoid-operated pintle valve. Technician B says that the EVO actuator controls fluid flow from the power steering pump. Who is right?
   (A) A only
   (B) B only
   (C) Both A and B
   (D) Neither A nor B

7. Technician A says that all steering control modules store diagnostic trouble codes that can be retrieved with a scan tool. Technician B says that all control modules contain a self-diagnostic program. Who is right?
   (A) A only
   (B) B only
   (C) Both A and B
   (D) Neither A nor B

8. Technician A says an electronically controlled power assist steering system provides more assist at higher speeds. Technician B says it provides greater assist at lower speeds. Who is right?
   (A) A only
   (B) B only
   (C) Both A and B
   (D) Neither A nor B

9. Which of the following components is NOT a part of the Mazda 4-wheel steering system?
   (A) sub steering angle sensors
   (B) steering angle transfer shaft
   (C) hydraulic phase control unit
   (D) two speed sensors

10. Technician A says that the rear wheels of a 4-wheel steering system steer in an

opposite direction from the front wheels when the vehicle is traveling below a specified speed. Technician B says that this increases turning radius to make parking easier. Who is right?

(A) A only

(B) B only

(C) Both A and B

(D) Neither A nor B

11. Which of the following components is NOT a part of the Honda 4-wheel steering system?

(A) rear wheel steering actuator

(B) front and rear main steering angle sensors

(C) front and rear sub steering angle sensors

(D) front-to-rear steering ratio sensor

12. Technician A says the Honda 4-wheel steering module can detect up to 48 malfunctions. Technician B says the speed sensor in the Honda system is a hydraulic pump. Who is right?

(A) A only

(B) B only

(C) Both A and B

(D) Neither A nor B

UNITS CONVERSION
-- TRADITIONAL TO METRIC/SI

The Technical Standards Board Document SAE/TSB 003 Jun92 (formerly SAE J916) of the Society of Automotive Engineers (SAE) has established the rules for the use of the International System of units (SI) in SAE technical reports/publications, including standards and recommended practices. The content of the TSB 003 is consistent with international and US national authoritative resource documents for SI: ISO 1000; NIST SP330; ANSI/IEEE Std. 268; ASTM E 380, and the US Federal Register Notice, "Metric System of Measurement," Dec 20, 1990.

As an automotive technician, you will encounter several units of weights and measures in your day-to-day work, and a knowledge of the metric/SI units will enable you determine the equivalences of the specifications of various hydraulic/mechanical/electrical/electronic components as well as test conditions for different North American and import cars. Also, most current periodicals in your technical specialty will be in metric/SI units, and a good grasp of this system of units enables you benefit from the published literature.

MAJOR FEATURES OF THE SI

- The system is comprehensive -- the base units are only seven, but cover all fields of science and technology.
- The system is coherent -- the derived units come from the base units and have NO numerical factors or arbitrary constants.
- Derived units in common use are given internationally agreed names.
- Multiples/sub-multiples of units are used for adequate coverage in practice.

THE SEVEN BASE UNITS OF SI

Length	meter, m
Mass	kilogram, kg
Time	second, s
Electric current	ampere, A
Thermodynamic temperature	kelvin, K
Amount of substance	mole, mol
Luminous intensity	candela, cd

THE TWO SUPPLEMENTARY UNITS OF SI

Plane angle	radian, rad
Spherical angle	steradian, sr

NINETEEN DERIVED UNITS OF SI

Absorbed dose	gray (Gy), J/kg
Activity (of a radionuclide)	becquerel (Bq), $1/s$, s^{-1}
Celsius temperature	degree Celsius, (°C)
Dose equivalent	sievert (Sv), J/kg
Electric capacitance	farad (F), C/V
Electric conductance	siemens (S), A/V
Electric inductance	henry (H), Wb/A
Electric potential difference	volt (V), W/A
Electric resistance	ohm (Ω), V/A
Energy, work	joule (J), N.m
Force	newton (N), $kg.m/s^2$
Frequency	hertz (Hz), $1/s$, s^{-1}
Illuminance	lux (lx), lm/m^2
Luminous flux	lumen (lm), cd.sr
Magnetic flux	weber (Wb), V.s
Magnetic flux density	tesla (T), Wb/m^2
Power	watt (W), J/s
Pressure or stress	pascal (Pa), N/m^2
Quantity of electricity	coulomb (C), A.s

OTHER PRACTICAL UNITS ACCEPTABLE

Plane angle	degree (°) (decimalized)
Time	minute (min), hour (h), day (d), week, and year
Mass	metric ton (t)
Area	hectare (ha)
Sound pressure level	decibel (dB)
Volume	liter (L)
Navigation velocity	knot (kn)
distance	nautical mile (nmi)

MULTIPLES AND SUB-MULTIPLES OF SI

Value	Prefix	Symbol
10^{18}	exa	E
10^{15}	peta	P
10^{12}	tera	T
10^{9}	giga	G
10^{6}	mega	M
10^{3}	kilo	k
10^{2}	hecto	h
10^{1}	deka	da
10^{-1}	deci	d
10^{-2}	centi	c
10^{-3}	milli	m
10^{-6}	micro	μ
10^{-9}	nano	n
10^{-12}	pico	p
10^{-15}	femto	f
10^{-18}	atto	a

REPRESENTATION OF UNITS AND DATA

Names of units (including those named after persons such as kelvin, ampere, joule, and watt) and **prefixes** (such as micro-, mega-) begin with lower case letters. Symbols of units (except those named after a person as Hz for hertz, K for kelvin, N for newton, Pa for pascal) and of prefixes (except E, P, T, G, M, and μ) are lower case letters. Exception — SAE permits the upper case (L) to represent the unit 'liter' because of the confusion that can occur between the lower case unit symbol (l) and the number one (1).

The 'liter' which is internationally accepted as a special name for the cubic decimeter, is approved for SAE use. The only prefixed use allowed by SAE is mL. However, SAE preference is to use cubic centimeter (cm^3) rather than milliliter (mL); and cubic decimeter (dm^3) rather than liter (L).

The units used with specific numbers (for example: 45 s, 18 m) are abbreviated or designated by symbol, except where a potential exists for misinterpretation -- in which case the units are spelled out. For example, unit symbol 'in' is spelled out as 'inch(es)' or, if style permits, its alternative symbol (") used.

Pressure units themselves should NOT be modified to indicate whether the pressure is absolute (above zero) or gage (above atmospheric). If the context leaves any doubt as to which is meant, the word pressure must be qualified appropriately. For example: " .... at a gage pressure of 300 kPa," or " .... attained an absolute pressure of 75 kPa."

Use of prefixes representing 10 raised to a power that is multiple of 3 is recommended. In the case of prefixed units that carry exponents, such as units of area and volume, this may not be practical, and any listed prefix may be used. Compound prefixes, should NOT be used. For example, nm for nanometer should be used, and NOT mμm or milli-micrometer; Mg for megagram but NOT kkg or kilokilogram. The prefix becomes part of the symbol or name with NO separation (meganewton, MN). When the multiple of a base unit is raised to a power, the power applies to the whole number and NOT to the base unit alone. For example, km^2 is $(km)^2$ or $10^6 \, m^2$ and NOT $k(m^2)$ or $10^3 \, m^2$.

Quantity symbols must NOT be confused with unit symbols. Quantity symbols are single letters representing physical quantities (f - frequency, F - force, m -mass, M - moment of force). Quantity symbols are single letters of the English (Latin) or Greek alphabet, and are *italicized*. The form of symbols and abbreviations is the SAME for singular or plural. Thus, write 10 m for 10 meters and NOT 10 ms (10 ms means 10 milliseconds). Periods are NOT used after symbols or abbreviations. Thus, 10 kg is correct and 10 kg. is NOT. When writing a quantity, a space should be left between the numerical value and a unit symbol — for example, write 20 mm, NOT 20mm; write 20 °C, NOT 20°C. Exception — No space is left between numerical values and symbols for degree, minute, and second of plane angle. For example, use 60°. In SAE practice, the degree symbol (°) is not used; it is spelled out.

The letter style must be followed for SI unit symbols and prefixes even in applications (such as technical drawings) where all other lettering is upper case.

To facilitate the reading of large numbers having five or more digits, the digit should be placed in groups of three separated by a space instead of a comma, counting both to the left and to the right of the decimal point. For example, write: 123 456.789 12 instead of 123,456.78912. In the case of four digits, the spacing is optional. For example, use: 7 494 or 7494 instead of 7,494. This style also avoids confusion from use elasewhere of the comma to express the decimal point. SAE uses the dot on the line (.) for quantities in either US customary or SI units.

UNITS CONVERSION

All conversions must depend upon an intended precision of the original quantity — either implied by a specific tolerance, or by the nature of the quantity. The first step in conversion is to establish this precision. If accuracy of measurement is known, this will provide a convenient lower limit to the precision of the dimension, and in some cases may be the only basis for establishing it. The implied precision should never be smaller than the accuracy of measurement.

A rule of thumb often helpful for determining implied precision of a toleranced value is to assume it is one-tenth of the tolerance. Since the implied precision of the converted value should be no greater than that of the original, the total tolerance is divided by 10, converted, and the proper significant digits retained in both the converted value and converted tolerance such that total implied precision is not reduced — that is, the last significant digit retained is in units no larger than one-tenth the converted total tolerance.

In rounding a toleranced quantity, the quantity may be first converted to limits and each limit rounded appropriately depending on the nature of the individual limit. For absolute maintenance of the original limits, the upper limit should be rounded down and the lower limit rounded up.

Temperatures expressed in a whole number of degrees Fahrenheit should be converted to the nearest 0.5 kelvin (or degree Celsius). As with other quantities, the number of significant digits to retain depends on the implied accuracy of the original value.

Worked Examples

A. 500 psi ± 25 psi. Tolerance is 50 psi, divided by 10 is 5 psi, converted is about 34.5 kPa. The value (500 psi) converted is 3 447.378 5 kPa ± 172.368 93 kPa which should be rounded to units of 10 kPa, since 10 kPa is the largest unit smaller than one-tenth the converted tolerance. The conversion should be 3 450 kPa ± 170 kPa.

B. 10 oz ± 0.1 oz of brake fluid. Tolerance is 0.2 oz, one-tenth of tolerance is 0.02 oz, converted is about 0.6 cm^3. The converted value (295.735 3 cm^3 ± 2.957 4 cm^3) should be rounded to units of 0.1 cm^3, and becomes 295.7 cm^3 ± 3.0 cm^3.

C. 3.527" length. Estimate of tolerance is 0.001" (significant digits judged correct). Converted tolerance 0.0254 mm. Units to use 0.01 mm. 3.527" equals 89.5858 mm, round to 89.59 mm.

D. Rounding of a converted dimension of 123.452 3 mm to two decimal places under different situations. Normal dimension, untoleranced — round to 123.45 mm (closest to original). Dimension stated as minimum — round to 123.46 mm (rounded up). Dimension stated as maximum — round to 123.45 (rounded down).

E. 200 °F ± 10°F, implied accuracy estimated 2 °F. The conversion is 93.3333 °C ± 5.5555 °C, rounds to 93 °C ± 6 °C.

With **nominal sizes** that are not measurements but are names for items, NO conversion should be made: for example, 1/4-20 UNC thread, 1 in pipe, 2x4 lumber.

In the case of **interchangeable dimensions** on engineering drawings, the approach outlined in SAE J390, should be consulted.

The tabulation (adapted from: SAE Handbook 1994) that follows should be useful for **conversion of units of measurement -- from traditional to metric/SI.**

QUANTITY	FROM TRADITIONAL UNITS	TO METRIC/SI UNITS	MULTIPLY BY
Acceleration, angular	rad/s^2	rad/s^2	1
Acceleration, linear	(mile/h)/s	(km/h)/s	1.609 344
	ft/s^2	m/s^2	0.304 8
	in/s^2	m/s^2	0.025 4
Angle, plane	r (revolution)	r (revolution)	1
	rad	rad	1
	°(deg)	°	1
	' (min)	°(decimalized)	1/60
	" (sec)	°(decimalized)	1/3600
Angle, solid	sr	sr	1
Area	acre	ha	0.404 687 3
	acre	m^2	4 046.873
	ft^2	m^2	0.092 903 04
	in^2	cm^2	6.451 6
	in^2	m^2	0.000 645 16
	in^2	mm^2	645.16
	$mile^2$	km^2	2.589 998
	rod^2	m^2	25.292 95
	yd^2	m^2	0.836 127 4
Area per time	acre/h	ha/h	0.404 687 3
	ft^2/s	m^2/s	0.092 903 04
Bending moment	(*See* Moment of force)		
Capacitance, electric	μF	μF	1
Capacity, electric charge	A.h	A.h	1
Capacity, heat	Btu/°F	kJ/K	1.899 101
Capacity , heat, specific	Btu/(lb.°F)	kJ/(kg.K)	4.186 8
Capacity, volume	(*See* Volume)		
Charge, electric	C	C	1
Coefficient of heat transfer	$Btu/(h.ft^2.°F)$	$W/(m^2.K)$	5.678 263
Coefficient of linear expansion	$°F^{-1}$, (1/°F)	$°C^{-1}$, (1/°C)	1.8
Conductance, electric	mho	S	1
Conductance, thermal	(*See* Coefficient of heat transfer)		
Conductivity, electric	mho/ft	S/m	3.280 840
Conductivity, thermal	$Btu.in/(h.ft^2.°F)$	W/(m.K)	0.144 227 9
	$Btu.ft/(h.ft^2.°F)$	W/(m.K)	1.730 735
Consumption, fuel	(*See* Efficiency, fuel)		
Consumption, oil	qt/1000 miles	L/1000 km	0.588 036 4
Consumption, specific, fuel	(*See* Efficiency, fuel)		

QUANTITY	FROM TRADITIONAL UNITS	TO METRIC/SI UNITS	MULTIPLY BY
Consumption, specific, oil	oz/(hp.h)	g/MJ	10.560 37
	lb/(hp.h)	g/(kW.h)	608.277 4
	lb/(hp.h)	g/MJ	168.965 9
Current, electric	A	A	1
Damping, coefficient	$lb_f.s/ft$	N.s/m	14.593 90
Density, current	A/in^2	kA/m^2	1.550 003
Density, magnetic flux	gauss	T	0.0001
Density, (mass)	lb/ft^3	kg/m^3	16.018 46
	lb/gal	kg/L	0.119 826 4
	lb/in^3	kg/m^3	27 679.90
	lb/yd^3	kg/m^3	0.593 276 3
	ton (long)/yd^3	kg/m^3	1 328.939
	ton (short)/yd^3	kg/m^3	1 186.553
Density of heat flow rate	$Btu/(h.ft^2)$	W/m^2	3.154
Diffusivity, thermal	ft^2/h	m^2/h	0.092 903 04
Drag	(*See* Force)		
Economy, fuel or oil	(*See* Efficiency, fuel or oil)		
Efficiency, fuel	gal/h	L/h	3.785 412
	hp.h/gal	kW.h/L	0.196 993 1
	mile/gal	km/L	0.425 143 7
	lb/(hp.h)	g/(kW.h)	608.277 4
	lb/(hp.h)	g/MJ	168.965 9
	lb/(hp.h)	kg/(kW.h)	0.608 277 4
	$lb/(lb_f.h)$	mg/(N.s)	28.325 26
Efficiency, oil	mi/qt	km/L	1.700 575
Energy, work, enthalpy. quantity of heat	Btu	kJ	1.055 056
	Chu	kJ	1.899 101
	erg	J	0.000 000 1
	kcal	kJ	4.186 8
	kW.h	kW.h	1
	kW.h	MJ	3.6
	ft.pdl	J	0.042 140 11
	$ft.lb_f$	J	1.355 818
	hp.h	MJ	2.684 520
Energy per area	Btu/ft^2	MJ/m^2	0.011 356 53
Energy, specific	Btu/lb	kJ/kg	2.326
	cal/g	J/g	4.186 8
Enthalpy	(*See* Energy)		
Entropy	(*See* Capacity, heat)		
Entropy, specific	(*See* Capacity, heat specific)		
Floor loading	(*See* Mass per area)		
Flow, heat, rate	(*See* Power)		

QUANTITY	FROM TRADITIONAL UNITS	TO METRIC/SI UNITS	MULTIPLY BY
Flow, mass, rate	oz/min	g/min	28.349 52
	lb/min	kg/min	0.453 592 4
	lb/s	kg/s	0.453 592
Flow, volume	ft^3/min	L/min	28.316 85
	ft^3/s	m^3/min	1.699 011
	ft^3/s	m^3/s	0.028 316 85
	gal/min	L/min	3.785 412
	gal/s	L/s	3.785 412
	gal/s	m^3/s	0.003 785 412
	oz/min	mL/min	29.573 53
	oz/s	mL/s	29.573 53
Flux, luminous	lm	lm	1
Flux , magnetic	maxwell	Wb	0.000 000 01
Force, thrust, drag	dyne	N	0.000 01
	kg_f	N	9.806 650
	oz_f	N	0.278 013 9
	pdl	N	0.138 255 0
	lb_f	kN	0.004 448 222
	lb_f	N	4.448 222
	ton force (2000 lb_f)	kN	8.896 444
Force loading	(*See* Pressure)		
Force per length	(*See also* Spring rate) lb_f/ft	N/m	14.593 90
Force per mass	lb_f/ton (short)	N/Mg, N/t	4.903 326
Frequency	Hz, c/s	Hz	1
	kc/s	kHz	1
	Mc/s	MHz	1
Hardness	(Conventional hardness numbers, BHN, R, etc., not affected by change to SI)		
Heat	(*See* Energy)		
Heat capacity	(*See* Capacity, heat)		
Heat capacity, specific	(*See* Capacity, heat specific)		
Heat flow rate	(*See* Power)		
Heat flow, density of	(*See* Density of heat flow)		
Heat (enthalpy), specific	Btu/lb	kJ/kg	2.326
	cal/g	kJ/kg	4.186 8
Heat transfer, coefficient	(*See* Coefficient of heat transfer)		
Illuminance, illumination	fc	lx	10.763 91
Impact strength	(*See* Strength, impact)		
Impedance, mechanical	(*See* Damping coefficient)		

QUANTITY		FROM TRADITIONAL UNITS	TO METRIC/SI UNITS	MULTIPLY BY
Inductance, electrical		H	H	1
Intense, luminous		candlepower	cd	1
Intensity, radiant		W/sr	W/sr	1
Leakage	(*See* Flow, volume)			
Length or Distance		ft	m	0.304 8
		in	cm	2.54
		in	mm	25.4
		micron	μm	1
		mil	μm	25.4
		mile	km	1.609 344
		mile (nautical)	km	1.852
		rod	m	5.029 210
		yd	m	0.914 4
		μin	nm	25.4
		μin	μm	0.025 4
Load	(*See* Mass)			
Luminance		footlambert	cd/m^2	3.426 259
Magnetization		A/in	A/m	39.370 08
Mass		grain	g	0.064 798 91
		oz (avoir)	g	28.349 52
		oz (troy)	g	31.103 48
		lb	kg	0.453 592 4
		slug	kg	14.593 90
		ton (long)	Mg, t	1.016 047
		ton (short)	Mg, t	0.907 184 7
Mass per area		oz/ft^2	g/m^2	305.151 7
		oz/yd^2	g/m^2	33.905 75
		lb/acre	kg/ha	1.120 851
		lb/ft^2	kg/m^2	4.822 428
		ton (short)/acre	t/ha	2.241 702
Mass per length or per distance		g/mi	g/km	0.621 371 2
		lb/ft	kg/m	1.488 164
		lb/yd	kg/m	0.496 054 7
Mass per time		ton (short)/h	t/h, Mg/h	0.907 184 7
Modulus, bulk	(*See* Pressure)			
Modulus of elasticity		lb_f/in^2	MPa	0.006 894 757
Modulus of rigidity	(*See* Modulus of elasticity)			
Modulus, section		in^3	cm^3	16. 387 06
		in^3	mm^3	16 387.06
Moment, bending	(*See* Moment of force)			
Moment of area, second		in^4	mm^4	416 231.4
		in^4	cm^4	41.623 14

QUANTITY	FROM TRADITIONAL UNITS	TO METRIC/SI UNITS	MULTIPLY BY
Moment of force, torque, bending moment	$kg_f.cm$	N.m	0.098 066 5
	$oz_f.in$	mN.m	7.061 552
	$lb_f.ft$	N.m	1.355 818
	$lb_f.in$	N.m	0.112 984 8
Moment of inertia	$oz.in^2$	$g.m^2$	0.018 289 98
	$lb.ft^2$	$kg.m^2$	0.042 140 11
	$lb.in^2$	$g.m^2$	0.292 639 7
Moment of Mass	$oz.in^2$	kg.mm	0.720 077 8
Moment of momentum	(*See* Momentum, angular)		
Moment of section	(*See* Moment of area, second)		
Momentum	lb.ft/s	kg.m/s	0.138 255 0
Momentum, angular	$lb.ft^2/s$	$kg.m^2/s$	0.042 140 11
Permeability	H/ft	H/m	3.280 840
Permeance	(*See* Inductance)		
Potential, electric	V	V	1
Power	Btu/h	W	0.293 071 1
	Btu/min	W	17.584 27
	hp (electric)	kW	0.746
	hp (550 $ft.lb_f/s$)	kW	0.745 699 9
	W	W	1
Power per area	$Btu/(ft^2.h)$	W/m^2	3.154 591
Power quotient			
	hp/ton (short)	kW/t	0.822 324 3
	lb/hp	kg/kW	0.608 032 7
Pressure	atm		
	(standard = 760 torr)	kPa	101.325
	bar	kPa	100
	ft H_2O (60°F)	kPa	2.986 08
	in Hg (60°F)	kPa	3.376 85
	in H_2O (60°F)	kPa	0.248 84
	kg_f/cm^2	kPa	98.066 5
	mm Hg (0°C) (torr)	kPa	0.133 322
	lb_f/ft^2	kPa	0.047 880 26
	lb_f/in^2	kPa	6.894 757
	lb_f/in^2 (absolute)	kPa	6.894 757
	torr (mm Hg, 0°C)	kPa	0.133 322
Pressure, sound, level	dB	dB	1
Radiant intensity	(*See* Intensity, radiant)		
Reflectance	cd/fc	mcd/lux	92.903 04
Resistance, electric	Ω	Ω	1
Resistivity, electric	Ω.ft	Ω.cm	30.48
	Ω.ft	Ω.m	0.304 8

QUANTITY	FROM TRADITIONAL UNITS	TO METRIC/SI UNITS	MULTIPLY BY
Sound pressure level	(*See* Pressure, sound level)		
Speed	(*See* Velocity)		
Spring rate, linear	lb_f/in	N/mm	0.175 126 8
(R) Spring rate, torsional	$lb_f.ft/deg$	N.m/°	1.355 818
Strength, field, electric	V/ft	V/m	3.280 840
Strength, field, magnetic	oersted	A/m	79.577 47
Strength, impact (energy absorption)	$ft.lb_f$	J	1.355 818
Stress	lb_f/in^2	mPa	0.006 894 75
Surface tension	(*See* Tension, surface)		
Temperature	°F	°C	$t_{°C} = (t_{°F} - 32)/1.8$
	°R	K	$T_K = T_{°R}/1.8$
Temperature interval	°F	K	$1\ K = 1°C = 1.8°F$
Tension, surface	dyne/cm	mN/m	1
	lb_f/in	mN/m	175 126.8
Thrust	(*See* Force)		
Time	h	h	1
	min	min	1
	s	s	1
Torque	(*See* Moment of force)		
Toughness, fracture	ksi.√in	$mPa.m^{1/2}$	1.098 843
Vacuum	(*See* Pressure)		
Velocity, angular	(*See* Velocity, rotational)		
Velocity, linear	ft/min	m/min	0.304 8
	ft/s	m/s	0.304 8
	in/s	mm/s	25.4
	knot (international)	km/h	1.851 999 8
	mile/h	km/h	1.609 344
Velocity, rotational	r/min	$r/min, r.min^{-1}$	1
	r/s	$r/s, r.s^{-1}$	1
	rad/s	rad/s	1
Viscosity, dynamic	centipoise	mPa.s	1
Viscosity, kinematic	centistokes	mm^2/s	1
Volume	acre.ft	dam^3	1.233 489
		m^3	1 233.489
	bushel	m^3	0.035 239 07
	ft^3	L	28.316 85
	ft^3	m^3	0.028 316 85

QUANTITY	FROM TRADITIONAL UNITS	TO METRIC/SI UNITS	MULTIPLY BY
	gal	L	3.785 412
	in^3	cm^3	16.387 06
	in^3	L	0.016 387 06
	in^3	m^3	0.000 016 387 06
	oz	mL	29.573 53
	peck (U.S. day)	m^3	0.008 097 68
	pt	L	0.473 176 5
	qt	L	0.946 352
	yd^3	m^3	0.764 554 9
Volume per area	gal/acre	L/ha	9.353 958
Weight	(May mean either Mass or Force)		
Work	(*See* Energy)		
Young's modulus	(*See* Modulus of elasticity)		

FASTENERS
-- TRADITIONAL AND METRIC

Selection of threaded fasteners for a given application — either initial selection or selection of a replacement — is generally based on specifications of mechanical properties as tensile strength, yield strength, proof load, and hardness. The fasteners should be of the correct strength, as well as the correct nominal diameter, thread pitch, length, and finish.

Original equipment fasteners are usually identified with numbers or symbols representing the strength of the fastener. These markings enable the technician to ascertain proper replacements are being used. Some metric fasteners, particularly nuts, are colored blue, to serve as a temporary aid for identification during production. This color will fade away with time.

The nomenclature and location of labeling on **bolts** is shown in Figure A2-1. The physical location of the markings are the same, whether the bolts are of traditional (British)/ SAE system, or of metric system. The strength of a bolt is denoted by the marking on the bolt head (Figure A2-2). SAE strength grades range from 2 to 8, with the increasing numbers indicating increasing strength. The embossed markings correspond to two lines less than the actual grade. A grade of 5 is indicated by three lines separated by 120° (Figure A2-2). A grade 8 bolt has 6 lines. Typical metric bolt strength classes are 9.8 and 12.9.

Nuts are marked in a similar way as bolts. Hex nuts (Figure A2-3) in the SAE classification are marked with dots, and those in the

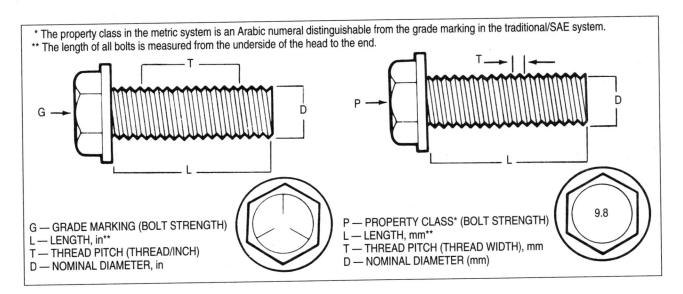

* The property class in the metric system is an Arabic numeral distinguishable from the grade marking in the traditional/SAE system.
** The length of all bolts is measured from the underside of the head to the end.

G — GRADE MARKING (BOLT STRENGTH)
L — LENGTH, in**
T — THREAD PITCH (THREAD/INCH)
D — NOMINAL DIAMETER, in

P — PROPERTY CLASS* (BOLT STRENGTH)
L — LENGTH, mm**
T — THREAD PITCH (THREAD WIDTH), mm
D — NOMINAL DIAMETER (mm)

Figure A2-1 Nomenclature for bolts. (Ford Motor)

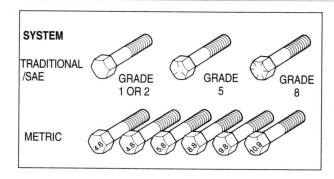

Figure A2-2 Bolt strength identification. (Ford Motor)

metric classification are embossed with an Arabic number. Again, increasing numbers mean increasing strengths.

Marking of **other types of parts** is often a variation of that used of bolts and nuts (A, Figure A2-4). In the metric system, **larger studs** bear a property class number, but **smaller studs** are embossed with a geometric code on the end (B, Figure A2-4).

Many types of traditional/SAE and metric fasteners have NO special identification if they are otherwise unique.

SAE and metric **thread notations** differ slightly. In the SAE system, the notation 5/16-18 indicates a thread major diameter of 5/16 inch and 18 threads per inch. In the metric system, M8 x 1.25 indicates a thread major diameter of 8 mm and a distance of 1.25 mm between threads.

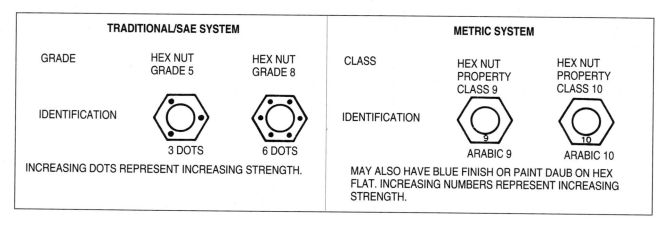

Figure A2-3 Hex nut strength identification. (Ford Motor)

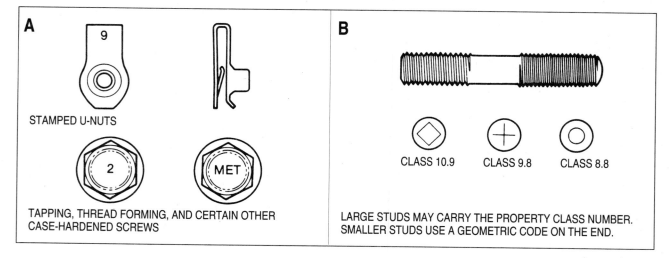

Figure A2-4 Other types of parts. (Ford Motor)

INDUSTRY STANDARDS -- SAE AND ASTM

The Society of Automotive Engineers (SAE) and the American Society for Testing and Materials (ASTM) have established industry standards for the production/servicing/testing of automobiles and parts. The latest standards (as of 1994) relevant to automotive front-end systems are listed here and one should refer to the original standards for detailed information. SAE standards recognized by the American National Standards Institute (ANSI) are indicated by an asterisk (*) preceding the acronym SAE.

SAE STANDARDS

(Ref: SAE Handbook 1994)

ACCELERATION TEST

Vehicle Acceleration Measurement — SAE J1491 Jun90

Electric Vehicle Acceleration, Gradeability, and Deceleration Test Procedure — SAE J1666 May93

AXLES

Axle Efficiency Test Procedure — *SAE J1266 Jun90

Passenger Cars and Light Truck Axles — *SAE J2200 Jan91

Trailer Axle Alignment — *SAE J875 Jun85

BALL JOINTS

Ball Joints — SAE J490 Oct81

Metric Ball Joints — *SAE J2213 Jun91

Metric Spherical Rod Ends — SAE J1259 Jun89

Performance Test Procedure — Ball Joints and Spherical Rod Ends — *SAE J1367 Sep81

Spherical Rod Ends — SAE J1120 Jun89

BALL STUDS

Ball Stud and Socket Assembly — Test Procedures — *SAE J193 Feb87

Steering Ball Studs and Socket Assemblies — *SAE J491 Nov87

BEARINGS

Performance Test Procedure — Ball Joints and Spherical Rod Ends — *SAE J1367 Sep81

CORROSION

Prevention of Corrosion of Motor Vehicle Body and Chassis Components — SAE HS-J447 Jun81

DAMPING

Laboratory Measurement of the Composite Vibration Damping Properties of Materials on a Supporting Steel Bar — SAE J1637 Feb93

DATA COMMUNICATION

Chrysler Sensor and Control (CSC) Bus Multiplexing Network for Class 'A' Applications — SAE J2058 Jun90

Class A Application/Definition — *SAE J2507/1 Jun91

Class A Multiplexing Architecture Strategies — SAE J2057/4 Jun93

Class A Multiplexing Sensors — SAE J2057/3 Jun93

Class B Data Communication Network Interface — SAE 1850 Aug91

Class B Data Communication Network Messages Part 2: Data Parameter Definitions — SAE J2178/2 Jun93

Class B Data Communication Network Messages: Detailed Header Formats and Physical Address Assignments — SAE J2178/1 Jun92

Class C Application Requirement Considerations — SAE J2056/1 Jun93

Collision Detection Serial Data Communications Multiplex Bus — SAE J1567 Aug87

Controller Area Network (CAN), An In-Vehicle Serial Communication Protocol — SAE J1583 Mar90

E/E Data Link Security — SAE J2186 Sep91

E/E Diagnostic Data Communications — *SAE J2054 Nov90

Enhanced E/E Diagnostic Test Modes — SAE J2190 Jun93

Initial Graphics Exchange Specification — *SAE J1881 Feb93

Off-Board Diagnostic Message Formats — *SAE J2037 Nov90

Selection of Transmission Media — *SAE J2056/3 Jun91

Survey of Known Protocols — SAE J2056/2 Apr93

Token Slot Network for Automotive Control — *SAE J2106 Apr91

Universal Interface for OBD II Scan — SAE J2201 Jun93

A Vehicle Network Protocol with a Fault Tolerant Multiplex Signal Bus — SAE J1813 Aug87

DECELERATION

Sound Level for Passenger Cars and Light Trucks — SAE J986 Oct88

DIAGNOSTICS

Diagnostic Connector — SAE J1962 Jun93

Diagnostic Trouble Code Definitions — SAE J2012 Mar92

E/E Diagnostic Data Communications — *SAE J2054 Nov90

E/E Diagnostic Test Modes — SAE J1979 Dec91

Enhanced E/E Diagnostic Test Modes — SAE J2190 Jun93

OBD II Scan Tool — SAE J1978 Mar92

Off-Board Diagnostic Message Formats — *SAE J2037 Nov90

DIMENSIONS

Automobile

Curb Clearance Approach, Departure, and Ramp Breakover Angles — Passenger Car and Light Truck — *SAE J689 Dec89

Motor Vehicle Dimensions — *SAE J182 Nov90

Motor Vehicle Fiducial Marks and Three Dimensional Reference System — *SAE J182 Nov90

Ball Joints

Metric Ball Joints — *SAE J2213 Jun91

Belts and Pulleys

SI (Metric) Synchronous Belts and Pulleys — SAE J1278 Mar93

Clamps

Hose Clamp Specifications — SAE J1508 Jun93

Type 'F' Clamps for Plumbing Applications — SAE J1670 May93

Clutch Housings

Housing Internal Dimensions for Single- and Two-Plate Spring-Loaded Clutches — *SAE J373 Apr93

Fittings

Automotive Pipe Fittings — SAE J530 Jun93

Automotive Tube Fittings — SAE J512 Jun93

Beaded Tube Hose Fittings — SAE J1231 Jun93

Clip Fastener Fitting — SAE J1467 Jun93

Fitting — O-ring Face Seal — SAE J1453 Jun93

Hydraulic Hose Fittings — SAE J516 Jun93

Hydraulic Tube Fittings — SAE J514 Jun93

Lubrication Fittings — *SAE J534 Jun93

Spherical and Flanged Sleeve (Compression) Tube Fittings — SAE J246 Jun93

Flanges

Companion Flanges, Type A (External Pilot) and Type S (Internal Pilot) — *SAE J1946 Jan91

Hoses

Fuel and Oil Hoses — *SAE J30 May93

Hydraulic Hose — SAE J517 Jun 93

Mounts

Fastener Hardware for Wheels for Demountable Rims — *SAE J1835 Mar90

Hydraulic Pump and Motor Mounting and Drive Dimensions — *SAE J744 Jul88

Starting Motor Mountings — *SAE J542 Jun91

O-Rings

Hydraulic O-Ring — SAE J515 Jun92

Passenger Compartments

Devices for Use in Defining and Measuring Vehicle Seating Accommodation — SAE J826 Jun92

Pulleys

V-Belts and Pulleys — SAE J636 May92

Rims

Wide Base Tire Rims and Wheels — *SAE J876 Jan91

Seals

Application Guide to Radial Lip Seals — SAE J876 Oct91

ELECTROMAGNETIC COMPATIBILITY (EMC)

Electromagnetic Susceptibility Measurements of Vehicle Components Using TEM Cells (14 kHz - 200 MHz) — SAE J1448 Jan84

Electromagnetic Susceptibility Procedures for Common Mode Injection (1 - 400 MHz) Module Testing — SAE J1547 Jan84

Function Performance Status Classification for EMC Susceptibility Testing of Automotive Electronic and Electrical Devices — SAE J1812 Oct88

ELECTROMAGNETIC INTERFERENCE (EMI)

Collision Detection Serial Data Communications Multiplex Bus — SAE J1567 Aug87

Electromagnetic Susceptibility Measure Procedures for Vehicle Components (Except Aircraft) — *SAE J1113 Aug87

ELECTRONIC EQUIPMENT

Design/Process Checklist for Vehicle Electronic Systems — SAE J1938 Oct88

Performance Levels and Methods of Measurement of Electromagnetic Radiation from Vehicles and Devices, Narrowband, 10kHz to 1000 MHz — *SAE J1816 Oct87

ELECTROSTATIC DISCHARGE (ESD)

Electrostatic Discharge Test for Vehicles — SAE J1595 Oct88

ENVIRONMENTAL EFFECTS

Bonded Assemblies

Accelerated Environmental Testing for Bonded Automotive Assemblies — SAE J2100 Aug92

Electronic Equipment

General Qualification and Production Acceptance Criteria for Integrated Circuits in Automotive Applications — SAE J1879 Oct88

Recommended Environmental Practices for Electronic Equipment Design — SAE J1211

Trim

Accelerated Exposure of Automotive Interior Trim Components Using a Controlled Irradiance Water Cooled Xenon-Arc Apparatus — SAE J1885 Mar92

FASTENERS

Aluminum

Wrought Aluminum Applications Guidelines — SAE J1434 Jan89

Gasket Materials

Fastener Hardware for Wheels for Demountable Rims — *SAE J1835 Mar90

Standard Classification System for Nonmetallic Automotive Gasket Materials — *SAE J90 Jun90

Steel

Clip Fastener Fitting — SAE J1467 Jun93

Decarburization in Hardened and Tempered Threaded Fasteners — *SAE J121 Aug83

Mechanical and Chemical Requirements for Nonthreaded Fasteners — SAE J430

Mechanical and Material Requirements for Externally Threaded Fasteners — *SAE J429 Aug83

Mechanical and Material Requirements for

Metric Externally Threaded Steel Fasteners — *SAE J1199 Sep83

Mechanical and Material Requirements for Wheel Bolts — SAE J1120

Metric Countersunk Holes for Cutting Edges and End Bits — *SAE J1580 DEC89

Surface Discontinuities on Bolts, Screws, and Studs — SAE J123c

Surface Discontinuities on General Application Bolts, Screws, and Studs — SAE J1061 OCT92

Test Methods for Metric Threaded Fasteners — *SAE J1216

Torque-Tension Test Procedure for Steel Threaded Fasteners — SAE J174

FATIGUE

Springs

Fatigue Testing Procedure for Suspension-Leaf Springs — *SAE J1528 Jun90

Manual on Design and Application of Helical and Spiral Springs — SAE HS-J795 Apr90

Manual on Design and Application of Leaf Springs — SAE HS-788 Apr80

Manual on Design and Manufacture of Torsion Bar Springs — SAE HS-796 Jul90

Wheels

Spoke Wheels and Hub Fatigue Test Procedures — *SAE J1095 Jan91

Wheels — Passenger Cars — Performance Requirements and Test Procedures — *SAE J328 Mar90

FIBER OPTICS

Selection of Transmission Media — *SAE J2056/3 Jun91

FLANGES

Balance Weight and Rim Flange Design Specifications, Test Procedures, and Performance Recommendations — SAE J1986 Feb93

Companion Flanges, Type A (External Pilot) and Type S (Internal Pilot) — *SAE J1946 Jan91

Cross-Tooth Companion Flanges, Type T — *SAE J1945 Jan90

Starting Motor Mountings — *SAE J542 Jun91

FRICTION MATERIALS

Band Friction Test Machine (SAE) Test Procedure — SAE J1499 Feb87

SAE No.2 Clutch Friction Test Machine Test Procedure — *SAE J286 Nov83

FUSES

Blade Type Electric Fuses — *SAE J1284 Apr88

Electric Fuses (Cartridge Type) — *SAE J554 Aug87

Fusible Links — *SAE J156 Apr86

High Current Time Lag Electric Fuses — *SAE J1888 Nov90

Miniature Blade Type Eelctrical Fuses — *SAE J2077 Nov90

HYDRAULIC FLUIDS

Assessing Cleanliness of Hydraulic Fluid Power Components and Systems — *SAE J1227 Mar86

Hydraulic Power Circuit Filtration — SAE J931 Mar86

Method for Assessing the Cleanliness Level of New Hydraulic Fluid — *SAE J1227 Jul90

Recording Cleanliness Levels of Hydraulic Fluids — *SAE J1165 Mar86

Standardized Fluid for Hydraulic Component Tests — *SAE J1276 Mar86

HYDRAULIC SYSTEMS — COUPLINGS

Connections for Fluid Power and General Use — Ports and Stud Ends with ISO 261 Threads and O-Ring Sealing. Part 1: Port with O-Ring Seal in Truncated Housing — SAE J2244/1 Dec91; Part 2: Heavy-Duty (S Series) Stud Ends — Dimensions, Design, Test Methods, and Requirements — SAE J2244/2 Dec91

Hydraulic Diagnostic Couplings — *SAE J1502 Apr86

Metallic Tube Connections for Fluid Power and General Use Test Methods for Threaded Hydraulic Fluid Power Connectors — SAE J1644 May93

— CYLINDERS

Cylinder Rod Wiper Seal Ingression Test — *SAE J1195 Mar86

Hydraulic Cylinder Integrity Test — SAE J1334 Jun87

Hydraulic Cylinder Leakage Test — SAE J1336 Jun87

Hydraulic Cylinder No-Load Friction Test — *SAE J1335 Apr90

Hydraulic Cylinder Rod Corrosion Test — *SAE J214 Mar86

Hydraulic Cylinder Rod Seal Endurance Test Procedure — *SAE J1374 May85

Hydraulic Cylinder Test Procedure — *SAE J214 Mar86

Rubber Cups for Hydraulic Actuating Cylinders — *SAE J1601 Nov90

— DIAGNOSTICS

Hydraulic Systems Diagnostic Port Sizes and Locations — *SAE J1298 Sep88

— HOSES

Beaded Tube Hose Fittings — SAE J1231 Jun93

Clip Fastener Fitting — SAE J1467 Jun93

Cumulative Damage Analysis for Hydraulic Hose Assemblies — SAE J1927 Oct88

Fluid Conductors and Connectors — SAE HS-150 Jun92

Fuel and Oil Hoses — *SAE J30 May93

Hydraulic Hose — SAE J517 Jun93

Hydraulic Hose Fittings — SAE J516 Jun93

Optional Impulse Test Procedures for Hydraulic Hose Assemblies — SAE J1405 Jun90

Road Vehicle — Hydraulic Brake Hose Assemblies for Use with Nonpetroleum-Base Hydraulic Fluids — *SAE J1401 Jun93

Selection, Installation, and Maintenance of Hose and Hose Assemblies — SAE J1273 Nov91

Tests and Procedures for SAE 100R Series Hydraulic Hose and Hose Assemblies — *SAE J343 Jun93

Clamps

Hose Clamp Specifications — SAE J1508 Jun93

Type 'F' Clamps for Plumbing Applications — SAE J1670 May93

Numbering Systems

Coding Systems for Identification of Fluid Conductors and Connectors — SAE J846 Jun89

Power Steering

High-Temperature Power Steering Pressure Hose — SAE J2050 Feb93

High-Temperature Power Steering Return Hose — Low Pressure — SAE J2076 Feb93

Power Steering Pressure Hose — High Volumetric Expansion Type — *SAE J188 Oct89

Power Steering Pressure Hose — Low Volumetric Expansion Type — *SAE J191 Oct89

Power Steering Pressure Hose — Wire Braid — SAE J190

Power Steering Pressure Hose — Low Pressure — SAE J189 Dec89

— INSTRUMENTATION

Instrumentation for Impact Test — *SAE J211 Oct88

— LEAKAGE

External Leakage Classifications for Hydraulic Systems — *SAE J1176 Mar86

— MOTORS

Hydraulic Motor Test Procedure — *SAE J746 Mar86

— OPERATOR PROTECTIVE STRUCTURES

Rear Underride Guard Test Procedure — *SAE J260 Jun90

— PIPE/TUBE FITTINGS

Automotive Pipe Fittings — SAE J530 Jun93

Automotive Tube Fittings — SAE J512 Jun93

Flares for Tubing — SAE J533 Jun92

Hydraulic Tube Fittings — SAE J514 Jun93

Lubrication Fittings — *SAE J534 Jun93

Pressure Ratings for Hydraulic Tubing and Fittings — SAE J1065 Mar92

Seamless Copper-Nickel 90-10 Tubing — SAE J1650 Mar93

Spherical and Flanged Sleeve (Compression) Tube Fittings — SAE J246 Jun93

O-rings

Connections for General Use and Fluid Power-Ports and Stud Ends with ISO 725 Threads and O-Ring Sealing — Part 1: Threaded Port with O-Ring Seal in Truncated Housing — SAE J1926/1 ISO 11 Mar93; Part 2: Heavy-Duty (S Series) Stud Ends — SAE J1926/2 ISO 11 Mar93; Part 3: Light-Duty (L Series) Stud Ends — SAE J1926/3 ISO 11 Mar93

Fitting — O-Ring Face Seal — SAE J1453 Jun93

Hydraulic O-Ring — SAE J515 Jun92

Rubber Rings for Automotive Applications — SAE J120a

— PUMPS

Hydraulic Pump and Motor Mounting Drive Dimensions — *SAE J744 Jul88

— STEERING GEARS

Performance Assurance of Remanufactured, Hydraulically-Operated Rack and Pinion Steering Gears — *SAE J1890 Jun88

— VALVES

Control Valve Test Procedure — *SAE J747 May90

Hydraulic Directional Control Valves, 3000 psi Maximum — *SAE J748 Mar86

Measuring and Reporting Internal Leakage of a Hydraulic Fluid Power Valve — *SAE J1235 Mar86

Method of Measuring and Reporting the Pressure Differential - Flow Characteristics of a Hydraulic Fluid Power Valve — *SAE J1117 Mar86

INSTRUMENT PANELS

Design Criteria — Driver Hand Controls Location for Passenger Cars, Multi-Purpose Passenger Vehicles, and Trucks (10,000 GVW and Under) — SAE J1138

Photometric Guidelines for Instrument Panel Displays That Accommodate Older Drivers — SAE J2217 Oct91

Supplemental Information — Driver Hand Controls Location for Passenger Cars, Multi-Purpose Passenger Vehicles, and Trucks (10,000 GVW and Under) — SAE J1139

INTEGRATED CIRCUITS

Collision Detection Serial Data Communications Multiplex Bus — SAE J1567 Aug87

General Qualification and Production Acceptance Criteria for Integrated Circuits in Automotive Applications — SAE J1879 Oct88

LIQUID LEVEL INDICATORS

Guidelines for Liquid Level Indicators — SAE J48 May93

LUBRICANTS

Automotive Lubricating Greases — SAE J310 Jun93

The Automotive Lubricant Performance and Service Classification Maintenance Procedure

— *SAE J1146 JUN86

Axle and Manual Transmission Lubricants — SAE J308 Jun89

Axle and Manual Transmission Lubricant Viscosity Classification — SAE J306 Oct91

Effective Dates of New or Revised Technical Reports — *SAE J301 Mar93

Fuels and Lubricants Standards Manual — SAE HS-23 Feb93

PARKING

Trailer Grade Parking Performance Test Procedure — SAE J1452 Oct88

Vehicle Grade Parking Performance Requirements — *SAE J293 Oct88

Wheel Chocks — SAE J348 Jun90

PINS

Rod Ends and Clevis Pins — SAE J493

Unhardened Ground Dowel Pins — SAE J497

Grooved Straight Pins — SAE J497

Spring Type Straight Pins — SAE J496

Straight Pins (Solid) — SAE J495

PLUGS

Automotive Pipe, Filler, and Drain Plugs — SAE J531 Jun93

PRINTED CIRCUITS

Automotive Printed Circuits — *SAE J771 Apr86

PROGRAMMABLE CONTROLLERS

OEM/Vendor's Interface Specifications for Vehicle Electronic Programming Station — SAE J1924 Dec92

SCREWS

Decarburization in Hardened and Tempered Threaded Fasteners — *SAE J121 Aug83

Mechanical and Material Requirements for Externally Threaded Fasteners — *SAE J429 Aug93

Mechanical and Material Requirements for Metric Externally Threaded Steel Fasteners — *SAE J1199 Sep83

Mechanical and Quality Requirements for Machine Screws — SAE J82 Jun79

Mechanical and Quality Requirements for Tapping Screws — SAE J933 Jun79

Metric Thread Rolling Screws — SAE J1237

Screw Threads (ANSI B1.1) — SAE J475a

Steel Self-Drilling Tapping Screws — SAE J78 Jun79

Surface Discontinuities on Bolts, Screws, and Studs — SAE J123c

Surface Discontinuities on General Application Bolts, Screws, and Studs — SAE J1061 Oct92

Test Methods for Metric Threaded Fasteners — *SAE J1216

Thread Rolling Screws — SAE J81 Jun79

SEALS

Cast Iron Sealing Rings — SAE J281 Sep80

Cast Iron Sealing Rings (Metric) — SAE J1236 Apr93

Cylinder Rod Wiper Seal Ingression Test — *SAE J1195 Mar86

Hydraulic Cylinder Leakage Test — SAE J1336 Jun87

Hydraulic Cylinder Rod Seal Endurance Test Procedure — *SAE J1374 May85

Fitting — O-Ring Face Seal — SAE J1453 Jun93

Front-Wheel Drive Constant Velocity Joint Boot Seals — SAE J2028 Jun92

Seals — Testing of Radial Lip — SAE J110 Dec91

Test Method for Evaluating the Sealing Capability of Hose Connections with a PVT Test Facility — SAE J1610 Apr93

SENSORS

Accelerator Pedal Position Sensor for Use with Electronic Controls in Medium- and Heavy-Duty Vehicle Applications — SAE J1843 Apr93

Automatic Vehicle Speed Control — Motor Vehicles — SAE J195 Dec88

Chrysler Sensor and Control (CSC) Bus Multiplexing Network for Class 'A' Applications — SAE J2058 Jun90

Collision Detection Serial Data Communications Multiplex Bus — SAE J1567 Aug87

Equivalent Temperature — SAE J2234 Jan93

Transmission Mounted Vehicle Speed Signal Rotor Specification — SAE J1377 Jan89

SLACK ADJUSTER

Automatic Slack Adjuster Performance Requirements — SAE J1513 Apr90

Automatic Slack Adjuster Test Procedure — *SAE J1462 May87

Manual Slack Adjuster Performance Requirements — *SAE J1512 Apr90

Manual Slack Adjuster Test Procedure — SAE J1461 Apr91

SPRINGS

Hard Drawn Mechanical Spring Wire and Springs — SAE J113 Dec88

Music Steel Spring Wire and Springs — SAE J178 Dec88

Oil Tempered Carbon Steel Spring Wire and Springs — SAE J316 Dec88

Oil Tempered Chromium-Silicon Alloy Steel Wire and Springs — SAE J157 Dec88

Special Quality High Tensile, Hard Drawn Mechanical Spring Wire and Springs — SAE J271 Dec88

Stainless Steel 17-7 PH Spring Wire and Springs — SAE J217 Dec88

Stainless Steel, SAE 30302, Spring Wire and Springs — SAE J230 Dec88

Coil/Helical

Helical Compression and Extension Spring Terminology — *SAE J1121 Jul88

Helical Springs: Specification Check Lists — *SAE J1122 Jul88

Manual on Design and Application of Helical and Spiral Springs — SAE HS-J795 Apr90

Conical

Conical Spring Washers — SAE J773b

Nut and Conical Spring Washer Assemblies — SAE J238

Leaf

Fatigue Testing Procedure for Suspension-Leaf Springs — *SAE J1528 Jun90

Leaf Springs for Motor Vehicle Suspension — Made to Metric Units — SAE J1123 Nov92

Leaf Springs for Motor Vehicle Suspension — Made to Customary US Units — SAE J510 Nov92

Pneumatic

Manual for Incorporating Pneumatic Springs in Vehicle Suspension Designs — SAE HS-1576

Pneumatic Spring Terminology — SAE J511 Jun89

Torsion Bar

Manual on Design and Manufacture of Torsion Bar Springs — SAE HS-J96 Jul90

Valves

Hard Drawn Carbon Steel Valve Spring Quality Wire and Springs — SAE J172 Dec88

Oil Tempered Carbon Steel Valve Spring Quality Wire and Springs — SAE J351 Dec88

Oil Tempered Chromium-Vanadium Valve Spring Quality Wire and Springs — SAE J132 Dec88

STEERING

Describing and Measuring the Driver's Field of View — SAE J1050a

Performance Assurance of Remanufactured, Hydraulically-Operated Rack and Pinion Steering Gears — *SAE J1890 Jun88

STOP LAMPS

Central High Mounted Stop Lamp Standard for Use on Vehicles Less than 2032 mm Overall Width — SAE J1957 Jun93

SAE Ground Vehicle Lightning Standards Manual — SAE HS-34 Jan93

Stop Lamps for Use on Motor Vehicles Less Than 2032 mm in Overall Width — *SAE J586 Dec89

Supplemental High Mounted Stop and Rear Turn Signal Lamps for Use on Vehicles Less than 2032 mm in Overall Width — *SAE J186 Dec89

Tail Lamps (Rear Position Lamps) for Use on Motor Vehicles Less Than 2032 mm in Overall Width — SAE J585 Dec91

TERMINOLOGY

Vehicle Aerodynamics Terminology — *SAE J1594 Jun87

Vehicle Dynamics Terminology — SAE J670e Jun76

Handbook of Motor Vehicle Safety and Environmental Terminology — SAE HS-215

Driveshafts

All Wheel Drive Systems Classification — *SAE J1952 Jan91

Universal Joints and Driveshafts — Nomenclature — Terminology — Application — *SAE J901 Oct 90

Electrical/Electronic

Electrical/Electronic Systems Diagnostic Terms, Definitions, Abbreviations, and Acronyms — SAE J1930 Jun93

Glossary of Automotive Electronic Terms — SAE J1213 Nov82

Glossary of Automotive Inflatable Restraint Terms — SAE J1538 Apr88

Glossary of Reliability Terminology Associated with Automotive Electronics — SAE J1213/2 Oct88

Glossary of Vehicle Networks for Multiplexing and Data Communications — *SAE J1213/1 Jun91

Heat Treatment

Definitions of Heat Treating Terms — SAE J415 Jun83

Hydrodynamic Drives

Hydrodynamic Drives Terminology — *SAE J641 Jul88

Symbols for Hydrodynamic Drives — *SAE J640 Apr93

Springs

Helical Compression and Extension Spring Terminology — *SAE J1121 Jul88

Pneumatic Spring Terminology — SAE J511 Jun89

Tires

Military Tire Glossary — *SAE J2013 May91

Towing

Towability Design Criteria and Equipment Use — Passnger Cars, Vans, and Light Duty Trucks — *SAE J1142 Jun91

Universal Joints

Universal Joints and Driveshafts — Nomenclature — Terminology — Application — *SAE J901 Oct90

Wheels

Nomenclature — Wheels for Passenger Cars, Vans, and Light Trucks, and Multipurpose Vehicles — SAE J1982 Dec91

TIRES

Factors Affecting Accuracy of Mechanically Driven Automotive Speedometer and Odometers — SAE J862 Jan89

Laboratory Speed Test Procedure for Passenger Car Tires — SAE J1561 Feb93

Laboratory Testing Machines and Procedures for Measuring the Steady State Force and Moment Properties of Passenger Car Tires — SAE J1107 Feb75

Laboratory Testing Machines for Measuring the Steady State Force and Moment Properties of Passenger Car Tires — SAE J1106 Feb75

Measurement of Passenger Car, Light Truck, and Highway Truck and Bus Tire Rolling Resistance — SAE J1270 Mar87

Passenger Car and Light Truck Tire Traction Device Profile Determination and Classification — SAE J1232

Passenger Car and Light Truck Tire Dynamic Driving Traction in Snow — *SAE J1466 Oct85

Passenger Car and Light Truck Performance Requirements and Test Procedures — SAE J918c

Rolling Resistance Measurement Procedure for Passenger Car, Light Truck, and Highway Truck and Bus Tires — *SAE J1269 Mar87

Subjective Rating Scale for Evaluation of Noise and Ride Comfort Charateristics Related to Motor Vehicle Tires — SAE J1060

Test Procedure for Measuring Passenger Car Tire Revolutions per Mile — SAE J966

Testing Machines for Measuring the Uniformity of Passenger Car and Light Truck Tires — *SAE J332 Aug81

Wet or Dry Pavement Passenger Car Tire Peak and Locked Wheel Braking Traction — SAE J345a

Valves

Method for Testing Snap-In Tubeless Tire Valves — SAE J1206

Performance Requirements for Snap-In Tubeless Tire Valves — SAE J1205

VISCOSITY

Method of Viscosity Test for Automotive Type Adhesives, Sealers, and Deadeners — SAE J1524 Nov88

Method of Tests for Automotive-Type Sealers, Adhesives, and Deadeners — SAE J243

WARNING SYSTEMS

Combination Turn Signal Hazard Warning Signal Flashers — *SAE J2068 Jan90

Emergency Warning (Triangular Shape) — *SAE J774 Dec89

Flasher Test — *SAE J823 Jun91

Hazard Warning Signal Switch — *SAE J910 Oct88

Minimum Requirements for Wheel Slip Brake Control System Malfunction Signals — SAE J1230 Oct79

SAE Ground Vehicle Lighting Standards Manual — SAE HS-34 Jan93

Vehicular Hazard Warning Signal Flashers — *SAE J945 Jun93

Warning Lamp Alternating Flashers — *SAE J1054 Oct89

WEAR

Abrasive Wear — SAE J965 Aug66

WHEELS

Balance Weight and Rim Flange Design Specifications, Test Procedures, and Performance Recommendations — SAE J1986 Feb93

Disc Wheel Radial Runout Low Point Marking — SAE J2133 Jun93

Mechanical and Material Requirements for Wheel Bolts — SAE J1102

Road Vehicles — Wheels for Commercial Vehicles and Multipurpose Passenger Vehicles — Fixing Nuts — Test Methods — SAE J1965 Feb93

Wheel Chocks — SAE J348 Jun90

Wheels — Impact Test Procedures — Road Vehicles — *SAE J175 Jun88

Wheels — Passenger Cars — Performance Requirements and Test Procedures — *SAE J328 Mar90

WINDSHIELDS

Passenger Car Windshield Defrosting Systems — SAE J902 Apr93

Passenger Car Windshield Washer Systems — SAE J942b

Passenger Car Windshield Wiper Systems — SAE J903c

ASTM STANDARDS

(Ref: 1993 Annual Book of ASTM Standards)

Calibration of systems used for measuring vehicular response to pavement roughness, practice, ASTM E1448

Longitudinal peak skid resistance of paved surfaces, using standard reference tire, test — ASTM E1337

Lined journal bearings, for locomotive tenders/passenger cars/freight equipment, UNS C94100, spec., ASTM B67

Simulating vehicular response to longitudinal profiles of a vehicular traveled surface, practice — ASTM E1170

Speed/distance calibration of fifth wheel equipped with either analog/digital instrumentation, method, ASTM F457

Trailer used for measuring vehicle response to road roughness, spec., ASTM E1215

Vehicular response to traveled surface roughness, test — ASTM E1082

FRICTION COEFFICIENTS

Friction coefficients — measuring/reporting/selecting tests, guide, ASTM G115

TIR (TOTAL INDICATED RUNOUT)

Photoplate surface flatness, by interferometric non-contact technique, test, ASTM F508

TIRES

Accelerometer use in vehicles for tire testing, practice, ASTM F811

Discernment capability — tire x-ray imaging system, using rubber-cord pie disc, practice, ASTM F1035

Establishing road test distance (using a fifth wheel), method, ASTM F559

Groove (void) area of passenger car tires, method, ASTM F870

Longitudinal peak skid resistance of paved surfaces, using standard reference tire, test, ASTM E1337

Preparing artificially worn passenger car/light truck tires for testing, guide, ASTM F1046

Rib or lug height, test, ASTM F421

Rubber deterioration — dynamic fatigue, test, ASTM D430

Skid resistance of paved surfaces, using full-scale tire, test, ASTM E274

Stopping distance on paved surfaces, using passenger vehicle with full-scale tires, test, ASTM E445/445M

Tires- determining precision for test method standards, practice, ASTM F1082

Tires- performance/characteristics, terminology, ASTM F538

Tire tread depth (change in groove (or void) depth) determination, test, ASTM F762

Tire tread water data analysis, practice, ASTM F1016

Tubeless pneumatic tires — static testing for rate of loss of inflation pressure, test, ASTM F1112

Use of calibration device to demonstrate inspection capability of interferometric laser imaging nondestructive tire inspection system, practic, ASTM F1364

— STANDARD

Radial standard reference test tire, spec., ASTM E1136

Standard rib tire for pavement skid-resistance tests, spec., ASTM E501

Standard smooth tire (for pavement skid-resistance testing), spec., ASTM E524

Using a nominal 67.23-in. (1.707 m) diameter laboratory test roadwheel in testing tires, practice, ASTM F551

— WET TRACTION

Straight-ahead motion, using highway vehicles, testing, ASTM F424

Tires for wet traction performance in cornering, method, ASTM F376/376M

VELOCITY TRANSDUCER

Non-destructive testing of pavements, using cyclic-loading dynamic deflection equipment, guide, ASTM D4602

WHEEL BEARINGS

Low-temperature torque of grease lubricated wheel bearings, test, ASTM D4693

SAFETY AND HEALTH STANDARDS -- FMVSS AND OSHA

Federal Motor Vehicle Safety Standards (FMVSS) are concerned with the safety of motorists, and prescribe the requirements of a road-worthy vehicle. Occupational Safety and Health Administration (OSHA) Standards prescribe the work practices and engineering controls related to the manufacturing and repair/service operations. A responsible automotive technician will be familiar with the salient features of these Federal Standards that address the Safety and Health aspects affecting motorists and technicians.

FEDERAL MOTOR VEHICLE SAFETY STANDARDS (FMVSS)

The National Traffic and Motor Vehicle Safety Act (the Act), 15 USC 1381, was passed by Congress in 1966 aiming to improve highway safety. Congress empowered the National Highway Traffic Safety Administration (NHTSA) to develop and enforce motor vehicle safety standards. These standards, called Federal Motor Vehicle Safety Standards (FMVSS) as contained in the Code of Federal Regulations (CFR), Title 49 Part 571, cover specifications that a manufacturer must comply with for building cars, trucks, buses, multi-purpose passenger vehicles, trailers, and motorcycles. The Standards also cover various equipment or components concerning the safe operation of the vehicle, as lighting, brakes, fuel system, and cab or occupant safety. The Act also imposes certain obligations as notification, recall, and remedy on manufacturers of motor vehicles. A responsible automotive technician is expected to be familiar with the various Federal Standards related to the Safety and Health aspects affecting motorists and technicians.

For the purposes of the Act, a dealer, truck equipment distributor, or body/accessory manufacturer that installs a body or other equipment on an incomplete vehicle or that alters a certified completed vehicle before the first purchase of the vehicle in good faith for purposes other than resale is deemed a '**manufacturer**' that must ensure the vehicle's conformance with applicable Standards.

When the ultimate customer purchases an incomplete vehicle and installs additional equipment, the **customer**, in effect, **becomes a manufacturer** and is subject to the certification provisions of the Act. However, a minor finishing operation like painting does NOT come under manufacturing.

Every manufacturing firm is required by NHTSA (49 CFR Part 566) to submit a description of the items it produces. Depending on the stage in the manufacturing sequence of the vehicle, a manufacturer may be categorized as an incomplete, intermediate, final-stage, or altering manufacturer — each having certain obligations under the Act.

The provision of '**Due Care**' allows one vehicle type to be certified on the basis of testing a similar vehicle type. Due Care also allows a *small* manufacturer to employ one or a combination of alternating testing methods in order to certify the vehicle. However, the manufacturer must be reasonably certain that a particular vehicle configuration will conform to all applicable Standards.

All incomplete-vehicle manufacturers must provide subsequent-stage manufacturers with an **incomplete-vehicle document** (IVD), containing the information as required in 49 CFR Part 568.4. The intermediate-stage manufacturer must provide an addendum to the document that includes company (or individual's) name and address, and an indication of all changes to be made in the IVD to reflect the alterations made to the vehicle.

Section 114 of the Act (15 USC 1403) requires that every manufacturer or distributor of a motor vehicle or related equipment provide the distributor or dealer at the time of delivery with a certification that each such vehicle or item of motor vehicle equipment conforms to all applicable FMVSS's. The **certification responsibilities** of each type of manufacturer are specified in 49 CFR Part 567.

The Act's **recall and remedy requirements** (Part B of the Act, 15 USC 1411 etc., and regulations at 49 CFR Parts 573, 577, and 579) apply to all manufacturers of automobiles, including vehicle alterers, and to manufacturers of original as well as replacement automotive equipment.

A recall is warranted when:

- the vehicle fails to comply with any applicable Safety Standards, or
- it is determined that the vehicle has safety-related defect (which may or may not be associated with a Standard).

In compliance, the manufacturer must report certain information to NHTSA, notify the vehicle owner, and either repair or replace the vehicle at no cost to the customer, or refund the purchase price of the vehicle minus any reasonable depreciation.

The Act provides for **civil penalties** of up to $1,000 per violation, with a maximum penalty of up to $800,000. Each vehicle not conforming to relevant Safety Standards, or not certified properly, and each such occurrence of **non-compliance**

with the recall and remedy requirements could constitute a separate violation of the Act. **Two important points** to note:

1. Every vehicle must have a final-stage certification.
2. Every manufacturing performed on a motor vehicle prior to the first retail sale for use must be certified.

Additional information on this topic, including detailed instructions on completing the certification label, can be found in the NTEA Certification Guide.

The paragraphs below outline the important aspects of **selected FMVSS's**. FMVSS's related to protection from impact and flammability are listed first, followed by those that specify the requirements for tires, accelerator, and steering in that order. Lastly, the titles of selected FMVSS's for brake systems are also given, efficient brakes being the most important safety item in a motor vehicle.

FMVSS's FOR PROTECTION FROM IMPACT AND FLAMMABILITY

FMVSS 101, Controls and Displays

This standard specifies the requirements for the location, identification, and illumination of motor vehicle controls. It applies to multipurpose passenger vehicles (MPVs), trucks, and buses manufactured effective September 01, 1989. For older vehicles, FMVSS 100 applies.

FMVSS 125, Warning Systems

This standard specifies the requirements for traffic warning devices — that have no self-contained power sources — designed to be carried in the vehicle and used to warn approaching traffic of the presence of a stopped vehicle.

FMVSS 201, Occupant Protection in Interior Impact

Applicable to MPVs, trucks, and buses with a GVWR of ≤10,000 lb, this standard requires the use of appropriate energy-absorbing materials on interior components such as instrument panels, seat backs, interior doors, arm rests, and sun visors.

FMVSS 214, Side Door Strength and FMVSS 216, Roof Crush Resistance

These standards, applicable to passenger cars, specify the impact strength requirements for the side doors and the roof, respectively.

FMVSS 220, School Bus Rollover Protection

This standard aims at reducing the number of deaths and the severity of injuries resulting from failure of the school bus body structure to withstand the forces involved in rollover crashes.

FMVSS 302, Flammability of Interior Materials

This standard stipulates that NO interior material shall burn or transmit a flame front across its surface at a rate >4 inches per minute.

FMVSS's ON TIRES, ACCELERATOR, STEERING, AND WHEELS

FMVSS 119, New Pneumatic Tires for Vehicles Other Than Passenger Cars

This standard specifies the performance and marking requirements for tires used on vehicles other than passenger cars.

FMVSS 120, Tire Selection and Rims for Motor Vehicles Other Than Passenger Cars

Applicable to MPVs, trucks, buses, and trailers, this standard requires that details of tire size(s), rim designation, and cold inflation pressure be given on the certification label or on a separate tire information label.

FMVSS 124, Accelerator Control Systems

This standard applies to MPVs, trucks, and buses. It requires the return of a vehicle's throttle to the idle position when the driver removes the actuating force from the accelerator or in the event of a breakage or disconnection in the accelerator control system.

FMVSS 203, Impact Protection for the Driver from the Steering Control System

This standard is applicable to MPVs, trucks, and buses with a GVWR of ≤10,000 lb, but not to walk-in vans. It requires that the steering column assembly transmit a force <2,500 lb when a body block impacts it at 15 mph.

FMVSS 204, Steering Control Rearward Displacement

This standard is applicable to MPVs, trucks, and buses with a GVWR of ≤10,000 lb with an unloaded weight of ≤5,500 lb. It is not applicable to walk-in vans. It requires that the steering column must NOT move rearward into the occupant compartment by more than 5 inches in a frontal barrier crash at 30 mph. Prior to September 01, 1991, the applicable unloaded vehicle weight was ≤4,000 lb.

FMVSS 211, Wheel Nuts, Wheel Discs, and Hub Caps

As per this standard, the items — wheel nuts, wheel discs, and hub caps — on MPVs shall NOT contain any winged projections.

FMVSS's ON BRAKE SYSTEMS

Major FMVSS's on brake systems include — **FMVSS 105, Hydraulic Brake Systems; FMVSS 106 Brake Hoses; FMVSS 116, Motor Vehicle Brakefluids; FMVSS 135, Intended Replacement (proposed by NHTSA) for FMVSS 105.**

OCCUPATIONAL SAFETY AND HEALTH ADMINISTRATION (OSHA) STANDARDS

The OSHA, a division of the US Department of Labor establishes standards on occupational exposure to hazardous materials like asbestos fibers and organic solvents, typically encountered in an automotive workshop handling repairs of brakes and front-end systems.

Exposure to Airborne Asbestos Fibers

OSHA's asbestos risk assessment shows that a 20-year exposure at 0.2 fiber per cubic centimeter (f/cc) of air offers a cancer risk of 4.5 per 1000 workers. Reduction in the exposure level to 0.1 f/cc is expected to reduce the risk to 2.3 per 1000. The latest revision of **OSHA Standard 1910.1001** published in Federal Register Volume 59, Number 153, dated August 10, 1994 specifies a time-weighted-average permissible exposure limit (PEL) of 0.1 f/cc for all asbestos work in an automobile repair shop.

Exposure to Airborne Solvent Vapors

Inhalation of airborne **solvent vapors** is also quite hazardous and causes cancer. Though not as severe a problem as asbestos exposure in an automotive workshop, it is still a matter of concern to technicians. The major sources of solvent vapor hazard are the liquids and aerosols used in cleaning of components. These fluids contain chlorinated hydrocarbon solvents, like 1,1,1-trichloroethane, trichloroethylene, and tetrachloroethylene (also known as perchloroethylene or 'perk'). The current **OSHA standard 1910.1000** for airborne trichloroethylene is 100 ppm in the ambient air averaged over an 8-hour work shift. The ceiling level for exposure is 200 ppm, and there is a maximum acceptable peak level of 300 ppm for 5 minutes in any 3-hour period. The limits for other chlorinated hydrocarbon solvents are similar.

Contact Address

Detailed information on pertinent OSHA standards may be obtained from: Director of Information and Consumer Affairs, Occupational Safety and Health Administration, US Department of Labor, Room N3647, 200 Constitution Avenue, NW, Washington DC 20210.

J1930 -- SAE NOMENCLATURE FOR ELECTRICAL/ELECTRONIC SYSTEMS

J1930 (last revised in June 1993) is an industry-wide nomenclature standard for diagnostic terms applicable to electrical/electronic systems, and also includes related mechanical terms and acronyms. This standard is recommended by the Society of Automotive Engineers (SAE) and is adopted into government regulations. It requires that various components with the same functions be known by the same terminology, regardless of the carmaker.

EXISTING USAGE	SAE RECOMMENDED USAGE	
	Term	Acronym
3GR (Third Gear)	Third Gear	3GR
4GR (Fourth Gear)	Fourth Gear	4GR
A/C (Air Conditioning)	Air Conditioning	A/C
A/C Cycling Switch	Air Conditioning Cycling Switch	A/C Cycling Switch
A/T (Automatic Transaxle)	Automatic Transaxle	A/T
A/T (Automatic Transmission)	Automatic Transmission	A/T
AC (Air Conditioning)	Air Conditioning	A/C
ACC (Air Conditioning Clutch)	Air Conditioning Clutch	A/C Clutch
Accelerator	Accelerator Pedal	AP
ACCS (Air Conditioning Cyclic Switch)	Air Conditioning Cycling Switch	A/C Cycling Switch
ACH (Air Cleaner Housing)	Air Cleaner Housing	ACL Housing
ACL (Air Cleaner)	Air Cleaner	ACL
ACL (Air Cleaner) Element	Air Cleaner Element	ACL Element
ACL (Air Cleaner) Housing	Air Cleaner Housing	ACL Housing
ACL (Air Cleaner) Housing Cover	Air Cleaner Housing Cover	ACL Housing Cover
ACS (Air Conditioning System)	Air Conditioning System	A/C System
ACT (Air Charge Temperature)	Intake Air Temperature	IAT
Adaptive Fuel Strategy	Fuel Trim	FT
AFC (Air Flow Control)	Mass Air Flow	MAF
AFC (Air Flow Control)	Volume Air Flow	VAF
AFS (Air Flow Sensor)	Mass Air Flow Sensor	MAF Sensor
AFS (Air Flow Sensor)	Volume Air Flow Sensor	VAF Sensor
After Cooler	Charge Air Cooler	CAC
AI (Air Injection)	Secondary Air Injection	AIR
AIP (Air Injection Pump)	Secondary Air Injection Pump	AIR Pump

EXISTING USAGE	SAE RECOMMENDED USAGE	
	Term	**Acronym**
AIR (Air Injection Reactor)	Pulsed Secondary Air Injection	PAIR
AIR (Air Injection Reactor)	Secondary Air Injection	AIR
AIRB (Secondary Air Injection Bypass)	Secondary Air Injection Bypass	AIR Bypass
AIRD (Secondary Air Injection Diverter)	Secondary Air Injection Diverter	AIR Diverter
Air Cleaner	Air Cleaner	ACL
Air Cleaner Element	Air Cleaner Element	ACL Element
Air Cleaner Housing	Air Cleaner Housing	ACL Housing
Air Cleaner Housing Cover	Air Cleaner Housing Cover	ACL Housing Cover
Air Conditioning	Air Conditioning	A/C
Air Conditioning Sensor	Air Conditioning Sensor	A/C Sensor
Air Control Valve	Secondary Air Injection Control Valve	AIR Control Valve
Air Flow Meter	Mass Air Flow Sensor	MAF Sensor
Air Flow Meter	Volume Air Flow Sensor	VAF Sensor
Air Intake System	Intake Air System	IA System
Air Flow Sensor	Mass Air Flow Sensor	MAF Sensor
Air Management 1	Secondary Air Injection Bypass	AIR Bypass
Air Management 2	Secondary Air Injection Diverter	AIR Diverter
Air Temperature Sensor	Intake Air Temperature Sensor	IAT Sensor
Air Valve	Idle Air Control Valve	IAC Valve
AIV (Air Injection Valve)	Pulsed Secondary Air Injection	PAIR
ALCL (Assembly Line Communication Link)	Data Link Connector	DLC
Alcohol Concentration Sensor	Flexible Fuel Sensor	FF Sensor
ALDL (Assembly Line Diagnostic Link)	Data Link Connector	DLC
ALT (Alternator)	Generator	GEN
Alternator	Generator	GEN
AM 1 (Air Management 1)	Secondary Air Injection	BypassAIR Bypass
AM 2 (Air Management 2)	Secondary Air Injection	Diverter AIR Diverter
APS (Absolute Pressure Sensor)	Barometric Pressure Sensor	BARO Sensor
ATS (Air Temperature Sensor)	Intake Air Temperature Sensor	IAT Sensor
Automatic Transaxle	Automatic Transaxle	A/T
Automatic Transmission	Automatic Transmission	A/T
B+ (Battery Positive Voltage)	Battery Positive Voltage	B+
Backpressure Transducer	Exhaust Gas Recirculation Backpressure Transducer	EGR Backpressure Transducer
BARO (Barometric Pressure)	Barometric Pressure	BARO
Barometric Pressure Sensor	Barometric Pressure Sensor	BARO Sensor
Battery Positive Voltage	Battery Positive Voltage	B+
Block Learn Matrix	Long Term Fuel Trim	Long Term FT
BLM (Block Learn Memory)	Long Term Fuel Trim	Long Term FT
BLM (Block Learn Multiplier)	Long Term Fuel Trim	Long Term FT
BLM (Block Learn Matrix)	Long Term Fuel Trim	Long Term FT
Block Learn Memory	Long Term Fuel Trim	Long Term FT
Block Learn Multiplier	Long Term Fuel Trim	Long Term FT
BP (Barometric Pressure) Sensor	Barometric Pressure Sensor	BARO Sensor

EXISTING USAGE

SAE RECOMMENDED USAGE

	Term	Acronym
C3I (Computer Controlled Coil Ignition)	Electronic Ignition	EI
CAC (Charge Air Cooler)	Charge Air Cooler	CAC
Camshaft Position	Camshaft Position	CMP
Camshaft Position Sensor	Camshaft Position Sensor	CMP Sensor
Camshaft Sensor	Camshaft Position Sensor	CMP Sensor
Canister	Canister	Canister
Canister	Evaporative Emission Canister	EVAP Canister
Canister Purge Valve	Evaporative Emission Canister Purge Valve	EVAP Canister Purge Valve
Canister Purge Vacuum Switching Valve	Evaporative Emission Canister Purge Valve	EVAP Canister Purge Valve
Canister Purge VSV (Vacuum Switching Valve)	Evaporative Emission Canister Purge Valve	EVAP Canister Purge Valve
CANP (Canister Purge)	Evaporative Emission Canister Purge	EVAP Canister Purge
CARB (Carburetor)	Carburetor	CARB
Carburetor	Carburetor	CARB
CCC (Converter Clutch Control)	Torque Converter Clutch	TCC
CCO (Converter Clutch Override)	Torque Converter Clutch	TCC
CDI (Capacitive Discharge Ignition)	Distributor Ignition	DI
CDROM (Compact Disc Read Only Memory)	Compact Disc Read Only Memory	CDROM
CES (Clutch Engage Switch)	Clutch Pedal Position Switch	CPP Switch
Central Multiport Fuel Injection	Central Multiport Fuel Injection	Central MFI
CFI (Continuous Fuel Injection)	Continuous Fuel Injection	CFI
CFI (Central Fuel Injection)	Throttle Body Fuel Injection	TBI
Charcoal Canister	Evaporative Emission Canister	EVAP Canister
Charge Air Cooler	Charge Air Cooler	CAC
Check Engine	Service Reminder Indicator	SRI
Check Engine	Malfunction Indicator Lamp	MIL
CID (Cylinder Identification) Sensor	Camshaft Position Sensor	CMP Sensor
CIS (Continuous Injection System)	Continuous Fuel Injection	CFI
CIS-E (Continuous Injection System-Electronic)	Continuous Fuel Injection	CFI
CKP (Crankshaft Position)	Crankshaft Position	CKP
CKP (Crankshaft Position) Sensor	Crankshaft Position Sensor	CKP Sensor
CL (Closed Loop)	Closed Loop	CL
Closed Bowl Distributor	Distributor Ignition	DI
Closed Throttle Position	Closed Throttle Position	CTP
Closed Throttle Switch	Closed Throttle Position Switch	CTP Switch
CLS (Closed Loop System)	Closed Loop	CL
Clutch Engage Switch	Clutch Pedal Position Switch	CPP Switch
Clutch Pedal Position Switch	Clutch Pedal Position Switch	CPP Switch
Clutch Start Switch	Clutch Pedal Position Switch	CPP Switch
Clutch Switch	Clutch Pedal Position Switch	CPP Switch
CMFI (Central Multiport Fuel Injection)	Central Multiport Fuel Injection	Central MFI

EXISTING USAGE

SAE RECOMMENDED USAGE

Term	Acronym

Existing Usage	Term	Acronym
CMP (Camshaft Position)	Camshaft Position	CMP
CMP (Camshaft Position) Sensor	Camshaft Position Sensor	CMP Sensor
COC (Continuous Oxidation Catalyst)	Oxidation Catalytic Converter	OC
Condenser	Distributor Ignition Capacitor	DI Capacitor
Continuous Fuel Injection	Continuous Fuel Injection	CFI
Continuous Injection System	Continuous Fuel Injection System	CFI System
Continuous Injection System-E	Electronic Continuous Fuel Injection System	Electronic CFI System
Continuous Trap Oxidizer	Continuous Trap Oxidizer	CTOX
Coolant Temperature Sensor	Engine Coolant Temperature Sensor	ECT Sensor
CP (Crankshaft Position)	Crankshaft Position	CKP
CPP (Clutch Pedal Position) Switch	Clutch Pedal Position Switch	CPP Switch
CPS (Camshaft Position Sensor)	Camshaft Position Sensor	CMP Sensor
CPS (Crankshaft Position Sensor)	Crankshaft Position Sensor	CKP Sensor
Crank Angle Sensor	Crankshaft Position Sensor	CKP Sensor
Crankshaft Position	Crankshaft Position	CKP
Crankshaft Position Sensor	Crankshaft Position Sensor	CKP Sensor
Crankshaft Speed	Engine Speed	RPM
Crankshaft Speed Sensor	Engine Speed Sensor	RPM Sensor
CTO (Continuous Trap Oxidizer)	Continuous Trap Oxidizer	CTOX
CTOX (Continuous Trap Oxidizer)	Continuous Trap Oxidizer	CTOX
CTP (Closed Throttle Position)	Closed Throttle Position	CTP
CTS (Coolant Temperature Sensor)	Engine Coolant Temperature Sensor	ECT Sensor
CTS (Coolant Temperature Switch)	Engine Coolant Temperature Switch	ECT Switch
Cylinder ID (identification) Sensor	Camshaft Position Sensor	CMP Sensor
D-Jetronic	Multiport Fuel Injection	MFI
Data Link Connector	Data Link Connector	DLC
Detonation Sensor	Knock Sensor	KS
DFI (Direct Fuel Injection)	Direct Fuel Injection	DFI
DFI (Digital Fuel Injection)	Multiport Fuel Injection	MFI
DI (Direct Injection)	Direct Fuel Injection	DFI
DI (Distributor Ignition)	Distributor Ignition	DI
DI (Distributor Ignition) Capacitor	Distributor Ignition Capacitor	DI Capacitor
Diagnostic Test Mode	Diagnostic Test Mode	DTM
Diagnostic Trouble Code	Diagnostic Trouble Code	DTC
DID (Direct Injection- Diesel)	Direct Fuel Injection	DFI
Differential Pressure Feedback EGR (Exhaust Gas Recirculation) System	Differential Pressure Feedback Exhaust Gas Recirculation System	Differential Pressure Feedback EGR System
Digital EGR (Exhaust Gas Recirculation)	Exhaust Gas Recirculation	EGR
Direct Fuel Injection	Direct Fuel Injection	DFI
Direct Ignition System	Electronic Ignition System	EI System

EXISTING USAGE

SAE RECOMMENDED USAGE

Term	Acronym

EXISTING USAGE	Term	Acronym
DIS (Distributorless Ignition System)	Electronic Ignition System	EI System
DIS (Distributorless Ignition System) Module	Ignition Control Module	ICM
Distance Sensor	Vehicle Speed Sensor	VSS
Distributor Ignition	Distributor Ignition	DI
Distributorless Ignition	Electronic Ignition	EI
DLC (Data Link Connector)	Data Link Connector	DLC
DLI (Distributorless Ignition)	Electronic Ignition	EI
DS (Detonation Sensor)	Knock Sensor	KS
DTC (Diagnostic Trouble Code)	Diagnostic Trouble Code	DTC
DTM (Diagnostic Test Mode)	Diagnostic Test Mode	DTM
Dual Bed	Three Way + Oxidation Catalytic Converter	TWC+OC
Duty Solenoid for Purge Valve	Evaporative Emission Canister Purge Valve	EVAP Canister Purge Valve
E2PROM (Electrically Erasable Programmable Read Only Memory)	Electrically Erasable Programmable Read Only Memory	EEPROM
Early Fuel Evaporation	Early Fuel Evaporation	EFE
EATX (Electronic Automatic Transmission/Transaxle)	Automatic Transmission	A/T
	Automatic Transaxle	A/T
EC (Engine Control)	Engine Control	EC
ECA (Electronic Control Assembly)	Powertrain Control Module	PCM
ECL (Engine Coolant Level)	Engine Coolant Level	ECL
ECM (Engine Control Module)	Engine Control Module	ECM
ECT (Engine Coolant Temperature)	Engine Coolant Temperature	ECT
ECT (Engine Coolant Temperature) Sender	Engine Coolant Temperature Sensor	ECT Sensor
ECT (Engine Coolant Temperature) Sensor	Engine Coolant Temperature Sensor	ECT Sensor
ECT (Engine Coolant Temperature) Switch	Engine Coolant Temperature Switch	ECT Switch
ECU4 (Electronic Control Unit 4)	Powertrain Control Module	PCM
EDF (Electro-Drive Fan) Control	Fan Control	FC
EDIS (Electronic Distributor Ignition System)	Distributor Ignition System	DI System
EDIS (Electronic Distributorless Ignition System)	Electronic Ignition System	EI System
EDIS (Electronic Distributor Ignition System) Module	Distributor Ignition Control Module	Distributor ICM
EEC (Electronic Engine Control)	Engine Control	EC
EEC (Electronic Engine Control) Processor	Powertrain Control Module	PCM
EECS (Evaporative Emission Control System)	Evaporative Emission System	EVAP System
EEPROM (Electrically Erasable Programmable Read Only Memory)	Electrically Erasable Programmable Read Only Memory	EEPROM

EXISTING USAGE

SAE RECOMMENDED USAGE

Term	Acronym

EXISTING USAGE	Term	Acronym
EFE (Early Fuel Evaporation)	Early Fuel Evaporation	EFE
EFI (Electronic Fuel Injection)	Multiport Fuel Injection	MFI
EFI (Electronic Fuel Injection)	Throttle Body Fuel Injection	TBI
EGO (Exhaust Gas Oxygen) Sensor	Oxygen Sensor	O2S
EGOS (Exhaust Gas Oxygen Sensor)	Oxygen Sensor	O2S
EGR (ExhaustGas Recirculation)	Exhaust Gas Recirculation	EGR
EGR (Exhaust Gas Recirculation) Diagnostic Valve	Exhaust Gas Recirculation Diagnostic Valve	EGR Diagnostic Valve
EGR (Exhaust Gas Recirculation) System	Exhaust Gas Recirculation System	EGR System
EGR (Exhaust Gas Recirculation) Thermal Vacuum Valve	Exhaust Gas Recirculation Thermal Vacuum Valve	EGR TVV
EGR (Exhaust Gas Recirculation)	Exhaust Gas Recirculation Valve	EGR Valve
EGR TVV (Exhaust Gas Recirculation Thermal Vacuum Valve)	Exhaust Gas Recirculation Thermal Vacuum Valve	EGR TVV
EGRT (Exhaust Gas Recirculation Temperature)	Exhaust Gas Recirculation Temperature	EGRT
EGRT (Exhaust Gas Recirculation Temperature) Sensor	Exhaust Gas Recirculation Temperature Sensor	EGRT Sensor
EGRV (Exhaust Gas Recirculation Valve)	Exhaust Gas Recirculation Valve	EGR Valve
EGRVC (Exhaust Gas Recirculation Valve Control)	Exhaust Gas Recirculation Valve Control	EGR Valve Control
EGS (Exhaust Gas Sensor)	Oxygen Sensor	O2S
EI (Electronic Ignition) (With Distributor)	Distributor Ignition	DI
EI (Electronic Ignition) (Without Distributor)	Electronic Ignition	EI
Electrically Erasable Programmable Read Only Memory	Electrically Erasable Programmable Read Only Memory	EEPROM
Electronic Engine Control	Electric Engine Control	Electronic EC
Electronic Ignition	Electronic Ignition	EI
Electronic Spark Advance	Ignition Control	IC
Electronic Spark Timing	Ignition Control	IC
EM (Engine Modification)	Engine Modification	EM
EMR (Engine Maintenance Reminder)	Service Reminder Indicator	SRI
Engine Control	Engine Control	EC
Engine Coolant Fan Control	Fan Control	FC
Engine Coolant Level	Engine Coolant Level	ECL
Engine Coolant Level Indicator	Engine Coolant Level Indicator	ECL Indicator
Engine Coolant Temperature	Engine Coolant Temperature	ECT
Engine Coolant Temperature Sender	Engine Coolant Temperature Sensor	ECT Sensor

EXISTING USAGE	SAE RECOMMENDED USAGE Term	Acronym
Engine Coolant Temperature Sensor	Engine Coolant Temperature Sensor	ECT Sensor
Engine Coolant Temperature Switch	Engine Coolant Temperature Switch	ECT Switch
Engine Modification	Engine Modification	EM
Engine Speed	Engine Speed	RPM
EOS (Exhaust Oxygen Sensor)	Oxygen Sensor	O2S
EPROM (Erasable Programmable Read Only Memory)	Erasable Programmable Read Only Memory	EPROM
Erasable Programmable Read Only Memory	Erasable Programmable Read Only Memory	EPROM
ESA (Electronic Spard Advance)	Ignition Control	IC
ESAC (Electronic Spard Advance Control)	Distributor Ignition	DI
EST (Electronic Spark Timing)	Ignition Control	IC
EVAP CANP	Evaporative Emission Canister Purge	EVAP Canister Purge
EVAP (Evaporative Emission)	Evaporative Emission	EVAP
EVAP (Evaporative Emission) Canister	Evaporative Emission Canister	EVAP Canister
EVAP (Evaporative Emission) Purge Valve	Evaporative Emission Canister Purge Valve	EVAP Canister Purge Valve
Evaporative Emission	Evaporative Emission	EVAP
Evaporative Emission Canister	Evaporative Emission Canister	EVAP Canister
EVP (Exhaust Gas Recirculation Valve Position) Sensor	Exhaust Gas Recirculation Valve Position Sensor	EGR Valve Position Sensor
EVR (Exhaust Gas Recirculation Vacuum Regulator) Solenoid	Exhaust Gas Recirculation Vacuum Regulator Solenoid	EGR Vacuum Regulator Solenoid
EVRV (Exhaust Gas Recirculation Vacuum Regulator Valve)	Exhaust Gas Recirculation Vacuum Regulator Valve	EGR Vacuum Regulator Valve
Exhaust Gas Recirculation	Exhaust Gas Recirculation	EGR
Exhaust Gas Recirculation Temperature	Exhaust Gas Recirculation Temperature	EGRT
Exhaust Gas Recirculation Temperature Sensor	Exhaust Gas Recirculation Temperature Sensor	EGRT Sensor
Exhaust Gas Recirculation Valve	Exhaust Gas Recirculation Valve	EGR Valve
Fan Control	Fan Control	FC
Fan Control Module	Fan Control Module	FC Module
Fan Control Relay	Fan Control Relay	FC Relay
Fan Motor Control Relay	Fan Control Relay	FC Relay
Fast Idle Thermo Valve	Idle Air Control Thermal Valve	IAC Thermal Valve
FBC (Feed Back Carburetor)	Carburetor	CARB
FBC (Feed Back Control)	Mixture Control	MC
FC (Fan Control)	Fan Control	FC
FC (Fan Control Relay)	Fan Control Relay	FC Relay
FEEPROM (Flash Electrically Erasable Programmable Read Only Memory)	Flash Electrically Erasable Programmable Read Only Memory	FEEPROM

EXISTING USAGE

SAE RECOMMENDED USAGE

Term	Acronym

Existing Usage	Term	Acronym
FEPROM (Flash Erasable Programmable Read Only Memory)	Flash Erasable Programmable Read Only Memory	FEPROM
FF (Flexible Fuel)	Flexible Fuel	FF
FI (Fuel Injection)	Central Multiport Fuel Injection	Central MFI
FI (Fuel Injection)	Continuous Fuel Injection	CFI
FI (Fuel Injection)	Direct Fuel Injection	DFI
FI (Fuel Injection)	Indirect Fuel Injection	IFI
FI (Fuel Injection)	Multiport Fuel Injection	MFI
FI (Fuel Injection)	Sequential Multiport Fuel Injection	SFI
FI (Fuel Injection)	Throttle Body Fuel Injection	TBI
Flash EEPROM (Electrically Erasable Programmable Read Only Memory)	Flash Electrically Erasable Programmable Read Only Memory	FEEPROM
Flash EPROM (Erasable Read Only Memory)	Flash Erasable Read Only Memory	FEPROM
Flexible Fuel	Flexible Fuel	FF
Flexible Fuel Sensor	Flexible Fuel Sensor	FF Sensor
Fourth Gear	Fourth Gear	4GR
FP (Fuel Pump)	Fuel Pump	FP
FP (Fuel Pump) Module	Fuel Pump Module	FP Module
FT (Fuel Trim)	Fuel Trim	FT
Fuel Charging Station	Throttle Body	TB
Fuel Concentration Sensor	Flexible Fuel Sensor	FF Sensor
Fuel Injection	Central Multiport Fuel Injection	Central MFI
Fuel Injection	Continuous Fuel Injection	CFI
Fuel Injection	Direct Fuel Injection	DFI
Fuel Injection	Indirect Fuel Injection	IFI
Fuel Injection	Multiport Fuel Injection	MFI
Fuel Injection	Sequential Multiport Fuel Injection	SFI
Fuel Injection	Throttle Body Fuel Injection	TBI
Fuel Level Sensor	Fuel Level Sensor	Fuel Level Sensor
Fuel Module	Fuel Pump Module	FP Module
Fuel Pressure	Fuel Pressure	Fuel Pressure
Fuel Pressure Regulator	Fuel Pressure Regulator	Fuel Pressure Regulator
Fuel Pump	Fuel Pump	FP
Fuel Pump Relay	Fuel Pump Relay	FP Relay
Fuel Quality Sensor	Flexible Fuel Sensor	FF Sensor
Fuel Regulator	Fuel Pressure Regulator	Fuel Pressure Regulator
Fuel Sender	Fuel Pump Module	FP Module
Fuel Sensor	Fuel Level Sensor	Fuel Level Sensor
Fuel Tank Unit	Fuel Pump Module	FP Module
Fuel Trim	Fuel Trim	FT
Full Throttle	Wide Open Throttle	WOT
GCM (Governor Control Module)	Governor Control Module	GCM
GEM (Governor Electronic Module)	Governor Control Module	GCM
GEN (Generator)	Generator	GEN
Generator	Generator	GEN
Governor	Governor	Governor

EXISTING USAGE

SAE RECOMMENDED USAGE

Term	Acronym

EXISTING USAGE	Term	Acronym
Governor Control Module	Governor Control Module	GCM
Governor Electronic Module	Governor Control Module	GCM
GND (Ground)	Ground	GND
GRD (Ground)	Ground	GND
Ground	Ground	GND
Heated Oxygen Sensor	Heated Oxygen Sensor	HO2S
HEDF (High Electro-Drive Fan) Control	Fan Control	FC
HEGO (Heated Exhaust Gas Oxygen) Sensor	Heated Oxygen Sensor	HO2S
HEI (High Energy Ignition)	Distributor Ignition	DI
High Speed FC (Fan Control) Switch	High Speed Fan Control Switch	High Speed FC Switch
HO2S (Heated Oxygen Sensor)	Heated Oxygen Sensor	HO2S
HOS (Heated Oxygen Sensor)	Heated Oxygen Sensor	HO2S
Hot Wire Anemometer	Mass Air Flow Sensor	MAF Sensor
IA (Intake Air)	Intake Air	IA
IA (Intake Air) Duct	Intake Air Duct	IA Duct
IAC (Idle Air Control)	Idle Air Control	IAC
IAC (Idle Air Control) Thermal Valve	Idle Air Control Thermal Valve	IAC Thermal Valve
IAC (Idle Air Control) Valve	Idle Air Control Valve	IAC Valve
IACV (Idle Air Control Valve)	Idle Air Control Valve	IAC Valve
IAT (Intake Air Temperature)	Intake Air Temperature	IAT
IAT (Intake Air Temperature) Sensor	Intake Air Temperature Sensor	IAT Sensor
IATS (Intake Air Temperature Sensor)	Intake Air Temperature Sensor	IAT Sensor
IC (Ignition Control)	Ignition Control	IC
ICM (Ignition Control Module)	Ignition Control Module	ICM
IDFI (Indirect Fuel Injection)	Indirect Fuel Injection	IFI
IDI (Integrated Direct Ignition)	Electronic Ignition	EI
IDI (Indirect Diesel Injection)	Indirect Fukel Injection	IFI
Idle Air Bypass Control	Idle Air Control	IAC
Idle Air Control	Idle Air Control	IAC
Idle Air Control Valve	Idle Air Control Valve	IAC Valve
Idle Speed Control	Idle Air Control	IAC
Idle Speed Control	Idle Speed Control	ISC
Idle Speed Control Actuator	Idle Speed Control Actuator	ISC Actuator
IFI (Indirect Fuel Injection)	Indirect Fuel Injection	IFI
IFS (Inertia Fuel Shutoff)	Inertia Fuel Shutoff	IFS
Ignition Control	Ignition Control	IC
Ignition Control Module	Ignition Control Module	ICM
In Tank Module	Fuel Pump Module	FP Module
Indirect Fuel Injection	Indirect Fuel Injection	IFI
Inertia Fuel Shutoff	Inertia Fuel Shutoff	IFS
Inertia Fuel - Shutoff Switch	Inertia Fuel Shutoff Switch	IFS Switch
Inertia Switch	Inertia Fuel Shutoff Switch	IFS Switch
INT (Integrator)	Short Term Fuel Trim	Short Term FT

EXISTING USAGE

SAE RECOMMENDED USAGE

Term	Acronym

Existing Usage	Term	Acronym
Intake Air	Intake Air	IA
Intake Air Duct	Intake Air Duct	IA Duct
Intake Air Temperature	Intake Air Temperature	IAT
Intake Air Temperature Sensor	Intake Air Temperature Sensor	IAT Sensor
Intake Manifold Absolute Pressure Sensor	Manifold Absolute Pressure Sensor	MAP Sensor
Integrated Relay Module	Relay Module	RM
Integrator	Short Term Fuel Trim	Short Term FT
Inter Cooler	Charge Air Cooler	CAC
ISC (Idle Speed Control)	Idle Air Control	IAC
ISC (Idle Speed Control)	Idle Speed Control	ISC
ISC (Idle Speed Control) Actuator	Idle Speed Control ACtuator	ISC Actuator
ISC BPA (Idle Speed Control By Pass Air)	Idle Air Control	IAC
ISC (Idle Speed Control) Solenoid Vacuum Valve	Idle Speed Control Solenoid Vacuum Valve	ISC Solenoid Vacuum Valve
K-Jetronic	Continuous Fuel Injection	CFI
KAM (Keep Alive Memory)	NonVolatile Random Access Memory	NVRAM
KAM (Keep Alive Memory)	Keep Alive Random Access Memory	Keep Alive RAM
KE-Jetronic	Continuous Fuel Injection	CFI
KE-Motronic	Continuous Fuel Injection	CFI
Knock Sensor	Knock Sensor	KS
KS (Knock Sensor)	Knock Sensor	KS
L-Jetronic	Multiport Fuel Injection	MFI
Lambda	Oxygen Sensor	O2S
LH-Jetronic	Multiport Fuel Injection	MFI
Light Off Catalyst	Warm Up Three Way Catalytic Converter	WU-TWC
Light Off Catalyst	Warm Up Oxidation Catalytic Converter	WU-OC
Lock Up Relay	Torque Converter Clutch Relay	TCC Relay
Long Term FT (Fuel Trim)	Long Term Fuel Trim	Long Term FT
Low Speed FC (Fan Control) Switch	Low Speed Fan Control Switch	Low Speed FC Switch
LUS (Lock Up Solenoid) Valve	Torque Converter Clutch Solenoid Valve	TCC Solenoid
M/C (Mixture Control)	Mixture Control	MC
MAF (Mass Air Flow)	Mass Air Flow	MAF
MAF (Mass Air Flow) Sensor	Mass Air Flow Sensor	MAF Sensor
Malfunction Indicator Lamp	Malfunction Indicator Lamp	MIL
Manifold Absolute Pressure	Manifold Absolute Pressure	MAP
Manifold Absolute Pressure Sensor	Manifold Absolute Pressure Sensor	MAP Sensor
Manifold Differential Pressure	Manifold Differential Pressure	MDP
Manifold Surface Temperature	Manifold Surface Temperature	MST
Manifold Vacuum Zone	Manifold Vacuum Zone	MVZ
Manual Lever Position Sensor	Transmission Range Sensor	TR Sensor

EXISTING USAGE

SAE RECOMMENDED USAGE

Term	Acronym

EXISTING USAGE	Term	Acronym
MAP (Manifold Absolute Pressure)	Manifold Absolute Pressure	MAP
MAP (Manifold Absolute Pressure) Sensor	Manifold Absolute Pressure Sensor	MAP Sensor
MAPS (Manifold Absolute Pressure Sensor)	Manifold Absolute Pressure Sensor	MAP Sensor
Mass Air Flow	Mass Air Flow	MAF
Mass Air Flow Sensor	Mass Air Flow Sensor	MAF Sensor
MAT (Manifold Air Temperature)	Intake Air Temperature	IAT
MATS (Manifold Air Temperature Sensor)	Intake Air Temperature Sensor	IAT Sensor
MC (Mixture Control)	Mixture Control	MC
MCS (Mixture Control Solenoid)	Mixture Control Solenoid	MC Solenoid
MCU (Microprocessor Control Unit)	Powertrain Control Module	PCM
MDP (Manifold Differential Pressure)	Manifold Differential Pressure	MDP
MFI (Multiport Fuel INjection)	Multiport Fuel Injection	MFI
MIL (Malfunction Indicator Lamp)	Malfunction Indicator Lamp	MIL
Mixture Control	Mixture Control	MC
Modes	Diagnostic Test Mode	DTM
Monotronic	Throttle Body Fuel Injection	TBI
Motronic	Multiport Fuel Injection	MFI
MPI (Multipoint Injection)	Multiport Fuel Injection	MFI
MPI (Multiport Injection)	Multiport Fuel Injection	MFI
MRPS (Manual Range Position Switch)	Transmission Range Switch	TR Switch
MST (Manifold Surface Temperature)	Manifold Surface Temperature	MST
Multiport Fuel Injection	Multiport Fuel Injection	MFI
MVZ (Manifold Vacuum Zone)	Manifold Vacuum Zone	MVZ
NDS (Neutral Drive Switch)	Park/Neutral Position Switch	PNP Switch
Neutral Safety Switch	Park/Neutral Position Switch	PNP Switch
NGS (Neutral Gear Switch)	Park/Neutral Position Switch	PNP Switch
Nonvolatile Random Access Memory	Nonvolatile Random Access Memory	NVRAM
NVRAM (Nonvolatile Random Access Memory)	Nonvolatile Random Access Memory	NVRAM
O2 (Oxygen) Sensor	Oxygen Sensor	O2S
O2S (Oxygen Sensor)	Oxygen Sensor	O2S
OBD (On Board Diagnostic)	On Board Diagnostic	OBD
OC (Oxidation Catalyst)	Oxidation Catalytic Converter	OC
Oil Pressure Sender	Oil Pressure Sensor	Oil Pressure Sensor
Oil Pressure Sensor	Oil Pressure Sensor	Oil Pressure Sensor
Oil Pressure Switch	Oil Pressure Switch	Oil Pressure Switch
OL (Open Loop)	Open Loop	OL
On Board Diagnostic	On Board Diagnostic	OBD
Open Loop	Open Loop	OL
OS (Oxygen Sensor)	Oxygen Sensor	O2S
Oxidation Catalytic Converter	Oxidation Catalytic Converter	OC

EXISTING USAGE

SAE RECOMMENDED USAGE

Term	Acronym

EXISTING USAGE	Term	Acronym
OXS (Oxygen Sensor) Indicator	Service Reminder Indicator	SRI
Oxygen Sensor	Oxygen Sensor	O2S
P/N (Park/Neutral)	Park/Neutral Position	PNP
P/S (Power Steering) Pressure Switch	Power Steering Pressure Switch	PSP Switch
P - (Pressure) Sensor	Manifold Absolute Pressure Sensor	MAP Sensor
PAIR (Pulsed Secondary Air Injection)	Pulsed Secondary Air Injection	PAIR
Park/Neutral Position	Park/Neutral Position	PNP
PCM (Powertrain Control Module)	Powertrain Control Module	PCM
PCV (Positive Crankcase Ventilation)	Positive Crankcase Ventilation	PCV
PCV (Positive Crankcase Ventilation) Valve	Positive Crankcase Ventilation Valve	PCV Valve
Percent Alcohol Sensor	Flexible Fuel Sensor	FF Sensor
Periodic Trap Oxidizer	Periodic Trap Oxidizer	PTOX
PFE (Pressure Feedback Exhaust Gas Recirculation) Sensor	Feedback Pressure Exhaust Gas Recirculation Sensor	Feedback Pressure EGR Sensor
PFI (Port Fuel Injection)	Multiport Fuel Injection	MFI
PG (Pulse Generator)	Vehicle Speed Sensor	VSS
PGM-FI (Programmed Fuel Injection)	Multiport Fuel Injection	MFI
PIP (Position Indicator Pulse)	Crankshaft Position	CKP
PNP (Park/Neutral Position)	Park/Neutral Position	PNP
Positive Crankcase Ventilation	Positive Crankcase Ventilation	PCV
Positive Crankcase Ventilation Valve	Positive Crankcase Ventilation Valve	PCV Valve
Power Steering Pressure	Power Steering Pressure	PSP
Power Steering Pressure Switch	Power Steering Pressure Switch	PSP Switch
Powertrain Control Module	Powertrain Control Module	PCM
Pressure Feedback EGR (Exhaust Gas Recirculation)	Feedback Pressure Exhaust Gas Recirculation	Feedback Pressure EGR
Pressure Sensor	Manifold Absolute Pressure Sensor	MAP Sensor
Pressure Transducer EGR (Exhaust Gas Recirculation) System	Pressure Transducer Exhaust Gas Recirculation System	Pressure Transducer EGR System
PRNDL (Park, Reverse, Neutral, Drive, Low)	Transmission Range	TR
Programmable Read Only Memory	Programmable Read Only Memory	PROM
PROM (Programmable Read Only Memory)	Programmable Read Only Memory	PROM
PSP (Power Steering Pressure)	Power Steering Pressure	PSP
PSP (Power Steering Pressure) Switch	Power Steering Pressure Switch	PSP Switch
PSPS (Power Steering Pressure Switch)	Power Steering Pressure Switch	PSP Switch
PTOX (Periodic Trap Oxidizer)	Periodic Trap Oxidizer	PTOX
Pulsair	Pulsed Secondary Air Injection	PAIR

EXISTING USAGE

SAE RECOMMENDED USAGE

Term	Acronym

EXISTING USAGE	Term	Acronym
Pulsed Secondary Air Injection	Pulsed Secondary Air Injection	PAIR
Radiator Fan Control	Fan Control	FC
Radiator Fan Relay	Fan Control Relay	FC Relay
RAM (Random Access Memory)	Random Access Memory	RAM
Random Access Memory	Random Access Memory	RAM
Read Only Memory	Read Only Memory	ROM
Recirculated Exhaust Gas Temperature Sensor	Exhaust Gas Recirculation Temperature Sensor	EGRT Sensor
Reed Valve	Pulsed Secondary Air Injection Valve	PAIR Valve
REGTS (Recirculated Exhaust Gas Temperature Sensor)	Exhaust Gas Recirculation Temperature Sensor	EGRT Sensor
Relay Module	Relay Module	RM
Remote Mount TFI (Thick Film Ignition)	Distributor Ignition	DI
Revolutions per Minute	Engine Speed	RPM
RM (Relay Module)	Relay Module	RM
ROM (Read Only Memory)	Read Only Memory	ROM
RPM (Revolutions per Minute)	Engine Speed	RPM
SABV (Secondary Air Bypass Valve)	Secondary Air Injection Bypass Valve	AIR Bypass Valve
SACV (Secondary Air Check Valve)	Secondary Air Injection Control Valve	AIR Control Valve
SASV (Secondary Air Switching Valve)	Secondary Air Injection Switching Valve	AIR Switching Valve
SBEC (Single Board Engine Control)	Powertrain Control Module	PCM
SBS (Supercharger Bypass Solenoid)	Supercharger Bypass Solenoid	SCB Solenoid
SC (Supercharger)	Supercharger	SC
Scan Tool	Scan Tool	ST
SCB (Supercharger Bypass)	Supercharger Bypass	SCB
Secondary Air Bypass Valve	Secondary Air Injection Bypass Valve	AIR Bypass Valve
Secondary Air Check Valve	Secondary Air Injection Check Valve	AIR Check Valve
Secondary Air Injection	Secondary Air Injection	AIR
Secondary Air Injeciton Bypass	Secondary Air Injection Bypass	AIR Bypass
Secondary Air Injection Diverter	Secondary Air Injection Diverter	AIR Diverter
Secondary Air Switching Valve	Secondary Air Injection Switching Valve	AIR Switching Valve
SEFI (Sequential Electronic Fuel Injection)	Sequential Multiport Fuel Injection	SFI
Self Test	On Board Diagnostic	OBD
Self Test Codes	Diagnostic Trouble Code	DTC
Self Test Connector	Data Link Connector	DLC
Sequential Multiport Fuel Injection	Sequential Multiport Fuel Injection	SFI
Service Engine Soon	Service Reminder Indicator	SRI
Service Engine Soon	Malfunction Indicator Lamp	MIL

EXISTING USAGE

SAE RECOMMENDED USAGE

Term	Acronym

Existing Usage	Term	Acronym
Service Reminder Indicator	Service Reminder Indicatol	SRI
SFI (Sequential Fuel Injection)	Sequential Multiport Fuel Injection	SFI
Short Term FT (Fuel Trim)	Short Term Fuel Trim	Short Term FT
SLP (Selection Lever Position)	Transmission Range	TR
SMEC (Single Module Engine Control)	Powertrain Control Module	PCM
Smoke Puff Limiter	Smoke Puff Limiter	SPL
SPI (Single Point Injection)	Throttle Body Fuel Injection	TBI
SPL (Smoke Puff Limiter)	Smoke Puff Limiter	SPL
SRI (Service Reminder Indicator)	Service Reminder Indicator	SRI
SRT (System Readiness Test)	System Readiness Test	SRT
ST (Scan Tool)	Scan Tool	ST
Supercharger	Supercharger	SC
Supercharger Bypass	Supercharger Bypass	SCB
Sync Pickup	Camshaft Position	CMP
System Readiness Test	System Readiness Test	SRT
TAB (Thermactor Air Bypass)	Secondary Air Injection Bypass	AIR Bypass
TAD (Thermactor Air Diverter)	Secondary Air Injection Diverter	AIR Diverter
TB (Throttle Body)	Throttle Body	TB
TBI (Throttle Body Fuel Injection)	Throttle Body Fuel Injection	TBI
TBT (Throttle Body Temperature)	Intake Air Temperature	IAT
TC (Turbocharger)	Turbocharger	TC
TCC (Torque Converter Clutch)	Torque Converter Clutch	TCC
TCC (Torque Converter Clutch) Relay	Torque Converter Clutch Relay	TCC Relay
TCM (Transmission Control Module)	Transmission Control Module	TCM
TFI (Thick Film Ignition)	Distributor Ignition	DI
TFI (Thick Film Ignition) Module	Ignition Control Module	ICM
Thermac	Secondary Air Injection	AIR
Thermac Air Cleaner	Air Cleaner	ACL
Thermactor	Secondary Air Injection	AIR
Thermactor Air Bypass	Secondary Air Injection Bypass	AIR Bypass
Thermactor Air Diverter	Secondary Air Injection Diverter	AIR Diverter
Thermactor II	Pulsed Secondary Air Injection	PAIR
Thermal Vacuum Switch	Thermal Vacuum Valve	TVV
Thermal Vacuum Valve	Thermal Vacuum Valve	TVV
Third Gear	Third Gear	3GR
Three Way + Oxidation Catalytic Converter	Three Way + Oxidation Catalytic Converter	TWC+OC
Three Way Catalytic Converter	Three Way Catalytic Converter	TWC
Throttle Body	Throttle Body	TB
Throttle Body Fuel Injection	Throttle Body Fuel Injection	TBI
Throttle Opener	Idle Speed Control	ISC
Throttle Opener Vacuum Switching Valve	Idle Speed Control Solenoid Vacuum Valve	ISC Solenoid Vacuum Valve
Throttle Opener VSV (Vacuum Switching Valve)	Idle Speed Control Solenoid Vacuum Valve	ISC Solenoid Vacuum Valve
Throttle Position	Throttle Position	TP

EXISTING USAGE	SAE RECOMMENDED USAGE	
	Term	**Acronym**
Throttle Position Sensor	Throttle Position Sensor	TP Sensor
Throttle Position Switch	Throttle Position Switch	TP Switch
Throttle Potentiometer	Throttle Position Sensor	TP Sensor
TOC (Trap Oxidizer - Continuous)	Continuous Trap Oxidizer	CTOX
TOP (Trap Oxidizer - Periodic)	Periodic Trap Oxidizer	PTOX
Torque Converter Clutch	Torque Converter Clutch	TCC
Torque Converter Clutch Relay	Torque Converter Clutch Relay	TCC Relay
TP (Throttle Position)	Throttle Position	TP
TP (Throttle Position) Sensor	Throttle Position Sensor	TP Sensor
TP (Throttle Position) Switch	Throttle Position Switch	TP Switch
TPI (Tuned Port Injection)	Multiport Fuel Injection	MFI
TPS (Throttle Position Sensor)	Throttle Position Sensor	TP Sensor
TPS (Throttle Position Switch)	Throttle Rosition Switch	TP Switch
TR (Transmission Range)	Transmission Range	TR
Transmission Control Module	Transmission Control Module	TCM
Transmission Position Switch	Transmission Range Switch	TR Switch
Transmission Range Selection	Transmission Range	TR
TRS (Transmission Range Selection)	Transmission Range	TR
TRSS (Transmission Range Selection Switch)	Transmission Range Switch	TR Switch
Tuned Port Injection	Multiport Fuel Injection	MFI
Turbo (Turbocharger)	Turbocharger	TC
Turbocharger	Turbocharger	TC
TVS (Thermal Vacuum Switch)	Thermal Vacuum Valve	TVV
TVV (Thermal Vacuum Valve)	Thermal Vacuum Valve	TVV
TWC (Three Way Catalytic Converter)	Three Way Catalytic Converter	TWC
TWC + OC (Three Way + Oxidation Catalytic Converter)	Three Way + Oxidation Catalytic Converter	TWC+OC
VAC (Vacuum) Sensor	Manifold Differential Pressure Sensor	MDP Sensor
Vacuum Switches	Manifold Vacuum Zone Switch	MVZ Switch
VAF (Volume Air Flow)	Volume Air Flow	VAF
Vane Air Flow	Volume Air Flow	VAF
Variable Fuel Sensor	Flexible Fuel Sensor	FF Sensor
VAT (Vane Air Temperature)	Intake Air Temperature	IAT
VCC (Viscous Converter Clutch)	Torque Converter Clutch	TCC
Vehicle Speed Sensor	Vehicle Speed Sensor	VSS
VIP (Vehicle In Process) Connector	Data Link Connector	DLC
Viscous Converter Clutch	Torque Converter Clutch	TCC
Voltage Regulator	Voltage Regulator	VR
Volume Air Flow	Volume Air Flow	VAF
VR (Voltage Regulator)	Voltage Regulator	VR
Volume Air Flow	Volume Air Flow	VAF
VR (Voltage Regulator)	Voltage Regulator	VR
VSS (Vshicle Speed Sensor)	Vehicle Speed Sensor	VSS
VSV (Vacuum Solenoid Valve) (Canister)	Evaporative Emission Canister Purge Valve	EVAP Canister Purge Valve

EXISTING USAGE

SAE RECOMMENDED USAGE

EXISTING USAGE	Term	Acronym
VSV (Vacuum Solenoid Valve) (EVAP)	Evaporative Emission Canister Purge Valve	EVAP Canister Purge Valve
VSV (Vacuum Solenoid Valve) (Throttle)	Idle Speed Control Solenoid Vacuum Valve	ISC Solenoid Vacuum Valve
Warm Up Oxidation Catalytic Converter	Warm Up Oxidation Catalytic Converter	WU-OC
Warm Up Three Way Catalytic Converter	Warm Up Three Way Catalytic Converter	WU-OC
Wide Open Throttle	Wide Open Throttle	WOT
WOT (Wide Open Throttle)	Wide Open Throttle	WOT
WOTS (Wide Open Throttle Switch)	Wide Open Throttle Switch	WOT Switch
WU-OC (Warm Up Oxidation Catalytic Converter)	Warm Up Oxidation Catalytic Converter	WU-OC
WU-TWC (Warm Up Three Way Catalytic Converter)	Warm Up Three Way Catalytic Converter	WU-TWC

J670E -- SAE TERMINOLOGY FOR VEHICLE DYNAMICS

SAE J670e helps understand the terminology used in the technical literature for the automotive technician specializing in suspension, steering, and wheel alignment. This appendix is an adaptation of the SAE standard rearranged in a glossary format for the convenience of the user. Categories of terms included are: •Mechanical Vibration — Qualitative Terminology; •Mechanical Vibration — Quantitative Terminology; •Vibrating Systems; •Components and Characteristics of Suspension Systems; •Vibrations of Vehicle Suspension Systems; •Suspension Geometry; •Tires and Wheels; •Kinematics — Forces and Moments; and •Directional Dynamics. Aerodynamics Nomenclature is beyond the scope of coverage of the text, and is therefore excluded. *Italicized* words and phrases appearing in various definitions are themselves defined elsewhere in this appendix. It is important that the reader first becomes familiar with the terminology related to *angular orientation, earth-fixed axis system, tire axis system, vehicle axis system*, and various *forces* and *moments* illustrated in Figures D2-1 to D2-4 on the last two pages of this appendix.

acceleration. The time rate of change of the *velocity*.

Ackerman steer angle (δ_a). The angle whose tangent is the wheelbase divided by the radius of turn.

Ackerman steer angle gradient. The rate of change of *Ackerman steer angle* with respect to change in *steady-state lateral acceleration* on a level road at a given *trim* and test conditions. Equals the wheelbase divided by the square of the vehicle speed (rad/ft/s^2).

aligning stiffness (aligning torque stiffness). The rate of change of *aligning torque* with respect to change in *slip angle*, usually evaluated at zero *slip angle*.

aligning stiffness coefficient (aligning torque coefficient). The ratio of *aligning stiffness* of a *free straight-rolling tire* to the *vertical load*.

aligning torque (aligning moment) (M_z). The component of the tire moment vector tending to rotate the tire about the Z'-axis. Positive clockwise when looking in the positive direction of Z'-axis.

amplitude. The largest value of displacement that the point attains with reference to its equilibrium position. Related terms — *peak-to-peak amplitude, static amplitude, amplitude ratio*.

amplitude ratio (relative magnification factor). Ratio of a *forced vibration amplitude* to the *static amplitude*.

angular orientation. The orientation of the *vehicle axis system* (x, y, z) with respect to the *earth-fixed axis system* (X,Y, Z) is given by a sequence of three angular rotations. The following sequence of rotations, starting from a condition in which two sets of axis are initially aligned, is defined to be the standard: a **yaw rotation**, about the aligned z- and Z-axis; a **pitch rotation**, about the vehicle y-axis; and a **roll rotation**, about the vehicle x-axis. NOTE: Angular rotations are positive clockwise when looking in the positive direction of the axis about which rotation occurs.

asymptotic stability. Asymptotic stability exists at a prescribed trim if, for any small temporary change in disturbance or control input, the vehicle will approach the motion defined by the *trim*.

axle fore-and-aft shake. Oscillatory motion of an axle involving only longitudinal displacement.

axle side shake. Oscillatory motion of an axle involving transverse displacement.

axle vibration modes. Related terms — *axle side shake, axle fore-and-aft shake, axle yaw, axle windup.*

axle windup. Oscillatory motion of an axle about the horizontal transverse axis through its center of gravity.

axle yaw. Oscillatory motion of an axle around the vertical axis through its center of gravity.

bead. The portion of the tire which fits onto the rim of the wheel. Related terms — *bead base, bead toe.*

bead base. The nearly cylindrical portion of the bead that forms its inside diameter.

bead toe. The portion of the bead that joins the bead base and the inside surface of the tire.

beaming. A mode of *vibration* involving predominantly bending deformations of the *sprung mass* about the vehicle x-axis.

boom. A high intensity vibration (25-100 Hz) perceived audibly and characterized as sensation of pressure by the ear.

bounce. The translational component of *ride* vibrations of the *sprung mass* in the direction of the vehicle z-axis. (See Figure D2-2)

brake hop. Wheel hop that occurs when brakes are applied in forward or reverse motion of the vehicle.

braking force. The negative *longitudinal force* resulting from *braking torque* application.

braking force coefficient (braking coefficient). The ratio of the *braking force* to the *vertical load.*

braking (driving) squeal. The *squeal* resulting from *longitudinal slip.*

braking (driving) stiffness. The rate of change of *longitudinal force* with respect to change in *longitudinal slip,* usually evaluated at zero *longitudinal slip.*

braking (driving) stiffness coefficient. The ratio of *braking (driving) stiffness* of a *free straight-rolling tire* to the *vertical load.*

braking torque. The negative *wheel torque.*

braking traction coefficient. The maximum of the *braking force coefficient* that can be reached without locking a wheel on a given tire and road surface for a given environment and operating condition. Related term — *sliding braking traction coefficient.*

bump stop. An elastic member that increases the *wheel rate* toward the end of the *compression* travel. The bump stop may also act to limit the compression travel.

camber angle. The inclination of the wheel plane to the vertical. Considered positive when the wheel leans outward at the top and negative when it leans inward.

camber force (camber thrust). The *lateral force* when the *slip angle* is zero and the *plysteer* and *conicity forces* are subtracted.

camber stiffness. The rate of change of *lateral force* with respect to change in *inclination angle,* usually evaluated at zero *inclination angle.*

camber stiffness coefficient (camber coefficient). The ratio of *camber stiffness* of a *free straight-rolling tire* to the *vertical load.*

caster angle. The angle in side elevation between the steering axis and the vertical. Considered positive when the steering axis is inclined rearward (in the upward direction) and negative when the steering axis is inclined forward.

caster offset. The distance in side elevation between the point where the steering axis intersects the ground, and the *center of tire contact*. Taken as positive when the intersection point is forward of the *center of tire contact* and negative when it is rearward.

center of parallel wheel motion. The center of curvature of the path along which each of a pair of *wheel centers* moves in a longitudinal vertical plane relative to the *sprung mass* when both wheels are equally displaced.

center of tire contact. The intersection of the *wheel plane* and the vertical projection of the *spin axis* of the wheel onto the road plane. NOTE: The center of tire contact may NOT be the geometric center of the tire contact area due to distortion of the tire produced by applied forces.

central force. The component of the *tire force* vector perpendicular to the direction of travel of the *center of tire contact*. Central Force is equal to *lateral force* times cosine of *slip angle* minus *longitudinal force* times sine of *slip angle*.

centrifugal caster. The unbalance moment about the steering axis produced by a lateral acceleration equal to gravity acting at the combined center of gravity of all the steerable parts. Considered positive if the combined center of gravity is forward of the steering axis and negative if rearward of the steering axis.

centripetal acceleration. The component of the vector *acceleration* of a point in the vehicle perpendicular to the tangent to the path of that point and parallel to the road plane.

characteristic speed. That forward speed for an understeer vehicle at which the steering sensitivity at zero *lateral acceleration trim* is one-half the steering sensitivity of a *neutral steer* vehicle.

complex damping. The force opposing the vibratory motion is variable, but NOT proportional, to the *velocity*.

compliance camber. The camber motion of a wheel due to compliance in suspension linkages and produced by forces and/or moments applied at the tire-road contact.

compliance camber coefficient. The rate of change in wheel *inclination angle* with respect to change in forces or moments applied at the tire-road contact.

compliance oversteer. *Compliance steer* which decreases vehicle *understeer* or increases vehicle *oversteer*.

compliance steer. The change in *steer angle* of front or rear wheels resulting from compliance in suspension and steering linkages and produced by forces and/or moments applied at the tire-road contact. Related terms — *compliance understeer, compliance oversteer*.

compliance understeer. *Compliance steer* which increases vehicle *understeer* or decreases vehicle *oversteer*.

compliance steer coefficient. The rate of change in *compliance steer* with respect to change in forces or moments applied at the tire-road contact.

componenents and characteristics of suspension systems. Related terms — *vibrating mass and weight, spring rate, resultant spring rate, static deflection, damping devices.*

compression. The relative displacement of *sprung* and *unsprung masses* in the suspension system where the distance between the masses decreases from that at static condition. Related terms — *ride clearance, metal-to-metal position, bump stop.*

conicity force. The component of *lateral force offset* that changes sign (with respect to the *Tire Axis System*) with a change in direction of rotation (positive away from the serial number or toward the whitewall). The force is positive when it is directed away from the serial number on the right side tire and negative when it is directed toward the serial number on the left side tire.

control modes. Related terms — *position control, force control.*

cornering squeal. The *squeal* produced by a *free-rolling tire* resulting from *slip angle.*

cornering stiffness — The negative of the rate of change of *lateral force* with respect to change in *slip angle,* usually evaluated at zero *slip angle.*

cornering stiffness coefficient (cornering coefficient). The ratio of *cornering stiffness* of a *free straight-rolling* tire to the *vertical load.* NOTE: Although the term 'cornering coefficient' has been used in technical literature, for consistency with definitions of other terms using the word 'coefficient', the term 'cornering stiffness coefficient' is preferred by SAE.

Coulomb damping. A constant force opposes the vibratory motion.

course angle (υ). The angle between the trace of the vehicle velocity vector on the X-Y plane and X-axis of the *earth-fixed axis system.* A positive course angle is shown in Figure D2-3. Course angle is the sum of *heading angle* and *sideslip angle.*

critical damping. The minimum amount of *viscous damping* required in a *linear system* to prevent the displacement of the system from passing the equilibrium position upon returning from an initial displacement.

critical speed. The forward speed for an oversteer vehicle at which the steering sensitivity at zero *lateral acceleration trim* is infinite.

cycle of oscillation. The complete sequence of variations in displacement which occur during a *period.*

damped system. Energy is dissipated by forces opposing the vibratory motion. Any means associated with a vibrating system to balance or modulate exciting forces will reduce the vibratory motion, but may not be considered 'damping'. The term is applied to an inherent characteristic of the system without reference to the nature of the excitation. Related terms — *viscous damping, critical damping, damping ratio, coulomb damping, complex damping, undamped system.*

damping devices. Actual mechanisms used to obtain damping of suspension systems. Related terms — *shock absorber, snubber.*

damping ratio. Ratio of the amount of *viscous damping* present in a system to that required for *critical damping.*

deflection (static). The radial difference between the undeflected tire radius and the static loaded radius, under specified loads and inflation. Percent Deflection — The static deflection expressed as a percentage of the unloaded section height above the top of the rim flange.

degree of freedom. The sum total of ALL ways in which the masses of the system can be independently displaced from their respective equilibrium positions. Examples — A single rigid body constrained to move only vertically on supporting springs is a system of one degree of freedom. If the same mass is also permitted angular displacement in one vertical plane, it has two degrees of freedom: one being vertical displacement of the center of gravity; the other, angular displacement about the center of gravity.

directional dynamics. Related terms — *control modes, vehicle response, stability, suspension steer and roll properties, tire load transfer.*

disturbance response. The vehicle motion resulting from unwanted force or displacement inputs applied to the vehicle. Examples of disturbances — wind forces or vertical road displacements.

divergent instability. Exists at a prescribed if any small temporary disturbance or control input causes an ever increasing vehicle response without oscillation. NOTE: Divergent instability may be illustrated by operation above the critical speed of an *oversteer* vehicle. Any input to the steering wheel will place the vehicle in a turn of ever decreasing radius unless the driver makes compensating motions of the wheel to maintain general equilibrium. This condition represents divergent instability.

drag force. The negative *tractive force*.

driving force. The *longitudinal force* resulting from *driving torque* application.

driving force coefficient. The ratio of the *driving force* to the *vertical load*.

driving torque. The positive *wheel torque*.

driving traction coefficient. The maximum value of *driving force coefficient* that can be reached on a given tire and road surface for a given environment and operating condition.

dynamic index. The ratio k^2/ab, where k is the radius of gyration of the *sprung mass* about a transverse axis through the center of gravity, and a and b are the two longitudinal distances from the center of gravity to the front and rear *wheel centers*.

dynamic rate. The rate measured during rapid deflection where the elastic member is not allowed to reach static equilibrium.

earth-fixed axis system (X, Y, Z). This system is a right-hand orthogonal axis system fixed on the earth. The trajectory of the vehicle is described with respect to this earth-fixed axis system. The X- and Y-axes are in a horizontal plane and the Z-axis is directed downward.

effective rolling radius. Ratio of the linear velocity of the *wheel center* in the X'-direction to the *spin velocity*. (See *Tire Axis System*)

effective static deflection. Equals the *static load* divided by the *spring rate* of the system at that load. Equals the *total static deflection* when the *spring rate* is constant.

exciting frequency. *Frequency* of variation of the exciting force.

first order lateral force variation. The *peak-to-peak amplitude* of the fundamental frequency component in the mathematical expression for *lateral force variation*. Its *frequency* is equal to the rotational *frequency* of the tire.

first order radial force variation. The peak-to-peak *amplitude* of the fundamental frequency component in the mathematical expression for *radial force variation*. Its *frequency* is equal to the rotational *frequency* of the tire.

fixed control. That mode of vehicle control wherein the position of some point in the steering system (front wheels, Pitman arm, steering wheel) is held fixed. This is a special case of *position control*.

flat tire radius. The distance from the spin axis to the road surface of a loaded tire on a specified rim at zero inflation.

force control. That mode of vehicle control wherein inputs or restraints are placed upon the steering system in the form of forces, independent of the displacement required. Related term — *free control*.

forced vibration. *Vibration* during which variable forces OUTSIDE the system determine the period of the *vibration*. Related term — *resonance*.

forces. The external forces acting on the vehicle can be summed into one force vector having the components — *longitudinal force*, *side force*, and *normal force*.
NOTE: To make axis transformations and resolve the forces with respect to the direction of vehicle motion, it is essential to measure ALL six force and *moment* components — F_X, F_y, F_z, M_X, M_y, and M_z.

forward velocity. The component of the vector *velocity* perpendicular to the y-axis and parallel to the road plane.

free control. That mode of vehicle control wherein no restraints are placed upon the steering system. This is a special case of *force control*.

free-rolling tire. A loaded rolling tire operated without application of *driving* or *braking torque*.

free vibration. *Vibration* during which variable forces INSIDE the system determine the period of the *vibration*.

frequency. Frequency of *vibration* is the number of periods occurring in unit time. Related terms — *natural frequency, exciting frequency, frequency ratio, resonant frequency.*

frequency ratio. Ratio of the *exciting frequency* to the *natural frequency.*

general nomenclature, tires/wheels. Related terms — *standard loads and inflations, rim diameter, rim width, tire section width, tire overall width, tire section height, tire outside diameter, flat tire radius, deflection, tire rate, sidewall, bead, tread.*

gross contact area. The total area enclosing the pattern of the tire *tread* in contact with a flat surface, INCLUDING the area of grooves of other depressions.

harshness. High frequency (25-100 Hz) vibrations perceived tactually and/or audibly, produced by interaction of the tire with road irregularities.

heading angle (ψ). The angle between the trace on the X-Y plane of the vehicle x-axis and the X-axis of the *earth-fixed axis system.* (See Figure D2-3)

hop. The vertical oscillatory motion of a wheel between the road surface and the *sprung mass.* Related terms — *parallel hop, tramp, brake hop, power hop.*

inclination angle. The angle between the Z'-axis and the *wheel plane.*

jerk. A concise term for the time rate of change of *acceleration* of a point.

kinematics, forces/moments. Related terms — *earth-fixed axis system, vehicle axis system, angular orientation, motion variables, sideslip angle, forces.*

kingpin geometry. Related terms — *wheel plane, wheel center, center of tire contact, kingpin inclination, kingpin offset.*

kingpin inclination. The angle in front elevation between the steering axis and the vertical.

kingpin offset. The kingpin offset **at the**

ground is the horizontal distance in front elevation between the point where the steering axis intersects the ground and the *center of tire contact.* The kingpin offset **at the wheel center** is the horizontal distance in front elevation from the *wheel center* to the steering axis.

lateral acceleration. The component of the vector *acceleration* of a point in the vehicle perpendicular to the vehicle x-axis and parallel to the road plane. In *steady-state* condition, the lateral acceleration is equal to the product of *centripetal acceleration* times the cosine of the vehicle's *sideslip angle.* Typically, the *sideslip angle* is small, so that the *lateral acceleration* may be equated to *centripetal acceleration.*

lateral force (F_y). 1. The component of the *tire force* vector in the Y'-direction.

lateral force coefficient. The ratio of the *lateral force* to the *vertical load.*

lateral force offset. The average *lateral force* of a *free straight-rolling tire.* Related terms — *ply steer force, conicity force.*

lateral force variation. The periodic variation of *lateral force* of a *straight free-rolling tire* which repeats each revolution, at a fixed *loaded radius*, given mean *normal force*, constant speed, given inflation pressure and test surface curvature. Related terms — *peak-to-peak (total) lateral force variation, first order lateral force variation.*

lateral run-out. Related terms — *peak-to-peak lateral wheel run-out, peak-to-peak lateral tire run-out.*

lateral traction coefficient. The maximum value of *lateral force coefficient* attainable on a *free-rolling tire* for a given road surface, environment and operating condition.

lateral velocity. The component of the vector *velocity* perpendicular to the x-axis and parallel to the road plane.

linear system, vibrating. That in which all the variable forces are directly proportional to the displacement, or to the derivatives of the displacement, with respect to time.

loaded radius. The distance from the *center of tire contact* to the *wheel center* measured in the *wheel plane*.

longitudinal acceleration. The component of the vector *acceleration* of a point in the vehicle in the x-direction.

longitudinal force (F_X). 1. The component of the *tire force* vector in the X'-direction. 2. The component of the *force* vector in the x-direction.

longitudinal slip (percent slip). The ratio of the *longitudinal slip velocity* to the *spin velocity* of the *straight free-rolling tire* expressed as a percentage. NOT to be confused with the 'slip number' that frequently appears in kinematic analysis of tires in which the *spin velocity* appears in the denominator.

longitudinal slip velocity. The difference between the *spin velocity* of the driven or braked tire and the *spin velocity* of the *straight free-rolling tire*. Both *spin velocities* are measured at the same linear *velocity* at the *wheel center* in the X' direction. A positive value results from *driving torque*.

longitudinal velocity (u). The component of the vector *velocity* in the x-direction.

mechanical vibration, qualitative terminology. Related terms — *vibration, oscillation, free vibration, forced vibration, self-excited vibration, simple harmonic vibration, steady-state vibration, periodic vibration, random vibration, transient vibration*.

mechanical vibration, quantitative terminology. Related terms — *period of oscillation, cycle of oscillation, frequency, amplitude, velocity, acceleration, jerk, transmissibility*.

metal-to-metal position (compression). The point of maximum *compression* travel limited by interference of substantially rigid members.

metal-to-metal position (rebound). The point of maximum *rebound* travel limited by

interference of substantially rigid members.

moments. The external moments acting on the vehicle can be summed into one moment vector having the components — *rolling moment, pitching moment, yawing moment*. (See Figure D2-1)

motion variables. Related terms — *vehicle velocity, vehicle acceleration*.

natural frequency. *Frequency* of *free vibration*.

normal acceleration. The component of the vector *acceleration* of a point in the vehicle in the z-direction.

net contact area. The area enclosing the pattern of the tire *tread* in contact with a flat surface, EXCLUDING the area of grooves of other depressions.

neutral stability. Neutral stability exists at a prescribed *trim* if, for any small temporary change in disturbance or control input, the resulting motion of the vehicle remains close to, but does NOT return to, the motion defined by the *trim*.

neutral steer. A vehicle is neutral steer at a given *trim* if the ratio of the *steering wheel angle gradient* to the *overall steering ratio* equals the *Ackerman steer angle gradient*.

neutral steer line. The set of points in the x-z plane at which external *lateral forces* applied to the *sprung mass* produce NO *steady-state yaw velocity*.

nonlinear system, vibrating. None of the variable forces are directly proportional to the displacement, or to its derivatives with respect to time. Example — A system having a variable *spring rate*.

normalized tire force and moment stiffnesses (coefficients). Related terms — *cornering stiffness coefficient, camber stiffness coefficient, braking stiffness coefficient, aligning stiffness coefficient*.

normal force (F_Z). 1. The component of the *tire force* vector in the Z'-direction. 2. The component of the *force* vector in the z-direction.

normal velocity (w). The component of the

vector *velocity* in the z-direction.

oscillation (vibration), general. The variation with time of the displacement of a body with respect to a specified reference dimension when the displacement is alternately greater and smaller than the reference. Related terms — *period of oscillation, cycle of oscillation, vibration.*

oscillatory instability. Exists if a small temporary disturbance or control input causes an oscillatory vehicle response of ever increasing *amplitude* about the initial *trim*. May be illustrated by the free control response following a pulse input of displacement or force to the steering wheel. Some vehicles will turn first in one direction, and then the other, and so on, until the *amplitude* of the motion increases to the extent that the vehicle 'spins out'. In this event, the vehicle does not attempt to change its general direction of motion, but does not achieve a *steady-state* condition and has an oscillatory motion.

overall steering ratio. The rate of change of *steering wheel angle* at a given steering wheel *trim* position, with respect to change in average *steer angle* of a pair of steered wheels, assuming an infinitely stiff steering system with no roll of the vehicle. For *nonlinear* steering systems, this ratio is presented as a function of *steering wheel angle* in order to be compatible with the definition of *understeer/oversteer gradient.*

oversteer. A vehicle is oversteer at a given *trim* if the ratio of the *steering wheel angle gradient* to the *overall steering ratio* is less than the *Ackerman steer angle gradient.*

overturning couple. The *overturning moment* on the vehicle with respect to a central, longitudinal axis in the road plane due to *lateral acceleration* and *roll* acceleration.

overturning couple distribution. The distribution of the total *overturning couple* between the front and rear suspensions expressed as the percentage of the total.

overturning moment (M_X). The component of the *tire moment* vector tending to rotate the tire about the X'-axis, positive clockwise when looking in the positive direction of the X'-axis.

parallel hop. A pair of wheels *hop* in phase.

parallel springing. Describes the suspension of a vehicle in which the *effective static deflections* of the two ends are equal; that is, the *spring center* passes through the center of gravity of the *sprung mass.*

peak-to-peak amplitude (double amplitude). The sum of the extreme values of displacement in both directions from the equilibrium position.

peak-to-peak (total) lateral force variation. The difference between the maximum and minimum values of the *lateral force* during one revolution of the tire.

peak-to-peak lateral tire run-out. The difference between maximum and minimum indicator readings, measured parallel to the *spin axis* at the point of maximum tire section, on a true running wheel (measured separately for each sidewall).

peak-to-peak lateral wheel run-out. The difference between maximum and minimum indicator readings, measured parallel to the *spin axis* on the inside vertical portion of a rim flange (measured separately for each flange).

peak-to-peak (total) radial force variation. The difference between maximum and minimum values of the *normal force* during one revolution of the tire.

peak-to-peak loaded radial tire run-out. The difference between maximum and minimum values of the *loaded radius* on a true running wheel.

peak-to-peak radial wheel run-out. The difference between the maximum and minimum values of the wheel bead seat radius, measured in a plane perpendicular to the *spin axis* (measured separately for each bead seat).

peak-to-peak unloaded radial tire run-out.

The difference between maximum and minimum undeflected values of the tire radius, measured in plane perpendicular to the *spin axis* on a true running wheel.

period of oscillation. The smallest increment of time in which one full sequence of variation in displacement occurs.

periodic vibration. Exists when recurring cycles occur in equal time intervals.

pitch. The angular component of *ride* vibrations of the *sprung mass* about the vehicle y-axis.

pitch velocity (q). The angular velocity about the y-axis.

pitching moment (M_y). The component of the *moment* vector tending to rotate the vehicle about the y-axis, positive clockwise when looking in the positive direction of the y-axis.

ply steer force. The component of *lateral force offset* which does not change sign (with respect to the *Tire Axis System*) with a change in direction of rotation (positive along positive Y'-axis). The force remains positive when it is directed away from the serial number on the right side tire and toward the serial number on the left side.

position control. That mode of vehicle control wherein inputs or restraints are placed upon the steering system in the form of displacements at some control point in the steering system (front wheels, Pitman arm, steering wheel), independent of the force required. Related term — *fixed control*.

power hop. Wheel *hop* that occurs when tractive force is applied in forward or reverse motion of the vehicle.

radial force variation. The periodic variation of the *normal force* of a loaded *straight free-rolling tire* that repeats each revolution at a fixed *loaded radius*, given mean *normal force*, constant speed, given inflation pressure and test surface curvature. Related terms — *peak-to-peak (total) radial force variation, first order radial force variation*.

radial run-out. Related terms — *peak-to-peak radial wheel run-out, peak-to-peak unloaded radial tire run-out, peak-to-peak loaded radial tire run-out*.

random vibration. The *oscillation* is sustained but irregular both as to period and *amplitude*.

rate of camber change. The change of camber angle per unit vertical displacement of the *wheel center* relative to the *sprung mass*. Related terms — *swing center, swing-arm radius*.

rate of caster change. The change in *caster angle* per unit vertical displacement of the *wheel center* relative to the *sprung mass*.

rate of track change. The change in wheel track per unit vertical displacement of both *wheel centers* in the same direction relative to the *sprung mass*.

rebound. The relative displacement of the *sprung* and *unsprung masses* in a suspension system in which the distance between the masses increases from that at static condition. Related terms — *rebound clearance, metal-to-metal position, rebound stop*.

rebound clearance. The maximum displacement in *rebound* of the *sprung mass* relative to the *wheel center* permitted by the suspension system, from the normal load position.

rebound stop. An elastic member that increases the *wheel rate* toward the end of the *rebound* travel. The *rebound stop* may also act to limit the rebound travel.

resonance. A *forced vibration* phenomenon that exists if any small change in *frequency* of the applied force causes a decrease in the amplitude of the vibrating system.

resonant frequency. *Frequency* at which resonance exists.

resultant spring rate. Related terms — *suspension rate, tire rate, ride rate*.

ride. Low frequency (≤ 5 Hz) vibrations of the

sprung mass as a rigid body. Related terms — *bounce, pitch, roll.*

ride clearance. The maximum displacement in compression of the *sprung mass* relative to the *wheel center* permitted by the suspension system, from the normal load position.

ride rate. The change of wheel load, at the *center of tire contact*, per unit vertical displacement of the *sprung mass* relative to the ground at a specified load.

rim diameter. The diameter at the intersection of the *bead* seat and flange. Nominal rim diameter (i.e., 14, 15, 16.5, etc.) is commonly used.

rim width. The distance between the inside surfaces or the rim flanges.

roll. The angular component of *ride* vibrations of the *sprung mass* about the vehicle x-axis.

roll axis. The line joining the front and rear *roll centers*.

roll camber. The camber displacements of a wheel resulting from *suspension roll*.

roll camber coefficient. The rate of change in wheel *inclination angle* with respect to change in *suspension roll angle*.

roll center. The point in the transverse vertical plane through any pair of *wheel centers* at which lateral forces may be applied to the *sprung mass* without producing *suspension roll*. NOTE: The *roll center* as defined here is an idealized concept and does NOT necessarily represent a true instantaneous center of rotation of the *sprung mass*.

roll oversteer. *Roll steer* which decreases vehicle *understeer* or increases vehicle *oversteer*.

roll steer. The change in *steer angle* of front or rear wheels due to *suspension roll*. Related terms — *roll understeer, roll oversteer.*

roll steer coefficient. The rate of change in *roll steer* with respect to change in *suspension roll angle* at a given *trim*.

roll stiffness distributions. The distribution of the *vehicle roll stiffness* between front and rear suspension expressed as percentage of the *vehicle roll stiffness*.

roll understeer. *Roll steer* which increases vehicle *understeer* or decreases vehicle *oversteer*.

roll velocity (p). The angular velocity about the x-axis.

rolling characteristics. Related terms — *loaded radius, static loaded radius, spin axis, spin velocity, free-rolling tire, straight free-rolling tire, longitudinal slip velocity, longitudinal slip, effective rolling radius, wheel skid.*

rolling moment (M_x). The component of the moment vector tending to rotate the vehicle about the x-axis, positive clockwise when looking the positive direction of the x-axis.

rolling resistance force. The negative *longitudinal force* resulting from energy losses due to deformations of a rolling tire. Can be computed from the *forces* and *moments* acting on the tire by the road. NOTE: This definition applies to wheels either driven or braked. The wheel torque can be expressed in terms of the *longitudinal force*, *rolling resistance force*, and *loaded radius* by $T_w = (F_x + F_r) R_l$. For a free-rolling wheel, the rolling resistance force is thus the negative of the *longitudinal force*.

rolling resistance force coefficient (coefficient of rolling resistance). The ratio of the *rolling resistance* to the *vertical load*.

rolling resistance moment (M_y). The component of the *tire moment* vector tending to rotate the tire about the Y'-axis. Positive clockwise when looking in the positive direction of the Y'-axis.

roughness. *Vibration* (15-100 Hz) perceived tactily and/or audibly, generated by a rolling tire on a smooth road surface and producing the sensation of driving on a coarse or irregular surface.

self-excited vibration. The vibratory motion produces cyclic forces which sustain the *vibration*.

shake. The intermediate frequency (5-25 Hz) vibrations of the *sprung mass* as a flexible body. Related terms — *torsional shake, beaming, harshness.*

shimmy. A self-excited oscillation of a pair of steerable wheels about their steering axes, accompanied by appreciable tramp.

shock absorber. A generic term for hydraulic mechanisms that produce damping of suspension systems.

side acceleration. The component of the vector *acceleration* of a point in the vehicle in the y-direction.

side force (F_y). The component of the force vector in the y-direction.

side velocity (v). The component of the vector *velocity* in the y-direction.

sideslip angle (attitude angle) (ß). The angle between the traces on the X-Y plane of the vehicle x-axis and the *vehicle velocity* vector at some specified point in the vehicle. Sideslip angle is shown negative in Figure D2-3. Related terms — *sideslip angle gradient, course angle, vehicle roll angle, vehicle roll gradient, vehicle pitch angle.*

sideslip angle gradient. The rate of change of *side-slip angle* with respect to change in *steady-state lateral acceleration* on a level road at a given *trim* and test conditions.

sidewall — The portion of either side of the tire which connects the bead with the tread. Related term — *sidewall rib.*

sidewall rib. A raised circumferential rib located on the sidewall.

simple harmonic vibration. The displacement with respect to time is described by a simple sine function.

sizzle. A *tread noise* (up to 4000 Hz) characterized by a soft frying sound, particularly noticeable on a very smooth road surface.

slap. Airborne smacking noise produced by a tire traversing road seams such as tar strips and expansion joints.

sliding braking traction coefficient. The value of the *braking force coefficient* of a tire obtained on a locked wheel on a given tire and road surface for a given environment and operating condition.

squeal. Narrow band airborne tire noise (150-800 Hz) resulting from either *longitudinal slip* or *slip angle* or both. Related terms — *cornering squeal, braking squeal.*

slip angle. The angle between the X'axis and the direction of travel of the *center of tire contact.*

slip angle force. The *lateral force* when the inclination angle is zero and *plysteer* and *conicity forces* have been subtracted.

snubber. A generic term for mechanisms that use dry friction to produce damping of suspension systems.

spring center. The vertical line along which a vertical load applied to the *sprung mass* will produce only uniform vertical displacement.

spin axis. The axis of rotation of the wheel. (See Figure D2-1)

spin velocity (Ω). The angular velocity of the wheel on which the tire is mounted, about its *spin axis*. Positive spin velocity is shown in Figure D2-1.

spring rate. The change of load of a spring per unit deflection, taken as a mean between loading and unloading at a specified load. Related terms — *static rate, dynamic rate.*

sprung mass. Considered a rigid body having equal mass, the same center of gravity, and the same moments of inertia about identical axes as the total *sprung weight.*

sprung mass vibrations. Related terms — *ride, shake, boom.*

sprung weight. All weight supported by the suspension, including portions of the weight of the suspension members. Generally defined as the total weight less the weight of unsprung parts.

stability. Related terms — *asymptotic stability, neutral stability, divergent instability, oscillatory instability.* NOTE: Passenger vehicles exhibit varying characteristics depending upon test conditions and *trim*. Test conditions refer to vehicle conditions like wheel loads, front wheel alignment, tire inflation pressure, and also atmospheric and road conditions that affect vehicle parameters. For example, temperature may change *shock absorber damping* characteristics and a slippery road surface may change tire cornering properties. *Trim* may be specified in part by *steer angle, forward velocity*, and *lateral acceleration*. As all these factors change the vehicle behavior, the vehicle stability must be examined separately for each environment and *trim*.

For a given set of vehicle parameters and test conditions, the vehicle may be examined for each theoretically attainable *trim*. The conditions which most affect stability are the *steady-state* values of *forward velocity* and *lateral accelerations*. In practice, it is possible for a vehicle to be stable under one set of operating conditions and unstable in another.

standard loads and inflations. Those combinations of loads and inflations up to the maximum load and inflation as recommended by the Tire and Rim Association, and published in their Yearbook.

static amplitude. That displacement of the point from its specified equilibrium position which would be produced by a static force equal to the maximum value of exciting force.

static deflection. Related terms — *total static deflection, effective static deflection, spring center, parallel springing*.

static loaded radius. The *loaded radius* of a stationary tire inflated to normal recommended pressure. NOTE: In general, static loaded radius is different from the radius of slowly rolling tire. Static radius of a tire rolled into position may be different from that of the tire loaded without being rolled.

static margin. The horizontal distance from the center of gravity to the *neutral steer line* divided by the wheelbase. It is positive if the center of gravity is forward of the *neutral steer line*.

static rate. The rate measured between successive stationary positions at which the elastic member has settled to substantially equilibrium condition.

static toe angle (degrees). The angle between a longitudinal axis of the vehicle and the line of intersection of the *wheel plane* and the road surface. The wheel is 'toed-in' if its forward portion is turned toward a central longitudinal axis of the vehicle, and 'toed-out' if turned away.

static toe-in or toe-out (in. or mm) of a pair of wheels. The difference in the transverse distances between the *wheel planes* taken at the extreme rear and front points of the tire treads. When the distance at the rear is greater, the wheels are 'toed-in' by this amount; and where smaller, the wheels are 'toed-out'. NOTE: The static toe (inches) is equal to the sum of the toe angles (degrees) of the left and right wheels multiplied by the ratio of tire diameter (inches) to 57.3. If the toe angles on the left and right wheel are the same and the outside diameter of tire is 28.65 in (727.7 mm), the static toe (inches) is equal to *static toe angle* (degrees).

steady-state. Exists when periodic (or constant) vehicle responses to periodic (or constant) control and/or disturbance inputs do not change over an arbitrarily long time. The motion responses in steady-state are referred to as steady-state responses. This definition does NOT require the vehicle to be operating in a straight line or on a level road surface. It can also be in a turn of constant radius or on a cambered road surface.

steady-state response gain. The ratio of change in the *steady-state* response of any motion variable with respect to change in input at a given *trim*.

steady-state vibration. Exists in a system if

the displacement at each point recurs for equal increments of time.

steer angle (δ). The angle between the projection of a longitudinal axis of the vehicle and the line of intersection of the *wheel plane* and the road surface. Positive angle is shown in Figure D2-3.

steering response. The vehicle motion resulting from an input to the steering (control) element. NOTE: Although the steering wheel is the primary directional control element, it should be recognized that *longitudinal forces* at the wheels resulting from driver inputs to brakes or throttle can modify directional response.

steering sensitivity (control gain). The change in *steady-state lateral acceleration* on a level road with respect to change in *steering wheel angle* at a given *trim* and test conditions.

steering system vibrations. Related terms — *wheel flutter, wheel wobble, shimmy, wheelfight.*

steering wheel angle. Angular displacement of the steering wheel measured from the straight-ahead position (that corresponds to zero average *steer angle* of a pair of steered wheels).

steering wheel angle gradient. The rate of change in the *steering wheel angle* with respect to change in *steady-state lateral acceleration* on a level road at a given *trim* and test conditions.

steering wheel torque. The torque applied to the steering wheel about its rotational axis.

steering wheel torque gradient. The rate of change in the *steering wheel torque* with respect to change in *steady-state lateral acceleration* on a level road at a given *trim* and test conditions.

straight free-rolling tire. A *free-rolling tire* moving in a straight line at zero *inclination angle* and zero *slip angle*.

suspension geometry. Related terms — *kingpin geometry, wheel caster, wheel camber, wheel toe, compression, rebound,* *center of parallel wheel motion, torque arm.*

suspension rate (wheel rate). The change of wheel load, at the *center of tire contact*, per unit vertical displacement of the *sprung mass* relative to the wheel at a specified load. If the *wheel camber* varies, the displacement is measured relative to the lowest point on the rim centerline.

suspension roll. The rotation of the vehicle *sprung mass* about the x-axis with respect to a transverse axis joining a pair of *wheel centers*.

suspension roll angle. The angular displacement produced by *suspension roll*.

suspension roll gradient. The rate of change in the *suspension roll angle* with respect to change in *steady-state lateral acceleration* on a level road at a given *trim* and test conditions.

suspension roll stiffness. The rate of change in the restoring couple exerted by the suspension of a pair of wheels on the *sprung mass* of the vehicle with respect to change in *suspension roll angle*.

suspension steer and roll properties (Figure D2-4). Related terms — *steer angle, Ackerman steer angle, Ackerman steer angle gradient, steer wheel angle, steering wheel angle gradient, overall steering ratio, understeer/oversteer gradient, neutral steer, understeer, oversteer, steering wheel torque, steering wheel torque gradient, characteristic speed, critical speed, neutral steer line, static margin, suspension roll, suspension roll angle, suspension roll gradient, roll steer, roll steer coefficient, compliance steer, compliance steer coefficient, roll camber, roll camber coefficient, compliance camber, compliance camber coefficient, roll center, roll axis, suspension roll stiffness, vehicle roll stiffness, roll stiffness distributions.* NOTE: It is possible for a vehicle to be *understeer* for small inputs and *oversteer* for large inputs (or the opposite), since it is a *nonlinear* system and does not have the same characteristics at all *trims*. Therefore, it is necessary to specify the range of inputs and *velocities* when determining the vehicle's steer characteristics. A set of equivalent definitions in terms of *yaw velocity* or curvature (reciprocal of radius of curvature) are also used, which are applicable only to two-axle vehicles.

swing-arm radius. The horizontal distance from the *swing center* to the *center of tire contact*.

swing center. That instantaneous center in the transverse vertical plane through any pair of *wheel centers* about which the wheel moves relative to the *sprung mass*.

tire angles. Related terms — *slip angle, inclination angle*.

tire axis system (Figure D2-1) — The origin of the tire axis system is the *center of tire contact*. The X'-axis is the intersection of the *wheel plane* and the road plane with a positive direction forward. The Z'-axis is perpendicular to the road plane with a positive direction downward. The Y'-axis is in the road plane, its direction being chosen to make the axis system orthogonal and right-hand.

tire forces. The external force acting on the tire by the road. Related terms — *longitudinal force, driving force, driving force coefficient, braking force, braking force coefficient, rolling resistance force, rolling resistance force coefficient, lateral force, lateral force coefficient, slip angle force, camber force, normal force, vertical load, central force, tractive force, drag force*.

tire forces and moments. Related terms — *tire axis system, tire angles, tire forces, tire moments*.

tire lateral load transfer. The *vertical load* transfer from one of the front tires (or rear tires) to the other that is due to *acceleration*, rotational, or inertial effects in the lateral direction.

tire lateral load transfer distribution. The distribution of the total *tire lateral load transfer* between front and rear tires expressed as the percentage of the total.

tire load transfer. Related terms — *tire lateral load transfer, tire lateral load transfer distribution, tire longitudinal load transfer, overturning couple, overturning couple distribution*.

tire longitudinal load transfer. The *vertical load* transferred from a front tire to the corresponding rear tire that is due to *acceleration*, rotational, or inertial effects in the longitudinal direction.

tire moments. The external moments acting on the tire by the road. Related terms — *overturning moment, rolling resistance moment, aligning torque, wheel torque, driving torque, driving torque, braking torque*.

thump. A periodic vibration and/or audible sound generated by the tire and producing a pounding sensation which is synchronous with wheel rotation.

tire associated noise and vibrations. Related terms — *tread noise, squeal, thump, roughness, harshness, slap*.

tire force and moment stiffness. May be evaluated at any set of operating conditions. Related terms — *cornering stiffness, camber stiffness, braking stiffness, aligning stiffness*.

tire outside diameter. The maximum diameter of the new unloaded tire inflated to the normal recommended pressure and mounted on a specified rim.

tire overall width. The width of the unloaded new tire, mounted on specified rim, inflated to the normal recommended pressure — including protective rib, bars, and decorations.

tire rate (static). The *static rate* measured by the change of wheel load per unit vertical displacement of the wheel relative to the ground at a specified load and inflation pressure.

tire section height. Half the difference between the tire outside diameter and the nominal rim diameter.

tire section width. The width of the unloaded new tire mounted on specified rim, inflated to the normal recommended pressure — including the normal sidewalls but NOT including protective rib, bars, and decorations.

tire and wheel non-uniformity characteristics. Related terms — *radial run-out, lateral run-out, radial force variation, lateral force variation, lateral force offset.*

tires and wheels. Related terms — *general nomenclature, rolling characteristics, tire forces and moments, tire force and moment stiffness, normalized tire force and moment stiffnesses, tire traction coefficients, tire associated noise and vibrations, tire and wheel non-uniformity characteristics.*

tire traction coefficients. Related terms — *lateral traction coefficient, driving traction coefficient, braking traction coefficient.*

torque arm. Related terms — *torque-arm center, torque-arm radius.*

torque-arm center. The instantaneous center in a vertical longitudinal plane through the *wheel center* about which the wheel moves relative to the *sprung mass* when the brake is locked **(torque-arm center in braking)** or when the drive mechanism is locked at the power source **(torque-arm center in drive)**.

torque-arm radius. The horizontal distance from the *torque-arm center* to the *wheel center.*

torsional shake. A mode of *vibration* involving twisting deformations of *sprung mass* about the vehicle y-axis.

total static deflection. The overall deflection under the static load from the position at which all elastic elements are free of load. Equals the *effective static deflection* when the *spring rate* is constant.

track change. The change in wheel track due to vertical suspension displacements of both wheels in the same direction.

tractive force. The component of the *tire force* vector in the direction of travel of the *center of tire contact*. Tractive force is equal to *lateral force* times sine of *slip angle* plus *longitudinal force* times cosine of *slip angle.*

tramp. A pair of wheels hop in opposite phase.

transient state. Exists when the motion responses, the external forces relative to the vehicle, or the control positions are changing with time. NOTE: Transient responses are described by the terminology normally used for other dynamic systems. Some terminology is described in the "Control Engineers' Handbook," but a more complete terminology is contained in ANS C85.1-1963.

transient vibration. One or more component *oscillations* are discontinuous.

transmissibility. Ratio of the transmitted force to the applied force.

tread (tire). The peripheral portion of the tire, with its exterior designed to contact the road surface. Related terms — *tread contour, tread radius, tread arc width, tread chord width, tread contact width, tread contact length, tread depth, gross contact area, net contact area, tread pattern.*

tread arc width. The distance measured ALONG the tread contour of an unloaded tire between one edge of the tread and the other. For tires with rounded tread edges, the point of measurement is at the intersection of the *tread radius* extended until it meets the prolongation of the upper sidewall contour.

tread chord width. The distance measured PARALLEL to the spin axis of an unloaded tire between one edge of the tread and the other. The point of measurement is the same as for *tread arc width.*

tread contact length. The perpendicular distance between the tangent to edges of the leading and following points of road contact and parallel to the *wheel plane.*

tread contact width. The distance between

the extreme edges of road contact at a specified load and pressure measured parallel to the Y'-axis at zero *slip angle* and zero *inclination angle*.

tread contour. The cross sectional shape of tread surface of an inflated unloaded tire neglecting the tread pattern depressions.

tread depth. The distance between the base of tire tread groove and a line tangent to the surface of the two adjacent *tread* ribs or rows.

tread noise. Airborne sound (up to 5000 Hz) except *squeal* and *slap* produced by the interaction between the tire and the road surface. Related term — *sizzle*.

tread pattern. The molded configuration on the face of the *tread*. Usually composed of ribs, rows, grooves, bars, lugs, etc.

tread radius. The radius or combination of radii describing the tread contour.

trim. The *steady-state* (or equilibrium) condition of the vehicle with constant input which is used as the reference point for analysis of dynamic vehicle *stability* and control characteristics.

undamped system. No forces opposing the vibratory motion to dissipate energy.

understeer. A vehicle is understeer at a given *trim* if the ratio of the *steering wheel angle gradient* to the *overall steering ratio* is greater than the *Ackerman steer angle gradient*.

understeer/oversteer gradient. The quantity obtained by subtracting the *Ackerman steer angle gradient* from the ratio of the *steering wheel angle gradient* to the *overall steering ratio*.

unsprung mass(es). The equivalent masses that reproduce the inertia forces resulting from the motions of the corresponding unsprung parts.

unsprung mass vibrations. Related terms — *wheel vibration modes, axle vibration modes, steering system vibrations*.

unsprung weight. All weight NOT carried by the suspension system, but is supported directly by the tire or wheel, and considered to move with it.

vehicle acceleration. The vector quantity expressing the acceleration of a point in the vehicle relative to the *earth-fixed axis system* (X, Y, Z). The following motion variables are components of this vector, resolved with respect to the moving *vehicle axis system* (x, y, z) — *longitudinal acceleration, side acceleration, normal acceleration, lateral acceleration, centripetal acceleration, heading angle*.

vehicle axis system (x, y, z) (Figure D2-2). This system is a right-hand orthogonal axis system fixed in a vehicle such that with the vehicle moving steadily in a straight line on a level road, the x-axis is substantially horizontal, points forward, and is in the longitudinal plane of symmetry. The y-axis points to the driver's right and the z-axis points downward.

vehicle pitch angle. The angle between the vehicle x-axis and the ground plane.

vehicle response. The vehicle motion resulting from some internal or external input to the vehicle. Response tests can be used to determine the stability and control characteristics of a vehicle. Related terms — *steering response, disturbance response, steady-state, transient state, trim, steady-state response gain, steering sensitivity*.

vehicle roll angle. The angle between the vehicle y-axis and the ground plane.

vehicle roll gradient. The rate of change in *vehicle roll angle* with respect to change in *steady-state lateral acceleration* on a level road at a given *trim* and test conditions.

vehicle roll stiffness. Sum of the separate *suspension roll stiffnesses*.

vehicle velocity. The vector quantity expressing *velocity* of a point in the vehicle relative to the *earth-fixed axis system* (X, Y, Z). The following motion variables are components of this vector resolved with respect to the moving *vehicle axis system* (x, y, z)

— *longitudinal velocity, side velocity, normal velocity, forward velocity, lateral velocity, roll velocity, pitch velocity, yaw velocity.*

velocity. The time rate of change of displacement.

vertical load. The normal reaction of the tire on the road which is equal to the negative of *normal force*.

vibration (oscillation), general. The variation with time of the displacement of a body with respect to a specified reference dimension when the displacement is alternately greater and smaller than the reference. Related terms — *free vibration, forced vibration, self-excited vibration, simple harmonic vibration, steady-state vibration, periodic vibration, random vibration, transient vibration.*

vibrations, vehicle suspension systems. Related terms — *sprungmass vibrations, unsprungmass vibrations.*

vibrating mass and weight. Related terms — *sprung weight, sprung mass, dynamic index, unsprung weight, unsprung mass.*

vibrating systems. Related terms — *degree of freedom, linear system, nonlinear system, undamped system, damped system.*

viscous damping. The force opposing the motion is proportional and opposite in direction to the *velocity*.

wheel camber. Related terms — *camber angle, rate of camber change, wheel track, track change, rate of track change.*

wheel caster. Related terms — *caster angle, rate of caster change, caster offset, centrifugal caster.*

wheel center. The point at which the spin axis of the wheel intersects the wheel plane.

wheel flutter. Forced oscillation of steerable wheels about their steering axes.

wheel plane. The central plane of the tire, normal to the spin axis.

wheelfight. A rotary disturbance of the steering wheel produced by forces acting on the steerable wheels.

wheel skid. The occurrence of sliding between the tire and road interface which takes place within the entire contact area. Skid can result from braking, driving and/or cornering.

wheel toe. Defined at a specified wheel load or relative position of the *wheel center* with respect to the *sprung mass*. Related terms — *static toe angle, static toe-in or toe-out.*

wheel torque (T_W). The external torque applied to the tire from the vehicle about the *spin axis*. Positive wheel torque is shown in Figure D2-1.

wheel track (wheel tread). The lateral distance between the *center of tire contact* of a pair of wheels. For dual-wheeled vehicles, it is the distance between the points centrally located between the *centers of tire contact* of the inner and outer wheels.

wheel vibration modes. Related term — *hop.*

wheel wobble. A self-excited oscillation of steerable wheels about their steering axes, occurring without much tramp.

yaw velocity (r). The angular velocity about the z-axis.

yawing moment (M_Z). The component of the moment vector tending to rotate the vehicle about the z-axis, positive clockwise when looking in the positive direction of the z-axis.

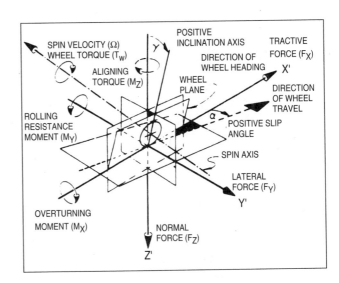

Figure D2-1 Tire axis system. (SAE)

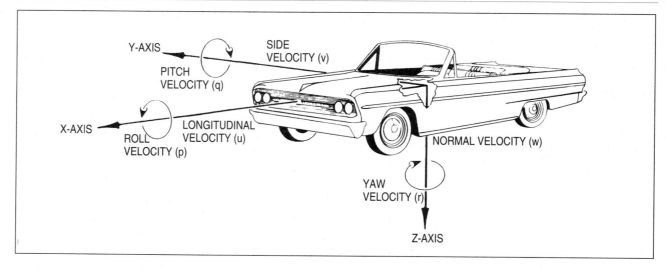

Figure D2-2 The vehicle axis system — x, y, and z directions. (SAE)

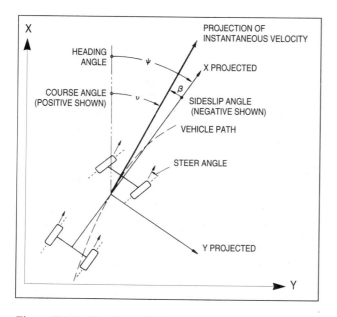

Figure D2-3 Heading, sideslip, and course angles. (SAE)

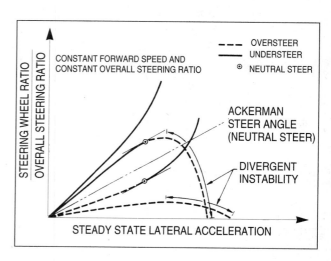

Figure D2-4 Suspension steer and roll properties. (SAE)

TECHNICIAN CERTIFICATION -- ASE

GENERAL INFORMATION

Why is certification important?

- Certification protects both the consumer and the technician.
- It assures the consumer and the employer that certain basic standards of performance have been met.
- It offers recognition in the profession.
- It is an effective marketing tool for employer's business promotion.
- It provides increased opportunities for professional advancement.

What is the name of the organization that certifies technicians?

National Institute for Automotive Service Excellence (ASE). ASE automotive certification program is both industry-wide and national in scope, and is endorsed by forty professional associations and trade groups.

Who will administer these certification tests? How many technicians take these tests annually?

ASE tests are administered under strict security conditions by ACT (American College Testing), a professional testing organization. Presently, well over 100,000 technicians take these tests annually.

How many times a year are these tests administered?

Twice a year, May and November, at some 500 testing sites. The registration deadline is approximately six weeks before the test.

What are the specialties of certification?

ASE offers certification tests (totaling 23) in the following specialties — Automobile (8), Medium/Heavy Truck (6), Body/Paint (4), Engine Machinist (3), Light Vehicle Compressed Natural Gas (1), and Advanced Engine Performance Specialist (1).

In the area of **automobile,** there are eight specialties of certification — engine repair, automatic transmission/transaxle, manual drivetrain and axles, **suspension and steering**, brakes, electrical/electronic systems, heating and air conditioning, and engine performance.

If you pass one or more tests, and have at least two years of hands-on working experience in automotive repair, then you will be certified as an **ASE Automobile Technician**. If you are already certified in Automobile Engine Performance, you are eligible to take the new Advanced Engine Performance Specialist test.

If you pass ALL eight tests in the series and meet the experience requirement, you will earn the certificate of **ASE Master Automobile Technician**.

What is the minimum score for passing? May I register for more than one test?

Information on the passing score is not published. A candidate scoring around 70% seems to have a fair chance of being declared successful. You may register for as many as four regular tests on one day.

What is the experience requirement for receiving the certification?

You should have at least two years of full time, hands-on working experience to *receive* the certification. However, you may take the tests before you have two years of experience and you will receive a score report. If you pass the test, you will be issued a certificate after you have met the required experience requirement. Vocational training may be substituted for part of the experience requirement. High school or post high school training may count for up to one year of work experience.

Once I pass, what do I receive to prove that I am ASE Certified?

You will receive the *blue seal of excellence* — the nationally recognized ASE emblem on a certificate suitable for framing. Included will be an insignia (*See* Figure) for your sleeve or pocket, a wallet card, display card and pocket credentials card complete with plastic pocket protector. Each card lists your area(s) of certification and expiration date(s).

Are there any accommodations for candidates with special needs?

Yes. Technicians who have been professionally diagnosed with a physical or mental impairment as defined by the Americans With Disabilities Act, may receive assistance when taking the tests. The type of help required should be identified and the request must be received by ASE/ACT by a specified due date. Certificates/transcripts awarded on the basis of special arrangements or reader/translator assistance will be noted to show that such help was given.

When should I take recertification tests?

Certification credentials are valid for 5 years, in view of the rapidly changing technologies in the automotive field. If it has been 5 years since you took a particular test(s), it is time to register for the *corresponding* Recertification Test(s). They are one-half the length of the corresponding regular test. If you prefer, you may also take the regular test instead of the recertification tests to re-certify.

Figure E-1   When certified, you earn the right to wear the ASE insignia appropriate to the level of your certification.

What is the contact address for more detailed information?

National Institute for Auto Service Excellence (ASE)
13505 Dulles Technology Drive
Herndon, VA 22071-3415
Phone (703)713-0727

ASE TEST — SUSPENSION & STEERING

SPECIFICATIONS

Content Area	Questions No.	%
A. Steering Systems Diagnosis and Repair	9	22.5
1. Steering Columns and Manual Steering Gears (2)		
2. Power-Assisted Steering Units (4)		
3. Steering Linkage (3)		
B. Suspension Systems Diagnosis and Repair	13	32.5
1. Front Suspensions (6)		
2. Rear Suspensions (5)		
3. Miscellaneous Service (2)		
C. Wheel Alignment Diagnosis, Adjustment, and Repair	13	32.5
D. Wheel and Tire Diagnosis and Repair	5	12.5
Total	40*	100%

*This is the number of scored questions. There could be up to 10 additional pre-test questions. Your answers to these questions will not affect your score, but since you do not know which they are, you should answer ALL questions in the test.

TASK LIST

It is to be noted that the number of questions in each content area may not equal the number of tasks listed below. Some of the tasks are complex and broad in scope and may be covered by several questions. Other tasks are simple and narrow in scope; one question may cover several tasks. The main purpose for listing the tasks is to describe accurately what is done on the job, NOT to make each task correspond to a particular test question.

A. Steering Systems Diagnosis and Repair (9 questions)

1. Steering Columns and Manual Steering Gears (2 questions)

1. Diagnose steering column noises, looseness, and binding problems (including tilt mechanisms); determine repairs.
2. Diagnose manual steering gear (non-rack-and-pinion type) noises, binding, uneven turning effort, looseness, hard steering, and lubricant leakage problems; determine repairs.
3. Diagnose rack-and-pinion steering gear noises, vibration, looseness, and hard steering problems; determine repairs.
4. Inspect and replace steering shaft U-joint(s), flexible coupling(s), collapsible columns, steering wheels, including steering wheels with air bags.
5. Remove and replace manual steering gear (non-rack-and-pinion type).
6. Adjust manual steering gear (non-rack-and-pinion type) worm bearing preload and sector lash.
7. Remove and replace rack-and-pinion steering gear.
8. Adjust rack-and-pinion steering gear.
9. Inspect and replace rack-and-pinion steering gear inner tie rod ends (sockets) and bellows boots.
10. Inspect and replace rack-and-pinion steering gear mounting bushings and brackets.

2. Power-Assisted Steering Units (4 questions)

1. Diagnose power steering gear (non-rack-and-pinion type noises, binding, uneven turning effort, looseness, hard steering, and fluid leakage problems; determine repairs.
2. Diagnose power rack-and-pinion steering gear noises, vibration, looseness, hard steering, and fluid leakage problems; determine repairs.
3. Inspect power steering fluid level and condition; adjust level as per vehicle manufacturers' recommendations.
4. Inspect, adjust tension and alignment, and replace power steering pump.
5. Remove and replace power steering pump; inspect pump mounts.
6. Inspect and replace power steering pump seals and gaskets.

7. Inspect and replace power steering pump pulley.

8. Perform power steering system pressure test; determine repairs.

9. Inspect and replace power steering hoses, fittings, and O-rings.

10. Remove and replace power steering gear (non-rack-and-pinion type).

11. Remove and replace power rack-and-pinion steering gear; inspect and replace mounting bushings and brackets.

12. Adjust power steering gear (non-rack-and-pinion type) worm bearing preload and sector lash.

13. Inspect and replace power steering gear (non-rack-and-pinion type) seals and gaskets.

14. Adjust power rack-and-pinion steering gear.

15. Inspect and replace power rack-and-pinion steering gear inner tie rod ends (sockets), seals, gaskets, O-rings, and bellows boots.

16. Diagnose, inspect, and adjust, repair or replace components of electronically controlled steering systems.

17. Flush, fill, and bleed power steering system.

18. Diagnose, inspect, repair or replace components of variable assist steering systems.

3. Steering Linkage (3 questions)

1. Inspect and adjust (where applicable) front and rear steering linkage geometry including attitude and parallelism.

2. Inspect and replace Pitman arm.

3. Inspect and replace relay (center link/intermediate) rod.

4. Inspect, adjust (where applicable), and replace idler arm and mountings.

5. Inspect, replace, and adjust tie rods, tie rod sleeves, clamps, and tie rod ends (sockets).

6. Inspect and replace steering linkage damper.

B. Suspension Systems Diagnosis and Repair (13 questions)

1. Front Suspensions (6 questions)

1. Diagnose front suspension system noises, body sway, and ride height problems; determine repairs.

2. Inspect and replace upper and lower control arms, bushings, shafts, and rebound bumpers.

3. Inspect, adjust, and replace strut rods/radius arm (compression/tension) and bushings.

4. Inspect and replace upper and lower ball joints.

5. Inspect and replace steering knuckle/spindle assemblies.

6. Inspect and replace front suspension system coil springs and spring insulators (silencers).

7. Inspect and replace front suspension system leaf spring(s), leaf spring insulators (silencers), shackles, brackets, bushings, and mounts.

8. Inspect, replace, and adjust front suspension system torsion bars; inspect mounts.

9. Inspect and replace stabilizer bar (sway bar) bushings, brackets, and links.

10. Inspect and replace MacPherson strut cartridge or assembly.

11. Inspect and replace MacPherson strut upper bearing and mount.

2. Rear Suspensions (5 questions)

1. Diagnose suspension system noises, body sway, and ride height problems; determine repairs.

2. Inspect and replace rear suspension system coil springs and spring insulators (silencers).

3. Inspect and replace rear suspension system transverse links (track bars), control arms, stabilizer bars (sway bars), bushings, and mounts.

4. Inspect and replace rear suspension system leaf spring(s), leaf spring insulators (silencers), shackles, brackets, bushings, and mounts.

5. Inspect and replace rear MacPherson strut cartridge or assembly, and upper mount assembly.

6. Inspect non-independent rear axle assembly for bending, warpage, and misalignment.

7. Inspect and replace rear ball joints and tie rod assemblies.

3. Miscellaneous Service (2 questions)

1. Inspect and replace shock absorbers.

2. Inspect and replace air shock absorbers, lines, and fittings.
3. Diagnose and service front and/or rear wheel bearings.
4. Diagnose, inspect, adjust, repair or replace components of electronically controlled suspension systems.

C. Wheel Alignment Diagnosis, Adjustment, and Repair (13 questions)

1. Diagnose vehicle wander, drift, pull, hard steering, bump steer, memory steer, torque steer, and steering return problems; determine repairs.
2. Measure vehicle ride height; determine repairs.
3. Check and adjust front and rear wheel camber on suspension systems with a camber adjustment.
4. Check front and rear wheel camber on non-adjustable suspension systems; determine repairs.
5. Check and adjust caster on suspension systems with a caster adjustment.
6. Check caster on non-adjustable suspension systems; determine repairs.
7. Check and adjust front wheel toe.
8. Center steering wheel.
9. Check toe-out-on-turns (turning radius); determine repairs.
10. Check SAI/KPI; determine repairs.
11. Check included angle; determine repairs.
12. Check rear wheel toe; determine repairs or adjustments.
13. Check rear wheel thrust angle; determine repairs or adjustments.
14. Check for front wheel setback; determine repairs or adjustments.
15. Check front cradle (subframe) alignment; determine repairs or adjustments.

D. Wheel and Tire Diagnosis and Repair (5 questions)

1. Diagnose tire wear patterns; determine repairs.
2. Inspect tires; check and adjust air pressure.
3. Diagnose wheel/tire vibration, shimmy, and noise problems; determine repairs.
4. Rotate tires/wheels according to manufacturers' recommendations.

5. Measure wheel, tire, axle, and hub runout; determine repairs.
6. Diagnose tire pull (lead) problems; determine corrective actions.
7. Balance wheel and tire assembly (static and/or dynamic).

TYPICAL TEST QUESTIONS

1. The front end of a vehicle vibrates up and down while traveling at most road speeds. Technician A says too much radial runout of the front tires is the cause. Technician B says static out-of-balance of the front tires is the cause. Who is right?
   (A) A only
   (B) B only
   (C) Both A and B
   (D) Neither A nor B

2. From the alignment settings shown in the tabulation below, indicate which of the conditions would result.

	Readings		Specs
	Left	Right	Left or Right
Camber	+3/4° (+45')	-1 1/2° (-1° 30')	0 to +1/2° (0 to +30')
Caster	0°	0°	0° to +1°
Toe-In	0.16 mm (1/16")		0.16 to 0.48mm (1/16" to 3/16")

   (A) Left tire wear on inside; vehicle does not pull to either side
   (B) Right tire wear on inside; vehicle pulls to left
   (C) Right tire wear on outside; vehicle pulls to left
   (D) Right tire wear on outside; left wear on inside; vehicle pulls to left

3. A vehicle wanders while being driven on a level road. Technician A says too much negative camber could be the cause. Technician B says too much positive caster could be the cause. Who is right?
   (A) A only
   (B) B only
   (C) Both A and B
   (D) Neither A nor B

4. A vehicle with manual rack-and-pinion steering has a shimmy. Technician A

says worn rack-to-frame mounting bushings could be the cause. Technician B says loose inner or outer tie-rod ends (sockets) could be the cause. Who is right?
(A) A only
(B) B only
(C) Both A and B
(D) Neither A nor B

5. During a wheel alignment, a technician finds the toe-out-on-turns (turning radius) to be incorrect. Which of these could be the cause?
(A) Bent Pitman arm
(B) Bent tie rod
(C) Bent idler arm
(D) Bent steering arm

6. A vehicle pulls to the right during braking. Technician A says a worn strut rod bushing could be the cause. Technician B says a bent right wheel could be the cause. Who is right?
(A) A only
(B) B only
(C) Both A and B
(D) Neither A nor B

7. The ball joints on the MacPherson strut suspension system (Figure E-2) are being replaced. Technician A says a coil spring compressor should be installed before separating the control arm and spindle. Technician B says the wheel alignment should be checked after replacing the ball joints. Who is right?
(A) A only
(B) B only
(C) Both A and B
(D) Neither A nor B

8. The suspension in Figure E-3 is being checked for ball joint wear. Technician A says the check can be made with the front end jacked up at 'X'. Technician B says the check can be made with the front end jacked up at 'Y'. Who is right?
(A) A only
(B) B only
(C) Both A and B
(D) Neither A nor B

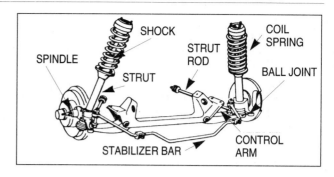

Figure E-2 MacPherson Strut. (ASE)

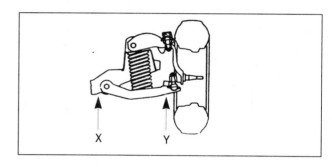

Figure E-3 Checking suspensions for ball joint wear. (ASE)

9. A pressure test is being performed on a vehicle with power steering. The pressure readings taken when the wheels are at the right and left stops are below specs. The readings are normal when the tester shutoff valve is closed. Technician A says these readings could be caused by a bad steering gear. Technician B says they are caused by a bad pump. Who is right?
(A) A only
(B) B only
(C) Both A and B
(D) Neither A nor B

10. All of these could cause tire wear if not within manufacturer's specs, EXCEPT:
(A) caster.
(B) wheel balance.
(C) toe-in.
(D) camber.

Answer Key
1. C   2. B   3. D   4. C   5. D
6. A   7. B   8. B   9. A   10. A

REFERENCE MATERIALS/SOURCES

With more than 600 different models on the road and over 450 different types of on-board computers under the hood, the information needs of today's technician are immense. The technician has to understand a system, diagnose the problem by appropriate tests, and fix the problem. All this has to be accomplished within the time and budgetary constraints, often set by the customer. The technician seeks help from a variety of information sources — videotapes, CD-ROMs, vehicle manufacturers' service manuals, comprehensive shop manuals, trade magazines, and manuals/catalogs from manufacturers of vehicle systems, parts, and tools. This appendix attempts to identify some of these reference materials available to the front-end technician.

VIDEOS

Videos constitute a very effective training medium in the field of automotives. They help the technician understand clearly the operation of a specific tool/instrument or the step-by-step procedure for the diagnosis and repair of an automobile problem. Some videos are published by the manufacturers of automobiles/parts, and others by independent publishers. All videos listed are in VHS format.

Arrow Automotive Industries, Farmingham, MA.
- *The Men Under the Hood* (14 minutes). Diagnosis and installation.
- *Power Rack-and-Pinion Steering* (14 minutes). Diagnosis and installation.

Bergwall Productions, Chadds Ford, PA.
- *Automotive Suspension Explained* (4 videos, 60 minutes). *Frames, Wheels and Tires; Steering Angles; Steering Systems; Suspension Systems.* Provide a comprehensive introduction to the fundamentals of basic suspension systems.

Bergwall Productions, Uniondale, NY.
- *Automotive Electronics Explained* (5 videos, 17 minutes each). *Comparing Old and New systems; Basic Concepts and Equipment; Microprocessor Design and Usage; Schematics and Components; Troubleshooting Techniques.*
- *Electronic Wheel Balancing* (3 videos).
- *The Front End* (4 videos).
- *Front Wheel Drive: Transaxle Overhaul* (5 videos).

Cardone Industries, Inc., Philadelphia, PA
- *Troubleshooting and Repair of GM Electronic Control Modules* (30 minutes). Fundamentals of electronic control computer systems; engine control subsystems; troubleshooting procedures for electronic control modules. Describes General Motors electronic control modules, and the various diagnostic tests involved in their maintenance.

Chrysler Corporation, Tech Authority, CIMS 423-21-06, 26001 Lawrence Avenue, Center Line, MI 48015 (in Canada: Chrysler Canada, Tech Authority, CIMS 240-01-10, PO Box 1621, Windsor, Ontario, N9A 4H6).
- *Multiplex Electronics and Body/Chassis Diagnosis* (30 minutes).
- *1990 Daytona and Lebaron Instrument Cluster Service and Body Electronics* (30 minutes).

C 365

Cliff Berry, Madison, WI
- *Wisconsin Pre-trip Inspection Procedures, Chevrolet Forward Control Chassis, Capenter Body* (42 minutes). Using standard form, shows details of pre-trip inspection procedures.

Collector Car Restoration Video, Inc., Elsmere, KY
- *Chassis & Running Gear* (120 minutes). Processes of dismantiling, inspecting, rebuilding and restoring the frame, suspension, brakes, and the rest of the chassis.

The Corporation, Detroit, MI.
- *FCA Fab. Report I; Chassis Report II; and Bodyshop Report III.* (60 minutes).

Dana Corporation, Ottawa Lake, MI.
- *4x4 Alignment Correction* (9 minutes). Demonstrates alignment procedure.
- *Honda 4-Wheel Steer* (9 minutes). Discusses alignment angles and procedures of a Honda steering system.
- *Front Wheel Drive Wheel Bearing Service* (8 minutes). Gives tips on troubleshooting and service for front wheel drive wheel bearings.

Ford Service Publications, PO Box 07150, Detroit, MI 48207.
- *Automotive Suspensions* (*basic suspension* 28:20 minutes; *4-wheel alignment* 19:00 minutes). Covers fundamentals of suspension systems and procedures for completing a total, 4-wheel alignment for front-wheel drive vehicles.
- *Automotive Suspensions — Large Cars & Light Trucks* (25 minutes). Provides general directions for service and repair work.
- *Automotive Suspensions* (25:14 minutes). Covers front-wheel alignment on rear-wheel drive vehicles and the front and the rear suspension systems on F-150 and F-250 light trucks.
- *Basic Automotive Electronics* (23 minutes). Covers the use of electronics in modern vehicle systems. Reviews electron theory and explains the application of microprocessor circuitry.
- *Basic Automotive Electronics* (23 min-

utes). Provides general directions for service and repair work.
- *Brakes, Steering and Suspension Systems* (14:50 minutes). Introduces principles of braking, hydraulics and steering; describes various brake, steering and suspension systems. Provides information on tires and wheels.
- *EEC System Operation* (45:31 minutes). Describes the Ford Electronic Engine Control System, identifies engine systems and operations controlled by the EEC System. Describes operation of electronic control assembly (ECA). Illustrates the function and operation of all EEC input and output components.
- *Electronic Steering System* (32:39 minutes). Describes electronically controlled steering systems in Ford vehicles. Includes Electronic Variable Orifice (EVO) Steering and Variable Assist Power Steering (VAPS) systems. Contains instructions for testing and diagnosis.
- *Electrical Systems* (17:50 minutes). Covers basic circuit construction and components. Includes principles of starting, ignition, charging and lighting systems.
- *Fastening Devices and Torquing Techniques* (25:23 minutes). Provides information related to fastening devices, bolt identification, torque, torque wrench usage, de-torque methods and torque methods. Concepts apply to all fastener applications, emphasis on engine-related components.
- *The Ford World of Automotive Technology* (99:40 minutes). Provides overviews of the internal combustion engine, fuel and emission control systems, electricity, instruments and climate control, drivetrains, transmissions, wheels and brakes, steering, suspension and future trends in body designs.
- *1991 New Model Service Features Pre-Delivery Chassis & Electrical* (26 minutes).
- *Noise and Vibrations* Explains diagnosing noise and vibration concerns. Presents source identification procedures, using the Reed Tachometer, Electronic Vibration Analyzer (EVA), Chassis Ear*TM* and Engine Ear*TM*.
- *Rack and Pinion Power Steering Gears and Pumps* (25:02 minutes). Covers the

operation, diagnosis and repair of rack and pinion steering systems used on Ford and other domestic vehicles. The use of special tools is also described.

- *Rear Axle Diagnosis and Overhaul* (26:00 minutes). Provides complete overhaul and parts replacement procedures for integral carrier axles. Includes making and interpreting disassembly checks and inspections.
- *Servicing Supplemental Air Bag Restraint Systems* (19:55 minutes). Discusses the operation and test procedures for keyless entry and illumination systems on Ford and Lincoln-Mercury vehicles. Coverage includes Auto Lock.
- *Shop Practices* (15:30 minutes). Explains procedures and precautions for shop safety, including the Hazard Communication Program. Contains descriptions and safety guidelines for basic tools and measuring devices.

General Motors Training Materials, MascoTech Marketing Services, 1972 Brown Rd, Auburn Hills, MI 48326-1701.

- *ABC of the Automobile: The Chassis* (15 minutes). Illustrates and explains the flow of power from engine to wheels in an automobile, using cutaway models and animation.
- *Basic Electronics* (Expertec, 4 tapes, 120 minutes). Theory and application of basic electronics. Ohm's Law, magnetism, current flow, circuits, semiconductors, diodes, meters, resistors, transistors, and computer logic. Vehicle computers.
- *Controlling Electrostatic Discharge* (20 minutes).
- *Vibration Correction* (13 minutes). Classroom supplement. Explains centrifugal force, cycles, frequency, amplitude, phasing and force variation. Focus is on tires, wheels and driveline.

Kirkwood Community College, Cedar Rapids, IA

- *Typical Frame Design* (6 minutes). Describes typical damge to an auto frame from a collision.

Monroe Auto Equipment Co., Monroe, MI
- *Strut Installations.*

Northern Virginia Community College, Manassas, VA

- *Auto 169 — Frame Repair* (30 minutes). Shows frame and unit construction straightening processes. Includes segments on setting up frame gauges and pull chains.

The Office, Washington, D.C.
(Marketed by: National Audiovisual Center, Washington, D.C.)

- *Steering, Wheels, Front and Rear Axles* (19 minutes). Shows how to check for play in the steering wheel and the front end assembly of an automobile; correct wheel runout; make a toe-in test; and test springs, axles, and overall backlash.

Rockwell International, Troy, MI.

- *Parts Counter Sales and Product Training Program* (2 tapes) — *Selling in the Trenches* (26 minutes); *"Q" Brakes, Drive Lines, Front Axles, Gearing* (32 minutes).

Ross Roy, Inc., Detroit, MI

- *Chassis and Drive-line Highlights* (13 minutes). Describes the design features and repair procedures of the chassis and drive-lines on Trail Dusters and Ramchargers.

Specialty Products Co., Longmont, CO

- *Light Truck Alignments.* Removal and installation of bushings and sleeves available for aligning 2WD and 4WD light truck vehicles. *Rear Wheel Alignment Procedures. MacPherson Strut Spring Compressing and Replacement. Split Boot Procedures.*

Standard Motor Products, Inc., Detroit, MI.

- *Body Control Computers* (30 minutes). Basic background on the function and operation of a body control computer. Interaction of computer with the engine control computer and various other systems — air conditioning, suspension, braking, fuel injection, electronic ignition, and automatic transmission control.
- *Power Steering Diagnostics* (30 minutes). Diagnosing problems in power rack-and-pinion and integral power

steering systems. Visual inspection procedures. Power rack diagnostics using pressure and flow gauge test apparatus. Step-by-step replacement procedures for power steering pump assembly, hoses, and rack-and-pinion unit. Procedure for assembling a short rack replacement unit.

- *Wiring of the Future — Multiplexing* (30 minutes). Principles of multiplexing. Multiplexing and computer systems. Review of how auto control systems communicate, sensors with computers and computers among themselves. Multiplexing in '88 and '89 Chrysler vehicles. Trouble shooting and repair.

Teaching Aids, Costa Mesa, CA

- *Pre-alignment Checks* (1 video). Teaches the procedures for chencking the suspension and steering for problems that may prevent proper wheel alignment.
- *Steering Geometry* (30 minutes). Teaches the theory of steering geometry as it applies to front-end alignment, including the caster, camber, steering axis inclination, toe-in, and turning radius angles.

CD-ROMS

The Compact Disk Read-Only Memory (CD-ROM) is the most recent distribution medium through which vast amounts of data are made accessible using a microcomputer. Typically, a 650 MB CD-ROM can hold data equivalent of about 1500 floppy disks — that is more than one quarter-million pages of text, or 12,000 scanned images.

The following are some major CD-ROM databases for the automobile service/repair shops. CD-ROM databases are updated periodically, quarterly updates being most usual.

ALLDATA Corporation, 9412 Big Horn Blvd., Elk Grove, CA 95758.

- *ALLDATA Automotive Diagnostic and Repair Database*
  Contents — manufacturers' technical service bulletins, diagnostic and repair procedures, component test procedures, component locations, PROM updates, part numbers and prices, flat rate figures,

wiring diagrams, maintenance schedules, and warranty and recall information.
  Coverage — most North American and import cars, back to 1982. Includes — computerized engine controls; fuel and ignition systems; tune up; emissions systems; starting/charging systems, power and ground distributions; body electrical, safety, entertainment, communication; heating, ventilation, air conditioning; engine mechanical, cooling, exhaust; transmissions; clutches, differentials, driveshafts, axles; steering, suspension, chassis, body parts; brakes, antilock brakes, traction control systems.

Bell and Howell Co., 5700 Lombardo Center, Suite 220, Seven Hills, OH 44131, USA; 230 Barmac Drive, Weston, M98 2X5, Canada.

- *Automobile Parts Information System (Nissan)* in Japanese
- *Chrysler Parts Access Info System (PAIS) Catalog*
- *General Motors Electronic Parts Catalog*
- *Honda/Acura Electronic Parts Catalog*
- *Parts and Service Manuals — General Motors, Chrysler, Honda, and Mercedes Benz.*

Chilton On Disc, One Chilton Way, Radnor, PA 19089.

- *Chilton-On-Disc* (initial release, Nov '94) Automotive repair database, in a relational database format.
  Contents — component locations; customer review, technician safety, 'how it works', identification placards, labor times, maintenance intervals, repair procedures, wiring and vacuum schematics, special tools, specifications, training/certification information, diagnostics, technical information, and technical service bulletins.
  Coverage — most North American and import cars and light trucks, 1985-92 (initial release), and 1982-current (later releases). The initial release **excludes** the following systems/manufacturers — A/C, ABS, parts, transmission repair and electronic suspension diagnostics; BMW, Hyundai, Mitsubishi, Subaru, Volkswagen, Audi, Isuzu, Mercedes-Benz, Volvo, Porsche, Saab, and Suzuki.

Ford New Holland, Inc., 500 Diller Avenue, PO Box 1895, New Holland, PA 17557.

- *Parts Master File OSI Information*

Mitchell International, 9889 Willow Creek Road, PO Box 26260, San Diego, CA 92196.

- *On-Demand*
  A comprehensive automotive repair information system.
  Contents — over 1 million pages of service and repair procedures; 175,000 illustrations; 50,000 technical service bulletins; 250 Mitchell manuals. The *Expertec* information in the system contains thousands of GM authorized technical service bulletins, the latest ECM/PROM updates, service data, vehicle and system specifications for major makes and models plus a data communications link for the Tech-1 hand-held diagnostic computer. Includes labor estimating data for vehicles back to 1974.
  Coverage — most North American and import cars, light trucks, and vans back to 1983. Includes — air bags; air conditioning and heating; brakes; clutches; diagnostics; drive axles; electrical; emissions; engine cooling; engine performance; engine repairs; maintenance; recalls; safety and accessory equipment; steering; suspension; transmission; wheel alignment; wiring diagrams.
  Option — Triad *ServiceCat* Electronic Parts Catalog and labor estimating guide. *ServiceCat* gives instant access to over 1.9 million parts, 9.6 million applications, and 3,000 graphic illustrations, and lets ordering of parts electronically. Also confirms and prints order for parts at the jobber's site.

VEHICLE MANUFACTURERS' SERVICE MANUALS

These manuals, typically system specific, explain the function and operation of the system and related subsystems/components, as well as describe diagnosis and testing procedures. Usually safety precautions are also covered. They serve well as training materials.

Acura Manuals

- Helm Incorporated, Publications Div., PO Box 07130, Detroit, MI 48207.

Chrysler Manuals

- Chrysler Corporation, Tech Authority, CIMS 423-21-06, 26001 Lawrence Avenue, Center Line, MI 48015.
- Chrysler Canada, Tech Authority, CIMS 240-01-10, PO Box 1621, Windsor, Ontario N9A 4H6, Canada.

Ford Manuals

- Ford Service Publications, PO Box 07150, Detroit, MI 48207.

GM Manuals

- **Chevrolet, Pontiac, Cadillac**
  Helm Incorporated, Publication Div., PO Box 07130, Detroit, MI 48207.
- **Oldsmobile**
  Lansing Lithographers, Inc., PO Box 23188, Lansing, MI 48909.
- **Buick**
  Tuar Company, PO Box 354, Flint, MI 48501; Service Publications, PO Box 1901, Flint, MI 48501.
- **GMC Truck**
  Adistra Corporation, attn - GMC Service Publications, PO Box 56006, Pontiac, MI 48506.

Honda, Isuzu, and Mazda Manuals

- Helm Incorporated, Publications Div., PO Box 07130, Detroit, MI 48207.

Nissan Manuals

- Nissan Corporation, 20770 Westwood Drive, Cleveland, OH 44136.

Toyota Manuals

- Toyota Service Publications, 750 West Victoria Street, Compton, CA 90220.

Volvo Manuals

- Volvo Cars of North America, PO Box 25577, Milwaukee, WI 53225.

COMPREHENSIVE SHOP MANUALS

These contain information on the most common specifications and procedures for the most often performed service operations for various late-model cars. These are annual publications and constitute excellent single source of reference material you need in your day-to-day job. Three major sources of comprehensive shop manuals serving the automotive repair industry are:

- *Chilton Auto Repair Manuals*
  Chilton Book Company, Chilton Way, Radnor, PA 19087.

- *Mitchell Service and Repair Manuals*
  Mitchell International, PO Box 26260, San Diego, CA 92196-0260.
- *Motor Auto Repair Manuals*
  Hearst Business Publishing, Inc., 5600 Crooks Rd, Troy, MI 48098.

The Chilton and Mitchell manuals are also stored electronically and are incorporated into the CD-ROM automotive diagnostic and repair databases from these publishers.

TRADE MAGAZINES

Trade magazines help the technician keep current with the latest developments in automotive technology. The technical and how-to features will be of immediate relevance to the day-to-day work at the service/repair shop. Two popular trade magazines are the *Motor Age* and the *Motor*, published monthly.

Motor Age Magazine (Chilton) has three sections — 'technical', 'making money', and 'for your information'. Typical topic area headings include — face-to-face, troubleshooting, servicing imports, product showcase, training resources, free literature, industry notes, classified, calendar, and service dealer spotlight. **Motor** Magazine (Motor) has three sections — 'technical', 'reports', and 'departments'. Typical topic area headings include — trouble shooter, trade secrets, foreign service, eye on electronics, a special topic, and service slants; editor's report, a special topic, and newsbreak; tools of the trade, after market monitor, reader service card, classified, and advertiser index. *Motor* Magazine issues an annual source guide as well.

Typical **special topic articles** published in the **Motor** Magazine which should be of interest to the front-end technician include: "Sizing It Up," (July '94); "Diagnostic Overload," (July '94); "Choosing Diagnostic Equipment," (Aug '94); "Shop Management Software," (a series of 4 articles, Feb/Mar/June/Aug '94). Typical articles that appeared in **Motor Age** Magazine include: "Fluid Maintenance — Time for a Change," (July '94); "Using the Multimeter," (Aug '94); "A New Way to Look at Automotive Waveforms" (Nov '94). This list is only a quick sampling, not based on any detailed search.

Another monthly magazine for the automotive repair technician is the **Import**

Service (Gemini Communications), devoted to import cars. Its March '95 issue is a 'Tech Tips Special', containing repair tips on various automobile parts — brakes, drivetrain, electrical, engine/mechanical, fuel & emissions, general, steering & suspension, and temperature control. Tech tips on steering/suspension include — alignment, power steering noises, Pitman seal removal, handling improvement, camber adjustment, steering rack caution, wheel balance (Honda), ball joint replacement (Saab), and steering race removal (VW).

The **Automotive Engineering**, published monthly by the Society of Automotive Engineers is an important professional journal intended for an advanced readership.

MANUALS/CATALOGS BY MANUFACTURERS OF BRAKE SYSTEMS/PARTS/TOOLS

The manufacturers of various parts, tools, and diagnostic and measuring instruments you use in servicing suspension, steering, and braking systems offer a variety of reference materials. Usually these materials are available free upon request.

Abex Corpn., American Brakeblock Div., Troy, MI
AC-Delco Div., General Motors, Detroit, MI
Allied Signal, Inc., Aftermarket Brake Div., Bendix, East Providence, RI
Airtex Automotive Div., Fairfield, IL
ALLDATA, Elk Grove, CA
Alltest, Inc., Schaumburg, IL
Apple Motors Fiat, Yugo & Lancia, Denver, CO
Arrow Automotive Industries, Framingham, MA
Auto Force, Huntington Beach, CA
Automation, Inc., Miamisburg, OH
Autometer Products, Inc., Sycamore, IL
Automotive Electronics Services, Fresno, CA
Barrett Brake Service Equipment, John Bean Div., FMC, Lansing, MI
Baum Tools Unlimited, Inc., Longboat Key, FL
Bayless, Inc., Marietta, GA
Bear Mfg. Corpn., Rock Island, IL
Beck/Arnley Worldparts Corpn., Nashville, TN
Bendix Corpn., South Bend, IN
Big A Auto Parts, APS Inc., Houston, TX
Black & Decker Mfg. Co., Towson, MD
Blackhawk Handtools, Div. Stanley-Proto, Covington, GA
Brembo Kelsey-Hayes, S.p.A., Ibraco, Inc., Costa Mesa, CA

British Auto, Macedon, NY
Brooks Enterprises of Brevard, Inc., Melbourne, FL
Car Care Auto Parts, Inc., Lake Charles, LA
Cardone Industries, Philadelphia, PA
CARQUEST Corpn., Tarrytown, NY
CAS, San Jose, CA
Central Tools, Inc., Cranston, RI
Clayton Mfg. Co., El Monte, CA
Coastal Test Equipment, Inc., North Miami, FL
CPS Products, Hialeah, FL
Crown Remanufacturing, Philadelphia, PA
DeJaye Electronics, Des Moines, IA
Dana Parts Corpn., Hagerstown, IN
Dresser Inds., Hand Tools, Franklin Park, IN
Dura Corpn., Weaver Div., Springfield, IL
E. Edelmann & Co., Skokie, IN
EDGE Diagnostic Systems, Sunnyvale, CA
Environmental Systems Products, Inc., East
    Granby, CT
Everco Industries, Moog Automotive, St. Louis, MO
Ferret Instruments, Inc., Cheboygan, MI
John Fluke Mfg. Co., Inc., Everett, WA
Ford Parts & Service Div., Ford Motor, Co.,
    Dearborn, MI
Gatke Corpn., Chicago, IL
Goodyear Tire & Rubber Co., Akron, OH
Hein-Werner Corpn., Waukesha, WI
Hennessy Industries, Inc., Ammco Tools,
    North Chicago, IL
Ingersol Rand/Proto Tool Div., Los Angeles, CA;
    Schiller Park, IL
ITM Automotive Parts, Inc., Cerritos, CA
ITT Aimco, Auburn Hills, MI
JGM Automotive Tooling, Huntington Beach, CA
Kelsey-Hayes Co., Romulus, MI
KD Tools, Lancaster, PA
Kent-Moore Div., SPX Corporation, Warren, MI
K-Line Industries, Inc., Holland, MI
Lazorlite Import Parts, Fremont, CA
Lisle Corpn., Clarinda, IA
Lockheed Products, Wagner Electric Corpn.,
    St. Louis, MO
Lucas Automotive, Troy, MI
Mercedes-Benz of North America, Montvale, NJ
Midland-Grau Heavy Duty Systems, Kansas
    City, MO
Mac Tools, Stanley Works, Washington Court
    House, OH
Matco Tools, Stow, OH
Mighty Distributing System of North America,
    Inc., Norcross (Atlanta), GA

Moog Automotive, St. Louis, MO
Mopar Parts / Chrysler, Farminghills, MI
Morak Brakes, Inc., Brooklyn, NY
Mustang Dynamometer, Twinsburg, OH
NAPA Hand/Service Tools, Atlanta, GA
Neward Enterprises/Mityvac, Cucamonga, CA
Owatonna Tool Co., Owatonna, MN
Parts, Inc., Memphis, TN
Parts Plus /AAAD, Memphis, TN
P&C Hand Tool Company, Portland, OR
Raybestos/Brake Parts, Inc., McHenry, IL
Rinda Technologies, Chicago, IL
Robert Bosch Corpn., Broadview, IL
Robinair Division, SPX Corpn., Montpelier, OH
Rockwell International, Troy, MI
Rolero-Omega, Inc., Gibson Products,
    Cleveland, OH
Russell Mfg. Co., Middletown, CT
Sherco Automotive Warehouse, Ashland, VA
Snap-On Tools Corpn., Kenosha, WI;
    Stevensville, MI
SPX Corpn., OTC Div., Owatonna, MN
Standard Motor Products, Inc., Long Island
    City, NY
Star Machine and Tool Co., Minneapolis, MN
L.S. Starrett Co., North Charleston, SC
Subaru of America, Parts Dept., Cherry Hill, NJ
Sun Electric Corpn., Crystal Lake, IL
The Technician's Company, Inc., Houston, TX
TIF Instruments, Inc., Miami, FL
Tokico (USA), Inc., Torrance, CA
Toyota Racing Development, Gardena, CA
Undercar Specialists, Inc., Roseville, MN
United Brake Parts, McHenry, IL
Van Norman Machine Co., Springfield, MA
Vetronix, Santa Barbara, CA
Walker Mfg. Co., Racine, WI
SK Wellman Corpn., Bedford, OH
World Wide Trading Co., Inc., Hayward, CA

This compilation of videos, CD-ROMs, and printed materials is neither complete nor selective. Listing here is for information only, and is NOT an endorsement of an item. It is the reader's responsibility to make an independent evaluation of a specific item prior to any purchase/lease decision.

GLOSSARY OF TECHNICAL TERMS

This glossary is compiled based on information from different sources, including — Society of Automotive Engineers (SAE Standards J656, J1213), Institute of Electrical and Electronic Engineers (IEEE), Instrument Society of America (ISA), McGraw-Hill Dictionary of Scientific and Technical Terms, and various service/training manuals by Chrysler, Ford, and General Motors. The terms relate to the suspension and steering systems, and electrical and electronic systems.

A-arm suspension. A short-long-arm (SLA) suspension.

acceleration. The rate of change of velocity with respect to time. Acceleration may be positive or negative depending upon whether the object is speeding up or slowing down.

accelerating force. The rapid change in the speed of rotation of a tire from zero mph at the point of road contact to twice the speed of the vehicle, at the top of the rolling tire.

accelerator. Pedal, which when depressed causes the vehicle to accelerate. Controls the fuel flow to the engine.

accumulator. A part of a hydraulic system filled with nitrogen gas and used to store high pressure fluid to provide pressure assistance for system operation.

Ackerman angle. The angle between the planes of the steered wheels of a vehicle, particularly when steering lock is applied. Usually measured in the horizontal plane. With steered wheels in the ahead position (zero steering angle), the Ackerman angle is a measure of toe-in or toe-out.

actuator. An electromechanical device that follows instructions from the control module and puts them into action. Its output is a force or torque and usually involves motion.

adapter. A bracket on disc brakes on which the caliper mounts, or slides or floats. Bolted to the spindle or steering knuckle, or the rear axle or control arm.

adder. Switching circuit that combines binary bits to generate the sum and carry of these bits.

address. An expression, usually numerical, that designates a specific location in a storage or memory device.

adhesion. Grip between road and tire, proportional to the static coefficient of friction.

aerodynamics. The science concerned with the motion of air and other gaseous fluids and with the forces acting on objects when they move through such fluids or when such fluids move against or around the objects.

air bag. A large nylon bag, compactly stored in the steering wheel or the passenger's side of the dashboard, that is automatically inflated with gas in a fraction of a second to provide cushioned protection against the impact of a collision. Typically, an **air bag module** includes the steering wheel with an air bag, ignitor, flammable-gas canister, and some sodium azide pellets.

air hammer. A tool, operated by compressed air, used to cut, chisel, shear, or punch rivets, nuts, bolts, or sheet metal.

air shock absorber. A heavy duty shock absorber stiffened by the addition of an air chamber at the top of the cylinder.

air spring. A type of automotive suspension spring that relies on a membrane filled with air to perform the same function of a typical leaf or coil spring.

air suspension system. An air-operated, microprocessor-controlled suspension system that replaces the conventional coil spring suspension and provides automatic front and rear load leveling.

algorithm. A prescribed sequence of well-defined rules or operations for the solution of a problem in a specified number of steps.

alignment. The proper positioning of parts, as in paralel lines.

allen wrench. A hexagonal-shaped tool or bit that fits into a hexagonal-shaped hole in the head of a bolt or screw.

alphanumeric code. A code whose code set consists of letters, digits, and associated special characters.

alternating current (AC). An electric current whose polarity is constantly changing from positive to negative and back again.

alternator. A unit that produces AC current and converts it to DC current by using diodes and provides electricity for vehicle operation.

ALU (arithmetic logic unit). A computational subsystem which performs the mathematical operations of a digital system.

ammeter. An instrument for measuring current flow. It may be constructed to measure alternating or direct current.

ampere (A). The standard unit for measuring the strength of an electric current. The rate of flow of a charge in a conductor or conducting medium of one coulomb per second.

amplifier. A device, circuit, or component that produces as an output an enlarged reproduction of the essential features of its input.

amplitude modulation (AM). Modulation in which the amplitude of a wave is the characteristic subject to variation.

analog. A signal that varies proportionally with the data it measures.

analog computer. A computer that represents numerical quantities as electrical and physical variables and manipulates these variables in solving mathematical problems.

analog output. Transducer output which is a continuous function of the measurand except as modified by the resolution of the transducer.

analog representation. A representation that does not have discrete values but is continuously variable.

analog-to-digital (A/D) converter. Circuitry to convert analog information into numeric form for use in a digital computer.

anchor plate. A bracket, solidly attached to the vehicle suspension, on which a floating or sliding caliper mounts.

AND gate. A combinational logic element such that the output channel is in its '1' state, if and ONLY IF, each input channel is in its '1' state.

angstrom. The angstrom is a common unit of length for light wavelength measurements equal to 10^{-10} m. Nanometer (10^{-9} m) is the preferred SI unit.

anode. The positive (+) pole in batteries, galvanic cells, or plating apparatus. In diodes, the positive lead.

anodize. A method of electrolytically coating a metal surface with a protective oxide.

anti-rattle springs. A device that attach to disk-brake pads to keep them from rattling when the brakes are not applied.

antiroll bar. A transverse suspension link that transfers some of the load on one wheel to the opposite wheel. Prevents body roll during cornering. Also called an **antisway bar** or **stabilizer bar**.

aquaplaning. Synonym for **hydroplaning**. Floating of vehicle tire on a thin surface of water, thereby losing contact with the road surface, and resulting in sudden loss of traction and control.

arbor. The rotating shaft of a lathe on which a drum or rotor is mounted for machining.

arcing. Machining of drum brake shoe linings to the proper curvature for a given drum size and brake design.

armature. A current-carrying conductor inside a motor, that reacts to the motor's magnetic field by moving to weaker area of the field. This movement provides mechanical energy for work. In a braking system, it is the rotating part of the electric actuating mechanism to which the magnet is attracted.

asbestos. A fibrous substance that does not burn or conduct heat. Used in combination with bonding materials like asphalts and resins to make brake linings. Airborne asbestos is a health hazard.

aspect ratio. The ratio of tire section height to section width expressed as a percentage. For example, a G78 tire is 78% as high as it is wide. The lower the number, the wider is the tire.

asymmetrical rear springs. A type of rear leaf spring, used with the torsion bar suspension, in which the rear axle is mounted ahead of the center of the spring.

atmospheric pressure. The force due to atmosphere per unit area. Atmospheric pressure at sea level is 14.7 psi absolute; it decreases as altitude increases.

atmospheric-suspended power chamber. A booster power chamber with atmospheric pressure on both sides of its diaphragm when the brakes are not applied.

atom. The individual structure that constitutes the basic unit of any chemical element.

automatic level control (air suspension system). Consists of four air-chamber shock absorbers on the front and rear of the car. Compressed air is fed by an electronic compressor. The pressure in the air chambers is determined automatically by a sensing system to keep the car's body at a predetermined height (trim height), irrespective of the load it is carrying.

automatic ride control (ARC). A modified/updated version of the Programmed Ride Control (PRC) system used on the Ford's Thunderbird Turbo Coupe. Allows the driver to select either continuous firm (sport) suspension tuning or system-determined setting.

avalanche diode. Also called **breakdown-diode**. A silicon diode having a high ratio of reverse-to-forward resistance until avalanche breakdown occurs. After breakdown, the voltage drop across the diode is essentially constant and is independent of the current. Used for voltage regulating and voltage limiting. Originally called **Zener diode** before it was found that the Zener effect had no significant role in the operation of diodes of this type.

axial play. Movement along, or parallel to, the axis of a shaft. Measured in linear dimension.

axis. A line about which an object rotates.

axle. A shaft that transmits driving torque to the wheels. It is a vehicle cross support carrying the mass of the car. Depending on the suspension design, the axle may or may not link the two wheels directly.

axle offset. A condition of vehicle tracking, that occurs when the rear axle position has changed so that the thrust line is no longer parallel with the vehicle center line.

axle sideset. A condition of vehicle tracking, that occurs when axle centers are not aligned with the vehicle centerline, but all four wheels remain parallel to each other.

axle spindle. Shaft machined to carry wheel bearings and seals and with means for securing the wheel to the axle.

axle windup. 1. Torsional deflection of an axle shaft, as due to sudden application of power or brakes. 2. Rotation of an axle casing due to flexure of semi-elliptical springs in reacting torsional loads. 3. Oscillatory motion of an axle about the horizontal transverse axis through its center of gravity.

B⁺(battery positive voltage). Acronym used to designate positive voltage at or near the battery level.

bail. The spring-wire loop used to secure the cover on most master cylinder reservoirs.

balance. State of equipoise, as between weights, different elements or opposing forces.

ball-and-cage CV joint. A constant velocity joint, typically consisting of an inner race, six balls 60° apart, a ball cage, and an outer race.

ball bearing. An antifriction bearing that uses a series of steel balls held between inner and outer bearing races.

ball joint. A design that joins two components by means of a ball on one side and a matching socket on the other, permitting rotation. In a front suspension, the wheel spindle is directly attached to the upper and lower suspension arms, through ball joints.

ball joint inclination. Inclination or angle of the steering axis as viewed from the front of the vehicle. Also called **kingpin inclination (KPI)** or **steering axis inclination (SAI)**.

ball nut. A part of a recirculation ball steering gear, it has a groove cut inside it that matches with the groove on the worm gear, creating a tunnel through which steel balls roll to move the ball nut and sector gear.

ball stud. Stud with a ball on the end, normally used in the steering linkage to connect the Pitman arm to the linkage, or to connect tie rods.

banjo fitting. A banjo-shaped connector with a hollow bolt through its center that enables brake lines to exit hydraulic components at a right angle.

bar mount. A shock absorber mounting bar extending across the top or bottom of the shock and bolted to the frame or suspension.

bayonet mount. A shock absorber mounting stud that extends straight out of the top or bottom of the shock.

bearing. A device that acts to reduce friction between two moving parts.

bearing cone. The inner race for a ball or roller bearing.

bearing cup. The outer race for a ball or roller bearing.

bearing race. The inner or outer ring that provides the smooth, hard contact surface for the balls or rollers in a bearing.

bellmouth. A form of brake drum distortion in which the open edge of the drum has a larger diameter than the closed edge.

bellows seal. An expanding diaphragm used as a seal between the master cylinder reservoir and the reservoir cover. It prevents air from contacting the fluid, yet it allows the fluid to change in volume.

belt. In a tire, a layer of fiber glass, rayon, or woven steel located under the tread around the circumference of a tire.

belted-bias tire. A tire in which the plies are laid on the bias, crisscrossing each other, with a circumferential belt on top. The rubber tread is vulcanized on top of the belt and plies.

belted-radial tire. A tire in which the plies run parallel to each other and vertical to the tire bead. Over this radial section, belts running parallel to the tire tread are applied.

bias-ply tire. A conventionally constructed tire in which the plies are laid on the bias, crisscrossing each other at an angle of about 30 to 40 degrees.

binary coded decimal (BCD). A binary numbering system for coding decimal numbers in groups of 4 bits. The binary value of these 4-bit groups ranges from 0000 to 1001, and codes the decimal digits '0' to '9' . To count to 9 takes 4 bits; to count to 99 takes two groups of 4 bits; to count to 999 takes three groups of 4 bits, etc.

bipolar. Having to do with a device in which both majority and minority carriers are present. A bipolar transistor contains both positive and negative charge carriers, and can be operated in either polarity of collector voltage. Bipolar and MOS are the two common types of IC construction.

bit (binary digit). The smallest element of information in the binary language. A contraction of binary digit, these characters in system (computer) language signify 'on' and 'off' (1 and 0). Word length, memory capacity, etc., can be expressed in number of 'bits'.

bleeding. Removing air from the hydraulic system.

body-over-frame (BOF) design. Used on North American vehicles until mid-1970's. Consisted of an independent frame. The powertrain and other major components were mounted on the frame, with the body installed over them and bolted to the frame.

bonded linings. Linings which attach to the lining table or backing plate with a high-temperature adhesive cured under heat and pressure.

boom. A cycling, rhythmic sound that may also cause a sensation of pressure on the ear drums.

booster holding position. The point at which a booster maintains a constant level of power assist.

boot. A flexible rubber or plastic cover used over the open ends of master cylinders and wheel cylinders to keep out water and other foreign matter. When pleated to allow for compression and expansion, it is called **bellows**.

bore. The inner surface of a cylinder along which a piston travels back and forth. May also refer to the walls or the inside diameter of a cylinder.

bounce. Vertical motion of the vehicle on its suspension system.

bound electron. An electron whose orbit is near the nucleus of an atom and is strongly attracted to it.

bridge bolt(s). The bolt(s) holding the two halves of a fixed caliper together.

bump stop. Rubber blocks fitted to some suspension systems to limit the amount of spring travel when a vehicle hits a bump or dip in the road.

bus. One or more conductors used as a path over which data is transmitted.

bushing. A removable metal, rubber or plastic sleeve placed between two parts, either or both of which may move. The bushing may absorb shock, act as a bearing, or help to position parts.

byte. An IBM developed term used to indicate a specific number of consecutive bits treated as a single entity. Consists of eight bits which as a unit can represent one character or two numerals.

calibration. A fixed setting.

cam. A stepped or curved eccentric wheel mounted on a rotating shaft. As a cam is turned, objects in contact with it are raised or lowered.

cam bolt. A bolt fitted with an eccentric that will cause parts to change position when the bolt is turned.

camber. The inward or outward tilt of the wheels from the true vertical as seen from the front of the vehicle. When the wheel tilts outward at the top, the camber is positive. If the wheel tilts inward, the camber is negative. The difference between the tilt of the wheel and the true vertical is measured directly in degrees, and is called the **camber angle**.

camber roll. An inherent characteristic of independent suspension vehicles to change camber angle when cornering.

camber wear. Wear on one side of a tire tread caused by the angle of the tire tread to the road surface.

capacitance (C). In a system of layered conductors and dielectrics, the property that permits storage of electrical charges when a potential difference exists between the conductors. A value expressed as the ratio of a quantity of electricity to a potential difference (Q/V).

capacitor. (formerly called a **condenser**) A device consisting of two electrodes separated by a dielectric, which may be air, for introducing capacitance into an electric circuit.

castellated nut. A nut having slots through which a cotter pin can be passed to secure the nut to its bolt or stud.

caster. The angle at which the steering axis leans forward (negative) or rearward (positive) from a perpendicular position.

cathode. A negative electrode.

center of gravity. The point about which the mass of a car is evenly distributed. It is the point of balance.

center link (drag link). A part of the steering linkage that connects to both tie-rod assemblies and moves them equally, as the steering gear arm moves.

central processor unit (CPU). The section of a computer that contains the arithmetic, logic, and control circuits. In some systems, it may also include the memory unit and the operator's console. Also called main frame in larger systems. Performs arithmetic operations, control instructions processing, and provides timing signals and various housekeeping operations.

centrifugal force. A force acting outward from the center of a turn on a turning body, such as an automobile following a curve in the road or rounding a corner.

channel. A path along which signals can be sent or received; e.g. data channel, output channel.

chassis. The part of an automobile structure consisting of the frame, running gear, steering and suspension systems, and wheels and tires.

check ball. A type of hydraulic valve consisting of a ball that seals an orifice when it is seated and can be unseated to open the orifice.

check valve. A one-way valve which passes fluid in one direction, but prevents passage in the other direction.

    closed type. A valve which allows fluid flow in one direction only.

    open type. A valve, normally open to fluid flow in both directions, which closes when fluid flow in one direction exceeds a predetermined value.

chip. 1. A single substrate on which all the active and passive elements of an electronics circuit have been fabricated. 2. A leadless discrete component like a resistor or capacitor intended for surface mounting to printed circuit boards or film hybrid substrates.

circuit. The complete path provided for current flow.

clevis. A U-shaped bracket with holes in each end through which a retaining pin or bolt is inserted. Often used to attach the brake pedal pushrod to the pedal arm.

clock. 1. A device that generates periodic signals used for synchronization. 2. A device that measures and displays time.

closed loop. A control system configuration in which information on output parameter is used to improve the system accuracy and/or response.

clunking. Heavy metallic noise accompanied by a jarring sensation.

code. 1. A set of clear rules specifying the way in which data may be represented; e.g., the set of correspondence in the standard code for information interchange. Synonymous with coding schemes. 2. In data processing, to represent data or a computer program in a symbolic form that can be accepted by a data processor.

coefficient of friction. A ratio of the force required to slide an object over a surface to the mass of the object, and is always less than 1.00.

coil spring. A spring-steel bar formed into a cylindrical coil. In suspensions, they are used to support the mass of the vehicle and provide springing of the wheels.

collector (transistor). A region through which primary flow of charge carriers leaves the base.

commutator. A part of a DC motor or generator which, in combination with brushes, provides an electrical connection between the rotating armature winding and the stationary terminals, and also allows reversal of the current in the armature windings.

compensating port. The passage through which excess fluid returns to the reservoir when the brakes are released.

complementary MOS (CMOS). Pertaining to N- and P-channel enhancement-mode devices fabricated compatibly on a silicon chip and connected into push-pull complementary digital circuits. These circuits offer low quiescent power dissipation and potentially high speeds, but are more complex than circuits with only one channel type.

computer. An electronic device capable of accepting information, applying prescribed processes to the information, and supplying the results of the process. Typical features include — provision for data input, a control unit, a storage or memory capability, an arithmetic logic section, and a provision for discharging its output in usable form.

compliance steer. A rear toe change resulting from suspension links and bushings giving way to cornering force. Specially designed suspension bushings distort under certain conditions to provide compliance steer.

concentric. Having the same center.

conductivity. The ability to transmit heat or electricity. Electrical conductivity is expressed in terms of the current per unit of applied voltage. The reciprocal is resistivity.

consistency. The degree of solidity or fluidity of a material such as grease or oil.

constant-rate spring. A spring that continues to compress at the same rate as more weight is applied to it.

contact or patch area. The portion of a tire that touches the road surface.

control arms. Structural members of independent front suspension designs, shaped like 'A'. They form a moving link between the vehicle's underbody structure and the king pin or ball joints upon which the steering knuckle pivots.

control module. A semiconductor microprocessor device that is used to control the action of a steering and/or suspension.

cornering wear. A type of tire-tread wear due to taking turns at excessive speeds.

corrosion. The gradual wearing away of a metal surface by chemical reaction. Also, the name given the residue left by the process.

cotter pin. A round locking pin formed by a folded semicircular steel wire. Locked by spreading the paired ends of the wire.

counter-balancing torsion spring. Provides an outward force on the MacPherson strut to offset the twisting forces induced by the road on the wheel. First used by Ford on the 1988 Continental.

critical damping. Provides the most rapid transient response without overshoot. Operation between underdamping and overdamping.

crocus cloth. Cloth material with iron oxide. Contains no grit material and is used to remove slight blemishes from machined surfaces.

crossmember. A lateral, or transverse, steel rail in the automobile frame, running from one side member to the other.

cross steering linkage. A single-tie-rod steering linkage in which the drag link reaches from the Pitman arm on the driver's side of the vehicle to the tie-rod end on the opposite side.

cup. The common hydraulic piston seal in master and wheel cylinders. Hydraulic pressure assists the sealing action.

curb weight. The mass of the vehicle with a full supply of oil, water and fuel (no driver or passengers).

current density. The amount of electric current passing through a given channel but has its origin in another channel.

CV (constant velocity) joint. Universal joint in which the output shaft rotates at constant angular velocity with no cyclic variations, at a constant input shaft speed.

cycle. Any set of operations repeated regularly in the same sequence. The operations may vary on each repetition.

cylinder hone. A rotating instrument fitted with abrasive material, used to remove roughness and deposits, and to polish bores of wheel cylinders and master cylinders.

cylinder housing. The working part of the master cylinder housing that contains the piston bore and pistons.

dampening belt. A rubber belt wound around the outside of a brake drum or rotor prior to machining the drum or rotor. The belt dampens out vibrations that might affect the quality of the finished surface.

damping. The transitory decay of the amplitude of a free oscillation of a system, involving energy loss from the system. In a hydraulic shock absorber, it is the physical control of unwanted spring vibrations by means of resistance due to a forced flow of confined fluid through passages in the piston and base of the shock absorber.

damping constant. The component of applied force 90° out of phase with the deformation, divided by the velocity of deformation.

damping ratio. The ratio of the degree of actual damping to the degree of damping required for critical damping.

data. 1. A representation of facts, concepts, or instructions in a format sutiable for communication, interpretation, or processing by manual or automatic means. 2. Any representations such as characters or analog quantities to which meaning may be assigned.

databus. Most microprocessors communicate externally through a databus, usually bi-directional — capable of transferring data to and from the CPU, storage, and peripheral devices.

data link connector (DLC). Provides access and/or control of the vehicle information, operating conditions, and diagnostic data.

data processing. Performing a systematic sequence of operations upon data. Synonymous with information processing.

deflection. The initial movement of spring, in response to any force acting on it. Deflection may take the form of flexing (leaf spring) or twisting (torsion bar). The lb$_f$ required to bend a spring by one inch is termed the **deflection rate**.

delay. 1. The amount of time by which an event is retarded. 2. The amount of time by which a signal is delayed.

denatured alcohol. Ethyl alcohol that contains methanol to make it unfit for consumption. Used to clean components.

desiccant. A drying agent, that absorbs moisture and so removes moisture from surrounding elements.

diagnostic sensor. Any sensing device used partly or exclusively for diagnostic purposes, to provide information on conditions of a motor-vehicle or parts of it. Different types include — built-in, plug-in, and clip-on.

diagnostic test modes. Various levels of diagnostic capabilities in on-board-diagnostic (OBD) systems — different functional states to observe signals, a base level to read diagnostic trouble codes, a monitor level that includes information on signal levels, bi-directional control with on/off board aids, and the ability to interface with remote diagnosis.

diagnostic trouble codes. A numeric identifier for a fault condition identified by the on-board diagnostic system.

diagonal wipe. A tire wear pattern caused by excessive toe. Usually occurs on the rear tires of a front-wheel-drive car, if the wheels have severe toe.

diaphragm. A flat but flexible membrane that separates a chamber into two zones and moves according to the volume and pressure of both zones.

dielectric. A medium in which it is possible to maintain an electric field with little or no supply of energy from outside sources.

digital. A signal that is either 'on' or 'off'. In a computer, the signal is translated into binary digits 0 and 1 and is interpreted by the microprocessor as a voltage signal that is either 'low' or 'high', or current flow that is 'on' or 'off'.

digital computer. A computer that processes information in numerical form. Generally uses binary or decimal notation and processes information by repeated high speed use of the fundamental arithmetic operations.

diode. A semiconductor device having two terminals and exhibiting a non-linear voltage-current characteristic.

diode-transistor logic (DTL). A logic circuit that uses diodes at the input to perform the electronic logic function that activates the circuit transistor output. In monolithic circuits, the DTL diodes are a positive level logic AND function or a negative level OR function. The output transistor acts as an inverter to result in the circuit becoming a positive NAND or a negative NOR function.

DIP (dual inline package). A black, rectangular housing for memory chips. Has a row of legs or pins on each side that connect the chip to the printed circuit board. Late-model computers use a square housing called 'quad pac'.

direct addressing. Method of programming with the address pointing to the location of data or the instruction to be used.

direct-acting shock absorber. That attached directly to the frame and to the suspension.

directional stability. Ability of a vehicle to move forward in a straight line with a minimum of driver control. A car with good directional stability will not be unduly affected by side wind or road irregularities.

distortion (deflection). A twisting, twisted, or bending condition.

dive. A suspension system condition caused by heavy braking. When it happens, the front suspension is severely compressed by rapid deceleration.

dog-tracking. A driving condition in which the rear wheels of a vehicle follow a path parallel to the path of the front wheels.

DOT. Department of Transportation. A government agency that establishes vehicle standards.

double-cardan universal joint (U-joint). A shaft coupling, consisting of two sets of yokes with two crosspieces joining them together. Allows changes in the angle between two rotating shafts with minimal effect on the rate of rotation.

double-offset joint. A plunging, ball-and-cage CV joint using long grooves in the outer race to allow plunge.

double wishbone suspension. Another name for an SLA suspension or for a strut/SLA suspension.

drag link. The tube or rod connecting the steering gear Pitman arm to the tie rods or steering knuckle arms.

drive-away shudder. A strong vibration felt in the floorpan and seat, usually during heavy acceleration; usually present between 0 and 25 mph.

drive axle. One that transmits torque from a differential or transaxle to the wheels.

drone/moan. A low frequency (90-200 Hz) sound that does not cycle.

drum web. The metal plate or structure that

fills the closed edge of the drum.

dual dampening. A shock or strut which has two separate calibrations.

dump. To copy the contents of all or part of a storage, usually from an internal storage into an external storage. The data resulting from the process.

dust covers. Small plugs made of rubber or metal, used to cover the access holes in backing plates and drums.

duty cycle. The ratio of the time 'on' of a device or system divided by the total cycle time (i.e. time 'on' plus time 'off'). For a device that normally runs intermittently, it is the amount of time the device operates as opposed to its idle time.

dynamic balance. Balance in motion, such as the balance of a wheel while rotating. The total mass distributed evenly in reference to both the axis of rotation and center line of the wheel.

dynamic imbalance. Occurs when the centerline of the weight mass of a revolving object is not in the same plane as the centerline of the object.

dyne. A metric unit of force. 1 dyne of force is applied when a 1 gram object is accelerated 1 cm/s^2.

ECA. Electronic Control Assembly.

eccentric. Off center. A drum defect caused by unequal wear, drum distortion, or both.

eddy currents. Those currents that exist as a result of voltages induced in the body of a conducting mass by a variation of magnetic flux. The variation of magnetic flux is the result of a varying magnetic field or of a relative motion of the mass with respect to the magnetic field.

edge code. A manufacturer's code used to identify friction materials.

edgebrand. A series of codes on the side of a brake lining that identify the manufacturer, the specific lining material, and the friction coefficient of the lining. Only meant for identification and comparison; does not indicate lining quality.

elastic limit. The point beyond which a deformed piece of metal will no longer return to its original shape.

electric. Any device or system operating on the direct flow of electrons or the low frequency (<1 kHz) alternating flow of electrons.

electrically erasable programmable read only memory (EEPROM). A non-volatile memory used for storing information permanently. This device can have all or selected parts of its memory erased electrically and reprogrammed.

electrically programmable read only memory (EPROM). A non-volatile memory used for storing information permanently. This device can have its contents changed if the entire contents are first 'erased' through exposure to ultraviolet light (providing the device has a means of allowing light to reach the silicon level) and electronically reprogrammed.

electromagnet. A magnet that consists of a coil wound around a soft iron or steel core. The core is strongly magnetized when current flows through the coil, and is almost completely demagnetized when the current is interrupted.

electromagnetic compatibility (EMC). The ability of electronic systems to operate in their intended environments without suffering or causing unacceptable degradation of performance as a result of unintentional electromagnetic radiation or response.

electromagnetic interference (EMI). An electromagnetic phenomenon that can contribute to the degradation in performance of an electronic receiver or system.

electromagnetic waves. The radiant energy produced by the oscillation of an electric charge.

electromotive force (EMF). The force that may cause current to flow when there is a difference of potential between two points.

electron. One of the natural or elementary constituents of matter. Carries a negative electric charge of one electronic unit.

electronic. Any device or system in which electrons flow through a vacuum, gas, or semiconductor. Normally operative in frquency range >1 kHz.

element, chemical. The combination of atoms that forms a primary substance that cannot, by chemical means, be divided into simpler substances.

Elliott axle. Arrangement of axle whereby the axle beam terminates in a yoke or fork-end that holds the kingpin, the axle pivoting on an eye-end within the yoke.

emitter. A region from which charge carriers that are minority carriers in the base are injected into the base.

encode. To apply a set of clear rules specifying the way in which data may be represented such that subsequent decoding is possible. Synonymous with code.

endplay. Axial play, as measured at the end of a shaft.

energy. The ability to do work. Energy available to do work but not actually being used is called potential energy.

equalizer. A device attached to the front parking brake cable that divides force equally to each rear wheel cable.

equalizer beam. Pivoted beam joining the fore and aft springs of an interactive (reactive) tandem axle suspension.

EVO (electronic variable orifice). Provides varying levels of power-assist based on speed and steering wheel rotation. Designed to adjust steering effort for an optimum road feel.

exclusive OR. A logic operator having the property that if P is a statement and Q is a statement, then P exclusive OR Q is true if either statement is true but not both, and false if both statements are true or both are false.

exhaust gas recirculation (EGR) valve. A valve which admits exhaust to the incoming air/fuel mixture.

expanders. Discs used in a wheel cylinder which help seal the fit between the cup lips and cylinder walls when there is no pressure in the system.

feedback. The recycling of a portion of the output to the input of a system. Systems using feedback are closed-loop systems.

feedback amplifier. An amplifier that uses a passive network to return a portion of the ouput signal to modify the performance of the amplifier.

feeler gauge. A thin strip of metal of known thickness used for measuring the clearance between two parts.

ferromagnetic material. Material whose permeability is greater than unity and depends upon the magnetizing force. Usually exhibits hysteresis.

FET (field effect transistor). A semiconductor device in which the resistance between the source and the drain depends on a field produced by a voltage applied to the gate terminal.

field. In a record, a specified area used for a particular category of data — e.g., a set of bit locations in a computer word used to express the address of the operand.

filler port. The passage through which brake fluid flows from the reservoir to the cylinder bore, refilling the low pressure ahead of the cup on the return stroke. Also called an inlet or intake port.

filter. A selective network that may contain resistors, inductors, capacitors or active elements, and offers comparatively little opposition to certain frequencies or to direct current, while blocking or attenuating other frequencies.

firewall. The bulkhead that separates the engine bay from the passenger compartment.

first law of thermodynamics. The natural law that states energy can neither be created nor destroyed, and that energy can only be converted into another form.

fixed anchor. A non-adjustable anchor pin.

Can be riveted/welded to the backing plate, or can pass through the backing plate and attach to a part of the suspension system.

fixed-anchor grind. A variation of undersize grinding that compensates for the size and location of a fixed shoe anchor.

fixed joint. A CV joint that does not allow plunging movement of a shaft, but allows a sharper angle between the shafts. Always used at the outboard end of a front axle shaft, and can be used at the inboard end or outboard end of a rear axle shaft.

fixed-point binary number. A binary number represented by a sign bit and one or more number bits with a binary point fixed somewhere between two adjacent bits.

flare. The expanded, funnel-shaped end of a piece of tubing.

flat ride tuning. Varying the natural frequency between the front and rear suspensions to avoid pitch.

flip-flop (storage element). A circuit having two stable states and the capability of changing from one state to another with the application of a control signal and remaining in that state after removal of signals.

floating-point binary number. A binary number expressed in exponential notation. That is, a part of the binary word represents the mantissa and is part of the exponent.

flow chart. A graphical representation for the definition, analysis, or solution of a problem, in which symbols are used to represent operations, data, flow, equipment, etc.

fluid. A gas (compressible) or a liquid (incompressible), that flows. In an automotive hydraulic system, a liquid that conveys pressure from one surface to another. Automotive fluids also include lubricants and coolants of moving parts.

flux (magnetic). The sum of all the lines of force in a magnetic field crossing a unit area per unit time.

FMVSS. Federal Motor Vehicle Safety Standards.

follow-up-type valve. A unit which responds to fluid displacement or mechanical linkage movement, to modulate pressure in a cylinder or chamber.

footcandle (fc). The unit of illumination given by the illumination on a surface one ft^2 in area on which there is a flux of one lumen. A surface all points of which are one foot from a one candela source has an illumination of one footcandle.

footlambert (fl). The unit of brightness (luminance) equal to the uniform brightness of a perfectly diffusing surface emitting or reflecting light at the rate of one lumen per ft^2. The average brightness of a reflecting surface is the product of the illumination in fc times the reflection factor of the surface. A one ft^2 surface, all points of which are one ft from a one candela source has a luminance of one fl.

force. That influence on a body which causes it to accelerate.

forward voltage (V_f). The voltage across a semiconductor diode associated with the flow of forward current. The P-region is at a positive potential relative to the N-region.

frame. An assembly of steel components, typically including two long rails, that supports a vehicle's body and engine, and is supported by the suspension system.

free diameter. The outer diameter of a tire that is not under load.

freeplay. The portion of brake pedal travel not converted into piston movement in the master cylinder.

frequency (Hz, hertz). 1. The number of times in a given interval that a suspended object springs back and forth to dissipate the energy imparted to it by an applied force. Automotive springs have certain 'natural' frequencies at which they vibrate in response to the force of road shocks. 2. The number of times that an electric signal occurs, or repeats, in cycles per second.

frequency modulation (FM). A scheme for modulating a carrier frequency in which the amplitude remains constant but the carrier frequency is displaced in frequency proportial to the amplitude of the modulating signal. An FM broadcast system is practically immune to external disturbances.

frequency, natural. 1. The frequency at which an object is most prone to vibration. Large heavy objects have low natural frequencies and small light objects have high natural frequencies. 2. The frequency of free (NOT forced) oscillations of the sensing element of a fully assembled transducer.

frequency output. An output in the form of frequency which varies as a function of the applied measurement — e.g., angular velocity or flow rate.

frequency, resonant. The measured frequency at which a transducer responds with maximum output amplitude.

frequency response. A measure of how the gain or loss of a circuit device or system varies with the frequencies applied to it. Also, the portion of the frequency spectrum which can be sensed by a device within specified limits of error.

friction. The resistance to motion between two bodies in contact with each other.

front-end alignment. Wheel alignment, steering alignment. The systematic procedure for checking/adjusting certain steering system factors to specifications using a special equipment. Camber, caster, and toe-in are set to specifications by simple adjustments, but toe-out on turns and steering axis inclination or king pin slant can be corrected only by replacing faulty components.

front-end geometry. The angular relationship of the front wheels, wheel-attaching parts, and car frame, including camber, caster, steering axis inclination, toe-in, and toe-out on turns.

front suspension. The linkage used to attach the front wheels to the vehicle, support the mass, and keep the front wheels in proper alignment.

front spring eye. The opening at the front end of a leaf spring main leaf where the spring is attached to the vehicle frame.

full-floating axle. An axle whose only job is the transmission of power. It does not support any of a vehicle's weight.

g-force. A force such that a body subjected to it would have the acceleration of gravity at sea level. Used as a unit of measurement for bodies undergoing the stress of acceleration.

gear lash. A lack of mesh between two gears.

gear pump. A rotary pump that uses two meshing gear wheels which contrarotate so that the fluid is entrained on one side and discharged on the other.

gravitational acceleration. The acceleration imparted to a body by the attraction of the earth. Approximately equal to 32.2 ft/s^2 (9.807 m/s^2).

grommets. Ring-shaped parts made of a third material that prevent problems where two other dissimilar materials come into contact. Plastic brake fluid reservoirs attach to metal master cylinders with rubber grommets.

gross vehicle weight rating (GVWR). The manufacturer's specified maximum allowable mass for a vehicle including passengers and cargo.

ground. The wiring and connections that return electrical current to the battery. The ground is common to all circuits in a vehicle's electrical system.

grunt. Ruspy sound, accompanied by a vibration in the floor pan during acceleration or deceleration.

half-adder. A logic circuit capable of adding two binary numbers with no provision for a carry-on from a preceding addition.

Hall-effect. The development of a transverse electric potential gradient in a current carrying conductor or semiconductor upon the application of a magnetic field.

handling. Evaluation of a vehicle's stability in turns and on rough roads. NOT to be confused with 'ride'.

hardware. Mechanical, magnetic, electrical, or electronic devices; physical equipment (contrasted with software).

harshness. A term generally used to describe vehicle ride quality.

heat checks. Small cracks on the friction surface of the drum or rotor. They do not penetrate through the friction surface, and can usually be machined out of it.

height sensor. Device used in the air suspension system to monitor vehicle trim height and provide information to the microprocessor.

henry. The inductance of a closed circuit in which an electromotive force of one volt is produced when the electric current in the circuit varies uniformly at the rate of one ampere per second.

hertz (Hz). The unit of frequency, one cycle per second.

high speed shake. Visible shaking and a bumpy feel in the steering wheel along with vibrations in the floor pan, seat, and front end sheet metal at over 45 mph.

hole. In the electronic valence structure of a semiconductor, a mobile vacancy that acts like a positive electronic charge with a positive mass.

hole conduction. The apparent movement of a hole to the more negative terminal in a semiconductor. Since the hole is positive, this movement is equivalent to a flow of positive charges in that direction.

homogeneous. Being of a similar nature. Homogeneous liquids blend together completely; no part of either liquid remains separate.

hone. To remove metal with a fine abrasive stone.

hop. Occurs when a tire repeatedly loses contact with the road surface, then lands again harshly. A ride problem, resulting from radial runout.

hotchkiss drive. Suspension design in which the motive force of the drive wheels is transmitted forward through the rear springs.

hub. A rotating component at the center of a wheel that contains the wheel bearings. It is attached to, or integral with, the brake drum or rotor.

humming. A pure tone at a constant frequency, like that made by an electric motor in an electric fuel pump, window motor or electronic steering actuator.

hybrid circuit. A circuit that combines the thin-film (or thick-film) and semiconductor technologies. Generally, thin film techniques are used for passive components, and the semiconductor techniques for the active components.

hydraulic booster. A master cylinder containing a separate hydraulic chamber and spool valve operated by power steering fluid. Hydraulic pressure in the booster pressure chamber operates the master cylinder piston.

hydraulic circuit. The path of hydraulic fluid from the master cylinder to the wheels, through all valves, lines, hoses, and fittings.

hydraulic piston. A piston in a cylinder, acted upon by or acting on a hydraulic fluid.

hydraulic pressure. The force per unit area exerted in all parts of a hydraulic system by a liquid.

hydraulics. The science of the use of fluids to transmit force and motion.

hydroplane. Tire rolls upon a layer of water instead of staying in contact with the road surface. Occurs when all of the water on the pavement cannot be displaced from under the tire tread.

hygroscopic. Readily absorbing and retaining moisture.

hysteresis. The difference between the response of a unit or system to an increasing and a decreasing signal. Hysterical behaviour is characterized by inability to tretrace exactly on the reverse swing a particular locus of input/output conditions.

idler lever (arm). A lever or arm that can rotate about its support and is used to support one end of a tube or rod. A component of the steering linkage that supports the tie rod and transmits steering force. One end attaches to the car frame.

IGFET (insulated gate field effect transistor). Another name for **MOSFET**, **metal oxide semiconductor field effect transistor**.

illumination (illuminance). The density of luminous flux on a surface. It is the flux divided by the area when the surface is uniformly illuminated.

immediate address mode. Pertains to an instruction in which an address part contains the value of an operand rather than its address.

impedance (Z). The total opposition offered by a component or circuit to the flow of alternating or varying current. Expressed in ohms and is similar to the actual resistance in a direct current circuit. May be computed as $Z = I/E$, where E is the applied AC voltage and I is the resulting alternating current flow in the circuit.

inboard constant velocity (CV) joint. Joins an axle shaft to the transaxle, differential, or transfer case. In a front axle, it is always a plunging joint.

in-cab drone. A low-pitched, pulsating rumble inside the passenger compartment on any road surface; usually occurs between 30 and 45 mph.

included angle. The steering axis inclination angle plus or minus the camber angle.

independent suspension. A suspension system in which the movement of two opposite wheels is NOT interdependent. One wheel does not force the other wheel to deflect or react to movement in the vertical plane.

indicator. A device that makes information available about a measured characteristic but does not store the information nor initiate a responsive or corrective action.

indirect addressing. Programming method in which the initial address is the storage location of a word that contains another address. Used to obtain the data to be operated upon.

inductance. The property of an electric circuit by which a varying current in it produces a varying magnetic field that induces voltage in the same circuit or in a nearby circuit. Measured in henrys.

inductor. A device consisting of one or more associated windings, with or without a magnetic core, for introducing inductance into an electric circuit.

inert. A substance that exhibits no chemical activity, or does so only under extreme conditions.

inertia. The property of a body at rest to remain at rest, and a body in motion to remain in motion in a straight line unless acted upon by an outside force.

inline steering gear. A type of integral power steering, using a recirculating-ball steering gear to which are added a control valve and an actuating piston.

input impedance. The impedance a transducer presents to a source. The effective impedance seen looking into the input terminals of an amplifier, circuit details, signal level, and frequency.

input/output (I/O) devices. Computer hardware through which data are entered into or transmitted from a digital system or by which data are recorded for immediate or future use.

insulator. 1. A material that prevents or slows the transfer of heat from one area to another. 2. A high resistance device that supports or separates conductors to prevent a flow of current between them or to other objects.

integral power steering system. That in which the control valve and power piston are integrated into the steering gear construction.

integrated circuit (IC). A combination of interconnected circuit elements inseparably associated on or within a continuous substrate. NOTE: To further define the nature of an integrated circuit, additional modifiers may be prefixed. Examples — dielectric-isolated monolithic IC; beam lead monolithic IC; and silicon-chip tantalum thin-film hybrid IC.

inter-cable adjuster. An adjuster built into some parking brake cables that allows the outer housing to be made longer or shorter to adjust the parking brake.

inverse voltage. The effective voltage across a rectifier during the half-cycle when current does not flow.

ion. An electrically charged atom or group of atoms. An ion may be either positively charged (having a deficiency of electrons) or negatively charged (having a surplus of electrons).

ion implantation. A method of semiconductor doping in which impurities that have been ionized and accelerated to a high velocity penetrate the semiconductor surface and get deposited in the interior.

ISO flare. The type of brake line flare made popular by the International Standards Organization.

jack. A device for raising a car.

jam nuts. Two nuts tightened against each other to lock them in position.

jerk. The time rate of change of acceleration.

JFET. Abbreviation for junction field effect transistor.

joule. The unit of energy in the SI system.

jounce. The suspension condition that causes spring compression. The upward movement of a wheel usually caused by a road bump or weight transfer onto the wheel.

keep alive memory (KAM). A memory device that will lose information if power is off, but is usually supplied continuous power (through battery backing when main power is lost) so that the information is retained.

kickback. Vibrations and road shocks transmitted through the steering system, and felt by the driver at the steering wheel.

kinetic. Pertaining to or producing motion. Referring to an electronic wheel balancer, the radial forces on a spinning tire.

kinetic balance. Balance of the radial forces on a spinning tire; determined by an electronic wheel balancer.

kinetic energy. The energy of mass in motion. All moving objects possess kinetic energy.

kinetic friction. The amount of friction between two surfaces in motion.

kingpin (spindle bolt). A pin or bolt on which the steering spindle assembly pivots.

kingpin inclination (steering axis inclination). The tilt of the upper end of the king pin or steering axis centerline toward the center of the car.

knock sensor. A sensor that provides information on engine 'knock' conditions.

knuckle. Steering gear component that is also part of the suspension. It has a spindle that supports the wheel and it pivots (typically on ball joints) allowing the wheels to be steered.

lack of parallelism. A measurement of brake rotor thickness variation at various points around a rotor.

lambert. The lambert is a unit of luminance equal to 1 candela/cm^2 which is equal to 1 stilb. A one centimeter square surface, all points of which are one centimeter from a one candela source, has a luminance of one lambert.

language. A set of representations, conventions, and rules to convey information.

lash. Movement or play between parts. The clearance between moving parts, such as meshing gear teeth.

lateral. Forces or uneven movement on a wheel or tire from side to side.

LCD (liquid crystal display). A passive display whose operating principle is the change in light transmission or polarization in a liquid crystal under the influenece of an electric field.

lead (drift, pull, wander). A condition caused by misalignment of one of the factors affecting steering stability, resulting in a stabilizing force that tends to hold the car in a slight turn instead of straight ahead. In contrast to 'drift', 'pull', or 'wander', which are essentially unstable conditions, 'lead' is a stable condition that constantly steers the car in one direction.

leaf spring. A type of suspension spring containing a number slightly arched steel strips of varying lengths stacked together. Absorbs road shocks by flexing, or bending in the middle. The longest strip (or leaf) is called the main leaf. 'Eyes' are formed at both ends of this leaf to provide a means for attaching the spring to the underbody structure of the automobile.

LED (light emitting diode). An active display whose operating principle is the emission of light due to current flow in a semiconductor diode.

leverage. The use of a lever and fulcrum to create a mechanical advantage. The brake pedal is an automotive part that employs leverage.

lift. A condition in which air pressure beneath a vehicle lifts part of the vehicle weight off the wheels.

limited-slip differential. A differential which uses a clutch device to provide power to either rear wheel when the opposite wheel is spinning. Drives both rear wheels equally with little slippage.

linearity. The relationship between two quantities when a change in a second quantity is directly proportional to a change in the first quantity. Also, deviation from a straight-line response to an input signal.

linkage. A system of rods and levers used to transmit motion or force.

load. 1. The force in weight units applied to a body. 2. The element or circuit driven by the output of a device or circuit.

load compensation. Action of a suspension system to maintain vehicle trim height when weight is placed on the vehicle.

loaded runout. Radial runout that appears only when the tire is supporting the mass of the car. Caused by stiff sections accidentally built into the tire sidewall.

lockup. A condition where the wheel and tire is prevented from rotating. Braking power overcomes the traction of the tires and skidding occurs.

logic. A mathematical approach to solving complex situations, using symbols to define basic concepts. In computers and information-processing networks, it is the sequence of operations performed on the information, usually with each step affecting the one that follows.

logic controller. A part of the control system which interprets input signals from the sensor(s) and transmits the controlling output signals to the modulator(s).

long and short arm suspension. An independent suspension system with the wheels linked to the frame through 'A'-shaped control arms.

longitudinal axis. An imaginary line, running the length of a vehicle front to rear and intersecting the front and rear roll centers, around which the car body tilts during cornering.

look-up. A technique to utilize data in a table; to execute that technique.

loop. A sequence of instructions that is executed repeatedly until a terminal condition prevails.

lubricant. Any material, typically a petroleum product like grease or oil, placed between two moving parts to reduce friction.

lumen (lm). The unit for **luminous flux**, the amount of light energy emitted per unit time. It is equal to the flux through a unit solid angle from a point source of one candela. The flux on a unit surface, all points of which are at unit distance from a one candela source, is one lumen.

machining. The process of using a machine to remove metal from a metal part.

MacPherson strut. Suspension design which combines the shock absorber and a spring in a single assembly linking the lower control arm and chassis.

magnet. The part of the electric actuating mechanism, which when energized is attracted to the armature, creating a controlled force to apply the brake(s).

magnetic field. The field produced by a magnet or a magnetic influence. It has force and direction.

manifold absolute pressure sensor. A sensor that measures absolute air pressure in the intake manifold.

manifold vacuum sensor. A sensor that senses the difference between barometric pressure and intake manifold pressure.

manifold vacuum zone switch. A type of manifold vacuum sensor (MVS) that dramatically changes the sensor output signal level upon reaching a preselected level or zone of manifold vacuum.

mass. The amount of matter in an object. A quantitative measure of a body's resistance to being accelerated. Unlike weight, an object's mass remains constant and independent of the location of the object. For example, an astronaut in space is weightless but still possesses the same mass as he/she would on earth.

master cylinder. The device that converts mechanical pressure from the brake pedal into hydraulic pressure that is routed to the wheels to operate the friction assemblies.

match mounting. A method that involves mounting of the tire with its point of highest runout at the point of lowest wheel runout. Minimizes runout of a wheel and tire assembly.

matrix. In computers, a logic network in the form of array of input leads and output leads with logic elements connected at some of their intersections. By extension, an array of any number of dimensions.

measurand. A physical quantity, property, or condition which is measured.

mechanical advantage. The ratio of the force exerted to the force applied. The force is multiplied by applying it to the longer arm of a lever pivoted on a fulcrum (or by other means that give the same basic result). The shorter arm of the lever will move with increased force, but over a smaller distance than the longer arm. Typically, a manual brake pedal has a mechanical advantage, or pedal ratio of 5 to 1.

mechanical-hydraulic booster. A power booster that uses hydraulic pressure from the power steering pump to increase brake application force.

memory. Electronic **storage**.

memory steer. Steering pull due to rubber bonded socket joints installed without centering the steering system. The joints try to return to their initial position, as if they 'remembered' it.

metalization. The deposition of a thin-film pattern of a conductive material onto a substrate to provide interconnection of electronic components or to provide conductive pads for interconnections.

microcomputer. A complete system capable of performing minicomputer functions, with a much lower power range. It is a combination of chip sets; interface I/O along with the auxiliary circuits, power supply, and control console.

micron. A unit of length equal to 10^{-6} m.

microprocessor. A digital computer built on

a single IC chip. Capable of performing arithmetic and control logic functions, it is the basic component of any microcomputer system.

mill-and-drill pads. Welded to the space frame at strategic points mechanically fasten the body panels in place.

mixture control solenoid. An electronically controlled device which regulates bleed air, fuel, or both, on carbureted vehicles.

modified strut. A strut solidly mounted to the knuckle, but with no suspension spring as part of its construction.

modulator. A unit in a wheel slip brake control system that adjusts brake actuating force in response to input signals.

modulator valve. The valve in a power steering pump which controls fluid flow into the pressure hose.

molecule. Two or more atoms joined together to form an element or compound.

molylube. Grease containing molybdenum. A special plating ingredient with excellent lubricating characteristics unaffected by moisture.

monolithic. An integrated circuit built on a single slice of silicon substrate.

MOSFET (metal-oxide semiconductor field effect transistor). An active semiconductor device in which a conducting channel is induced in the region between two electrodes by a voltage applied to an insulated electrode on the surface of the region.

multi-link suspension. Unique suspension designs, used at the rear of sports or performance cars.

multiplier vacuum booster. A vacuum brake power booster that installs between the master cylinder and the wheel friction assemblies. Actuated by hydraulic pressure from the master cylinder.

multiplexing. The process of combining several measurements for transmission over the same signal path. Two usual methods of multiplexing are — time division and frequency division. Time division utilizes the principle of time sharing among measurement channels. Frequency division utilizes the principle of frequency sharing among information channels where the data from each channel are used to modulate sinusoidal signals (subcarriers) so that the resultant signal for each channel contains only frequencies in a limited narrow range.

NAND gate. The grouping of an AND gate followed by an inverter is called a NOT-AND or NAND gate. If all the inputs have a value of 1, the output is 0, and if any of the inputs have a value of 0, the output will be 1. The opposite of an AND gate.

nave. Hollow or dished center part of a road wheel on which the rim is mounted.

negative charge. The condition when an element has more than a normal quantity of electrons.

negative feedback (degeneration). A process by which a part of the output signal of an amplifer circuit is fed back to the input.

negative ion. An atom with more electrons than normal. It has a negative charge.

negative logic. Logic in which the more-negative voltage represents the '1' state, and the less-negative voltage the '0' state.

neutral. Neither positive nor negative, or in a neutral condition. Having the normal number of electrons; that is the same number of electrons as protons.

newton. An SI unit describing force. A force of 1 newton is applied when an object of mass 1 kg is accelerated 1 m/s^2. The symbol for newton is N.

neutron. A particle within the nucleus of an atom. It is electrically neutral.

nibble. A low-frequency vibration, associated with the steering wheel, that is characterized by a slight or partial oscillation of the steering wheel at speeds of 40-50 mph. Caused mainly by radial or lateral runout in a wheel/tire axle or rotor assemblies.

nibs. Small indentations on the edge of the brake shoe lining table that contact the shoe support pads on the backing plate.

NIOSH. National Institute for Occupational Safety and Health.

nip. Gap at mid-point between adjacent leaves of a loosely stacked leaf spring.

NMOS (N-type MOS). MOS devices made on P-type silicon substrates where the active carriers are electons flowing between N-type source and drain contacts.

noise. 1. Unpleasant sound. 2. Unwanted disturbances superimposed on a useful signal and obscure its data content.

noise immunity. A measure of the insensitivity of a logic circuit to triggering or reaction to spurious/undesirable electrical signals or noise, largely determined by the signal swing of the logic. Noise can be in either direction — positive or negative.

non-directional finish. The recommended machine finish on a face of a rotor.

non-volatile random access memory (NVRAM). A non-volatile memory used to store information for either short or long term usage. This type of memory can be written to. If external energy is removed from the device, the contents in memory are not destroyed.

NOR gate. An OR gate followed by an inverter to form a binary circuit in which the output is a logic zero if any of the inputs is one, and vice-versa.

NPN transistor. A transistor with a P-type base and N-type collector and emitter.

N-type material. A crystal of pure semiconductor material to which has been added an impurity so that electrons serve as the majority charge carriers.

Null. A condition (typically of balance) that results in a minimum absolute value of output. Usually specified as the calibration point when the least error can be tolerated by the related control system.

nut rack — ball nut (steering nut). A component of the gear which rides on the worm shaft and converts rotational movement of the steering wheel to linear movement which is applied to the sector gear by means of the 'rack' gear teeth.

NVH. Noise, Vibration, and Harshness.

Ohm. The unit of resistance. One ohm is the value of resistance through which a potential of one volt will maintain a current of one ampere.

Ohm's law. The basic principle that amperage varies in direct proportion to voltage and in inverse proportion to resistance. For example, one ampere is equal to the amount of current forced by one volt through a resistance of one ohm.

on-board. Tools and/or equipment available as part of the delivered new vehicle.

operand. That which is operated upon. Usually identified by an address part of an instruction.

OR gate. A multiple-input gate circuit whose output is energized when any one or more of the inputs is in a prescribed state. Used in digital logic. The OR operator is represented in both electrical and FORTRAN terminology by a 'plus'. If P and Q are logic quantities, then the quantity 'P OR Q' is denoted by 'P+Q'.

oscillator. An electronic device that generates alternating current power at a frequency determined by the values of certain constants in its circuits.

OSHA. Occupational Safety and Health Administration. A division of the US Department of Labor that oversees and regulates matters affecting safety in the workplace.

on-board diagnostic (OBD) system. Monitors some or all computer input and control signals. Signal(s) outside predetermined limits implies a fault in the system or in a related system.

open circuit. An electric installation in which the circuit is not complete (no current flow).

open loop. A predetermined operating condition not based on output conditions.

output impedance. The impedance across the output terminals of a transducer presented by the transducer to the connected external circuitry.

output noise. The unwanted root mean square, peak or peak-to-peak (as specified) AC component of a transducer's DC output in the absence of variations. In the measurand and the environment.

overhaul. To dismantle, inspect, repair/ replace parts as required, reassemble, and test a vehicle or system to a level of functional performance satisfactory for continued use, but not necessarily equal to new system performance levels.

overinflation. The condition of a tire that is inglated to more than the recommended pressure.

overload (overrange). The maximum magnitude of measurand that can be applied to a transducer without causing a change in performance beyond specified tolerance.

overshoot. The amount of output measured beyond the final steady output value, in response to a step change in the measurand.

oversteer. A built-in characteristic of certain types of rear suspension geometry that causes the rear wheels to turn toward the outside of a turn. When a vehicle oversteers, it will turn sharper for a given amount of steering wheel motion than the vehicle that understeers.

over-travel spring. A special assembly on some cable-actuated starwheel automatic adjusters that prevents over-adjustment or damage.

oxidation. A form of corrosion caused by reacting a substance with oxygen. Rust (iron oxide) is a typical example.

oxygen sensor. A sensor that detects the amount of oxygen (O_2) content in the exhaust gases.

pal nut. A locking nut used to lock a retaining nut.

parallel circuit. A pattern of connecting units in an electrical circuit. All the units are connected negative-to-negative and positive-to-positive.

parallelism. A state in which two surfaces are an equal distance apart at every point.

parallelogram linkage. A steering system that uses a short idler arm on the right side, mounted so that it is parallel to the Pitman arm.

Pascal's law. A basic principle of hydraulics that a confined fluid transmits externally applied pressure uniformly in all directions, with no change in magnitude.

passive transducer. A transducer with NO source of power other than the input signal(s), and whose ouput signal-power can NOT exceed that of the input.

peening. A method of locking one part to another, using a ball-peen hammer.

penetrating oil. A very thin oil that is used to penetrate rust and corrosion, and to free rusted parts.

phase-reverse operation. An operational mode of some four-wheel-steering systems, in which the rear wheels turn first in the opposite direction of the front wheels, then in the same direction.

phenolic. This refers to wheel cylinder or caliper pistons made of plastic (phenolic) material rather than metal.

photocell (photoelectric cell). 1. A solid-state photosensitive electron device involving the variation of current-voltage characteristics as a function of incident radiation. 2. A device exhibiting photovoltaic or photoconductive effects.

photodiode. A light-emitting or light-sensitive diode generally used in sensing or switching circuits.

photometer. An instrument used for the measurement of photometric quantities as luminance or luminous intensity measurements. Spectral and time response are important characteristics. The candela and the lumen are the basic photometric units.

piezoelectric. The property of certain crystals which produce a voltage when subjected to a mechanical stress, or undergo mechanical stress when subject to a voltage.

pinion. A small gear wheel, or the smaller of a meshing pair of gear wheels.

pinion angle. The angle between the centerline of the drive shaft and the centerline of the pinion gear.

pinion bearing preload. The resistance exerted by the bearings in a rack-and-pinion steering gear against the pinion gear and shaft, or the force needed to overcome that resistance.

pinion torque. The force required to move the pinion of a rack-and-pinion steering gear against the resistance exerted by the rack.

piston. A moveable plug that fits into the inside diameter of a cylinder.

piston cup. A rubber cup-shaped part that seals a cylinder and eliminates leakage between the piston and the cylinder walls.

piston stops. Tabs, or protrusions, on a backing plate positioned to prevent the wheel cylinder pistons from leaving the wheel cylinder.

pitching (bobbing). A fore-and-aft rocking motion of an automobile. As the front end rises, the rear end falls, and vice versa. 'Bobbing' is usually considered a pitching motion occurring at only one end of the car, while the other end remains relatively steady.

Pitman arm (steering gear arm). The arm connected to the steering gear cross shaft to transfer the rotating motion of the cross shaft to lateral motion of the drag link.

pits. The holes or surface irregularities left on a surface as a result of rust or corrosion.

PLA (progammable logic array). An integrated circuit that employs ROM matrices to combine sum and product terms of logic networks.

play. Possible free movement of a mechanical part, without encountering another part.

plunging joint. A CV joint that allows plunging, or in-and-out, movement of a shaft. Always used at the inboard end or the outboard end of a rear axle shaft.

PMOS (P-type MOS). MOS devices made on an N-type silicon substrate where the active carriers are holes flowing between P-type source and drain controls.

PNP transistor. A transistor having two P-type regions separated by an N-type region.

PNPN diode. A semiconductor device that may be considered a two transistor structure with two separate emitters feeding a common collector.

polar moment of inertia. The tendency of a vehicle to maintain the same speed and direction. A high polar moment of inertia gives straight-ahead stability; a low polar moment of inertia gives more control during cornering and other changes in direction.

polarity. Having two opposite charges — one positive and one negative.

positive logic. Logic in which the more positive voltage represents the '1' state, and the less positive voltage represents the '0' state.

potential. The difference in voltage between two points of a circuit. Frequently, one point is assumed to be ground that has zero potential.

pound(s)force-feet. A unit of measurement for torque. In tightening, 1 poundforce-foot is the torque obtained by a pulling force of 1 pound applied to a wrench handle 12 inches long. Commonly referred to as foot-pounds or ft-lb.

power chamber. The main housing of a vacuum booster internally partitioned in half by a flexible diaphragm. Pressure differentials between the halves move the diaphragm and create application force.

power steering. A device that uses hydraulic pressure from a pump to multiply the driver's effort as an aid in turning the steering wheel.

power steering fluid. Petroleum-based hydraulic fluid used in automotive power steering systems. Contains additives which raise its boiling point, lower its viscosity, and make it non-corrosive and compatible with the seals and materials of construction of a power steering system.

preload. The resistance exerted by one mechanical part against the movement of another; and also, the force required to overcome that resistance. Measured in lbf.in, lbf.ft, or N.m.

preloaded ball joint. A condition of tightness between the ball and socket of a ball joint. Upper ball joints on most vehicles are pre-loaded.

pressure. Force per unit area. The load placed on an object based on the amount of force applied to a specific area.

processor. 1. In hardware, a data processor. 2. In software, a computer program that includes the compiling, assembling, translating, and related functions, for a specific programming language, COBOL processor or FORTRAN processor.

program. A series of instructions to the computer in order to achieve a certain result. Also, design, write, and test a program. Loosely, a routine or to write a routine.

programmable read only memory (PROM). An electronic memory, permanent (non-volatile) or semi-permanent (erasable electronically or with ultra-violet light) and therefore able to be programmed one or more times.

programmed ride control (PRC). A system that adjusts the dampening action of the front and rear shock absorbers, in earlier models of Ford's vehicles. On the 1987 and 1988 Thunderbird Turbo Coupe, the PRC system is automatic. On the Probe, the system allows the driver to select from thrre settings — soft, firm, and very firm.

proportioning valve. A hydraulic valve that reduces pressure to the rear wheel to obtain balanced braking.

proton. One of the positive-charged particles in the nucleus of an atom.

P-type material. A semiconductor material doped with an excess of acceptor impurity atoms, so that free holes are produced in the material.

pull (lead). The tendency of a vehicle to pull or lead to one side (to the right or left of the roadway) when brakes are applied. It may be caused by a malfunctioning brake, or even by unequal caster adjustments or a lower control arm strut that is not properly tightened, allowing caster to change at one wheel when brakes are applied. A weak or broken rear spring can also be a cause.

pulse-width modulated (PWM). A continuous on-and-off cycling of an actuator for a fixed number of times per second. Pulse width is usually measured in milliseconds.

quick-take-up valve. The part of a quick-take-up master cylinder that controls fluid flow between the reservoir and the primary low-pressure chamber.

race. The inner or outer ring that provides the smooth, hard contact surface for the balls or rollers in a bearing.

rack-and-pinion steering gear. A steering gear in which the pinion gear attached to the steering shaft transfers steering wheel motion to a rack. The rack is attached to a steering linkage.

rack-and-sector gear. Component parts of the steering gear. The rack is a series of gear teeth arranged in a straight line on the rack nut. The sector is a segment of a conventional circular gear that meshes with the teeth on the rack. Linear motion of the rack is translated into rotational motion of the sector.

radial bound. Runout of a tire measured at the center of the tread diameter.

radial cooling fins. Brake drum cooling fins that are parallel to the centerline of the axle.

radial load. A load perpendicularly applied to the axis of rotation.

radial-ply tire. A tire in which the plies are laid on radially, or perpendicular to the rim, with a circumferential belt on top of them. The rubber tread is vulcanized on top of the belt and plies.

radial runout. A variation in true rotation of the tire tread, an out-of-round condition.

radii adapter. A mounting device that is used to center a drum or rotor on the arbor of a lathe. A radii adapter centers the drum or rotor through contact with the bearing races.

rag joint. A flexible coupling that contains a rubberized fabric disc, or wafer. Usually used in steering systems.

random access memory (RAM). A volatile memory that has stored information immediately available when addressed regardless of the previous memory address location. Memory words can be selected in any order, and the access time is equal for all words. This type of memory can be written to. It is temporary, and if energy is removed from the RAM device, the contents in memory are destroyed.

range. The measurand values, over which a transducer is intended to measure, specified by their upper and lower limits.

rate. The softness or stiffness of a spring. The load required to cause the spring to deflect one inch.

reaction time. The interval between the beginning of a stimulus and the beginning of the response of an observer.

reactionary type valve. A unit which responds to fluid displacement and pressure, or mechanical linkage movement and force, to modulate pressure in a brake cylinder or chamber.

read only memory (ROM). A non-volatile memory that stores information perma-nently. Information is placed into the memory at the time of manufacture and cannot be altered after the manufacturing process. A ROM is analogous to a dictionary where a certain address results in predetermined information output.

real time. 1. Pertaining to the actual time during which a physical process occurs. 2. Pertaining to the performance of a computation during the actual time that the related physical process occurs, so that results of the computation can be used in guiding the physical process.

rear-end torque. Reactionary torque applied to the rear axle housing as torque is applied to the wheels. Attempts to turn the axle housing in a direction opposite to wheel rotation.

rebound. Downward movement of a wheel opposite the direction of spring compression. In other words, the expansion of a suspension spring resulting from jounce.

recirculating ball steering gear. A steering gear that utilizes a series of recirculating balls on a worm gear to transfer steering wheel movement to an internal rack. The rack in turn applies this movement to a sector shaft attached to the steering linkage.

rectifier. A device with its asymmetrical conduction characteristic, converts an alternating current into a unidirectional current.

reference pressure. The pressure relative to which a differential-pressure device measures pressure.

relay. An electromagnetic switch using a small amount of current in one circuit to control a second circuit using a greater current flow.

relief valve. Limits the power steering pump output when the steering wheel is held 'hard over'. Protects the system against excessive pressure buildup.

replenishing port. The opening between the fluid reservoir and the low-pressure chamber that keeps the chamber filled with fluid.

reservoir diaphragm gasket. The gasket under the master cylinder reservoir cap separating the fluid from the atmosphere. Moves with fluid to allow venting above the fluid.

resilience. The ability of a strained object to recover its original size and shape, following deformation.

resistance. The opposition offered to the free flow of an electric current. The unit of measurement is ohm (Ω).

resistivity. The electrical resistance offered by a material to the flow of current, times the cross-sectional area of current flow and per unit length of current path. The reciprocal of conductivity. Also known as electrical resistivity; specific resistance.

resistor. A device designed to have a definite amount of resistance; used in electric circuits to limit current flow or to provide a voltage drop.

response time. The time required for the output of a transducer to reach a specified fraction of its final value as a result of a step change of measurand.

retaining spring. A spring used to connect the lower ends of a pair of brake shoes and to hold them in contact with the star wheel adjuster.

retracting spring. Used to pull the brake shoes away from the drum when the brake pedal is released. Also pushes the wheel cylinder piston back into its bore, returning the brake fluid to the master cylinder.

returnability. The natural tendency of certain front-end alignment factors, notably steering axis inclination, to bring the front wheels back to their straight-ahead position and hold them there following a turn.

return springs. Springs used on drum brakes to pull the brake shoes away from the drums when the brakes are released.

reverse bias. An external voltage applied to a semiconductor junction to reduce the flow of current through the junction.

reverse bleeding. A method of purging air from a hydraulic system by forcing fluid into the system at a bleeder valve and allowing the air to escape at the master cylinder.

ride control switch. Switch used to change the suspension setting on an electronically controlled suspension system.

ride height. The distance from a specified point on the car to the road surface when the car is at a curb weight condition.

rivet. A semipermanent fastener used to hold two pieces together.

road crown. The downward slope of a road from its center to its edge.

road shock. A shock or movement transmitted from the road surface to the steering wheel through the steering gear and linkages.

roll. A suspension system condition caused by high speed maneuvers. When it occurs, the suspension on one side of the vehicle is severely compressed while the other side is extended. Caused by centrifugal force.

roller bearing. An anti-friction bearing that uses a series of steel rollers held between inner and outer bearing races.

rolling diameter. The diameter of a tire under load as measured from the inner deflection point.

rolling radius. A measurement from the center of an axle to the ground.

rotary valve. Component within the power steering gear that controls the application of fluid pressure.

rotor. The rotating part of a device, such as a disc-brake rotor.

rotor hat. The raised center section of some brake rotors which gives the rotor the shape of a hat.

runout. On disc brakes, it is the measure of wobble in the disc as it rotates. Measured with a dial indicator.

saddle. That portion of an axle housing that mounts on the spring.

scrub radius. The distance between the extended center line of the steering axis or pivot center line, and the center line of the tire at the point where the tire contacts the road.

scuff wear. A type of tire wear that has feathered edges across the tire tread, caused by the tire scuffing sideways.

secondary piston. In a dual or tandem master cylinder, it is this piston normally pushed forward by fluid trapped between it and the primary piston.

section width. The dimension obtained when a tire is measured from one sidewall to the other across its widest point.

sector gear. The gear of the cross shaft that meshes with the recirculating ball nut.

sector shaft. Part of the power train in the power steering gear assembly. Connected by the steering arm to the steering linkage. Its teeth mate with the teeth on the power piston. The sector shaft initiates a right or left turn as the piston is moved upward (for a left turn) or downward (for a right turn).

select-low principle. The controlling principle for rear-wheel anti-lock systems which states that pressure to both wheels shall be limited to the level required by the wheel with the least traction.

semiconductor. An electronic conductor, with resistivity in the range between metals and insulators. The electric-charge-carrier concentration increases with temperature over a temperature range. Certain semi-conductors possess two types of carriers — negative electrons and positive holes.

semiconductor controlled rectifier (SCR). Another name for the reverse-blocking triode-thyristor. The name of the actual semiconductor material (selenium, silicon, etc.) may be substituted for the word 'semiconductor' in naming the components.

semi-elliptical spring. Leaf spring operating as a pin-ended beam reacting loads acting at its mid-length in bending, and so called originally because of its unloaded shape. Recent designs approximate a shallow arc or catenary. May be of single or multi-leaf design. The traditional means of suspending a beam axle.

sensing element. A transducer part that responds directly to the measurand.

sensitivity. Measure of the ability of a device or circuit to respond to a change in input. Also, the minimum or required level of an input that gives rated output. The ratio of the change in transducer output to a change in the value of the measurand.

sensor. A device directly responsive to the value of the measured quantity. A transducer which converts a parameter (at a test point) to a form suitable for measurement (by the test equipment). Sends an input signal to a computer.

serial operation. Data manipulation within circuitry wherein the digits of a word are transmitted one at a time along a single line. Slower than parallel operation but utilizes less complex circuitry.

serial transmission. Transmission of groups of elements of a signal in time intervals that follow each other without overlapping. The bits of a character occur serially in time. Implies only a single transmission channel. Also called serial by bit.

series. A method of connecting several parts in a row so that one feeds into the next.

series circuit. An electric circuit in which the units are consecutively connected or wired positive-to-negative, and current flows through all units.

servo. A transducer type in which the output of the transduction element is amplified and fed back so as to balance the forces applied to the sensing element or its displacements. The output is a function of the feedback signal.

set-up time. The minimum amount of time that data must be present at an input to ensure data acceptance when the device is clocked.

shackle. A flexible connecting link between one end of a leaf spring and the chassis.

shake. Low frequency vibration with visible movement of components.

shim. A spacer used to adjust the distance between two parts.

shimmy. A rapid oscillation or wobble of the wheel/tire assembly about the steering axis.

shock absorber. Usually, a hydraulic cylinder placed at each vehicle wheel to dampen spring action by preventing excessive spring oscillation. Other types of shock absorbers include — adjustables, gas-charged, coil-over, and air shock absorbers, and steering dampers.

shock absorber grommet. A rubber bushing used as part of the mounting assembly of a shock absorber.

shock strut. A component in the suspension of some vehicles that acts as a structural member and as a shock absorber. Its function is to guide, dampen, and limit vehicle motion to control the fore-aft, in-out loads that are placed on a vehicle body on uneven road surfaces.

short-long-arm (SLA) suspension. A suspension system which uses (at each wheel) a shorter upper arm, a longer lower arm, and a coil spring, a torsion bar, or a transverse leaf spring.

shudder. A low-frequency vibration that causes a fore-and-aft lateral movement. Usually caused by the power train or brake systems, and is felt, not heard.

signal. The event or phenomenon that conveys data from one point to another. Information about a variable that can be transmitted in a system.

signal generator. A shielded source of voltage or power, the output level and frequency of which are calibrated, and are usually variable over a range. The output of known waveform is usually subject to one or more forms of calibrated modulation.

signal-to-noise ratio. The ratio of the value of the signal to that of the noise. This ratio is usually in terms of peak values in the case of impulse noise and in terms of root-mean-square values in the case of random noise. To avoid any ambiguity, definitions of the signal and noise should be associated with the terms as, for example, root-mean-square to root-mean-noise ratio; peak-to-peak signal to peak-to-peak noise ratio, etc. This ratio may be a function of the bandwidth of the transmission system.

simulator. A device, system or computer program representing certain behavioral features of a physical or abstract system.

single arm front suspension. A modified MacPherson strut design used on some vehicles. The design utilizes shock struts with coil springs mounted between the lower arm and the frame.

sintering. The process of fusing a metal-powder mixture together under high heat and pressure.

sliding spool. Part of the power steering valve, its sliding action controls oil flow from the oil pump.

slip angle. The angle between the true center line of the tire and the actual path followed by the tire when rounding a turn.

slip yoke. Two pieces of a shaft, splined together, which can slide axially and allow variation in overall length.

slipper pump. A pump using a rotor and spring-loaded slippers inside an elliptic cam ring to effect fluid flow. Slippers create fluid chambers of different volumes.

slope. The percentage of full hydraulic system pressure supplied to the rear brakes by the proportioning valve. Expressed as the ratio of rear pressure to front pressure.

snap ring. A split ring held in a groove by its own tension. Internal split rings are used in grooves cut around the bore of a hole. External snap rings are used in grooves cut around a shaft.

software. Computer programs, routines, programming languages and systems.

solenoid. A coil surrounding a movable iron core that is pulled to a central position with respect to the coil when the coil is energized by allowing current through it.

solenoid valve. Electromagnetic valve assembly.

solid-axle suspension. A suspension system in which the wheels are mounted at each end of a solid, or undivided, axle or axle housing.

solid-state device. Any element that can control current without moving parts, heated filaments, or vacuum gaps. All semi-conductors are solid-state devices, although NOT all solid-state devices (e.g., transformers) are semiconductors.

solvent. A liquid capable of dissolving another substance.

source impedance. The impedance that a source of energy presents to the input terminal of a device.

space frame. A specific type of unit body design that first appeared on European race cars. Consisted of many small diameter tubes welded together so that it looked very much like a birdcage. Individually, each tube was weak, but when they were all welded together with only a few inches separating the tubes, the strength was impressive.

specific gravity. The ratio comparing the mass of a solid or fluid to that of an equal volume of water. A scientifically more appropriate term is the **relative density**. Dimensionless.

speed nuts. Spring-steel clips used to hold floating drums and rotors in place during vehicle assembly.

spindle (stub axle). A short, tapered axle that supports a free-rolling wheel.

spline. A tooth or serration cut on a shaft or in a hole. Used where a part must fit on a shaft without turning.

spongy pedal. Soft pedal.

spool valve. A hydraulic control valve shaped somewhat like a spool on which sewing thread is wound.

spring. An elastic device that yields under stress or pressure but returns to its original state or position when the stress or pressure is removed. The operating component of the automotive suspension system that absorbs the force of road shock by flexing and twisting.

spring rate. The load required to move a spring or a suspended wheel a given distance. A measure of the softness or firmness of a spring or suspension.

spring windup. A twisting effect that pushes up on one end of the rear springs and pulls down on the other end. Reaction to the torque forces applied to the rear wheels on acceleration or braking tends to rotate the rear axle housing in the opposite direction. As the rear springs are attached to the housing, this reaction pushes upward on the front of the spring, and pulls downward on the rear, during acceleration. On braking, the reaction is opposite — it pulls down on the front of the spring, and pushes up at the rear.

sprung mass. A rigid body having equal mass, the same center of gravity, and the same moments of inertia about identical axes as the total sprung weight.

sprung weight. All weight supported by the suspension, including portions of the weight of the suspension members. Total weight minus the weight of unsprung parts.

squat. A suspension system condition caused by road undulations. When it occurs, all springs bottom out.

squeak. Constant or intermittent sound that is high pitched and of a short duration.

stability. 1. The property of a body that causes it, when disturbed from a condition of equilibrium or steady motion, to develop forces or tendencies to restore the body to its original condition. 2. The ability of a device to maintain its nominal operating characteristics after being subjected to changes in operating conditions.

stabilizer. A device using the torsional resistance of a steel bar to reduce vehicle side roll and to prevent too great a difference in the spring action at the two front wheels.

stabilizer bar. A bar linking the two sides of the vehicle in order to help minimize sway. Also called an **anti-roll bar**, **anti-sway bar**, and **sway bar**.

stake. To secure a part by burring or distorting adjacent surfaces.

state. The condition of an input or output of a circuit as to whether it is a logic '1' or a logic '0'. The state of a circuit (gate or flip-flop) refers to its output. A gate is in the '1' state when its output is '1'. A flip-flop is in the '1' state when its '0' output is '1'.

static balance. Balance at rest. A distribution of mass around the axis of rotation so that the wheel has no tendency to rotate by itself, irrespective of its position.

static electricity. Electrical charges temporarily contained in objects with an excess of electrons until discharged.

static friction. The friction existing between two surfaces at rest.

stator. In an alternator, the part that contains the conductors within which the field rotates.

steady-state. A condition in which circuit values do not change with time, after initial transients or fluctuating conditions have disappeared.

steering. Mechanism or means to control the direction of a vehicle.

steering arm. An arm protruding from the steering knuckle, that is connected to the tie-rod and turns the steering knuckle in response to tie-rod movement.

steering axis. The centerline of the ball joints in a front suspension system.

steering axis inclination (SAI). The lean of an imaginary line drawn through the upper and lower pivot points. Simply, it is the inward or outward tilt of the steering axis. Before the development of strut suspensions, the term **kingpin inclination** or **ball joint inclination** was used to denote the angle formed by the centerline of the kingpin or suspension ball joints and the true vertical centerline.

steering gear. A device with gears and rollers to transmit driver steering effort to the steering linkage for guiding the vehicle. A fairly high mechanical advantage is normally designed into the steering gear.

steering gear arm (Pitman arm). The arm linking the cross shaft in the steering gear with the steering linkage.

steering gear ratio. The number of degrees the input gear or a steering gear must turn so as to turn the output gear one degree. The major determining factor of the overall steering ratio.

steering geometry. The geometric arrangement of the components and linkages of a steering system, and the numerical specifications of related lengths and angles.

steering kickback. Sharp and quick movements of the steering wheel as front wheels face obstructions in the road. The resulting shocks 'kickback' to the steering wheel.

steering knuckle. The front-wheel spindle supported by the upper and lower ball joints and the wheel. The part mounting the wheel that is turned for steering.

steering linkage. A system of links, rods, tubes, and levers used to transmit motion from the steering gear to the front wheel steering spindles.

steering pressure sensor. A sensor that provides information on the steering pump pressure for idle speed control.

steering ratio. The number of degrees a steering wheel must rotate so as to move the wheels one degree. High ratios are slower ratios, and low ratios are faster.

steering system. The combination of steering gear, steering wheel, and steering linkage designed to enable the driver to turn the front wheels and direct the vehicle.

steering wheel rotation sensor. A sensor that informs the control module of steering wheel position and also how fast the steering wheel is being turned.

storage. A device that can accept, retain, and read back one or more times. In a computer, a section used primarily for storing information. The physical means of storing information include — electronic, electrostatic, electric, ferroelectric, magnetic, optical, acoustic, chemical, mechanical, etc.

straddle mounted. Mounting a rotating part on bearings such that the part is supported on two sides.

strain gauge. Converting a change of measurand into change or resistance due to strain.

stroking seal. A disc brake hydraulic seal that is set in a piston groove and moves in the caliper bore with the piston.

strut. A bar or rod that keeps two components in a fixed relationship. A combination shock absorber and spring assembly.

stud. A headless bolt that is threaded on both ends.

substrate. The physical material upon which an electronic circuit is fabricated. Used primarily for mechanical support but may serve a useful electrical, thermal, or chemical function.

support arms. The front suspension horizontal arms connecting the front wheels to the vehicle and supporting the mass of the front end.

support yoke. The part of a rack-and-pinion steering gear that braces the pinion against the reaction force of the rack.

surge bleeding. A bleeding method designed to remove air from wheel cylinders by creating turbulence in the wheel cylinder.

suspension. The system of springs, arms, shock absorbers, and related components that connect a vehicle's body and frame to its wheels and axles.

suspension arm. In the front suspension, an arm pivoted at one end to the frame and at the other to the steering-knuckle support.

suspension geometry. The geometric arrangement of components and linkages in a suspension system, and the numerical specs of related lengths and angles.

swaged. A method of locking a part in place by permanently deforming a portion of it or the surrounding material.

sway bar. Another name for **stabilizer bar**.

swept area. The area of a brake drum or rotor that contacts the brake linings.

symmetrical idler arm. A steering linkage component supporting the right side of the steering center link that operates the two tie-rods. A geometric duplicate of the steering gear arm. The steering linkage configuration that results eliminates front wheel toe changes during jounce and rebound caused by changes in the effective tie-rod length of earlier designs.

system. A combination of several equipment integrated to perform a specific function.

table, look-up. A procedure for obtaining the function value corresponding to an argument from a table of function values.

taper. A lack of parallelism. A defect in which the thickness of the drum or rotor at the outer edge differs from its thickness at the inner edge.

tapered roller bearing. An antifriction bearing with a series of tapered steel rollers held between tapered inner and outer races. Used where both radial and thrust loads are to be handled.

tire carcass. The foundation of the tire, consisting of plies forming the basic shape of the tire and beads around the inner circumference of each side of the tire.

torque steer. A driving condition in which the car steers to one side during hard acceleration from high speed, and to the oppostie side during sudden deceleration.

thermal vacuum switch. A vacuum switch that controls vacuum levels or routing based on coolant or ambient air temperature.

thermistor. A solid-state semi-conducting device, the electrical resistance of which varies with the temperature. Its temperature coefficient of resistance is unusually high, and is also nonlinear and negative. Acts as a sensor for temperature change.

thermodynamics. The area of the physical sciences that deals with the interactions of heat energy and mechanical energy.

three-way valve. A hydraulic system component incorporating metering, proportioning, and warning light activation.

threshold. The minimum driving signal level at which a noticeable change in a specified optical property occurs. A multiplexed display requires that a threshold exists.

throttle position sensor. A sensor which provides information on the position of the throttle actuation system.

thrust angle. The angle between the geometric centerline and the rear axle thrust line. If the thrust line deviates to the right of the vehicle (as seen from the top), the thrust angle is positive. A deviation to the left of the vehicle is considered negative.

thrust load. A load applied in line with an axis of rotation.

thyristor. A bistable semiconductor device consisting of three or more junctions that can be switched from the 'off' state to the 'on' state or vice-versa — such switching occurring within at least one quadrant of the principal voltage-current characteristic.

tie rod. A rod-like component of the steering linkage, consisting of strong steel tubing, that links a steering arm to the center link. Two tie rods are used to transfer steering forces to both steering knuckles. Tie rods 'tie' both front wheels together so the wheels will turn simultaneously to steer the vehicle.

tip in moan. Light moan heard upon light acceleration between 20-50 mph.

TIR. Total Indicator Reading. In disc brakes, this refers to a rotor runout reading of the entire swing of the dial indicator's needle, both above and below zero.

tire. The rubber and cord donut on the wheel rim that is filled with pressurized air and transmits vehicle forces (including braking forces) to the road.

tire patch area. The small portion of tire tread, nearly oval in shape, that provides the only contact the car has with the road at a given instant. All directional, starting and stopping control lies in the tire patch areas of the four tires.

tire print. The pattern made by the tire at the point of road contact.

tire tube. An inflatable rubber device mounted inside some tires to contain air at sufficient pressure to inflate the casing and support the vehicle weight.

tire casing. Layers of cord, called plies, shaped in a tire form and impregnated with rubber, to which the tread is applied.

tire patch area. The small portion of tire tread, roughly oval in shape, that actually touches the road at a given instant. All directional, starting and stopping control is concentrated in the tire patch areas of the four tires.

tire rotation. Moving the wheel and tire assemblies to different locations to equalize wear patterns.

tire sidewall. The portion of a tire between the tread and the bead.

tire slip. The difference between vehicle speed and the speed at which the tire tread moves along the pavement. Tire slip is usually expressed as a percentage.

tire tread. The portion of a tire that contacts the road surface.

tire wear indicator. Extra rubber molded into the bottom of the tire tread groove, that appears as a strip of smooth rubber 1/2" (12.7 mm) wide extending across the tire when the tire tread depth decreases to 1/16" (1.59 mm).

toe. Denotes the comparison of the distance between the extreme front of both tires and the distance between the extreme rear of both tires, measured at the front wheels, at a specified height from the road surface. If the front wheel tires are closer together at the front than at the rear, it is called **toe-in**. If they are farther apart at the front than at the rear, it is called **toe-out**. If the distance is exactly equal at front and rear, that the wheels run parallel, it is called **zero toe**.

toe-out on turns (turning angle). The difference between the turning angle of the inside wheel and outside wheel on a turn to the right or left. Normally measured with the outside wheel turned 20 degrees.

tolerance. A permissible variation, usually stated as limits of a specification.

tool bit. The hardened steel or carbide blade that cuts away metal during machining.

torque. The turning or twisting force applied at the end of a rotating shaft. It is force applied multiplied by the torque arm. In the traditional system the units are pound-force-foot (or foot-poundforce). The units in the SI and metric systems are newton•meter or dyne•centimeter respectively.

torque arm. Defined as the distance from the center-point of rotation to the point at which the force is applied. If torque is being applied using a wrench, the length of the torque arm is the same as the length of the wrench.

torque sequence. The order in which a series of bolts or nuts should be tightened.

torque wrench. A wrench or handle which indicates the amount of torque applied to a bolt or nut. A tool used to tighten bolts and nuts to a specific torque.

torsion. Twisting action, particularly as applied to turning one end of a rod while the other end is kept from turning.

torsion bar. A long spring steel rod attached in such a way that one end is anchored while the other is free to twist.

torsional vibration. 1. The back-and-forth twisting of a shaft along its length. 2. Vibration in seat and floor pan during steady to heavy acceleration at 25-45 mph.

track (tread). The distance between the centerline of the wheels from one side of the car to the other.

tracking. The following of the rear wheels directly behind, or in the tracks of, the front wheels.

traction. The amount of grip between the tire tread and the road surface. Higher traction allows greater braking and cornering force to be generated.

tramp. The up- and down- 'hopping' action of a wheel. Usually caused by static imbalance. Sometimes called **shimmy**.

transducer. Any device that converts an input signal into an output signal of a different form. Converts energy from one form or power level to another. Often used to interface unit under test with test or diagnostic equipment.

transformer. A device consisting of a winding with tap or taps, or two or more coupled windings with or without a magnetic core for introducing mutual coupling between electric circuits.

transient. A phenomenon caused in a system by a sudden change in conditions and that persists for a relatively short time after the change. A temporary increase or decrease of voltage or current. Transients may take the form of spikes or surges.

transistor. An active element semiconductor device with three or more terminals.

transistor-transistor logic (TTL or T^2L). Also called multi-emitter transistor logic. A logic circuit design is similar to DTL, with the diode inputs replaced by a multi-emitter transistor. In a 4-input DTL gate, there are 4 diodes at the input. A 4-input TTL gate will have 4 emitters of a single transistor as the input element. TTL gates using NPN transistors are positive-level NAND gates or negative-level NOR gates.

triangulation. A three-point connection between the frame and wheel. Effectively braces the wheel against road forces from all directions, and still allows the wheel to pivot on the steering axis.

trim height. The normal no-load height of a vehicle. It is also called the curb height or chassis height, since it is defined as the distance between the vehicle frame, or the bottom of the front and rear suspensions, and a level surface.

trouble codes. Numerical codes created by an electronic module with self-diagnostic capabilities and usually stored in the module memory. They result from a system self-test that indicates a circuit or subsystem malfunction, or a condition that is beyond range. Often called fault or service codes, the new term is 'diagnostic trouble codes'.

truth table. A chart that tabulates and summarizes all the combinations of possible states of inputs and outputs of a circuit. It tabulates what will happen at the output for a given input combination.

tube seat. An insert or machined face, against which a flared tube end seals.

tubing bender. A tool used to bend tubing without kinking or deforming its walls.

tubing wrench. A wrench to turn fittings on tubing. A tubing wrench distributes the turning forces evenly around the fitting and minimizes the possibility of damage.

two-stage control. Provided by means of a valve on the power steering pump to regulate fluid flow in the system at various engine speeds. Allows sufficient flow at low engine speed, and then restricts the flow at higher speeds to that needed for power steering operation.

U-bolt. A rod bent to the shape of the letter 'U' having threads on both ends.

understeer. A feature of rear suspension geometry that causes the rear wheels to turn slightly toward the inside of a turn.

Offers additional resistance to the tendency of the rear wheels to lose traction and skid outward on a turn.

unitized body design. A design feature that combines body and frame structures into one integrated welded assembly. Replaces the earlier practice of bolting the body to a separate frame.

undulation. A rapid dip or rise in the road surface.

unijunction transistor (UJT). A three-element terminal semiconductor device exhibiting stable open-circuit negative resistance characteristics.

unsprung mass(es). The equivalent masses that reproduce the inertia forces resulting from the motions of the corresponding unsprung parts.

unsprung weight. All weight not carried by the suspension system, but is supported directly by the tire or wheel, and considered to move with it. High unsprung weight makes suspension movement more difficult to control. Low unsprung weight makes the ride smoother.

vacuum. Technically, a complete absence of pressure (0 psi), although the term is commonly used to describe any pressure less than atmospheric.

vacuum-assist unit. An actuating mechanism that uses vacuum on one side of a diaphragm as a source of power.

vacuum servo. A flexible diaphragm with a linkage attached to it installed in a sealed housing. When vacuum is applied to one side of the diaphragm, atmospheric pressure on the other side moves the diaphragm and linkage to perform work.

vacuum switch. A switch that closes or opens its contacts in response to changing vacuum conditions.

valence. The extent to which an atom combines with other atoms. Believed to depend on the arrangement and number of electrons in its outer shell.

valve. Any device used to control the

direction, volume, or pressure of a fluid flowing through a hydraulic system. The word preceding valve usually designates the type of valve (e.g. needle valve) or the function it performs (e.g. check valve).

valve seat. The surface against which a valve comes to rest to provide a seal against leakage.

valve spool. A spool-shaped valve, such as in the power-steering unit.

vane. A thin plate attached to a rotating unit to either throw off air or liquid, or to receive the thrust imparted by moving air or liquid striking the vane. The first is the action of a pump and the second is that of a motor.

vapor. Any substance in the gaseous state, as distinguished from the liquid or solid state.

VAPS (variable-assist power steering). Provides more assist at low speeds and for sharp cornering, and less assist at high speeds and for wider turns. May be controlled hydraulically or electronically.

vehicle speed sensor. Input to the control module that informs it of the speed the vehicle is traveling.

vent solenoid. A solenoid assembly placed on an air compressor in an air suspension system that vents excess pressure from the system when instructed by the control module. Also maintains a minimum pressure within the system.

vibration. A constant or variable high-frequency trembling, shaking or grounding condition that is felt or heard.

viscosity. The resistance that a fluid offers to flow, when it is subjected to a shear stress. The more viscous a fluid is, the thicker it is, and the less it tends to flow. Usually varies with temperature.

volatile memory. An electronic memory (RAM) which temporarily stores data that is lost when the power is turned off.

volt. The unit of voltage or potential difference. It is the voltage between two points of a conducting wire carrying a constant current of one ampere, when the power dissipated between these points is one watt.

voltage regulator. A unit which controls alternator output voltage as needed for vehicle operation.

vulcanizing. The process of bonding rubber by means of chemical action (with sulfur or other vulcanizing agent) under heat and pressure. Increases strength and resilience of rubber.

waddle. Side-to-side movement of a car, usually caused by a tire with a belt installed crookedly.

wallowing. A slow pitching motion of a car driven over a smooth road with only slight undulations on crosswise tar strips at regular intervals. One cause is shock absorbers having too little control over minor spring deflections.

wander (drift, weave). The tendency of a vehicle to veer from a straight path without driver control. Usually indicates the need for front end alignment.

warning light valve. A valve in the hydraulic circuits of a dual brake system that switches on a dash warning light when one system fails.

watt. A unit of electric power required to do work at the rate of one joule per second. It is the power expended when one ampere of direct current flows through a resistance of one ohm.

ways. Special sliding surfaces machined into the anchor plate and caliper body where these parts of a sliding caliper make contact and move against one another.

wear indicator. 1. A projection from a ball joint that recedes into the joint as the joint wears. 2. A projection on the inner brake pad that contacts the disc and creates a squealing noise when pad replacement is necessary. Gradually being replaced by an electrical sensor that illuminates a warning lamp.

weight. The mass of an object under the

influence of gravity. Unlike mass, the weight changes with the location of the object. As the force of gravity is relatively constant on earth, we use the terms weight and mass interchangeably.

weight bias. An element of vehicle design that results in either the front or rear suspension having to support more than half of the vehicle's weight. Most cars have a forward weight bias.

weight transfer. The shift of weight toward the front of a vehicle that occurs when the brakes are applied while driving forward.

wheel. The disc and rim assembly onto which the tire mounts and which turns on the axle or spindle.

wheel alignment. The adjustment of suspension and steering parts, particularly at the front wheels, bringing the wheels into a specified relationship with the road and with each other. Rear-wheel alignment must be performed on some wheels with independent rear suspension.

wheel balance. The weight distribution of a wheel and tire. A wheel and tire are out of balance if their weight is not evenly distributed around the hub and side-to-side.

wheelbase. Longitudinal distance between the front and rear wheel axes of a vehicle. The longer the wheelbase, the smoother the vehicle ride. Correctly established when the vehicle leaves the factory, but can change as a result of suspension wear or damage, or as a result of collision. Any change in the wheelbase will affect vehicle tracking, and thus the directional control and stability.

wheel bearing seals. Rubber or leather seals used at wheel hubs to keep wheel bearing grease from getting into a brake drum or onto a brake disc.

wheel flutter. Oscillation of steered wheel about its steering axis, usually at a frequency grteater than that of rotation.

wheel friction assemblies. The axle-mounted components of a brake system that create the friction necessary to stop a vehicle.

wheel lockup. Condition of 100% wheel slip.

wheel offset. The distance between the rim centerline and the mounting plane of the wheel.

wheel setback. Occurs when the two wheels on one axle do not share a common centerline or wheelbase. Generally results from collision damage and can be measured on an alignment machine.

wheel slip sensor. Used with the wheel slip brake control system. Senses the rate of angular rotation of the wheel(s) and transmits signals to the logic controller.

wheel speed sensor. A variable reluctance device whose signal to the computer module is used to determine the possibility of wheel lockup.

wheel spindle. The part of the front suspension about which the front wheel rotates.

wheel torque. Torque applied to the wheel from the vehicle about the spin axis.

wheel tramp. Tendency for the wheel to move up and down so it repeatedly bears hard, or 'tramps' on the pavement. Also called high-speed shimmy.

whine. Pure tone, constant frequency sound.

wide open throttle switch. A switch which senses a wide open throttle condition. Existing methods of sensing this condition are manifold vacuum and mechanical travel of the throttle.

wiring harness. The complete wiring assembly of a vehicle, specifically when installed as an integrated unit.

wishbone. Two-armed or V-shaped frame, mounted in horizontal plane for locating an independently suspended wheel.

wobble. 1. Oscillation of a wheel at rotational frequency usually resulting from unbalance or misalignment. 2. Self-excited oscillation of steerable wheels about their steering axes, occurring without appreciable tramp.

word. A character string or a bit string considered as an entity.

work. The transfer of energy from one system to another, particularly through the application of force. Expressed as the magnitude of a force times the distance through which that force is applied.

worm shaft. A shaft in the steering gear, coupled to the shaft from the driver's steering wheel. A special type of spiral gear, called a worm gear, is machined into the wormshaft. This gear resembles the threads on a bolt and transfers steering forces to the nut rack. A revised practice is to machine the threads in the worm gear and nut rack in the form of a channel to accommodate steel ball bearings that reduce friction.

write time. The time that the appropriate level must be maintained on the write enable line and that data must be presented to guarantee successful writing of data in the memory.

writing enable. Also called read/write or R/W. The control signal to a storage element or a memory that activates the 'write' mode or operation. Conversely when not in the 'write' mode, the 'read' mode is active.

yaw. Swaying movement of the car body, rotating the body around the vertical axis. Occurs when road forces push the front or the rear of the car to one side.

yoke. A fork-ended component, as of a tow bar or universal joint.

Zener diode. A two-layer device, above a certain reverse voltage (the 'Zener value'), has a sudden rise in the current. If forward-biased, the diode is an ordinary rectifier, but when reverse-biased, the diode exhibits a typical sharp break, in its current-voltage graph. The voltage across the device remains essentially constant for any further increase of reverse current, up to the allowable dissipation rating. The Zener diode is a good voltage regulator, over-voltage protector, voltage reference, level shifter, etc. True Zener breakdown occurs at <6V. Also called **avalanche** or **breakdown diode**.

Zener effect. Nondestructive breakdown in a semiconductor, occurring when the electric field across the junction region becomes high enough to produce a form of field emission that suddenly increases the number of carriers in this region.

zerk fittings. Grease fittings

Subject Index

AUTOMOTIVE UNDERCAR

SUSPENSION STEERING AND ELECTRONIC SYSTEMS

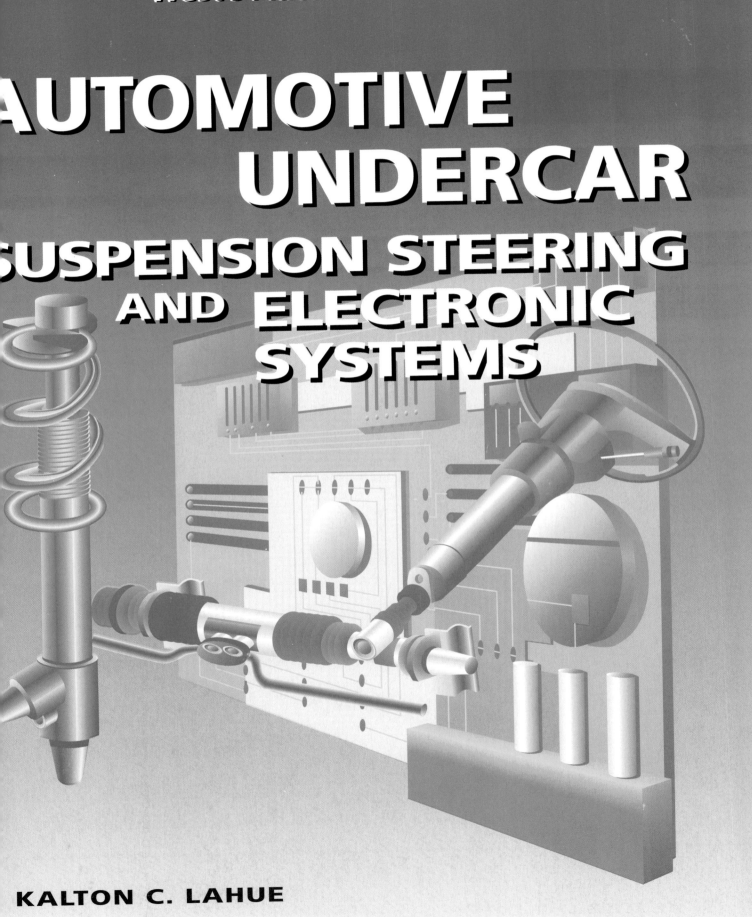

KALTON C. LAHUE

AUTOMOTIVE UNDERCAR: SUSPENSION, STEERING & ELECTRONIC SYSTEMS

SHOP MANUAL

SAFETY AND THE SHOP ENVIRONMENT

OBJECTIVES

After completion of this chapter, you should be able to:

- Relate good safety practices to the shop environment and list at least five safety rules, describing the consequences of ignoring them.

- Describe three features of an organized work area and explain how each contributes to your efficiency.

- List two types of shop equipment found in a front end shop, and briefly describe what each is used for.

- Explain briefly the term 'essential special tool' as it applies to servicing suspension and steering systems.

- List four examples of 'general' special tools used for servicing suspension and steering systems.

- Explain why electronic supension and steering systems require the use of special test equipment.

- Identify various specifications as descriptive, service, operating, or parts specifications.

- Use a factory service manual to locate the correct procedure for overhaul of a specific suspension or steering system.

- Use either a factory service manual or an independent service and repair manual to locate overhaul specifications for a specific suspension or steering system.

- Use a flat-rate manual to correctly determine flat-rate time requirements for various suspension or steering system service and repair jobs.

The successful automotive front end shop of tomorrow will differ considerably from those of today. The shop of the future will be a clean, orderly, and safe workplace capable of servicing the increasingly complex electronic controls used with suspension and steering systems. It will be staffed by highly trained technicians who can troubleshoot and solve electronic problems quickly and efficiently, using sophisticated test equipment.

The technician of tomorrow will be highly skilled and project an image of competence to his customers. The corner jack-of-all trades auto repair facility will NOT attract customers who want high-tech automotive service for their high-tech vehicles. The shops that survive will be clean and organized, with neatly dressed service personnel who are comfortable with electronics.

The field of electronics has enlarged the size of all automotive tool chests. To service the many new electronic suspension and steering systems in use, the tool chest now contains the specialized test equipment required to diagnose, troubleshoot, and repair a variety of such systems. Instead of a handful of torque specifications, you will now have to deal increasingly with diagnostic trouble codes, electrical specifications, and many new test and repair procedures.

Today's automotive technician has become a victim of the information age; no longer able to remember all the data, specifications, and procedures required to keep pace with the field. To do the job, the technician must know where to locate the information required. Once the information is in hand, the ability to use a service manual, service bulletin, or booklet to quickly and accurately find the necessary information about a specific system is equally necessary.

SAFETY PRACTICES

Good safety practices are recognized by professional automotive technicians as both basic and common sense. Accidents can be prevented if you 'think safety'. This means avoiding potential hazardous situations, such as working with the wrong tools, shortcutting a procedure, or tempting fate by using unsafe equipment. Accidents mean personal injury, damage to vehicles or equipment, and possible time lost from the job. While no technician deliberately wants an accident to happen, all too many of us often gamble that while it may happen to the 'other guy', it won't happen to us. You should be aware that all too often, it does. Before undertaking a procedure, think the process through and ask yourself what precautions should be taken. Nothing beats clear, logical thinking and a liberal use of common sense.

This volume contains service and repair procedures for both electronic and conventional suspension and steering systems. Servicing these systems will bring you in contact with other automotive areas that are filled with potential hazards. The procedures in this manual contain specific CAUTIONS and WARNINGS. CAUTIONS focus attention on hazards that can damage a vehicle or equipment. WARNINGS focus attention on hazards that can cause personal injury.

SAFETY RULES

Safety should be an instinctive part of every service procedure. While many of the following precautions apply to your technical specialty, they do NOT cover all aspects of safety that should be practiced when working in a shop. You can probably name many others that should be followed when working on or near a vehicle.

- Know where the shop's first-aid supplies and equipment are located, as well as how and where to obtain emergency medical help.
- Know where the shop fire extinguisher is located and how to use it correctly.
- If you are unsure about the operation of any tool or machine, ask your instructor how to safely use it before proceeding.
- Before you turn on any machine, make certain the machine is correctly set up and adjusted. Be sure all safety equipment has been installed and is working properly on any machine you use.
- ALWAYS use the correct tool for the job. If the correct tool is not available, check with your instructor.

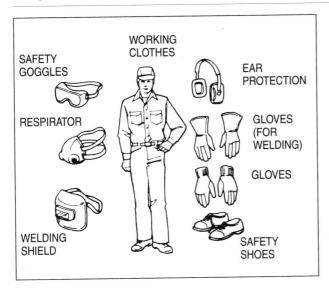

Figure 1-1   Safety equipment and protective clothing should be used when performing a job where personal injury is possible. (General Motors)

- ALWAYS wear safety items appropriate to the job when performing a task that involves possible injuries, such as grinding, welding, or working around hot components (Figure 1-1).
- Before starting an engine, set the parking brake and put the transmission in 'park' or 'neutral'. If the parking brake is vacuum-operated, disconnect and plug the vacuum lines.
- NEVER work underneath a vehicle when the engine is running.
- Before running an engine, make sure the vehicle exhaust is connected to shop exhaust ducts. If the shop has none, open the doors and windows as necessary to assure good ventilation.
- NEVER bend at the waist and lift heavy objects with your back. Bend your knees and lift with your back straight.
- Do NOT use a bumper jack to lift or support a vehicle in the shop.
- If you do not know the correct lifting or jacking points for a vehicle, ask your instructor or consult a service manual.
- When lifting one end of a vehicle, block the

wheels at the other end securely to prevent the vehicle from rolling off the jack.
- ALWAYS use safety stands under the axle, suspension, or frame when raising a vehicle with a jack.
- Clean up spilled hydraulic fluid and other liquids immediately. Keep your work area free of oily rags and paper.
- Make sure that any part clamped in a vise is held securely.
- Do NOT drive a vehicle faster than 5 mph (8 km/h) when entering, leaving, or driving inside the shop area.
- When working under the vehicle, keep your hands away from hot exhaust components or wear protective gloves.
- If an electronic control system contains accumulators or other parts that are under pressure, be sure to depressurize them as described by the carmaker before starting work.
- Some electronic suspension systems automatically change vehicle height when the engine is started or shut off. Do NOT get under the vehicle or place any part of your body between the car body and wheelhouse. Wait a minimum of three minutes after the ignition is turned on or shut off before attempting any work on such vehicles.
- Wait at least three minutes after stopping the engine on such vehicles before raising it with a jack. Do NOT get under the vehicle unless safety stands are in place, and do NOT start the engine.
- Follow the carmaker's torque specifications when installing fasteners that require a torque value. Fasteners that are improperly torqued can result in damage to the part or system.
- If wheel/tire diagnosis requires spinning the drive wheels with the vehicle on safety stands:
  a. All four wheels of an all-wheel drive vehicle or a 4WD vehicle locked in

4WD must be off the ground to prevent the vehicle from driving off the safety stands.

b. If the vehicle is equipped with a posi-traction or limited-slip differential, do NOT spin one drive wheel with the other wheel on the ground. The vehicle may move unexpectedly and drive off the safety stands.

c. AVOID excessive speeds when spinning wheels. Do NOT exceed 35 mph (56 km/h) when spinning one drive wheel with the other drive wheel stopped, or 70 mph (112 km/h) if both drive wheels are spinning at the same speed.

• When spinning wheels on or off the vehicle, make sure other personnel stay clear of rotating components and balance weight areas.

Every technician needs to be aware of in-shop hazards and safety regulations, as well as the proper methods to be used in the disposal of toxic, hazardous, and flammable materials. This includes solvents used in the parts cleaning machine and elsewhere in the shop area, as well as used hydraulic fluids. Such substances must be properly handled and disposed of according to local environmental regulations. If the shop does not have a copy of the practices recommended by the Occupational Safety and Health Administration (OSHA) and the Environmental Protection Agency (EPA) to be used in handling and disposition of such by-products, obtain a set and see that they are prominently displayed where everyone in the shop will be aware of them.

THE SHOP ENVIRONMENT

As an automotive technician, you will spend a good part of your working day in one small area of the shop. To make your work both efficient and profitable, this area should be as comfortable, organized, and convenient as

possible. You do not make money searching for tools and equipment, or trying to locate service literature for specifications and procedures.

ORGANIZING YOUR WORK AREA

The area in which you work should be large enough to accommodate all the different activities you will need to perform. The best way to increase the efficiency of your work area is to keep it clean and organized. Working in this kind of environment reduces unnecessary and tiring motion to a minimum.

You should have a sturdy tool chest that can stand up under occasional rough handling and still protect your investment in tools (Figure 1-2). Clean your tools and put them away when you are finished with them. A clean, dry tool will not slip out of your hand, or off the fastener, the next time you use it. If you follow this practice, you can locate the tools you need when you want them, and they will be ready for use. The most expensive tool set in the world is worthless if you cannot find

Figure 1-2 Keep your tools clean, organized, and stored in a tool chest where you can find them when needed.

the right wrench when it is needed.

There should be some part of your work area where service manuals, technical service bulletins, and specifications can be stored and used. Whether these materials are kept on a shelf or in a bookcase, they should be available for use without coming in contact with hydraulic fluids, or grease, dirt, and other contamination. By reserving a part of your workbench for their use, you also have space for doing any necessary paperwork.

Sectioned trays or pans are useful to store small parts and fasteners while you are working. They will keep such parts from being lost or misplaced during disassembly, and you will be able to find them during reassembly. You'll find that muffin tins (Figure 1-3) are ideal for this purpose.

Your workbench should be large enough to let you lay out the parts of a steering rack in order as you disassemble it. Keeping the parts in proper order is important, since it is the most efficient way of assuring that you reinstall them correctly. The workbench also should have some provision for containing and collecting any fluids that drain from components during disassembly. If the bench does not have a built-in drain, keep a large

Figure 1-3 Keeping small parts and tools in a sectioned container like a muffin tin helps keep your work area clean and lets you find them when needed.

pan or container handy to hold the fluid. Another container should be available to store shop cloths used to clean fluid from the components or bench surface.

Keep your workbench and the area around it clean and dry. Clean up any fluids that spill on the floor before they can cause an accident or get tracked around the shop. A bucket of soapy water and a mop, or a bag of absorbant to soak up spilled fluid, should be within easy reach.

Remember that cleanliness is a high priority when working with a hydraulic steering system. Dirt or contamination that gets into such systems while you are working on them virtually guarantees that the vehicle will come back, and that you will work on it a second time. Keep your hands, components, and workbench clean. You'll have fewer problems, and fewer jobs that come back for rework.

SHOP EQUIPMENT

All shops have certain equipment, such as hoists, hydraulic jacks, a hydraulic press, grinders, welders, and parts cleaning machines, that are required to do the job. This equipment generally is shared by all the technicians in the shop. You must know how to use this equipment, and do your part in keeping the shop clean and safe.

VEHICLE HOISTS

The shop should be equipped with a hoist for each work stall. It may be a single-post, frame-contact hoist or a twin-post, suspension contact hoist. Some shops might be equipped with a twin-post, double-runner hoist. How a hoist is used, and whether it requires adapters to safely support a vehicle's weight will be determined by the type of vehicle you are servicing. Service manuals contain the necessary diagrams and information showing the correct vehicle lift points (Figure 1-4). You should refer to these

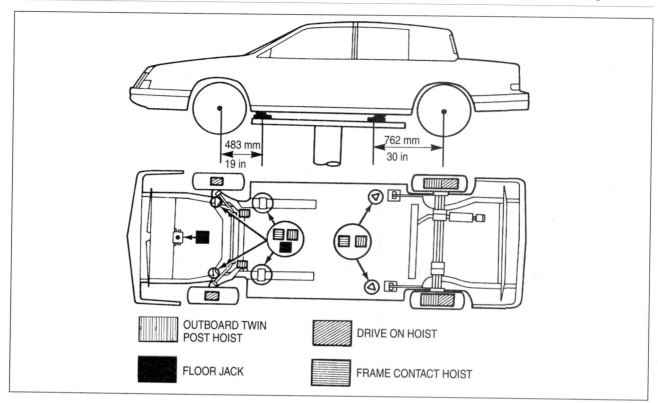

483 mm
19 in

762 mm
30 in

OUTBOARD TWIN POST HOIST

DRIVE ON HOIST

FLOOR JACK

FRAME CONTACT HOIST

Figure 1-4 A typical lift point diagram showing hoist points for various types of hoists and jacks. (Chrysler)

diagrams and information if you have any doubts. Hoisting a vehicle at other points can cause frame or suspension damage. If the hoist has a safety latch, it should be securely engaged.

Floor Jacks and Safety Stands

When necessary, some suspension or steering work can be performed without the use of a hoist. A hydraulic floor jack will raise the vehicle enough to do the job. However, NEVER work around a vehicle supported only by a floor jack. Always install safety stands (often called jack stands) as a protective measure in case of jack failure (Figure 1-5).

Parts Cleaning Machines

Most cleaning is done in a cold-solution cleaning tank that recirculates solvent or mineral spirits (Figure 1-6). Use it to clean the outside of steering pumps, gearboxes, and

Figure 1-5 Safety stands should be used to support the vehicle while you are working on it.

Figure 1-6 Use a parts cleaning machine to clean the outside of calipers and other components. This keeps dirt off your workbench and makes disassembly faster.

other components before disassembly. Cleaning exterior dirt and grease from the component makes disassembly faster and cleaner, and keeps much of the contamination out of your work area. Once you have disassembled the parts, clean them individually in the cleaning tank and blow dry with shop air.

> **WARNING:** Solutions used in cleaning tanks can cause serious skin reactions for some people. ALWAYS wear protective gloves and safety glasses when cleaning parts.

PARTS CLEANING BUCKETS

Heavily varnished disassembled parts that will NOT clean up in the wash tank should be submerged in a basket in parts cleaning solution. This cleaner, which usually comes in a five-gallon or smaller bucket with a

basket, is highly caustic. Do NOT use a brush in those caustic solutions that are meant for a basket. The brush will spatter the solution, which will burn skin and eat holes in clothes.

After cleaning parts with the caustic solution, allow the basket to drain back into the bucket, then follow your instructor's directions for rinsing the parts. Some technicians rinse in mineral spirits or water. Hot water is a good rinse, if available. All rinsing must be safe for the environment, so follow your instructor's directions to avoid contaminating drains or vacant lots.

Dry with compressed shop air after rinsing. NEVER blow off caustic solutions until after they have been rinsed. Be sure to direct the compressed air to blow any remaining cleaning agent away from you.

Do NOT wipe the parts dry with shop cloths. They can leave particles of lint that can cause problems after reassembly.

> **WARNING:** ALWAYS wear safety glasses when drying parts with compressed air to prevent any solution from blowing into your eyes.

GRINDERS

Grinders are used to remove metal rapidly (Figure 1-7), but a grinding wheel rotating at 10,000 rpm is dangerous if you do not wear the proper protective gloves and glasses, or if you do not pay attention to what you're doing. When using a grinder, treat it as a piece of equipment that can cause serious injury in the blink of an eye.

HYDRAULIC PRESS

Every shop will have one or more hydraulic presses. These are required to separate components or remove bearings (Figure 1-8) with the proper tools and adaptors. They also are

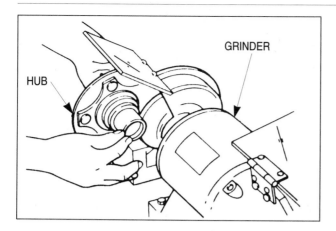

Figure 1-7 Grinders used to remove excess metal revolve at high speeds, and can cause serious injuries unless used properly. (Ford Motor)

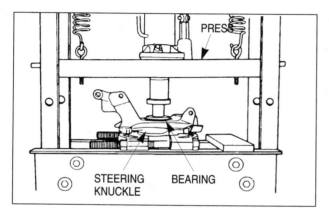

Figure 1-8 A hydraulic press is used to remove and install bearings, separate the hub from the steering knuckle, and many other jobs requiring a large amount of force. (Ford Motor)

used to install bearings or reassemble components. Hydraulic presses exert tremendous pressure, and their use often is the only way to complete the job. Separating or installing parts by striking them with a heavy hammer is NOT efficient, seldom works, and can damage the parts.

WELDING UNITS

The shop should have one or more oxyacetylene and metal inert gas (MIG) welders available for your use (Figure 1-9). You should know when and how to use each type,

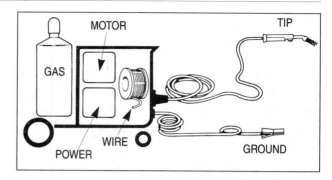

Figure 1-9 One type of welding equipment found in shops, the MIG welder produces a high-energy electric arc when the wire contacts the metal. (General Motors)

> ⚠ **WARNING:** Exposure to a welding arc is dangerous to the eyes and skin, since prolonged exposure can cause blindness and burns. NEVER weld without the proper eye protection and protective clothing.

as well as the proper protective measures to be followed when welding. On vehicles with electronic control systems, ALWAYS disconnect the battery negative (-) cable and remove any electronic control module or component located between the ground clamp and weld area to avoid possible damage. If the vehicle is equipped with an airbag, be sure to disconnect the airbag control module.

SPECIAL TOOLS AND TEST EQUIPMENT

In addition to the general automotive tools in your tool chest, such as wrenches, pliers, and screwdrivers, there are two catagories of special tools you will use when servicing automotive suspension and steering systems. You will also use specialized tools and test equipment.

ESSENTIAL SPECIAL TOOLS

Suspension and steering system components have their own special service requirements. To meet these service needs, the manufacturer

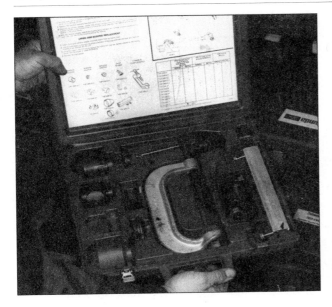

Figure 1-10 Essential tools for servicing automotive electronic systems should be kept in their protective case with the instructions for their use.

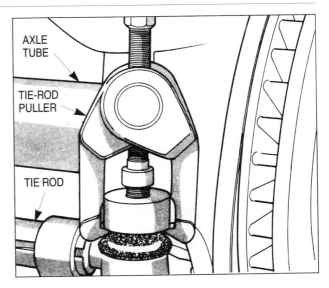

Figure 1-11 A tie rod end remover is a safer and easier method of separating ball joints than the use of the old-fashioned (but commonly available) pickle fork. (Chrysler)

makes available a kit of 'essential' special tools (Figure 1-10). Such tools are designed to make correct disassembly and reassembly easy according to the factory procedure. For example, control arm bushings require special removers and installers. Other tools and procedures often can be used for disassembly and reassembly if you do not have the recommended essential tools. However, since the essential tools are designed for specific functions, they make the job easier, faster, and safer.

GENERAL SPECIAL TOOLS

The other catagory of special tools is more general in nature, since they can be used with a variety of systems. The following is only a small sampling of such equipment:

- Tie rod end removers come in a wide variety of styles (Figure 1-11).
- C-clamps often are used with bearing receiver and installer cups or when installing strut dampers (Figure 1-12).
- Pitman arm pullers are used to separate the Pitman arm from the steering gearbox sector shaft (Figure 1-13).

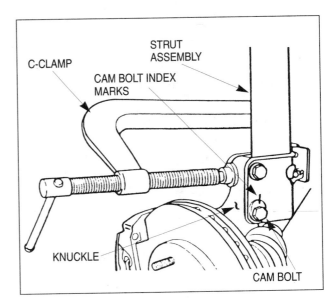

Figure 1-12 C-clamps have many uses, from holding parts in correct alignment to applying force. (Chrysler)

- Coil spring compressors are used to remove oil springs from struts (Figure 1-14).
- A vise is necessary to hold components securely when working on them (Figure 1-15).

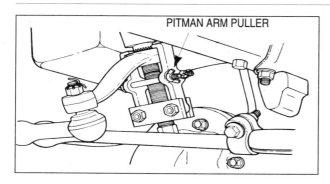

Figure 1-13 The Pitman arm puller separates the Pitman arm from the serrated sector shaft. (Ford Motor)

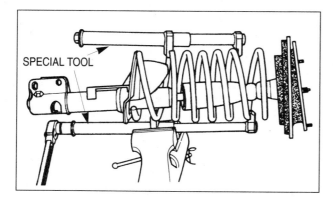

Figure 1-14 Carmakers and aftermarket spring manufacturers offer many different types of spring compressors to be used in removing the spring from a strut. (Chrysler)

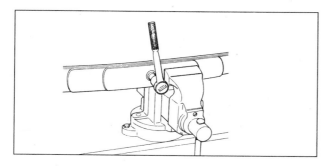

Figure 1-15 A vise has many purposes, from holding components such as a spring in alignment, to holding the components from moving when working on them. (Chrysler)

- Torque wrenches allow you to tighten fasteners to exact specifications and are used for many purposes, including wheel and tire installation (Figure 1-16).

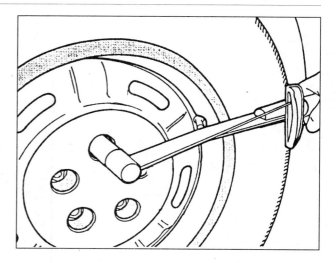

Figure 1-16 When wheels are reinstalled on the vehicle, they should be tightened by hand with a torque wrench to assure proper tightness of the lug nuts. (Chrysler)

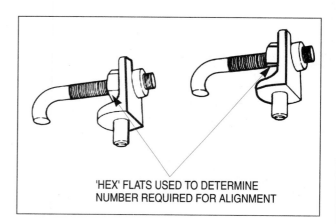

Figure 1-17 Different types of suspensions require different special tools to make alignment faster and easier. (Ford Motor)

- Caster/camber adjustment tools make alignment work faster and easier (Figure 1-17).
- Dial indicators are necessary to check wheel/tire runout (Figure 1-18).
- Wheel alignment racks or machines are used to determine and correct alignment problems (Figure 1-19).

TEST EQUIPMENT

You will use a variety of test equipment when diagnosing an electronic control system

Figure 1-18 Dials indicators with rotary wheels are used for some purposes; others use the standard plunger tip. (Chrysler)

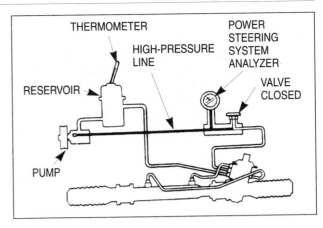

Figure 1-20 A typical power steering pressure tester. (Ford Motor)

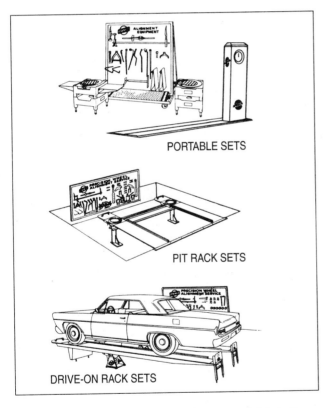

Figure 1-19 Wheel alignment racks are available in three general types — portable, those installed in a pit, and those installed above ground (often called drive-on racks). (Ammco Tools / ©Hennessy Industries)

problem. Some test equipment is general in nature, and can be used with many different systems. Other test equipment is specialized,

and can be used only with a specific system. General test equipment such as power steering analyzers, pressure gauges, and thermometers (Figure 1-20) are used when checking power steering pressure.

Specialized Test Equipment

Electronic control systems are designed to help the technician find the cause of a malfunction. The microcomputer constantly monitors sensor input/output signals used for system control. Each input/output must fall within a specified range to be accepted as correct by the microcomputer. If an input/output falls outside its range, the microcomputer sets a numeric trouble or fault code in memory. Each code denotes a different electrical, hydraulic, or mechanical malfunction. In order to read these codes with many electronic control systems, you must connect a special diagnostic tester to a diagnostic connector located on the vehicle.

Chrysler has designed its control systems to communicate through a diagnostic readout box or DRB II (Figure 1-21). This is basically a scan tool. It puts the control module into various test modes to diagnose the control system and components. The DRB II is used with chassis diagnostic procedure booklets to isolate the cause of a problem quickly.

Figure 1-21 The Chrysler DRBII scan tool is used to diagnose problems in Chrysler electronic control systems. (Chrysler)

Ford Motor Company units will communicate with its STAR and Super STAR II testers, as well as breakout boxes or pin testers used with its EEC engine management systems. The STAR tester (Figure 1-22) displays system trouble codes on a digital panel. It requires a special adapter cable to connect into the self-

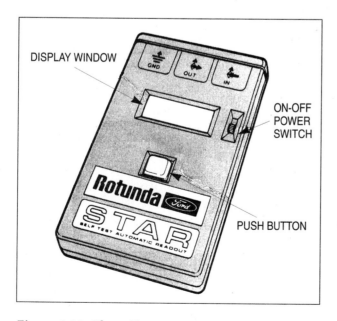

Figure 1-22 The self-test automatic readout (STAR) tester is used to retrieve trouble codes from Ford electronic control systems. (Ford Motor)

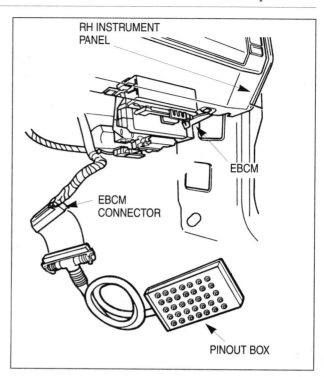

Figure 1-23 A breakout or pinout box connects to the control module and provides multiple test points when troubleshooting the system. (General Motors)

test input, self-test output (STAR) connector, and is powered by an internal 9-volt battery.

Breakout boxes, often called pin testers or pinout boxes (Figure 1-23), connect directly into a sensor circuit and display the actual sensor output—the same voltage signal sent to the microprocessor. They generally are used with quick check sheets (Figure 1-24) to determine the necessary test steps to perform.

Ford introduced the New Generation STAR (NGS) scan tool (Figure 1-25) for use with some 1993 models. By inserting the proper memory card in the slot at the rear of the tool, and connecting it to the vehicle's data link connector, this tester can be programmed to display trouble codes and perform diagnostic tests. Ford plans to expand its capabilities and use with subsequent model years.

The method used to retrieve trouble codes on General Motors vehicles differs according to the control system used. In general, GM

Item to be Tested	Ignition Mode	Measure Between Pin Numbers	Tester Scale/Range	Specification	Test Step
Battery Check	ON	60 + 53	V	10 minimum	A1
Main Relay Coil	ON	53 + 34	Ω	45 to 90 Ω	A3a
Jumper pins 60+34					
Power from Main Relay	ON	19 + 33	V	10 minimum	A2
Remove jumper from pins 60 + 34					
Main Relay Circuit	ON	60 + 33	continuity	continuity	A4
Sensor Resistance (RR)	ON	27 + 45	kΩ	0.8-1.4 kΩ	C3
Sensor Resistance (LF)	ON	30 + 48	kΩ	0.8-1.4 kΩ	C1
Sensor Resistance (LR)	ON	28 + 46	kΩ	0.8-1.4 kΩ	C4
Sensor Resistance (RF)	ON	29 + 47	kΩ	0.8-1.4 kΩ	C2
Valve Resistance (IFL)	OFF	3 + 20	Ω	5-8 Ω	BB2
Valve Resistance (IFR)	OFF	3 + 38	Ω	5-8 Ω	BB4
Valve Resistance (IRL)	OFF	3 + 54	Ω	5-8 Ω	BB8
Valve Resistance (IRR)	OFF	3 + 55	Ω	5-8 Ω	BB6
Valve Resistance (OFL)	OFF	3 + 2	Ω	3-6 Ω	BB3
Valve Resistance (OFR)	OFF	3 + 21	Ω	3-6 Ω	BB5
Valve Resistance (ORR)	OFF	3 + 18	Ω	3-6 Ω	BB7
Valve Resistance (ORL)	OFF	3 + 36	Ω	3-6 Ω	BB9
Reservoir Warning (FLS#2)	OFF	8 + 26	Ω	<5 Ω	A6
Pedal Travel Switch: Pedal NOT Applied	OFF	5 + 26	continuity	continuity	D1
With minimum 3 Inch Apply	OFF	5 + 26	continuity	no continuity	D2
Sensor Cable Continuity Wiring to Ground (RR)	OFF	27 + 60	continuity	no continuity	B2
(LF)	OFF	30 + 60	continuity	no continuity	B4
(LR)	OFF	28 + 60	continuity	no continuity	B1
(RF)	OFF	29 + 60	continuity	no continuity	B3
Sensor Voltage: Rotate wheels (RR)	OFF	27 + 45	AC mV	100-1400 mV	C11
@ 1 revolution (LF)	OFF	30 + 48	AC mV	100-1400 mV	C9
per second. (LR)	OFF	28 + 46	AC mV	100-1400 mV	C12
(RF)	OFF	29 + 47	AC mV	100-1400 mV	C10
Pump Motor Speed Sensor Resistance	OFF	31 + 49	Ω	5-100 Ω	EE7
Valve Resistance (SV1)	OFF	3 + 37	Ω	5-8 Ω	BB10
Valve Resistance (SV2)	OFF	3 + 40	Ω	5-8 Ω	BB11
Pressure Switch (Brake Pedal Not Applied)	OFF	13 + 26	continuity	continuity	K3

Figure 1-24 The quick check sheet used when troubleshooting a Ford electronic control system with the 60-pin breakout box tells you which pins to be checked when measuring a particular circuit and provides the required specifications. (Ford Motor)

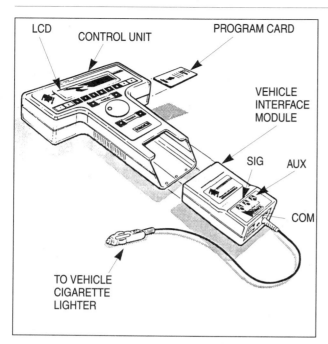

Figure 1-25 The Ford New Generation STAR or NGS tester performs diagnostic tests on Ford electronic control systems. (Ford Motor)

Figure 1-26 Independent tool manufacturers also make scan tools like the OTC Monitor 2000 and 4000 for use in testing electronic control systems.

trouble codes can be retrieved manually through a diagnostic connector and a lamp in the instrument cluster, through a digital display in the Driver Information Center or Fuel Data Center and Climate Control Panel (if so equipped), or with a bidirectional scan tool, such as the Tech 1. While some GM control systems permit the use of multiple retrieval methods, codes in other systems can only be retrieved with a scan tool.

Independent test equipment companies manufacture a variety of special testers called scan tools or scanners (Figure 1-26). Scan tools vary widely in their capabilities, which are contained within their operating software cartridges. They are most useful with GM and Chrysler vehicles because they can monitor the continuous data stream between the engine computer and its sensors and actuators. When properly used, a scan tool can provide information about a component or particular part of a circuit through the digital display on its face.

A digital volt-ohmmeter (DVOM) is required to make electrical checks of the circuits involved in control system operation (Figure 1-27). Electronic circuitry in the DVOM senses current, voltage, or resistance and displays it digitally (Figure 1-28). You should NOT use the older analog volt-ohmmeter with a swinging needle. Electronic circuits operate on very low current of only a few milliamperes. When connected across an electronic circuit, the low input impedance of an analog meter can draw excessive current and may damage the circuit. The DVOM is safe to use because its high input impedance will not harm electronic circuits.

Before testing any electronic circuit, always read the manufacturer's service

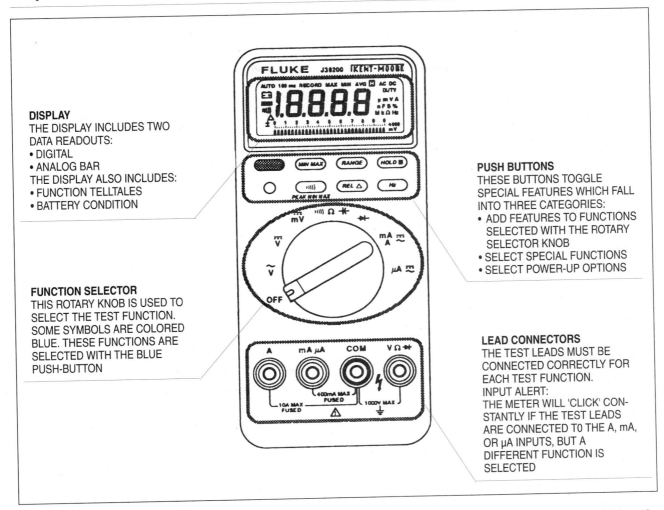

DISPLAY
THE DISPLAY INCLUDES TWO
DATA READOUTS:
• DIGITAL
• ANALOG BAR
THE DISPLAY ALSO INCLUDES:
• FUNCTION TELLTALES
• BATTERY CONDITION

PUSH BUTTONS
THESE BUTTONS TOGGLE
SPECIAL FEATURES WHICH FALL
INTO THREE CATEGORIES:
• ADD FEATURES TO FUNCTIONS
  SELECTED WITH THE ROTARY
  SELECTOR KNOB
• SELECT SPECIAL FUNCTIONS
• SELECT POWER-UP OPTIONS

FUNCTION SELECTOR
THIS ROTARY KNOB IS USED TO
SELECT THE TEST FUNCTION.
SOME SYMBOLS ARE COLORED
BLUE. THESE FUNCTIONS ARE
SELECTED WITH THE BLUE
PUSH-BUTTON

LEAD CONNECTORS
THE TEST LEADS MUST BE
CONNECTED CORRECTLY FOR
EACH TEST FUNCTION.
INPUT ALERT:
THE METER WILL 'CLICK' CON-
STANTLY IF THE TEST LEADS
ARE CONNECTED T0 THE A, mA,
OR µA INPUTS, BUT A
DIFFERENT FUNCTION IS
SELECTED

Figure 1-27 The Fluke 87 is an advanced DVOM for use in checking control system electrical circuits. (General Motors)

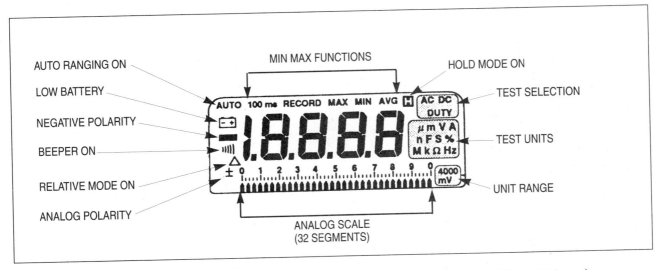

AUTO RANGING ON

LOW BATTERY

NEGATIVE POLARITY

BEEPER ON

RELATIVE MODE ON

ANALOG POLARITY

MIN MAX FUNCTIONS

HOLD MODE ON

TEST SELECTION

TEST UNITS

UNIT RANGE

ANALOG SCALE
(32 SEGMENTS)

Figure 1-28 Some of the many different readings provided by the Fluke 87 digital readout. (General Motors)

manual for the proper procedure and equipment to be used. You will learn more about trouble codes and the use of specialized test equipment in the shop manual chapter on electronic control system diagnosis.

SPECIFICATIONS AND PROCEDURES

Specifications and procedures are additional 'tools of the trade'. Automotive service and repair involves the use of four types of specifications — descriptive, service, operating, and parts.

Descriptive specifications give you general information about a vehicle or its components. If the shop manager tells you to check the air suspension system on a Lincoln Continental in the next stall, he is using a descriptive specification. When the manager suggests the right front wheel pulls to the left, he is using another descriptive specification.

Service specifications tell you something about a component adjustment. A front trailing link bolt torque of 49-69 lbf•ft. is one example. Another example is a caster angle of 1°55'± 55'.

Operating specifications include the recommended type or quantity of lubricant, preventive maintenance intervals, or the resistance range of a sensor or actuator at a given temperature.

Parts specifications identify a specific component or tool by a series of numbers and letters. D78P-5310-A is the tool number specification of a coil spring compressor tool used with Ford single arm front suspensions. N801623-S100 is the part number specification for a Torx head bolt used to secure shock absorbers on some Ford vehicles. You will use one or more types of specifications whenever you work on an automotive suspension or steering system.

A **procedure** is a series of step-by-step instructions used to perform a specific job. In logical order, a procedure directs you in the use of a trouble code to diagnose a control system problem, or how to disassemble and reassemble a front suspension. When using a procedure to disassemble and reassemble a component, you also may have to use specifications. If so, the adjustment specifications may vary according to the vehicle application.

The procedures given throughout this book are general in nature, and can be used for basic diagnosis, service, and overhaul. When servicing a particular system using any service manual, be sure to use a manual that covers the specific year and model of vehicle you are servicing. This is very important, as the service manual for another make and model year of vehicle that uses the same suspension or steering system may contain a different procedure and specifications because of the location of other components. Also, do NOT assume that a later manual may be used to service earlier models unless the manual specifically lists the different years.

REFERENCE MANUALS

Every technician should have a library of reference materials in the form of factory service literature, and manuals available from independent publishers and trade associations. In addition to traditional printed materials, electronic media reference materials are becoming commonplace in shops.

FACTORY SERVICE MANUALS

Each year, vehicle manufacturers publish service manuals for each line of cars and trucks they produce. These publications also are called 'shop' manuals. A manual may cover only a single vehicle line, like all models of the Oldsmobile Cutlass Supreme. Others cover one or more lines, like the Ford Aerostar/Ranger/Explorer manual. Multiple coverage is possible when all of the vehicles are built on the same chassis, using the same powertrains, suspensions, and steering systems, and share many other components.

During the model year, changes in service

procedures and specifications appear in technical service bulletins (TSB) published at specified intervals. Because service manuals are published only once a year, always use the manual for the specific year and model vehicle, along with any applicable TSBs, to be sure you have the latest and most accurate information.

Factory service manuals contain test and repair procedures and complete specifications for all vehicle systems. The service manuals and TSBs are designed for use by dealership service departments, but are available for purchase by vehicle owners and independent repair shops.

Carmakers maintain a national network of service training centers. These training centers offer a regular schedule of classes, and provide training materials in the form of booklets and video tapes. If a manufacturer announces a new electronic control system, its training centers will provide classes for dealership service personnel. The training booklets used in such classes are an excellent source of reference information until the material can be incorporated in the service manual. Although attendance is limited to dealership technicians, independent companies offer similar training courses and seminars for independent shops.

Independent Repair Manuals

Independent publishers compile the service information and specifications of all manufacturers into their own service and repair manuals. In most cases, domestic vehicles will be covered in one volume, with a separate volume for import vehicles. While the procedures are often condensed, the specs are complete.

The value of such manuals is in keeping your library space to a minimum. An independent shop that had every service manual of every manufacturer for a single year would soon have a shop full of books and an empty checkbook.

Major manufacturers of test and shop equipment, as well as automotive suppliers,

often maintain service training facilities. For example, Unocal Oil certifies technicians who work in Unocal stations through its ProTech program. AC-Delco offers similar classes for independent technicians. These facilities function much like the manufacturers' training centers, and provide those who attend with useful information and specifications.

Flat-rate Manuals

Flat-rate manuals are offered by all automotive manufacturers and some independent manual publishers. This type of publication contains a comprehensive listing of various automotive services, and the factory-allowed time to complete them. A flat-rate manual is used by dealerships and independent shops to determine the amount of time necessary to perform specific jobs on a particular vehicle. Flat-rate time is the factory-allowed time in which a skilled repairman should be able to do a particular job. It takes considerable skill and practice to complete a job within the allowed flat rate time. However, a skilled technician who specializes in one particular job can often beat the flat rate time. Time standards are listed in hours and tenths of hours.

It may be necessary to perform other flat-rate jobs to provide access for the main task, such as alternator removal and installation for access to a power steering pump. The manual will list each required sub-task and its flat-rate time. These times must be added to that given for the main job to determine the total time allowed. Shops generally use the flat-rate times shown in the manual to determine a customer's labor charge by multiplying the time by the shop's hourly rate. Carmakers pay dealerships for warranty work based on flat-rate times.

Technicians often are paid a percentage of the flat-rate labor charge. If they can do a job in less than the flat-rate time, they make more money per hour. If they take more than flat-rate time to complete the job, they earn less money per hour. If you are new to the field, you probably will require more than flat-rate time to do a job. However, as you become more experienced, you will find it takes less time to do the same job. It is also easier to work on a fairly new, clean vehicle and stay within the flat-rate time, than to work on an older vehicle whose fasteners are likely to be rusted or frozen.

Critics of the flat-rate system worry that repairs will be done fast and incorrectly, but on a comeback a shop does NOT get paid for correcting work that was not done right. Thus, the technician who did the job, and works for flat-rate wages, does NOT get paid for the rework on a comeback.

Electronic Media Materials

Service, repair, and parts manuals have been available on microfiche for several years now. Use of this technology reduces both storage space requirements and costs to the shop. With the recent development of CD ROM technology, a number of information retrieval systems such as Mitchell's On-Demand and the All-Data systems now can provide the independent shop with service manual and bulletin information that can be displayed on a computer screen.

Other Reference Information

Diagnostic procedures and electrical diagrams are provided in service and repair manuals. Each of these contains information you will need to do your work.

Diagnostic Procedures

Whether provided by the manufacturer or an independent publisher, service manuals contain numbered, step-by-step diagnostic procedures to be followed. These procedures are arranged in a logical manner and allow you to perform the job safely and efficiently.

Test procedures for diagnosis of electronic control systems often are provided in the form of troubleshooting charts or diagrams. These are useful when troubleshooting a problem that has more than one variable, such as determining the most likely cause of a problem when working with an air suspension or shock dampening system.

Troubleshooting charts can be designed in several different ways. The most traditional is a 3-column table (Figure 1-29) that lists a symptom, its possible causes, and corrective steps required. There are several variations of this design, with cause and condition columns, or condition and action columns. The flow chart (Figure 1-30) is another common form, with 'yes/no' or 'pass/fail' decisions at various points. When working on some electronic control systems, you may even use a pictorial troubleshooting chart for many test and repair procedures.

Electrical Diagrams

Circuit diagrams and schematics are a vital part of the troubleshooting reference materials necessary when diagnosing an electronic control system. Sensor input reaches the microcomputer through electrical circuits. Once the microcomputer digests the inputs, it sends signals to the output solenoids through electrical circuits. You must be able to locate and follow these electrical circuits to determine the cause of numerous problems. An electrical diagram or schematic is your road map for diagnosis (Figure 1-31).

CONDITION	POSSIBLE CAUSE	CORRECTIVE ACTION
• Heavy Steering Efforts, Poor Assist or Loss of Assist: A condition recognized by the driver while turning corners and during parking maneuvers	• Low pump fluid • Gear assembly external or internal leakage • Pump external leakage • Improper drive belt tension • Hose or cooler external leakage • Improper engine idle speed • Pulley loose or warped • Pump flow/pressure not to specifications • Hose or cooler line restriction • System contamination • Plugged valve screen	• Fill as required and check for system leaks. • Refer to Section x-xx for Rack and Pinion Power Gear Diagnosis. • Refer to Section x-xx, Pump Diagnosis. • Adjust belt tension. • Service/replace as necessary. • Adjust idle. • Replace pulley. • Refer to Section x-xx • Clean or replace as necessary. • Inspect system for foreign objects, kinked hose, etc. — Flush System — Refer to Section x-xx. • Prior to rebuilding a CII pump, examine the valve screen for contamination. Replace all valves which have plugged or contaminated valve screens.
• Fluid Leakage	• Overfilled system. • Component leakage	• Correct fluid level as required. • Locate suspect component, and refer to appropriate section for service.
• System Noise: Chirp or squeal when steering wheel is cycled lock to lock. • Pump Whine or Moan	• Loose or worn pump belt • Fluid aeration • Low fluid • Pump brackets loose or misaligned • Power steering hose(s) grounded	• Adjust to specification, or replace as required. • Purge system of air. Refer to Purging Procedures in this Section. • Check fluid level. Correct as required. • Check bracket(s), bolt torques, and bracket alignment. Correct as required. • Check for component grounding, and correct as required.
• Other Suspected Pump Noises	• Internal pump discrepancies	• Refer to Section x-xx

Figure 1-29 A traditional 3-column troubleshooting chart. (Ford Motor)

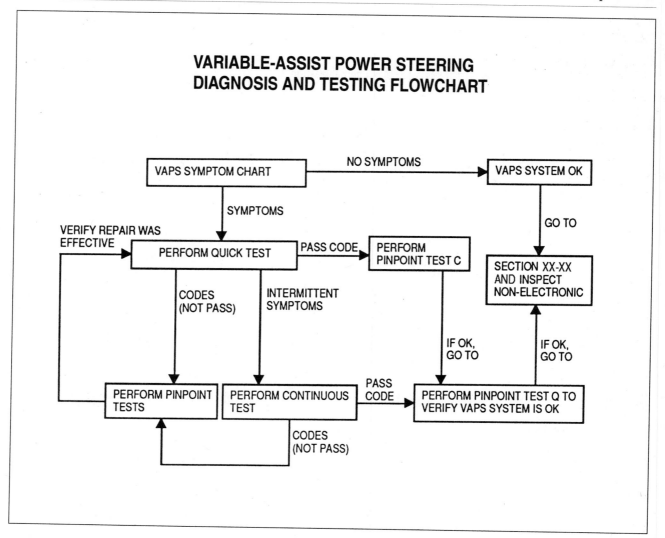

Figure 1-30 A troubleshooting chart arranged in the familiar flow chart pattern walks you through a diagnostic procedure. (Ford Motor)

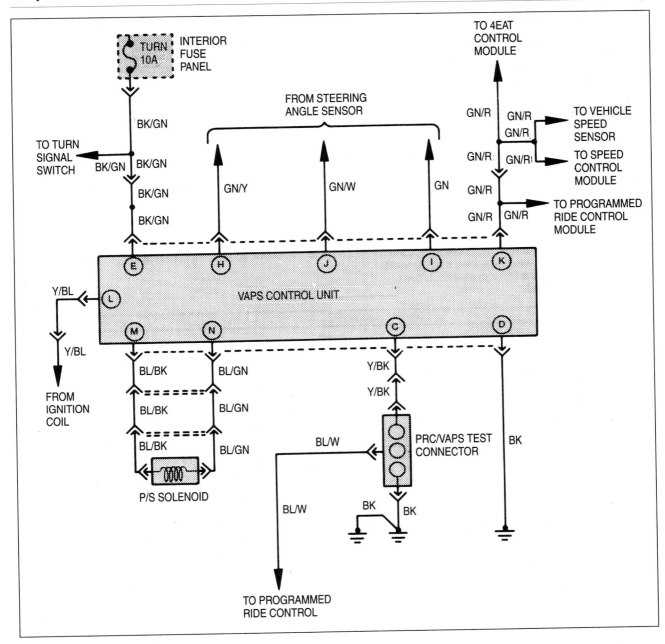

Figure 1-31 A typical Ford electronic control system electrical schematic. (Ford Motor)

? REVIEW QUESTIONS

1. All of the following statements are correct EXCEPT:
   (A) A good automotive technician thinks safety.
   (B) Cleanliness is very important when dealing with hydraulic systems.
   (C) Keep all parts in order of removal to help in reassembly.
   (D) Clean up all fluid spills at the end of each day.

2. Technician A says that you should wear protective gloves and safety glasses when grinding or cleaning parts. Technician B says parts should be wiped dry with shop cloths after cleaning. Who is right?
   (A) Technician A
   (B) Technician B
   (C) Both A and B
   (D) Neither A nor B

3. Small parts that will NOT clean up in the solvent tank should be cleaned in:
   (A) water.
   (B) the parts cleaner bucket.
   (C) the hot tank.
   (D) the steam cleaner.

4. Technician A says that a bumper jack can be used to make a quick inspection of the control arm ball joints without using safety stands. Technician B says it is NOT safe to work around a vehicle with the engine running if its exhaust is connected to shop exhaust ducts. Who is right?
   (A) Technician A
   (B) Technician B
   (C) Both A and B
   (D) Neither A nor B

5. Technician A says that a high-impedance digital volt-ohmmeter must be used to check electronic circuits. Technician B says that an analog volt-ohmmeter can be used. Who is right?
   (A) Technician A
   (B) Technician B
   (C) Both A and B
   (D) Neither A nor B

6. Technician A says most electronic control systems have a trouble code function for diagnosing problems. Technician B says the code function of some control modules must be accessed with special diagnostic testers. Who is right?
   (A) Technician A
   (B) Technician B
   (C) Both A and B
   (D) Neither A nor B

7. Descriptive specifications provide:
   (A) information on parts interchangeability.
   (B) step-by-step instructions.
   (C) general information.
   (D) information on component adjustment.

8. Troubleshooting charts and diagrams are useful because they give you:
   (A) warranty labor cost allowances.
   (B) the estimated time required to do a job.
   (C) easily followed pictures.
   (D) a method of dealing with numerous variables.

9. Service specifications provide:
   (A) information on component adjustment.
   (B) general information.
   (C) information on parts interchangeability.
   (D) step-by-step instructions.

10. Technician A says that diagnostic procedures help estimate the time required for a job. Technician B says that electrical diagrams are useful in locating specific electrical circuits in an electronic control system. Who is right?
    (A) Technician A
    (B) Technician B
    (C) Both A and B
    (D) Neither A nor B

11. When you select a special tool to check wheel and tire runout, you are using:
    (A) service and operating specifications.
    (B) descriptive and operating specifications.

(C) service and parts specifications.

(D) descriptive and parts specifications.

12. Procedures contain:

    (A) information on parts interchangeability.

    (B) step-by-step instructions.

    (C) general information.

    (D) information on component adjustment.

13. Technician A says that flat-rate is a suggested factory time to complete a job. Technician B says that it is the maximum time required for a job. Who is right?

    (A) Technician A

(B) Technician B

(C) Both A and B

(D) Neither A nor B

14. Technician A says that factory service manuals contain the latest procedures and specifications. Technician B says that technical service bulletins should be consulted for the latest specifications. Who is right?

    (A) Technician A

    (B) Technician B

    (C) Both A and B

    (D) Neither A nor B

SERVICING WHEELS AND TIRES

 OBJECTIVES

After completion of this chapter, you should be able to:

- Remove and install a wheel/tire assembly following the specified procedure and observing all appropriate safety rules.

- Define radial and lateral runout.

- Balance correctly a wheel/tire assembly off the vehicle.

- Perform a visual check and correctly indicate the faulty wheel/tire, given a vehicle with one wheel/tire that has a runout problem.

- Measure correctly the wheel/tire runout on a spin-type wheel balancer.

- Explain the concept of vectoring as a means of correcting runout problems.

- Visually inspect a tire mounted on a vehicle and report your findings to the instructor.

- Dismount, inspect, and correctly remount the tire on the wheel, given a wheel/tire assembly and the proper equipment.

SERVICING WHEEL AND TIRE ASSEMBLIES

Wheels and tires often require separate service, but are so closely related that we will begin by considering them as a unit. Certain procedures, such as removal and installation, wheel balance, or checking runout specifications, involve both components.

REMOVAL

Wheels are mounted to the hubs with studs. To make sure the wheel and hub surfaces mate properly when the wheel is secured in place, the wheel's mounting holes are machined with tapered seats to match the tapered lug nuts.

> **TECH TIP:** Some aftermarket wheels are mounted with a flat lug nut and washer. The washer must fit into a corresponding flat in the wheel mounting boss.

S 25

To remove a wheel/tire assembly from a vehicle:

1. Remove any trim ring, hubcap, or wheel cover from the wheel with a wide bladed screwdriver or hubcap tool, being careful NOT to scratch or chip the paint on the wheel. Some wheel covers may be equipped with anti-theft locking systems (Figure 2-1). Be sure to use the correct tools when working with such wheel covers to avoid damaging the locking mechanism.

2. Some vehicles, usually very expensive performance cars, may have had their wheels balanced on the car because of extreme sensitivity to any unbalance. The car owner can usually tell you if this is the case. On those vehicles, unless the tire is to be rotated, replaced, or repaired, make chalk marks on the wheel and the end of the lug nut stud nearest the tire valve stem. If the valve stem is located between two lug nuts, mark both studs. This enables you to reinstall the wheel in its original location on the vehicle without a change in its balance. Since all ordinary wheel balancing is done off the car, marking the studs is usually not necessary.

3. Loosen the wheel lug nuts with an appropriate lug wrench or six-point lug nut socket. This step is not necessary if you are going to remove the lug nuts with a power impact wrench.

4. Raise the end of the vehicle from which the wheel is to be removed with a jack and support it safely on stands made for that purpose.

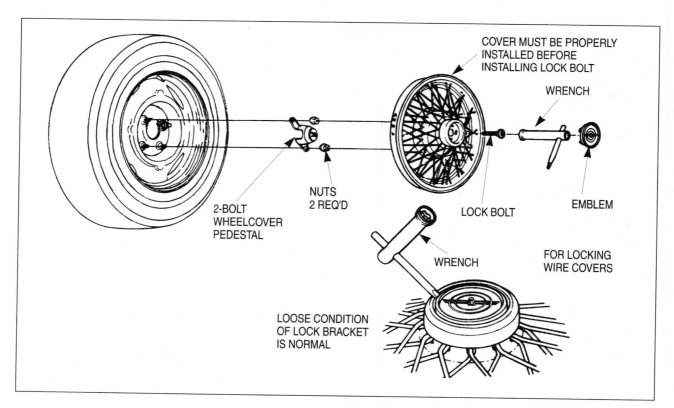

Figure 2-1 Some types of wheel trim are equipped with anti-theft locking devices and should NOT be removed without the proper tools. (Ford Motor)

> **TIP TECH TIP:** If you are not familiar with the vehicle, check the carmaker's shop manual for lifting points to determine where the jack and stands should be placed before raising the vehicle. Raising the rear of some FWD vehicles by placing the jack at the center of the axle can cause the rear axle to bend. Know what you are doing before you do it.

5. Finish removing the lug nuts, either by hand or with a power impact wrench.

> **TIP TECH TIP:** Some imported vehicles use a lug bolt to attach the wheel instead of the more conventional wheel stud and lug nut. The tapered bolt head replaces the lug nut on such vehicles.

6. Remove the wheel/tire assembly from the vehicle.

You may encounter a wheel that will NOT come off the vehicle after the lug nuts have been removed. This is caused either by corrosion or a tight fit between the center hole of the wheel and the hub or disc. Avoid the use of penetrating oil, heat, or excessive hammering to loosen a tight wheel. Although penetrating oil can be effective on occasion, any oil that gets on the vertical surfaces between the wheel and drum or disc can cause the wheel to work loose when the vehicle is driven after wheel installation. Applying heat to the wheel or excessive hammering on the wheel or tire can adversely affect the life of the wheel, studs, or hubs and bearing assemblies.

Use the following procedure to remove a tight wheel without damage:

1. Retighten the wheels snug, but NOT to full torque, on the problem wheel, then loosen each nut two full turns.

2. Lower the vehicle to the ground.

3. With at least two people helping, rock the vehicle from side-to-side to loosen the wheel. The more helpers you can enlist for this step, the more likely the wheel will loosen quickly.

4. If Step 3 does NOT work, start the engine and shift the vehicle from 'drive' to 'reverse', allowing it to move several feet in each direction while you apply the brake pedal with quick, sharp jabs to loosen the wheel. Remember that the problem wheel or wheels are loose, so do NOT move the vehicle more than a few feet.

5. Raise the vehicle in the air and reinstall the safety stands. Remove the lug nuts, then remove the wheel/tire assembly.

INSPECTION

With the wheel/tire assembly removed from the vehicle, visually inspect the wheel for signs of heavy rust, warpage, dents, and worn or elongated holes in the wheel nut bosses. If any of these defects are noted, replace the wheel. When excessive lateral or radial runout is suspected, check runout as described in this chapter. Clean any corrosion buildup from the wheel, brake drum, or disc mounting surfaces with a wire brush, steel wool, or other suitable material.

INSTALLATION

1. Fit the wheel over the wheel studs, aligning the chalk marks made during removal.

2. Manually install the lug nuts and tighten them finger tight.

3. Make sure the tapered part of the lug nut enters the tapered opening in the wheel nut boss.

4. Tighten the remaining lug nuts with a hand wrench, making sure the tapers

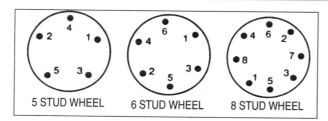

Figure 2-2 Wheel nut tightening numbered sequences. (Ford Motor)

engage correctly. Snug all lug nuts enough to hold the tire in the correct position. If you have a power impact wrench, final tightening may be done with the vehicle still on stands. Be sure to tighten each nut partially using a star-shaped or criss-cross pattern (Figure 2-2), then continue the pattern while applying full torque from the impact wrench. The impact wrench must have a torque limiting device or air pressure regulator to avoid overtightening. Using an extension bar between the socket and the wrench will reduce the applied torque because the bar twists and absorbs some of the force. Some carmakers suggest using a special extension bar called a torque stick, to prevent overtightening.

WARNING: Make sure all lug nuts are tightened evenly to the correct torque. Overtightening is serious because it may prevent the car owner from removing the wheel with the lug wrench that comes with the vehicle. Over-tightened lug nuts can also cause wheel or brake disc distortion and vibration at highway speeds and may damage the wheel tapered seats, lug nuts, hub, brake drums, or discs. Under-tightened nuts can back off their studs, allowing the wheel to wobble and possibly slide off the hub while rotating.

5. If you are hand tightening, lower the vehicle to the ground and tighten the lug nuts to the specified torque using a star-shaped or criss-cross pattern.

WHEEL AND TIRE BALANCING

Correct balance of the wheel/tire assemblies is extremely important because of their effect on the steering and suspension systems. The wheels and tires rotate as assemblies, with the tires cushioning the ride, developing traction, and providing firm support to the vehicle. The tires also absorb the stress of acceleration, braking, and centrifugal force during cornering. A wheel/tire that is out-of-balance, or heavier at any one point, will vibrate at highway speeds. Since the front wheels are a part of the suspension and steering systems, any vibrations caused by wheel rotation will be transmitted to both systems, affecting directional control and handling, as well as the service life of suspension and steering components.

Wheel and tire balance is corrected by the use of additional weight attached to the wheel rim across from heavy spots in the assembly. A wheel balancer machine indicates the amount of weight required and where to place it. These weights are available in one-quarter ounce increments and are provided in several clip-on designs for use with steel and aluminum rims. Be sure that you have the correct weight for the wheel. A weight with the wrong clip may go on, but it will soon fly off because the clip isn't designed to fit the wheel. Premolded stick-on weights are used with alloy rims. A wheel weight tool or hammer is used to install or remove the clip-on weights.

STATIC VS. DYNAMIC BALANCE

There are two types of balance — static or single-plane balance, and dynamic or two-plane balance. Static balance is concerned

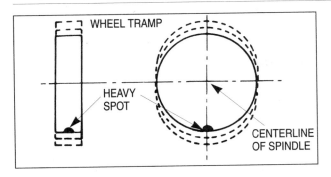

Figure 2-3 Static imbalance. (Chrysler)

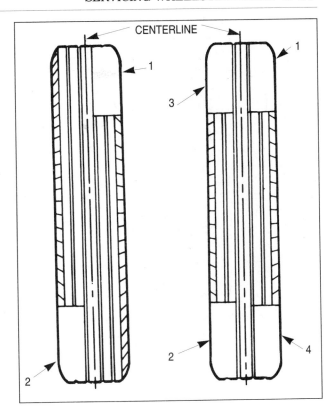

Figure 2-4 Dynamic balance. (Chrysler)

with the weight distribution around the wheel circumference (one-plane). When a wheel in static balance is raised off the ground, it should NOT rotate by itself. If it does, the wheel is out-of-balance and will rotate until the heaviest spot is at the bottom. When the vehicle is driven, centrifugal force acting on the heavy spot of a statically imbalanced wheel causes a vertical or bouncing motion of the wheel (sometimes called 'tramp' or 'hop') as it rotates (Figure 2-3). The greater the degree of imbalance, the lower the speed at which this bouncing motion will occur.

Dynamic balance means balance on each side of the wheel/tire centerline (two-plane). A wheel/tire that is in static balance is NOT necessarily in dynamic balance. If static balance is obtained by placing weights in segments 1 and 2 (Figure 2-4), the wheel/tire will wobble or shimmy as it rotates. Since the weights are on opposite sides of the center point, the wheel/tire wobbles each half revolution as the weights try to align with the rotation center or spindle. Weights installed in segments 3 and 4 will compensate for this dynamic imbalance without affecting static balance.

> **TIP TECH TIP:** In general, vehicles are more sensitive to static imbalance. As little as 1/2 to 3/4 of an ounce can induce a vibration with some vehicles.

BALANCING MACHINES

Wheel/tire assemblies can be balanced on the vehicle or off the vehicle. A computerized off-vehicle balancer that spins the wheel is the type used in most shops. Although there are many types of off- and on-vehicle balancers available, we will discuss only those most commonly used.

Off-Vehicle Balancers

The simplest off-vehicle balancer is a single-plane static balancer called a bubble balancer because it uses a spirit level with a bubble (Figure 2-5). The bubble balancer was very popular in the past because it could be moved wherever necessary with little effort and was relatively inexpensive, simple to use, and reasonably accurate. To use a bubble balancer, set the control lever to the 'off' position and adjust the legs of the unit until the spirit level bubble is

Figure 2-5 Bubble balancers use a spirit level (arrow) to determine how much weight is necessary and where it should be attached.

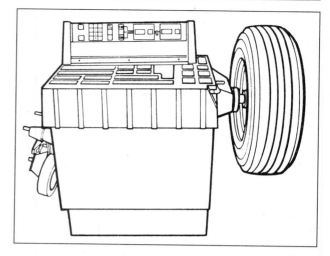

Figure 2-6 A computerized spin-type off-vehicle wheel balancer. (General Motors)

centered. Align the tire's valve stem with a mark on the face of the spirit level and place the assembly on the balancer. When the control lever is moved to the 'on' position, the balancer head and wheel/tire will pivot as the heavier part of the tire lowers and the bubble moves off-center toward the lightest side. Place enough weight on the tire bead at the bubble to balance the tire and mark the tire sidewall with chalk or a tire crayon. Move the lever to the 'off' position or remove the wheel/tire from the balancer so that hammering the weights in place will NOT damage the balancer. Attach one-half of the weight to the inside of the tire rim at the chalk mark. Realign the valve stem with the level mark so that the wheel is in the same position as before and reinstall the wheel/tire on the balancer. Putting the wheel in exactly the same position avoids any slight difference in balance caused by wheel position. Place the other half of the weight at the chalk mark to see if the wheel is still in balance.

If NOT, increase or decrease the weight until balance is obtained. When balance is achieved, attach the weight to the wheel rim. Recheck the balance and remove the wheel/tire from the balancer.

Modern off-vehicle balancers are computerized spin-type, two-plane balancers (Figure 2-6). After mounting the wheel/tire assembly with the proper adapters, the computer must be programmed with certain information about the wheel and tire (machine-to-rim distance, rim width, wheel diameter, etc.) by entering it through the keyboard. Once the information has been entered and the start button

TECH TIP: To avoid incorrect readings when using a spin-type off-vehicle wheel balancer, make sure the wheel locates on the balancer with the correct size cone through the center pilot hole, as shown in the machine instructions. It is possible to mount a wheel on the machine without using the proper cone, but this will NOT give correct balance because the wheel is not centered properly.

depressed, the balancer will go into a short spin cycle and stop. The control panel display gives a readout of where and how much weight should be added to each side of the wheel.

When using a computerized balancer to balance a wheel/tire off the vehicle, make sure the machine is properly calibrated. These machines can drift out of calibration or lose their accuracy due to heavy use. A balancer machine can indicate that the wheel/tire is in balance when in fact, it is NOT. A quick calibration check of most such machines used in shops can be performed with the following procedure:

1. With all adapters removed from the machine, spin the balancer and note the reading. It should be zero ±1/4 oz (6.5 grams).

2. Install a previously balanced wheel/tire assembly with the proper adapters on the shaft. The wheel/tire used should be within radial and lateral runout tolerances. Spin the wheel and check the balance, which should be okay and NOT require any weight. If necessary, balance the wheel.

3. To the perfectly balanced wheel add a three-ounce (85 grams) test weight to the wheel and spin the balancer. The machine reading should specify the addition of three ounces (85 grams) of weight in both static and dynamic modes at a position 180° from the test weight.

4. Remove the test weight, reattach it in a different spot and make the same test five more times. The five readings should not vary by more than 1/4 oz (6.5 grams).

5. Move the position of the wheel on the balancer shaft to four separate locations 90 degrees apart. Run the machine after each change of wheel/tire location and note the

results. The readings obtained during this step should not vary more than 1/4 oz (6.5 grams).

6. If the balancer fails any of the steps above, have it checked by the manufacturer to determine the problem.

TECH TIP: A balancer should be recalibrated every 15 days, or whenever the readings are questionable. Read the machine instructions for proper calibration. Most late model machines have a pre-programmed calibration that is done automatically.

On-Vehicle Balancers

Mechanical on-vehicle balancers are single-plane spin-type units that attach to the wheel with an adapter (Figure 2-7). Non-drive wheels are rotated with the use of a wheel spinner. Driven wheel/tire assemblies are spun using the engine. Internal weights in the balancer head are adjusted while the wheel/tire is spinning (Figure 2-8). When the wheel/tire spins without vibration, the assembly is stopped. Slowly rotate the tire until the balancer arrow points upward. The balancer window will

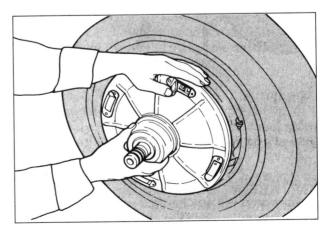

Figure 2-7 A typical mechanical on-wheel balancer installed on the wheel with adaptor. (Ford Motor)

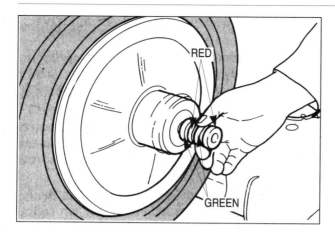

Figure 2-8 Colored knobs (4) on the balancer are used to adjust internal weights that determine the correct position and size of weight to be used. (Ford Motor)

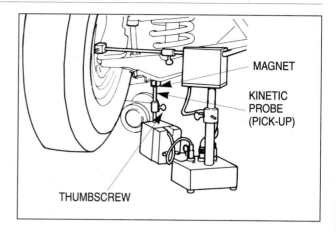

Figure 2-10 An electronic balancer uses a static pickup probe magnetically attached to the underside of the suspension. (Ford Motor)

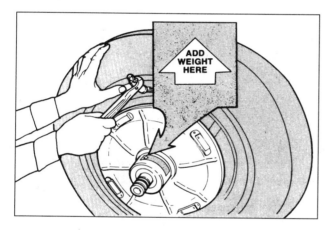

Figure 2-9 The balancer scale indicate the amount and location of weights necessary to balance the wheel. (Ford Motor)

pickup unit (Figure 2-11) senses side to side or dynamic imbalance. The strobe unit is placed on the floor about one foot from the wheel with the light facing the wheel (Figure 2-12). Suspension or brake backing plate vibrations cause the strobe light to flash, making the spinning wheel/tire appear to be stationary. The position of the wheel, indicated by the chalk mark, shows where the heavy spot is,

indicate the amount of weight to be added to the top of the wheel rim (Figure 2-9). If the required weight exceeds 3 oz (85 grams), add one-half of the weight to the outside of the rim and the other one-half to the inside of the rim.

The electronic or strobe light balancer is a two-plane spin-type unit. It senses static imbalance through a pickup unit that sits on the floor and is attached to the suspension with a magnet (Figure 2-10). The wheel must be chalk marked so the light will show wheel position. A separate

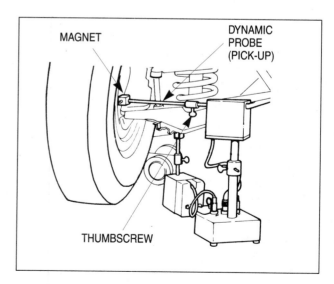

Figure 2-11 The electronic balancer also uses a dynamic pickup placed against the brake backing plate. (Ford Motor)

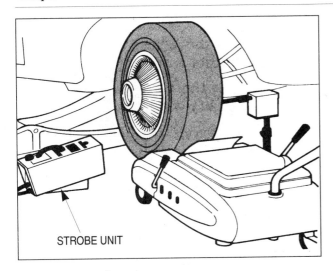

STROBE UNIT

Figure 2-12 The electronic balancer strobe light faces the wheel and flashes when the pickups sense vibration. (Ford Motor)

and the weight is added directly opposite. An indicator dial reading on the unit gives the approximate amount of weight required. Like the mechanical balancer, a wheel spinner is necessary when balancing non-drive wheels; driven wheels are spun with the engine.

Computerized on-vehicle balancers are two-plane spin-type units that combine the operating principles of the strobe light balancer with the digital readout of weight location and amount of the computerized off-vehicle balancer.

BALANCING PRECAUTIONS

- When doing an on-vehicle balance on an FWD vehicle, do not let the front suspension hang free. FWD vehicles use constant velocity (CV) joints in the drivetrain. When CV joints are run at very high angles, additional vibrations are created and damage to the joints and seals can result.
- Do NOT remove the balance weights from an off-vehicle dynamic balance when on-vehicle balancing. You want to fine-tune the balance already obtained, NOT to start all over.

- Do NOT spin one drive wheel with the other wheel on the ground if the vehicle is equipped with a posi-traction or limited-slip differential. The vehicle may move unexpectedly and drive off the safety stands.
- When one drive wheel is spinning and the other wheel is stopped, do NOT spin the drive wheels in excess of 35 mph (56 km/h) as indicated by the speedometer. In this situation, the speedometer indicates only one-half of the actual wheel speed.
- If the vehicle is equipped with a posi-traction or limited-slip differential and you are performing an on-vehicle balance of the rear wheels, remove the wheel/tire assembly not being balanced from the axle. Leave the drum in place and reinstall the wheel lug nuts. Balance the remaining wheel, then reinstall and balance the wheel you removed.
- Before balancing a wheel/tire assembly, clean the inside of the wheel to remove any foreign material. Remove all stones and debris from the tread to obtain a true balance. Inspect the tire for signs of any damage. If none are found, balance the assembly according to the equipment manufacturer's procedure.

> **TIP TECH TIP:** If a solid locking lug nut is used in place of a standard lug nut, install it next to the valve stem and add a 1/2 oz (14 grams) balance weight 180° from the locking nut on the inside of the wheel. When rotating the tires, always use the locking nut next to the valve stem to keep it 180° from the balance weight. This method of compensating for the locking nut will improve on-vehicle wheel balance.

OFF-VEHICLE VS. ON-VEHICLE BALANCING

As a rule, electronic off-vehicle balancers (Figure 2-6) are more accurate than the on-vehicle spin balancers. Since most off-vehicle balancers will perform dynamic as well as static balancing, off-vehicle balancing is recommended because the balance is NOT affected when the tires are rotated. Also, off-vehicle computerized balancers are much easier to use in a tire shop because the wheels are already off the vehicle to put on the new tires.

On-vehicle balancers do NOT provide a true dynamic balance unless they specify exactly how much weight should go inside and how much outside. Simply splitting the weight half and half between inside and outside is a valid precaution so that the dynamic balance is NOT affected, but is NOT really dynamic balance. However, in defense of on-vehicle balancers, they were used for many years on millions of wheels before computerized dynamic off-vehicle balancers were available. The big advantage of on-vehicle balancers is that you can see the results. As a vibrating, shaking wheel becomes as smooth as glass, it is obvious that the balance job has been done correctly.

Hub, drums, and discs also can cause imbalance. If an off-wheel balance does NOT correct vibration problems, perform an on-vehicle high-speed balance to determine if these components are properly balanced. Use the following procedure to check RWD brake drums and FWD discs for imbalance:

1. Support the driving axle with an appropriate hoist or safety stands.
2. Remove the wheel/tire assemblies from the driving axle and reinstall the lug nuts to hold the drums or discs in place.
3. Start the engine and run it at the vibration complaint speed, taking care NOT to overheat the engine.
4. If the vibration is present, remove both drums or discs and run the engine up to speed again.
5. If there is no vibration in Step 4, retest with one drum or disc at a time to locate the defective component.
6. Before installing the new drum or disc, check it for imbalance.

If the procedure above does not correct the vibration, mount the wheel/tire assemblies on the vehicle and use an on-vehicle high-speed spin balancer to balance the hubs, drums or discs, and wheels at the same time. On a strobe balancer the wheel covers or trim rings may also be installed so that the wheel spins exactly the way it does during driving. Covers and trim may have to be removed to install the weights. If the covers or trim do NOT locate on the valve stem, be sure to put them back in the same position. Use the procedure specified by the balancer manufacturer, but do NOT remove the off-vehicle balance weights. If the on-vehicle balance requires more than two ounces (56 grams) of extra weight, split the additional weight between the inner and outer wheel flanges to maintain the dynamic balance obtained during the off-vehicle balance.

> **TIP TECH TIP:** Wheel trim can induce static imbalance in some cases. This is particularly true of wire wheel covers. If the wheel cannot be balanced with the trim in place, road test the vehicle or spin the wheel with it removed to eliminate it as a possible cause of vibrations.

WHEEL AND TIRE RUNOUT

Runout is a term used to describe abnormal up-and-down (radial) or side-to-side (lateral) movement of the wheel/tire

Figure 2-13 Radial runout.

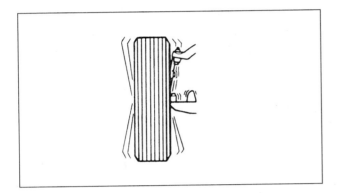

Figure 2-14 Lateral runout.

assembly. Radial runout results in an egg-shaped or oval rotation instead of a perfect circle (Figure 2-13). Lateral runout is a horizontal variation that causes the wheel/tire to twist or wobble (Figure 2-14). Runout has a direct effect on imbalance and radial force variation. The radial force is the amount that unbalanced or out of round tires push outward in a radial direction. The smaller the amount of runout, the less imbalance and force variation or vibrations will occur. Since runout consists of a tire or wheel that is not perfectly round, correcting a runout condition generally involves one of the following:

- wheel or tire remounting
- wheel or tire replacement
- wheel bearing replacement
- hub replacement

A quick visual check often can confirm the presence of runout by simply lifting the vehicle off the ground and spinning the suspect wheel/tire assembly. Watch the tire rotate relative to a stationary object. If the tire seems to move during rotation, runout measurements should be taken with a dial indicator and fixture. You can also perform this visual check with the wheel/tire assembly mounted on a tire balancing machine. If measured on the vehicle, the wheel bearings must be in good condition and properly adjusted. When measured off the vehicle, use a spin-type tire balancer and rotate the wheel by hand.

MEASURING RUNOUT

Before you measure runout or attempt to correct excessive runout, always check the tire carefully for an uneven bead seat (Figure 2-15). This is usually caused by mounting a tire without bead lubricant. Make sure the distance from the edge of the

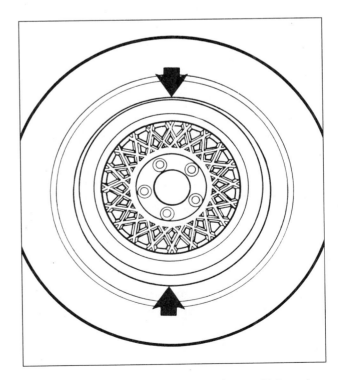

Figure 2-15 Improper bead seating. (General Motors)

rim to the concentric rim locating ring is equal around the entire circumference of the tire. Remount the tire with bead lubricant if the beads are not seated correctly.

1. Check tire pressure and inflate to specifications, if necessary.

2. Drive the vehicle long enough to warm up the tires. This will eliminate any flat spots that exist when the vehicle has been sitting in one place for a length of time.

3. Lift the vehicle on a hoist or raise with a hydraulic jack and support safely with stands made for that purpose.

4. Spin each wheel/tire by hand to visually check for runout.

5. Mark the location of suspect wheel/tire assemblies relative to the wheel studs and to their position on the vehicle for reinstallation reference.

6. Remove the suspect wheel/tire assemblies one at a time and mount on a spin-type wheel balancer. Use a cone through the center pilot hole to correctly locate the wheel/tire assembly on the balancer.

7. Install a dial indicator with a roller contact point (Figure 2-16) to measure tire runout as shown in Figure 2-17.

Figure 2-16 The dial indicator used for checking runout should have a roller wheel instead of the conventional plunger tip. (Chrysler)

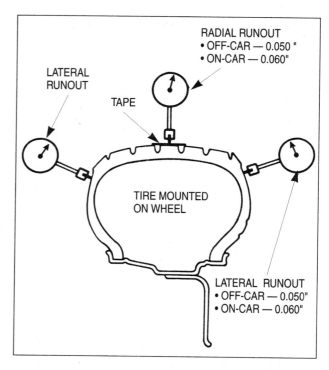

Figure 2-17 Measuring radial and lateral runout of the wheel/tire assembly. (General Motors)

TIP TECH TIP: Before measuring radial runout on tires without a continuous rib, wrap the center of the tread with tape to provide a flat surface for the dial indicator roller. When measuring lateral runout, position the indicator to contact a smooth area of the sidewall as near the tread as possible. Ignore any indentations in the sidewall caused by normal ply splices and determine the average amount of runout.

8. Slowly rotate the wheel/tire one complete revolution and set the dial indicator to zero on the low spot. Mark the location of the low point on the tire.

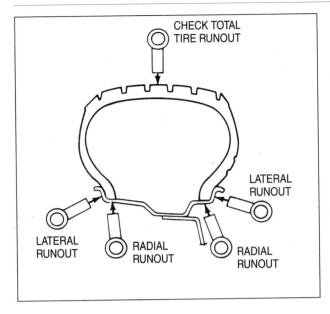

Figure 2-18 Measuring wheel runout at the wheel bead seats. (General Motors)

9. Slowly rotate the assembly another complete revolution and record the total amount of runout indicated. Mark the location of the high point of runout on the tire. Compare the reading to the carmaker's specifications.

10. Reposition the dial indicator to measure wheel runout at the wheel bead seats as shown in Figure 2-18.

11. Repeat Step 8 and Step 9. Mark the location of the high point of runout on the rim and compare the reading to the carmaker's specifications.

VECTORING

If the runout measurements are excessive, you must determine whether the problem exists in the wheel, tire, or a combination of both before you can correct it. The procedure used to make this determination is called vectoring or match-mounting. It consists of measuring carefully to determine where the high and low spots are, and then remounting so the tire high spot corresponds with the wheel low spot.

1. Mark the tire sidewall at the tire stem. This is called the 12:00 position. The location of the high spot is referred to relative to its 'clock location' on the wheel.

2. Install the wheel/tire on a tire machine. Deflate the tire and break loose the tire bead, but do NOT remove the tire from the wheel.

3. Rotate the tire 180 degrees on the rim until the valve stem reference mark is at 6:00 relative to the valve stem. Reinflate the tire and use lubricant, making sure the bead is seated properly.

4. Reinstall the wheel/tire assembly on the tire balancer and remeasure the runout. Mark the new location of the runout high point on the tire:

   a. If runout is now within specifications, balance the tire and remount on the vehicle.

   b. If the high spot remains the same (Figure 2-19), the wheel is probably at fault. Remove the tire and remeasure the wheel for excessive runout. Replace the wheel if required.

   c. If the high spot moves to a position approximately 180° from the original high spot (Figure 2-20), replace the tire.

5. If the high spot moves to a point between the two extremes, both wheel and tire are contributing to the problem. Rotate the tire on the wheel another 90° in both clockwise and counterclockwise directions. Mea-

TECH TIP: When replacing an old wheel with a new one, do NOT assume that the new wheel is within runout specifications. ALWAYS measure the replacement wheel for runout before using it.

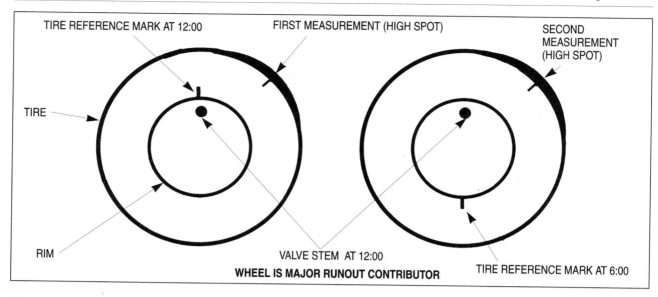

Figure 2-19 Vectoring — The high spot remains the same. (General Motors)

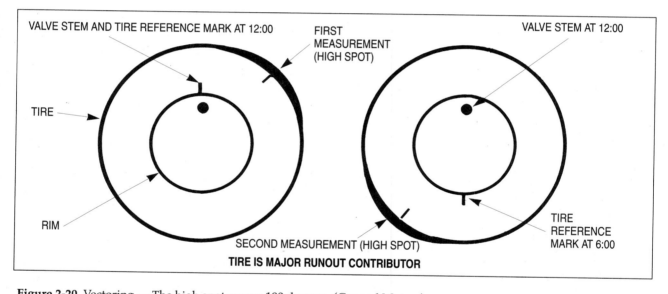

Figure 2-20 Vectoring — The high spot moves 180 degrees. (General Motors)

sure runout after each rotation to pinpoint whether the wheel or tire is the major problem. If this does not clarify the cause, it may be necessary to replace both wheel and tire.

6. If vectoring does not bring runout within specifications, remove the tire from the wheel and measure wheel rim runout on the inside bead area of the wheel as shown in Figure 2-21.

a. If wheel runout is beyond the carmaker's specification, replace the wheel.
b. If wheel runout is within specifications, but the wheel/tire runout cannot be brought to an acceptable level by vectoring, replace the tire.
c. If runout cannot be reduced to an acceptable level, check wheel stud circle runout and wheel hub/axle flange runout as described below.

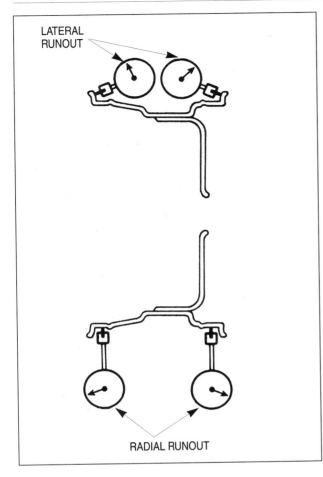

Figure 2-21 Wheel rim runout is more accurately measured on the inside bead area of the wheel. (General Motors)

Vectoring is the preferred method of correcting a properly balanced tire that causes a vibration. Another method is called 'truing' the tire. When a tire is trued, a machine is used to remove rubber from the high spots in an effort to return the tire to a perfectly circular condition. Using a blade-type machine to true the tire reduces the tread life somewhat and does not always correct the problem permanently. Another method of truing is to buff small amounts of rubber from high spots in the outer two tread rows. When done correctly, this method will NOT affect tread life and generally is a permanent solution to the problem.

WHEEL STUD CIRCLE RUNOUT

If the radial runout differs significantly between off-vehicle and on-vehicle measurements, but other attempts to correct a wheel/tire vibration problem have NOT worked, follow the procedure below to check stud circle runout:

1. Install a suitable dial indicator with an appropriate fixture to contact the wheel mounting studs (Figure 2-22).

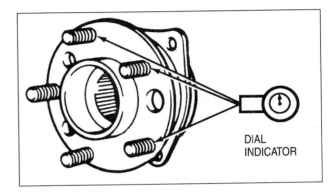

Figure 2-22 Measuring wheel stud runout. (General Motors)

2. Position the indicator button against one of the wheel studs and set it to zero.
3. Carefully lift the indicator button from the stud and rotate the hub flange to position the next stud against the indicator button.
4. Repeat Step 3 with each remaining stud, recording the runout on each stud. The indicator dial should read zero when repositioned on the stud checked in Step 2.
5. Compare your readings with the carmaker's specifications. Generally, stud runout measurements of 0.010" are acceptable; replace the hub or axle shaft if runout exceeds 0.030".

WHEEL HUB/AXLE FLANGE RUNOUT

Lateral runout of the wheel/tire assembly that can be measured on the vehicle, but

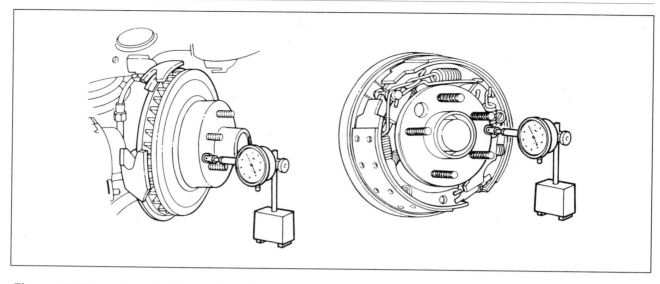

Figure 2-23 Measuring wheel hub and axle flange runout. (General Motors)

does NOT appear in off-vehicle testing, is an indication of possible hub/axle flange runout. To check for this condition:

1. Install a roller-type dial indicator with an appropriate fixture to contact the machined surface of the hub, axle flange, or disc on the area outside the wheel studs (Figure 2-23).
2. Slowly rotate the hub to locate the low spot, then set the indicator dial to zero.
3. Rotate the hub one complete revolution to check the total amount of runout. Most carmakers consider 0.005" runout as acceptable.

TIRE SERVICE

Tires support a vehicle, cushion the ride, and develop traction. In addition, they absorb the stresses of acceleration, braking, and cornering forces. To perform these functions satisfactorily, they must be properly maintained. If NOT, they can make the vehicle unsafe to drive.

DIAGNOSIS

Inspect the tires before trying to diagnosis a wheel/tire problem. This tire inspection should include:

- an inflation pressure check
- a visual inspection
- tread depth measurement

Make sure the tires are inflated to their recommended pressure. Tire inflation specifications generally are found on a decal on the driver's front door jamb, inside the glovebox door, or on the inner side of the trunk lid. During the visual inspection, look for signs of uneven wear (Figure 2-24). Tires can be further evaluated by running a hand over the tread to detect feathered edges (Figure 2-25). A feathered edge pointing out means there is too much toe-out. If it points in, there is too much toe-in. Cupped or scalloped tread wear can be confirmed by running your hand lengthwise along the tread. Use a tread depth gauge to measure tire wear (Figure 2-26).

Tire wear patterns (Figure 2-24) can be useful in diagnosing mechanical problems. Some vehicles wear the tires more than others, so the wear you see may be characteristic of the vehicle. Properly inflated tires usually wear evenly, if they have been rotated at recommended intervals. If NOT rotated, front drive vehicles usually wear out two sets of front tires for each set of rears. If you determine that the tire wear

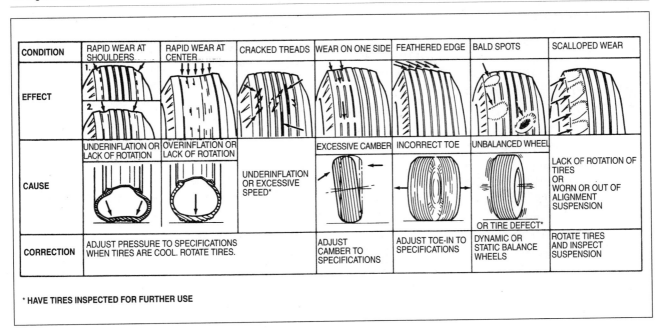

CONDITION	RAPID WEAR AT SHOULDERS	RAPID WEAR AT CENTER	CRACKED TREADS	WEAR ON ONE SIDE	FEATHERED EDGE	BALD SPOTS	SCALLOPED WEAR
EFFECT							
CAUSE	UNDERINFLATION OR LACK OF ROTATION	OVERINFLATION OR LACK OF ROTATION	UNDERINFLATION OR EXCESSIVE SPEED*	EXCESSIVE CAMBER	INCORRECT TOE	UNBALANCED WHEEL OR TIRE DEFECT*	LACK OF ROTATION OF TIRES OR WORN OR OUT OF ALIGNMENT SUSPENSION
CORRECTION	ADJUST PRESSURE TO SPECIFICATIONS WHEN TIRES ARE COOL. ROTATE TIRES.			ADJUST CAMBER TO SPECIFICATIONS	ADJUST TOE-IN TO SPECIFICATIONS	DYNAMIC OR STATIC BALANCE WHEELS	ROTATE TIRES AND INSPECT SUSPENSION

* HAVE TIRES INSPECTED FOR FURTHER USE

Figure 2-24 Tire wear patterns. (Chrysler)

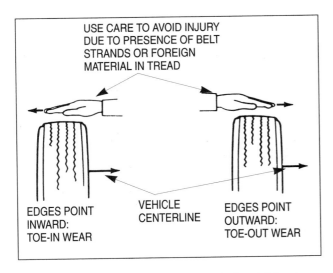

Figure 2-25 Feeling the tire tread should be done carefully to avoid injury. (General Motors)

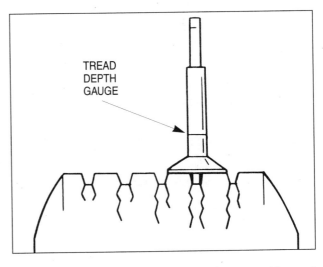

Figure 2-26 Using a tire tread depth gauge. (General Motors)

is excessive for the vehicle, it should be inspected to find the cause.

Uneven tire wear is an indication of a problem in the tires, steering, suspension, or wheel alignment. Excessive positive or negative wheel camber causes the tire to run at an angle to the road and results in one side of the tread wearing more than the other. Excessive toe-in or toe-out moves the tire sideways slightly as it rolls down the road. This produces the feathered edge mentioned above. Tire cupping or scalloping is the result of imbalance and lack of proper tire rotation. A cupped tire must be balanced and rotated to the rear, or tire cupping will continue despite corrective wheel alignment.

Tires that exhibit signs of unusual wear can cause tire growl, howl, slapping noises, and vibrations throughout the vehicle. If a customer complaint involves noise or vibration, you can determine if the tires are at fault by driving the vehicle over a smooth road at different speeds while listening to the effect of acceleration and deceleration on the noise level. In most cases, tire noise remains constant, but the intensity of exhaust and axle noise will vary with changes in speed. If you suspect the tires are at fault after road testing the vehicle, balance all tires, inflate them to 50 psi, and repeat the road test. If the noise or the vibration changes or disappears, lower the tire pressure to normal (one wheel at a time) and continue the road test. If the noise or vibration returns, the last tire you deflated generally is the cause of the problem and should be replaced.

ROTATION

To equalize wear, tires should be rotated at the periodic intervals specified by the carmaker (Figure 2-27). In addition to the scheduled rotations, the tires should be rotated whenever inspection indicates uneven tire wear. When rotating, pay particular attention to any tires with a direction of rotation arrow on the sidewall. Also check the tire manufacturer's recommendations for rotation to see if rotating from side to side is permitted. Moving a tire from one side of the vehicle to the other reverses the direction of rotation, and is NOT recommended by some tire companies. The following factors make regular tire rotation important in obtaining minimum tread wear:

- Radial tires tend to wear faster in the shoulder area, particularly when used on the front wheels.

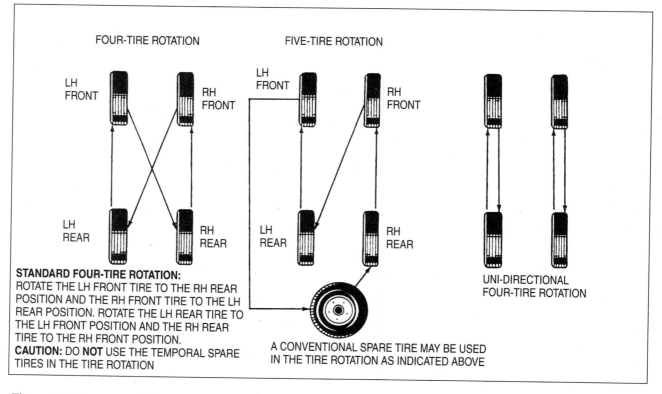

Figure 2-27 Recommended tire rotation patterns. (Ford Motor)

- Front tires on FWD vehicles drive as well as steer, and tend to wear faster than rear tires.
- Radial tires used in non-drive positions can develop irregular wear patterns that will create tire noise.
- Misalignment or suspension defects will wear tires on one end of the car more than the other. Rotation will even out the wear between front and rear, but is a poor substitute for repairing the real problem.

TIRE DISMOUNTING AND MOUNTING

Many vibration diagnosis and wheel/tire repair procedures involve removing the tire from the rim. Use a tire mounting machine to avoid any damage to the tire beads or wheel rim flanges. When working on custom or styled wheels, use the special cone adapters and plastic end clips provided with the mounting tool.

1. Position the wheel/tire assembly on the mounting machine. Remove the valve core to deflate the tire and remove any old wheel weights.
2. Install the center cone on the mounting machine (Figure 2-28). Tighten the cone securely against the rim to prevent it from shifting and damaging the center hole.
3. Using the appropriate tools, carefully break the beads loose from the rim (Figure 2-29).
4. To prevent damage to the tire beads, swab both beads with a recommended mounting lubricant before removing the tire from the rim.

> ⚠ **CAUTION:** Do NOT use oil or silicone as a lubricant. Oil may deteriorate the rubber, and silicone is too slippery and may cause the bead to slip on the rim during driving.

Figure 2-28 Thread the center cone tightly against the wheel rim to prevent the wheel from shifting.

Figure 2-29 Break the tire bead with the proper equipment.

5. Work the tire off the rim. Before removing the second side of the tire, position the part of the bead across from your demounting tool in the

Figure 2-30 Cleaning the bead seats on the wheel rim. (General Motors)

wheel's drop center to prevent the tool from hanging up and damaging the bead.

6. Before remounting the tire, inspect and clean the wheel (Figure 2-30) to make sure both bead seats are free of dirt, rust, and corrosion. Use a wire brush or steel wool on steel wheel rims; on aluminum wheels, a non-abrasive cleaner should be used. If the bead seats are not clean, air seepage at the bead area may occur after the tire has been mounted. While cleaning the wheel, check for bent, distorted, or damaged flanges. If any defects are noted, measure runout and replace the wheel if required.

7. Lubricate the bead areas on the tire you are mounting.

8. Before mounting the second side of the tire, position the part of the bead across from your mounting tool in the wheel's drop center to prevent the tool from hanging up and damaging the bead (Figure 2-31).

9. Once the beads are properly positioned, loosen the center cone one turn and inflate the tire with NO more than 40 psi. As the tire is inflated, the beads should slowly

TIP TECH TIP: If too little lubricant is used, the tire may be difficult to seat and result in damage to the bead. Too much lubricant can cause the bead to slip on the rim when the vehicle is driven. If you are having a problem with wheels going out of balance in a few days of driving, make a paint mark on the rear of the wheel and tire to check for slippage. After a few more days of driving, check to see if the mark is still aligned.

work toward the rim and then pop into place. If they do NOT, deflate the tire and break the bead loose from the rim. Relubricate the beads and rim, then reinflate the tire.

⚠ WARNING: Use a long air hose extension if necessary to avoid standing over or in front of a tire when inflating it to seat the beads.

A defective tire that comes apart can result in serious personal injury. This text does not cover locking rims used on large trucks, but if you should ever inflate one of

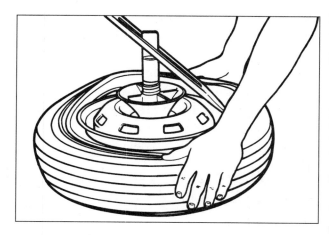

Figure 2-31. Mounting the tire on the rim. (General Motors)

them, be sure the tire and wheel are enclosed in a safety cage to prevent injury.

10. Once the beads have seated properly, let the tire deflate and install the valve core. Reinflate the tire to the recommended pressure and install the valve cap.

11. Check the tire carefully for uneven bead seating, as shown in Figure 2-15. If the distance from the rim edge to the concentric rim locating ring is NOT equal around the entire circumference, loosen the beads, lubricate, and inflate again.

12. If the tire is correctly mounted on the rim, reinstall it on the vehicle and tighten the lug nuts to the specified torque using a star-shaped or criss-cross pattern, as shown in Figure 2-2.

TIRE REPAIRS

The tools, materials, and methods used to repair a tire will differ according to the type of tire. Instructions regarding their use are provided by manufacturers of tire repair materials. When dealing with a tire that leaks, there are certain general guidelines to be followed in determining the cause of the leak.

You can repair a punctured tire from the outside with a suitable plug without removing it from the wheel. This method of repair has been used for many years by many different professional shops without any problems, but it should be avoided for two reasons:

1. It is only a temporary repair and is NOT recommended by tire manufacturers.

2. If the repaired tire fails in use, you could be held liable for damages from using a not-recommended repair.

A repair made from the inside of the tire, using a patch, is permanent and allows you to inspect the rest of the tire to make certain it is safe. For example, if the inner liner is not properly sealed, the air under pressure in the tire might cause the ply layers to separate. If this happens, the tire is unsafe to use and should be replaced. When a tire is repaired from the outside, there is no way to make this determination until the tire fails, maybe with disastrous consequences.

The first step in repairing a leaking tire is to visually inspect it for punctures in the tread area. If none are found, remove the wheel/tire from the vehicle and place it in a test tank of water. A stream of air bubbles should indicate the cause of the leak:

- If the bubbles come from the wheel flange, check the wheel for signs of cracking or other damage.
- If the bubbles appear at the valve stem, the stem or valve core is leaking and must be replaced.
- If the bubbles are seen around the bead, dismount the tire from the wheel and inspect the bead for defects.
- If the leak is in the sidewall, discard the tire and install a new one.
- If the leak appears to be from the tread area, the tire can be repaired and reused.

When you have located the leak, mark its location with a tire marking crayon so you can find it without difficulty once the tire has been dismounted from the rim. The exact method of repair will depend on the shop's equipment and materials used.

❓ REVIEW QUESTIONS

1. Technician A says that on some cars a wheel should be reinstalled on the hub in the same position from which it was removed to avoid a possible change in balance. Technician B says that wheel removal can be made difficult by corrosion between the wheel and drum or disc. Who is right?
   (A) A only
   (B) B only
   (C) Both A and B
   (D) Neither A nor B

2. Which is the most efficient method to loosen a tight wheel?
   (A) Penetrating oil
   (B) Heat
   (C) Hammering
   (D) None of these

3. Technician A says that overtightening wheel studs makes them work better. Technician B says that the lug nuts should be torqued to the carmaker's specification using a star-shaped pattern. Who is right?
   (A) A only
   (B) B only
   (C) Both A and B
   (D) Neither A nor B

4. Technician A says that the tires support the vehicle and cushion the ride. Technician B says that the tires develop traction and provide road adhesion. Who is right?
   (A) A only
   (B) B only
   (C) Both A and B
   (D) Neither A nor B

5. Under-tightened lug nuts can cause:
   (A) the wheel to fall off the vehicle.
   (B) distortion of the brake drum or disc.
   (C) wheel distortion.
   (D) no problems.

6. Technician A says that vibration from an out-of-balance wheel/tire assembly will affect directional control. Technician B says that wheel/tire balance is corrected by weights installed on the wheel rim. Who is right?
   (A) A only
   (B) B only
   (C) Both A and B
   (D) Neither A nor B

7. Technician A says that a statically imbalanced wheel/tire assembly will wobble. Technician B says that a dynamically imbalanced wheel/tire causes tramp or hop. Who is right?
   (A) A only
   (B) B only
   (C) Both A and B
   (D) Neither A nor B

8. Technician A says that off-vehicle balancing generally is more accurate than on-wheel balancing and overall balance is usually NOT affected when tires are rotated. Technician B says that on-vehicle balancing balances the hubs, drums or discs, and wheel trim at the same time. Who is right?
   (A) A only
   (B) B only
   (C) Both A and B
   (D) Neither A nor B

9. Technician A says that when a wheel raised off the ground rotates by itself, it is statically imbalanced. Technician B says the wheel is dynamically imbalanced. Who is right?
   (A) A only
   (B) B only
   (C) Both A and B
   (D) Neither A nor B

10. Technician B says that a wheel/tire in static balance also is in dynamic balance. Technician B says dynamic balance is achieved with the use of a

single-plane balancer. Who is right?
(A) A only
(B) B only
(C) Both A and B
(D) Neither A nor B

11. Which of the following statements is NOT true of a bubble balancer?
(A) It is a single-plane balancer.
(B) It is a static and dynamic balancer.
(C) It is an off-vehicle balancer.
(D) It uses a spirit level.

12. Technician A says that a computerized off-vehicle balancer should be calibrated periodically to avoid errors. Technician B says the electronic balancer uses a strobe light and two pickups to sense imbalance. Who is right?
(A) A only
(B) B only
(C) Both A and B
(D) Neither A nor B

13. Technician A says that all balance weights should be removed before doing an on-vehicle balancing. Technician B says that the drive wheels should NOT be spun faster than 35 mph (56 km/h) when one drive wheel is stopped. Who is right?
(A) A only
(B) B only
(C) Both A and B
(D) Neither A nor B

14. Technician A says that radial runout causes a sideways or wobble condition. Technician B says that lateral runout causes an abnormal up-and-down motion of the wheel/tire. Who is right?
(A) A only
(B) B only
(C) Both A and B
(D) Neither A nor B

15. Which of the following will NOT correct a runout condition?
(A) Wheel alignment

(B) Wheel or tire remounting
(C) Wheel replacement
(D) Tire replacement

16. Technician A says that radial runout is measured at the center of the tire tread. Technician B says that lateral runout is measured at the sidewall just below the tread line. Who is right?
(A) A only
(B) B only
(C) Both A and B
(D) Neither A nor B

17. The procedure used to determine whether excessive runout is caused by the tire, wheel, or a combination of both is called:
(A) dismounting.
(B) vectoring.
(C) truing.
(D) balancing.

18. Technician A says that runout often can be corrected by repositioning the tire on the wheel. Technician B says that the most accurate place to measure wheel rim runout is the inside bead area of the wheel. Who is right?
(A) A only
(B) B only
(C) Both A and B
(D) Neither A nor B

19. Technician A says that incorrect camber can cause one side of the tire tread to wear more than the other side. Technician B says that underinflation results in a tapered or feathered edge on the outer tread ribs. Who is right?
(A) A only
(B) B only
(C) Both A and B
(D) Neither A nor B

20. Which of the following is the recommended maximum air pressure to be used when seating a tire bead?
(A) 30 psi

(B) 40 psi
(C) 50 psi
(D) 60 psi

21. Which of the following is the recommended inflation pressure to be used when road testing to locate a tire thump condition?
(A) 30 psi
(B) 40 psi
(C) 50 psi
(D) 60 psi

22. Technician A says that tire beads should be lubricated with recommended tire lubricant when removing and installing a tire on a wheel. Technician B says that rusted wheel bead seats can cause air seepage after the tire has been mounted. Who is right?
(A) A only
(B) B only
(C) Both A and B
(D) Neither A nor B

23. Technician A says that a puncture in the sidewall can be repaired safely with a plug inserted from the outside of the tire. Technician B says that all tire repairs should be made from the inside. Who is right?
(A) A only
(B) B only
(C) Both A and B
(D) Neither A nor B

SERVICING WHEEL AND AXLE BEARINGS

 OBJECTIVES

After completion of this chapter, you should be able to:

- Road test a vehicle assigned by the instructor and diagnose the condition of the wheel and axle bearings.

- Correctly remove, repack, and adjust conventional rear wheel bearings on an FWD vehicle.

- Correctly remove, repack, and adjust front wheel bearings on an RWD vehicle or adjustable rear wheel bearings on an FWD vehicle.

- Replace an integral or non-integral front wheel bearing assembly on an FWD vehicle using the appropriate procedure and tools.

WHEEL BEARING SERVICE

RWD vehicles use serviceable front wheel bearings and rear axle bearings; FWD vehicles use front and rear wheel bearings that may or may not be serviceable. Serviceable bearings require periodic cleaning and inspection, repacking or replacement, and adjustment. Rear axle bearings on most RWD vehicles with rigid axle housings require no adjustment. Rear axle bearings are commonly called rear wheel bearings because they are next to the wheels. A few seldom seen rear axle bearings on rigid housings can be repacked with grease or are sealed and the bearing contains its own lubricant. Most rear axle bearings are not sealed. They receive lubrication from the lube in the differential housing. A separate seal between the bearing and the outer end of the axle prevents the axle lube from running out of the housing.

FWD vehicles use two types of non-serviceable front wheel bearings — integral or non-integral. Since integral bearings are a part of the factory-sealed hub assembly, the entire assembly must be replaced to correct a wheel bearing problem. Non-integral (cartridge) bearings are a separate component pressed into the hub or steering knuckle, and can be replaced individually.

WHEEL BEARING DIAGNOSIS

Proper wheel bearing adjustment is important, as it controls bearing end play. Wheel bearings that are too tight will overheat and fail prematurely. If the bearings are too loose or defective, the excessive end play will allow the wheel to wobble and change alignment angles. This will cause pounding that results in uneven tire wear or cupping, wheel shake and excessive play in the steering, or inefficient braking. You must be able to determine **when** bearings are the cause of a problem, **which** bearings are causing the problem, and **how** to service them properly.

To diagnose wheel bearing problems, or suspension, steering or braking problems that might involve wheel bearings, first check the condition of the tires and their inflation pressures. Adjust the inflation pressures, if necessary, and then road test the vehicle in an area where traffic is moderate. Conduct your road test at differing speeds until the problem appears. During the road test, make several left and right turns while listening carefully. Turning the vehicle causes weight transfer which shifts the load on the bearings. If the bearings are defective or out-of-adjustment, the noise level will change. Before completing the road test, gently apply and release the brakes several times. If the noise level changes as a result of brake application, suspect a wheel bearing problem.

After completing the road test, lift the vehicle on a hoist and check for loose bearings. This involves pushing, pulling, and rocking the wheel in different directions—up and down, in and out, and sideways. There should be NO vertical motion, only about 0.001-0.005" endplay with serviceable tapered roller bearings, and 0.005" endplay with non-serviceable bearings (Figure 3-1).

As a final step, spin the wheel/tire and listen for a grating or grinding noise (Figure 3-2). For personal safety, have your instructor check your setup before attempting to spin any wheels. Spin a nondrive wheel/tire with a wheel spinner; spin a drive wheel/tire with the engine. When spinning with the engine, do NOT exceed 35 mph on the speedometer at any time, to avoid damage to the vehicle. Independent suspension drive axles, front or rear, must be supported close to the wheels so that the axles hang down as little as possible to avoid universal joint damage.

While spinning a wheel, stay away from the wheel to avoid injury. If you hear a noise but are NOT certain where it comes from, lightly touch the steering knuckle or axle housing as close as possible to the bearing location with your finger tips. A rough or irregular feeling when the wheel is spun indicates the bearing is at fault.

CONVENTIONAL WHEEL BEARING ADJUSTMENT

The front wheels of RWD vehicles and rear wheels of many FWD vehicles use conventional wheel bearings (Figure 3-3) that are adjustable. These should be cleaned, repacked, and adjusted according to the carmaker's specified intervals, or whenever the brake shoes or pads are serviced. Bearing end play specified by the carmaker usually ranges between 0.001-0.005" on tapered roller bearings and allows for heat expansion during operation. The following procedure is general in nature, as you will need the carmaker's specifications. Figure 3-4 summarizes front wheel bearing adjustment on late-model Ford RWD vehicles.

1. With the vehicle off the ground and the hub cap or wheel cover removed, carefully pry the grease or dust cap from the hub (Figure 3-5) and wipe any excess grease from the spindle end.
2. Straighten the bent leg of the cotter

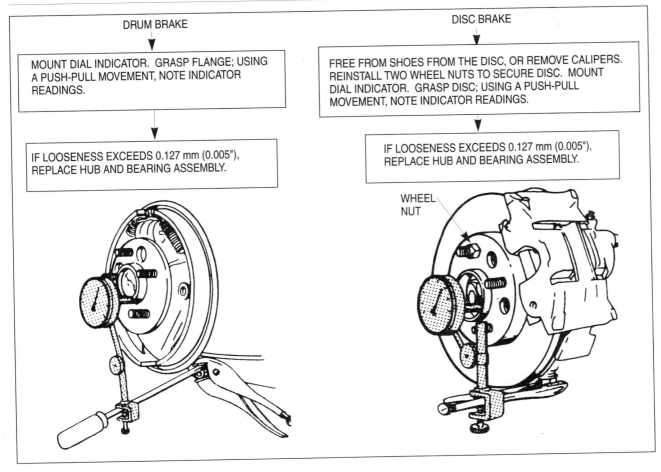

Figure 3-1 Wheel bearing looseness diagnosis. (General Motors)

NOTE Bearing adjustment is normally performed after removing, cleaning, inspecting, and repacking the bearings, and installing a new grease seal.

pin, then remove and discard it. Remove the nut lock and washer (Figure 3-6), then wipe any excess grease from the hub or adjusting nut.

3. Use a torque wrench to tighten the adjusting nut to the carmaker's specifications (usually about 25 lbf•ft) while rotating the wheel in the opposite direction to seat the bearings.

4. Back off the adjusting nut as specified by the carmaker (usually 1/4 to 1/2 turn), then retighten the nut to specifications or finger tight. The preferred setting is a slight amount of endplay. Hold the adjusting nut to prevent it from moving and install the nut lock.

5. Align the spindle hole with the nearest notch in the nutlock. If there is a castle nut without a nut lock, loosen the nut slightly if necessary to line up the hole. NEVER tighten the nut to line up the hole on tapered roller bearings. This would apply a preload to the bearing and shorten its life. Install a new cotter pin without bending the ends of the pin over.

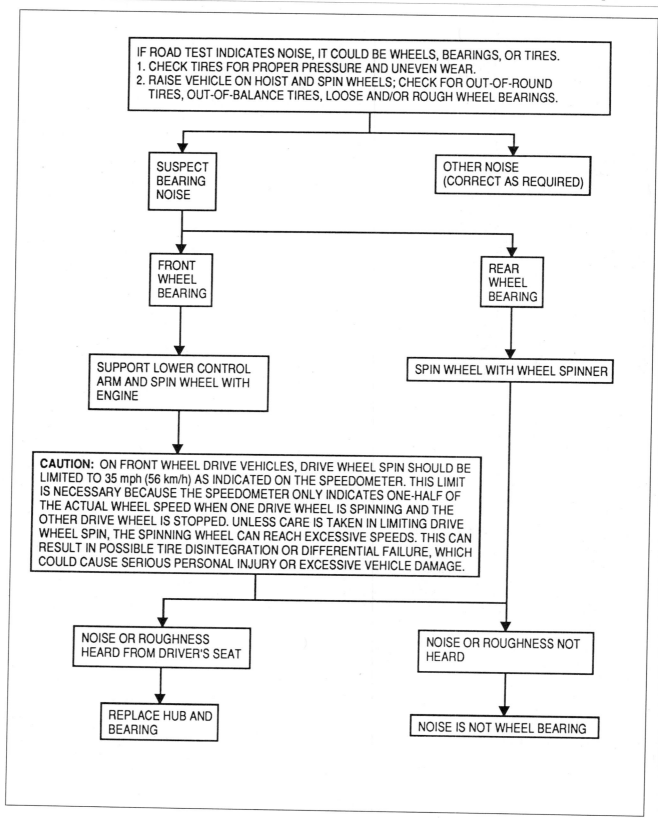

Figure 3-2 Wheel bearing noise diagnosis. (General Motors)

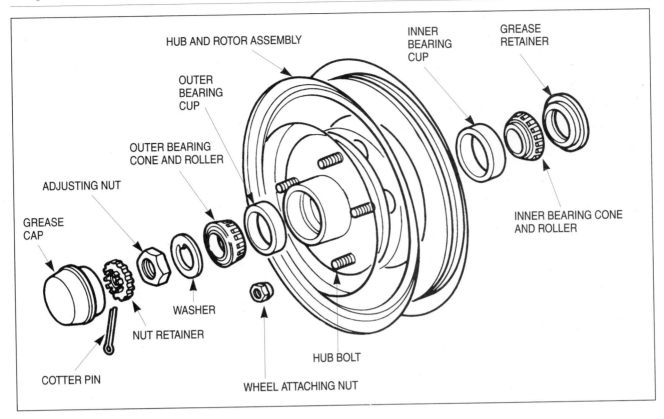

Figure 3-3 A typical front wheel using adjustable tapered roller wheel bearings. (Ford Motor)

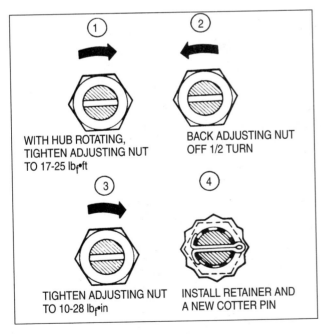

Figure 3-4 The wheel bearing adjustment procedure used on the front wheels of Ford RWD vehicles. (Ford Motor)

Figure 3-5 If a grease cap removal tool is not available, pry it off with a screwdriver or use a pair of channel-lock pliers, but be careful NOT to crush the cap.

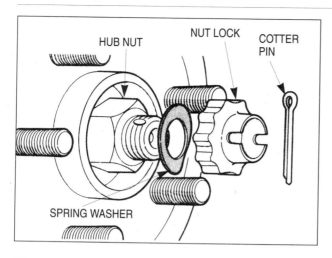

Figure 3-6 A cotter pin holds the nut lock and washer in place on the hub or adjusting nut. This type of nut lock uses a wave or spring washer. Others do not use any washer. (Chrysler)

6. Rock the wheel from top to bottom to make sure there is NO excessive endplay. If necessary, repeat the adjustment procedure.

7. When adjustment is satisfactory, bend the ends of the cotter pin over to lock it in place (Figure 3-7) and reinstall the grease or dust cap by lightly tapping in place with a soft-faced hammer.

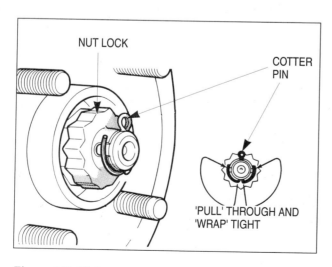

Figure 3-7 Unique cotter pin wrapping procedure used with nut locks that have a wave washer. (Chrysler)

WHEEL BEARING INSPECTION AND REPLACEMENT

1. With the vehicle off the ground remove the wheel cover, wheel lugs and the wheel. If the drum is a slip fit on the hub, remove it. Carefully pry the grease or dust cap from the hub (Figure 3-5).

2. Straighten the cotter pin, and then remove and discard it. Remove the nut lock, hub or adjusting nut, and washer (Figure 3-6).

NOTE It is possible to remove the wheel, drum, and hub as a unit without first removing the wheel, but it makes a very heavy lift that is hard to handle. It is better to remove the wheel lugs and wheel first until you have more experience.

3A. Drum brakes — Pull the hub toward you to move the outer bearing out far enough on the spindle so it can be removed (Figure 3-8), then pull the

Figure 3-8 Pulling the tire toward you will free the outer wheel bearing.

hub and drum off the brake assembly.

3B. Disc brakes — Remove the wheel/tire assembly. Remove the brake caliper and suspend it to prevent stressing the hose. Pull the disc toward you to move the outer bearing out, then remove the bearing and disc. Do NOT get grease or fingerprints on the braking surface of the disc.

4. Pry out the grease retainer or seal from the rear of the drum or disc hub, using a seal removal tool. NEVER reuse a seal, regardless of its condition. Remove the inner bearing assembly (Figure 3-9).

5. Thoroughly clean the bearings and inside of the drum or disc hub with solvent. Rotate the bearings by hand to check for the defects shown in Figure 3-10. With safety in mind, wear safety goggles and use shop air to blow the bearing dry without spinning.

Figure 3-9 Remove and discard the grease seal, then remove the inner bearing from the hub.

⚠ WARNING: Do NOT spin bearings with compressed air in Step 5; it is capable of rotating the bearings at speeds far greater than those for which they were designed. The bearing may disintegrate, causing damage and injury.

6. Inspect the bearing cups for scoring, pitting, cracking, scratching, or excessive wear. If any of these defects are found, replace the bearings and cups as a set.

7. If the bearings are to be replaced, carefully drive the inner and outer cups from the drum or disc. Fit each new cup squarely in the drum or disc hub and use a bearing cup installer tool to seat it properly (Figure 3-11). If an installer tool is not available, place a piece of wood on the cup and start it in the hub squarely by carefully tapping around the circumference of the cup. Then use a brass drift to seat the cup.

8. Carefully clean the spindle with a cloth moistened in solvent. Be careful NOT to get any solvent on the brake components.

9. Pack the bearings with a good quality, high-temperature, wheel bearing grease. Use a bearing packer and follow the procedure specified by the equipment manufacturer. If a bearing packer is not available, place a small quantity of wheel bearing grease in the palm of one hand. Insert the bearing in the grease with the open side of its cage facing the palm and carefully work the grease into the bearing by hand with a rotating motion until the grease fills the entire cage (Figure 3-12).

10. Some carmakers recommend packing the inside of the hub with wheel bearing grease until it is level with

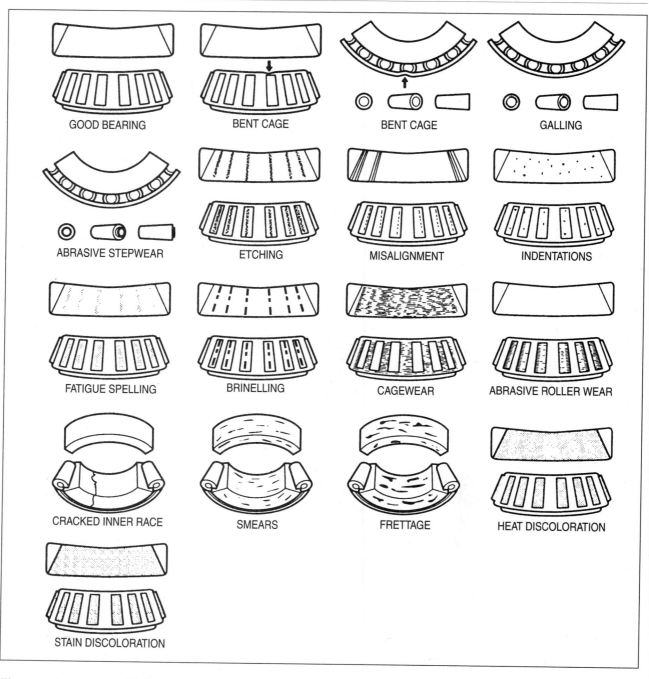

Figure 3-10 Tapered roller bearing diagnosis. (General Motors)

the inside diameter of the outer bearing cup (Figure 3-13). This will assure that the bearings stay lubricated. Others recommend only that the inside of the hub be lightly greased to prevent rust. Do NOT fill the entire inside of the hub with grease. To do so will only overload the seals and waste grease.

11. Grease the bearing surface of the inner cup, then install the inner bearing in the cup and place a new retainer or seal squarely in the hub.

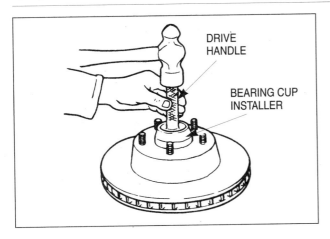

Figure 3-11 Installing an outer bearing cup with an installer tool. (Ford Motor)

Figure 3-12 If a bearing packer is not available, pack the bearing with fresh grease by hand, working it into every crevice while rotating the bearing in its race.

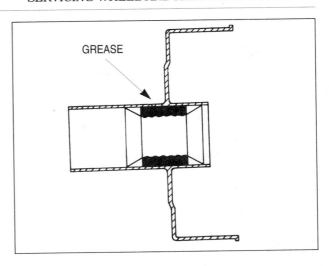

Figure 3-13 The inside of the hub should be packed with grease in the area shown, up to the inner edge of each bearing cup. (Ford Motor)

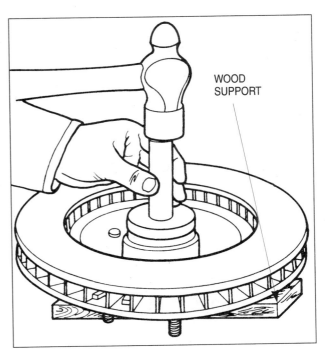

Figure 3-14 Installing a grease seal with an installer tool. (Ford Motor)

Seat the seal in the hub with a seal installer tool and hammer (Figure 3-14), or by tapping evenly around its circumference with a soft-faced hammer. Grease the seal lips.

12. Install the disc or drum and hub on the spindle, keeping the hub centered around the spindle to prevent damage to the seal.

13. Install the outer bearing and washer, then thread the adjusting nut in place.

14. Adjust the bearings as described under 'wheel bearing adjustment' in this section.

> ⚠️ **CAUTION:** Apply the brakes to be sure you have a normal pedal before moving the vehicle.

Reinstall the caliper and wheel/tire assembly on disc brakes. Replace the wheel/tire assembly on drum brakes.

CARTRIDGE WHEEL BEARING REPLACEMENT

Some FWD vehicles use a cartridge-type wheel bearing in the front axle hub (Figure 3-15) or steering knuckle assembly (Figure 3-16). This type of bearing is prelubricated and requires no adjustment or service. If a cartridge bearing is defective, it can be replaced using the following generalized procedure.

1. Raise the vehicle in the air. If a jack is used instead of a hoist, install jackstands for support and safety. Remove the wheel/tire, brake caliper, and disc. Disconnect the ABS speed sensor, if so equipped.

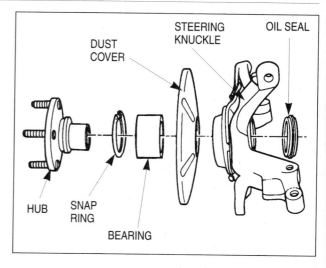

Figure 3-16 Exploded view of a front hub/steering knuckle using a cartridge bearing. (Ford Motor)

2. Unstake the nut holding the drive axle halfshaft to the hub with a hammer and chisel. Remove and discard the nut.
3. On some vehicles, the hub can be unbolted from the steering knuckle assembly without removing the

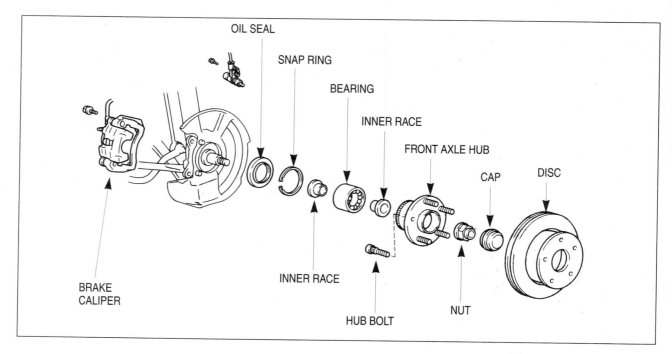

Figure 3-15 Exploded view of a front axle hub using a cartridge bearing. (Toyota)

knuckle from the vehicle (Figure 3-15). When servicing this type, omit Steps 4-6 and Step 9.

4. Separate the outer tie rod from the steering knuckle.

5. Remove the fasteners holding the shock strut to the steering knuckle. Separate the shock strut from the knuckle.

6. Disconnect the lower ball joint from the steering knuckle.

7. Remove the hub and steering knuckle assembly from the vehicle. Suspend the drive axle halfshaft from the suspension with a length of wire to prevent overextension of the CV joint.

8. Remove the oil seal from the back of the hub/steering knuckle assembly (Figure 3-16).

9. Place the hub and knuckle assembly on a press. Press the hub from the knuckle with an appropriate removal tool.

NOTE Follow press written instructions carefully. You should be behind a shield when full pressure is applied on the press.

10. If the inner race of the bearing remains on the hub when it is separated from the knuckle, use a grinder to cut the inner race and remove it from the hub with a chisel.

11. Compress and remove the snap ring from the front of the steering knuckle (Figure 3-16). Discard the snap ring.

12. Using the press and an appropriate bearing removal tool, press the bearing from the hub or knuckle.

13. Wipe the outer race of the new cartridge bearing with a threadlock compound as specified by the carmaker.

14. Press the new bearing into the hub or

knuckle with an appropriate bearing installer tool.

15. Install a new snap ring in the hub or knuckle. If necessary, press the hub into the knuckle assembly.

16. Press a new oil seal in the rear of the hub or knuckle assembly.

17. Reinstall the hub or knuckle assembly to the vehicle by reversing Steps 1-7. Use a new drive axle nut and tighten to the carmaker's specification.

INTEGRAL WHEEL BEARING/HUB REPLACEMENT

Many FWD vehicles use an integral wheel bearing/hub design. When used on the rear wheels, they are easily removed by unbolting the unit once the wheel/tire and brake drum has been removed. Replacing integral bearing/hub assemblies used on front wheels is more complicated (Figure 3-17). Use the following generalized procedure when replacement is necessary.

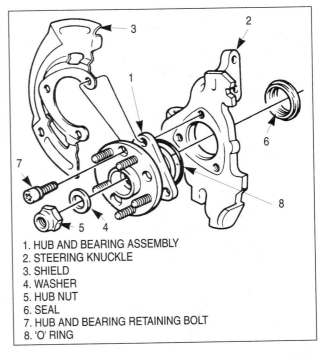

1. HUB AND BEARING ASSEMBLY
2. STEERING KNUCKLE
3. SHIELD
4. WASHER
5. HUB NUT
6. SEAL
7. HUB AND BEARING RETAINING BOLT
8. 'O' RING

Figure 3-17 A typical front wheel integral bearing/hub assembly. (General Motors)

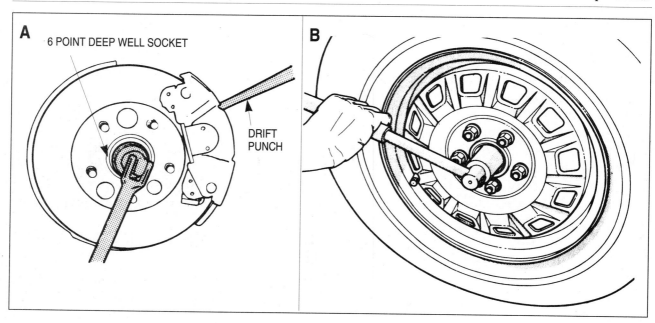

Figure 3-18 The front hub nut can be removed with the wheel off the ground by holding the disc with a drift punch (A). The hub nut also can be removed with the wheel on the ground and the brakes applied (B). (General Motors (A), and Chrysler (B))

1. Raise the vehicle in the air. If a jack is used instead of a hoist, install jackstands for support and safety. Remove the wheel/tire assembly and disconnect the ABS speed sensor, if so equipped.

2. Unstake the nut holding the drive axle halfshaft to the hub with a hammer and chisel. Insert a brass drift through the brake caliper to prevent the disc from moving, then remove the hub nut and washer (Figure 3-18); discard the nut.

TIP TECH TIP: The hub nut also can be removed with the vehicle wheels on the ground and the brake applied.

3. Remove the brake caliper and disc. Suspend the caliper from the suspension with a length of wire to prevent stressing the brake hose.

4. Like cartridge bearings, the hub can be unbolted from the steering

knuckle assembly on some vehicles without removing the knuckle (Figure 3-19). When servicing this design, omit Steps 5-7 and Step 9.

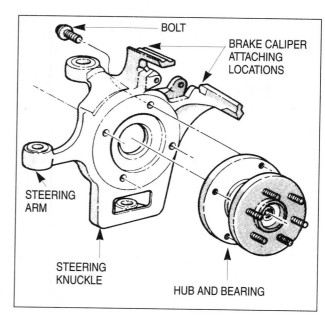

Figure 3-19 Some front wheel hub/bearing assemblies bolt to the steering knuckle. (Chrysler)

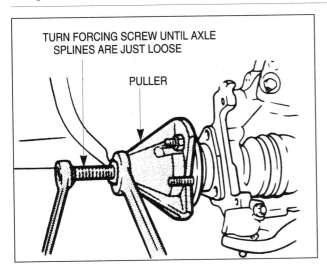

TURN FORCING SCREW UNTIL AXLE
SPLINES ARE JUST LOOSE

PULLER

Figure 3-20 Removing a front wheel hub/bearing assembly from the drive axle with a puller. (General Motors)

5. Attach an appropriate puller to the wheel studs (Figure 3-20) and separate the hub from the drive axle.
6. Unbolt the stabilizer bar from the control arm.
7. Disconnect the tie rod end and lower ball joint from the steering knuckle.
8. Remove the hub and steering knuckle assembly from the vehicle. Suspend the drive axle halfshaft from the suspension with a length of wire to prevent overextension of the CV joint.
9. Unbolt the hub/bearing assembly from the steering knuckle.
10. Remove and discard the seal at the rear of the knuckle. Install a new seal.
11. Reinstall the knuckle over the drive axle halfshaft and reconnect the ball joint and tie rod end to the knuckle.
12. Reattach the stabilizer bar to the control arm.
13. Lubricate the O-ring on the new hub/bearing assembly, then position the assembly against the knuckle and bolt in place. Tighten bolts to the carmaker's specifications.

14. Reinstall the disc and brake caliper. Insert the drift through the caliper to hold the disc stationary, then install the washer with a new hub nut and tighten the nut to the specified torque.

REAR WHEEL AXLE BEARING SERVICE

RWD axle bearings help support the vehicle mass and reduce the rotating friction of the axle shaft. Under normal circumstances, axle bearing replacement should NOT be required on low-mileage vehicles unless the grease seal fails, or the vehicle has been consistently subjected to overloading or pulling excessive mass.

DIAGNOSIS AND REPLACEMENT

Many rigid housing rear axles use C-locks on the inner end of the axles to retain the axles in the housing. Only RWD axle bearings used with C-lock axles should have end play; the amount allowed may vary between 0.001" and 0.030", depending on the carmaker's specifications. Loose or rough rear wheel axle bearings will cause a noise that can be easily confused with axle noises. A rough bearing produces a growling noise or vibration that remains the same whether the vehicle is in drive, or coasting at low speed with the transmission in neutral. Light application of the brakes while holding vehicle speed constant may cause rear wheel axle bearing noise to diminish. The rollers in these bearings do NOT rotate at the same speed as the rear axle. A defective bearing makes a knocking or clicking sound once in approximately two revolutions of the wheel.

Since tire and bearing noise is similar under many conditions, one of the best ways to determine whether the bearing is at fault is to raise the rear of the vehicle with a hydraulic jack and place the axle housing on jackstands. Make sure the parking brake is released and have an assistant manually rotate the suspected wheel while you hold a long screwdriver against the outside of the axle at the bearing location, or use an automotive stethoscope, and listen for a rough or clicking sound from the bearing.

To replace a defective bearing or leaking seal on an RWD axle, you must remove the axle. To do this properly, use the procedures specified in the factory service manual for the particular year and model of the vehicle you are servicing.

? REVIEW QUESTIONS

1. Technician A says that a defective wheel bearing will change noise levels during cornering maneuvers. Technician B says that serviceable tapered roller bearings should have NO endplay. Who is right?
   (A) A only
   (B) B only
   (C) Both A and B
   (D) Neither A nor B

2. Technician A says that wheel bearing end play should be checked by grasping the tire and using a rocking motion. Technician B says that a defective wheel bearing will be rough or noisy when you spin the wheel. Who is right?
   (A) A only
   (B) B only
   (C) Both A and B
   (D) Neither A nor B

3. An integral wheel bearing assembly is serviced by:
   (A) adjusting the hub/bearing assembly.
   (B) replacing the cartridge.
   (C) cleaning and repacking.
   (D) replacing the hub/bearing assembly.

4. Technician A says that wheel bearings must NOT be lubricated before they are installed. Technician B says wheel bearing adjustment controls bearing endplay. Who is right?
   (A) A only

   (B) B only
   (C) Both A and B
   (D) Neither A nor B

5. Technician A says that endplay of serviceable tapered roller bearings should NOT exceed 0.010". Technician B says that loose wheel bearings will overheat and fail. Who is right?
   (A) A only
   (B) B only
   (C) Both A and B
   (D) Neither A nor B

6. Technician A says that if a bearing cup is scored, the bearings and cups should be replaced as an assembly. Technician B says that a grease seal in good condition can be reused. Who is right?
   (A) A only
   (B) B only
   (C) Both A and B
   (D) Neither A nor B

7. Technician A says that the front hub nut of an FWD vehicle can be loosened with the wheels on the ground and the brake applied. Technician B says the nut can be loosened with the vehicle in the air and a brass drift inserted through the brake caliper. Who is right?
   (A) A only
   (B) B only
   (C) Both A and B
   (D) Neither A nor B

8. Technician A says that all RWD axle

bearings should have a slight amount of endplay. Technician B says that only rear axle bearings used with C-lock axles should have endplay. Who is right?

(A) A only
(B) B only
(C) Both A and B
(D) Neither A nor B

9. Technician A says that a defective wheel bearing can be detected by feeling the steering knuckle with your finger tips while spinning the wheel. Technician B says that a stethoscope also can be

used. Who is right?

(A) A only
(B) B only
(C) Both A and B
(D) Neither A nor B

10. Technician A says that cartridge bearings require NO adjustment after replacement. Technican B says that integral wheel bearings should be lubricated before installing. Who is right?

(A) A only
(B) B only
(C) Both A and B
(D) Neither A nor B

SUSPENSION HEIGHT, SPRINGS, SHOCK ABSORBERS, AND STRUTS — ADJUSTMENT/REPLACEMENT

 **OBJECTIVES**

After completion of this chapter, you should be able to:

- Use the appropriate service manual to locate the correct trim height specifications and measuring points for a vehicle.

- Use the trim height specifications and measuring points to determine the trim height of a vehicle.

- Remove and install any of the following, using the appropriate method and equipment — leaf spring, coil spring, torsion bar, and strut coil spring.

- Replace a leaf spring bushing, using the appropriate method and equipment.

- Replace a defective shock absorber, using the appropriate method and tools.

VEHICLE TRIM HEIGHT

Trim height describes the normal no-load height of a vehicle at rest. You will also see trim height described as chassis height, curb ride height, or curb height. Regardless of what it is called, trim height is the basis for static camber, caster, and toe settings. Since it also controls dynamic changes in caster and toe, maintaining trim height at its specified level is just as important as accurately setting camber and toe. Incorrect trim heights can cause symptoms similar to alignment problems.

If the springs are fatigued and have sagged, the vehicle height will drop, causing a change in the suspension geometry (Figure 4-1). When this occurs, the suspension components will bottom out (strike the jounce bumpers harshly) as the vehicle passes over severe road irregularities. Combined with the effect of road

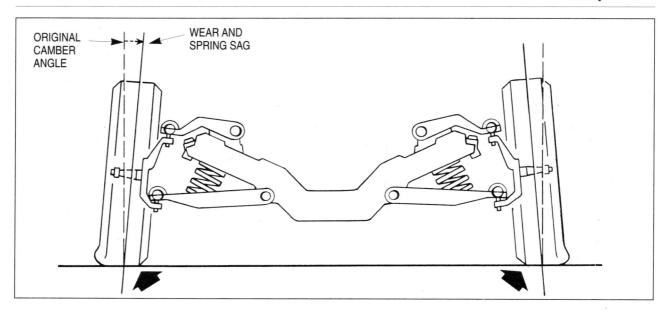

Figure 4-1 Suspension sag combines with wear to distort the front end relationship. (McQuay-Norris)

forces on the tires (Figure 4-2), both vehicle handling and tire wear are affected.

Specifications for trim height are published by many carmakers and can be found in factory shop manuals or specialized technical publications provided by the carmaker (Figure 4-3). They also can be found in specialized manuals provided by

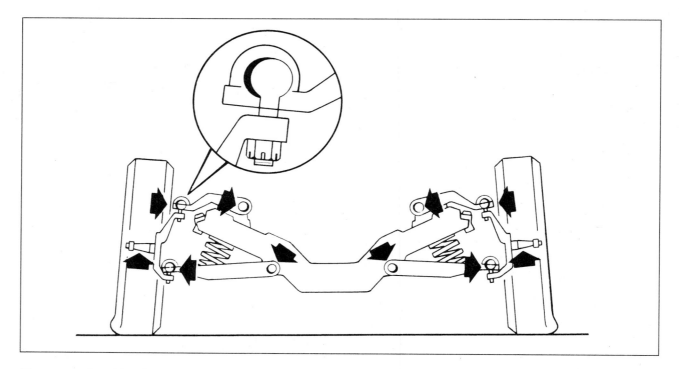

Figure 4-2 Road forces transmitted through the wheel spindles, ball joints, and bushing eventually cause wear. Note how one side of the ball and socket is worn, allowing excessive clearance. (McQuay-Norris)

SUSP	MODEL	ENGINE	STYLE	TIRE	Z (CURB)	D (CURB)
FE1	Z7P w/o BYP	LHO	2 DR	P205/70R15	72.2 mm (2.84 in.)	92.3 mm (3.63 in.)
FE1	Z7P with BYP	LHO	2 DR	P215/60R16	71.3 mm (2.81 in.)	92.3 mm (3.63 in.)
FE1	Z7P with BYP	L82	2 DR	P215/60R16	71.3 mm (2.81 in.)	92.3 mm (3.63 in.)
FE3	Z7P w/o BYP	LQ1	2 DR	P225/60R16	66.1 mm (2.60 in.)	87.4 mm (3.44 in.)
FE3	Z7P with BYP	LQ1	2 DR	P225/60R16	66.1 mm (2.60 in.)	87.4 mm (3.44 in.)
FE3	Z7Q w/o BYP	LHO	2 DR	P225/60R16	65.7 mm (2.59 in.)	87.4 mm (3.44 in.)
FE3	Z7Q w/o BYP	LQ1	2 DR	P225/60R16	66.9 mm (2.63 in.)	87.4 mm (3.44 in.)
FE3	Z7S w/o BYP	LHO	2 DR	P225/60R16	66.4 mm (2.62 in.)	89.0 mm (3.50 in.)
FE3	Z7S withBYP	LQ1	2 DR	P225/60R16	67.7 mm (2.67 in.)	89.0 mm (3.50 in.)
FE1	Z7P w/o BYP	LHO	4 DR	P205/70R15	72.8 mm (2.87 in.)	93.5 mm (3.68 in.)
FE1	Z7P with BYP	LHO	4 DR	P215/60R16	71.9 mm (2.83 in.)	93.3 mm (3.67 in.)
FE1	Z7P with BYP	L82	4 DR	P215/60R16	71.9 mm (2.83 in.)	93.3 mm (3.67 in.)
FE3	Z7P w/o BYP	LQ1	4 DR	P225/60R16	66.9 mm (2.63 in.)	87.9 mm (3.46 in.)
FE3	Z7P with BYP	LQ1	4 DR	P225/60R16	66.9 mm (2.63 in.)	87.9 mm (3.46 in.)
FE3	Z7Q w/o BYP	LHO	4 DR	P225/60R16	66.5 mm (2.62 in.)	88.0 mm (3.46 in.)
FE3	Z7Q w/o BYP	LQ1	4 DR	P225/60R16	66.9 mm (2.63 in.)	87.9 mm (3.46 in.)

- NOTE: ALL MEASUREMENTS ARE ±10 mm (0.39 in.)
- NOTE: 'J' AND 'K' CURB HEIGHTS ARE 249 mm (9.80 in.) FOR ALL MODEL COMBINATIONS.

Figure 4-3 Typical trim height specifications for a 1993 Oldsmobile Cutlass Supreme. (Oldsmobile Division, General Motors)

many aftermarket manufacturers of suspension components. In many cases, the specifications will be accompanied by the measuring locations recommended for a particular vehicle (Figure 4-4).

Knowing the correct places to measure trim height is important, because they vary among carmakers. To further complicate matters, their locations vary among the different models produced by a single carmaker. In general, they also vary from simple-to-make measurements such as the bottom of the rocker panel or bumper to the ground, to more difficult-to-make mea-

surements between the control arm and rubber jounce bumpers, or determining the difference in ground clearance between the inner control arm bushing and the ball joint. Most measurements are affected by tire diameter and inflation pressures; if the tires are over- or underinflated, or a different size than recommended by the carmaker, the readings will be incorrect. Even tire wear will affect height, and must be taken into consideration.

In cases where the carmaker or aftermarket publications do not provide the necessary specifications, a common rule of thumb can be used to determine if the front suspension height is too low. At normal ride height, the lower control arm should be parallel with the road surface, or slightly higher at the inner pivot than at the ball joint. If the outer end of the control arm is higher than the pivoting inner end, the springs probably are fatigued and should

TIP TECH TIP: The measurements specified by carmakers generally are minimum heights. Installing new springs on a vehicle usually results in measurements that are slightly higher than specified.

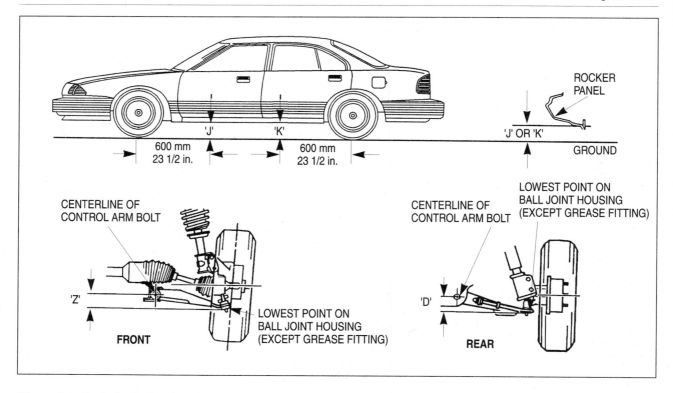

Figure 4-4 Typical trim height measuring points for a 1993 Oldsmobile 88. (Oldsmobile Division, General Motors)

be replaced. To verify this, check the condition of the rubber jounce bumpers to see if they are damaged.

TRIM HEIGHT MEASUREMENT AND CORRECTION

Checking trim height is the first step in diagnosing steering and vibration complaints. Use the following procedure:

1. Park the vehicle on a level surface, such as an alignment rack. This is an ideal location because it permits easy access to the suspension measuring and adjusting points.

2. Make sure the tires are the correct size and in good condition. Check and adjust tire inflation pressures to within ±3 psi of the specification on the door post.

3. Make sure there is NO unnecessary weight in the passenger compartment or trunk. The trunk must be empty except for the spare tire and jack. Ride height specifications apply to unloaded vehicles.

4. Check the fuel level. The fuel tank should be full. If not, place a weight in the trunk to simulate a full fuel load.

5. If the vehicle is equipped with an electronic level control (ELC) system, make sure it works correctly.

6. Bounce the vehicle at least three times at the front and three times at the rear to normalize the suspension.

7. Make sure you have the correct trim height specifications and measuring point locations for the vehicle being serviced. If you are not certain about the locations, ask your instructor for help.

8. Take the required measurements and compare them to the specifications. Measurements that are less than specified indicate sagged springs.

9. Compare the measurements taken on one side of the vehicle to those taken on the other. They should be within 1/2" to 3/4" of each other.

After completing the measurements, check the springs visually for signs of coil spring clash, collapsed coils, worn or split jounce bumpers, broken leafs, worn or missing shackle bushings, or any other damaged components. When one side of the vehicle is lower than the other (indicating a sagging spring), you must determine which spring is at fault — front, rear, or both. Height measurements cannot always determine which spring is at fault because one sagging spring will lower its own corner of the car and raise the diagonally opposite corner. To make this determination, raise the rear of the vehicle with a jack positioned at the center of the rear axle until the wheels just clear the ground. Be sure that the location you are jacking is an acceptable lift point to avoid damage to the vehicle. The jack should make point contact at the middle of the housing so the vehicle can tilt on the point. You may have to use spacers on the jack saddle to accomplish this. If the lean was caused by a sagging rear spring, the vehicle will tilt on the lifting point and straighten out as it is lifted. A vehicle that continues to lean after the rear end is lifted has a problem in the front springs. The jacking may also be done from the front, as long as the jack is in the exact center and the vehicle can pivot around the lift point. In any case, if the vehicle straightens out when it is lifted, the cause of the lean is in the end that was lifted. If it does NOT straighten out, it is in the other end, or possibly both ends. There may be some vehicles with a sagging spring on both ends, so the test should be done from both ends of the vehicle. This is only a test. Do NOT do any work under the vehicle while it is supported only by the jack. Always replace springs in front or rear pairs, because a new spring will never match up in height with a used spring.

SPRING SERVICE

Vehicle mass in a leaf or coil spring system is supported by the force of the leaf or coil spring, and is controlled by the spring rate. Torsion bars support vehicle mass by the twisting or torsional action of the bars. In a strut suspension, vehicle mass is supported by the coil spring component of the strut assembly. Because the stored energy in a spring can be released very quickly, working with springs can be very dangerous.

The technician must use the necessary special equipment and tools, while following the proper procedures and observing all safety precautions. Because spring service or replacement affects alignment angles, make sure to check wheel alignment once the suspension has been reassembled.

LEAF SPRINGS

When weight is added to a vehicle with a leaf spring suspension, or when the vehicle is driven over a bump, the main leaf is forced to flatten out from its normal slight curve, increasing the load on the secondary leaves. Some springs have only one leaf, which works the same as the main leaf in a multi-leaf spring. As the spring straightens out, the distance between the spring eyes at each end becomes longer. One spring eye, usually the front, is attached to the vehicle frame so it can only pivot. The other spring eye is attached to the rear pivot point on the frame with a shackle. The shackle permits the distance between the spring eyes to change as the spring flexes over bumps and dips. Without the shackle there would be NO spring action.

Leaf springs also absorb rear wheel torque on an open driveshaft rear wheel

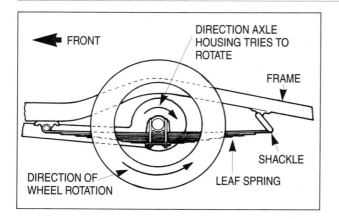

Figure 4-5 These are the forces that try to wind up the leaf spring during acceleration and result in torque dampening. (Chrysler)

drive vehicle. During acceleration and braking, drive line torque attempts to rotate the axle housing in a direction opposite to the wheel rotation (Figure 4-5). This results in the spring winding up, attempting to form an S curve, which absorbs and dampens some of the torque. The amount of damping or windup that occurs depends on the distance between the front spring eye and the center bolt of the spring where it is clamped to the axle housing. The longer the spring is from front eye to axle housing, the greater the damping force. The torque that is used up in bending the spring is wasted, and does NOT contribute to the acceleration of the vehicle. This softens acceleration and avoids rear tire spinning every time the driver steps on the gas. Shortening or stiffening the front half of the spring reduces the damping action, but makes the vehicle ride hard and can have a bad effect on overall handling.

The leaf spring front suspension originally used on passenger cars was replaced by independent coil springs or struts many years ago, but some RWD cars still use leaf spring rear suspensions. The major use of a leaf spring suspension today is primarily with pickup trucks and some sport utility vehicles, although some specialty vehicles like the Corvette continue to use transverse fiberglass leaf springs. Since leaf springs normally require little service, and their use has gradually diminished over the years, you probably will not work on them very often. Spring service usually involves removal, installation, and bushing or shackle replacement. Sometimes, you may find it necessary to replace a broken center bolt on a multi-leaf spring.

SPRING REMOVAL AND INSTALLATION

Leaf springs may be mounted above (Figure 4-6) or below the axle (Figure 4-7). Shackle position varies also, depending on whether the shackle pivot is above or below the spring. The following procedure is general in nature and the required steps may vary in sequence according to suspension design. Refer to Figures 4-6 and 4-7 (typical) for this procedure:

1. Raise the rear of the vehicle with a jack, then place safety stands under the frame side rails so that the frame is high enough to allow the suspension to hang free.
2. Remove the wheel/tire assembly and support the rear axle with a jack.
3. If the lower end of the shock absorber is fastened to the spring cap or U-bolt plate, or will otherwise interfere with spring removal, disconnect the shock absorber. Many times the shock absorber limits the amount that the suspension can hang down, and therefore it must be disconnected at the bottom end.
4. Make sure the rear axle is safely supported, and then remove the U-bolt nuts. Remove the U-bolts from the spring cap or U-bolt plate. Remove the cap or plate.
5. If the axle housing is above the spring, raise the housing with the jack until it is clear of the spring. When the housing is below the

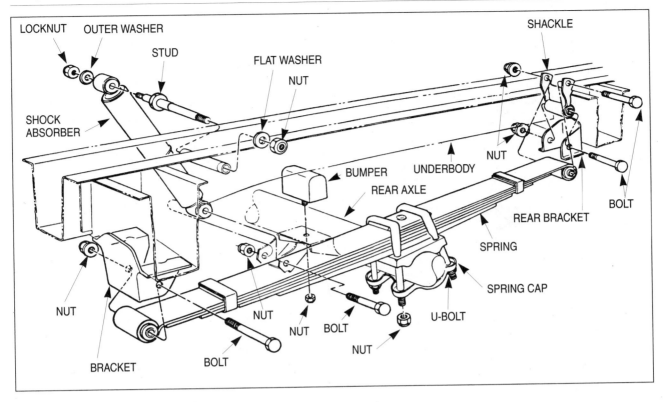

Figure 4-6 Typical leaf spring installed above the axle. (Ford Motor)

spring, lower it just enough to clear the spring. Watch the brake hose, axle housing vent hose, or any height sensing devices to be sure they are NOT stretched or broken when letting the axle housing down.

> ⬥ **CAUTION:** Safely support the spring or wire it to the frame so it cannot fall when the eyebolts are removed.

Remove the nut from the front spring eye bolt, then remove the bolt with a hammer and suitable drift.

6A. If only the spring is being removed, remove the nut from the shackle bolt. Drive the bolt from the hanger with a hammer and suitable drift. Springs are very heavy, so get some help to remove the spring from the vehicle.

6B. If the shackle is to be removed with the spring, remove the hanger nut and bolt instead. Drive the bolt from the hanger and remove the spring and shackle from the vehicle.

7. To reinstall the spring, use a helper and reposition the rear spring eye in the shackle, or the shackle in the hanger, and install the bolt and nut.

8. With a helper, position the front spring eye in the hanger or bracket and install the bolt and nut.

9. Raise or lower the axle to the spring as required with a jack and center the spring center bolt in the axle pilot hole.

10. Install the U-bolt plate or spring cap, U-bolts, and nuts, aligning the spring leaves. Tighten the nuts to the specified torque.

11. If the shock absorber was disconnected, raise the axle with the jack

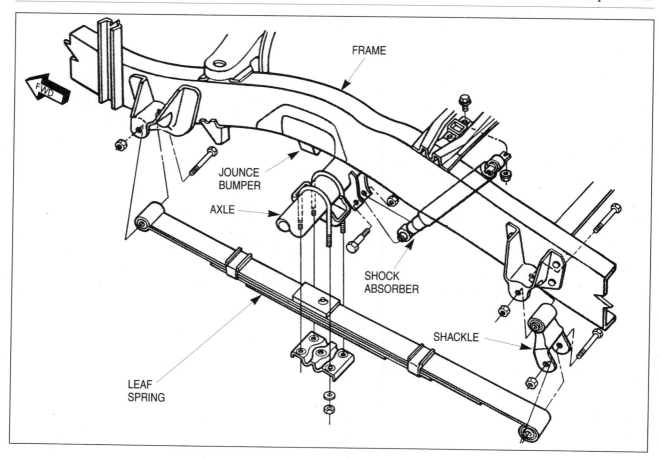

Figure 4-7 Typical leaf spring installed below the axle. (Chrysler)

enough to reattach the shock absorber.

12. Many spring eye bushings are rubber which compresses when the bolt is tightened. Do NOT tighten the bolt with the weight off the suspension. The movement of the spring from a completely unloaded to the loaded position is much greater than normal driving movement, and the bushing may be torn. Lower the vehicle to the ground and tighten the shackle and spring eye bolts with the normal weight on the suspension.

BUSHING REPLACEMENT

Two types of leaf spring bushings are used — a single metal-backed rubber bushing or a pair of rubber bushings installed in the spring eye from each side. To remove a metal-backed bushing, press the old one out and the new one in, much like control arm bushings are replaced (Figure 4-8). Remove two-piece bushings from the spring eye by prying out with a small prybar. Install new bushings by sliding one half into each side of the spring eye. To make two-piece bushing installation easier, lubricate them with soapy water or tire mounting lube.

SPRING LEAF REPLACEMENT

With the spring removed from the vehicle, remove the alignment clips and clamp the spring in a heavy-duty vise (Figure 4-9). After removing the nut and center bolt,

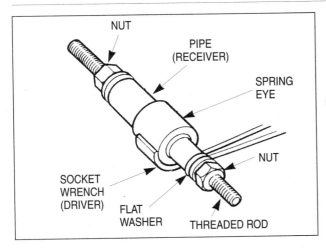

Figure 4-8 Leaf spring eye bushing removal tools. (Chrysler)

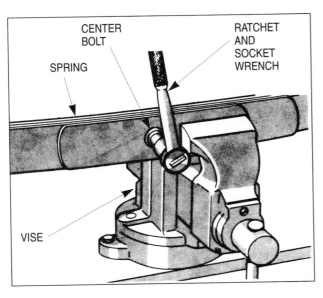

Figure 4-9 Removing the spring center bolt. (Chrysler)

install a long bolt with a nut on the end of it. There may be considerable spring action in the leaves, and the long bolt will help to keep the leaves from springing apart. Carefully release the vise. Remove the spring assembly from the vise.

Separate the leaves and replace the faulty one. Some springs may have full length pads between the leaves or at the end of each leaf. These pads either act as a lubricant so that the spring does NOT have

to be greased or are used with grease. Modern cars do not ordinarily have greased springs. Be sure that the pads and leaves go back together in the correct order. If the old center bolt is hollow and has a grease fitting, clean off the old grease and coat the leaves with new grease. Insert the long bolt through the spring center bolt hole to align the leaves, then reinstall the spring in the vise. It is usually easier to assemble the leaves on the floor with a long threaded bolt, then put the spring in the vise while you remove the long bolt. With the spring leaves properly aligned and clamped, remove the long bolt and insert a new center bolt and nut, if available, in its place. When the nut is tightened to specifications, there should be NO gaps between the leaves. After installing the alignment clips, remove the spring from the vise and reinstall in the vehicle.

TORSION BARS

Two types of torsion bar suspensions are used — longitudinal and transverse. Longitudinal (front-to-rear) torsion bars (Figure 4-10) are found primarily on older RWD vehicles and some import pickup trucks. The transverse (side-to-side) torsion bar suspension (Figure 4-11) is used mainly by Chrysler and Volkswagen. Torsion bar suspensions are subjected to many of the same conditions that affect coil springs.

TORSION BAR SERVICE

Torsion bars require periodic adjustment to maintain the proper vehicle trim height. In addition, they sometimes break and must be replaced. Height inspection and measurement procedures for vehicles with torsion bar suspensions are the same as for coil springs. Unlike coil spring suspensions, vehicle sagging generally can be corrected by adjusting the torsion bars.

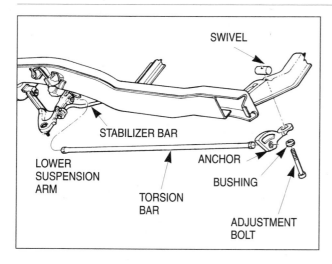

Figure 4-10 Typical longitudinal torsion bar installation. (Chrysler)

Procedures for torsion bar adjustment and replacement vary widely among carmakers using this type of suspension. For this reason, always refer to the recommended procedures in the carmaker's shop manual for the make and model of vehicle being serviced when working on a torsion bar suspension. The procedures below are general in nature and are given to acquaint you with the various steps involved.

Adjustment

1. Park the vehicle on a level surface, such as an alignment rack. This is an ideal location because it permits easy access to the suspension measuring and adjusting points.

2. Apply penetrating oil to the adjustment bolt threads on the end of each torsion bar. If the vehicle is several years old, it is a good idea to support the vehicle so that the weight is off the suspension. With no weight on the bars you can work the adjustment bolt back and forth several turns to free it up for the adjustment. Lower the vehicle onto a level surface before

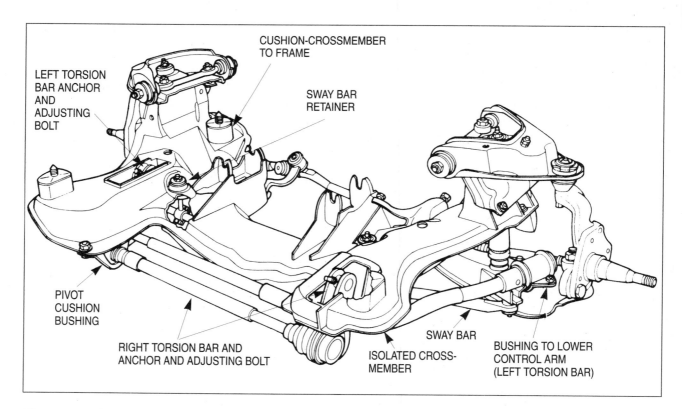

Figure 4-11 Typical transverse torsion bar installation. (Chrysler)

proceeding with the adjustment.

3. If you have access to torsion bar gauges, install one on each side of the vehicle to measure the front ride height as specified by the carmaker. If NOT, manually measure the ride height at the specified locations.

4A. Longitudinal torsion bars: rotate the torsion bar adjustment bolt (Figure 4-10) clockwise to increase or counterclockwise to decrease suspension arm height.

4B. Transverse torsion bars: rotate the anchor adjusting bolts located in the front crossmember (Figure 4-11). The right bar is adjusted from the left side; the left bar is adjusted from the right side.

5. After adjusting the bars, bounce the vehicle and recheck measurements on each side. Continue adjusting and measuring, if necessary, until the suspension height is correct at each side of the vehicle.

Replacement

Some carmakers specify removal of the suspension arm bumpers before raising the vehicle. This allows the suspension to drop further, taking most of the tension off the bars. When replacing torsion bars, refer to the appropriate shop manual to determine if other preliminary steps are required. Refer to Figure 4-10 and Figure 4-12 (typical) as required for this procedure.

1. Raise and support the vehicle with the front suspension hanging free.

2. Remove the wheel/tire assemblies, shock absorbers, and disconnect the stabilizer bar end links, if necessary.

3. Mark the adjustment bolt setting. A special tool is required to hold the adjustment arm on the torsion bar design shown in Figure 4-12 before removing the adjustment bolt (Figure 4-13).

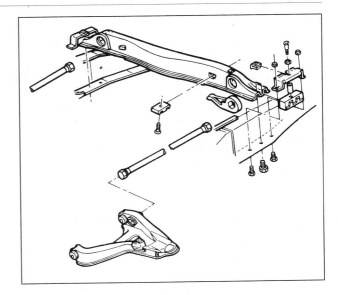

Figure 4-12 Adjustment arm tension must be held with a special tool before the torsion bars adjusting bolt can be removed in this suspension design. (General Motors)

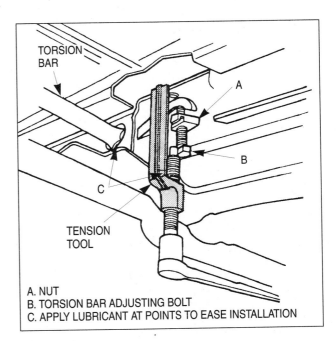

A. NUT
B. TORSION BAR ADJUSTING BOLT
C. APPLY LUBRICANT AT POINTS TO EASE INSTALLATION

Figure 4-13 One type of tool used to apply and release tension on the torsion bar during replacement. (Oldsmobile Division, General Motors)

4. Count and record the number of turns required to remove the torsion bar adjustment bolt. When the torsion bar is reinstalled, tightening

the bolt the same number of turns will provide a rough readjustment setting.

5. Remove the adjustment bolt swivel or retaining plate, if one is used.

6. Remove the torsion bar as specified by the carmaker:

   a. On the suspension shown in Figure 4-10, the bar is removed toward the rear of the vehicle by withdrawing it from the control arm. Remove the anchor and bushing from the torsion bar.

   b. On the suspension shown in Figure 4-12, slide the bars forward, remove the adjustment arms from the support crossmember, then unbolt and slide the crossmember to the rear to remove the torsion bars.

   c. On some designs, a locating clip or the mounting bolts must be removed at the splined end of the bar before it can be removed.

7. Clean the torsion bar and its attachment anchor or adjustment arm and inspect all components for wear, damage, or corrosion. Check for surface nicks or scratches that can create stress raisers (surface flaws) which result in cracks. If any defects are found, replace the bar.

> ⚠ **CAUTION:** Torsion bars take a set once they are used, and are NOT interchangeable from one side of the vehicle to the other. When the same bar is going to be replaced, it should be marked R or L before removal. Torsion bars that are NOT splined do NOT have a front or rear end, and can be installed with either end facing forward.

8. To reinstall the torsion bar in Figure 10, install the anchor and slide the bar into the control arm. Fit the anchor and bushing into the frame crossmember and install the adjustment bolt through the bushing to engage the swivel. Turn the adjustment bolt clockwise the number of turns counted in Step 4.

9. To reinstall the torsion bars in Figure 4-12, insert them through the control arms and slide the support crossmember forward until it engages the bars. Install the adjustment arms and move the crossmember into position, then install and tighten the crossmember fasteners. Install the special tool to hold the arm (Figure 4-13), then insert the retainer plate and adjustment bolt. Turn the bolt clockwise the number of turns counted in Step 4, then remove the special tool to allow the bolt to take up the load.

10. Reinstall the stabilizer bar end link (if disconnected), the shock absorbers, and the wheel/tire assemblies.

11. Measure the trim height and adjust the torsion bars to bring the vehicle into specifications.

COIL SPRINGS

When a coil spring breaks, which is rare, it generally results from a stress raiser (surface flaw) on a coil which leads to metal fatigue. Many late-model springs are coated with epoxy or painted to prevent rust that can lead to stress raisers, and should be handled carefully to avoid damage to the coating.

The most common problem that affects coil springs is sagging. As a coil spring sags, its length decreases and the resulting drop in the suspension affects front end geometry. Severe sag can result in constant bottoming of the suspension against the jounce bumpers.

Shims and spacers (Figure 4-14) are

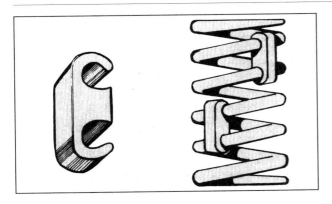

Figure 4-14 One type of spacer used to eliminate spring sag. (McQuay-Norris)

available to eliminate spring sag. Although there may be a savings in labor and parts by using such temporary measures, the only real correction of the problem is to install new springs. Among the several disadvantages of using shims and spacers:

- shim installation requires the same amount of work as spring replacement.
- since shim installation does NOT lengthen the spring, the coils can bottom and contact each other (coil clash) under severe conditions.
- spacers concentrate stresses on a single point of the coil instead of distributing the forces throughout the spring.
- metal spacers prevent spring action between the coils where they are installed.
- rubber spacers tend to fall out of place and get lost under the strain of hard driving.

In spite of all the disadvantages, many repair shops have been installing spacers for years, at considerably less cost than a new spring, with hundreds of satisfied customers.

When installing a new spring, make sure that you have the correct replacement. Carmakers often use a variety of different spring rates on the same vehicle, according

to its powertrain and accessories, and it is impossible to tell the difference visually. On many vehicles, the springs are rated separately for each side of the vehicle. The best way to assure that you have an exact replacement is to check the part number on the tag attached to the old spring. Some springs have a designated top and bottom, and should be installed accordingly.

As with all other types of springs, coils must be mounted on rubber bushings to prevent metal-to-metal contact that would raise the road noise transmitted to the passenger compartment to an intolerable level. These bushings are located at each end of the coil and should be checked for wear or damage when replacing the spring.

FRONT COIL SPRING REPLACEMENT (SPRING ON LOWER CONTROL ARM)

There are several different methods and tools that can be used to remove the spring. Which one you use will depend on the equipment you have available. The following procedure is typical of the steps involved. When possible, refer to the factory shop manual and use the procedure and tools recommended by the carmaker.

> **WARNING:** The spring used in this suspension is under considerable force. Work carefully and use the proper tools. It is a good idea to install a safety chain through the spring when installing the spring compressor tool. This will reduce the possibility of a serious injury if the spring should break during removal or installation.

1. Raise and support the vehicle by its frame, allowing the control arms to hang free.
2. Remove the wheel/tire assemblies, shock absorbers, and disconnect the stabilizer bar end links, if necessary.

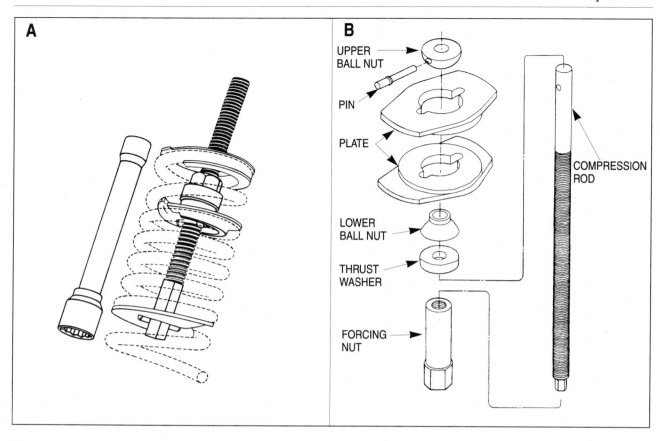

Figure 4-15 Coil spring compressors come in various designs and should be used according to the instructions provided by the tool manufacturer. (Moog Automotive (A), Ford Motor (B))

3. Disconnect the outer tie rod ends from the steering knuckle with a tie rod end remover tool.

4. Install a spring compressor (Figure 4-15) and tighten it until the spring has been compressed enough to provide a clearance at one end. Install a safety chain through the coil spring.

5. If the vehicle uses a strut rod, disconnect it at the control arm.

6. Disconnect the lower ball joint stud and carefully swing the control arm downward until the compressed spring can be removed. Some carmakers recommend removal of the control arm pivot bolts instead of disconnecting the ball joint. This allows the control arm to pivot downward at the ball joint. If this technique is used, work carefully. The control arm can twist and slip, allowing the spring to fall out. It is best to use a transmission jack with an adapter to support the control arm from slipping (Figure 4-16).

7. Remove the compressed spring. If it does not come out easily, use a pry bar to remove the spring from its lower seat.

8. Once the spring has been removed, check the upper and lower spring seats to make sure you understand how the spring should be positioned during installation. Each end of the spring generally fits into a pocket and the lower end must be positioned according to the inspection/drain holes in the control arm.

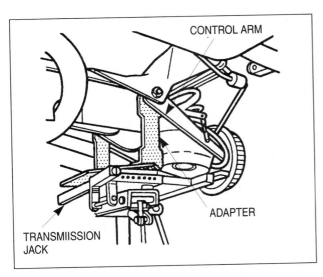

Figure 4-16 An adapter attached to the top of a transmission jack is used to support the lower control arm when the inner pivot bolts are removed. (Oldsmobile Division, General Motors)

9. Measure the length of the compressed spring before removing the compressor tool.

10. Clean and inspect the ball joint stud hole in the steering knuckle and align the cotter pin hole in the stud with the side of the vehicle.

11. Install the spring compressor on the new spring in the same location as on the old spring to assure that the tool can be removed once the new spring is installed. Install a safety chain and compress the new spring to the same length measured in Step 9.

12. Install the compressed spring in the control arm pocket. Pivot the control arm upward, guiding the spring into its seats, and fit the ball joint stud into the steering knuckle. Install and tighten the ball joint stud nut to specifications. If necessary, continue tightening the nut to the nearest cotter pin hole; do NOT back off the nut to align the cotter pin holes.

If the control arm was disconnected at the pivot bolts, move it upward until the holes align, then install the bolts and nuts. If necessary, use a punch to help align the control arm bushing holes with the frame/body holes. Do NOT torque the pivot bolts until the vehicle is on the ground with its mass on the tires.

13. Remove the spring compressor and safety chain. Connect the outer tie rod end to the steering knuckle.

14. Reattach the stabilizer bar end link and/or strut rod, if disconnected, then reinstall the shock absorber and wheel/tire assembly.

15. Repeat the procedure on the other side of the vehicle. When the vehicle is lowered to the ground, torque the control arm pivot bolts, if necessary.

FRONT COIL SPRING REPLACEMENT (SPRING ON UPPER CONTROL ARM)

Removing an upper arm spring is less complicated than removing a lower arm spring. As with the lower arm spring, refer to the factory shop manual and use the procedure and tools recommended by the carmaker. The following procedure is typical.

1. Raise the vehicle by its frame, install safety stands under the lower control arms, and remove the wheel/tire assemblies.

2. Remove the shock absorbers and the upper jounce bumper bracket.

3. Install a spring compressor (Figure 4-15) and compress the spring until it can be removed from the vehicle.

4. Once the spring has been removed, check the upper and lower spring seats to make sure you understand how the spring should be positioned during installation.

5. Measure the compressed length of the spring, then remove the spring compressor and install it on the replacement spring. Compress the new spring to the same length.

6. Install and position the spring, then gradually release the spring compressor until the spring is properly seated.

7. Remove the compressor tool from the spring. Reconnect the jounce bumper, shock absorber, and wheel/tire assembly.

8. Repeat the procedure on the other side of the vehicle.

REAR COIL SPRING SUSPENSIONS

Rear suspensions use a wide variety of spring installations. Since it is beyond the scope of this book to discuss each and every possible installation, the procedures provided below are typical. Before attempting to remove any rear spring, you should refer to the factory shop manual and use the procedure and tools recommended by the carmaker.

REAR COIL SPRING REPLACEMENT (SPRING ON REAR AXLE)

1. Raise the rear of the vehicle with a jack, then place safety stands under the frame side rails.

2. Remove the wheel/tire assemblies if necessary to allow the rear axle to drop far enough and still clear the floor. Support the rear axle with a hydraulic jack.

3. Disconnect the rear shock absorbers at their lower mounts.

4. Check to be sure that height sensing devices, brake hoses, or axle housing breather hoses will NOT be stretched or damaged by lowering the axle. Disconnect those parts if necessary. Try to disconnect brake pipe mountings to avoid actually disconnecting the brake hoses. If brake hoses must be disconnected, the brakes will have to be bled after reconnecting the hose. Lower the

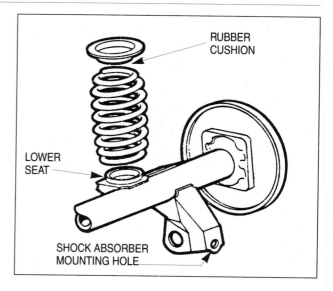

Figure 4-17 Coil spring installation on a rear axle. (Moog Automotive).

rear axle with the hydraulic jack until the spring can be removed.

5. Check the condition of the spring seat (Figure 4-17) and any spring pads that are used. If the old spring uses a rubber cushion, remove it and install on the new spring.

6. Install the new spring, making sure that the spring ends are in the correct position as recommended by a repair manual.

7. Raise the axle with the hydraulic jack and reconnect the shock absorber at the lower mount.

REAR COIL SPRING REPLACEMENT (SPRING ON TRAILING ARM)

The following procedure is used with the rear suspension on some RWD vehicles.

1. Raise the rear of the vehicle with a jack, then place safety stands under the frame side rails.

2. Remove the wheel/tire assemblies, if necessary, and support the rear axle with a hydraulic jack.

3. Check the routing of the rear brake line and hoses. If necessary, discon-

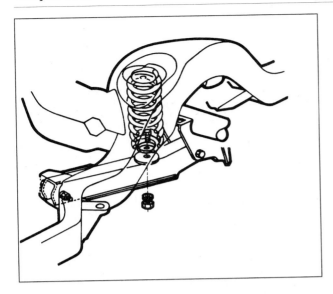

Figure 4-18 One type of coil spring installation on an RWD trailing arm suspension. (Moog Automotive)

nect the brake line brackets as required to avoid possible damage when the axle is lowered. Disconnect any other hoses or height sensing devices as required.

4. Disconnect both rear shock absorbers at their lower mounts.
5. Lower the rear axle with the hydraulic jack and remove the nut, bolt, and spring retainer (Figure 4-18) from each spring. Remove the old springs and lower plates from the vehicle.
6. Check the condition of the lower plates and spring retainers. Replace as necessary.
7. Install the new spring and lower plate on each trailing arm. Position the springs to assure they are properly positioned in the upper seat.
8. Insert each spring retainer, bolt, and nut. Finger-tighten the bolt and nuts, then raise the axle with the hydraulic jack.
9. Reposition the spring retainers as required, then tighten each spring bolt to specifications and reconnect the shock absorbers.

10. Remove the axle support and lower the vehicle to the ground. Tighten both shock absorber bolts to specifications with the suspension supporting the vehicle mass.

The following procedure is used with rear coil spring suspensions on some FWD vehicles. With some installations, you may need to use adhesive to temporarily hold upper insulators in place while raising the axle and spring assembly.

1. Raise the rear of the vehicle with a jack, then place safety stands under the frame side rails.
2. Remove the wheel/tire assemblies, if required, and support the rear axle with a hydraulic jack.
3. Check the routing of the rear brake line and hoses. If necessary, disconnect the brake line brackets as required to avoid possible damage when the axle is lowered. Disconnect any other hoses or height sensing devices as required.
4. Disconnect the rear shock absorbers at their lower mounts.
5. Lower the rear axle with the hydraulic jack and remove the screws holding the cup to the rail (Figure 4-19), and then remove the spring and upper isolator on each side.
6. Check the condition of the cups, upper isolators, and jounce bumpers. Replace as required.
7. Install the cup to the rail, then fit the isolator over the jounce bumper and install the spring. Repeat this step to install the spring on the other side.
8. Raise the axle with the hydraulic jack and connect both shock absorbers to the axle.
9. Remove the axle support and lower the vehicle to the ground. Tighten both shock absorber bolts to specifications with the suspension supporting the vehicle mass.

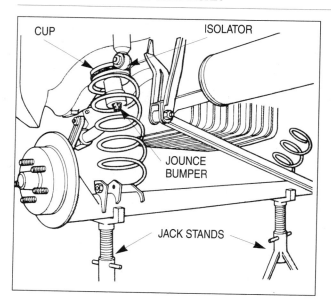

Figure 4-19 An example of a rear coil spring installation on a FWD trailing arm rear suspension. (Chrysler)

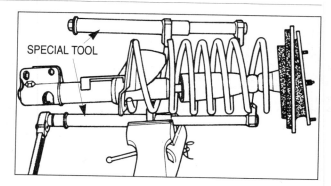

Figure 4-20 A typical strut coil spring compressor. (Chrysler)

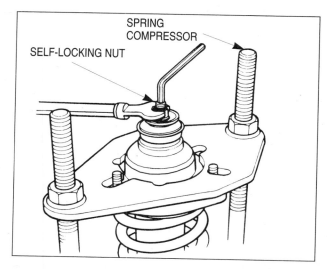

Figure 4-21 A hex wrench is used to hold the strut shaft on some designs. (Honda)

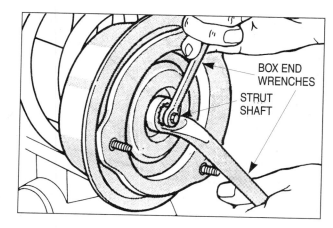

Figure 4-22 Other strut shafts are provided with wrench flats that can be used to prevent the shaft from moving when removing the nut. (Chrysler)

Strut Coil Spring Replacement

The coil spring on FWD vehicles using a modified strut rear suspension (spring on lower control arm) is removed with the same procedure as the front coil spring installed on the lower control arm described earlier. The following generalized procedure is used with a MacPherson strut (spring on strut) design.

1. With the strut removed from the vehicle and securely clamped horizontally in a holding fixture or vise, install an appropriate spring compressor according to the tool manufacturer's instructions (Figure 4-20).

2. Compress the spring enough to provide clearance between the spring and one of the mounts. Hold the end of the strut shaft from rotating and loosen the strut shaft nut. Strut piston rods generally have an internal hex opening (Figure 4-21) or wrench flats (Figure 4-22) to hold the rod from rotating during this step. If not, use an air wrench to spin the nut off. If the nut is a self-locking type,

discard it and install a new nut during reassembly.

3. Remove the upper strut mount from the strut assembly. Carefully inspect the mount for deterioration or damage. Mount designs used by carmakers differ considerably. If you are not familiar with the one you are working on, refer to the proper service manual. Some mounts may contain a steering pivot bearing that should be checked for smooth rotation without excessive clearance. Other mounts may consist of several components and their positioning should be noted as they are removed (Figure 4-23).

4. Remove the spring and compressor from the strut assembly. Mark the spring to identify it for reinstallation on the same side of the vehicle, measure the length of the compressed spring, and then carefully and slowly release the compressor and remove it from the spring.

5. To install the new spring, securely clamp the strut assembly vertically in the holding fixture or vise.

6. Install the spring compressor on the replacement spring and compress it to the same length as measured in Step 4.

7. Fit the compressed spring onto the strut assembly with the end of the coil properly seated in the lower spring mount recess (Figure 4-24).

8. Pull the piston rod upward to its completely extended position and install the dust shield and mount assembly on the end of the rod with the upper

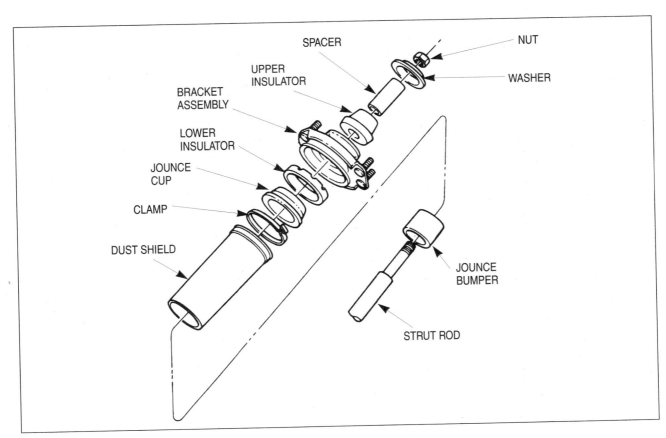

Figure 4-23 A typical upper strut mount consisting of several individual components. (Ford Motor)

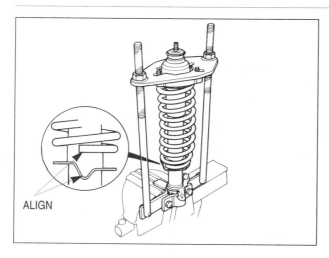

Figure 4-24 The bottom end of the coil spring must align with the recess in the lower spring mount. (Honda)

spring seat properly aligned. If the mount assembly consists of several components, be sure to install them in the proper order (Figure 4-23).

9. Install the rebound retainer and shaft nut. Hold the strut shaft from moving with the hex wrench (Figure 4-21) or special tool recommended by the carmaker (Figure 4-25) and tighten the nut to specifications. Some carmakers specify that the shaft nut on struts with rubber upper

Figure 4-25 A special tool must be used to tighten the shaft nut on some struts. (Chrysler)

mounts NOT be torqued until the strut has been reinstalled in the vehicle with its wheels straight ahead to eliminate pull.

10. Make sure the spring remains correctly aligned in its lower seat (Figure 4-24), then slowly release the compressor tool and remove it from the strut spring.

SERVICING SHOCK ABSORBER AND STRUT

Driving a vehicle with defective shock absorbers or struts is unsafe. Defective shocks or struts allow the springs to oscillate, affecting vehicle handling and directional control.

ON-VEHICLE INSPECTION AND TESTING

Shock absorbers and struts should be checked for three conditions — weakness, noise, and leaks. Use the following procedures to evaluate the performance of conventional shock absorbers and struts on the vehicle.

Weak Shocks or Struts

1. Check and adjust tire pressure to specifications.
2. Determine the normal driving and load conditions under which the vehicle is operated.
3. Test each front shock absorber or strut one at a time by rapidly pushing down and releasing the bumper nearest the shock or strut being checked. When released, the vehicle should move up beyond normal height, and then back to normal height. Some vehicles with extra stiff shock absorbers may move directly back to the normal height without going above it. If the vehicle moves up, then down, and back up again, the hydraulic damping is weak and

the shock absorber or strut is probably worn out. If in doubt, check another later model of the same vehicle, if available. Any vehicle that makes several up and down movements after being released definitely has shock absorbers or struts that should be replaced.

4. Repeat Step 3 with the rear shocks or struts.

5. If there is much difference between the left and right rear shock absorbers, support the rear axle enough to unload the shock mounts.

6. Disconnect the lower shock absorber mountings. Stroke each shock through its maximum travel in both directions at different rates of speed, comparing the compression and rebound resistance of the left and right units. Rebound resistance should be about twice that of compression resistance. A hissing noise heard during this step is normal; other types of sounds are NOT. If the two shocks do not feel comparable in both directions, or if a noise other than a slight hissing sound is heard, replace both shock absorbers.

TIP TECH TIP: Although only one shock absorber may appear to be defective, both should be replaced as a set to assure that they provide equal control.

Noisy Shocks or Struts

1. Raise and support the vehicle on a hoist or safety stands and check all shock or strut mounting fasteners for proper torque.

2. Check for shiny areas that indicate interference with other components.

3. Inspect the condition and appearance of the jounce bumpers. A shiny or deteriorated bumper indicates suspension bottoming, which may or may not be a defect, depending on the severity of the terrain and driving.

4. If NO defects are noted, lower the vehicle to the ground and isolate the suspected unit by performing the bounce test described in Step 3 and Step 4 of 'weak shocks or struts' above.

Hydraulic Fluid Leaks

1. Raise the vehicle with the wheels unsupported to fully extend the shocks or struts and allow inspection of the seal cover area at the top of the reservoir.

2. Inspect the seal cover area for leakage. A slight amount of fluid is normal, since the seal allows some seepage to lubricate the piston rod. A built-in fluid reserve accommodates this seepage. If fluid is found around the seal cover, as well as considerable fluid on the shock or strut body, replace the unit.

3. If you are unsure about the fluid found in Step 2, wipe the shock or strut cartridge clean, activate the unit, and reinspect for leakage. If the unit is leaking, fluid will reappear as in Step 2. Replace the shock or strut cartridge.

Air Pockets in Shocks and Struts

Air pockets can develop when replacement shocks or struts are stored horizontally, as well as in units installed on a vehicle that has NOT been driven for a period of time. Before bench-checking a shock absorber or strut cartridge, it should be stroked (extended and compressed) vertically at least five times to purge or bleed any air pockets from the pressure chamber (Figure 4-26). Hold the unit with its top end facing

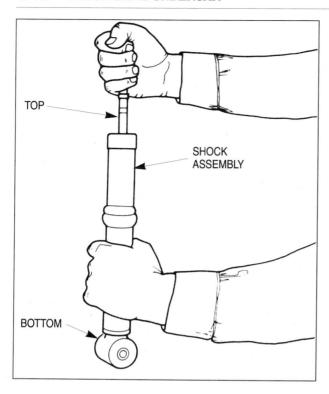

Figure 4-26 Stroking a shock absorber. (Chrysler)

up during extension, and facing down during compression. Use the following procedure to evaluate the performance of conventional shock absorbers and struts off the vehicle.

1. Secure the shock absorber or strut vertically in a vise. Do NOT clamp the unit by its mounting threads or reservoir tube.

2. Extend and compress the unit manually at different speeds and note the resistance. Rebound resistance should be about twice as great as compression resistance. Resistance also should be smooth and constant at each speed of movement.

3. If any of the symptoms below are noted, replace the shock or strut cartridge:
   a. clicking noise during a quick reversal in stroke direction
   b. skipping or lagging at mid-stroke

   reversal of pumping direction
   c. seizure of the piston rod at any point other than the extreme end of travel
   d. a noise (other than hissing) after a full stroke in each direction.

AIR-ADJUSTABLE SHOCK ABSORBERS

These are essentially conventional shock absorbers enclosed in an air chamber (Figure 4-27) and are used with RWD level control systems. A rubber sleeve connected to the dust tube and shock reservoir forms a flexible chamber that extends the shock absorber whenever air pressure inside the chamber increases. Checking this type of shock absorber requires an additional step to determine if it has an air leak. This involves pressurizing the shock absorber to approximately 90 psi and using a mild soap and water solution at all points where air

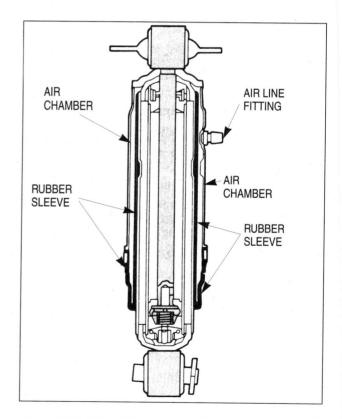

Figure 4-27 Potential air-adjustable shock absorber leak points. (General Motors)

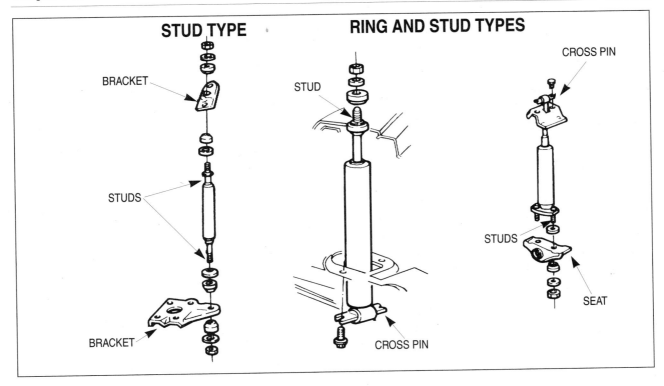

Figure 4-28 Stud and cross pin shock absorber mountings. (Ford Motor)

might leak, including the air line and its fitting. If air is leaking, bubbles will appear in the solution. This procedure is similar to that used to locate a tire leak.

SHOCK ABSORBER REPLACEMENT

Direct-acting or tubular shock absorbers generally are mounted in one of three ways. Figure 4-28 shows the stud type and cross pin mounts; the third type uses a mounting eye (Figure 4-29). Shock absorber placement and attachment method used depends upon suspension design, but in all cases, the vehicle must be raised and supported on a hoist or safety stands.

> **TIP TECH TIP:** Remove gas pressurized shocks with care, since they will extend to their full travel when released. If this happens, it will require considerable effort to compress the shock.

Removing the fasteners from cross pin and eye mounts present no problems, but the nut used on upper stud type mounts is prone to rust and can seize in place. If the

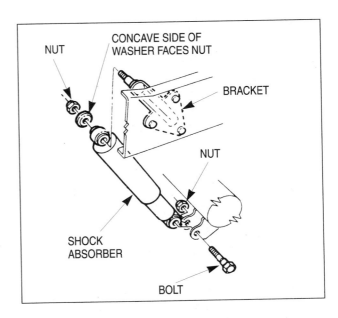

Figure 4-29 Shock absorber eye mounts.

stud nut has seized, the piston rod and stud will rotate with the nut as it turns. Although the stud generally has two flats to allow the use of a second wrench in holding the stud from rotating, inexperienced technicians are tempted to hold the piston with locking pliers. This technique has several disadvantages. It does NOT work, as the pliers will slip on the piston rod's smooth polished surface. It also is the surest way to ruin a shock absorber, as the pliers will damage the rod's polished surface. When the rod moves, it will destroy the upper shock absorber bushing and seal. Of course, if the shock absorber is being replaced, it does not matter if it is damaged during removal. But make sure the new shock absorbers are available before using techniques that would damage the old shock absorbers.

There are several methods of removing a seized stud nut easily and without damage. The preferred method is to start by applying a liberal amount of penetrating oil to the stud threads. If there is sufficient access to the nut, hold the stud from moving with a second wrench on its flats. When working space is limited, use one of the special tools designed to hold the stud from turning while the nut is unscrewed (Figure 4-30 and Figure 4-31). If the nut is rusted to a point where it cannot be loosened with penetrating oil and the special tool, it can be destroyed with a nut breaker tool, or with an air impact hammer and chisel.

Disconnect the shock at the bottom stud or hanger (Figures 4-32, 4-33, and 4-34), then at the top, and remove it from the vehicle. On some vehicles, the top mounting nut can be reached from under the hood (Figure 4-35) or through an opening in the trunk (Figure 4-36). When such access is available, disconnecting the upper fastener before lifting the vehicle will speed up the job. If the upper mounting

Figure 4-30 One type of special tool used to hold a shock absorber stud from rotating when removing the attaching nut.

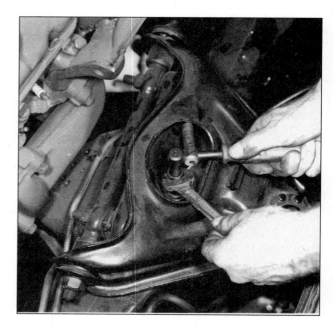

Figure 4-31 The tool fits over the shock stud and prevents it from turning while the nut is removed.

points are located in the wheelwells, remove the wheels and tires to provide sufficient working space. When installing new

Figure 4-32 Disconnecting an eye-type shock absorber.

Figure 4-34 Disconnecting a cross pin-type shock absorber.

Figure 4-33 Disconnecting a stud-type shock absorber.

Figure 4-35 The upper end of a front shock absorber can be disconnected in the engine compartment on some vehicles.

shocks, ALWAYS use the replacement bushings (Figure 4-37) and other mounting hardware furnished with the shock. Follow the instructions provided with the replacement unit to make certain the bushings, retainers, insulators, and other components are positioned properly.

In most cases, shock absorbers limit rear axle downward travel. Coil spring rear suspensions can be damaged if the wheels are not supported properly when the

Figure 4-36 The upper end of some rear shock absorbers can be disconnected in the trunk. The attaching nut generally is covered by a plastic cap.

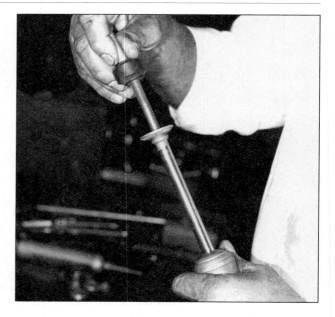

Figure 4-37 Follow the instructions provided with the replacement shock when installing the new bushings and hardware.

shocks are removed. Before removing the rear shocks, place safety stands under the rear axle housing to prevent it from dropping. This will prevent an excessive axle drop that might cause damage to the suspension or brake line, as well as a possible personal injury.

STRUT CARTRIDGE REPLACEMENT

The service life of the shock absorber component in a strut suspension is shorter than that of a conventional shock absorber due to the extreme loads it absorbs during operation. Until replacement strut cartridges were introduced, strut shock absorber service was limited to rebuilding the entire unit or installing a complete replacement strut assembly. The first choice was a difficult job, and both were expensive. It required a skilled technician to disassemble the strut, install all new internal components and seals, and reassemble the unit with the proper amount of oil. Even then, there was NO

way to assure that the rebuilt unit was up to performance requirements. With replacement cartridges now available, a technician can restore vehicle ride and handling to factory specs by removing the inner tube and piston rod assembly and inserting a sealed, calibrated cartridge in the OEM strut housing.

Strut cartridge service involves disconnecting or removing the strut and removing the spring for access to the shock absorber assembly. Experienced technicians with the necessary tools and equipment often can service a strut without disconnecting its lower end from the vehicle. While this method can save time and effort in some cases, removing the stut completely from the vehicle makes the technician's job easier by providing better access. The procedure used to remove and install a strut assembly depends on which method the carmaker uses to connect it to the control arm or steering knuckle. In the three most commonly used methods, the strut may be:

- bracket-mounted to the knuckle with two or three bolts.
- locked to the knuckle with a clamp and pinch bolt.
- attached to the top of the knuckle with three bolts.

Each of the above methods allows the strut to be disconnected from the steering knuckle without disconnecting the hub and CV joint. With the other two attachment methods, the strut is:

- integral with the knuckle and bolted to the steering arm.
- integral with the knuckle and connected to the steering arm by a ball joint.

Because of the variety in strut mounting methods, you should refer to the recommended procedure in a quality repair manual when removing and installing a strut assembly.

Once the strut has been removed from the vehicle, and the spring removed from the stut, a replacement shock absorber cartridge can be installed in most struts. Struts that are integral with the steering knuckle may be welded together in such a way as to discourage shock absorber replacement; this type of strut can be opened with a pipe cutter if replacement parts are available, but it generally is less expensive and time-consuming to replace the entire strut assembly.

> **WARNING:** Use extreme caution and follow the carmaker's procedure exactly when cutting a gas-charged shock open. The gas is under high pressure and can cause serious personal injury.

Use the following general procedure to install a replacement strut cartridge:

1. With the spring removed and the strut properly clamped in a vise, use a suitable spanner wrench to remove the retaining nut from the strut body. Save the nut for reuse if none is supplied with the replacement cartridge.

> **TECH TIP:** The retaining nut is an integral part of the cartridge in some strut designs (Figure 4-38).

2. Remove the O-ring (if so equipped) and withdraw the shock absorber from the strut body. Work slowly to prevent the suction created by the close fit between the components from pulling oil with the shock absorber that will splatter as the shock is removed.
3. If the strut is equipped with its original shock absorber, remove and discard the old piston and all internal strut components. If the strut contains a replacement cartridge, remove and discard the cartridge.

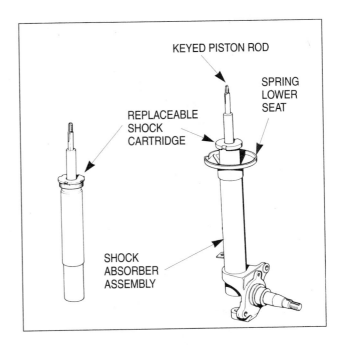

Figure 4-38 Some strut designs use replaceable cartridges with an integral retaining nut. (Ford Motor)

4. Drain the oil from the strut body. Clean the strut body and threads. Pour a spoonful or two of engine oil back into the strut body to help conduct heat away from the replacement cartridge.

5. Insert the replacement cartridge in

the strut body. Install the O-ring (if so equipped) and thread the retaining nut in place by hand to avoid cross-threading.

6. Use a spanner wrench and tighten the retaining nut to the carmaker's specification.

? REVIEW QUESTIONS

1. Technician A says that sagged springs will cause a change in suspension geometry. Technician B says that trim height is measured at the same points on all vehicles. Who is right?
   (A) A only
   (B) B only
   (C) Both A and B
   (D) Neither A nor B

2. Technician A says that trim height measurements are affected by tire inflation pressures. Technician B says they are affected by tire diameter. Who is right?
   (A) A only
   (B) B only
   (C) Both A and B
   (D) Neither A nor B

3. Technician A says that trim height measurements taken on both sides of a vehicle should be within 1/4" of each other. Technician B says that if vehicle lean is evident when the front end is raised, a rear spring is at fault.
   (A) A only
   (B) B only
   (C) Both A and B
   (D) Neither A nor B

4. Technician A says that as a leaf spring flexes, the distance between the spring eyes usually lengthens reduces the shock sent to the vehicle body. Technician B says that leaf springs may be mounted above or below the axle.

Who is right?
   (A) A only
   (B) B only
   (C) Both A and B
   (D) Neither A nor B

5. Technician A says that when installing a leaf spring, the shackle and front spring eye bolts should be torqued before lowering the wheels to the ground. Technician B says that a spring with a broken leaf must be replaced with a new spring. Who is right?
   (A) A only
   (B) B only
   (C) Both A and B
   (D) Neither A nor B

6. Technician A says that when the front end of a vehicle equipped with torsion bars sits low, the torsion bars should be replaced. Technician B says the torsion bars can be adjusted to correct the problem. Who is right?
   (A) A only
   (B) B only
   (C) Both A and B
   (D) Neither A nor B

7. Technician A says that both torsion bars and coil springs are subject to breaking from stress raisers. Technician B says that torsion bars without a splined end can be used on either side of the vehicle.
   (A) A only

(B) B only
(C) Both A and B
(D) Neither A nor B

8. Technician A says that coil springs may be factory coated with epoxy or paint to prevent rusting. Technician B says that rust is a primary cause of stress raisers. Who is right?
(A) A only
(B) B only
(C) Both A and B
(D) Neither A nor B

9. Technician A says that coil spring sag can be corrected by the use of shims or spacers. Technician B says that a coil spring can be replaced by any other coil spring of the same length and diameter. Who is right?
(A) A only
(B) B only
(C) Both A and B
(D) Neither A nor B

10. Technician A says that both front coil springs must have the same spring rating. Technician B says that the part number on the old spring should be used to select the correct replacement spring. Who is right?
(A) A only
(B) B only
(C) Both A and B
(D) Neither A nor B

11. Technician A says that when a new coil spring is installed on a vehicle with an SLA suspension, all fasteners should be torqued before lowering the vehicle to the ground. Technician B says that front end alignment should be checked and adjusted after installing the spring. Who is right?
(A) A only
(B) B only
(C) Both A and B
(D) Neither A nor B

12. Technician A says that a spring compressor should be installed before the control arm ball joint or inner pivot bolts are disconnected. Technician B says that pivoting the control arm downward after disconnecting the ball joint allows spring removal. Who is right?
(A) A only
(B) B only
(C) Both A and B
(D) Neither A nor B

13. Technician A says that before removing a coil spring, it is good practice to install a safety chain. Technician B says that when a control arm is disconnected at the inner pivot bolts instead of the ball joint, a jack and adapter should be used to support the control arm and prevent twisting. Who is right?
(A) A only
(B) B only
(C) Both A and B
(D) Neither A nor B

14. Technician A says that strut piston rods generally have an internal hex or wrench flats for use in holding the rod when removing the strut shaft nut. Technician B says that you should NEVER use an air wrench to spin the nut off. Who is right?
(A) A only
(B) B only
(C) Both A and B
(D) Neither A nor B

15. Technician A says that coil springs used with modified strut suspensions are removed with a procedure similiar to that used when removing a spring mounted on a lower control arm. Technician B says that strut upper mounts may consist of several different components. Who is right?
(A) A only
(B) B only

(C) Both A and B

(D) Neither A nor B

16. Technician A says that shock absorbers should be replaced in front or rear pairs instead of individually. Technician B says that rebound and compression resistance should be equal when testing a shock absorber. Who is right?

(A) A only

(B) B only

(C) Both A and B

(D) Neither A nor B

17. Technician A says that the best way to remove a rusted nut on upper stud-type shock mounts is to use vise grips. Technician B says that the nut can be removed by using a second wrench to hold the stud from rotating. Who is right?

(A) A only

(B) B only

(C) Both A and B

(D) Neither A nor B

18. Technician A says that the rear axle may drop unless properly supported when the shock absorbers are disconnected. Technician B says that the retaining nut is an integral part of some strut shock cartridges. Who is right?

(A) A only

(B) B only

(C) Both A and B

(D) Neither A nor B

SERVICING BALL JOINTS, CONTROL ARMS, STRUT RODS, AND STABILIZER BARS

 OBJECTIVES

After completion of this chapter, you should be able to:

- Use the required procedures to check ball joint clearance and condition on three different vehicles assigned by the instructor.

- Visually inspect a ball joint, report its condition to the instructor, and properly lubricate it with the approved procedure.

- Replace a defective control arm ball joint, using the appropriate method and tools.

- Remove a lower control arm, inspect and replace the bushings as required, then reinstall the arm on the vehicle.

- Inspect and replace strut rod and stabilizer bar bushing, when necessary.

BALL JOINT INSPECTION

Ball joint problems fall into two catagories — physical damage to the boot or seal, and excessive wear. Boot or seal damage allows the ball joint lubricant to leak out and contamination to enter the joint. Since ball joints with a damaged boot or seal will eventually fail, they should be checked periodically and replaced whenever a defect is found.

Ball joints should be visually inspected for leakage, boot damage, or control arm cracks at the carmaker's specified intervals, or whenever the vehicle is off the ground for other undercar service (Figure 5-1). Because you cannot see the entire ball joint circumference, check it by running a finger around the boot to feel for possible problems. If no damage is seen or felt, gently squeeze the boot to check the lubricant inside. If the boot does not feel firm, indicating it is full of grease, the ball joint should be lubricated, if lubrication is recommended by the carmaker.

S 95

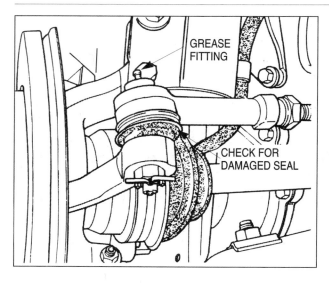

Figure 5-1 When inspecting ball joints, check the seal or dust boot and make sure it fits securely in place. (Chrysler)

Wear causes excessive ball joint clearance, but the amount considered excessive depends on the suspension design and how and where the ball joint is used. Since each carmaker establishes the permissible stud endplay, tolerances vary between different makes and models of vehicle. Load-carrying ball joints are made with a slight non-loaded clearance that disappears once vehicle mass is placed on the joint. Follower ball joints are friction-loaded and should have NO clearance. Although the follower joint is mounted on the unloaded control arm and does not carry any vehicle mass, both types of ball joints are subjected to the same twisting and pounding. For this reason, both types should be periodically checked, since a worn follower ball joint is just as dangerous as one that carries the load. When replacing a worn load-carrying ball joint, a technician should replace the follower joint at the same time.

The type of ball joint and how it is used will determine which of the methods below should be used to check for wear and excessive clearance:

- wear indicator ball joints
- friction-loaded ball joints
- load-carrying ball joints (spring on lower control arm)
- load-carrying ball joints (spring on upper control arm)
- load-carrying ball joints (twin I-beam or solid axle)

Like trim height specifications, allowable ball joint clearance specifications can be found in factory shop manuals or specialized technical publications provided by the carmaker or aftermarket manufacturers of suspension components.

TIP TECH TIP: Some states have regulations concerning ball joint replacement that require a shop to inform the customer of both the specified clearance and the actual clearance measured in a worn ball joint before replacing the defective joint.

There are two schools of thought regarding the proper method of determining excessive ball joint clearance. One recommends checking axial movement (A, Figure 5-2); the other recommends checking tire sidewall movement (B, Figure 5-2). Since axial movement is the actual movement of the ball joint stud in its housing, it is a direct movement measurement made at a single point. Tire sidewall movement is a multiplied reading taken at the wheel, and varies with the length of the arm (the upper ball joint as pivot point extending to the spot on the wheel or tire where the reading is made). The measurement obtained through this method will vary according to the spot on the wheel or tire where it is taken. Because inexperienced technicians can easily misinterpret a loose wheel bearing as a defective ball joint, this method should be used with care. If the vehicle has adjustable front wheel bearings

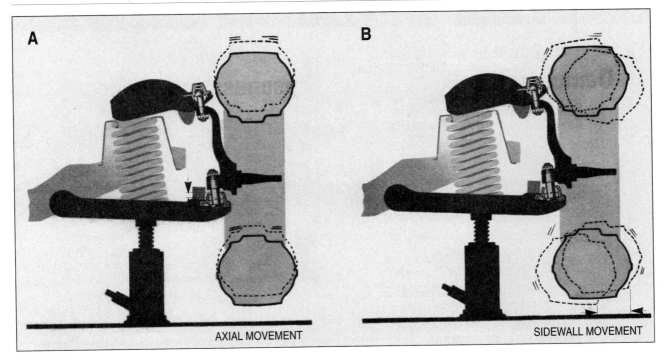

Figure 5-2 The two methods used to determine excessive ball joint clearance. (Moog Automotive)

you can eliminate the bearing movement by tightening the wheel bearings to eliminate endplay; but then you have to adjust the wheel bearings afterwards. And this technique will only work on those vehicles with adjustable front bearings.

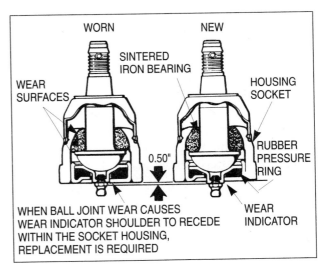

Figure 5-3 One type of wear indicator ball joint. (Moog Automotive)

> **TIP** **TECH TIP:** When using the tire sidewall method, you can avoid any possible confusion between wheel bearing looseness and ball joint clearance by having an assistant apply the brakes, which will prevent all types of wheel bearings from wobbling while you check the ball joints. If available, use a pedal jack and you will not need the assistant.

CHECKING WEAR INDICATOR BALL JOINTS

Introduced in 1973, wear indicator ball joints (Figure 5-3) are used primarily as load-carrying joints on RWD vehicles, although some FWD vehicles also use them. The exact inspection method used to determine wear on this type of ball joint depends on its design, but all require that the vehicle's mass rest on the wheels to

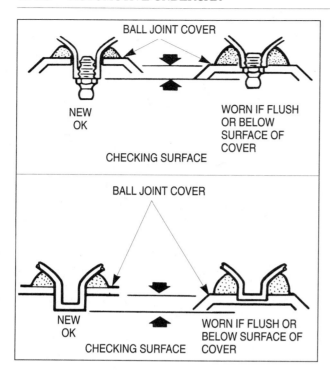

Figure 5-4 Replace the ball joint if there is no projection through the cover. (Ford Motor)

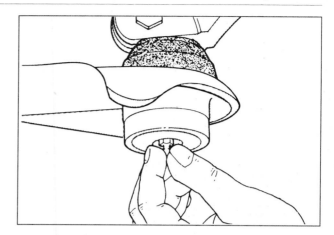

Figure 5-5 If the grease fitting can be rotated with this type of ball joint, clearance is excessive and the ball joint should be replaced. (Chrysler)

load the joint while making the inspection.

GM and some Ford vehicles have a protruding boss design, and are inspected to determine the position of a nipple into which the grease fitting is threaded. On some vehicles there may not be a grease fitting, but the nipple is still there. When new, this nipple projects 0.050" beyond the surface of the ball joint cover. Normal wear causes the nipple to gradually recede into the cover (Figure 5-3 and Figure 5-4).

When checking this type of wear indicator ball joint:

1. Park the vehicle on a level surface supported by the wheels to properly load the ball joints.
2. Clean the lower surface of the ball joint to remove all grease and dirt.
3. You should be able to see the nipple sticking out of the bottom of the joint. If not, scrape the ball joint cover with a flat-blade screwdriver tip or your fingernail. If the nipple or plug is

either flush with or inside the cover, wear is excessive and the ball joint must be replaced.

In the late 1970's, American Motor Corporation (AMC, now a part of the Chrysler Corporation) used a wear indicator ball joint design that is inspected by removing the lubrication plug and inserting a 2-3 inch length of stiff wire or thin rod until it contacts the ball stud. After marking the point on the wire or rod where it aligns with the outer edge of the plug hole, the wire or rod is removed and measured for comparison with specifications. Another type of wear indicator ball joint used by Chrysler is checked by trying to move or rotate the grease fitting (Figure 5-5). If it can be moved by finger pressure, the ball joint should be replaced.

CHECKING FRICTION-LOADED BALL JOINTS

This type of ball joint carries no mass and usually has a slight amount of preload, but no clearance. Its condition can be checked for free play or preload. In general, replacement of a friction-loaded or follower ball joint is recommended whenever a load-carrying ball joint is replaced. The follower joint is on the arm that does not support the mass. If the spring is on the upper arm, that arm supports the mass of the vehicle, and the follower joint is on the lower arm. If the spring is on the lower arm, the follower joint is on the upper arm. On a strut suspension, the bearing at the top of the strut usually carries the load, so the follower joint is at the bottom of the steering knuckle. There are many variations in suspension design, some seldom seen. ALWAYS consult a good repair manual if you are working on a suspension that is not familiar to you.

Free Play Check

To check the follower ball joint for free play, raise the vehicle on a frame-contact hoist, or with floor jacks beneath the underbody until the wheels drop to their fully-down position (this unloads the mass-carrying ball joint). Have an assistant rock the wheel in and out while you check for movement between the lower end of the steering knuckle and the control arm (Figure 5-6). If any movement is noted, the ball joint has excessive clearance and must be replaced. Be careful when making this check, because there is a lot of flexibility in modern lightweight suspensions. You may be able to shake the wheel in and out a considerable distance, but you are only concerned in this check with movement in the ball joint itself.

Preload Check

To measure the ball joint preload, disconnect the ball joint stud from the steering knuckle (with some vehicles, you may have to remove the lower control arm to perform this check). Move the ball joint stud back and forth several times (Figure 5-7), then thread the nut back on the stud. Run the nut down to the end of the stud threads or install a second nut to act as a jam nut that will force the stud to rotate with the

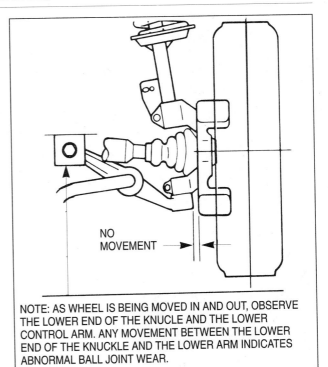

NOTE: AS WHEEL IS BEING MOVED IN AND OUT, OBSERVE THE LOWER END OF THE KNUCLE AND THE LOWER CONTROL ARM. ANY MOVEMENT BETWEEN THE LOWER END OF THE KNUCKLE AND THE LOWER ARM INDICATES ABNORMAL BALL JOINT WEAR.

Figure 5-6 Checking lower ball joints on a MacPherson strut suspension. The vehicle must be supported on the frame (arrow), allowing the suspension to hang free. (Ford Motor)

nut. Use a pound force-inch (commonly known as inch-pound) torque wrench to slowly turn the nut (Figure 5-7) and measure the amount of turning torque required to rotate the stud against the internal resistance of the ball joint. Compare the torque reading against the carmaker's specifications. If it exceeds specifications, replace the ball joint.

CHECKING LOAD-CARRYING BALL JOINTS (SPRING ON LOWER CONTROL ARM)

When the vehicle's mass is transferred to the steering knuckle through the spring and lower control arm, the lower ball joint becomes the load-carrying joint. Vehicle mass either forces the joint together (compression) or tries to pull it apart (tension) depending on whether the design places the

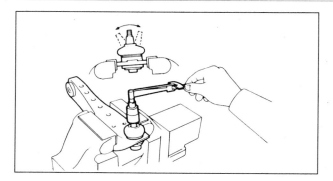

Figure 5-7 Checking ball joint preload or turning torque with a torque wrench. (Toyota)

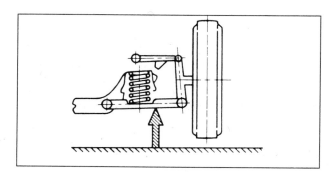

Figure 5-8 Placement of the lifting force to unload the ball joint when the spring is on the lower arm. (Moog Automotive)

steering knuckle socket below or above the arm. Figures 5-9 and 5-10 shows ball joints that are in compression when the vehicle is on the ground because the steering knuckle joint is below the arm. Lower ball joint clearance cannot be measured properly unless the joint is unloaded, that is, the vehicle and spring mass is removed. This is done by placing the lifting force or axle stand under the lower control arm as close as possible to the ball joint (Figure 5-8), which will compress the spring and unload the joint. If you should incorrectly lift the vehicle by the frame it allows the spring to push downward and hold both ball joints tightly loaded. A ball joint checked under this condition will appear to be good because it is held tight by the spring.

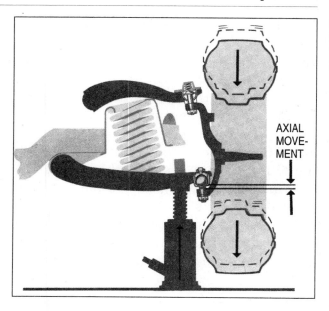

Figure 5-9 A lower compression-loaded ball joint — coil spring suspension. The jack is placed to unload the lower joint for checking. (Moog Automotive)

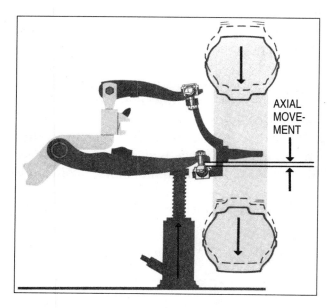

Figure 5-10 A lower compression-loaded ball joint — torsion bar suspension, supported for lower ball joint checking. The torsion bar attaches to the lower arm. (Moog Automotive)

Various ball joint checking gauges are offered by numerous manufacturers of aftermarket suspension components. These gauges generally consist of a dial indicator attached to a length of flexible tubing that clamps to a point on the suspension with vise-grip pliers.

To check the clearance of this type of ball joint:

1. Raise the vehicle wheel with a jack or stand positioned under the lower control arm close to the ball joint (Figure 5-9 and Figure 5-10). If a suspension contact hoist is used instead of a jack, the hoist lift pad should be located in a similar position.

2. With the tire raised off the ground, check to make sure the jounce or rebound bumper does NOT contact the suspension.

3A. Tire sidewall movement measurement: make sure the wheel bearings are properly adjusted or apply the brakes, then install a dial indicator on the lower control arm. Position its stylus against the inner side of the wheel rim next to the lower ball joint (Figure 5-11) and set the gauge to zero. Grasp the tire and rock it gently at the top and the bottom. Compare the dial indicator reading to specifications. Replace the ball joint if the reading is out of specification.

3B. Axial movement measurement: install the dial indicator so it can read the up-and-down movement of the ball joint, then set the gauge to zero. Use a pry bar placed under the tire to raise the wheel and tire assembly as far as possible. With maximum force applied to the pry bar, note the dial indicator reading. Compare the reading to the carmaker's specification. Replace the ball joint if the reading is excessive.

CHECKING LOAD-CARRYING BALL JOINTS (SPRING ON UPPER CONTROL ARM)

A different method of unloading the ball joint must be used when the spring is above the upper control arm. To prevent spring pressure from being applied to the upper ball joint, a brace or support wedge must be installed as shown in Figure 5-12, and the vehicle raised by its frame. The brace or wedge holds the control arm in a relatively normal position and transfers spring pressure to the frame, unloading the joint to allow an accurate measurement. To prevent the stabilizer bar from twisting and loading the ball joints, brace both sides of the vehicle, even if you only plan to check one side. On some vehicles the upper arm is recessed above the frame, and a block of wood can be placed between the arm and the frame.

To check the clearance of this type of ball joint:

1. With the vehicle on a flat surface providing access to the upper control arms, install a support wedge or wood block on each side to hold the control arms up when the vehicle is raised in the air.

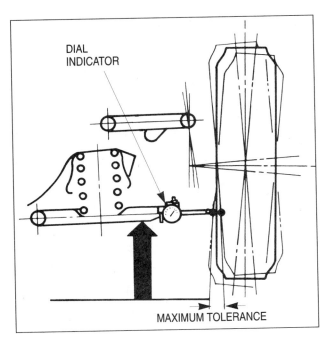

Figure 5-11 Lower ball joint movement inspection point — spring on lower arm. The arrow indicates where the jack should be placed. (Ford Motor)

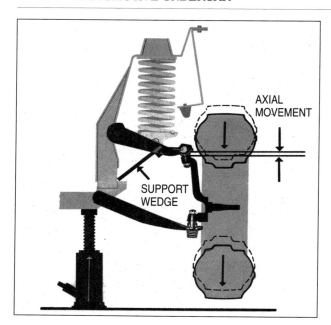

Figure 5-12 An upper compression-loaded ball joint — coil spring suspension, with spring on upper arm. The jack is on the frame, and the wedge holds the upper arm up. (Moog Automotive)

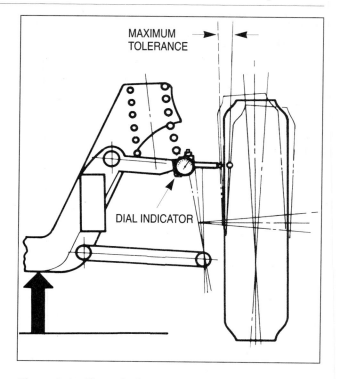

Figure 5-13 Upper ball joint movement inspection point — spring on upper arm. The arrow represents a jack on the frame. A wood block supports the upper arm. (Ford Motor)

2. Raise the vehicle wheels with jacks positioned under the frame (Figure 5-12). If a suspension contact hoist is used instead of jacks, the hoist lift pads should be positioned to lift the vehicle frame.

3. With the tires raised off the ground, check to make sure the jounce or rebound bumpers do NOT contact the suspension.

4A. Tire sidewall movement measurement: make sure the wheel bearings are properly adjusted or apply the brakes, then install a dial indicator on the upper control arm. Position its stylus against the inner side of the wheel rim next to the upper ball joint (Figure 5-13) and set the gauge to zero. Grasp the tire and rock it at the top and bottom. Compare the dial indicator reading to specifications. Replace the ball joint if the reading is excessive.

4B. Axial movement measurement: install the dial indicator so it can read the up-and-down movement of the ball joint, then set the gauge to zero. Use a pry bar placed under the tire to raise the wheel and tire assembly as far as possible. With maximum force applied to the pry bar, note the dial indicator reading. Compare the reading to the carmaker's specification. Replace the ball joint if the reading is excessive.

CHECKING LOAD-CARRYING BALL JOINTS (TWIN I-BEAM OR SOLID AXLE)

This type of axle is used on light duty trucks and some 4WD sport utility vehicles. Both ball joints on each side carry a share of the vehicle load, and are checked either for side clearance or turning torque. The method to be used will be specified by the carmaker.

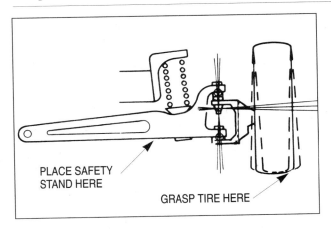

Figure 5-14 Upper and lower ball joint inspection — twin I-beam axles. (Ford Motor)

> ⚠️ **WARNING:** Be sure to remove the support wedges from both sides of the vehicle.

To check ball joint side clearance:

1. Raise the vehicle and place jack-stands under the axles at the location shown in Figure 5-14.
2. Have an assistant grasp the wheel at the bottom and move it in and out while you watch for any movement between the axle jaw and the steering knuckle at the lower ball joint. Replace the lower ball joint if movement exceeds specifications (generally 1/32").
3. Repeat Step 2, grasping the wheel at the top and moving it in and out while watching for movement between the axle jaw and the steering knuckle at the upper ball joint. The maximum allowable movement generally is the same as the lower ball joint.

To check ball joint turning torque:

1. Raise the vehicle with a hoist or jack. Support the vehicle with jackstands, as required.
2. Separate the tie rod end from the steering arm.
3. Using a socket on the ball joint nut and an pound force-inch torque wrench, measure the force required to turn the steering knuckle. In place of the torque wrench, some carmakers may specify the use of a spring scale attached to the end of the steering arm to determine the amount of pull necessary to turn the steering knuckle.
4. If the force or pull exceeds the carmaker's specifications, replace both ball joints.

BALL JOINT SERVICE

In addition to periodic inspection of ball joints, as mentioned earlier, carmakers also provide specified lubrication intervals. At one time, ball joint lubrication was a standard automotive service recommended with every other oil change, but those used on modern vehicles require lubrication at 30,000 miles (48,000 km), if at all. Many vehicles are equipped with sealed ball joints that cannot be lubricated, but must be checked for wear like other ball joints.

LUBRICATION

1. Use a clean shop cloth to wipe all accumulated dirt and grease from around the grease fitting and ball joint boot. Remove the grease fitting cap, if so equipped.
2. If a small plug is installed in the ball joint instead of a grease fitting (Figure 5-15), unscrew and remove the plug. Thread a grease fitting in its place (Figure 5-16), or use a grease gun with an adapter that threads directly into the ball joint.
3. Use a grease gun filled with the correct type of grease specified by the carmaker to fill the ball joint until the boot starts to swell or grease can be

Figure 5-15 Some carmakers install threaded plugs instead of grease fittings. These must be removed and replaced by a grease fitting to lubricate the ball joint.

Figure 5-17 Lubricating the ball joint grease fitting.

Figure 5-16 Installing a grease fitting in place of the plug.

seen at the boot bleed area (Figure 5-17). Incorrect use of an air-powered grease gun may balloon the boot or even rupture it.

4. Disconnect the grease gun from the ball joint fitting and wipe any excess grease from the fitting. Reinstall the grease fitting cap, if so equipped. If the fitting was installed in place of a plug, be sure to remove it and reinstall the plug. Grease fittings often leak, allowing water to get into the joint.

> **TECH TIP:** Although the grease fittings on vehicles equipped with kingpins are accessible with the wheels on the ground, ALWAYS lift the wheels off the ground before lubricating the kingpins.

DUST BOOT OR SEAL REPLACEMENT

Some ball joints, especially those on import vehicles, are designed with a replaceable boot or seal that can be changed, if damaged. Generally, they are used with integral control arm/ball joint assemblies that cannot be serviced separately. Boots on this type of ball joint are held in place by a circlip or wire spring furnished with the replacement boot. To replace this type of ball joint boot:

1. Disconnect the ball joint at the steering knuckle.
2. Remove the wire spring or circlip holding the boot in place, then remove and discard the old boot.
3. Use a clean lint-free shop cloth or a paper towel to carefully wipe any old grease from the ball joint stud.
4. Lightly lubricate the dust cover plate area (Figure 5-18) with the appropriate grease. Keep the grease away from the boot installation area or the tapered part of the stud.

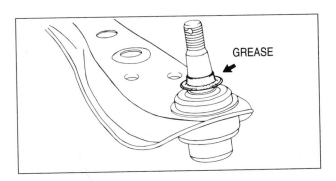

Figure 5-18 Lubricate the ball joint dust cover plate before installing a new dust boot or seal. (Toyota)

5. Fill the inside of the new boot with fresh grease and carefully install it in the boot installation groove with the bleed hole or escape area facing the rear of the vehicle (Figure 5-19). Gently squeeze the boot to bleed any air from inside.
6. If a wire spring is used to retain the boot, slip it over the top of the dust cover and slide it down into place. When a circlip is used to retain the

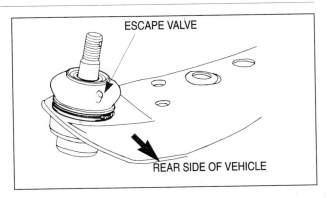

Figure 5-19 The bleed hole or escape area of the new dust boot should face to the rear. (Toyota)

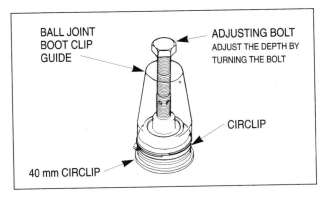

Figure 5-20 Replacement dust boots retained by circlips require special tools to install the circlip without damaging the new boot. (Honda)

boot, a special tool provided by the carmaker is required to install the circlip without damaging the new boot (Figure 5-20).

7. Wipe the tapered section of the stud with the shop cloth or paper towel to remove any grease contamination. If the ball joint is fitted with a plug, remove it and install a grease fitting.
8. Lubricate the ball joint with fresh grease until it appears at the bleed hole or escape area.

BALL JOINT REPLACEMENT

Ball joints are attached to the control arm in one of three ways; they are threaded, riveted/bolted, or pressed in place. The riveted/bolted ball joint has replaced the pressed-in ball joint as the attachment method most commonly used today. Replacements for riveted OEM ball joints are installed with bolts supplied with the new joint.

Ball joints can be replaced with the control arm on the vehicle, or with the control arm removed and installed in a vise. Working with the control arm on the vehicle has the advantage of holding the arm securely in place, while saving the time required to remove and reinstall it. Replacing the ball joint with the control arm in a vise has the advantage of providing complete access to the ball joint. Which method you use will depend on your preference, the circumstances involved, and the type of equipment available.

> **⚠ CAUTION:** During ball joint replacement, make certain that the control arm is NOT cracked or damaged, and that the ball joint opening is NOT distorted; if necessary, replace the control arm.

Some vehicles require that you replace the entire control arm if the ball joint is defective, since the control arm and ball joint are manufactured as a single unit and replacement ball joints are NOT provided. Procedures for control arm removal and installation are given later in this chapter.

Threaded Ball Joints

This type of ball joint has wrench flats and threads on the joint housing. It is removed with a special ball joint socket which fits the wrench flats (Figure 5-21) and a long socket handle or breaker bar to provide sufficient leverage. If an air wrench is used with the socket, it should be operated at a low speed to prevent tearing the ball joint and control arm threads. Once the joint

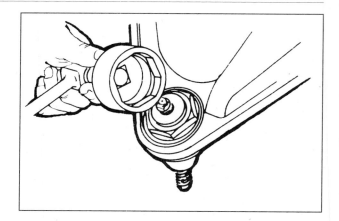

Figure 5-21 A ball joint removal socket engages the flats provided on a threaded-type joint. (Moog Automotive)

breaks loose, a small quantity of penetrating oil will help remove it without damaging the control arm threads. Before reinstalling the new ball joint, wipe its threads with a small quantity of engine oil, then thread it in place by hand to avoid cross-threading. Tighten the ball joint to the specified torque. If you cannot reach the required torque, the opening in the control arm is damaged and the control arm must be replaced.

Riveted/Bolted Ball Joints

Many FWD vehicles use control arms to which the lower ball joint assembly is either riveted or bolted. Bolted ball joints are replaced by disconnecting the joint from the steering knuckle, unbolting the ball joint and bracket assembly, and then bolting a new ball joint and bracket in place. Riveted ball joints are more difficult to replace, since the rivets have to be drilled out before the old ball joint and bracket can be removed.

> **⚠ WARNING:** NEVER use an acetylene torch to remove the rivet heads; the heat can weaken the control arm and cause it to fail.

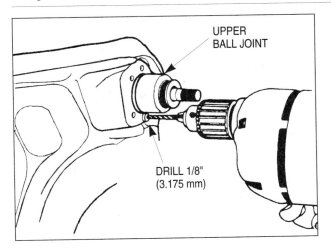

Figure 5-22 Drilling pilot holes in ball joint rivets. (General Motors)

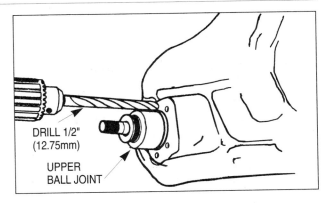

Figure 5-23 Removing the ball joint rivet heads by drilling. (General Motors)

Experienced technicians sometimes use a sharp chisel and air hammer to remove the rivet heads, but all carmakers recommend that they be drilled and removed with a pin punch. The approved technique is to disconnect the ball joint from the steering knuckle and use a center punch to make a pilot point on the head of each rivet. Working with a 1/8" drill, make a 1/4" deep hole in the center of each rivet (Figure 5-22). Use a 1/2" drill to remove the rivet heads (Figure 5-23), and then remove the rivets with a pin punch (Figure 5-24).

> **◆ CAUTION:** When using a drill with the control arm on the vehicle, work carefully to avoid damage to the drive axle boot.

Once the rivets are removed, separate the ball joint and bracket assembly from the control arm. Place the new ball joint and bracket in position and secure with the bolts and nuts provided in the replacement ball joint kit. Be sure to consult the instruction sheet that accompanies the kit regarding proper bolt head positioning; some are installed with the bolt head facing

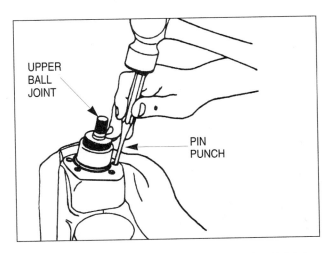

Figure 5-24 Use a pin punch to remove the ball joint rivets after drilling off the heads. (General Motors)

up (Figure 5-25), and others specify that the bolt head face down (Figure 5-26).

Pressed-In Ball Joints

Pressed-in ball joints can be removed in several ways using special pressing and support tools. The pressing tools remove and install the ball joint; support tools prevent the control arm from distorting under the pressure applied. When the control arm is removed from the vehicle, the tools generally are used with a press to remove the old ball joint and press the new one in place (Figure 5-27). Carmakers and independent tool suppliers also provide a

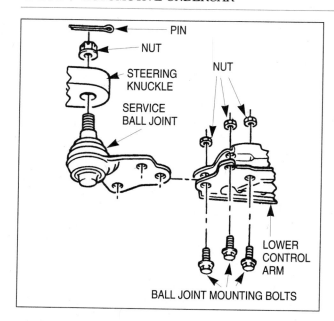

Figure 5-25 Some replacement ball joints are installed with the capscrew heads facing upward. (General Motors)

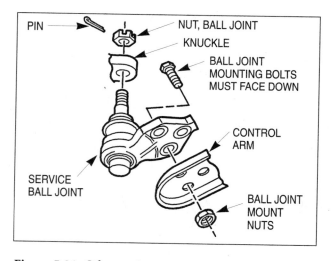

Figure 5-26 Other replacement ball joints are installed with the capscrew heads facing downward. (General Motors)

wide variety of tools to remove a ball joint with the control arm on the vehicle (Figure 5-28). Some carmakers use press-in ball joints with a peened ball joint housing retainer (Figure 5-29). The retainer sections must be pried upward before trying to press the joint out.

> ⚠ **CAUTION:** Do NOT use a hammer to remove or install a ball joint. Applying force in this way can distort the control arm and damage the replacement ball joint.

SERVICING KINGPINS

Some pickup trucks and vans with solid axles or twin I-beam axles still use kingpins or spindle pins (Figure 5-30). Since the function of kingpins is similar to that of ball joints, excessive clearance can be determined by measuring tire side movement.

INSPECTION

Kingpins are inspected by raising the vehicle axle enough to grasp the wheel and rock it back and forth. Apply the brakes to remove any wheel bearing looseness. If this preliminary check shows wheel side movement, install a dial indicator with its stylus positioned at the extreme bottom edge of the inside of the tire. Push in and out on the bottom of the tire and note the indicator reading. Excessive kingpin or spindle pin wear is indicated if the reading exceeds the following general specifications:

- 1/4" for wheel diameters up to 16".
- 3/8" for 17" or 18" wheel diameters.
- 1/2" for wheel diameters in excess of 18".

Note that the amount of movement at the bottom edge of the tire is much greater than the movement at the kingpin.

REPLACEMENT

With the axle raised off the ground and supported by stands, the tire, brake drum, brake backing plate, and steering arm removed, kingpins can be replaced with the following procedure:

1. Remove the lock pin nut and washer, and then drive the lock pin from the

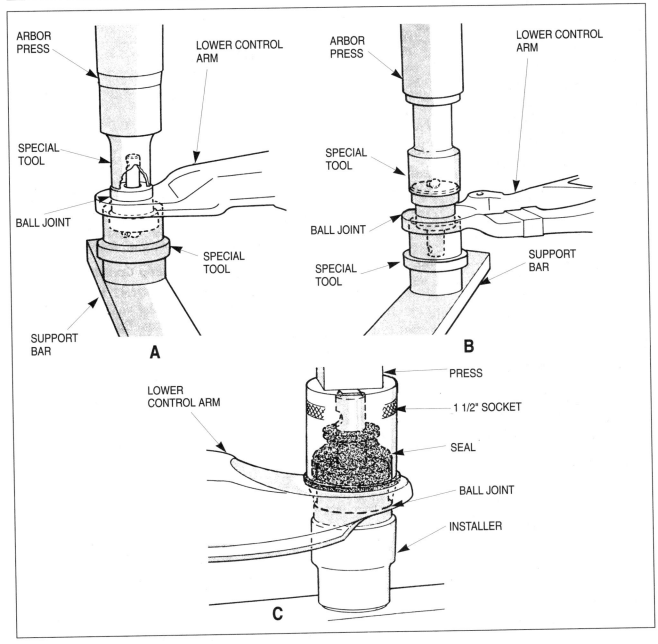

Figure 5-27 Removing (A) and installing (B) a control arm ball joint with special tools and a press. After the ball joint is installed, the dust boot or seal is pressed in place (C). (Chrysler)

spindle with a suitable punch and hammer.
2. Remove the upper and lower kingpin end caps or bolt plugs.
3. Rap the axle several times with a hammer near the kingpin to loosen any rust or binding.

4. Drive the kingpin out from the top of the axle with a suitable brass drift and hammer.
5. Carefully separate the spindle from the axle, saving any shims found between the top of the axle and the spindle.

6. Clamp the spindle in a vise with protective jaws. If protective jaws are NOT available, wrap the spindle in shop cloths.

7. Remove and discard the top bushing seal, if so equipped.

8. Drive the old bushings from the spindle with a drift slightly smaller than the spindle bore. If a suitable

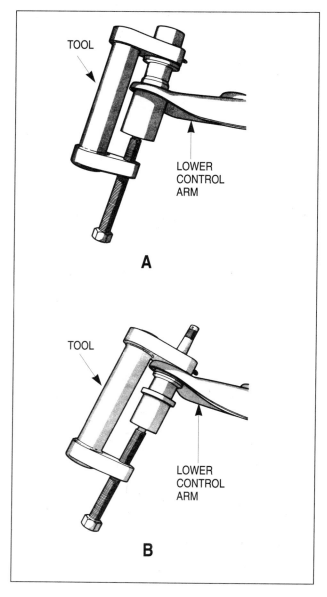

A

B

Figure 5-28 Removing (A) and installing (B) a lower control arm ball joint on the vehicle without removing the arm. (Chrysler)

drift is NOT available, the bushing can be collapsed by driving a small center punch between the bushing and spindle at the bushing split, then removing the bushing from the spindle bore.

9. Clean the spindle bore with solvent and compressed air. Make sure the lubricating holes are NOT plugged.

10. Inspect the axle and spindle for any cracks or out-of-round condition. Make sure the axle hole through which the kingpin passes is clean and free of nicks, burrs, or corrosion.

11. Install new upper and lower bushings in the spindle, seating to the depth specified by the carmaker. Position the open end of the bushing oil grooves to face the axle and align the lubrication holes with the spindle grease fittings. If specified by the carmaker, ream or hone the bushings to the specified fit on the kingpins. A properly fitted kingpin will fall through the installed bushings from its own mass, and when pushed side to side should NOT have any sideplay.

12. If an O-ring is used, place the new O-ring in the upper spindle below the bushing and make certain it is recessed enough to prevent it from being cut during spindle installation.

13. Pack the bearing with grease and install it on top of the lower hole in the spindle with its open area facing down. The bearing supports the mass of the vehicle, so it must be between the bottom of the axle and the lower spindle hole.

14. Position the original shim pack on top of the axle and slide the spindle in place carefully to avoid cutting the O-ring, if so equipped.

15. Try to insert a 0.005" feeler gauge

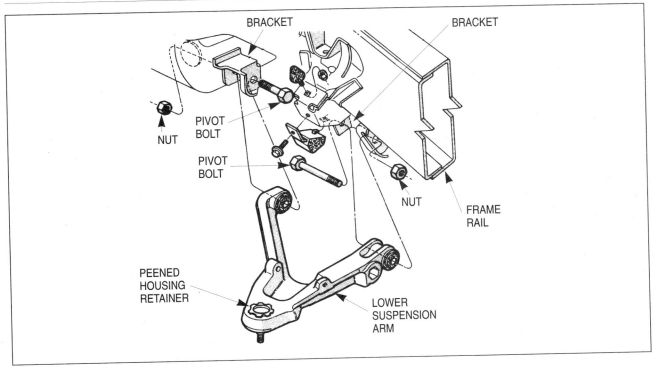

Figure 5-29 The peened sections of some ball joints must be pried upward before the ball stud can be pressed from the control arm. (Chrysler)

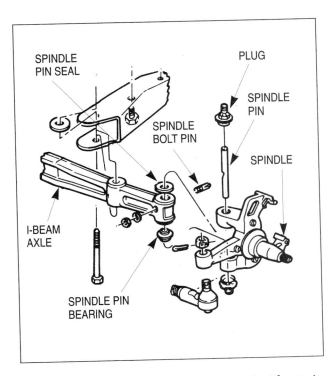

Figure 5-30 The kingpin components used with a twin I-beam axle. The part called a spindle here is called a steering knuckle by other carmakers. (Ford Motor)

between the shims and spindle. If the gauge fits, add shims to the shim pack until the gauge will not fit.

16. Wipe the kingpin with grease and position it in the axle, aligning its notch with the axle lock pin hole. Slide the kingpin into the spindle and axle if possible, or drive it carefully into place with a hammer and suitable drift until the notch and lock pin holes align. Test the fit by swinging the spindle side to side. It must swing freely. If there is any binding, it must be corrected.

TIP TECH TIP: Many replacement kingpins have the letter 'T' stamped on one end to indicate the top of the pin.

17. Drive the lock pin into the axle beam with its threads facing forward and the wedged groove facing the kingpin

notch. Install the lock washer and nut, tightening the nut to specifications.

18. Install the end caps and lubricate the grease fittings.

19. Once the kingpin is installed, reinstall the steering arm, brake backing plate, brake drum, and wheel/tire assembly.

CONTROL ARM SERVICE

Control arms act as the inner pivot or hinge for the spring-supporting link between the frame and the front wheels. With an SLA suspension, upper and lower control arms connect each front wheel to the frame. A strut suspension uses the strut mount and a lower control arm for the same purpose. This provides directional stability and lets the wheels move up and down with the irregularities in the road. Working together, the two control arms (or upper mount and control arm) assure that the wheels will rotate perfectly true, while minimizing the amount of scrubbing that affects tire wear.

The control arms are connected to the vehicle frame by pivot bolts and bushings. The bushings may be a metal screw-together type, or a metal-clad rubber torsion type. Some vehicles use a control arm shaft that bolts to the frame (Figure 5-31). Since the bushings are pressed into each end of the control arm, they pivot on the bolts or the control arm shaft. A ball joint installed on the outer end of the control arm provides the pivot point between the arm and spindle.

Some lower control arms have a single inner mounting point, which by itself would NOT hold the outer end of the arm in position. A strut rod from the outer end of the arm ties to the frame and prevents fore and aft movement of the arm, but still allows the arm to go up and down with spring action.

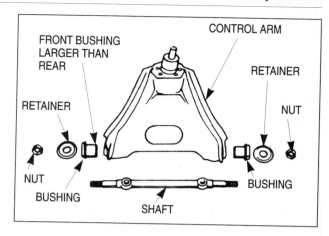

Figure 5-31 Some GM control arms are attached to the frame with a shaft instead of pivot bolts. (General Motors)

Because the position of the control arm affects both caster and camber angles, the control arm bushings must be in good condition or alignment settings cannot be maintained. Worn control arm bushings permit excessive movement, causing excessive tire wear and vehicle handling problems. Loose bushings can cause clunking noises while driving or when the brakes are applied.

Control arms are seldom replaced unless the arm itself is cracked or damaged, or the ball joint opening is distorted. Control arm problems generally result from worn or deteriorated bushings. Rubber torsilastic bushings tend to develop checks and cracks, then extrude or extend from their metal casing where the edges become torn or frayed. Metal screw-together bushings wear from the metal-to-metal contact.

CONTROL ARM AND BUSHING INSPECTION

To inspect the control arms and bushings:

1. If the vehicle is equipped with upper control arm bushings, use a bright light and inspect the bushings from the engine compartment. If the

rubber is springy and solid, bushing condition is acceptable even if hairline cracks have developed. If the bushing rubber is distorted or breaking up, replace the bushings.

2. Raise the vehicle until the wheels hang free. Rapidly swing the wheel/tire assemblies back and forth between the steering stops, watching the control arms for movement.

3. Remove the wheel/tire assemblies and visually inspect the lower control arm bushings for the same conditions as in Step 1.

4. Grasp the control arm firmly and try to move it up-and-down, and side-to-side. Replace the bushings if any looseness is seen or felt.

5. Check the control arm and frame for signs of metal-to-metal contact. Such contact indicates bushing failure.

6. If the vehicle is equipped with struts, move the inner ends of the lower control arm sideways with a suitable pry bar while watching the arm for movement. Replace the bushings if excessive movement is noted.

CONTROL ARM REMOVAL AND INSTALLATION

Each carmaker provides recommended procedures for removing the upper and lower control arms on its various models. When removing a control arm, ALWAYS consult the proper service manual and follow the specified procedure. To acquaint you with the various steps involved, a general procedure used to remove the lower control arm with the spring on the lower arm is provided below. A variation of this procedure can be used to remove the upper control arm with the spring mounted on it, or the lower control arm on a strut suspension. To avoid injury, talk the job over with your instructor before removing any parts, to be sure that the energy in the spring is kept under control.

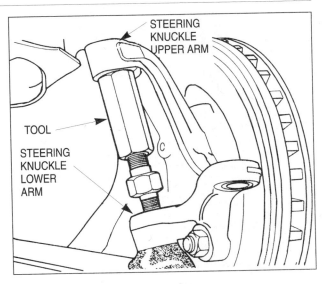

Figure 5-32 Using a ball stud remover to separate the stud from the steering knuckle. This tool can only be used when the ball joint studs face each other. (Chrysler)

Removal

1. Raise the vehicle with a hoist or jack. Support the vehicle with safety stands, as required.

2. Remove the wheel/tire assembly, brake caliper, shock absorber, and stabilizer bar end link.

3. Remove the torsion bar, if so equipped.

4A. If the lower ball joint is tension-loaded, loosen the ball joint stud nut a few turns and break the ball joint stud taper loose with an appropriate tool (Figure 5-32). It may be necessary to rap the steering knuckle sharply with a hammer to loosen the stud in the knuckle.

4B. If the lower ball joint uses a steering knuckle clamp and pinch bolt (Figure 5-33), remove the pinch bolt and separate the ball stud from the steering knuckle.

5. Install a spring compressor tool (Figure 5-34) and compress the spring until it moves freely or the control arm can be moved upward.

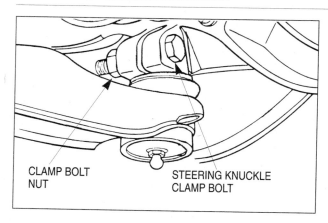

Figure 5-33 Steering knuckle clamp bolt. (Chrysler)

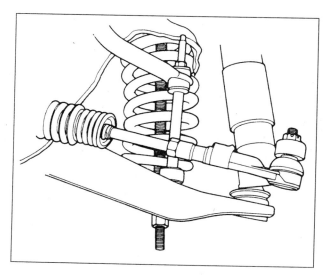

Figure 5-34 Installing one type of spring compressor. Have your work supervised by the instructor when using this tool, to avoid injury. (Ford Motor)

6. If the lower ball joint is compression-loaded, use the correct tools to free the ball joint stud from the steering knuckle arm.

7. Remove the ball joint stud nut and separate the stud from the steering knuckle.

8. Raise the upper control arm and steering knuckle, then wedge a suitable wooden block between the frame and control arm to hold the assembly out of the way.

9. Pivot the lower control arm down and

remove the spring and compressor assembly. At this point, the lower ball joint can be replaced with the control arm on the vehicle.

10. After removing the control arm pivot bolts (Figure 5-29), remove the control arm from the frame rail brackets.

The upper control arm on many General Motors RWD vehicles is mounted on a pivot shaft bolted to a vehicle frame bracket. Removing an upper control arm mounted in this way generally involves removal of the pivot shaft mounting bolts and removing the shaft with the arm because of lack of clearance in the engine compartment.

Installation

1. Fit the control arm in place in its frame rail brackets and install the pivot bolts, tightening the nuts finger-tight. Final tightening must be done with the suspension in the normal trim height position.

2. Rotate the ball joint stud until the cotter pin hole or notch in the side of the stud (Figure 5-35) is positioned horizontally with the vehicle body. This will make cotter pin installation

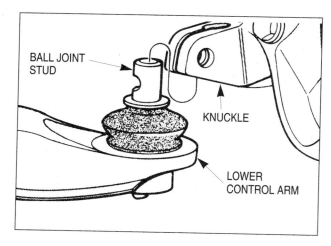

Figure 5-35 The ball stud notch must be aligned in the steering knuckle clamp to accept the pinch bolt. (Chrysler)

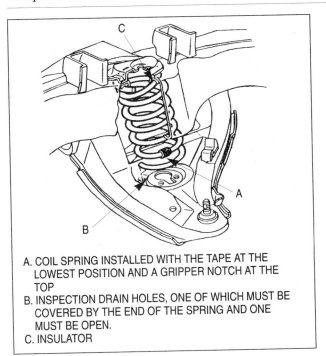

A. COIL SPRING INSTALLED WITH THE TAPE AT THE
   LOWEST POSITION AND A GRIPPER NOTCH AT THE
   TOP
B. INSPECTION DRAIN HOLES, ONE OF WHICH MUST BE
   COVERED BY THE END OF THE SPRING AND ONE
   MUST BE OPEN.
C. INSULATOR

Figure 5-36 When the coil spring is installed, it must be aligned as specified by the carmaker. (General Motors)

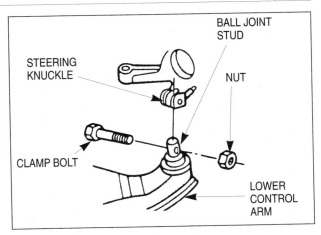

Figure 5-37 Tightening the steering knuckle clamp pinch bolt. (Chrysler)

easier, and is necessary to install the pinch bolt through a steering knuckle clamp design.

3. Reinstall the compressed spring and align it as specified by the carmaker (Figure 5-36).

4. Pivot the control arm upward until the ball joint stud enters the steering knuckle boss or clamp.

5A. Install the pinch bolt through the clamp and stud notch and finger-tighten the nut, and then tighten the bolt to specifications (Figure 5-37).

5B. Thread the nut on the ball stud, tighten the stud nut to the carmaker's specified torque and install a new cotter pin. If the ball joint uses a self-locking or prevailing torque nut, use a plain nut to seat the taper, then replace it with a new self-locking nut.

6. Carefully remove the spring compressor and make certain the spring

seats in place properly.

7. Reinstall and adjust the torsion bar, if so equipped.

8. Reinstall the brake caliper, shock absorber, stabilizer bar end link, and wheel/tire assembly.

9. Lower the vehicle to the ground and torque the control arm pivot bolts to specifications.

Bushing Replacement

Special tools are available to remove and install bushings without removing the control arm from the vehicle, but in most cases, it is best to remove the control arm because of the lack of space to work in. To remove threaded steel bushings, secure the control arm in a vise and use a suitable socket and breaker bar. Rubber bushings can be driven or pressed out. Appropriate tools for rubber bushing replacement are provided both by the carmaker and manufacturers of aftermaket suspension components (Figure 5-38). When replacing the pivot bushings in a lower control arm, most carmakers recommend that the large bushing be removed first and installed last. Replacement bushings can be installed with a suitable socket or bushing driver and an arbor press or vise.

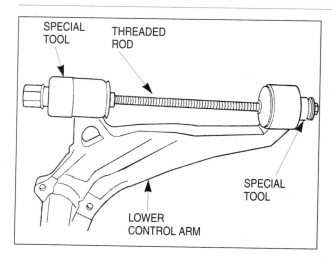

Figure 5-38 Typical control arm pivot bushing remover/installer tool. There usually is not enough room to use this tool with the control arm on the car. (Chrysler)

Figure 5-39 Strut rod mounting between the frame and lower control arm.

The vehicle must be at normal trim height when rubber suspension and steering bushings are torqued. These bushings are torsilastic, that is, they function by twisting in a torsional manner. Since the rubber in the bushing is squeezed tightly between its inner and outer metal sleeves, the rubber twists to allow control arm motion. If tightened with the vehicle wheels off the ground, torsilastic bushings will twist and may be torn when returned to normal trim height. This shortens the life of the bushing.

TIP TECH TIP: The bushings in some late-model control arms are welded in place and cannot be serviced. If the bushings are defective, the control arm must be replaced as an assembly.

STRUT ROD AND STABILIZER BAR SERVICE

Strut rods are bolted between the lower control arm at one end, and bracket-mounted to the frame with a strut rod

bushing at the other (Figure 5-39). Depending on the suspension design, the bushing end of some strut rods may be threaded to permit caster adjustment. The strut rod and bushing helps control ball joint wear and the caster setting.

To help equalize wheel loads during turns and spring action on the straightaway, stabilizer or sway bars are installed between the lower control arms with a link assembly at each end (Figure 5-40). Each

Figure 5-40 Typical stabilizer bar mounting with link assembly.

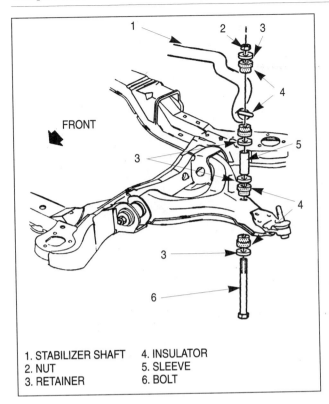

1. STABILIZER SHAFT
2. NUT
3. RETAINER
4. INSULATOR
5. SLEEVE
6. BOLT

Figure 5-41 Typical stabilizer link assembly components. (Oldsmobile Division, General Motors)

Figure 5-42 A simple clamp bracket is the most common method used to secure the stabilizer bar bushings or isolators to the crossmember.

link assembly consists of a bolt, nut, metal sleeves, and rubber bushings (Figure 5-41). The stabilizer bar is isolated from the crossmember by a pair of clamps or brackets containing bushings or insulators (Figure 5-42). Some rear suspension designs also use a stabilizer bar to help control body motion.

Except for collision damage, these components seldom require replacement; service most often involves replacement of worn or deteriorated bushings. To check the strut rod bushings for looseness, grasp the strut rod firmly and try to move it up-and-down, and side-to-side. Replace the bushings if any looseness is seen or felt. Check the bushings visually for wear, cracks, or a squeezed appearance that indicates distortion. If in doubt, remove the strut rod and check the bushings for internal wear. To replace a strut rod

bushing:

1. Raise the vehicle with a hoist or jack. Support the vehicle with safety stands, as required. Do NOT let the wheels hang free.
2. Remove the large nuts at the rear of the strut rod.
3. Remove the fasteners holding the strut rod to the lower control arm.
4. With the strut rod disconnected, slide it out of the frame bracket and remove the bushings.
5. Install the new bushings. Follow the instruction sheet provided with the bushing kit, since the exact procedure will vary according to bushing design.
6. Slide the strut rod into the frame bracket and tighten the strut rod nut to properly seat the bushings.
7. Pull the strut rod down, reconnect it to the lower control arm, and tighten the attaching bolts to specifications.
8. Follow the instruction sheet and torque the strut rod nut to specifications.

9. Lower the vehicle to the ground and check the wheel alignment.

Stabilizer link assemblies (Figure 5-40) should be inspected visually to determine the condition of the bushings and metal sleeves. Replace worn, missing, or deteriorated bushings, and broken or corroded metal sleeves and links. When removing a stabilizer link, note whether the bolt head faces up or down and install the new components in the same order the old ones were removed (Figure 5-41).

Stabilizer bar crossmember bushings tend to take a permanent set as they deteriorate. Since a split-type bushing is used, crossmember bushings can be replaced without removing the bar from the crossmember. Once the clamp bolts and clamp are removed, the old bushing can be twisted off the bar and the new one twisted on with its flat surface facing the frame. The usual method of mounting front stabilizer bar bushings is with the clamp shown in Figure 5-42, but various other methods are used. Some clamps are suspended from a frame bracket (Figure 5-43); other

clamps are attached with a single bolt and a tab that engages a slot in the crossmember (Figure 5-44). Rear stabilizer bar bushings may be attached to the axle housing with a U-bolt (Figure 5-45).

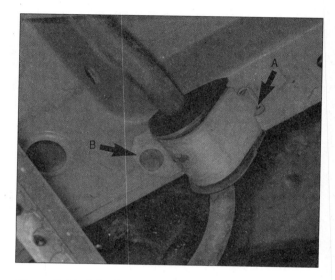

Figure 5-44 A bushing installed with a tabbed clamp is replaced by engaging the clamp tab in its slot (A), then forcing the clamp over the bushing until its bolt hole (B) aligns with the crossmember hole.

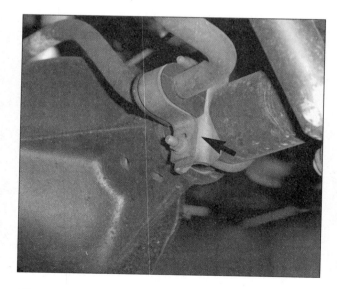

Figure 5-43 Some carmakers use suspended stabilizer bar bushings. With this design, the bushing at the top of the bracket bolt should also be checked.

Figure 5-45 Rear stabilizer bar bushings may be mounted on the axle housing with U-bolts.

⍰ REVIEW QUESTIONS

1. Technician A says that a ball joint with a damaged boot should be replaced. Technician B says that the control arm must be replaced on some vehicles if the ball joint is defective. Who is right?
   (A) A only
   (B) B only
   (C) Both A and B
   (D) Neither A nor B

2. Technician A says that load-carrying ball joints are friction-loaded and should have NO clearance. Technician B says that follower ball joints are manufactured with no preload and a slight amount of clearance. Who is right?
   (A) A only
   (B) B only
   (C) Both A and B
   (D) Neither A nor B

3. Technician A says the follower ball joint should also be replaced if the load-carrying joint is worn excessively. Technician B says all carmakers use the same ball joint wear specs. Who is right?
   (A) A only
   (B) B only
   (C) Both A and B
   (D) Neither A nor B

4. Technician A says that ball joint wear can be measured by checking axial movement. Technician B says that a tire sidewall movement test also will determine excessive wear. Who is right?
   (A) A only
   (B) B only
   (C) Both A and B
   (D) Neither A nor B

5. Technician A says you should apply the brakes when using the tire sidewall method to avoid confusion between wheel bearing looseness and ball joint play. Technician B says the axial method provides a direct measurement while the tire sidewall method is a multiplied measurement. Who is right?
   (A) A only
   (B) B only
   (C) Both A and B
   (D) Neither A nor B

6. Technician A says all wear indicator ball joints are checked in the same way. Technician B says wear indicator ball joints must be checked with the ball joints unloaded. Who is right?
   (A) A only
   (B) B only
   (C) Both A and B
   (D) Neither A nor B

7. Technician A says friction-loaded ball joints can be checked for wear by trying to rotate the grease fitting. Technician B says friction-loaded ball joints are checked for free play or preload to determine their condition. Who is right?
   (A) A only
   (B) B only
   (C) Both A and B
   (D) Neither A nor B

8. Technician A says ball joint axial play is checked by lifting the wheel with a pry bar. Technician B says a brace or support wedge is used when checking a load-carrying ball joint with the spring on the lower arm. Who is right?
   (A) A only
   (B) B only
   (C) Both A and B
   (D) Neither A nor B

9. Technician A says ball joints used with twin I-beam or solid axles are checked for side clearance. Technician B says they are checked for turning torque. Who is right?
   (A) A only
   (B) B only
   (C) Both A and B
   (D) Neither A nor B

10. Technician A says sealed, pre-lubricated ball joints do NOT require wear checks. Technician B says some ball joints are bolted to the control arm. Who is right?
    (A) A only
    (B) B only
    (C) Both A and B
    (D) Neither A nor B

11. Technician A says pressing a ball joint into the control arm is a common method of attachment. Technician B says riveted ball joints can be removed with an acetylene torch. Who is right?
    (A) A only
    (B) B only
    (C) Both A and B
    (D) Neither A nor B

12. Technician A says removing a ball joint with a hammer damages the control arm. Technician B says excessive kingpin clearance is determined by checking tire side movement. Who is right?
    (A) A only
    (B) B only
    (C) Both A and B
    (D) Neither A nor B

13. Technician A says control arms use metal screw-together bushings. Technician B says they use metal-clad rubber torsion bushings. Who is right?
    (A) A only
    (B) B only
    (C) Both A and B
    (D) Neither A nor B

14. Technician A says that defective control arm bushings will affect wheel alignment settings. Technician B says that the coil spring must be compressed before removing the lower control arm on an SLA suspension. Who is right?
    (A) A only
    (B) B only
    (C) Both A and B
    (D) Neither A nor B

15. Technician A says some ball joint studs are secured by a clamp and pinch bolts. Technician B says control arm bushing nuts must be torqued with the vehicle at normal trim height. Who is right?
    (A) A only
    (B) B only
    (C) Both A and B
    (D) Neither A nor B

16. Technician A says the stabilizer bar controls ball joint wear and camber. Technician B says strut rods equalize wheel loads during a turn. Who is right?
    (A) A only
    (B) B only
    (C) Both A and B
    (D) Neither A nor B

17. Technician A says stabilizer bar cross-member bushings or insulators can be replaced without removing the bar. Technician B says stabilizer bars distort easily and require frequent replacement. Who is right?
    (A) A only
    (B) B only
    (C) Both A and B
    (D) Neither A nor B

18. Technician A says strut rods use a split-type bushing. Technician B says the end of some strut rods is threaded to allow caster adjustments. Who is right?
    (A) A only
    (B) B only
    (C) Both A and B
    (D) Neither A nor B

WHEEL ALIGNMENT — MEASURING AND ADJUSTING

 OBJECTIVES

After completion of this chapter, you should be able to:

- Perform a preliminary alignment inspection and record any conditions that must be corrected before proceeding with wheel alignment.

- Demonstrate the use of one or more special tools required for caster or camber adjustment.

- Demonstrate the correct method of performing — a two-wheel alignment, a four-wheel alignment, and a four-wheel alignment with two-wheel equipment.

- Demonstrate an understanding of wheel alignment specifications.

- Describe caster and camber adjustments on a vehicle assigned by the instructor.

- Perform a front wheel toe adjustment on an RWD and an FWD vehicle.

- Measure the turning angle of a vehicle.

WHEEL ALIGNMENT

The process of aligning a vehicle's wheels starts with a preliminary inspection of the vehicle (Figure 6-1). Before any measurements are made, vehicle trim height and tire inflation pressures should be checked and corrected, if necessary. An incorrect trim height or improperly inflated tires will have an adverse effect on alignment angles. Also make certain that the suspension and steering systems are in good condition before measuring any angles. For example, if the linkage has excessive play or clearance, making a toe adjustment is a waste of time and effort. The play in the linkage will continue to allow changes in the toe setting as the vehicle is driven down the road.

Measurements should be taken and adjustments made with the vehicle on an alignment rack. This piece of equipment is designed (1) to provide a level platform for the vehicle, and (2) to assure that the

TIP TECH TIP: Toolboxes, sample cases, or other heavy items usually carried in the vehicle should remain in place during alignment. Since such items affect trim height and alignment angles, alignment adjustments made while the normal load is in the vehicle can compensate to some degree for the extra mass.

alignment system instruments or gauges measure the angles relative to a true vertical or horizontal.

Five alignment angles are measured:

- caster
- camber
- toe
- SAI
- turning angle

After the measurements are taken, they are compared with factory specifications for that particular vehicle, and any angles that do NOT agree with the specified tolerances are adjusted. Measuring most angles is not difficult, especially if you have access to a modern computerized alignment rack. The degree of difficulty encountered in adjusting incorrect angles depends on the adjustment method required by the suspension design. Some adjustment methods are quite easy; others can be complicated,

TREAD DEPTH

Left Front

Inside _____

Center _____

Outside _____

Right Front

Inside _____

Center _____

Outside _____

Left Rear

Inside _____

Center _____

Outside _____

Right Rear

Inside _____

Center _____

Outside _____

BEFORE: 0° 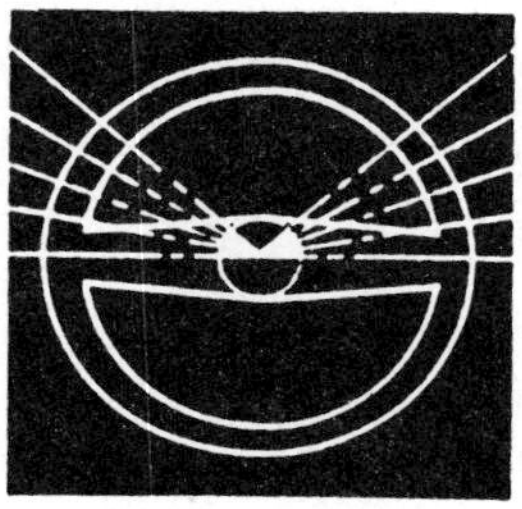 0°

AFTER: 0° 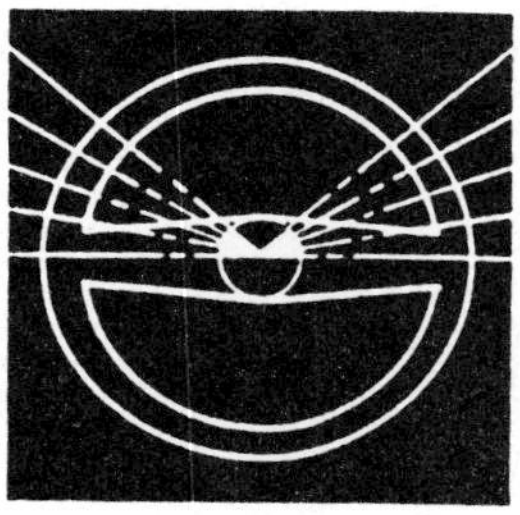 0°

☐ Worn King Pins
☐ Worn Tie-Rod Ends
☐ Worn Ball Joints
☐ Sagged Springs
☐ Excessive Gearbox Play
☐ Worn Steering Damper

☐ Worn Shock Absorbers
☐ MacPherson Strut
☐ Control Arm Bushings
☐ Brake Drag
☐ Worn Idler Arm
☐ Worn Pitman Arm

☐ Worn Center Link
☐ Worn Stabilizer Bushings
☐ Worn Tires
☐ Rotate Tires
☐ Worn Strut Rod Bushings

Figure 6-1 Many manufacturers provide pre-alignment check sheets which can be used to make sure that you have covered all required items prior to starting an alignment. (General Motors)

especially on older vehicles.

Although older RWD vehicles allowed adjustment of front wheel caster, camber, and toe, many late-model vehicles permit only a toe adjustment at the front. One reason for this lack of front wheel adjustment is the far more precise manufacturing technology used by carmakers in recent years; another is the result of simplification in design (i.e. the use of strut suspensions). It is faster and less expensive to build a vehicle with non-adjustable components that are correctly aligned during assembly, than to build one with adjustable components that must be aligned before the vehicle can leave the factory. Newer vehicles with non-adjustable front alignment angles are checked on an alignment rack and the readings compared to factory specifications. If one or more readings are not correct, proper alignment is restored by replacing the worn or damaged components. In some cases alignment shims or other devices may be used to provide adjustment where there was none originally. Front wheel alignment is referred to as 'two-wheel alignment'.

Note that one or more rear wheel angles can usually be adjusted on FWD vehicles because they usually have independent rear suspension. Rear wheel alignment and adjustments on RWD vehicles are seldom possible because the rigid rear axle housing has NO adjustments. Rigid rear axle housings can be aligned to correct dog tracking caused by a broken leaf spring center bolt or other problem. Rear wheel alignment can also be incorrect due to a bent frame or axle housing. Bent frames are most often straightened by a specialty shop. When rear axle housings are bent, they are usually replaced, although there are some shops that specialize in straightening them. When front and rear wheel alignment is checked/adjusted, we call it a 'four-wheel alignment'.

SPECIAL TOOLS AND EQUIPMENT

Performing an alignment often requires the use of special wrenches or other tools to reach and adjust the necessary bolts. These special wrenches and tools may be designed to make the required adjustments on only a few models in a carmaker's lineup (Figure 6-2), or they may be more general in nature, such as a tie rod adjusting sleeve wrench. In either case, they are available as special tools provided by carmakers, or from alignment equipment manufacturers.

ALIGNMENT SYSTEMS AND EQUIPMENT

Manufacturers offer a large variety of different systems and equipment for wheel alignment. How to use each of these systems is beyond the scope of this text, but you should understand that regardless of the system used, it is precision equipment that must be operated in accordance with the manufacturer's instructions. Wheel alignment systems basically fall into one of three different types.

The first type consists of magnetic caster-camber gauges with bubble levels. These devices attach to the front hubs and are used with portable turntables that allow the wheels to move. When wheel design does not permit the gauge to be attached magnetically, adapters are used to attach the gauge on the wheel rim. Magnetic gauges may also be used to measure rear wheel camber.

The second type consists of more sophisticated electronic alignment systems. These also attach to the wheels to measure alignment angles (Figure 6-3) and display their measurements with a light beam on a graduated screen (Figure 6-4) or a series of analog meters. This type of alignment system measures caster, camber, toe, and many can be used to do a four-wheel alignment.

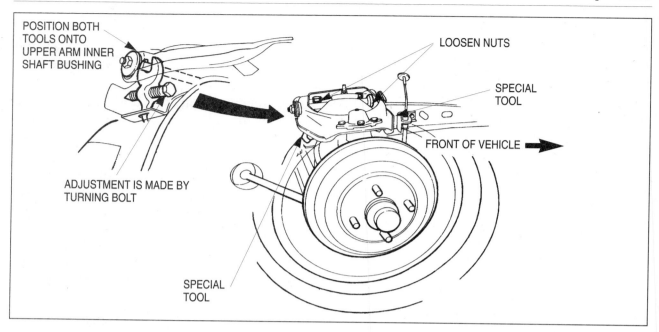

Figure 6-2 Caster and camber adjustments on Mustang II, Pinto, and Bobcat models are made by repositioning the upper control arm inner shaft. Without the use of special tools to keep the shaft from moving when loosened, accurate adjustment can be frustrating. With the tools holding the loosened shaft, it can be moved accurately by turning the tool bolts. (Ford Motor)

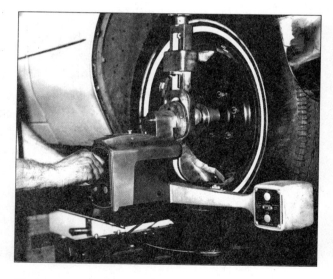

Figure 6-3 Locked onto the wheel by the frame, the alignment arm of this Bear system becomes an extension of the spindle.

Figure 6-4 The alignment arm sends an electrical signal to the monitor, which displays the reading on a graduated screen.

Computerized alignment systems make up the third type and offer the latest in modern equipment unmatched by the other systems. They do take longer to set up,

however, and may NOT be desirable when the technician wants only to make a quick check of the alignment. All instructions, alignment readings, and specifications are displayed on a computer screen with graphics (Figure 6-5). Alignment specifications for the majority of vehicles built over a decade or more are programmed into the computer memory and can be called up and displayed on the screen in seconds. When the system is correctly set up and adjusted, the computer reads the actual angles of a vehicle, compares them with specifications, and displays the results for the technician. Computerized alignment systems can read and display both front and rear angles at the same time, providing the technician with an instant overview of vehicle alignment condition. Special displays guide the technician through adjustment of each of the alignment angles to bring them within specifications (Figure 6-6). Some units also provide a printed readout.

Alignment systems are used with an alignment rack to maintain the vehicle on a flat, level surface during measurement and adjustment. Such racks are designed with turntables that allow movement of the front tires as required during alignment. Many different rack designs are available, but all provide a means of positioning a vehicle for quick and easy access to the suspension and steering components. Air-powered jacks are used with most racks to raise the vehicle or its suspension as required (Figure 6-7).

Although not all shops will have state-of-the-art alignment equipment, remember that the accuracy of the equipment and how it is used is far more important than the type of equipment. Regardless of the system or type of equipment used, it must be in good working condition, properly calibrated, and used correctly for accurate results.

ALIGNMENT SEQUENCE

The order in which alignment technicians take their measurements and make adjustments should be determined by alignment angle relationships, as some angles affect other angles. When doing a four-wheel alignment, for example, it is most efficient to measure thrust angle first, since the thrust angle controls all other angles. If the vehicle thrust angle differs from its centerline (Figure 6-8), measuring the front alignment angles first means that all measurements made during the alignment procedure will be incorrect (Figure 6-9). To some degree, the alignment sequence is determined by the type of equipment used, and whether the rear alignment angles of a vehicle can be adjusted.

When aligning only the front wheels, steering and suspension components are adjusted to the vehicle centerline to make certain that the front wheels relate correctly to one another (Figure 6-10). Aligning only the front wheels assumes that everything behind them is in good condition and proper alignment, but there are a number of problems that can affect rear wheel alignment:

- rear subframes and axles that have shifted from the vehicle centerline
- worn out control arm bushings
- sagging springs
- bent rear suspension components
- improper collision repairs.

During a four-wheel alignment, the rear angles (Figure 6-11) are measured and taken into account. If the rear suspension angles of a vehicle cannot be adjusted, determine the thrust angle and align the front wheels to it. When rear suspension angles are adjustable, adjust each rear wheel to the correct angle from the centerline. In this way, the vehicle will track properly when the front wheels are aligned with the centerline.

ALWAYS start at the rear wheels when doing a four-wheel alignment on a four-wheel alignment rack, regardless of whether you are working with an FWD or

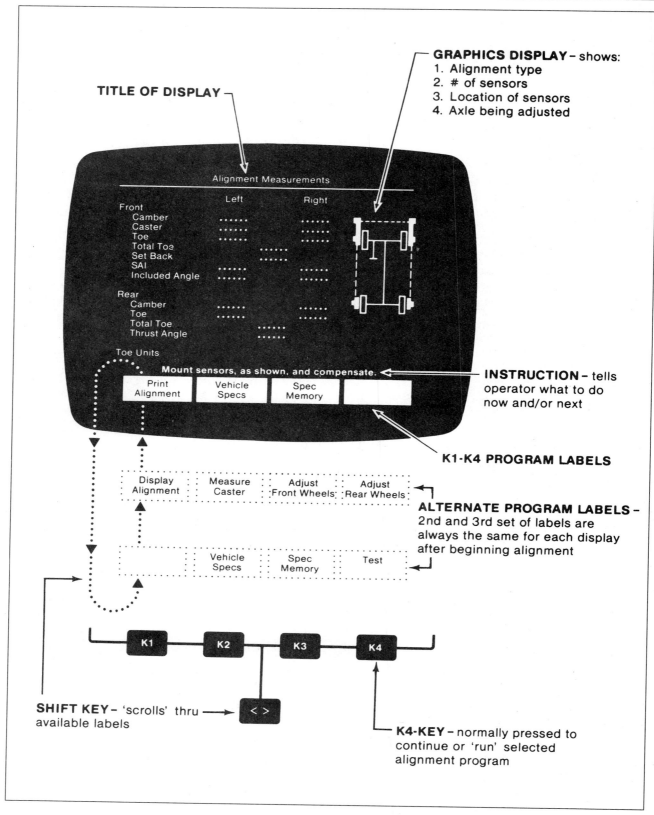

Figure 6-5 A typical computerized alignment machine CRT display. (Ford Motor)

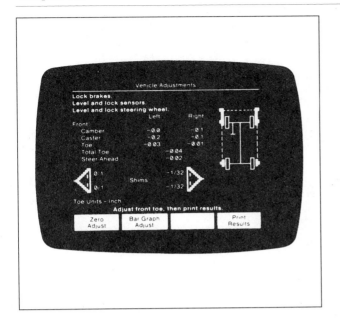

Figure 6-6 The CRT screen guides the technician through the alignment process, indicating the necessary shim size required and where to install it. (Ford Motor)

Figure 6-7 Portable air-powered jacks are used to lift the wheel for free rotation when checking camber.

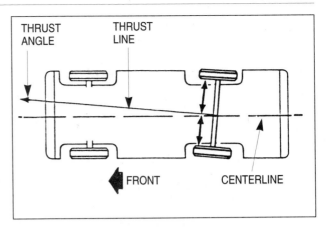

Figure 6-8 When the rear axle is out of square with the centerline, the vehicle dogtracks down the road because the rear axle directs the vehicle along the thrust line. (General Motors)

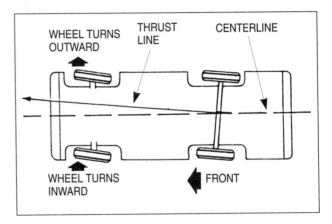

Figure 6-9 When the thrust line differs from the vehicle centerline, the front wheels must be steered parallel with the thrust angle if the vehicle is to travel in a straight line. (General Motors)

an RWD vehicle. Even though RWD vehicles seldom have adjustable rear alignment angles (fully independent rear suspensions are an exception), the thrust angle still determines the front alignment settings. Some types of two wheel alignment equipment can be used to perform a four-wheel alignment by changing the sequence of steps in which the procedure is done.

Most FWD vehicles have independent rear suspensions with adjustable rear camber and toe settings. After aligning the rear wheels so that the thrust angle and the vehicle centerline are the same, the front wheels can be aligned with the center-line. ALWAYS measure front wheel camber and caster before measuring toe, as these angles affect the toe setting. For example, adjusting camber to a more positive setting will move the top of the wheel outward. With the front-mounted steering linkage used on many RWD vehicles, this positive change in camber also changes the toe setting (Figure 6-12).

Four-Wheel Alignment (Using Four-Wheel Equipment)

When doing a four-wheel alignment with four-wheel equipment, refer to Figure 6-13 and use the following typical sequence.

1. Make a complete pre-alignment inspection.
2. Replace any worn or damaged components found during Step 1.
3. Follow the rack manufacturer's instructions and position the vehicle on the alignment rack. Jounce the front and rear of the vehicle three times to normalize the suspension.
4. Measure, read, and record the thrust angle at the rear axle.
5. If the vehicle has adjustable rear alignment angle, set the rear camber, then adjust rear toe to align the thrust angle to the vehicle centerline.
6. Measure and adjust the front alignment angles in the following sequence — caster, camber, and toe. On vehicles with power steering, start the engine and turn the steering wheel up to one-half turn in each direction before making any toe adjustment.

Four-Wheel Alignment (Using Two-Wheel Equipment and Rear Track Gauges)

When doing a four-wheel alignment with two-wheel equipment, use the following typical sequence. If the rear angles are not

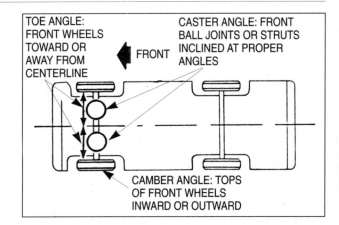

Figure 6-10 The angles checked during a front wheel alignment. (General Motors)

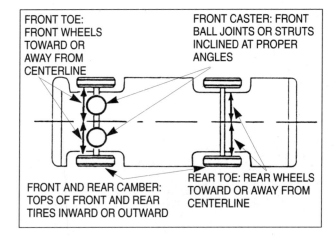

Figure 6-11 The angles checked during a front and rear wheel alignment. (General Motors)

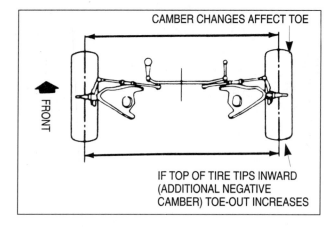

Figure 6-12 A change in positive camber can reduce the toe angle. (General Motors)

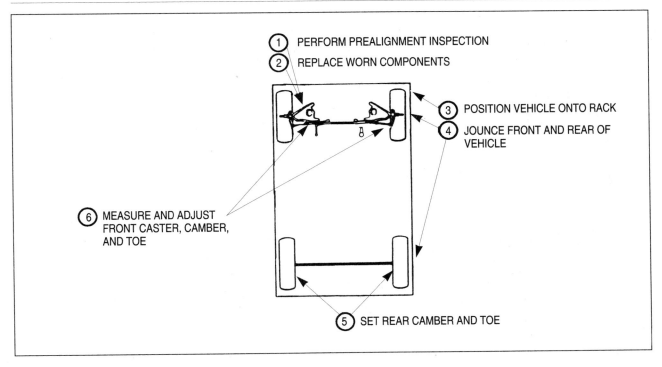

Figure 6-13 The alignment sequence used with four wheel alignment equipment. (General Motors)

adjustable, omit Steps 3 and 4.

1. Make a complete prealignment inspection.
2. Replace any worn or damaged components found during Step 1.
3. Back the vehicle onto the rack and install the alignment equipment onto the rear wheels following the manufacturer's instructions. With some equipment, the rear wheels can be measured and adjusted without backing the car onto the rack. It depends on whether there is room to work under the car at the back of the rack, and whether the alignment equipment can be moved to the back of the vehicle.
4. Adjust rear camber and toe as required. Remember that in this case, toe-in reads as toe-out and toe-out reads as toe-in when working with the rear of the vehicle on the rack.

5. Turn the vehicle around to position its front wheels on the rack.
6. Install the alignment equipment on the front wheels and adjust front caster and camber, if necessary. On vehicles with power steering, start the engine and turn the steering wheel up to one-half turn in each direction and back to center.
7. Use a suitable wheel locking tool to lock the steering wheel in a straight-ahead position, then turn off the engine.
8. Check and adjust toe as required. Check front and rear wheel track to make sure the steering wheel is properly positioned in a straight-ahead position.

ADUSTABLE ANGLES

Before discussing how to make the necessary adjustments, let us briefly review the angles involved and their effect on

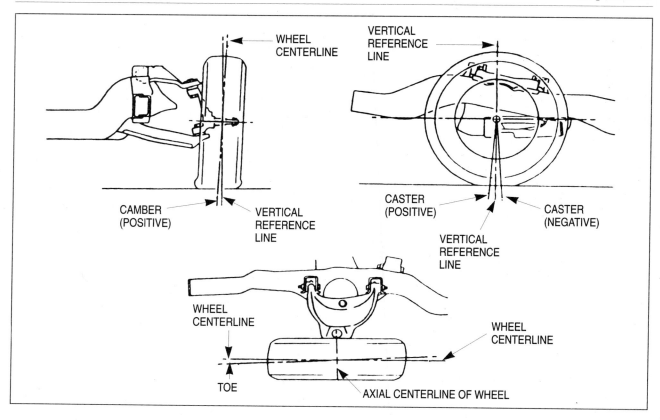

Figure 6-14 The three adjustable alignment angles — camber, caster, and toe. (General Motors)

wheel alignment and tire wear. Many vehicles have three adjustable alignment angles — camber, caster, and toe (Figure 6-14).

CAMBER

Camber is a comparison of the tire/wheel assembly's outward or inward tilt to a vertical reference. If the wheel tilts outward at the top, camber is positive; when the wheel tilts inward at the top, camber is negative. A wheel that is vertical has zero camber. The camber setting affects both vehicle directional control and tire wear. A slightly positive camber setting of 0.25 to 0.50 (1/4 to 1/2) degrees is used at the front wheels of most vehicles. This setting is used to maintain camber as close as possible to zero when the vehicle is driven, since the actual camber changes from slightly positive over dips in the road to

slightly negative over bumps (Figure 6-15).

Incorrect camber settings result in rapid, uneven tire wear, and can cause the vehicle to pull to one side. Excessively positive camber causes the outside of the tire tread to wear rapidly because the outer tread carries more of the vehicle weight than the inner tread. With excessively negative camber, the wear pattern reverses. Because the inner tread now carries more of the mass than the outer tread, it wears faster.

CASTER

Caster is a comparison of the forward or rearward tilt of the steering axis to a vertical reference, as viewed from the side of the vehicle. When the steering axis is vertical, the caster angle is zero (Figure 6-16). When the top of the steering axis tilts to

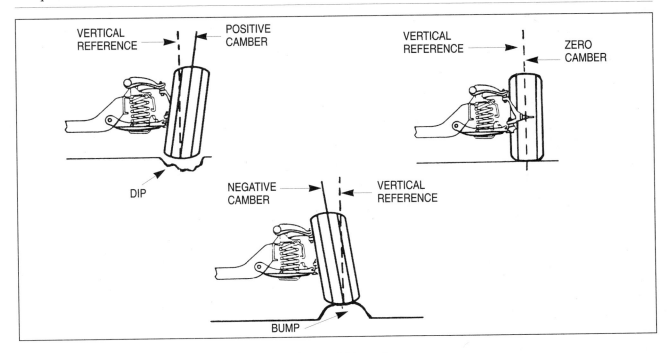

Figure 6-15 Camber changes over bumps and dips. (General Motors)

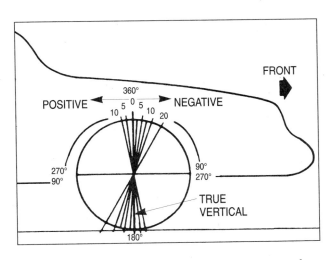

Figure 6-16 Positive and negative caster angles. (General Motors)

the rear, caster is positive; if the tilt is forward, caster is negative.

Positive caster angles project the vehicle mass to a point ahead of the tire contact patch. This increases the straight-line stability of the vehicle, as the tire naturally seeks this position, but at the same time, steering effort is increased because the tire resists turning in either direction. Negative caster angles direct the vehicle mass to a point behind the tire contact patch. This decreases the vehicle's straight-line stability, but allows the tire to change direction more easily.

Caster has no direct effect on tire wear, but it can cause wear indirectly by changing camber as the vehicle is driven. When a tire with excessive positive caster passes over a bump, front-end shimmy may result, causing the steering wheel to shake back and forth. A vehicle with insufficient caster will wander on the road, requiring constant steering corrections to travel in a straight line. Uneven caster can cause tire pull when the vehicle is moving. Under normal conditions, caster causes a camber change while turning, from positive to negative on one side, and negative to positive on the other side, depending upon which way the vehicle wheels are steered (Figure 6-17).

Many older vehicles were designed with

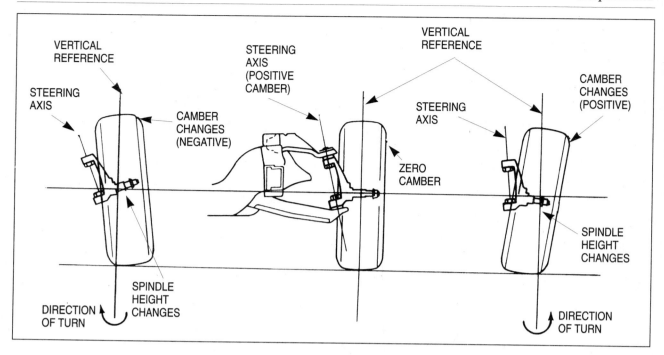

Figure 6-17 Positive caster changes the spindle angle and camber in turns. (General Motors)

one or two degrees of positive caster, which caused very little camber change in a turn. Some current models now have as much as 8° of positive caster, causing significant changes in camber during a turn. Vehicles designed with this much caster will eventually suffer excessive wear to both the inner and outer shoulders of both front tires. FWD vehicles are sometimes manufactured with variations in caster (and camber) from side to side and from vehicle to vehicle. Those vehicles may have NO provision for making adjustments, and the carmakers may advise against drilling or filing holes to make adjustments. Other carmakers provide instructions on exactly where to drill or file various holes. There are also aftermarket kits that will add caster or camber adjustment to these vehicles. Some automotive instructors or shop owners do NOT like to install the aftermarket kits because they feel that a vehicle should NOT be modified unless the carmaker approves. It is true that makeshift modifications

might weaken the structure of the vehicle. The kit or instructions should be properly engineered and come from a well known maker that has a history of producing quality products.

TOE

Toe is a measurement of how much a front wheel turns away from or toward the vehicle centerline. When the front of the wheels turn in toward the centerline, toe is said to be positive and is commonly called 'toe-in'. If the front of the wheels turn-out from the centerline, toe is negative and is called 'toe-out'. When the wheels are parallel, toe is zero (Figure 6-18).

Under ideal conditions, a toe angle of 0° is desirable during vehicle operation, but this cannot be achieved by setting toe to zero with the vehicle stationary on an alignment rack. As soon as the vehicle starts to move, suspension flex, tire drag, and various other factors cause toe angles to change (Figure 6-19). RWD vehicles use

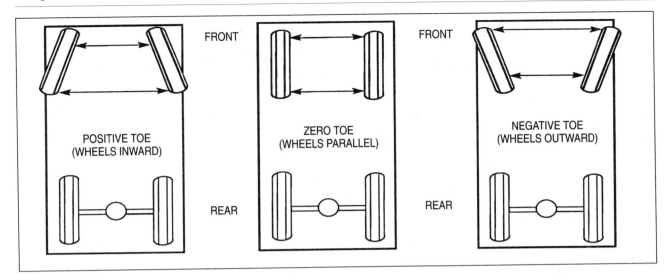

Figure 6-18 Positive, zero, and negative toe. (General Motors)

slightly positive toe settings to counter their normal tendency to toe out in motion. Because the torque developed by the front drive wheels of an FWD vehicle causes the wheels to toe in when driven, such vehicles generally use slightly negative toe settings.

NON-ADJUSTABLE ANGLES

Some alignment angles are NOT adjustable, but are used primarily as diagnostic angles. Checking them during wheel alignment can provide helpful information about potential problems.

TURNING ANGLE (TOE-OUT ON TURNS)

The turning angle of a vehicle changes front wheel toe during a turning maneuver (Figure 6-20). This occurs because the inside wheel is further into the turn than the outside wheel. The difference between the toe angles of the two front wheels usually amounts to only 1-2° during the turn.

Low-speed tire squeal generally is a symptom of an incorrect turning angle. As the tires try to travel different distances during a turn, they are forced to slip to accommodate the difference between their actual setting and the specified turning angle. This slippage causes the tires to squeal. The most likely cause of an incorrect turning angle is a bent steering arm.

SAI AND THE INCLUDED ANGLE

Steering axis inclination (SAI) refers to the inward tilt of the top of the steering axis, when seen from the front of the vehicle. The steering axis on a vehicle with unequal front control arms is an imaginary line drawn through the ball joints. With a strut suspension, the steering axis is a line extending from the upper strut bearing through the ball joint (Figure 6-21). The number of degrees that this line tips inward from a true vertical is called the steering axis inclination, or SAI angle. When kingpins are used instead of ball joints, the line is through the center of the kingpin, and the angle is called 'king pin inclination'.

The included angle is a combination of camber and SAI, and is calculated as SAI plus or minus camber (Figure 6-22). To determine the included angle, add positive camber to the SAI or subtract negative camber from the SAI. The included angle on each side of a vehicle normally should

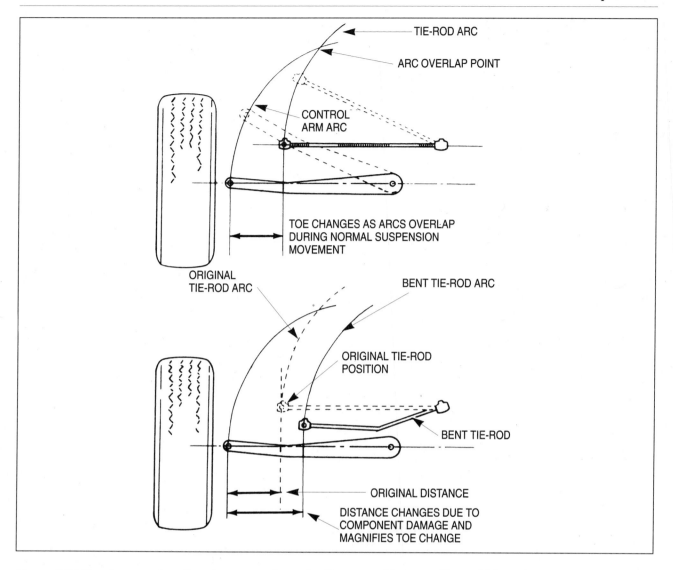

Figure 6-19 Toe changes when tie rod arcs are mismatched because of damage. (General Motors)

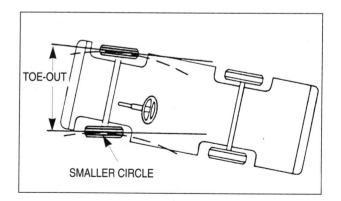

Figure 6-20 Turning angle or toe-out on turns. (General Motors)

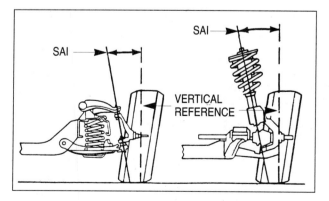

Figure 6-21 Steering axis inclination (SAI) with ball joint and strut suspensions. (General Motors)

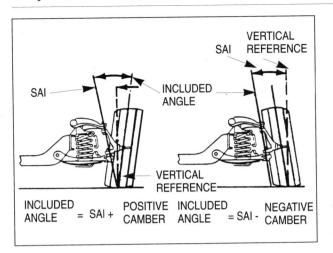

Figure 6-22 The included angle is the angle between the SAI and the centerline of the wheel. (General Motors)

be within 0.50° of one another. If they are not, the front spindle assembly or strut is probably bent as the result of a front-end collision. An incorrect included angle can cause vehicle wander, weave, rapid tire wear, or failure of the steering wheel to properly return to its center position after completing a turn.

ALIGNMENT SPECIFICATIONS

All carmakers and alignment equipment manufacturers publish wheel alignment specifications. Some specifications take the form of an alignment chart provided for all models in a given car line (Figure 6-23);

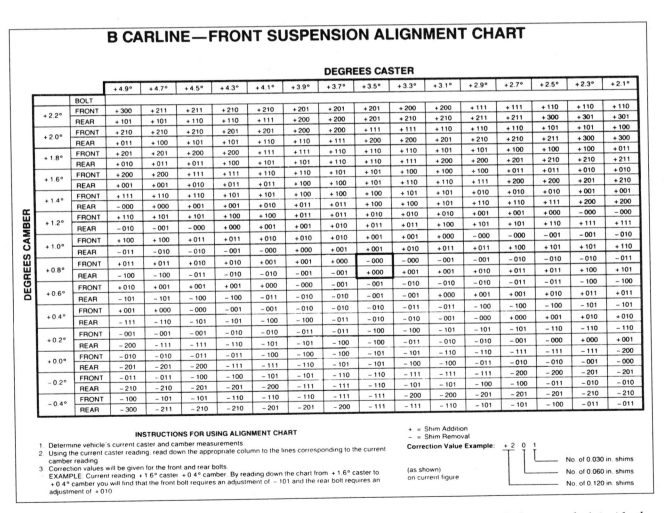

B CARLINE—FRONT SUSPENSION ALIGNMENT CHART

DEGREES CASTER

DEGREES CAMBER	BOLT	+4.9°	+4.7°	+4.5°	+4.3°	+4.1°	+3.9°	+3.7°	+3.5°	+3.3°	+3.1°	+2.9°	+2.7°	+2.5°	+2.3°	+2.1°
+2.2°	FRONT	+300	+211	+211	+210	+210	+201	+201	+201	+200	+200	+111	+111	+110	+110	+110
	REAR	+101	+101	+110	+110	+111	+200	+200	+201	+210	+210	+211	+211	+300	+301	+301
+2.0°	FRONT	+210	+210	+210	+201	+201	+200	+200	+111	+111	+110	+110	+110	+101	+101	+100
	REAR	+011	+100	+101	+101	+110	+110	+110	+200	+200	+201	+210	+210	+211	+300	+300
+1.8°	FRONT	+201	+201	+200	+200	+111	+111	+110	+110	+110	+101	+101	+100	+100	+100	+011
	REAR	+010	+011	+011	+100	+101	+101	+110	+110	+111	+200	+200	+201	+210	+210	+211
+1.6°	FRONT	+200	+200	+111	+111	+110	+110	+101	+101	+100	+100	+100	+100	+011	+011	+010
	REAR	+001	+001	+010	+011	+011	+011	+100	+100	+101	+110	+110	+111	+200	+200	+210
+1.4°	FRONT	+111	+110	+110	+101	+101	+100	+100	+100	+101	+101	+010	+010	+010	+001	+001
	REAR	−000	+000	+001	+001	+010	+011	+011	+100	+100	+101	+110	+110	+111	+200	+200
+1.2°	FRONT	+110	+101	+101	+100	+100	+011	+011	+010	+010	+010	+001	+001	+000	−000	−000
	REAR	−010	−001	−000	+000	+001	+001	+001	+010	+011	+011	+100	+101	+101	+110	+111
+1.0°	FRONT	+100	+100	+011	+011	+010	+010	+010	+001	+001	+000	−000	−000	−001	−001	−010
	REAR	−011	−010	−010	−001	−000	+000	+001	+001	+010	+011	+011	+100	+101	+101	+110
+0.8°	FRONT	+011	+011	+010	+010	+001	+001	+000	−000	−000	−001	−001	−010	−010	−010	−011
	REAR	−100	−100	−011	−010	−010	−001	−001	+000	+001	+001	+010	+011	+011	+100	+101
+0.6°	FRONT	+010	+001	+001	+001	+000	−000	−001	−001	−010	−010	−010	−011	−011	−100	−100
	REAR	−101	−101	−100	−100	−011	−010	−010	−001	−001	+000	+001	+001	+010	+011	+011
+0.4°	FRONT	+001	+000	−000	−001	−001	−010	−010	−010	−011	−011	−100	−100	−100	−101	−101
	REAR	−111	−110	−101	−101	−100	−100	−011	−010	−010	−001	−000	+000	+001	+010	+010
+0.2°	FRONT	−001	−001	−001	−010	−010	−011	−011	−100	−100	−101	−101	−101	−110	−110	−110
	REAR	−200	−111	−111	−110	−101	−101	−100	−100	−011	−010	−010	−001	−000	+000	+001
+0.0°	FRONT	−010	−010	−011	−011	−100	−100	−100	−100	−101	−101	−110	−110	−011	−010	−010
	REAR	−201	−201	−200	−111	−111	−111	−110	−101	−101	−100	−100	−011	−010	−001	−000
−0.2°	FRONT	−011	−011	−100	−100	−101	−101	−110	−110	−111	−111	−111	−200	−200	−201	−201
	REAR	−210	−210	−201	−201	−200	−111	−111	−110	−101	−101	−100	−100	−011	−010	−010
−0.4°	FRONT	−100	−101	−101	−110	−110	−110	−111	−111	−200	−200	−201	−201	−201	−210	−210
	REAR	−300	−211	−210	−210	−201	−201	−200	−111	−111	−110	−101	−101	−100	−011	−011

INSTRUCTIONS FOR USING ALIGNMENT CHART

1. Determine vehicle's current caster and camber measurements.
2. Using the current caster reading, read down the appropriate column to the lines corresponding to the current camber reading.
3. Correction values will be given for the front and rear bolts.
   - EXAMPLE: Current reading +1.6° caster +0.4° camber. By reading down the chart from +1.6° caster to +0.4° camber you will find that the front bolt requires an adjustment of −101 and the rear bolt requires an adjustment of +010

+ = Shim Addition
− = Shim Removal

Correction Value Example: + 2   0   1
(as shown)
on current figure

No. of 0.030 in. shims
No. of 0.060 in. shims
No. of 0.120 in. shims

Figure 6-23 A typical GM alignment correction chart used with 1991 RWD vehicles with the cross shaft inside the frame. (General Motors)

others are given for individual vehicles (Figure 6-24). Domestic vehicle alignment specifications generally are given in degrees (3°) or fractions of a degree (1/8°), although decimals may be used in place of a fraction of a degree (0.25° instead of 1/4°). Toe may be measured in inches, millimeters, or degrees (Figure 6-25). Import vehicle specifications also are given in degrees, but angles under one degree usually are measured in minutes or even seconds of arc (B, Figure 6-24).

> **TIP TECH TIP:** After adjusting alignment angles and torquing the fasteners to specifications, ALWAYS recheck your adjustments to make sure they did NOT change when the fasteners were torqued.

CASTER AND CAMBER ADJUSTMENT METHODS

Carmakers use many different methods for adjusting caster and camber (Figure 6-26).

A

	ACCEPTABLE ALIGNMENT RANGE	PREFERRED SETTING
Camber	0 to 1°	+1/2°
Caster*	-1/2° to +1 1/2°	+1/2°
Toe-in (at Hub Height)	0.0 to 0.50"	0.20"
Turning Angle (Base Tire) Left/Right	33°/33°	

* IF VEHICLE WANDERS, CASTER SHOULD BE INCREASED. IF STEERING EFFORT IS VERY HIGH, ESPECIALLY WHEN CORNERING, CASTER SHOULD BE DECREASED.

B

Cold tire inflation pressure	195/65 R15	222 kPa		2.2 kgf/cm²		32 psi
Vehicle height		Front			Rear	
	195/65 R15	231 mm	9.09"	245 mm		9.65"
Front wheel alignment						
Toe-in		0.2° ± 0.2°				
		2 mm ± 2 mm		0.08" ± 0.08"		
Camber	Left-right error	0° 30' ± 45'				
		30' or less				
Steering axis inclination		13° 10' ± 45'				
		30' or less				
Caster	Left-right error	7° 20' ± 45'				
		30' or less				
Side slip	Left-right error	3.0 mm/m (0.118"/3.3 ft) or less				
Wheel angle	Inside wheel	41° 28' (+1° or -2°)				
	Outside wheel	34° 17'				
	At 20°	21°				
	(Outside wheel)	(Inside wheel)				

Figure 6-24 Typical alignment specifications provided for Dodge light-duty trucks (A) and Toyota Cressida vehicles (B). (Chrysler (A) and Toyota (B))

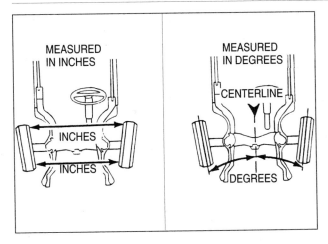

Figure 6-25 When toe is measured in inches or millimeters, the measurement is the difference in distance between the front and rear of the wheels. When measured in degrees, it is the angle between the wheel's plane of rotation and the vehicle centerline. (General Motors)

The adjustment method employed depends on the front end design used with a particular vehicle. The most common methods used to adjust caster and camber are:

- shims
- elongated (slotted) holes
- eccentric devices

On some vehicles, caster is adjusted by changing the length of a strut rod.

SHIM ADJUSTMENTS

Shims are small pieces of metal that are installed between the upper or lower control arm mounts and the frame. They vary widely in shape (Figure 6-27) according to the vehicle on which they are used, and generally are available in thicknesses of 1/64"-3/16" (0.4-5.0 mm). The total thickness of the shims installed on a control arm bolt determines how much the settings change. When working with a shim-type adjustment, adjust the caster angle first, then the camber. With experience, both adjustments can be made at the same time. Left- and right-side caster readings should be equal to each other within 0.50°.

Control Arm Cross Shaft Adjustments

Upper control arm cross shafts are designed to be mounted inside or outside the frame mounting bracket. When the cross shaft is located inside the frame bracket (A, Figure 6-28), add or subtract an equal number of shims at both front and rear of the cross shaft to decrease or increase positive camber. Caster is adjusted by transferring shims from the front to the rear to increase positive caster, or vice-versa to decrease positive caster.

On control arms with the cross shaft outside the frame bracket (B, Figure 6-28), the rules concerning shim placement are the opposite of the adjustments for cross shafts inside the frame bracket. Add or subtract an equal number of shims at both front and rear of the cross shaft to increase or decrease positive camber. Caster is adjusted by transferring shims from the rear to the front to increase positive caster, or vice-versa to decrease positive caster.

There are some vehicles with control arms that are NOT symmetrical. A shim at one mounting bolt may change the setting much more than the same shim at the other bolt. ALWAYS consult a good repair manual for the correct procedure before attempting to work on an unfamiliar vehicle.

Rear Wheel Spindle Adjustments

Some FWD vehicles have rear wheel spindles bolted to the rear axle. Rear wheel camber and toe adjustments can be made by installing adjustment shims between the spindle and axle (Figure 6-29).

Solid Beam or Rigid Housing Axle Adjustments

The caster angle on solid beam front axles or front wheel drive rigid axle housings is adjusted by tilting the axle. The most common method used is to loosen the leaf spring U-bolts and install tapered shims

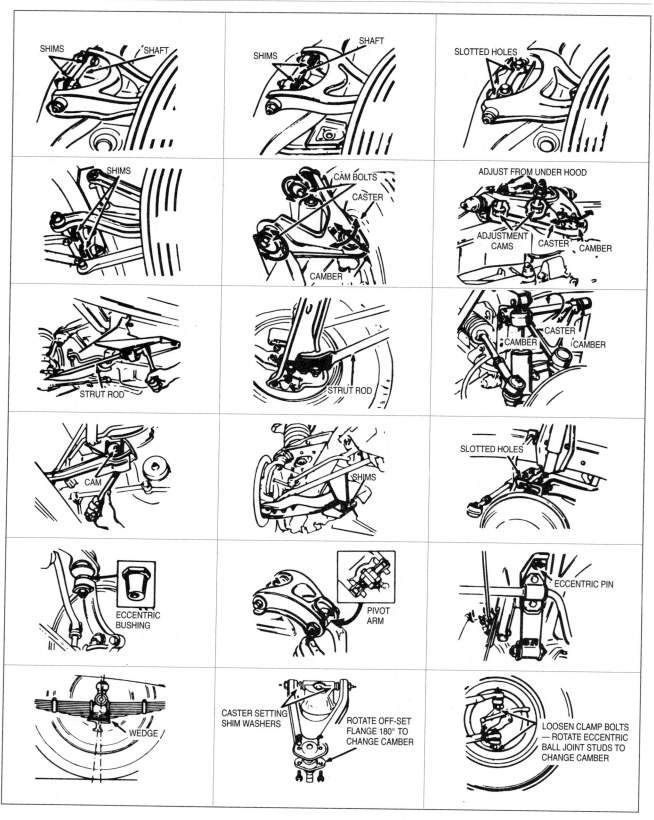

Figure 6-26 Typical methods of front wheel alignment. (Ammco Tools / ©Hennessy Industries)

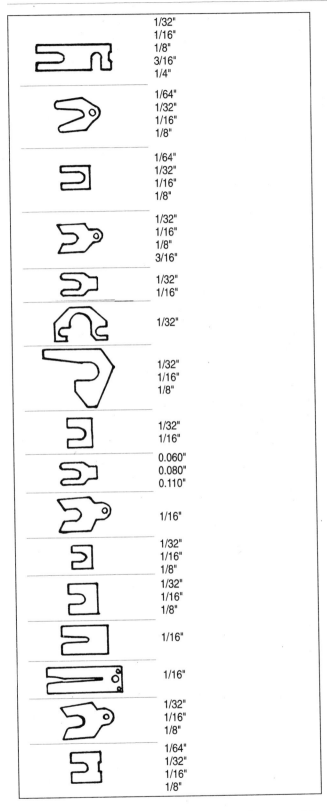

	1/32"
	1/16"
	1/8"
	3/16"
	1/4"
	1/64"
	1/32"
	1/16"
	1/8"
	1/64"
	1/32"
	1/16"
	1/8"
	1/32"
	1/16"
	1/8"
	3/16"
	1/32"
	1/16"
	1/32"
	1/32"
	1/16"
	1/8"
	1/32"
	1/16"
	0.060"
	0.080"
	0.110"
	1/16"
	1/32"
	1/16"
	1/8"
	1/32"
	1/16"
	1/8"
	1/16"
	1/16"
	1/32"
	1/16"
	1/8"
	1/64"
	1/32"
	1/16"
	1/8"

Figure 6-27 A sampling of the different shims used in front end alignment. (McQuay-Norris)

between the axle and spring to produce the desired angle (Figure 6-30). Removing shims from the rear will decrease positive caster; adding shims to the front will increase positive caster.

Sliding Adjustments (Elongated Holes)

Sliding adjustments through the use of elongated or slotted holes are used at the inner shaft of the upper control arm on some SLA suspensions. With strut suspensions, they may be used at the strut-to-steering knuckle connection, or at the strut-to-upper mount.

Upper Control Arm Adjustment

When a sliding adjustment is used to set both caster and camber, the upper arm mounting bolt holes are elongated and slotted. This mounting methods allows the upper arm to move inward and outward to set camber. At the same time, the upper arm can be angled left or right, which swings the ball joint forward or backward to set caster (A, Figure 6-31). To reduce the difficulty in making fine adjustments once the mounting bolts are loosened, special tools are available to hold, position, and move the upper arm (B and C, Figure 6-31). Even with the use of such tools, it may require several attempts to complete the adjustment because of the interaction between the caster and camber angle adjustments.

Strut-to-Knuckle Camber Adjustment

Camber typically is adjusted on front strut suspensions with a slotted lower strut-to-knuckle hole (Figure 6-32). Some carmakers use a strut that must be removed from the vehicle and modified by filing the lower strut hole to elongate it for camber adjustment (Figure 6-33). Use the following procedure to adjust camber (front or rear) when the strut has an elongated

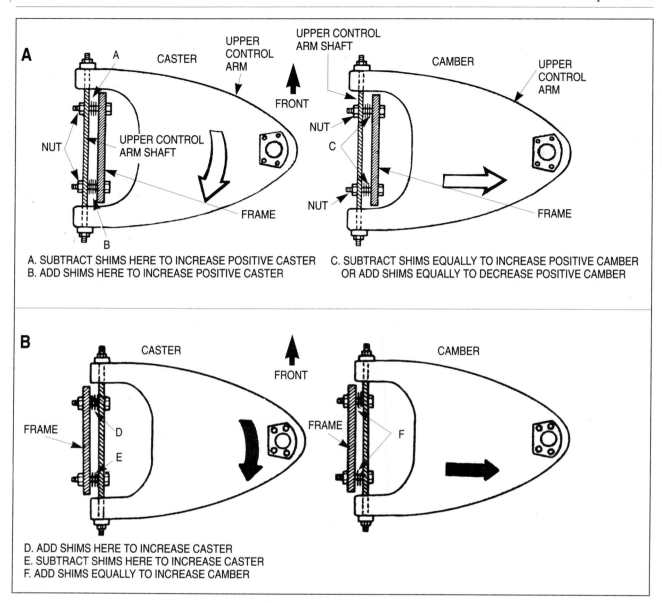

Figure 6-28 Typical RWD alignment adjustments with the cross shaft (A) inside the frame, and (B) outside the frame. (General Motors)

lower mounting hole:

1. Loosen both strut-to-knuckle nuts and install the carmaker's camber adjusting tool.
2. Adjust the tool as required to set camber to specifications.
3. Tighten both nuts to the specified torque and remove the camber adjusting tool.

Strut-to-Upper Mount Caster Adjustment

Caster can be adjusted on some front strut suspensions with the following procedure (Figure 6-34):

1. Loosen two of the three strut attaching nuts that cover the slotted mounting holes.
2. Remove the remaining nut over the

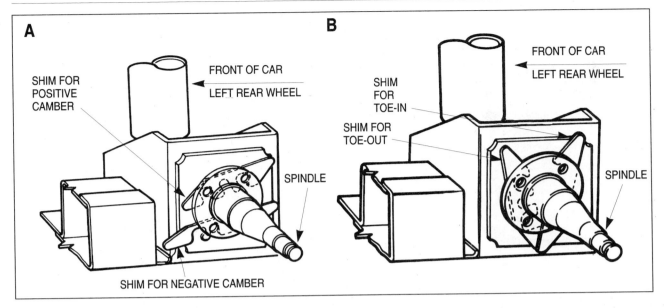

Figure 6-29 Adjustment shims are used to change rear wheel camber (A) and toe (B) on some FWD vehicles. (Chrysler)

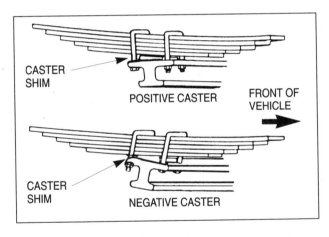

Figure 6-30 Using a shim to change caster on a beam axle. (Ford Motor)

oval strut mounting hole and move the washer away from the hole.

3. Raise the front of the vehicle enough to separate the strut from the inner wheelhouse.
4. Drill two 11/32" holes at the front and rear of the oval strut mounting holes. Remove any excess metal with a file.
5. Lower the front of the vehicle, making sure the strut returns to its position in the inner wheelhouse.
6. Reposition the washer over its hole and install the nut.
7. Move the top of the strut forward or rearward as required to set caster to specifications.
8. Tighten the top strut attaching bolts to specifications.

Strut-to-Upper Mount Camber Adjustment

A strut alignment template is required when making front camber adjustments on some FWD vehicles (Figure 6-35):

1. Remove the three nuts holding the strut cover plate in place, and then remove the cover plate.
2. Raise the front of the vehicle by its body enough to let the strut studs clear the front of the strut tower. Make sure the drive axle is NOT overextended.
3. Stuff a clean shop cloth around the top of the strut to prevent any metal filings from reaching the strut, and then position the strut alignment template (Figure 6-35) over the strut

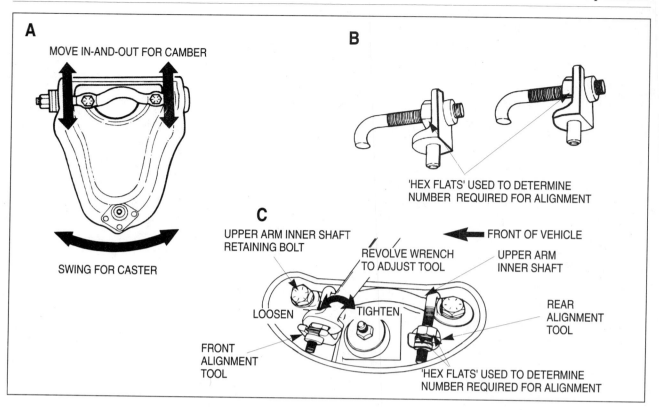

Figure 6-31 One type of special tool (A) used to set caster and camber when the upper control arm slides in slotted holes (B). (Ford Motor)

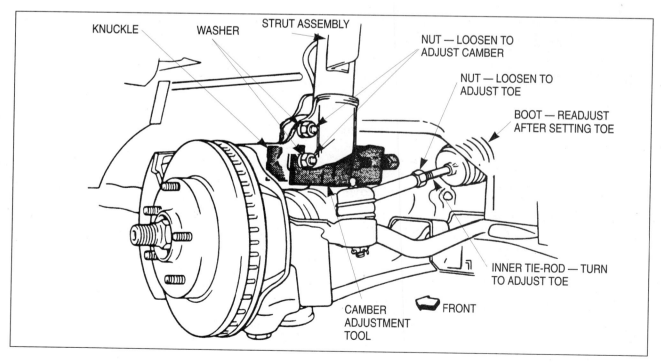

Figure 6-32 Typical front strut camber adjustment. (General Motors)

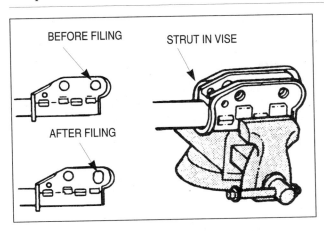

Figure 6-33 Modification of a strut for camber adjustment. (General Motors)

and file the inner or outer side of the existing holes as necessary. Do NOT file more than 0.20" in either direction.

4. Remove the template, clean off any filings, and paint the exposed metal with red oxide primer. Once the primer is dry, paint the area with touch-up paint that matches the body color.

5. Lower the front of the vehicle, guiding the strut studs into the newly slotted holes.

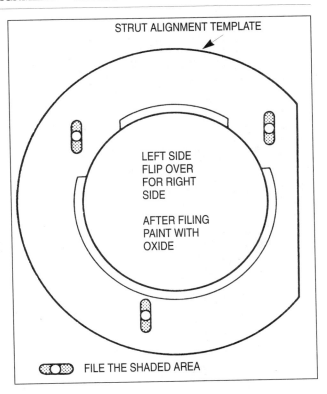

Figure 6-35 An alignment template used to adjust front camber on some strut suspensions. (General Motors)

6. Install the strut cover plate and nuts, then set the camber to the specified angle and torque the cover plate nuts to specifications.

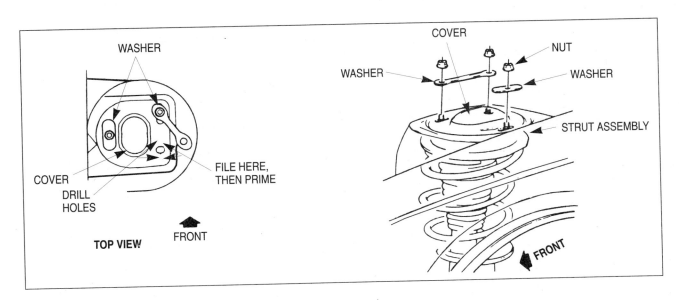

Figure 6-34 Typical front strut caster adjustment. (General Motors)

ECCENTRIC DEVICES

An eccentric is a device which causes the part or parts attached to it to move in an oval when rotated. Eccentric devices used to adjust caster or camber take one of four forms:

1. Eccentric pins — used during the 1950's and early 1960's on many GM and Studebaker models, eccentric pins are held in place by a lock bolt.

2. Eccentric bushings — used during the 1950's on many GM, Chrysler, Ford, Hudson, and Packard models, eccentric bushings also are held in place by a lock bolt.

3. Eccentric cams or washers — currently used on some vehicles, an eccentric cam consists of two washers offset-keyed to a bolt. The bolt passes through the control arm bushing, while the lobes of the washers or cams press against the vehicle frame (Figure 6-36). The bolt is held in place by a lock nut.

4. Upper ball joint eccentrics — used to position the upper ball joint stud in the upper spindle knuckle on many RWD Cadillacs (Figure 6-37). Camber is adjusted by loosening the ball joint stud nut and turning the bushing.

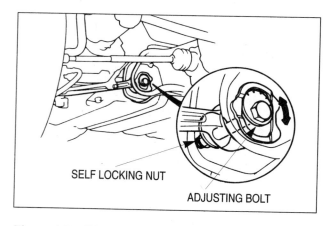

Figure 6-36 Eccentric cams are rotating off-set washers that apply pressure against a frame bracket to reposition a component. (Honda)

SELF LOCKING NUT

ADJUSTING BOLT

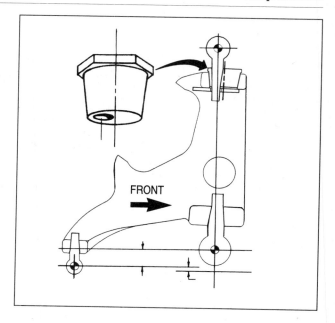

FRONT

Figure 6-37 Camber is adjusted on many RWD Cadillacs with an eccentric bushing. As the bushing is rotated around the upper ball joint stud, the upper spindle knuckle moves in and out. (Moog Automotive)

Front Control Arm Eccentric Cam Adjustment

The following procedure is typical when eccentric cams or washers are used to control front wheel caster and camber (Figure 6-38).

1. Loosen the upper control arm-to-frame attaching nuts.

2. To increase positive camber, rotate the bolt head to position both front and rear cam lobes inboard.

3. To increase positive caster, position the front cam lobe inboard and the rear cam lobe outboard.

4. When cams are properly positioned to obtain the desired camber and caster settings, tighten the nuts to specifications.

Front/Rear Struts with Eccentric Cam Bolts

Camber is adjusted on some strut suspensions with an eccentric cam bolt instead of a slotted lower mounting hole. After

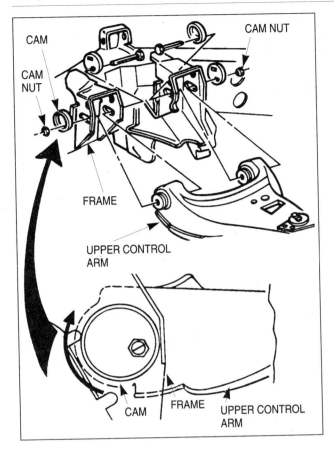

Figure 6-38 Caster and camber adjustment with an eccentric cam. (Oldsmobile Division, General Motors)

marking the position of the cam bolt on the strut mount, loosen the strut cam and knuckle bolts and nuts. Turn the cam bolt as required to move the top of the wheel/tire assembly in or out to the specified camber setting. Tighten the cam bolts and nuts to specifications, plus one-quarter turn beyond the specified torque.

Rear Control Arms with Eccentric Cams

Rear suspensions that use individual front and rear control arms on each side will have four eccentric cam adjustment to control camber adjustment (Figure 6-39).

Upper Ball Joint Camber Adjustment

Front camber is adjusted on Chevette,

Pontiac T1000, and early Fiero models by removing and rotating the upper ball joint by 180° (Figure 6-40). After ball joint rotation, the flat on the joint flange will face the inner side of the control arm and the camber will be increased by approximately 1°.

Strut Rod Caster Adjustment

Lower control arms with a single mounting point use a strut rod to maintain stability (Figure 6-41). Caster is controlled by changing the length of the strut rod through adjustment nuts (Figure 6-42) or by adding/subtracting shims or spacers (Figure 6-43). Since camber changes affect caster, the camber angle should be adjusted first.

Caster and Camber Adjustment Kits

Aftermarket manufacturers provide adjustment kits for vehicles that have NO provision for camber or caster adjustments (primarily import vehicles). Some kits will change a non-adjustable strut rod into one that can be adjusted to change caster. Other kits are designed to permit caster and camber corrections of non-adjustable struts (Figure 6-44). Kits are useful, but should NOT be installed to avoid replacing bent or damaged parts. A damaged part may fail sometime later.

When General Motors redesigned the Chevrolet/GMC C/K pickup truck in 1988, provision for caster and camber adjustment was built into the vehicle, but without the adjusting bolts. A separate eccentric cam and bolt kit is available through Chevrolet dealers to allow alignment adjustments. Alignment knockouts must be removed from the frame brackets to create slotted holes for adjustment (Figure 6-45). Installation is accomplished with the following procedure:

1. Raise the vehicle and support the

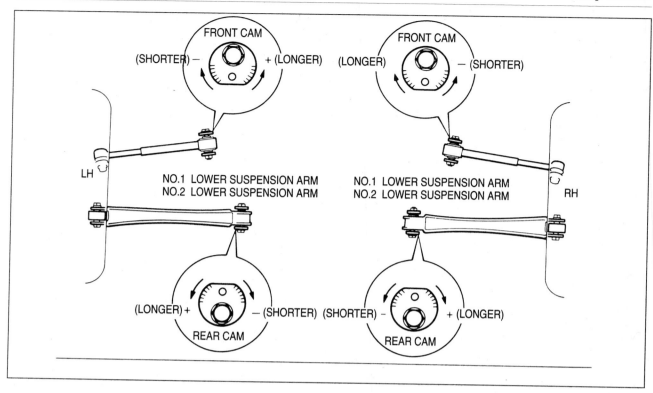

Figure 6-39 Typical rear suspension camber adjustment with individual control arms and eccentric cams. (Honda)

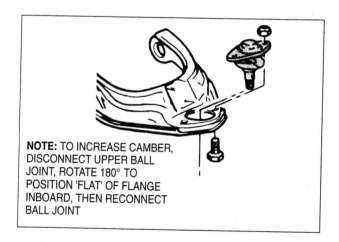

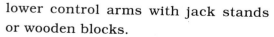

NOTE: TO INCREASE CAMBER, DISCONNECT UPPER BALL JOINT, ROTATE 180° TO POSITION 'FLAT' OF FLANGE INBOARD, THEN RECONNECT BALL JOINT

Figure 6-40 Rotating the upper ball joint on some GM models adjusts camber. (General Motors)

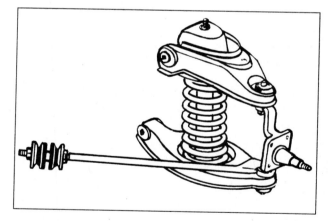

Figure 6-41 A strut rod is used to hold single pivot point lower control arms in the proper position. (Moog Automotive)

lower control arms with jack stands or wooden blocks.

2. Remove the front wheel/tire assemblies.

3. On 4WD (K) models, release tension on the torsion bars as described in

the chapter covering suspension height.

4. Remove the nut, bolt, and two cams from the upper control arm bracket.

5. Raise the upper control arm up and to one side to provide access to the

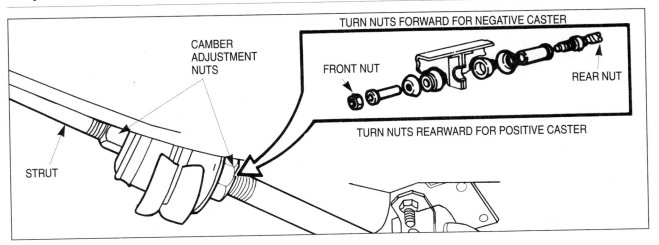

Figure 6-42 One method of caster adjustment on a lower control arm strut rod uses adjustment nuts to lengthen or shorten the strut rod. (Ford Motor)

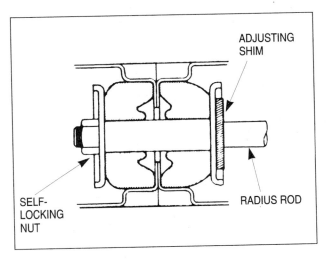

Figure 6-43 Other strut rods are adjusted with spacers or shims. (Honda)

inner part of the frame bracket.

6. Using a pry bar or other suitable tool, carefully remove the alignment knockouts from the frame brackets to avoid distorting the brackets.

7. Reposition the upper control arm in the frame brackets and install the bolt and one cam through one bracket and the control arm.

8. Install the second cam and nut, tightening the nut finger-tight.

9. Repeat Steps 7 and 8 to connect the other control arm leg to its bracket.

10. On 4WD models, re-tension and adjust the torsion bars as described in Chapter 4 of this shop manual.

11. Reinstall the front wheel/tire assemblies.

12. Position the vehicle on the alignment rack and measure trim height. Correct trim height as required.

13. Adjust caster and camber to specifications by rotating the bolt head installed through the adjuster cam. Tighten the upper control arm nuts to specifications.

14. Center the steering wheel with the front wheels in the straight-ahead position, and adjust toe to specifications with the tie rod adjuster sleeves.

TOE ADJUSTMENT METHODS

Regardless of the vehicle type or suspension, front wheel toe is adjusted by changing the length of the tie rods. Vehicles with an independent front suspension have two adjustable tie rods. Those with a solid axle have only one tie rod.

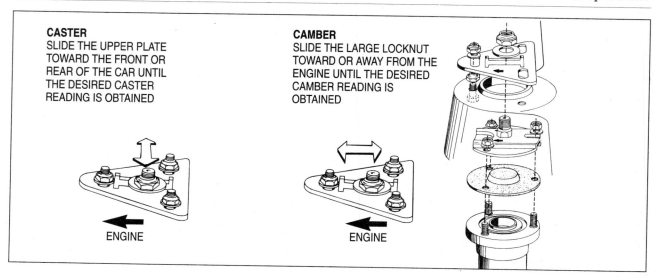

Figure 6-44 One example of the caster-camber adjustment kits used to permit adjustment of non-adjustable struts. (Moog Automotive)

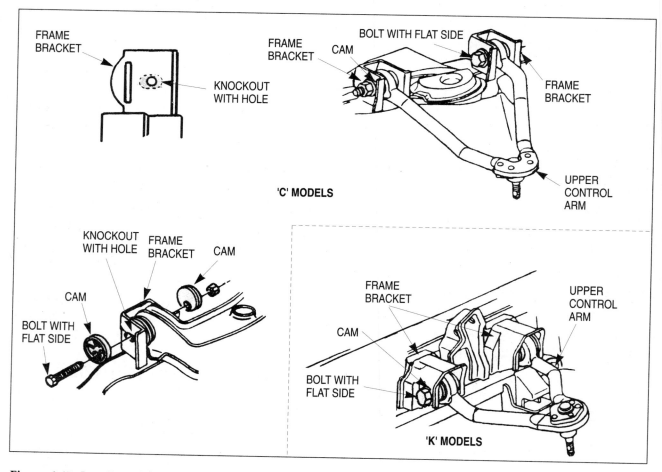

Figure 6-45 Installing the caster-camber adjustment kit on 1988 and later Chevrolet/GMC light-duty pickup trucks. (General Motors)

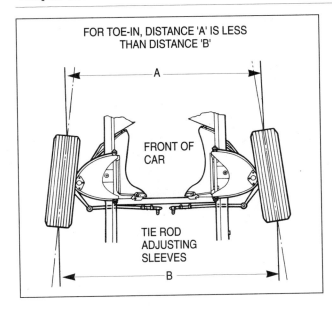

Figure 6-46 Tie rods located behind the steering knuckles are lengthened to increase toe-in, and shortened to increase toe-out. (General Motors)

Although the tie rods may be positioned ahead of the steering knuckles on some vehicles, most are located behind the knuckles (Figure 6-46). When the tie rods are mounted in front of the knuckles, they must be shortened to increase toe-in, or lengthened to increase toe-out. Those mounted behind the knuckles must be lengthened to increase toe-in, or shortened to increase toe-out. Before making any toe measurements or adjustments, the steering wheel should be centered and a steering wheel holder installed to prevent steering linkage movement.

Although alignment specifications provide a minimum and maximum toe setting, it is best to adjust the toe to the middle of the range (often called the 'preferred setting'). This is done to prevent tire wear that might occur when toe is adjusted to either end of the specified range. Toe specifications may be given as total or individual (one-half of total) measurements. If total toe is specified, each adjuster sleeve (RWD) or inner tie rod

(FWD) is rotated the same amount, unless the steering wheel requires centering. When individual toe settings are given, the sleeve or inner tie rod on one side is rotated to position the tire as specified, and then the procedure is repeated on the other side of the vehicle.

FRONT TOE ADJUSTMENT (RWD VEHICLES)

Tie rods used with conventional parallelogram steering on RWD vehicles consist of three parts — two ends and a center adjuster sleeve (Figure 6-47). One tie rod end and one end of the sleeve use right-hand threads; the other end of the tie rod and sleeve have left-hand threads. When the clamps are loosened, the sleeve can be rotated to increase or shorten the tie rod (Figure 6-48).

Because of their location underneath the vehicle, it is NOT uncommon for adjuster sleeves to freeze from rust, corrosion, or road dirt. Trying to rotate a frozen sleeve without the proper tools can damage it. Even when a sleeve does not appear to be frozen, it is best to apply penetrating oil in its slots and on the threads, then wait a few minutes for the oil to work

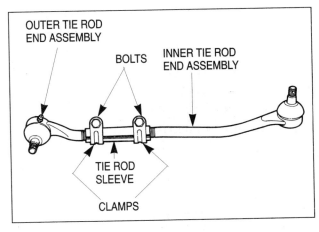

Figure 6-47 A typical recirculating ball steering tie rod assembly uses an adjuster sleeve to connect the inner and outer tie rods. (Chrysler)

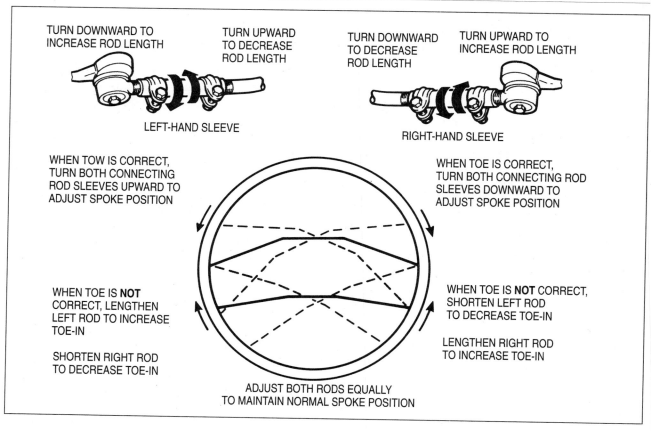

Figure 6-48 Typical tie rod adjustment and steering wheel centering. (Ford Motor)

before trying to rotate it. If it still will not rotate, use an air hammer and suitable blunt punch to vibrate the sleeve free. Special tie rod wrenches are available and should be used when the adjuster sleeve cannot be turned freely, instead of working with makeshift tools, such as a pipe wrench or slip joint pliers which can damage the sleeve. If clamp nut removal from the sleeve bolts requires more than 80 lbf•in torque, discard the nuts and install new ones after making the necessary toe adjustment.

TECH TIP: Do NOT heat a rusted or frozen adjuster sleeve with an acetylene torch unless the sleeve is to be removed and discarded.

Once the adjustment has been completed, make sure the adjuster clamps are properly located and the tie rod studs are positioned correctly. If the tie rod studs are not centered in their housings to permit full stud swing (Figure 6-49), the linkage can bind during steering or suspension movements. After lubricating the clamp bolts and nuts, refer to Figure 6-50 to assure proper positioning. The slot in the adjuster sleeve should NOT be within the clamp gap area (A), the clamp end may touch when tightened but a gap must be visible next to the adjuster sleeve (B), and the clamps must be between and clear of the dimples before tightening the nuts (C). Make sure the adjuster sleeve position does NOT change when tightening the clamp bolts, and that the clamps and bolts do NOT interfere with other components.

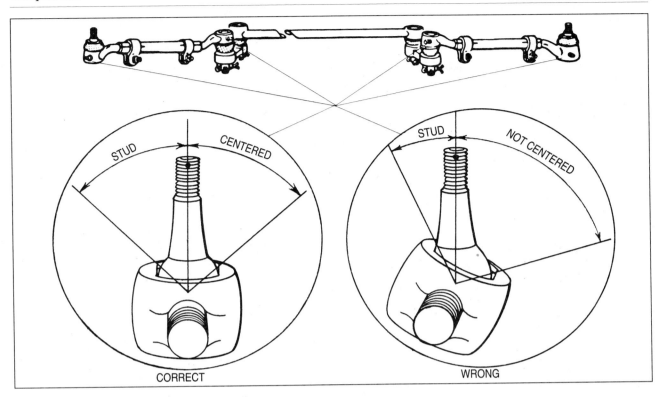

Figure 6-49 Tie rod studs not centered will limit linkage movement and can result in tie rod failure. (Moog Automotive)

FRONT TOE ADJUSTMENT (FWD VEHICLES)

Some FWD vehicles use a different type of three-piece tie rod (Figure 6-51). The inner and outer rod ends are threaded to accept a threaded adjuster rod. Wrench flats are provided in the center of the threaded rod for adjusting tie rod length. When this type of tie rod is used, the adjustment procedure is essentially the same as that used with RWD vehicles. After loosening the clamp bolts, the adjuster rod is rotated with a wrench on its flats until the toe setting is correct, then the clamp bolts are tightened to specifications.

Other FWD vehicles use a two-piece tie rod. The inner tie rod end is threaded to screw into the outer tie rod end. A jam nut on the inner tie rod end is loosened to allow adjustment, and tightened to maintain it (Figure 6-52). The tie rod end generally

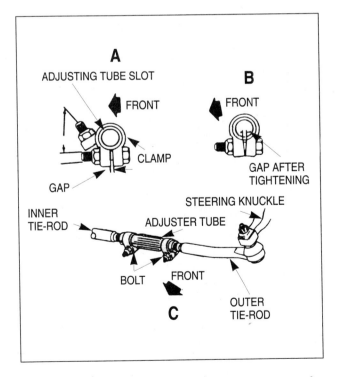

Figure 6-50 Tie rod adjuster sleeves and clamps must be properly positioned. (General Motors)

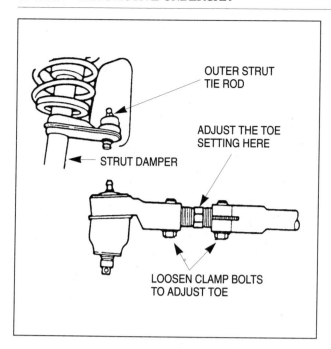

Figure 6-51 The three-piece tie rod used with FWD vehicles connects the two tie rods with a threaded adjuster rod. (Oldsmobile Division, General Motors)

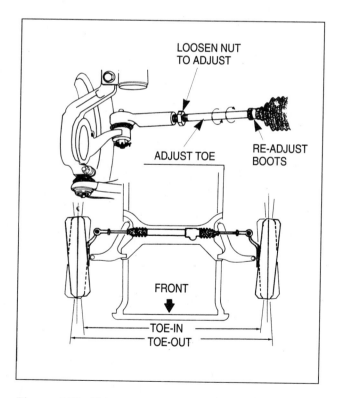

Figure 6-52 The two-piece tie rod uses a jam nut to maintain toe adjustment. (Chrysler)

has flats for use with an open-end wrench to prevent it from turning when loosening the jam nut. With this arrangement, the clamp or clip on the bellows/boot must be loosened to allow the inner tie rod to rotate without twisting the bellows/boot. With the jam nut and clamp loosened, the inner tie rod can be rotated as required with suitable pliers (do NOT grip tie rod threads with pliers) to bring toe within specifications, and the jam nut retightened. Check the boot to make sure it is NOT distorted, then reposition and tighten the clamp or reinstall the clip.

REAR TOE ADJUSTMENT (FWD VEHICLES)

Front wheel drive vehicles generally are designed with zero to slight toe-in at the rear wheels. Adjusting rear wheel toe on FWD vehicles involves some variation of the adjustment methods described earlier. Some vehicles have a jam nut arrangment similar to that used to adjust front toe (Figure 6-53), while others use an eccentric arrangement (Figure 6-54). Other methods of rear toe adjustment include the use of adjustment shims between the spindle and

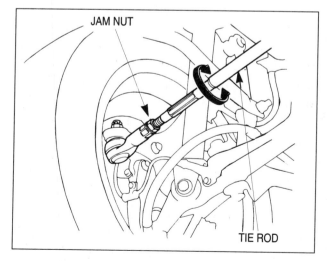

Figure 6-53 Rear wheel toe adjustment using a jam nut. (Honda)

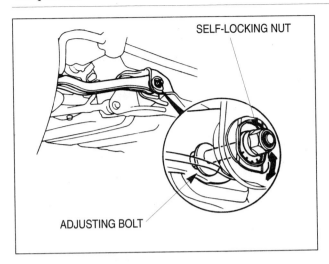

Figure 6-54 Rear wheel toe adjustment using an eccentric cam. (Honda)

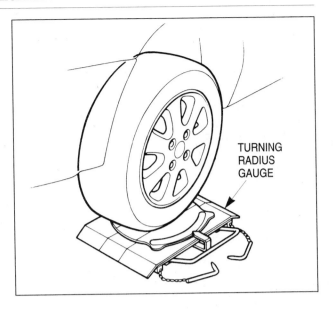

Figure 6-56 The front wheel is placed on a turning radius gauge or protractor turntable to check turning angle. (Honda)

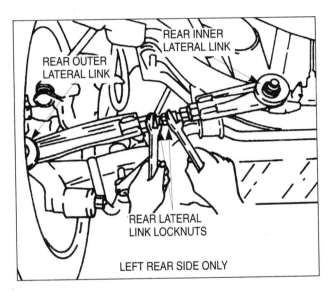

Figure 6-55 Rear wheel toe adjustment using an adjustable lateral link. (Ford Motor)

rear axle (B, Figure 6-29), or adjustment of a rear lateral link (Figure 6-55).

CHECKING TURNING ANGLE

Turning angle, or toe-out on turns, is checked after toe has been correctly adjusted. Most carmakers and equipment manufacturers specify turning one wheel by 20°, and then checking the increased

angle of turn on the other wheel. Be sure to check specifications for the vehicle, as some may require a higher setting. The higher specified angle applies to the inside wheel; the smaller angle is for the outer wheel.

1. Raise the front of the vehicle with its wheels positioned straight ahead, position a turning radius gauge or protractor turnplate set to zero under each front wheel (Figure 6-56), and lower the vehicle to the ground.

2. Raise the rear of the vehicle enough to place wooden boards the same thickness as the gauges or turnplates, and then lower the vehicle to the ground. This levels the vehicle to provide accurate readings. If your rack has built-in turning plates that are level with the rear wheels, this step is NOT necessary.

3. Turn the steering wheel to the right until the right (inner) wheel protractor reads 20°. Check the reading on the left (outer) wheel; it should be

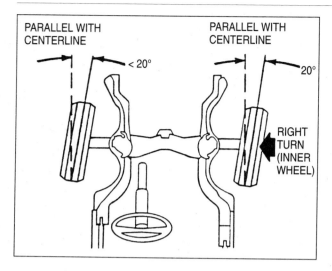

Figure 6-57 Checking the turning angle of the left front wheel. (General Motors)

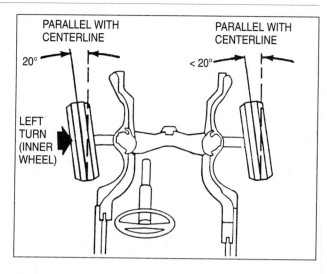

Figure 6-58 Checking the turning angle of the right front wheel. (General Motors)

less than 20°. This angle is the turning angle of the left (outer) wheel (Figure 6-57).

4. Recenter the wheels and turn the steering wheel to the left until the left (inner) wheel protractor reads 20°. Check the reading on the right (outer) wheel; it should be less than 20°. This angle is the turning angle of the right (outer) wheel (Figure 6-58).

5. Compare the two outer wheel readings. The two outer turning angle readings should be within

specifications (usually 1.5° of each other). For example, if the right outer wheel measurement is 16°, and the left outer wheel measurement is 19°, component damage is likely.

6. If component damage is indicated, it most likely will be found on the passenger side of the vehicle, as the curb side of any vehicle is subjected to the most abuse, such as running into curbs or stationary parking markers.

❓ REVIEW QUESTIONS

1. Technician A says that the front wheels must be positioned straight ahead when measuring camber and toe. Technician B says that the vehicle must be level and at the correct trim height during wheel alignment. Who is right?
   (A) A only
   (B) B only
   (C) Both A and B
   (D) Neither A nor B

2. Technician A says that setting the toe first will assure the wheels are properly positioned when adjusting caster and camber. Technician B says that alignment angles can be adjusted in any sequence the technician desires. Who is right?
   (A) A only
   (B) B only
   (C) Both A and B
   (D) Neither A nor B

3. Technician A says that a four-wheel alignment performed on a four-wheel alignment rack should start at the rear wheels. Technician B says that the four-wheel alignment should start with the front wheels. Who is right?
   - (A) A only
   - (B) B only
   - (C) Both A and B
   - (D) Neither A nor B

4. Technician A says that the steering wheel should be locked in a straight-ahead position when checking and adjusting toe. Technician A says that a four-wheel alignment cannot be done on two-wheel alignment equipment. Who is right?
   - (A) A only
   - (B) B only
   - (C) Both A and B
   - (D) Neither A nor B

5. Technician A says that caster should be set to maintain a setting as close as possible to zero with the vehicle in motion. Technician B says that excessive negative camber results in faster wear of the tire's inner tread. Who is right?
   - (A) A only
   - (B) B only
   - (C) Both A and B
   - (D) Neither A nor B

6. Technician A says that caster has a direct affect on tire wear. Technician B says that uneven caster can cause tire pull when the vehicle is moving. Who is right?
   - (A) A only
   - (B) B only
   - (C) Both A and B
   - (D) Neither A nor B

7. Technician A says that FWD vehicles may NOT have any provision for setting caster. Technician B says that setting toe to zero on the alignment rack will result in zero toe when the vehicle is in motion. Who is right?
   - (A) A only
   - (B) B only
   - (C) Both A and B
   - (D) Neither A nor B

8. Technician A says that an incorrect turning angle can cause low-speed tire squeal. Technician B says that when the included angle differs more than 0.50° side-to-side, a front strut or spindle is probably bent. Who is right?
   - (A) A only
   - (B) B only
   - (C) Both A and B
   - (D) Neither A nor B

9. Technician A says that toe measured in inches or millimeters represents the difference in distance between the front and rear of the wheels. Technician B says that toe measured in degrees represents the angle between the vehicle centerline and the wheel's rotational plane. Who is right?
   - (A) A only
   - (B) B only
   - (C) Both A and B
   - (D) Neither A nor B

10. Which of the following are NOT used to adjust camber?
    - (A) shims
    - (B) eccentric cams
    - (C) slotted holes
    - (D) strut rods

11. Technician A says that upper control arm cross shafts are mounted inside the frame bracket. Technician A says they are mounted outside the frame bracket. Who is right?
    - (A) A only
    - (B) B only
    - (C) Both A and B
    - (D) Neither A nor B

12. Technician A says that caster and camber often can be adjusted with the same shims. Technician B says that the camber angle should be adjusted first when working with a shim-type adjustment. Who is right?
    (A) A only
    (B) B only
    (C) Both A and B
    (D) Neither A nor B

13. Technician A says that when caster is adjusted by a strut rod, camber should be adjusted first. Technician B says that camber is adjusted on some vehicles by rotating the upper control arm ball joint 180°. Who is right?
    (A) A only
    (B) B only
    (C) Both A and B
    (D) Neither A nor B

14. Technician A says that lengthening one tie rod and shortening the other tie rod by an equal amount will decrease the toe. Technician B says that it will change the steering wheel position. Who is right?
    (A) A only
    (B) B only
    (C) Both A and B
    (D) Neither A nor B

15. Technician A says that the toe should be set to the middle of the specified range. Technician B says that a frozen tie rod sleeve should be loosened by applying heat. Who is right?
    (A) A only
    (B) B only
    (C) Both A and B
    (D) Neither A nor B

16. Technician A says that tie rod adjuster sleeve clamps must be properly positioned to avoid interference with other components. Technician B says that some three-piece tie rods use an adjuster rod instead of an adjuster sleeve. Who is right?
    (A) A only
    (B) B only
    (C) Both A and B
    (D) Neither A nor B

17. Technician A says that rack and pinion gear boots must be tightened to prevent distortion when making toe adjustments. Technician B says that a tight adjuster sleeve should be rotated with a pipe wrench or slip joint pliers. Who is right?
    (A) A only
    (B) B only
    (C) Both A and B
    (D) Neither A nor B

18. Technician A says that caster CANNOT be adjusted on solid beam axles. Technician B says that installing tapered shims between the axle and springs will change caster. Who is right?
    (A) A only
    (B) B only
    (C) Both A and B
    (D) Neither A nor B

STEERING SYSTEM SERVICING

 **OBJECTIVES**

After completion of this chapter, you should be able to:

- Use a troubleshooting guide to determine the condition of a recirculating ball steering box or a rack and pinion gear, as assigned by the instructor.

- Locate a fluid leak in a power steering system.

- Remove and install any of the following, as designated by the instructor, using the appropriate method and equipment — rack and pinion tie rod ends, parallelogram linkage tie rods or tie rod ends, worn or defective components of a parallelogram linkage, recirculating ball gearbox or rack and pinion steering gear, and steering wheel or steering column.

- Adjust a recirculating ball power steering gearbox for worm bearing preload and sector shaft gear lash.

- Check power steering system pressures and use the carmaker's specifications to determine if they are correct.

- Check and adjust the fluid level in a power steering system.

- Bleed air from the power steering system.

STEERING GEARBOXES

The manual recirculating ball gearbox can be disassembled, overhauled, and reassembled with a minimum of difficulty, provided the necessary parts and tools are available. The same type of gearbox equipped with power assist is similar in design, but somewhat more difficult to work on because of the control valve, the number of seals used, and the need to ensure that all pressure areas are properly sealed. If seal kits are available, recirculating ball and other similar gearboxes can usually be overhauled with success. The gearboxes are much stronger and longer lasting than many other parts of a vehicle.

Rack and pinion steering is much different. Service procedures are usually

S 157

restricted to replacing the boot seals and tie rod ends. When a rack and pinion gear has an internal problem, it is usually replaced as an assembly. There are a few rack and pinion steering gears that can be removed and disassembled to replace the pinion bearing, seals, and rack housing bushing.

When it is necessary to disassemble and overhaul a particular gear, refer to a good repair manual for the specific removal, overhaul, lubrication, and adjustment procedures.

With the continuing escalation in labor costs, and the length of time it takes to rebuild a gear, it often is less expensive for a shop to replace a defective gear with a rebuilt or remanufactured unit rather than to overhaul the old gear. Remanufactured units have been pretested to assure leak-free operation. In the shop, the only way to test for leaks is to install the gear, and then remove it for further repair if it leaks. A rebuilt unit saves time and money for both the shop and the customer.

MANUAL STEERING GEAR DIAGNOSIS

Problems connected with a manual steering gearbox generally fall into the following categories:

- Excessive steering wheel play — this can result from worn ball joints or loose tie rod ends, but may also be caused by excessive clearance between the contact faces of the ball nut and sector gear, insufficient worm shaft bearing preload, ball nut bearings that are missing, or loose gearbox mounting bolts. With rack and pinion gears, check for vertical movement of the tie rod ends, loose inner tie rod sockets, excessive clearance of the pinion shaft coupling, and incorrect rack-to-pinion gear preload.
- Noisy steering gear — this can be caused by a damaged gear face, a defective pinion shaft bearing, or an incorrect rack-to-pinion gear preload.
- Excessive effort required to turn the steering wheel — this generally results from a lack of sufficient lubricant in the gearbox, but it also can be caused by excessive preload on worm shaft bearings that have been torqued excessively.
- Rough steering wheel rotation — this is a rough feeling when the steering wheel is rotated and indicates problems with the worm shaft ball bearings or bearing races.
- Loss of gearbox lubricant — generally caused by a leaking sector shaft seal, but can result from excessive clearance between the sector shaft and its bushings.

POWER STEERING SYSTEM DIAGNOSIS

Problems associated with a power steering system are diagnosed according to the type of gearbox used. Many power steering problems are caused by the power steering pump rather than the steering gear.

Some noise is inherent in all power steering systems. One of the most common complaints is a hissing noise most noticeable when turning the steering wheel with the brakes applied, as during parking maneuvers. With recirculating ball steering systems, the noise results from the power steering pump relief valve. In rack and pinion steering systems, the gear valve and pinion assembly can make noise, but the pump is usually responsible for objectionable noise. Replacing the valve in either system may reduce, but will NOT eliminate, the noise since it results from high velocity fluid passing the valve orifice edges. Some power steering pumps are not what you could call quiet even after being overhauled or rebuilt. Sometimes the best that can be done is to get one that is less noisy, or try a new pump from the manufacturer. New pumps usually are much quieter than overhauled, rebuilt, or remanufactured pumps.

Recirculating Ball Gearboxes

Use the following guidelines to help diagnose problems with a recirculating ball power steering system. Be sure to check for loose, worn, or binding steering linkage, worn or incorrectly adjusted wheel bearings, misaligned front wheels, and correct tire inflation before blaming the steering gear.

1. Rattle or chuckle noise in steering gear — this can be caused by a loose steering gear or Pitman arm. It also may result from contact of the pressure hose with other vehicle components or from improper over-center adjustment of the gear.

2. Excessive wheel kickback or loose steering — generally results from air in the hydraulic system, but can be caused by a worn or improperly adjusted steering gear.

3. Vehicle leads to either side on a level road — if the front wheels are properly aligned, the steering gear valve probably is unbalanced and must be replaced. If the valve is at fault, the steering effort required will be very light in the lead direction, and quite heavy in the opposite direction.

4. Momentary steering effort increase when steering wheel is turned quickly to one side — can be caused by a low pump fluid level or slipping pump belt, but may also indicate high internal leakage either in the steering gear or pump.

5. Poor steering return — generally caused by a misaligned steering gear and column, but can result from a stuck or plugged spool valve or steering gear that is adjusted too tightly.

6. Steering wheel surge or jerk during parking — can be caused by a low pump fluid level, loose pump belt, or insufficient pump pressure, but may indicate a defective pump flow control or relief valve.

7. Hard steering effort or lack of assist in both directions — can result from a loose pump belt or low pump fluid level, but may also be caused by misalignment of the steering gear and column, steering shaft or coupling interference, a steering gear that is adjusted too tight, or a defective pump flow control valve.

8. Low hydraulic system pressure — may be caused by a hose restriction, a worn or leaking steering gear, or a defective power steering pump.

9. Squealing or chirping noise — caused by a slipping pump drive belt, especially when the belt is wet from rainwater.

10. Noisy power steering pump — depending on the type of noise, it may result from air in the hydraulic system, excessive back pressure in the steering gear or hoses, a low pump fluid level, or a defective pump. The design of some pumps makes them much noisier than others.

Rack and Pinion Gears

Use the following guidelines to help diagnose problems with a power rack and pinion steering system. Be sure to check for loose, worn, or binding steering linkage, worn or incorrectly adjusted wheel bearings, misaligned front wheels, and correct tire inflation before blaming the steering gear.

1. Rattle or chuckle noise in steering gear — this can be caused by loose tie rod ends or steering gear mounts. It also may result from contact of the pressure hose with other vehicle com-

ponents, incorrect rack bearing preload, or loose intermediate shaft U-joints.

2. Excessive wheel kickback or loose steering — usually results from air in the hydraulic system, but can be caused by a loose steering gear mount, loose steering coupling, loose tie rod ends, or an incorrect rack bearing preload.

3. Excessive wander or poor steering stability — if the front and rear wheels are properly aligned, the steering gear rack preload is too loose, or the steering gear valve is unbalanced.

4. Momentary steering effort increase when steering wheel is turned quickly to one side — can be caused by a low pump fluid level or slipping pump belt, but may also indicate high internal leakage either in the steering gear or pump.

5. Poor steering return — usually caused by a loose or binding steering coupling, but can result from a stuck or plugged valve and pinion, a binding tie rod end, tight or frozen steering shaft bearings, or a rack bearing preload that is too tight.

6. Steering wheel surge or jerk during parking — can be caused by a low pump fluid level, loose pump belt, or insufficient pump pressure, but may indicate a defective pump flow control or relief valve.

7. Hard steering effort or lack of assist in both directions — can result from a loose pump belt or low pump fluid level, but may also result from a loose steering gear mount, a loose or worn steering coupling, incorrect rack bearing preload, or high internal leakage either in the steering gear or pump.

8. Low hydraulic system pressure —

may be caused by a hose restriction, a worn or leaking steering gear, or a defective power steering pump.

9. Squealing or chirping noise in power steering pump — caused by a slipping pump drive belt, especially in wet weather.

10. Noisy power steering pump — depending on the type of noise, may result from air in the hydraulic system, excessive back pressure in the steering gear or hoses, a low pump fluid level, or a defective pump. The design of some pumps makes them much noisier than others.

LOCATING FLUID LEAKS

The power steering system is a completely closed circulation system with two main components, the pump and the steering gear, connected by two hoses. If an external seal on either component fails, there will be an obvious leak. Such a leak will not affect system operation until the fluid level drops to a critical point. Before the fluid level reaches this point, leakage can be seen on the floor or ground, or on the steering gear or pump. Once the fluid level does affect system operation, it can take several different forms, including growling noises, loss of steering assist during parking, and heavy steering effort.

The most difficult part of diagnosing an external leak is to determine exactly where it comes from, since the point from which the fluid drips is NOT necessarily the point at which the system is leaking. Tight underhood packaging makes locating the exact point of leakage difficult on some vehicles, but determining exactly which seal is leaking before removing any component can save considerable time and effort. Removing components for a bench check limits you to guesswork or reliance on a visual inspection. As long as the

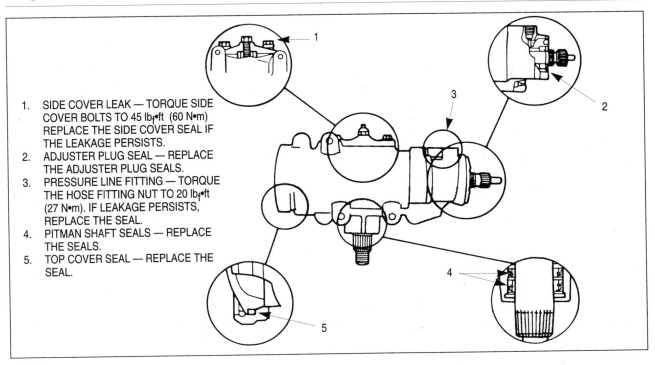

1. SIDE COVER LEAK — TORQUE SIDE COVER BOLTS TO 45 lbₜ•ft (60 N•m) REPLACE THE SIDE COVER SEAL IF THE LEAKAGE PERSISTS.
2. ADJUSTER PLUG SEAL — REPLACE THE ADJUSTER PLUG SEALS.
3. PRESSURE LINE FITTING — TORQUE THE HOSE FITTING NUT TO 20 lbₜ•ft (27 N•m). IF LEAKAGE PERSISTS, REPLACE THE SEAL.
4. PITMAN SHAFT SEALS — REPLACE THE SEALS.
5. TOP COVER SEAL — REPLACE THE SEAL.

Figure 7-1 Possible leakage points with a recirculating ball gearbox. (Chrysler)

system is intact on the vehicle, pump pressure can help you to locate the source of a leak.

Although seepage-type leaks are the most common, they also are the most difficult to locate. You can trace the cause of a seepage leak with the following procedure:

1. With the engine off and cold, wipe the power steering gear, pump, hoses, and connections dry. Depending on the system configuration, it may be necessary to place the vehicle on a hoist for this procedure.
2. Check and adjust the fluid level in the pump reservoir.
3. Start the engine and run at idle while an assistant turns the steering wheel several times from stop to stop. Do NOT hold the wheel at either stop, as this can cause pump overheating and damage.
4. Use a light and an inspection mirror,

if necessary, to check each seal or point of leakage while the steering wheel is rotated. Remember that fluid leaks travel due to gravity, normal fluid spreading, and engine or road drafts. Locate the source of the fluid leak path, not the location of the drip. Refer to Figure 7-1 (recirculating ball gearbox), Figure 7-2 and Figure 7-3 (typical rack and pinion gears), and Figure 7-4 and Figure 7-5 (typical power steering pumps). If no signs of leakage can be found, check the transmission cooler line or transaxle gaskets and seals since they are near power steering components on many vehicles.

LINKAGE SERVICE

The steering linkage used with recirculating ball gearboxes is called parallelogram linkage because the Pitman and idler arms move parallel to each other and, with the

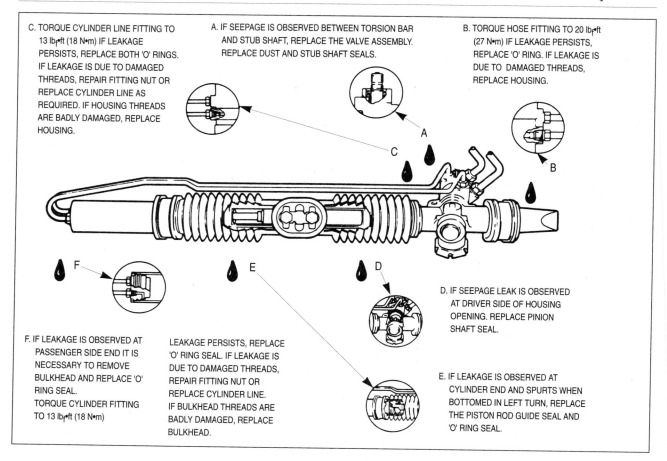

C. TORQUE CYLINDER LINE FITTING TO 13 lbₑft (18 N•m) IF LEAKAGE PERSISTS, REPLACE BOTH 'O' RINGS. IF LEAKAGE IS DUE TO DAMAGED THREADS, REPAIR FITTING NUT OR REPLACE CYLINDER LINE AS REQUIRED. IF HOUSING THREADS ARE BADLY DAMAGED, REPLACE HOUSING.

A. IF SEEPAGE IS OBSERVED BETWEEN TORSION BAR AND STUB SHAFT, REPLACE THE VALVE ASSEMBLY. REPLACE DUST AND STUB SHAFT SEALS.

B. TORQUE HOSE FITTING TO 20 lbₑft (27 N•m) IF LEAKAGE PERSISTS, REPLACE 'O' RING. IF LEAKAGE IS DUE TO DAMAGED THREADS, REPLACE HOUSING.

F. IF LEAKAGE IS OBSERVED AT PASSENGER SIDE END IT IS NECESSARY TO REMOVE BULKHEAD AND REPLACE 'O' RING SEAL. TORQUE CYLINDER FITTING TO 13 lbₑft (18 N•m)

LEAKAGE PERSISTS, REPLACE 'O' RING SEAL. IF LEAKAGE IS DUE TO DAMAGED THREADS, REPAIR FITTING NUT OR REPLACE CYLINDER LINE. IF BULKHEAD THREADS ARE BADLY DAMAGED, REPLACE BULKHEAD.

D. IF SEEPAGE LEAK IS OBSERVED AT DRIVER SIDE OF HOUSING OPENING. REPLACE PINION SHAFT SEAL.

E. IF LEAKAGE IS OBSERVED AT CYLINDER END AND SPURTS WHEN BOTTOMED IN LEFT TURN, REPLACE THE PISTON ROD GUIDE SEAL AND 'O' RING SEAL.

Figure 7-2 Possible leakage points with a tie rod center take-off power rack and pinion gear. (Oldsmobile Division, General Motors)

CAUTION: Fasteners such as nuts and washers used on steering linkage are made specifically to withstand high loads. Do NOT use hardware store fasteners on steering systems. To be sure of getting safe, correct fasteners, buy them from an auto parts store or new car dealer parts department.

center link, form three sides of a parallelogram (Figure 7-6). This type of linkage has tie rods or connecting links that can move up or down to follow the movement of the vehicle's suspension. Rack and pinion linkage is far less complicated, since the rack itself takes the place of the Pitman arm, idler arm, and center link. The tie rods are still used, but with the inner ball socket joint on each rod hidden by the boot (Figure 7-7).

Both linkage designs use ball sockets or ball studs of varying design at most connection points (Figure 7-8). Like control arm ball joints, service intervals have been reduced over the years with the use of improved seals and lubrication. Some ball stud designs used on late-model vehicles bond the stud in rubber (Figure 7-9). This type of connection uses the torsilastic nature of the rubber to twist and return, eliminates the need for lubrication, and does away with the problem of a damaged or leaking seal on the ball stud.

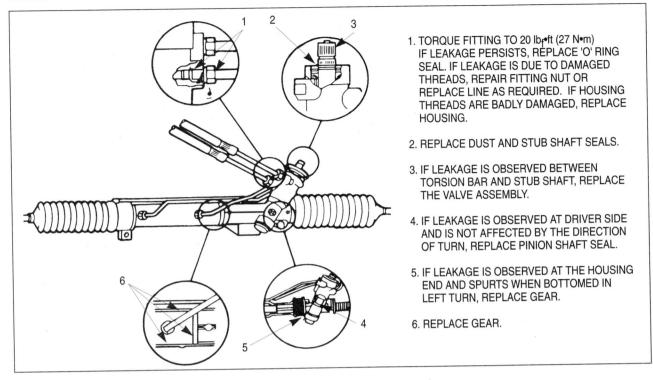

1. TORQUE FITTING TO 20 lbf•ft (27 N•m) IF LEAKAGE PERSISTS, REPLACE 'O' RING SEAL. IF LEAKAGE IS DUE TO DAMAGED THREADS, REPAIR FITTING NUT OR REPLACE LINE AS REQUIRED. IF HOUSING THREADS ARE BADLY DAMAGED, REPLACE HOUSING.

2. REPLACE DUST AND STUB SHAFT SEALS.

3. IF LEAKAGE IS OBSERVED BETWEEN TORSION BAR AND STUB SHAFT, REPLACE THE VALVE ASSEMBLY.

4. IF LEAKAGE IS OBSERVED AT DRIVER SIDE AND IS NOT AFFECTED BY THE DIRECTION OF TURN, REPLACE PINION SHAFT SEAL.

5. IF LEAKAGE IS OBSERVED AT THE HOUSING END AND SPURTS WHEN BOTTOMED IN LEFT TURN, REPLACE GEAR.

6. REPLACE GEAR.

Figure 7-3   Potential leak points with a typical power rack and pinion gear. (Oldsmobile Division, General Motors)

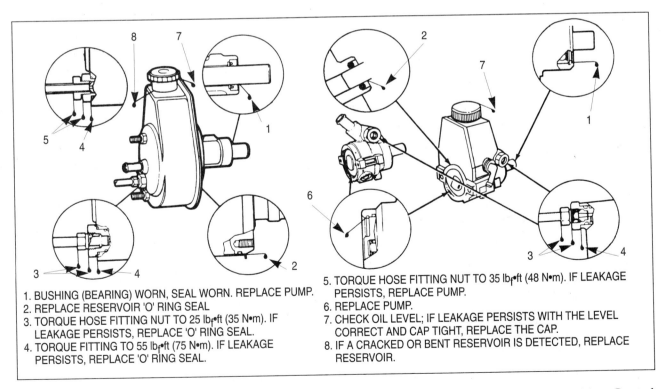

1. BUSHING (BEARING) WORN, SEAL WORN. REPLACE PUMP.
2. REPLACE RESERVOIR 'O' RING SEAL
3. TORQUE HOSE FITTING NUT TO 25 lbf•ft (35 N•m). IF LEAKAGE PERSISTS, REPLACE 'O' RING SEAL.
4. TORQUE FITTING TO 55 lbf•ft (75 N•m). IF LEAKAGE PERSISTS, REPLACE 'O' RING SEAL.
5. TORQUE HOSE FITTING NUT TO 35 lbf•ft (48 N•m). IF LEAKAGE PERSISTS, REPLACE PUMP.
6. REPLACE PUMP.
7. CHECK OIL LEVEL; IF LEAKAGE PERSISTS WITH THE LEVEL CORRECT AND CAP TIGHT, REPLACE THE CAP.
8. IF A CRACKED OR BENT RESERVOIR IS DETECTED, REPLACE RESERVOIR.

Figure 7-4   Typical leakage points with Saginaw reservoir-type power steering pumps. (Oldsmobile Division, General Motors)

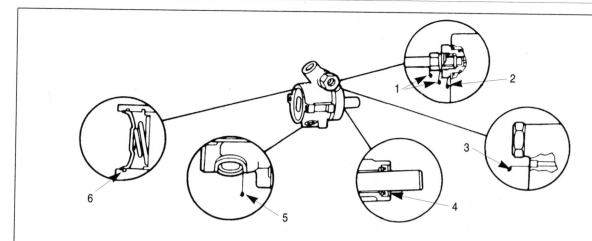

1. TORQUE FITTING TO 20 lb•ft (27 N•m). IF LEAKAGE PERSISTS, REPLACE 'O' RING SEAL.
2. TORQUE FITTING TO 55 lb•ft (75 N•m). IF LEAKAGE PERSISTS, REPLACE 'O' RING SEAL.
3. SEAT BALL IN HOUSING WITH BLUNT PUNCH. APPLY LOCTITE SAFETY SOLVENT AND LOCTITE 290 OR EQUIVALENT TO AREA.
4. REPLACE DRIVE SHAFT SEAL. MAKE CERTAIN THAT DRIVE SHAFT IS CLEAN AND FREE OF PITTING IN SEAL AREA.
5. SEAT PLUG IN HOUSING. APPLY LOCTITE SAFETY SOLVENT AND LOCTITE 290 OR EQUIVALENT TO AREA.
6. REPLACE 'O' RING SEAL.

Figure 7-5 Potential leakage points with a remote reservoir power steering pump. (Oldsmobile Division, General Motors)

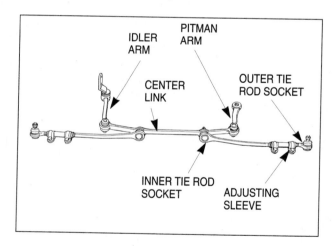

Figure 7-6 Typical parallelogram steering linkage. (McQuay-Norris)

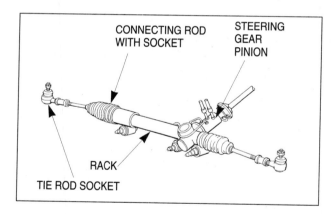

Figure 7-7 Typical rack and pinion steering linkage. (McQuay-Norris)

DIAGNOSING PARALLELOGRAM LINKAGE PROBLEMS

Linkage diagnosis starts with the vehicle wheels on the floor. If the vehicle has power steering, the engine must be idling and the wheels blocked as appropriate. With the steering wheel centered, have an assistant slowly rotate it back and forth while you watch the linkage for any signs of excessive clearance or slack (Figure 7-10). Since the linkage is moving under maximum stress, such clearance or slack

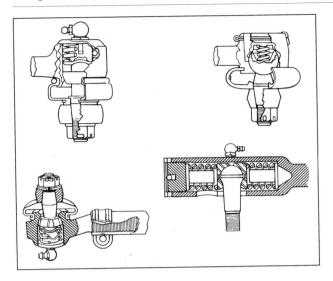

Figure 7-8   A variety of ball sockets used with tie rod ends. (Ford Motor)

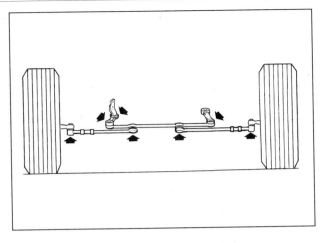

Figure 7-10 Road vibration and impact forces are transmitted to the linkage, causing wear and looseness at the connection points of a parallelogram linkage. (McQuay-Norris)

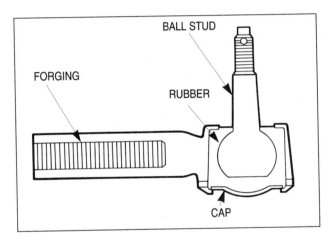

Figure 7-9   Bonded rubber outer tie rod ends use the torsilastic nature of rubber to apply a force that helps return the front wheels to their straight-ahead position. (Ford Motor)

indicates the need for replacement.

After completing this inspection, raise the vehicle in the air and place safety stands under the lower control arms so that the suspension is as close as possible to its running position. Putting stands under the frame allows the suspension to hang down, which may put a bind on the joints and eliminate the looseness you are looking for.

⬧ CAUTION: On some late model vehicles the control arms are so lightweight that jacking or supporting the vehicle on the arms will damage them. To avoid damage use a drive-on hoist or ramps to raise the vehicle.

Grasp each linkage component one at a time and push/pull on it to check for looseness. If no slack was noticed when the linkage moved with the wheels on the floor, you probably will NOT see any with the vehicle in the air, but this inspection also provides an opportunity to check the connections for damaged or deteriorated boots and other potential defects.

Be sure to check the idler arm. As the steering linkage moves, the idler arm pivots in a bracket attached to the frame. The pivot point between the arm and bracket is subjected to high stress and should be checked for looseness. Rubber bushings in the idler arm bracket twist as the wheels are turned, and provide a force that helps return the wheels to a center position. Grasp the center link or connecting rod near the idler arm and try to shake it up

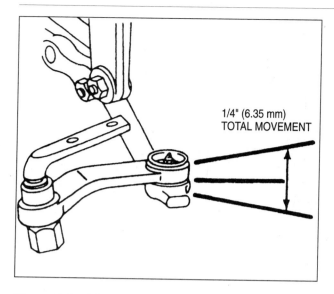

Figure 7-11 Idler arm movement should be compared with the carmaker's specifications to determine if it should be replaced. (General Motors)

Figure 7-12 Tie rod end inspection. (Chrysler)

and down. If any movement is noted, check the carmaker's specifications to determine if the idler arm should be replaced. For example, General Motors allows a 1/8" deflection in each direction (Figure 7-11) for an allowable total of 1/4"; some carmakers allow NO significant deflection.

DIAGNOSING RACK AND PINION LINKAGE PROBLEMS

Raise the vehicle on a hoist that is correct for the vehicle.

> ⚠ **CAUTION:** Some late model vehicles may be damaged by raising them on a twin-post hoist that contacts the front or rear lower control arms.

With the vehicle raised and safely supported, grasp each outer tie rod end and try to move it up and down (Figure 7-12). Tie rod ends must have zero free play, but still allow a swiveling action for suspension movement. Replace the tie rod end

if any slack is noted. Inspect the bellows or boots for damage or deterioration. If splits or cracks are found, or if leakage is noted, replace the bellows or boot. While inspecting the bellows or boot, carefully squeeze the outer end on each side of the vehicle until you can feel the inner tie rod socket, then push/pull on the tire to check for looseness in the socket. If looseness is felt in the socket, it may be necessary to remove the steering gear from the vehicle and service the inner tie rod. On some vehicles the boots and tie rods can be removed and replaced without removing the gear, but working under the vehicle is difficult, and the job will probably go faster and more efficiently if the gear is removed.

LINKAGE REPLACEMENT

Whenever any part of the steering linkage is separated or replaced, the toe adjustment must be checked and readjusted, if necessary. Steering linkage connections, like control arm ball joints, generally use a locking taper. The most efficient method of breaking the taper is to use a suitable

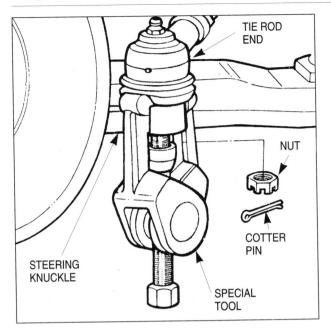

Figure 7-13 Break the stud taper with an appropriate puller. (Chrysler)

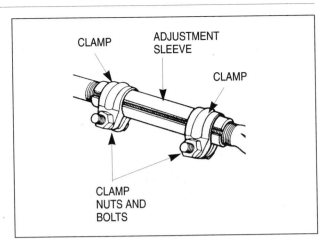

Figure 7-14 One type of outer tie rod threads into an adjuster sleeve and is secured by clamp bolts. (Chrysler)

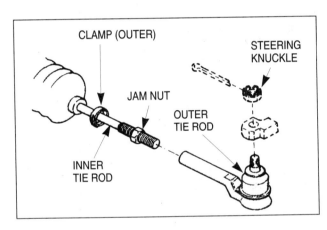

Figure 7-15 Another type of outer tie rod threads onto the inner tie rod and is positioned by a jam nut. (Chrysler)

puller (Figure 7-13). The use of pickle forks or other separators on FWD vehicles can result in damage to the bellows or boots, while hammering the joint stud on any vehicle can result in component damage.

Tie Rod End Replacement

A tie rod end or socket can be removed from a parallelogram linkage in one of two ways: individually or as part of the entire tie rod assembly. The outer tie rod end on a rack and pinion gear is removed individually. The gear housing must usually be removed to disconnect each tie rod at its inner ball socket under the boot and replace the entire tie rod. To remove the outer tie rod end individually:

1. Raise the vehicle in the air with a hoist. If a jack is used instead, support the vehicle safely with stands.
2. Apply penetrating oil and loosen the tie rod adjuster sleeve clamp bolt (Figure 7-14) or the jam nut (Figure 7-15).
3. Remove the ball stud cotter pin and nut. Disconnect the tie rod end ball stud from the steering knuckle arm with a suitable puller.
4. Count and record the number of turns required to unthread the tie rod end from the tie rod assembly. If the tie rod and adjuster sleeve are frozen by rust or corrosion, apply penetrating oil and support the rear of the sleeve with one hammer, then rap the front with another hammer to break the parts free.
5. Clean the adjuster sleeve to remove

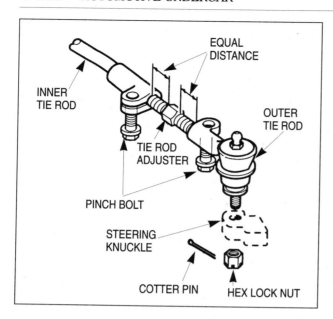

Figure 7-16 A third type of tie rod attachment in which the tie rod ends are clamped to an adjuster rod with adjusting hex. (Oldsmobile Division, General Motors)

all dirt, rust, and corrosion. Wire brush and lubricate the threads on an inner tie rod.

6. Thread the new tie rod end into the adjuster sleeve or onto the inner tie rod the same number of turn recorded in Step 4. If the tie rod is a three-piece assembly, each tie rod end should have approximately the same number of threads contacting the adjuster sleeve. If the tie rod assembly uses pinch bolts and a threaded tie rod adjuster, there should be an equal distance between the adjuster nut and each tie rod clamp (Figure 7-16).

7. Clean and check the tie rod stud hole in the steering knuckle for distortion.

8. If the tie rod stud dust boot is separate, fit it in place, then connect the stud to the knuckle and install the nut. Make sure the front wheels are positioned straight ahead before tightening the nut. Rubber-bonded studs like those shown in Figure 7-9

will develop a pull or memory steer when tightened with the wheels off-center. This can exceed the elastic limits of the rubber and result in premature failure, as well as difficulty in steering.

9. Tighten the nut to specifications and install a new cotter pin. If a castellated nut is used and the pin holes do not align, tighten the nut enough to install the pin.

> **⚠ CAUTION:** Do NOT back off the nut to install the cotter pin. Backing off the nut will allow the stud to loosen in the steering knuckle and result in distortion and eventual damage.

10. Check the toe setting and adjust to specifications, if required.

To remove the complete tie rod assembly (Figure 7-17) from a parallelogram linkage:

1. Raise the vehicle in the air with a hoist. If a jack is used instead, support the vehicle safely with stands.

2. Remove the cotter pins and nuts from the ball studs at the steering arm and center link. Disconnect each ball stud with a suitable puller.

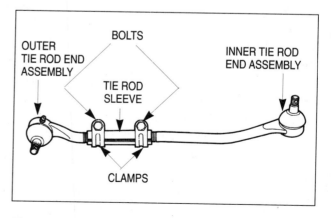

Figure 7-17 A typical tie rod assembly used with a parallelogram steering linkage. (Chrysler)

3. Remove the tie rod assembly from the vehicle. Measure and record the length of the assembly.

4. Assemble the new tie rod sockets and adjuster sleeve to equal the length of the old assembly. Both tie rod ends should be threaded into the adjuster sleeve the same number of turns, centering the sleeve on the two ends.

5. Perform Steps 7-10 of outer tie rod replacement, above.

To replace the inner tie rod end or ball socket on rack and pinion steering gears, refer to the carmaker's procedure in the factory shop manual for the make and model vehicle you are servicing. There are at least a half-dozen different methods of securing the inner tie rod ball socket in place. Some require drilling to remove the tie rod.

Pitman Arm Replacement

The Pitman arm is the most heavily stressed point in a parallelogram steering system. The steering gear end of a Pitman arm is splined to the steering gear sector shaft and held by a fastener. A blind tooth (missing spline) on both the sector shaft and inside the Pitman arm hole means it can be installed in only one position. The splined hole may be tapered so it can't be installed upside down. The other end has either a tapered hole or a stud-and-socket connection.

1. Raise the vehicle in the air with a hoist. If a jack is used instead, support the vehicle safely with stands.

2. Make sure the steering wheel and the front wheels are in the straight-ahead position.

3. Remove and discard the cotter pin from the center link at the Pitman arm. Remove the ball stud nut and separate the Pitman arm and center link with a tie rod end puller (Figure 7-13).

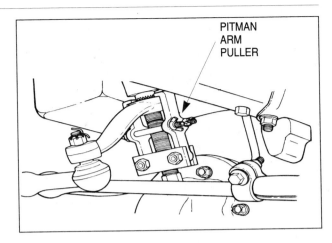

Figure 7-18 Use a suitable puller to separate the Pitman arm from the sector shaft. (Ford Motor)

4. Mark the Pitman arm-to-sector shaft position. Remove the Pitman arm nut and washer, if used. Install a suitable Pitman arm puller (Figure 7-18) and break the taper between the sector shaft and Pitman arm. Remove the puller and separate the arm from the shaft.

5. Clean and check the Pitman arm, the sector shaft splines, and the center link connection point.

6. Make sure the wheels are in a straight-ahead position and slide the Pitman arm on the sector shaft. The marks made in Step 4 should align.

7. Connect the other end of the Pitman arm to the center link and install the retaining nut finger tight.

8. Install the washer and nut on the sector shaft and tighten the nut to the specified torque.

9. Tighten the nut on the center link connection to its specified torque and install a new cotter pin.

Idler Arm Replacement

Several different types of idler arms have been used with parallelogram steering (Figure 7-19). Generally, the idler arm and the bracket are replaced as an assembly,

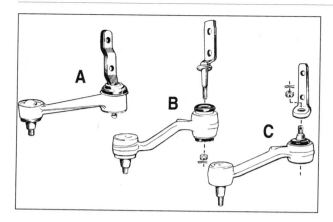

Figure 7-19 Different types of idler arms and mounting brackets illustrate various ways in which the assembly is installed. (Moog Automotive)

Figure 7-20 The lubricant in this manual recirculating ball gearbox lubricant is checked by removing the bolt (arrow). Other designs are checked by removing one of the end cap bolts. Many late-model gears are permanently lubricated at the factory and do not require a periodic check of lubricant level.

but idler arms with rubber bushings (B, Figure 7-19) must be tightened to the bracket with the wheels in a straight-ahead position. If not, the steering will pull in the direction in which the arm was positioned when tightened.

Replacement involves disconnecting the idler arm from the center link and unbolting the idler arm bracket from the frame, then bolting the new bracket to the frame and reconnecting the arm to the center link. Be sure to check the toe setting and adjust to specifications, if necessary.

Center Link Replacement

Some center links used in a parallelogram linkage have wearing sockets; others do not. Those without wearing sockets rarely need service unless they are bent or otherwise damaged. A center link that does have sockets must be replaced if the sockets are worn. Center links are replaced by disconnecting the sockets and removing the link.

STEERING GEAR SERVICE

Other than checking and topping up the lubricant in a manual recirculating ball

gearbox (Figure 7-20), steering gears generally should be removed from the vehicle for service. A rack and pinion gear removed for seal or bushing replacement should be bench tested on a steering gear analyzer, if possible, before it is reinstalled in the vehicle. When an analyzer is available, its use will assure that the gear works properly without leaking.

RECIRCULATING BALL GEARBOX ADJUSTMENTS

Periodic steering gear adjustments are not required at a specific time or mileage; they are performed only when needed. The recirculating ball gearbox requires two external adjustments, worm shaft bearing preload and sector gear lash (also called over-center adjustment). When a gearbox is overhauled, a third adjustment called lash adjuster endplay should be made internally.

Manual gearbox bearing preload and sector gear lash adjustments often can be performed with a manual gearbox in the vehicle. The Pitman arm should be disconnected at the center link and moved by hand to check the gear lash. While disconnected, the steering wheel can be turned easily to check the preload on the worm bearings. If any rough spots or binding can be felt, the gearbox should be removed and inspected to avoid a possible failure.

Power steering gearboxes can be adjusted on the vehicle, but it is difficult to get an accurate feel for preload and backlash. It may take several adjustments back and forth to get it right. Removal of the gearbox can be a major operation on some vehicles, so it might be a good idea to attempt adjustment in the vehicle first. Refer to your instructor or a good repair manual to find out if adjustment on the vehicle is recommended.

Worm Bearing Preload

Worm bearings should be adjusted to maintain just enough preload to eliminate any endplay between the worm shaft and bearings. This will result in a slight drag when the steering wheel is rotated. Excessive endplay allows the steering wheel to move up and down in line with the column. If you turn the wheel back and forth and can see it moving up and down, there is too much endplay. Preload can be measured by disconnecting the Pitman arm from the sector shaft, attaching a spring scale to the outer edge of a steering wheel spoke, and rotating the wheel one full revolution (Figure 7-21). Depending on the clearance under the vehicle, you may be able to do this by disconnecting the Pitman arm from the center link without removing it. Some carmakers specify preload measurement with the use of an poundforce-inch torque wrench and socket on the steering wheel attachment nut instead of

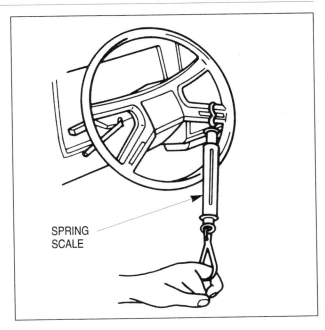

Figure 7-21 Using a spring scale to check turning effort. (Ford Motor)

the spring scale. Read the specifications carefully to determine if the specification includes the worm bearing preload and the drag from the sector gear as the gear mesh passes over center. If the specification is only for worm bearing preload, the sector gear lash adjustment must be loosened so it doesn't affect the reading. If the torque required for worm bearing preload only is not within the carmaker's specification:

1. Loosen the adjuster locknut at the bottom end of the wormshaft (Figure 7-22).
2. Turn the adjuster plug clockwise to increase preload, or counterclockwise to decrease preload. A special wrench is usually required.
3. Hold the adjuster plug from moving and tighten the locknut securely.
4. Recheck worm bearing preload.

If the gearbox has been removed from the vehicle, bearing preload can be measured as follows:

1. Remove the adjuster plug locknut and turn the adjuster plug inward to

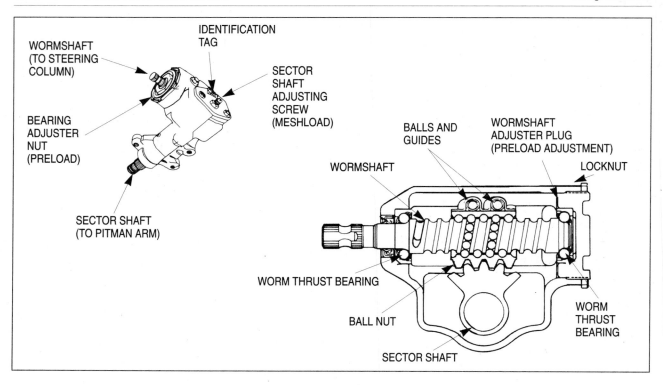

Figure 7-22 Recirculating ball steering gear adjustment points. (Ford Motor)

bottom the plug and bearing.

2. Mark the housing at a point across from one of the adjuster plug holes (Figure 7-23).

3. Measure back about 1/2" in a counterclockwise direction and make a second mark on the housing (Figure 7-24).

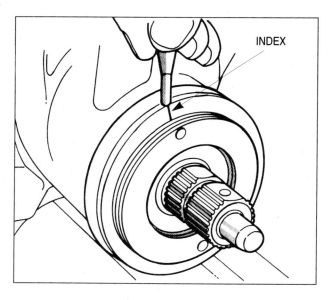

Figure 7-23 Gearbox housing alignment marking. (Chrysler)

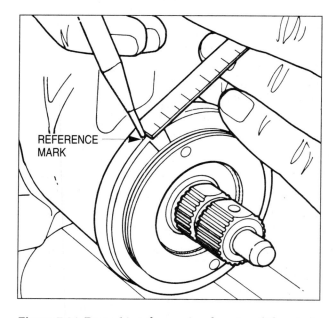

Figure 7-24 Remarking the gearbox housing. (Chrysler)

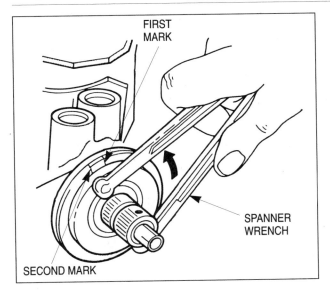

Figure 7-25 Rotating the adjuster plug to align with the second mark. Note the spanner wrench which has pins that fit into the holes in the plug. (Chrysler)

4. Rotate the adjuster plug counterclockwise to align the hole in the plug with the second mark (Figure 7-25), then install and tighten the locknut without moving the plug.

5. Use an poundforce-inch torque wrench as shown in Figure 7-26 and measure the torque required to turn

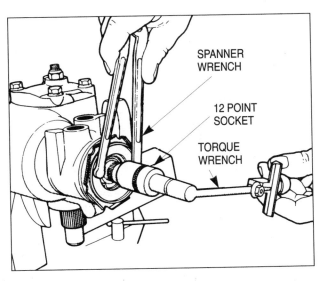

Figure 7-26 Adjusting worm shaft bearing preload. (Chrysler)

the stub shaft as specified by the carmaker.

6. If the reading is not within specifications, loosen the locknut and rotate the adjuster plug counterclockwise a small amount, then recheck torque. Repeat this step as required until the torque measurement falls within specifications.

> **TIP TECH TIP:** With the adjuster plug loose, the steering wheel should rotate with a torque wrench or spring scale measurement considerably below the specification. If not, something is binding inside the gear. It could be that the sector gear lash has been adjusted too tight, and only needs to be loosened. Or something else could be binding inside the gear, requiring disassembly.

Sector Gear Lash

The sector shaft adjusting screw is located in the housing cover, as shown in Figure 7-22. The screw raises or lowers the shaft to provide the correct mesh load between the tapered teeth of the ball nut and sector gear. Worm bearing preload must be correctly established before a sector gear lash adjustment can be made accurately.

1. With the Pitman arm disconnected from the sector shaft, count the number of revolutions required to turn the steering wheel gently from lock to lock, then rotate the wheel back exactly half the turns to center the gearbox. Do NOT force the wheel against the end of the travel, or the box may be damaged. Centering the gearbox should also approximately center the steering wheel. If the steering wheel is off center considerably when the gearbox is centered, the wheel may be installed on the

shaft in the wrong position, or the gearbox may have internal damage. Check with your instructor on this.

2. Remove all lash between the ball nut rack and sector gear teeth by turning the sector shaft adjusting screw clockwise, then tighten the screw locknut to specifications.

3. Rotate the steering wheel about 1/4 turn from the center position and install an poundforce-inch torque wrench with socket on the steering wheel attachment nut. Measure the torque required to return the steering wheel to its centered position and compare to the carmaker's specification. The measurement represents the total of worm shaft bearing preload and sector gear mesh load. If necessary, loosen the adjusting screw locknut and readjust the sector shaft screw.

4. Repeat Step 3 as required until the measurement reaches the specified torque, then tighten the adjusting screw locknut to specifications. Make sure the front wheels are in the straight ahead position and reattach the Pitman arm to the gearbox.

If the gearbox has been removed from the vehicle, sector gear lash can be measured as follows:

1. Count the number of rotations required to turn the stub shaft from stop to stop, then rotate the shaft back exactly half the turns. To make sure the gear is centered, check that the flat on the stub shaft faces upward and is parallel with the side cover (Figure 7-27). The master spline on the sector shaft also should align with the adjusting screw (Figure 7-28).

2. Loosen the locknut, and back the sector shaft adjusting screw fully out, then turn it back in one full turn.

3. Retighten the locknut and use an

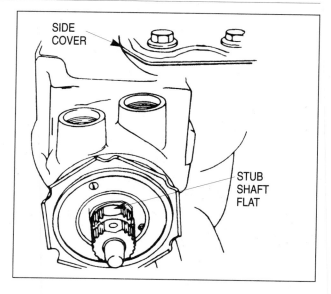

Figure 7-27 The steering gear is centered when the stub shaft flat aligns with the side cover. (Oldsmobile Division, General Motors)

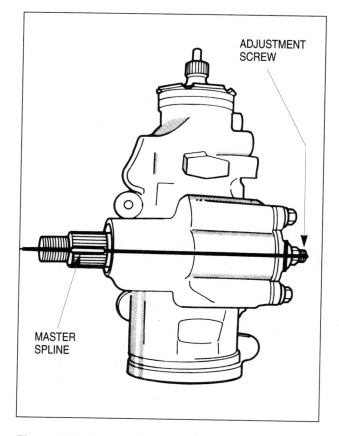

Figure 7-28 Aligning the sector shaft master spline with the adjuster screw is another way of centering the steering gear. (Chrysler)

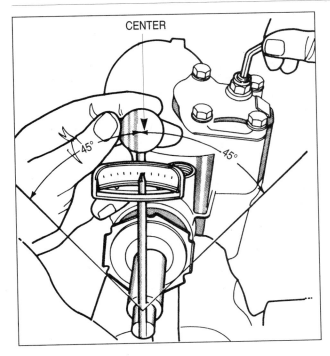

Figure 7-29 Measuring the over-center drag torque while adjusting the gear lash. (Chrysler)

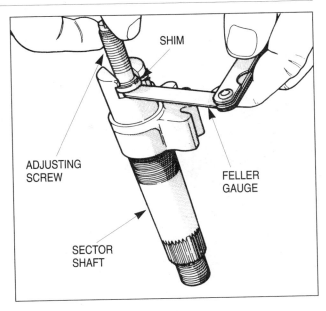

Figure 7-30 Checking lash adjuster end clearance. (Chrysler)

poundforce-inch torque wrench to rotate the stub shaft in a 45° arc on each side of center (Figure 7-29).

4. Turn the adjusting screw inward until the torque required to turn the stub shaft is within specifications. Make sure the locknut is tight when the reading is taken. The overcenter torque of a new gear will be somewhat higher than that of a used gear.

Lash Adjuster Endplay

The gearbox must be disassembled for this measurement. The lash adjuster screw fits into the slotted end of the sector shaft. The end clearance of the screw should be held to 0.002" or less. To check the clearance, try to insert a 0.002" feeler gauge between the screw and shaft (Figure 7-30). If the feeler gauge does not enter and the screw turns freely, the clearance is correct. Use a thicker or thinner shim between the screw and shaft as required to maintain proper clearance.

RACK AND PINION GEAR ADJUSTMENTS

Adjustment requirements and procedures for rack and pinion steering gears differ considerably among carmakers. Although some manual and power gears cannot be adjusted or overhauled, many units have a rack support bearing adjustment (Figure 7-31). A spring-loaded support yoke or rack

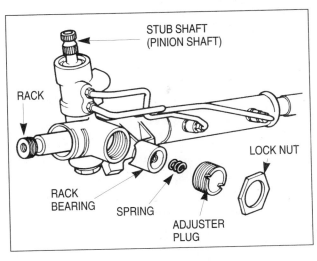

Figure 7-31 Typical rack bearing and adjuster plug. (Chrysler)

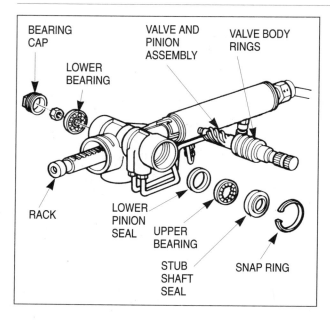

Figure 7-32 Typical pinion bearing assembly. (Chrysler)

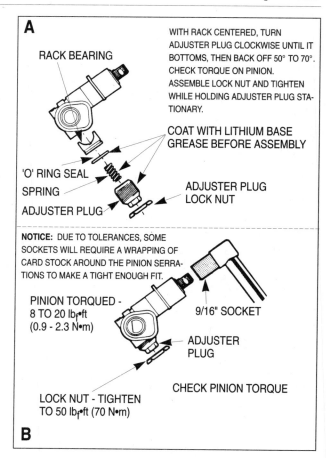

Figure 7-33 Some GM rack bearings can be adjusted with this procedure. If the adjustment (A) is made on the vehicle, checking pinion torque (B) is not required.

bearing maintains a constant pressure on the rack and pinion gears to eliminate gear lash. The adjustment is checked by measuring pinion shaft rotating torque with a torque wrench and socket, or a spring scale and adapter, and comparing the results to the carmaker's preload specifications. A few rack and pinion gears may require a pinion bearing adjustment (Figure 7-32). If either adjustment is required on a particular steering gear, the rack bearing or pinion bearing will have a threaded adjuster or shim pack at the bearing retainer. Figure 7-33 shows a typical procedure for adjusting the rack support on many rack and pinion gears used by General Motors. When diagnosis indicates the need for adjustment, refer to the carmaker's shop manual for the exact procedure and specifications.

With many rack and pinion gears, it is difficult, if not impossible, to properly adjust the unit in the vehicle due to lack of sufficient working space. While it is best to remove the gear from the vehicle for adjustment purposes, it is also difficult and time-consuming to remove the unit for adjustment, reinstall it to check the adjustment, and possibly have to remove it more than once for further adjustment or service. For this reason, many shops simply replace the gear with a rebuilt unit.

STEERING GEAR REPLACEMENT

Recirculating ball gearboxes are relatively easy to remove and install because they are bolted to the frame rail on the driver's side of the vehicle (Figure 7-34). Rack and pinion steering gears are more difficult to remove and install when located behind the engine/transaxle assembly (Figure 7-35). The rack and pinion gear usually is

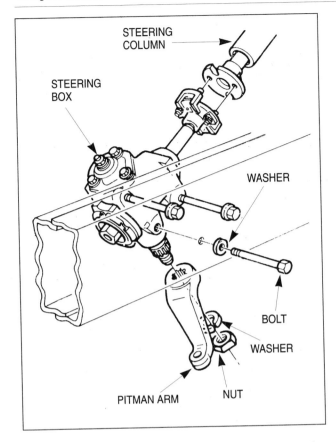

Figure 7-34 Recirculating ball gearbox mounting on the inside of the frame. Many early model gearboxes of other types use a similar mounting on the outside of the frame. (Ford Motor)

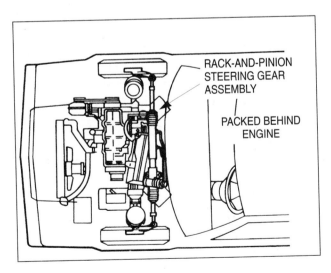

Figure 7-35 The location of rack and pinion steering gears make a compact installation, but one that can be difficult to service on the vehicle. (Chrysler)

mounted at the front of, or on top of, a front suspension crossmember (A, Figure 7-36), or on the engine compartment bulkhead (B, Figure 7-36). Consult with your instructor about the need for a helper to remove the gearbox. Gearboxes can be very heavy and cause injury if they fall.

REPLACING A RECIRCULATING BALL GEARBOX

1. With the vehicle on the ground, open and support the hood.
2. If the vehicle is equipped with power steering:
   a. Place a suitable drain pan or container under the steering gear.
   b. Disconnect the two fluid lines at the gearbox.
   c. Cap, plug, or tape the ends of the lines and fittings at the gearbox to prevent fluid loss and contamination from entering.
3A. When a flexible coupling is used (Figure 7-37), mark it with a grease pencil for reinstallation alignment reference, then unbolt the flex coupling.
3B. When an intermediate shaft or coupler is used (Figure 7-38), mark it for alignment reference and remove the pinch bolt or drive out the roll pin.
4. Raise the vehicle in the air with a hoist. If a jack is used instead, support the vehicle safely with stands.
5. Make sure the steering wheel and the front wheels are in the straight-ahead position, then disconnect the Pitman arm from the sector shaft.
6. Unbolt the gearbox from the frame and remove it from the vehicle, separating the coupler from the steering shaft in the process.
7. Remove the coupler from the gearbox stub shaft, check its condition, and

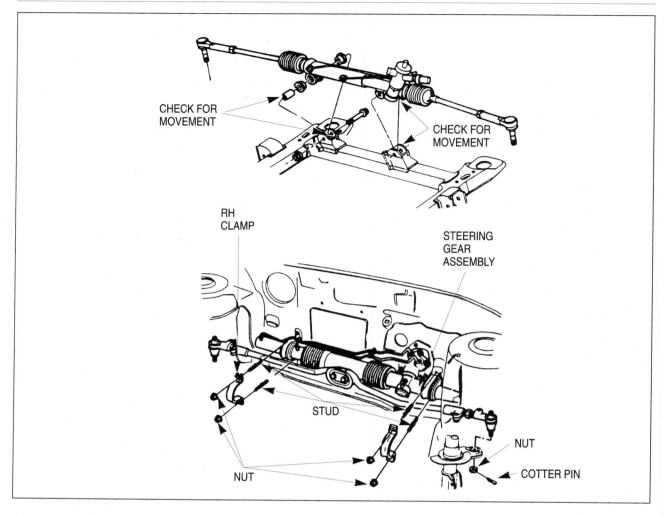

Figure 7-36 The rack and pinion gear may be mounted on the frame (A), or attached to the cowl (B). (General Motors)

replace if damaged.

8. To reinstall the gearbox, center the stub shaft by turning it from stop to stop, counting the number of turns required. Turn the shaft back one-half the number of turns counted when centering the shaft. If the shaft has an index flat, it should face downward. Position the gearbox against the frame and install the mounting bolts. If the coupler and steering shaft do not have a flat or other alignment method, align the marks made in Step 3.

9. Install the flex coupling pinch bolt.

Tighten the pinch bolt and gearbox mounting bolts to specifications.

10. Align the Pitman arm marks and reinstall the arm to the gearbox sector shaft. Tighten the nut to specifications.

11. Lower the vehicle to the ground and install the coupler pinch bolt and tighten to the correct torque, or drive a new roll pin in place.

12. If equipped with power steering, remove the caps, plugs, or tape from the lines and fittings.

13. Reconnect the lines to the gearbox, fill the system with fluid, bleed the

Figure 7-37 Flexible couplings are one method used to connect the steering gear with the steering shaft.

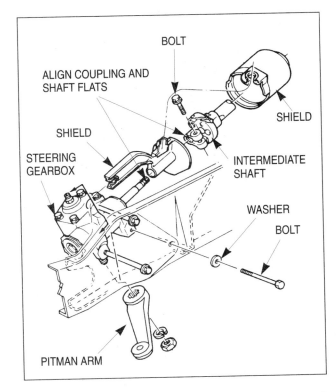

Figure 7-38 Some gearboxes and couplings are mated by flats and cannot be incorrectly connected. (Ford Motor)

system to remove any air, and road test the vehicle for proper operation.

14. After road testing, check for leaks and readjust the fluid level, if necessary.

REPLACING A RACK AND PINION GEAR

Due to the location of the steering gear mounts, engine compartment packaging will affect the sequence in which the steps are performed. For example, some steering gear couplers can be disconnected from under the hood with the vehicle on the ground. Others must be raised in the air to provide working access. On other installations, certain accessory units may have to be removed or repositioned to provide working access before the gear can be removed. The following procedure is generalized; when actually removing a rack and pinion gear from the vehicle, follow the carmaker's specified procedure in the appropriate shop manual, and ALWAYS consult with your instructor first.

1. With the vehicle on the ground, open and support the hood. Perform any of the following steps possible in the engine compartment.

2. Raise the vehicle in the air with a hoist. If a jack is used instead, support the vehicle with safety stands.

3. Remove the front wheel/tire assemblies.

4. If the vehicle is equipped with power steering:

   a. Place a suitable drain pan or container under the steering gear.

   b. Disconnect the two fluid lines at the gearbox.

   c. Cap, plug, or tape the ends of the lines and fittings at the gearbox to prevent fluid loss and contamination from entering.

5. Disconnect the tie rod ends from the steering knuckles.

6. Mark and disconnect the steering gear coupler to the steering shaft.

7. Unbolt the fasteners and/or brackets holding the steering gear to the crossmember or bulkhead, as shown in Figure 7-36. On some vehicles, it is necessary to remove the rear cradle bolts and support the cradle with a transmission jack to gain working access to the bolts and brackets.

8. Remove the steering gear assembly from underneath the vehicle.

9. Check the condition of the mounting bracket bushings or steering gear insulators. Replace as necessary during installation.

10. Installation is the reverse of removal, but a helper will be needed to guide the steering column coupling onto the steering shaft assembly. The attaching fasteners should be tightened as specified by the carmaker. One bolt or stud often acts as a pilot that locates and aligns the steering gear.

POWER STEERING SYSTEM SERVICE

The power steering pump provides and circulates the necessary hydraulic pressure for steering system operation. To assure proper operation, the system must be filled with the correct type of fluid and free of air. Normal system service involves checking the level and condition of the fluid, checking and adjusting drive belt tension, and correcting any leaks.

CHECKING AND ADDING FLUID

Some power steering systems are designed to use automatic transmission fluid (ATF), while others use power steering fluid. These fluids differ in viscosity and the additives used. In addition, ATF contains a reddish dye for identification; power steering fluid generally is green or greenish-yellow in color. Fluid color is useful in identifying the cause of a leak. The two fluids are NOT interchangeable, and any mixing of the two, or use of the wrong fluid will result in hose and seal damage within a short period of time. Some power steering fluids have a low boiling point and will actually boil or foam from the heat generated by the power steering pump. Some vehicles require a special fluid, with the name of the carmaker on the container. When adding fluid, or flushing and changing the fluid, always refer to the carmaker's specification for the correct type of fluid to use.

Fluid level in the power steering reservoir is checked either by marks on a translucent reservoir (Figure 7-39), or by a small dipstick attached to the fluid reservoir cap (Figure 7-40). The fluid level in translucent reservoirs can be checked visually without removing the cap. Systems that use an opaque reservoir and cap are checked by wiping the area around the cap free of contamination. With the engine 'off', remove the cap with dipstick

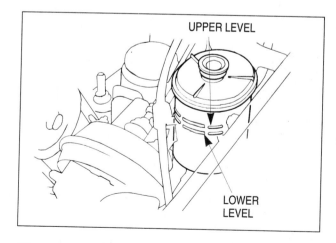

Figure 7-39 The fluid level in some power steering reservoirs can be checked visually without removing the cap. (Honda)

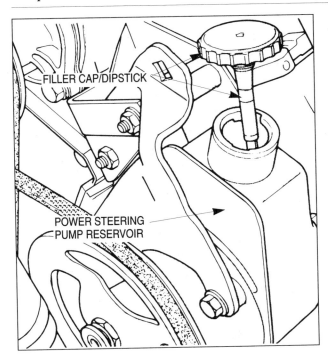

Figure 7-40 Opaque power steering reservoirs use a cap and dipstick to check fluid level. The cap must be fully installed and twisted to the lock position to get a valid measurement. (Chrysler)

and check the level. It should not be necessary to wipe off the dipstick. If the fluid is hot to the touch, the level should be at the upper mark; cool fluid should be at the lower mark. When the fluid level is low, add sufficient fluid of the proper type and replace the cap.

BLEEDING THE POWER STEERING SYSTEM

Whenever a power steering system hose has been disconnected, or the system has been flushed, air enters the system and must be removed by bleeding before operating the vehicle. If the air is NOT removed from the fluid, it will cause noisy, unsatisfactory system operation. Although some

> **TIP TECH TIP:** Power steering fluid contaminated with air has a lighter color and may look foamy.

carmakers recommend the use of an air evacuation tool, the following procedure can be used with most vehicles to bleed the power steering system.

1. Remove the reservoir cap and fill the pump to its proper level, allowing the fluid to settle for two or more minutes.
2. Start the engine and run at idle for several seconds, and then shut the engine off.
3. Repeat Step 1 and Step 2 until the fluid level remains constant after running the engine.
4. Raise the front end of the vehicle with a jack until the wheels are free to turn and install safety stands to support the vehicle safely.
5. Start the engine and run at idle. Slowly cycle the steering wheel to lightly contact both wheel stops.
6. Shut the engine off and lower the vehicle to the ground, and then check the level and refill is necessary.
7. With the wheels on the ground, restart the engine and slowly cycle the steering wheel gently from stop to stop, then shut the engine off.
8. Recheck the fluid level and refill as required. If the fluid is extremely foamy, let the vehicle stand for several minutes, then repeat the entire procedure. In cases of severe aeration, it may be necessary to repeat the procedure several times.

POWER STEERING SYSTEM FLUSHING

When a power steering gear or pump is replaced because of fluid contamination, the entire system must be flushed to remove all contaminated fluid.

1. Raise the front end of the vehicle with a jack until the wheels are free to turn, and then install safety stands to support the vehicle safely.
2. Disconnect the fluid return hose at

TIP TECH TIP: Many power steering pumps have a plastic reservoir which uses hose nipples and clamps to attach the hoses, similar to a radiator hose. If you are practicing flushing on an old pump, or removing the fluid because of contamination, the hose may have taken a set on the pump fittings and be difficult to remove. Prying or using any other than a straight pulling force to remove the hose from plastic fittings will result in breaking the fitting off the pump, requiring replacement of the pump. It may be necessary to cut the hose off of the pump.

the pump and plug the port. Use a piece of tubing and additional hose to lengthen the return hose so it can reach a container on the floor. Place a suitable container under the hose to catch the draining fluid.

3. Have an assistant continually add fresh fluid to the reservoir while you run the engine at idle. The assistant should watch the fluid coming out of the hose and signal you to turn off the engine when it is running clean. While the engine is running, smoothly cycle the steering wheel fully without touching the wheel stops. If the steering wheel is held in an off-center position without moving, fluid flow will cease as the pump switches to a pressure relief mode.

4. Continue draining until all of the old fluid has cleared the system. Most systems can be flushed with about one quart of fresh fluid.

5. Shut the engine off and unplug the pump port, and then reconnect the fluid return hose at the pump or install a new hose, as required. Fill the system to the reservoir cold mark with fresh fluid of the correct type.

6. Bleed the system and operate the engine for several minutes.

7. If fluid contamination was severe, repeat the procedure a second time and recheck the draining fluid. If contamination is still evident, the entire system should be removed, disassembled, and cleaned or replaced.

⚠ CAUTION: NEVER reuse drained power steering system fluid.

POWER STEERING SYSTEM PRESSURE TESTING

When diagnosis points to an internal pump or gear malfunction, a pressure test can be used to identify and isolate hydraulic circuit problems. The pressure test can help evaluate pump, rotary valve, and internal seals by providing a direct reading of pump pressure and flow, relief pressure, and seal integrity.

Pressure testing requires the use of a pressure gauge with shut-off valve (Figure 7-41). Some carmakers recommend the use of a tester that also measures pump flow (Figure 7-42). Regardless of the tester used, the procedure specified by most carmakers is essentially the same, other

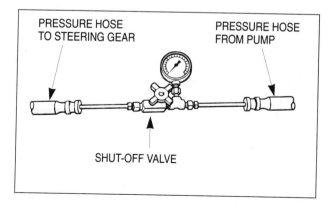

Figure 7-41 Typical power steering pressure test gauge. (Chrysler)

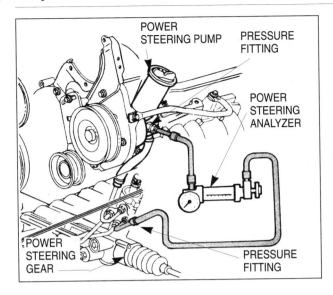

Figure 7-42 A power steering analyzer combines pressure testing with a flow meter. (Ford Motor)

than the pressure and flow specifications. The generalized procedure provided below is typical of that recommended by most carmakers.

1. Before connecting the pressure tester, check and correct (if necessary) the following:
   a. pump fluid level
   b. tire inflation pressure
   c. pump drive belt tension
   d. system condition, especially the hoses and whether or not they will have to be cut to disconnect them.
2. Place containers or shop cloths beneath the steering gear and pump connections to catch any fluid that leaks during hose disconnection and reconnection.
3. With the engine 'off', disconnect the pressure hose at the pump and steering gear. Install the pressure tester with its gauge between the pump and shutoff valve (Figure 7-42). Use any necessary adapters required, but do NOT overtighten the fittings. Make sure the shutoff valve is fully open (counterclockwise).

4. Bleed the system at this point, if specified by the carmaker.
5. Start and run the engine for approximately two minutes to bring the power steering fluid to normal operating temperature. Some carmakers specify the use of a thermometer in the reservoir filler opening while moving the steering wheel from stop to stop several times to bring the fluid to the operating temperature more quickly.
6. Once the fluid reaches the operating temperature, stop the engine and check the fluid level, adding fluid if necessary.
7. Restart the engine, run at idle and record the pressure (and flow) indicated by the tester.
   a. If the flow is less than specified by the carmaker, the pump may be defective, but testing should be continued.
   b. If the pressure exceeds specifications, discontinue the test and check for restricted hoses.
8. If the tester measures fluid flow, partially close the gate valve until the pressure reaches specifications, then record the flow. If the flow is below specifications, the pump is defective.
9. Fully close and open the gate valve three times, recording the highest pressure reached each time the valve is closed.

> ⚠ **CAUTION:** Do NOT leave the gate valve closed longer than specified by the carmaker or pump damage could occur.

   a. If the pressures attained are within specifications and do NOT vary by more than 50 psi, the pump is working properly.

b. If the pressures are constant but below the minimum pressure specified, replace the pump flow control valve if it is accessible, and recheck. The valve on many pumps is behind the metal fitting for the outlet (pressure) hose, and can be replaced without removing the pump from the vehicle. If the pressures remain low with the new flow control valve, the pump is defective.

c. If the pressures exceed the maximum pressure specified, the flow control valve is sticking. Remove and clean it with crocus cloth (Figure 7-43). Reinstall the valve and recheck; if pressures are still high, replace the valve.

d. If the fluid contains dirt, the system should be flushed. If exceptionally dirty, remove the pump and gear for disassembly, cleaning, flushing, and reassembly with new seals.

10. If the tester measures flow:

a. Open the gate valve fully and increase engine speed as specified by the carmaker. Fluid flow should be close to that measured in Step 8.

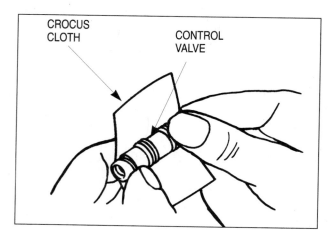

Figure 7-43 A sticking flow control valve can be cleaned with crocus cloth. (Chrysler)

If flow increases by more than 1 gpm, remove, clean, and retest the flow control valve. If flow is still above that measured in Step 8 by more than one gallon, replace the valve.

b. With the engine idling and the gate valve open, have an assistant lightly turn the steering wheel from lock to lock. When in each lock position, the pressure should be close to the maximum, as measured before with the tester gate valve closed. If the pressure is considerably lower, and the flow drops under 1/2 gpm, the steering gear has an internal leak.

11. Have the assistant partially turn the steering wheel in both directions, then release it quickly. The pressure should rise as the wheel is turned and fall back as it is released. If the pressure stalls or drops back slowly, the rotary valve is sticking.

12. Shut the engine off, remove the tester, reconnect the pressure hose, and recheck the fluid level. Some carmakers specify that the system be bled at this point.

PUMP REPLACEMENT

Power steering pumps are belt-driven. Many late-model pumps are rigidly mounted to the engine and driven by a self-adjusting serpentine belt that also drives the alternator, air conditioning compressor, and water pump. Other pumps are bracket-mounted to the engine and driven by poly-groove or V-belts that require periodic adjustment.

Some carmakers provide parts for pump overhaul; others do NOT, and recommend that the pump be replaced with a new, rebuilt or remanufactured unit. From a labor standpoint, pump overhaul may be more costly than the cost of a replacement pump and its installation. Although many vane-type pumps of the familiar Saginaw design (Figure 7-44) look alike externally, power steering pumps are designed internally to produce a specific displacement. For this reason, you should NOT replace a defective pump with one that is lying around the shop simply because it looks the same and happens to fit the mounting bracket.

Because power steering pump mounting varies widely, exact replacement procedures are beyond the scope of this book. Regardless of the mounting used, the drive belt must be removed from the pump pulley (Figures 7-45 and Figure 7-46), the pump inlet and outlet hoses disconnected and plugged (Figure 7-47), and the pump mounting fasteners removed. If the pump is part of an electronic variable orifice (EVO) steering system, an electrical connector must be disconnected from the EVO actuator installed at the pump outlet.

Before disconnecting the hoses from the pump, siphon the fluid from the reservoir

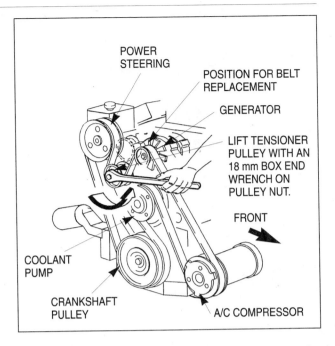

Figure 7-45 The tension on a serpentine belt must be relieved to remove the belt from the power steering pump. (Oldsmobile Division, General Motors)

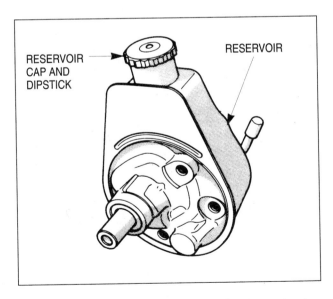

Figure 7-44 The external appearance of a power steering pump is no indication of its pumping capacity. Make sure to replace a defective pump with one of the same capacity. (Chrysler)

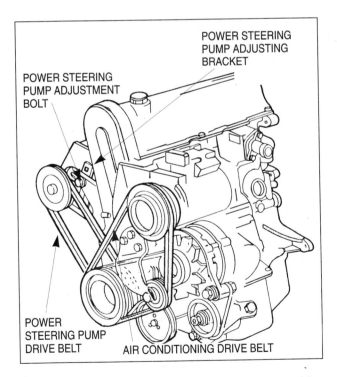

Figure 7-46 Poly-groove and V-belts are removed by loosening the pump adjustment bolt and moving the pump toward the engine to release belt tension. (Chrysler)

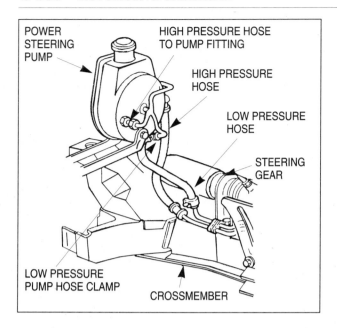

Figure 7-47 Power steering fluid hoses. (Chrysler)

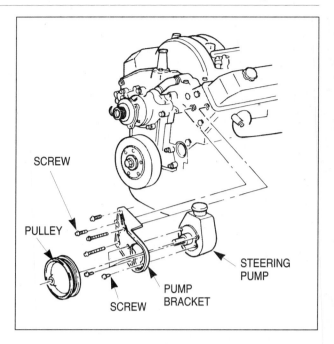

Figure 7-48 Some power steering pumps have the mounting bracket between the pulley and the pump body. The pulley must be removed before the pump and bracket can be separated. (Chrysler)

to avoid fluid spillage, then use shop cloths around the hoses to catch any remaining fluid. This is particularly important on engines where the pump is mounted near the timing belt cover, as fluid spills on the belt cover can cause damage to the timing belt.

With some pump installations, the pump and its mounting bracket must be removed as an assembly. In this design, the pump bracket is between the pump body and the pulley (Figure 7-48). To separate the pump from the bracket, the pulley must be removed with a suitable puller. Do NOT attempt to use an ordinary gear puller. The puller must be designed for pulley removal.

When reinstalling the pump, the drive belt must be adjusted to provide the proper tension. With serpentine belt installations, releasing the spring-loaded tensioner pulley after installing the belt applies the correct tension to the belt, as shown in Figure 7-45. Poly-groove or V-belts are adjusted by pivoting the pump in its mounting bracket until the correct belt tension is achieved

with a belt tension tool (Figure 7-49), then tightening the pump adjusting bolt, as shown in Figure 7-46. Some engines have limited clearance and require an adapter to use the belt tension tool.

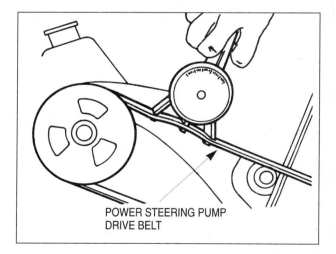

Figure 7-49 Checking power steering pump belt tension. An adapter may be required to use the belt tension tool on some engines. (Chrysler)

STEERING WHEEL AND COLUMN SERVICE

Over the past decade, the once-simple task of removing the steering wheel and/or steering column has become increasingly complicated. With the addition of multi-function switches, interlock devices, complex wiring harnesses, and airbag modules, the steering wheel/column assembly has become one of the vehicle's control centers in addition to its steering function.

In an attempt to simplify service procedures, carmakers have designed many late-model steering columns to permit service of their components with the column in the vehicle. This type of column generally requires removal from the vehicle only after collision damage. Due to the many design differences between the steering columns used by carmakers, it is recommended that you refer to the appropriate service manual before attempting to service the column components or remove and replace a steering column.

STEERING WHEEL REPLACEMENT

Two methods are used to attach the steering wheel to the upper steering shaft. While most vehicles use a nut that fits on the externally threaded shaft (Figure 7-50), the wheel may be attached to an internally threaded shaft with an integral washer head bolt (Figure 7-51). Steering wheels

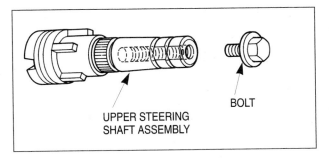

Figure 7-51 Some steering wheels are installed on an internally threaded shaft by a bolt with integral washer. (Ford Motor)

are drilled and tapped at the hub with two threaded holes to accept a puller to remove the wheel from the upper steering shaft. If the wheel and shaft do not have a blind spline to locate the wheel, marks on the end of the steering shaft and the wheel hub are used to properly index the two. Use the following procedures to remove and install a steering wheel.

Without an Airbag

Refer to Figure 7-52 (typical) for this procedure.

1. Turn the front wheels to a straight ahead position.
2. Disconnect the battery negative cable and tape the cable end to prevent accidental contact. Be aware that this will remove the radio preset station settings and disconnect the clock.
3. Remove the horn cap or pad. A cap can be pried off; a pad is retained by screws installed from the rear of the wheel (Figure 7-53).
4. Disconnect the horn lead and any other electrical connectors from the cap, pad, or column (Figure 7-54).
5. With the steering wheel centered, locate the alignment marks on the shaft and steering wheel hub. If none are found, make your own with a center punch or other suitable tool.

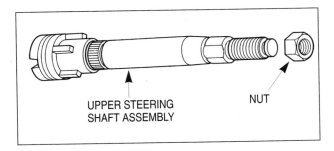

Figure 7-50 Steering wheels are secured on externally threaded upper steering shafts by a nut. (Ford Motor)

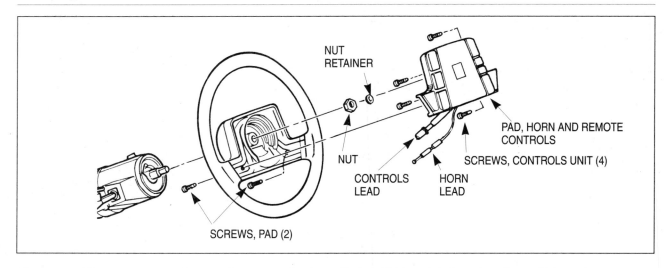

Figure 7-52 The components of a typical steering wheel installation. (Oldsmobile Division, General Motors)

6. Remove the steering wheel nut retainer, if so equipped.

TIP **TECH TIP:** When removing a steering wheel with electronic accessory controls under the hub, make sure the wheel puller bolts are installed flush with the bottom of the hub and not through it to prevent damage to electronic circuits.

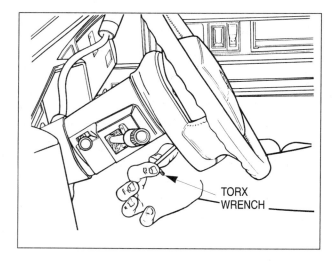

Figure 7-53 The horn pad on many steering wheels is secured by screws installed from behind the wheel. (General Motors)

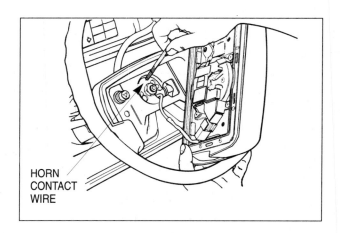

Figure 7-54 Disconnecting the horn contact wire. (General Motors)

7. Loosen the steering wheel nut (Figure 7-55) and back it off until it is flush with the end of the shaft. If the wheel is retained by a bolt, loosen the bolt four to six full turns. The bolt or nut must stay in place so that the wheel puller does not damage the shaft.

8. Install a suitable steering wheel puller (Figure 7-56), tighten the puller to break the wheel loose from the shaft, and remove the puller.

9. Remove the steering wheel nut or bolt and lift the wheel off the steering shaft.

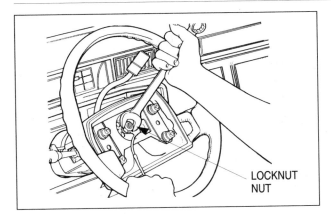

Figure 7-55 Use a socket wrench to loosen the steering wheel nut. This nut is already loose, and is being turned with an open end wrench until it is flush with the end of the shaft. (General Motors)

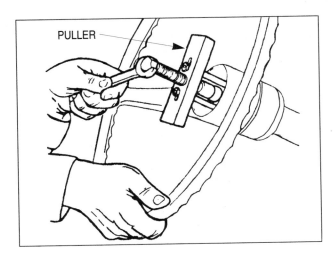

Figure 7-56 Remove the wheel from the steering shaft with a steering wheel puller. Do NOT hammer on the puller; you can damage the steering column. (Oldsmobile Division, General Motors)

10. To reinstall the steering wheel, position the wheel on the steering shaft splines with the hub and shaft marks or the blind spline aligned. Install the nut or bolt and tighten to specifications. This will draw the wheel onto the shaft properly. Install the nut retainer, if one is used.

11. Connect the horn lead and any other electrical connectors before installing the cap or pad.

12. Reconnect the battery negative cable and check the horn for proper operation. Reprogram the radio stations or leave a note for the customer that this will have to be done.

With an Airbag

Removal and installation of a steering wheel containing a live or undeployed airbag module is essentially the same as with a non-airbag wheel, but it requires strict attention to safety procedures to prevent module detonation during the procedure. Before starting wheel removal, the airbag system must be disabled temporarily according to the carmaker's procedure. Despite differences in carmaker's systems, disabling an airbag module generally involves the following steps:

- Ignition switch in the 'off' position.
- Removal of the airbag system fuse.
- Disconnecting the battery negative cable (tape the cable end to prevent accidental contact). Be aware that disconnecting the battery will require resetting radio stations, clocks, or any other memory features.
- Disconnecting the airbag module connector (generally located at the base of the steering column).

After the system has been disabled, wait for 10 to 15 minutes before starting the steering wheel removal procedure. The reserve capacitor in airbag systems contains enough electricity to discharge the module for periods of 2 to 10 minutes after the system has been disabled. The specific length of time involved differs according to the carmaker's system. While Chrysler's system discharges fully after two minutes, the system used by GM remains alive for up to 10 minutes. If you have instructions on how to do it, the airbag backup power supply may be removed to avoid waiting. Consult with your instructor before attempting this.

The fasteners used with airbag systems are specifically designed for such use and may have special coatings. NEVER replace a lost or damaged fastener with a substitute. Only appropriate OEM fasteners should be used. Once the module has been removed, do NOT handle it by the wires or connector; carry it by its edges and place face up on the work bench.

Gloves and safety glasses should be worn when removing a deployed airbag module. The sodium hydroxide dust remaining on the module can cause a skin irritation if allowed to remain for an extended period of time. After properly discarding the old module, wash with a mild soap.

Once the steering wheel and airbag module have been reinstalled, and electrical power restored to the system, turn the ignition switch to the 'run' position and watch the system indicator lamp. It should flash several times and then turn off. If it does not, there is a problem in the airbag system. Reprogram the radio stations, clocks, and any other memory features or leave a note for the customer that this will have to be done.

❓ REVIEW QUESTIONS

1. Technician A says that a hissing noise in a recirculating ball steering system is caused by the power steering pump relief valve. Technician B says that replacing the valve will eliminate the noise. Who is right?
   (A) A only
   (B) B only
   (C) Both A and B
   (D) Neither A nor B

2. Technician A says that excessive wander of an FWD vehicle with properly aligned wheels is caused by a loose steering gear preload. Technician B says that it is caused by an unbalanced steering gear valve. Who is right?
   (A) A only
   (B) B only
   (C) Both A and B
   (D) Neither A nor B

3. Technician A says that the best way to locate a power steering leak is to remove and check the components one at a time. Technician B says that pump pressure in an intact system can be used to find the leak. Who is right?
   (A) A only
   (B) B only
   (C) Both A and B
   (D) Neither A nor B

4. Technician A says that a low lubricant level in a manual recirculating ball gearbox indicates a leaking sector shaft seal. Technician B says that finding the location of a fluid drip does NOT mean you have found the source of a leak. Who is right?
   (A) A only
   (B) B only
   (C) Both A and B
   (D) Neither A nor B

5. Technician A says that the nut on tie rod end ball studs bonded in rubber can be tightened with the steering wheel in any position. Technician B says that this type of joint should be lubricated before installing and tightening the nut. Who is right?
   (A) A only
   (B) B only
   (C) Both A and B
   (D) Neither A nor B

6. Technician A says that parallelogram linkage should be checked for excessive wear or clearance with the full vehicle weight on the wheels. Technician B says that the linkage on FWD vehicles should be checked with the vehicle in the air. Who is right?
   (A) A only
   (B) B only
   (C) Both A and B
   (D) Neither A nor B

7. Technician A says that the tapered stud of a tie rod end should be loosened with a puller. Technician B says that using a pickle fork on an FWD vehicle can damage the bellows. Who is right?
   (A) A only
   (B) B only
   (C) Both A and B
   (D) Neither A nor B

8. Technician A says that wheel alignment should be checked after disconnecting and reconnecting any linkage component. Technician B says that a rack and pinion steering gear must usually be removed from the vehicle to replace the inner tie rod ball sockets. Who is right?
   (A) A only
   (B) B only
   (C) Both A and B
   (D) Neither A nor B

9. Technician B says that there should be an equal distance between a threaded tie rod adjuster and each tie rod clamp. Technician B says that a rack and pinion gear must be removed to replace the outer tie rod end. Who is right?
   (A) A only
   (B) B only
   (C) Both A and B
   (D) Neither A nor B

10. Technician A says that new tie rod sockets and the adjuster sleeve should be assembled to equal the length of the old assembly. Technician B says that the adjuster sleeve should be centered on the two socket ends. Who is right?
    (A) A only
    (B) B only
    (C) Both A and B
    (D) Neither A nor B

11. Which of the following is the most heavily stressed point in a parallelogram steering system?
    (A) idler arm
    (B) center link
    (C) tie rod ends
    (D) Pitman arm

12. Technician A says that one end of an idler arm is splined. Technician B says that the idler arm is bracket-mounted to the frame. Who is right?
    (A) A only
    (B) B only
    (C) Both A and B
    (D) Neither A nor B

13. Technician A says that power steering gearbox adjustments can be made on the car, but are easier if the gearbox is removed from the vehicle and drained before making any adjustments. Technician B says that worm shaft bearing preload and sector gear lash adjustments are required at periodic intervals. Who is right?
    (A) A only
    (B) B only
    (C) Both A and B
    (D) Neither A nor B

14. Technician A says that the steering wheel will rotate with a slight endplay when correctly adjusted. Technician B says the steering wheel will rotate with a slight drag. Who is right?
    (A) A only
    (B) B only
    (C) Both A and B

(D) Neither A nor B

15. Technician A adjusts worm bearing preload with a screw in the housing cover. Technician B adjusts sector gear lash with the adjuster plug. Who is right?
(A) A only
(B) B only
(C) Both A and B
(D) Neither A nor B

16. Technicians A and B center a gearbox to measure sector gear lash. To make sure it is properly centered, Technician A says that the stub shaft flat should face upward and be parallel with the side cover. Technician B says that the sector shaft master spline should align with the adjusting screw. Who is right?
(A) A only
(B) B only
(C) Both A and B
(D) Neither A nor B

17. Technician A says that lash adjuster endplay is maintained by a shim. Technician B says that lash adjuster endplay is checked with an poundforce-inch torque wrench. Who is right?
(A) A only
(B) B only
(C) Both A and B
(D) Neither A nor B

18. Technician A says that some rack and pinion steering gears are not adjustable. Technician B says that rack and pinion steering gears may require either a rack bearing or pinion bearing adjustment. Who is right?
(A) A only
(B) B only
(C) Both A and B
(D) Neither A nor B

19. Technician A says that the lubricant in a manual rack and pinion gear is checked through an oil plug located on

the top of the housing. Technician B says that a rack support bearing with too much preload can cause poor steering return. Who is right?
(A) A only
(B) B only
(C) Both A and B
(D) Neither A nor B

20. Technician A says that automatic transmission fluid is used as hydraulic fluid in a power steering system. Technician B says that power steering fluid is used. Who is right?
(A) A only
(B) B only
(C) Both A and B
(D) Neither A nor B

21. Which of the following is NOT considered as part of normal power steering system service?
(A) checking fluid level and condition
(B) checking and adjusting drive belt tension
(C) locating and correcting leaks
(D) pressure testing

22. Technician A says that the power steering system should be bled after it has been flushed. Technician B says that air is bled by disconnecting a hose and turning the steering wheel lock-to-lock until bubbles no longer escape. Who is right?
(A) A only
(B) B only
(C) Both A and B
(D) Neither A nor B

23. Technician A says that the system can be diagnosed with a special pressure tester. Technician B says that the tester must be installed between the pump outlet port and the steering gear inlet port with its gauge between the pump and shut-off valve. Who is right?
(A) A only

(B) B only
(C) Both A and B
(D) Neither A nor B

24. Technician A says that when replacing a power steering pump, the mounting bracket may have to be removed with the pump. Technician B says that the only requirement of a replacement pump is that it fit in the mounting bracket. Who is right?
(A) A only
(B) B only
(C) Both A and B
(D) Neither A nor B

25. Technician A says that a steering wheel is removed with a puller, regardless of whether it is retained by a nut or a bolt. Technician B says that once the nut or the bolt is removed, the wheel can be knocked free of the shaft with a brass hammer. Who is right?
(A) A only
(B) B only
(C) Both A and B
(D) Neither A nor B

26. When removing a steering wheel with an airbag module, Technician A says that the airbag system must be disabled. Technician B says that after the system is disabled, you must wait for the reserve capacitor in the system to discharge or the airbag may deploy accidentally. Who is right?
(A) A only
(B) B only
(C) Both A and B
(D) Neither A nor B

ELECTRONIC SUSPENSION AND STEERING CONTROL SYSTEM DIAGNOSIS

 OBJECTIVES

After completion of this chapter, you should be able to:

- Explain the difference between area and pinpoint tests.
- Explain the 3 ways a control module determines when a system problem exists.
- Retrieve stored diagnostic trouble codes through the appropriate method according to the system being diagnosed.
- List 6 precautions to be taken with all electronic suspension and steering control systems.

CONTROL SYSTEM TROUBLESHOOTING

Only a few electronic suspension or steering systems currently in use have an indicator or warning lamp that informs the driver of a system malfunction or failure. When a system without an indicator lamp does malfunction, the customer complaint generally involves a change in vehicle ride or steering effort. Do NOT assume that the electronics are at fault because the system does not work. Electronic control systems are designed to provide normal suspension or normal steering full power assist in the event of a component failure or system malfunction. If the system acts as if it did

not have electronic control, the control module has probably turned off the system because of mechanical or wiring failure. If the system does not work, first check the mechanical parts of the system to make sure they are in good condition. With power steering systems, make sure to check the pump reservoir fluid level before condemning the electronic part of the system.

The principles of troubleshooting an electronic suspension or steering system are the same as those used with an ABS system. Basically, you evaluate the driver's complaint and start with an area test to check the general operation of the system (Figure 8-1). The area test will direct you

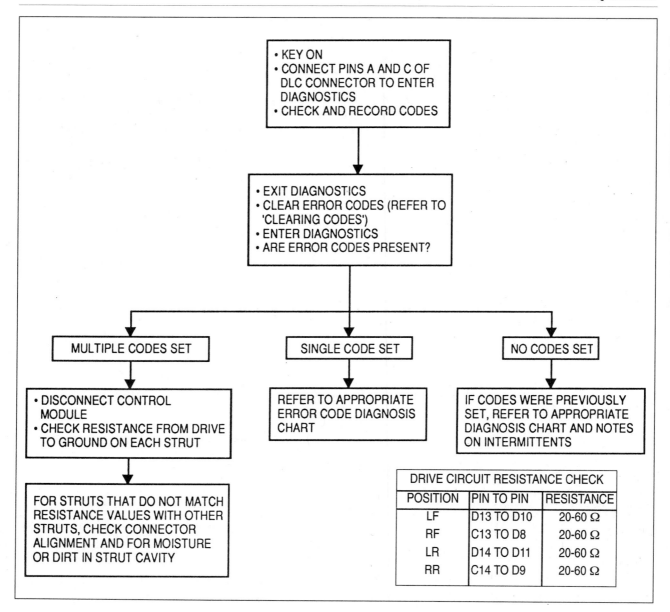

Figure 8-1 A system operational check, or area test, is the first step in diagnosing an electronic control system. (Oldsmobile Division, General Motors)

to the specific subsystems, circuits, and components to be tested (pinpoint tests). After making the necessary adjustments or repairs, check your work by performing the area test a second time.

To properly check and service an electronic control system, you must have the manufacturer's test procedures and specifications for the specific year and model of the vehicle. The internal operation of a particular component, the way it is controlled, or the system's electrical circuitry can vary from one vehicle application to another. In addition, the factory often makes small changes during a model year that can affect your diagnostic procedure.

A logical, common sense approach to electronic control system troubleshooting will serve you well. Remember that the electrical components in the control system operate on low voltages, and a high resistance in a circuit always causes problems. One of your first steps should be a visual check of the circuit for damaged wiring, and any signs of corroded, loose, or broken connectors.

SELF-DIAGNOSTIC SYSTEMS

Some suspension and steering control modules have no self-diagnostic programs; such systems are diagnosed by using a flow chart and digital volt-ohmmeter (DVOM) to check voltages at specified points. Other control modules are programmed to check their own operation, as well as the operation of each sensor and actuator circuit. They do this in the same way as an ABS control module:

- by recognizing the lack of an input or output signal from a given sensor or actuator
- by recognizing that a particular signal is not reasonable, or that it remains outside the specified limits for a period of time
- by checking circuit continuity or a return voltage signal through a test voltage signal sent to the sensors or actuators.

When a control module with a self-diagnostic program recognizes that something is wrong, it sets a trouble code in memory and lights an indicator lamp or light-emitting diode (LED). The indicator lamp or LED may be located in the instrument cluster, message center, or system select switch. When troubleshooting a system that sets trouble codes, the first step is to check the module memory to see if any codes are present. In some systems, any code set in memory is a hard or continuous code and will remain there until erased by the technician or displaced by a more recent one. In other systems, the module

memory is volatile, composed of soft or intermittent codes, which means that the codes are erased when the ignition is turned off. With any self-diagnostic electronic control system, code retrieval is your area test. Once the code is retrieved, it directs you to a pinpoint test. This takes the form of a troubleshooting chart similar to that shown in Figure 8-2. By following the steps in the pinpoint test, you can determine whether the problem is in a wiring circuit or is caused by a defective or malfunctioning component.

READING SUSPENSION OR STEERING SYSTEM TROUBLE CODES

Manufacturers have a specific list of trouble codes for each electronic control system, and provide specific procedures to read them. Most control systems have a diagnostic test connector to which test equipment is connected. Such systems require the use of an analog voltmeter, special test equipment, or a scan tool for code retrieval. Codes are retrieved as pulses of an analog voltmeter needle or as a digital numerical display with the special test equipment or scan tool. Some systems permit code retrieval through a lamp sequence check using the indicator lamp. When a lamp sequence check is used, the code is displayed as a flashing light or blinking LED.

CHRYSLER TROUBLE CODE RETRIEVAL

None of the electronically controlled suspension systems currently used by Chrysler display trouble codes on the vehicle instrument panel. Although the Automatic Air Suspension System module can set codes, they can be accessed only by Chrysler's DRB II tester or an equivalent scan tool. Since the module memory is volatile, the codes are erased when the ignition is turned 'off'.

STOP WARNING
You should enter this Pinpoint Test only when directed here from PRC Quick Test. To prevent the replacement of good components, be aware that the following non-electric areas may be at fault:
— Tires, front and rear struts, coils, stabilizer and steering components.

This Pinpoint Test is intended to diagnose only the following:
— Harness Circuit: Speed Sensor (GN/R)
— Speed Sensor (Analog instrument panel only)
— PRC Control Unit

TEST STEP	RESULT	▶ ACTION TO TAKE
A1 **System Integrity Check** • Visually inspect all wiring, wiring harness, connectors and components for evidence of overheating, insulation damage, looseness, shorting, or other damage. • Is there any cause for concern?	 YES NO	 SERVICE as required Go to A2
NOTE: Refer to the index for system component location illustration.		
A2 **Circuit Continuity Check** • Key 'off'. • VOM on 200 Ω scale. • Measure resistance between PRC Control Unit connector terminal M ('GN/R') and instrument panel connector terminal 2C ('GN/R') analog instrument cluster or 2S ('GN/R') digital instrument cluster. • Is resistance greater than 5 Ω ?	 YES NO	 SERVICE 'GN/R' wire between PRC control unit and instrument panel for opens. Go to A3

Figure 8-2 After performing an area test and retrieving any trouble codes, the next step in electronic control diagnosis is the pinpoint test which checks a specific component or circuit. (Ford Motor)

FORD TROUBLE CODE RETRIEVAL

Depending on the Ford suspension or steering system being tested, codes are retrieved in one of four ways:

1. A pulsing or sweeping movement of an analog volt-ohmmeter (VOM) needle (Figure 8-3). To check the Probe PRC or VAPS systems, the VOM connects to an engine compartment diagnostic connector (Figure 8-4). The diagnostic connector in a Continental VAPS system is located near the brake fluid reservoir (Figure 8-5). In both systems, codes are indicated by meter needle pulses, as shown in Figure 8-3. For example, a code 03 is indicated by three fast (0.5 s)

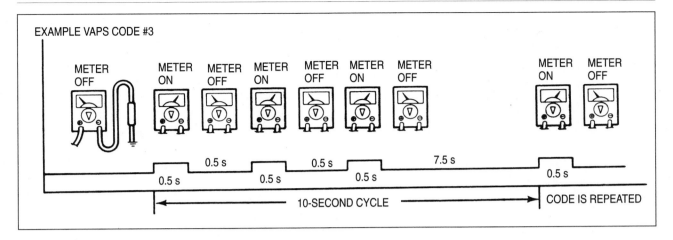

Figure 8-3 Reading trouble codes with an analog voltmeter. (Ford Motor)

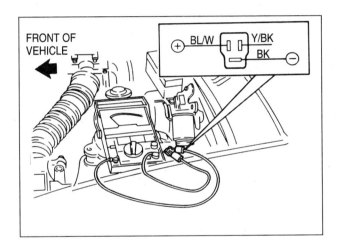

Figure 8-4 Trouble codes are retrieved through a diagnostic connector in many electronic control systems. (Ford Motor)

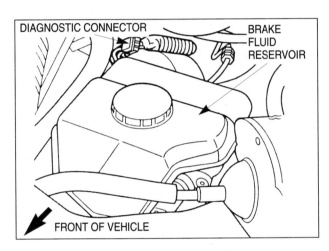

Figure 8-5 The Continental VAPS diagnostic connector is located near the brake fluid reservoir. (Ford Motor)

needle pulses, followed by a long pause (7.5 s) before the code is repeated.

2. A digital display on Ford's self-test automatic readout (STAR) tester or Super STAR II tester (Figure 8-6). The STAR or Super STAR II tester plugs into a diagnostic connector (Figure 8-7) located near the right shock tower in the engine compartment and displays codes in a digital format. Follow the operating procedures included with the tester and specified in the vehicle's service manual.

3. A flashing lamp located in the instrument cluster on some systems (Figure 8-8) that also accept the STAR tester. In the event of a malfunction, the lamp flashes on and off when the ignition is turned to the 'on' position. Since the lamp may start flashing in the middle of the code, wait until the first long flash is noted. Count the short flashes that follow and add them to the long flash. Since the code will continue to flash until the

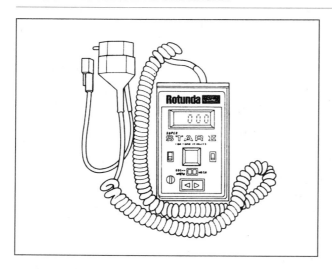

Figure 8-6 The STAR tester is used to retrieve trouble codes with many Ford electronic control systems. (Ford Motor)

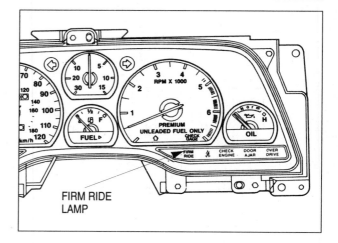

Figure 8-8 The 'FIRM RIDE' indicator lamp is one example of a warning lamp that alerts the driver to system problems and is used to retrieve trouble codes. (Ford Motor)

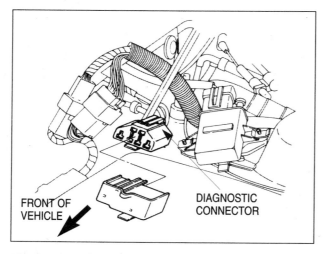

Figure 8-7 The STAR tester plugs into a diagnostic connector located near the right shock absorber tower. (Ford Motor)

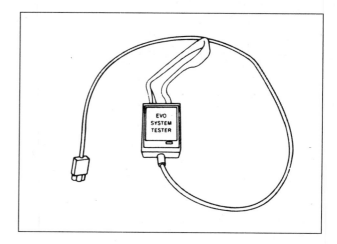

Figure 8-9 A separate test lamp is required to test some EVO systems. (Ford Motor)

ignition is turned off, read the code several times for verification.

4. A separate EVO service diagnostic test lamp (Figure 8-9) connected to a diagnostic connector located inside the glove compartment (Figure 8-10). The control module contains a lamp driver circuit that allows diagnostic codes to be flashed on the test lamp.

GM TROUBLE CODE RETRIEVAL

The GM Computer Command Ride (CCR) module can set and store trouble codes. If the vehicle is equipped with a Driver Information Center (DIC), the code is retrieved as a lamp flash sequence. On vehicles NOT equipped with a DIC, the two light-emitting diodes (LEDs) on the driver select switch glow to indicate a system problem. Whenever the module sets a

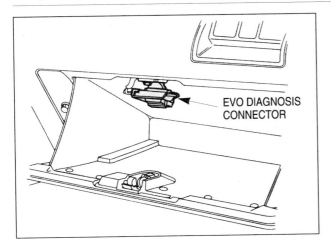

Figure 8-10 The separate test lamp connects to a diagnostic connector located inside the vehicle glove compartment. (Ford Motor)

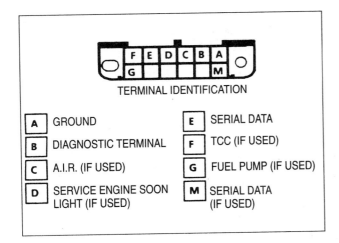

Figure 8-11 The GM diagnostic link connector (DLC). It is usually at the bottom edge of the instrument panel. (Oldsmobile Division, General Motors)

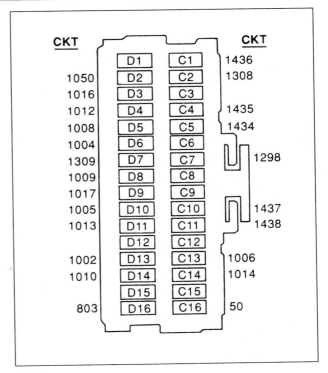

Figure 8-12 The CCR control module connector. (Oldsmobile Division, General Motors)

code, a one-second self-diagnostic test is activated at three-minute intervals until the problem is corrected. To determine the code, enter the CCR diagnostic mode by connecting a jumper between pins C and A of the diagnostic link connector (DLC) located under the instrument panel (Figure 8-11). Another way of doing it is by connecting pins D2 and D16 of the control module wiring harness connector (Figure 8-12) with a jumper wire.

Either method will cause the driver select switch LEDs to flash the code, which can be read by counting the number of times the LEDs glow. Once the connector pins are jumpered, the LEDs will remain off for three seconds, then flash one short flash, followed by a pause and two short, rapid flashes for a code 12. This indicates that the self-diagnostic function works properly. Code 12 will flash 3 times, then pause for 3 s. If the module has stored any trouble codes, the LEDs will flash each code 3 times in numeric order from lowest to highest, with a pause between each. The LEDs remain off for about a second after flashing the first digit of a code, then flash the second digit. Figure 8-13 shows how this flash sequence occurs.

After all codes have been retrieved, the LEDs will pause and the sequence will repeat, starting with code 12. At this point, turn the ignition key off and remove the

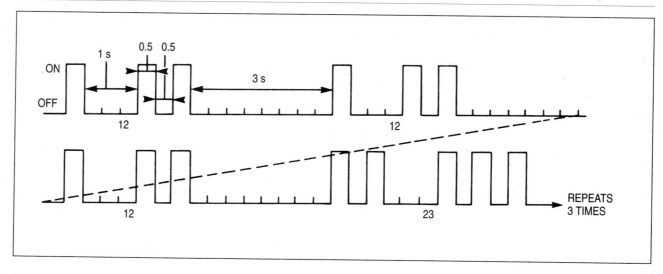

Figure 8-13 An example of trouble code 23 retrieval in the GM CCR system. The dotted line indicates that the code pulses are continued on the next line. (Oldsmobile Division, General Motors)

jumper wire from the connector pins. To clear the trouble codes from memory, connect one end of a jumper wire to pin 'A' of the DLC connector. Use the opposite end of the wire to alternately connect and disconnect pin 'C' of the connector three times, holding each connection for one second, and pausing one second between connections.

The GM EVO steering control modules are capable of disabling the system if a malfunction occurs, but set NO diagnostic trouble codes. Diagnosis of these systems relies on use of a Tech 1 or equivalent scan tool and a signal generator to monitor actuator duty cycle.

IMPORT TROUBLE CODE RETRIEVAL

Trouble codes on import suspension and steering systems generally are retrieved by grounding a diagnostic connector and counting the number of flashes from an instrument cluster indicator lamp. Since each carmaker uses different connector locations and terminals to be grounded, ALWAYS refer to the proper shop manual for the make and model being serviced.

PRELIMINARY SERVICE PROCEDURES

Before you can determine whether a customer complaint is real or imagined, you must understand the particular system and its components, how the system is supposed to operate, and what generally happens when something goes wrong with it. Although most conditions result from simple rather than complicated problems, you must know and remember the difference between 'impossible' and 'unlikely', and NOT rule out something unusual in your diagnosis. For example, many technicians assume that because a part is new, it will work as it is supposed to. While it is unlikely that a new part will fail, it is NOT impossible. Good technicians have wasted many hours in trying to diagnose problems because they forgot this.

VISUAL INSPECTION

Diagnosis of any electronic control system should start with a careful visual and physical inspection of the system. This often can result in correcting the problem without further troubleshooting. Assuming that you know and understand the system's operation, first check the condition of the system fuse(s), then inspect the system wiring for correct routing and connections, burned or chaffed insulation, and pinched, shorted, or grounded wires. Make any necessary repairs before continuing.

Electrical connectors are the weak points in any electronic control system. Corroded or poor electrical connections cause most problems with electronic circuits, NOT the solid state circuitry. Since intermittent problems also result from poor connections, pay particular attention to the system connectors and examine them carefully before replacing any system components. Many wiring harness connectors used in suspension and steering control systems are located underneath the vehicle where they are exposed to enviromental conditions (Figure 8-14). Corrosion, moisture, or other foreign material on terminal mating surfaces can act as an insulator, causing

erratic system operation. Also, the connector halves may have been disconnected earlier and incorrectly mated when reconnected, resulting in damage to the terminals. Before unplugging a connector to check for broken wires or loose connector terminals, clean it carefully to remove any accumulated road dirt.

The flexible tubes and hoses that connect system components are also exposed to environmental conditions and can develop leaks as a result of damage or deterioration. Before attempting to diagnose a problem, check the flexible air tubes and snap-together connectors for leakage. Clean each connector and the area around it to remove all dirt and contamination, and then use a mild soap solution to detect connector leakage. System tubes and hoses also should be checked carefully for brittleness or hardening from age or heat, softness caused by internal leakage, and loose or improperly fitted couplings. Air springs suspected of leaking can be checked for pinhole leaks or small cracks with a soap and water solution.

ELECTRONIC SYSTEM PRECAUTIONS

The following precautions must be observed when servicing vehicles with any electronic control system:

- Unplug the control module (and all other vehicle computers) when working on the vehicle with an electric welding unit.
- Do NOT subject the control module to high temperatures. If the vehicle is to be painted and dried with heat, either maintain the temperature below 180°F or remove the module from the vehicle.
- Do NOT let brake or suspension components hang by the sensor wires.
- NEVER disconnect the battery with the engine running.

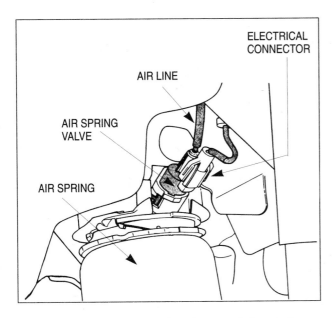

Figure 8-14 The location of air lines and electrical connectors underneath the vehicle makes them more prone to damage from environmental conditions. (Ford Motor)

- NEVER start the engine with a fast charger. Disconnect the battery from the electrical system before fast-charging it.

- NEVER connect or disconnect the control module harness with the ignition switch 'on'.

- Carefully note the position, routing, and location of control system wiring and make sure it is the same after servicing. Electronic components are extremely sensitive to electromagnetic interference (EMI). Incorrect sensor wire routing can result in false signals caused by electrical noise.

- Maintain the sealing integrity of electronic component connectors by disconnecting them ONLY when necessary. Before reconnection, make sure the connector cavity is clean and dry, and that the connector pins are properly aligned in the cavity.

- Measure the resistance at the terminals of a solid state component ONLY when a written diagnostic procedure instructs you to do so, or damage to the component can result.

- When using a voltmeter, ALWAYS connect the ground lead first.

Other precautions may be required by individual systems. For example, diodes are used in the compressor relay, air vent valve, and air spring valves of Ford air suspension and load leveling systems to suppress electrical noise. Since diodes are polarity sensitive, proper polarity must be followed during testing, or they may be damaged.

Air suspension systems must be shut off before hoisting, jacking, towing, or removing system components. Although some systems provide a separate on/off switch in the trunk (Figure 8-15), it is a good idea to disconnect the battery negative cable. This will prevent the possibility that

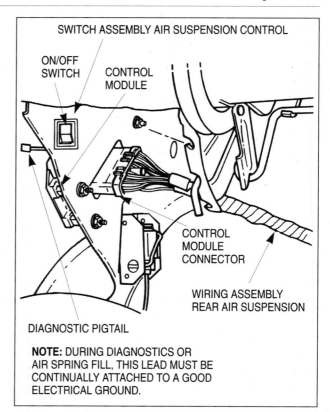

Figure 8-15 Air suspension systems have an on/off switch located near the module inside the trunk. The switch should be off whenever the vehicle is towed or hoisted to prevent accidental system operation. (Ford Motor)

the system will operate accidentally while you are working on it. Accidental operation can result in a shift of the component or vehicle position, causing possible component damage or serious personal injury.

VARIABLE SHOCK DAMPENING SYSTEMS

To illustrate the basic diagnostic procedures used with these systems, we will look at three different systems currently in use. Before starting diagnosis, perform all safety steps necessary to start and run the vehicle during testing, such as making sure the shift lever is in 'park', the wheels are blocked, or any other safety considerations that your instructor suggests.   Be sure to read the shop manual for the year of the car being tested. Diagnostic procedures may change from year to year.

PROGRAMMED RIDE CONTROL (PRC)

Ford currently uses three versions of the PRC system. First, the Probe PRC module does NOT store trouble codes in memory, nor does it signal any malfunction to the driver. When performing the self-test portion of the quick-test to verify system integrity, an analog voltmeter is connected between the two terminals of the suspension test connector shown in Figure 8-4.

Connect the red positive lead to the blue/white wire terminal, and the black negative lead to the black wire terminal. Any trouble codes retrieved through the VOM needle sweep pattern during self-test indicate that the problems were found during self-test.

The second system is on the Thunderbird Turbo Coupe. To ground this PRC diagnostic system, fabricate a special tool (Figure 8-16) and weld it to a screw-driver blade. With the engine off, insert the tool in the diagnostic connector located beneath the ash tray in the console (Figure 8-17). Start the engine and then remove the tool immediately. This will trigger the 'FIRM RIDE' lamp to blink the code four times, once every nine seconds.

The third version is called Automatic Ride Control when used on the Thunderbird Super Coupe and Cougar XR7. When installed on the Lincoln Mark VIII, it is called Shock Damping Control. Both systems are diagnosed using a STAR or Super STAR II tester. With the system select switch in the Auto position, and the tester switched off with the button in the 'hold' (up) position, attach the tester to the diagnostic connector. This is located under the hood near the passenger side shock tower and is marked ARC/EVO on the Super Coupe and XR7. On the Mark VIII, it

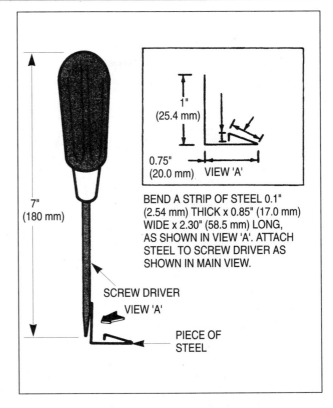

Figure 8-16 The fabricated jumper tool used to active self-test on some Ford PRC systems. (Ford Motor)

is located behind the right hand side trim panel in the trunk.

> **TIP TECH TIP:**   When using a Super STAR II tester, the mode switch on the tester must be in the EEC-IV MCU mode. If placed in the MECS mode, invalid error codes will appear.

Turn the STAR tester on and push the button down to the 'test' position. Start the engine, wait 10 s, then depress the tester button and let it come up to the 'hold' mode and push it back down to 'test' mode within 5 s. With Mark VIII models, firmly depress the brake pedal within 9s. The control module will initiate its self-test procedure and display any stored codes on the STAR tester. On Super Coupe and XR7

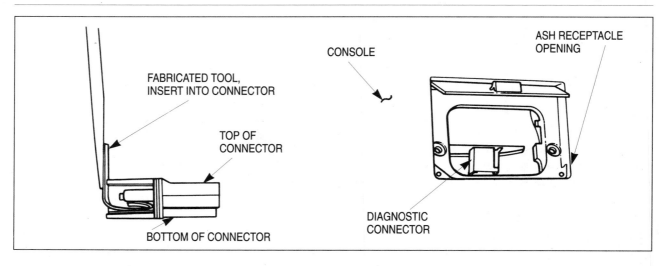

Figure 8-17 Fitting the jumper tool into a diagnostic connector located underneath the ash-tray activates the module self-test program. (Ford Motor)

models, the 'FIRM RIDE' lamp also will blink the code two times.

Code retrieval in all systems is the first step in the quick-test procedure. Once the code has been retrieved, it is used to determine which pinpoint test is required (Figure 8-18).

> **TIP TECH TIP:** Whenever a procedure requires circuit testing at the control module connector, a Rotunda EEC-IV 60-pin breakout box (or equivalent) will make testing faster and easier. A breakout box connects in series between the connectors and gives easy access for test connections while allowing current to flow for full system operation.

GM COMPUTER COMMAND RIDE (CCR)

The CCR module is capable of storing and displaying up to 12 diagnostic codes. These codes are retrieved as described above under 'GM Trouble Code Retrieval' as part of the CCR system check, as shown in Figure 8-1. The code will direct you to a diagnostic chart (Figure 8-19) which is used in conjunction with the system wiring schematic (Figure 8-20).

TOYOTA ELECTRONICALLY MODULATED SUSPENSION (TEMS)

Like many Honda, Nissan, and other Japanese vehicles, the TEMS system found on Toyota vehicles uses the control switch lamps as a diagnostic tool. With the control switch in the 'normal' position, and the ignition 'on' (engine 'off'), ground the engine compartment diagnostic connector terminals with a jumper wire.

Both lamps will light briefly before starting to flash. As the steering wheel is turned to the right, the left indicator lamp should go out, while the right lamp continues to flash. Turning the steering wheel to the left reverses the lamp sequence. If the lamps do not come on and go out according to the direction of steering wheel movement, the steering sensor is defective.

The automatic dampening function of the shock absorbers can be checked by bouncing the vehicle fenders with the control switch in different positions. If the

TEST STEP	RESULT	ACTION TO TAKE
A2 CHECK STEERING SENSOR		
NOTE: Steps A2 and A3 may be repeated as many times and in any order desired to ensure proper test results. However, once the engine is turned 'off' or the shock select switch is moved, you must proceed to Step A4 or start over at Step A1. • Wait until lamp has stopped blinking. • With the vehicle at rest and engine running, test the steering sensor by turning the steering wheel from lock in one direction to lock in other direction (3 full turns) or until 'FIRM RIDE' lamp turns on. NOTE: The lamp will usually turn on before the wheel has completed the lock turn. This is normal.	'FIRM RIDE' lamp turns 'on' for 5 s, then turns 'off' (OK) ▶ 'FIRM RIDE' lamp does NOT turn 'on' (∅) ▶	GO to A3 Fault in steering sensor circuit. GO to D13
A3 CHECK SPEED SENSOR		
• Wait until lamp has turned 'off' from Step A2 • Drive the vehicle at any desired speed above 15 mph (24 km/h)	'FIRM RIDE' lamp turns 'on' and stays 'on' until vehicle speed drops below 12 mph (19 km/h) (OK) ▶ 'FIRM RIDE' lamp does NOT turn 'on' (∅) ▶	GO to A4 Fault in speed sensor circuit. GO to D19
A4 PREPARE FOR REMAINING TESTS		
• Stop vehicle and turn engine 'off' • Move shock select switch to AUTO if it is not already there • Move the ignition switch to the RUN position leaving the engine 'off' • Wait until the 'firm ride' lamp has turned 'off' (usually after 4 s)	'FIRM RIDE' lamp turns 'on' for 4 s, then turns 'off' (OK) ▶ 'FIRM RIDE' lamp turns 'on' and stays 'on' even though switch is in AUTO position (∅) ▶ 'FIRM RIDE' lamp turns 'on' for 4 s, then flashes a code (∅) ▶	GO to A5 GO to D6 RECORD code and REFER to Step A1 for action to take

Figure 8-18 A portion of the ARC quick-test procedure designed to direct you to the appropriate pinpoint test. (Ford Motor)

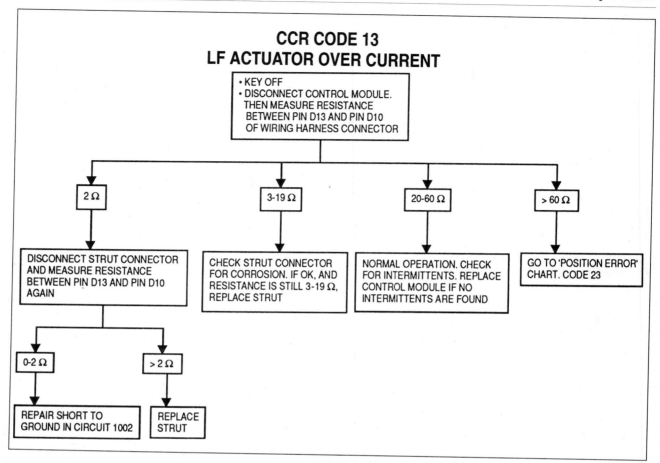

Figure 8-19 One of the pinpoint tests used to check the CCR strut actuators. (Oldsmobile Division, General Motors)

fenders are bounced with the switch in the 'normal' position, one indicator lamp should light. To check the 'sport' position, switch the jumper wire to a different terminal in the diagnostic connector. When the fender is bounced, both lamps should light. To check the shock absorbers, apply voltage to the actuator connector terminals and listen for a clicking sound.

ELECTRONIC LEVEL CONTROL SYSTEMS

These automatic leveling or ride height control systems operate only on the rear wheels and adjust vehicle trim height according to weight load. To point out the different approaches in diagnosis, we will look at typical ELC systems currently in use. These brief diagnostic procedures are only a small part of the many pages of diagnostic charts in the factory shop manuals.

CHRYSLER AUTOMATIC AIR LOAD LEVELING SYSTEM

This optional rear suspension system first appeared in 1986 as the Electronic Height Control (EHC) System and combined the control module with the rotary height sensor. Since the module/sensor stores NO trouble codes, the system is diagnosed by an operational check. To operate the system manually, raise the vehicle on a hoist and disconnect the sensor arm. With the ignition 'on', moving the arm upward should operate the compressor; moving the

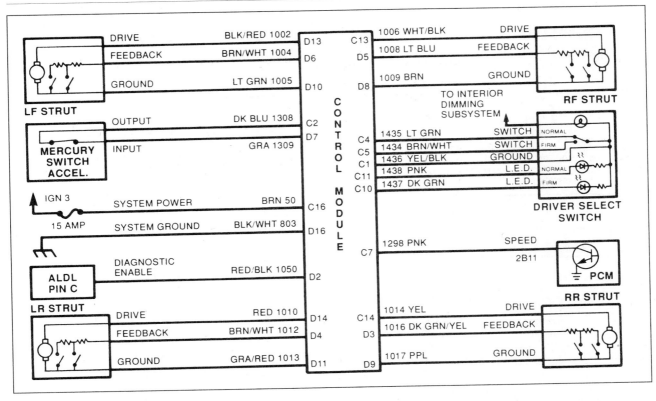

Figure 8-20 The CCR pinpoint test should be used with a CCR wiring diagram or schematic. (Oldsmobile Division, General Motors)

arm downward should operate the exhaust solenoid. If the system does not work correctly, use the appropriate diagnostic chart (Figure 8-21) with the circuit diagram (Figure 8-22) to check circuit voltages as directed.

The current Automatic Air Load Leveling System is a second generation version of the original EHC system. The combination rotary height sensor/control module is replaced by a magnetic switch sensor in the right rear air shock absorber and a separate control module containing a self-diagnostic program. To activate the self-diagnostic program:

1. Add a weight of approximately 300 lb to the rear of the vehicle.
2. Turn the ignition switch 'on' and remove the protective cover from the diagnostic connector.

3. Ground the connector ground pin (Figure 8-23) with one end of a jumper wire, then ground the other end of the jumper wire to the body or a control module fastener.
4. Connect a monitor (test) lamp between the connector test lamp feed and ground pins as shown in Figure 8-23.
5. Use the monitor lamp with the appropriate diagnostic chart (Figure 8-24) to diagnose the system.

FORD AUTOMATIC LEVELING REAR SUSPENSION SYSTEM

This ELC system is sometimes called the Rear Load Leveling System and uses a control module with a self-diagnostic capability. Troubleshooting the system requires the use of both digital and analog volt-

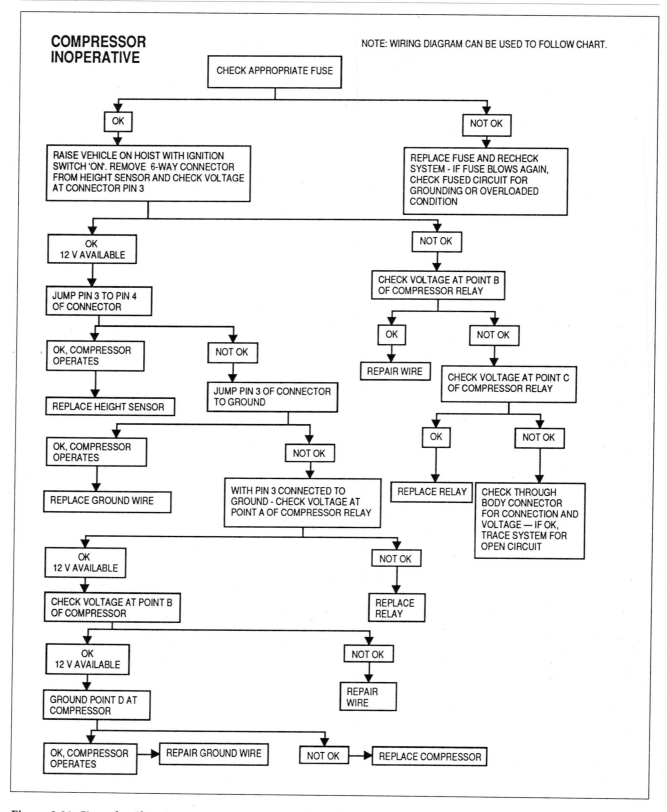

Figure 8-21 Since the Chrysler EHC system has no module diagnostic capabilities, a diagnostic chart is used for troubleshooting an air compressor that does not work. (Chrysler)

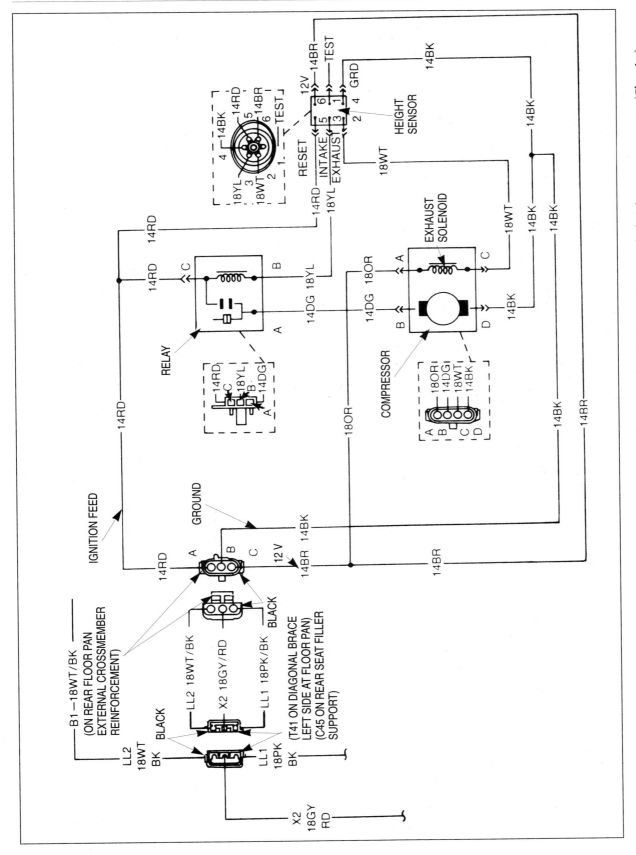

Figure 8-22 The Chrysler EHC circuit diagram should be used with the diagnostic chart when checking voltages at the height sensor connector. (Chrysler)

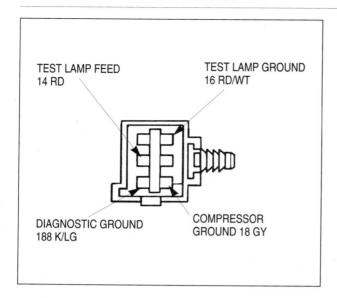

Figure 8-23 The Chrysler Automatic Air Load Leveling system diagnostic connector. (Chrysler)

meters, and a specially fabricated test lamp using a No. 194 bulb (use of any other bulb will damage the system).

As with all suspension systems using air lines, check the lines for leakage that can cause a pressure loss before testing or your results will be incorrect. Connect a battery charger set to slow charge to ensure that battery voltage remains at a high level during testing. Remember to maintain correct polarity at all times, as the compressor relay and vent solenoids are equipped with diodes to suppress electrical noise.

To initiate the self-diagnostic program, ground the diagnostic pigtail in the module harness (Figure 8-25) with the special test lamp. This activates the instrument cluster indicator (monitor) lamp for use in the area test sequence (Figure 8-26). The results of the area test will point you to the appropriate pinpoint tests to be performed (Figure 8-27). Unless otherwise stated in the pinpoint test directions, leave the module wiring harness connected and backprobe the terminals or use a Rotunda EEC-IV 60-pin breakout box (or equivalent).

GM ELECTRONIC LEVEL CONTROL (ELC) SYSTEM

Like the Chrysler Electronic Height Control system, the GM ELC system uses a combined height sensor/module that stores NO trouble codes. The system can be diagnosed only by an operational check with the help of a diagnostic test procedure chart from the shop manual (Figure 8-28) and a fused jumper wire with the vehicle raised in the air and the height sensor disconnected.

AIR SPRING SUSPENSION SYSTEMS

In this type of suspension system, air springs and/or air struts replace the conventional coil springs, providing load leveling at ALL four wheels. Air spring suspensions use more complex components, have more sophisticated electronics, and often are integrated with other systems such as spring damping and ride height control. All require a visual inspection of the air lines and air springs/struts, as well as maintaining sufficient battery voltage during testing through the use of a battery charger. Because air spring suspensions are more complicated, the circuit wiring and test procedures required to check these systems also are more complex. We will look at typical examples below.

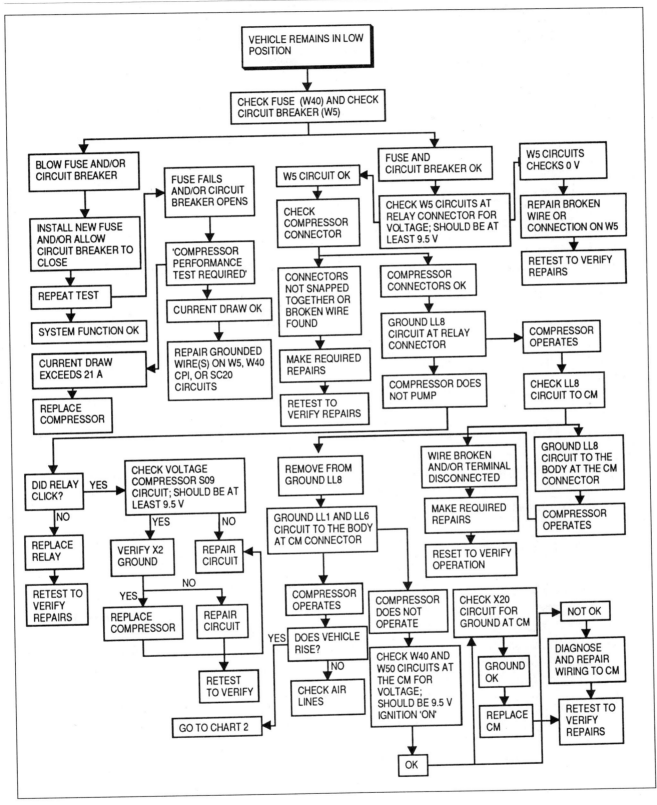

Figure 8-24 After connecting a test lamp to the connector, a diagnostic chart is used to troubleshoot the Automatic Air Load Leveling system. (Chrysler)

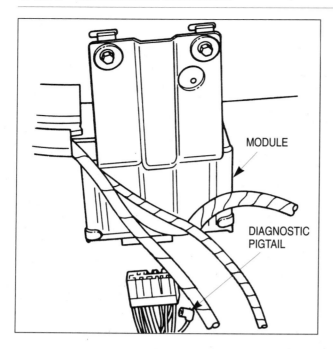

Figure 8-25 The diagnostic pigtail is part of the module harness in Ford ELC systems. (Ford Motor)

> **TIP TECH TIP:** Whenever a procedure requires circuit testing at a Ford control module connector, a Rotunda EEC-IV 60-pin breakout box (or equivalent) will make testing faster and easier.

FORD AIR SUSPENSION SYSTEM

The basic air suspension system used on Lincoln Mark VII and 1984-87 Continental models requires 10 specific diagnostic tests to check system operation. The system is equipped with an on/off switch located in the trunk (Figure 8-29) and an indicator lamp installed in the overhead console. During system diagnosis, the lamp lights to indicate that the module is in the diagnostic sequence, flashes the sequence test number, and indicates a subsystem problem during the first three of the 10 tests (Figure 8-30). Some tests in the sequence are automatically passed or failed by the module; others require that you

make a judgment. Once the judgment is made, the area test directs you to a specific pinpoint check of a particular component and its circuit (Figure 8-31).

LINCOLN CONTINENTAL ASARC SYSTEM

The Air Suspension and Automatic Ride Control system used on 1988 and later Continental models combines the programmed ride control and air suspension systems discussed above. The more complicated module diagnostic program (it can determine over 50 system failures) is divided into three different types:

- Drive cycle diagnostics
- Service bay diagnostics
- Spring fill diagnostics

The drive cycle diagnostic mode checks the entire system for problems that occur while the vehicle is being driven. The module can store up to 32 codes in memory for up to one hour after the ignition switch is turned off. After completing the drive cycle and turning the ignition switch off, connect the STAR tester and depress the test button. Any stored codes will be continuously displayed for up to an hour or until the tester is turned off. Record any displayed codes for comparison with codes obtained later during the service bay diagnostic mode. If the vehicle sits for more than an hour, or if the ignition switch is turned on, the drive cycle must be repeated to try and duplicate the problem(s).

The service bay diagnostic mode checks the system for problems when the vehicle is stationary, and is subdivided into three areas:

- Auto/manual diagnostics
- Trouble code display
- Functional (pinpoint) tests

When the diagnostic connector in the trunk (Figure 8-32) is grounded, the module automatically runs a self-test sequence. After performing this sequence, the module will display '12/OK do manual

TEST STEP	RESULT	ACTION TO TAKE
C3 INITIALIZE SYSTEM (CONTINUED) • Is lamp 'on' after first 60 s after ignition is switched to 'run'?	Lamp 'on', vent solenoid clicks within first 15 s and vehicle does / does NOT lower ▶	Normal operation. Vent solenoid timed out. GO to C4.
	Lamp 'off', vent solenoid does NOT click within first 15 s and vehicle does / does NOT lower ▶	CHECK test lamp. Vehicle may be in trim position. GO to C4.
C4 INITIALIZE SYSTEM (CONTINUED) • Apply a 300 lb (136 kg) load to rear of vehicle. • Does lamp turn 'off' within 15 seconds? NOTE: Compressor may run after this time. NOTE: Allow vehicle to vent and reach trim position before continuing to next Step.	YES (OK) ▶	Vent time out function OK. REMOVE load. GO to C5.
	NO (⊗) ▶	CHECK vent solenoid. REPLACE module. CYCLE ignition 'off'. PERFORM System Operational Check.
C5 INITIALIZE SYSTEM (CONTINUED) • Disconnect air line at dryer as outlined. NOTE: Lamp may turn 'off' and air may escape from removed line. • Cycle ignition switch from 'off' to 'run'. • Apply a 300 lb (136 kg) load to rear of vehicle. • Does lamp turn 'on' after 115-125 s and does compressor stop? NOTE: Time begins when compressor starts to run.	YES (OK) ▶	Compressor Run timer OK. RECONNECT air line. REMOVE weight. PERFORM System Operational Check.
	NO (⊗) ▶	REPLACE module. REPEAT C5. PERFORM System Operational Check.

Figure 8-26 A portion of an ELC quick-test used to select the proper pinpoint test. (Ford Motor)

checks' or '13/Faults detected do manual checks' on the STAR tester. The manual checks require technician input to check sensor, switch, and circuit operation. Once these are completed, the STAR tester will display any stored codes. These should be recorded and compared with those obtained during the drive cycle. Codes which appeared during both tests are hard faults; those appearing only in the drive cycle are intermittent faults. The code or codes are prioritized from 1 (highest) to 7 (lowest) and the pinpoint procedures assigned to each code should be performed in the order of priority, since one code may cause others to be displayed.

The spring fill diagnostic mode checks individual springs by allowing the techni-

TITLE	TEST
Vehicle Load at Curb	Quick Test A
Power Monitor Lamp	Quick Test B
Initialize Sytem	Quick Test C
Ignition Circuit	Pinpoint Test D
Battery Circuit	Pinpoint Test E
Vent Solenoid Circuit	Pinpoint Test F
Sensor Ground Circuit	Pinpoint Test G
Sensor Power Circuit	Pinpoint Test H
Sensor Logic Circuits	Pinpoint Test J
Compressor Relay Motor	Pinpoint Test K

Figure 8-27 The diagnostic test index used in troubleshooting Ford ELC systems. (Ford Motor)

cian to fill or vent each spring separately. Some pinpoint tests require that the technician enter this mode as part of the test sequence.

MARK VIII SPEED-DEPENDENT AIR SUSPENSION SYSTEM

Introduced on 1993 Mark VIII models, this system is diagnosed in a manner similar to that used with the ASARC system discussed above. The initial step in the diagnostic routine is a functional test 211, used to retrieve any stored codes with a Super STAR tester in the fast code mode. If

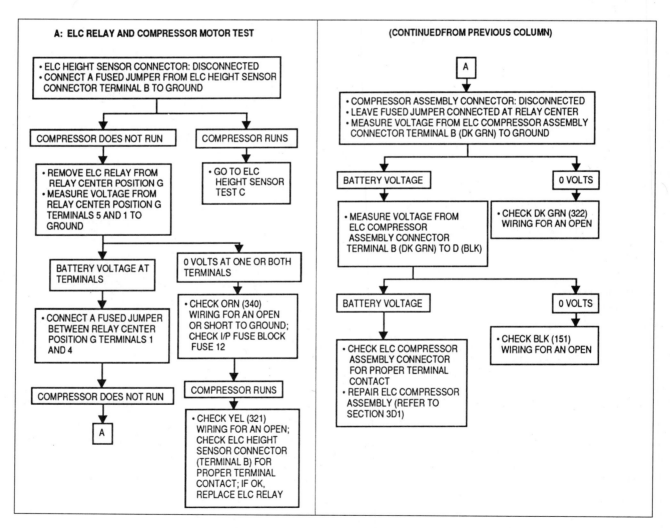

Figure 8-28 One of the diagnostic test procedures used to troubleshoot a GM ELC system with a fused jumper wire. (Oldsmobile Division, General Motors)

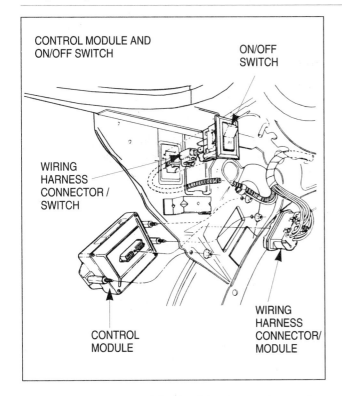

Figure 8-29 Location of the Ford Air Spring Suspension on/off switch in the trunk. (Ford Motor)

a code 15 appears, the module contains NO codes. This is followed by an auto test procedure in which the module self-tests the system for input/output errors and cycles all actuators. If no problems are found, the module executes a vehicle trim adjustment and then requests that the technician open and close each door, and turn the steering wheel at least 1/4 turn in each direction. If the module does not locate a problem during the auto test, the STAR tester will display a code 11. When a system problem is detected during the auto test, the module interrupts the test sequence and displays the appropriate trouble code. As with other electronic control systems, the code is used to determine the proper pinpoint test to be performed. After completing any service required, check your work by rerunning the auto test and erasing any stored codes.

CHRYSLER AUTOMATIC AIR SUSPENSION SYSTEM

Initial troubleshooting of this system is done at the control module connector with a circuit schematic (Figure 8-33), a diagnostic flow chart (Figure 8-34), and a DVOM. Complete diagnosis of the air suspension control module requires use of Chrysler's DRB II tester, the appropriate Chassis (Air Suspension) software cartridge, and Chassis Diagnostic Procedures manual. The DRB II is connected to a 6-pin connector under the instrument panel on the driver's side. With the software cartridge inserted in the DRB II and the ignition switch turned on, the DRB II asks you to identify the vehicle and the model year, and to select the system to be tested. After entering this information with the keypad, the DRB II automatically self-tests the air suspension circuits and lists the steps required to correct the failure.

ELECTRONIC VARIABLE-ASSIST POWER STEERING (VAPS)

Variable-assist or progressive power steering systems are relatively simple in design, operation, and diagnosis. The following are typical examples of the systems currently used.

TOYOTA PROGRESSIVE POWER STEERING (PPS)

Diagnosis of the PPS system does NOT involve indicator lamp or trouble codes; simple voltage and resistance checks are made at the solenoid, speed sensor, and control module (Figure 8-35). These checks will verify both component and system operation.

CONTINENTAL VARIABLE-ASSIST POWER STEERING (VAPS)

Diagnostics for this system involve a

TEST 1 — Rear Suspension System

Enter Test 1

☐ Open and Close the door once

The service indicator light will flash on and off with a pause between each flash. Watch the light and let the test proceed. If a failure occurs, this test can be repeated using the System Performance Checklist below to help isolate the subsystem problem, or Test 2 can be performed.

Test Results

☐ Test 1 completed and light continues to flash test number (one flash) ➤ Test 1 passed; proceed to Test 2

☐ Light on, no flash ➤ Test 1 failed; repeat Test 1 using System Performance Checklist below, or proceedto Test 2

☐ Light flashes rapidly (4/second) ➤ Test 1 failed; repeat Test 1 using System Performance Checklist below, or proceed to Test 2

System Performance Checklist

		YES	NO
1.	Compressor relay clicks closed (hand felt)..	☐	Page xx
2.	Compressor cuts in..	☐	Page xx
3.	Rear air spring valve click open...	☐	Page xx
4.	Vehicle rises for 8-30 seconds; sensor signals that vehicle is high (The compressor should cut out)...	☐	Page xx
5.	Air vent valve clicks open and vehicle lowers for a maximum of 30 seconds; sensor signals that vehicle is low. (The air vent valve should click closed and the compressor should cut in)...	☐	Page xx
6.	Vehicle rises back to trim height; sensor signals vehicle is at trim height (Rear air spring valve should click closed and compressor should cut out)......	☐	Page xx

Figure 8-30 One of the 10 tests in the Air Spring Suspension diagnostic sequence. These tests require technician input and judgment to determine the proper pinpoint test to be performed. (Ford Motor)

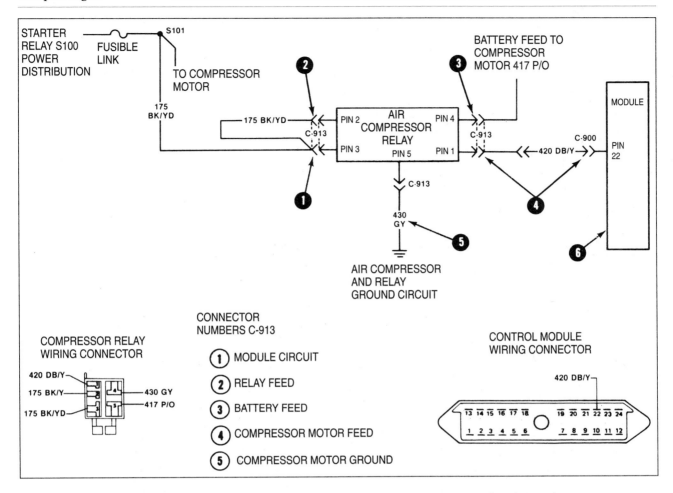

Figure 8-31 A sample pinpoint test used in checking the Air Spring Suspension system. (Ford Motor)

module self-test, trouble code retrieval, and various pinpoint tests. Self-test is activated by connecting a DVOM to the diagnostic connector near the brake fluid reservoir as shown in Figure 8-5. The self-test checks sensor and actuator operation, and circuit condition. Trouble codes are retrieved through the needle sweep pattern of an analog voltmeter. The self-test and trouble codes direct you to the appropriate pinpoint tests, which should be followed in the sequence indicated.

PROBE GT VARIABLE-ASSIST POWER STEERING (VAPS)

The self-test procedure used with the Probe GT system is more complicated than the other systems discussed. Before starting any diagnosis on this system, check the control module under the driver's seat to determine the position of the slide switch on the module (Figure 8-36). This switch permits a 10% harder or lighter steering effort compared to the normal production setting. It may be possible to correct the customer complaint by using the switch to provide a different setting feel.

The Probe VAPS control module does NOT store trouble codes in memory, nor does it signal any malfunction to the driver. When performing the self-test portion of the quick-test to verify system integrity, an analog voltmeter is connected between the two terminals of the suspension test

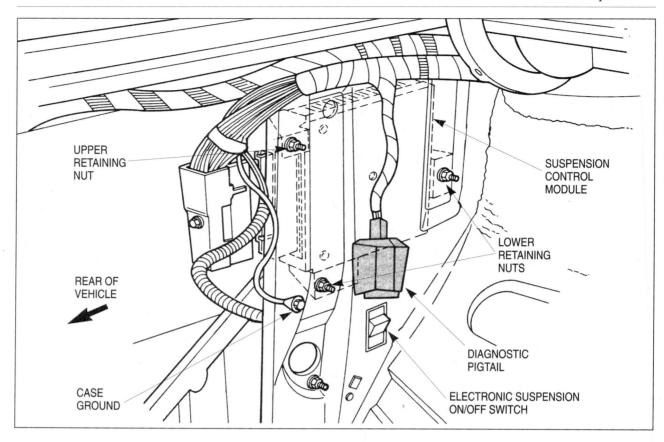

Figure 8-32 The Continental ASARC diagnostic pigtail location behind a trim panel in the trunk. (Ford Motor)

connector shown in Figure 8-37. Connect the red positive lead to the yellow/blue wire terminal, and the black negative lead to the black wire terminal. Any trouble codes retrieved through the VOM needle sweep pattern during self-test indicate that the problems were found during self-test.

TIP TECH TIP: This is the same diagnostic connector used to retrieve PRC codes through the blue/white terminal. Make sure the meter is connected to the proper terminals as described above or the code readout will be PRC codes instead of VAPS codes. Also note that VAPS codes are separated by a 10 s pause, while the PRC codes are repeated in two-second intervals.

ELECTRONIC VARIABLE ORIFICE (EVO) STEERING SYSTEMS

EVO power steering systems also are relatively simple in design and operation, but have a more complex control module and diagnostic procedure. We will discuss diagnostic procedures for representative systems currently in use.

FORD EVO POWER STEERING

Because of differences in control module programming between models, Ford's test procedures for the Thunderbird LX and Cougar LS differ from those used with the Thunderbird Super Coupe, Cougar XR7, and Lincoln Mark VIII. A stand-alone control module that controls only the EVO system is used with LX/LS models. This module contains a lamp driver circuit that

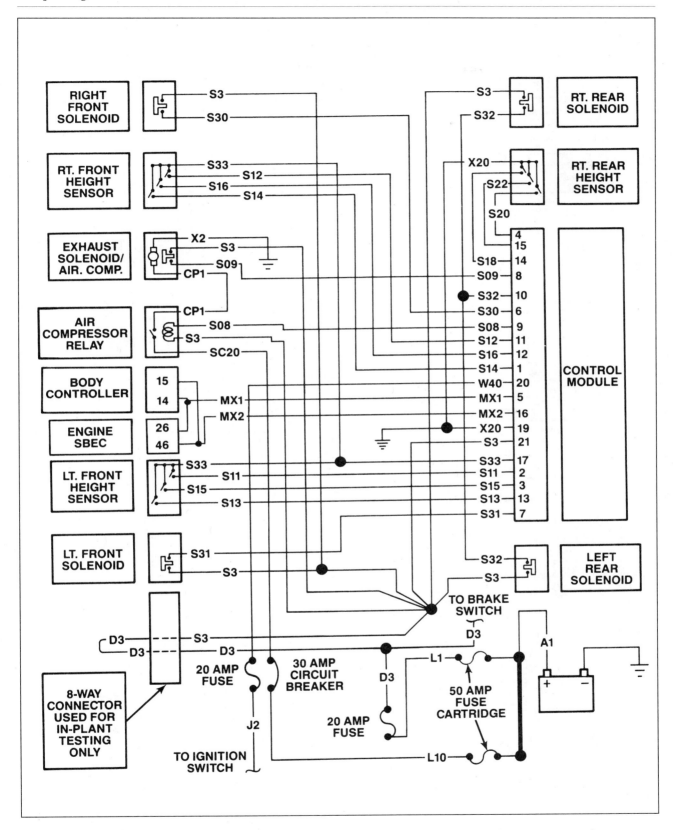

Figure 8-33 The Chrysler Automatic Air Suspension System circuit diagram. (Chrysler)

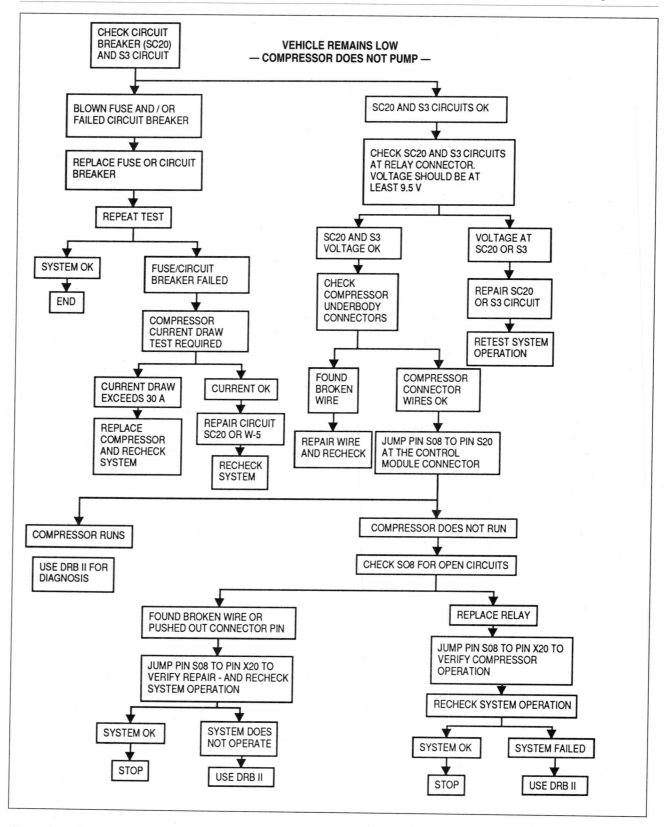

Figure 8-34 A typical diagnostic flow chart used in troubleshooting the Automatic Air Suspension System. (Chrysler)

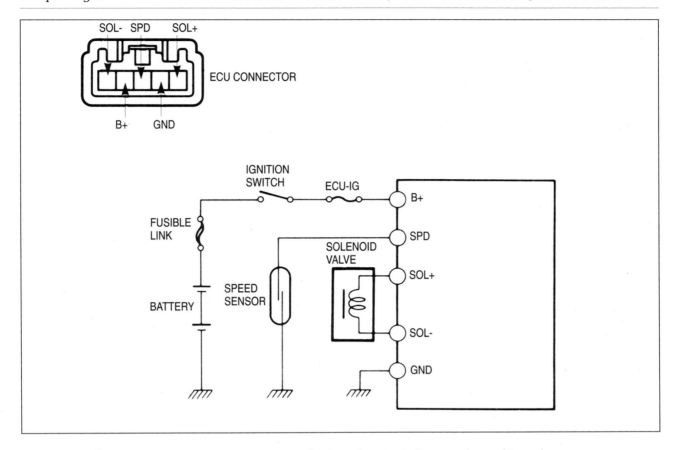

Figure 8-35 The Toyota PPS system is very simple to check, as this circuit diagram shows. (Toyota)

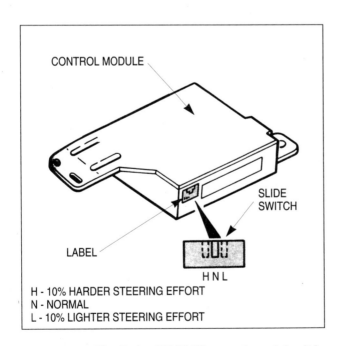

Figure 8-36 The Probe GT VAPS control module slide switch. The module is under the dash. (Ford Motor)

flashes trouble codes on a separate test lamp. The module used with Super Coupe and XR7 models also controls the automatic ride control (ARC) system and uses a STAR or Super STAR II tester instead of a test lamp for diagnosis. The Mark VIII module also controls the air spring suspension system and is diagnosed as described earlier under 'Mark VIII Speed-Dependent Air Suspension System'. The different test procedures for Thunderbird/Cougar models are described below. Use a shop manual for detailed testing.

THUNDERBIRD LX/COUGAR LS EVO SYSTEM

To retrieve trouble codes from the module, use a special diagnostic test lamp, as

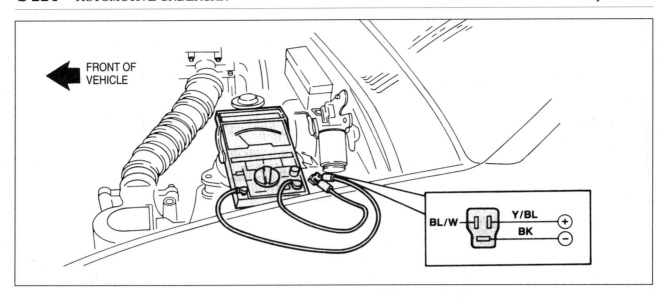

Figure 8-37 Different terminals of the same diagnostic connector are used to check the PRC and EVO systems on a Probe GT. (Ford Motor)

shown in Figure 8-9. It must be connected to the diagnostic connector located in the glove compartment as shown in Figure 8-10 with the ignition 'off'. Once the ignition is turned 'on', the module lamp driver circuit supplies current to the diagnostic test lamp for code retrieval. This output is short-circuit protected to the battery to prevent damage to the module. If a short exists, the module will NOT turn the lamp on until power is removed from and reapplied to the module by cycling the ignition switch off/on.

The self-test steps in the quick-test (Figure 8-38) directs you to the proper pinpoint tests to be performed. The pinpoint tests are used with the appropriate wiring diagrams and circuit schematics to check the components and the circuits.

TIP TECH TIP: Whenever a procedure requires circuit testing at the control module connector, a Rotunda EEC-IV 60-pin breakout box (or equivalent) will make testing faster and easier.

THUNDERBIRD SUPER COUPE/COUGAR XR7 EVO SYSTEM

Since the module used in this system also controls the ARC system, EVO diagnosis uses the STAR or Super STAR II tester and the same procedures described earlier under 'Programmed Ride Control'.

GM EVO-1, EVO-2, AND EVO-3 SYSTEMS

GM currently offers three versions of EVO power steering. EVO-2 has a steering wheel rotation sensor; EVO-1 does NOT. The simplest system, EVO-3 also is called Two-Flow Electronic (TFE) steering.

Diagnostic procedures used with EVO-1 and EVO-2 are fairly complex, requiring the use of a Tech 1 or equivalent scan tool, a signal generator to monitor EVO actuator duty cycle, a power steering system analyzer, digital multimeter, and jumper wires. The control module is capable of disabling the system if a malfunction occurs, but sets NO diagnostic trouble codes. The first step in diagnosis is a system check which involves connecting

TEST STEP	RESULT	▶ ACTION TO TAKE
A3 STEERING WHEEL SENSOR CHECK		
• Ignition switch in 'run' position • Vehicle speed 0 mph (0 km/h) • Turn steering wheel from lock to lock. The steering wheel must be rotated in one direction at least 220°	Diagnostic lamp turns 'on' for 3 s after the wheel has been sufficiently rotated.	▶ GO to A4
	Diagnostic lamp does NOT turn 'on'.	▶ GO to C1
A4 VEHICLE SPEED SENSOR CHECK		
• Ignition switch in 'run' position • Steering wheel rate 0 rpm • Operate vehicle on road and apply vehiicle speed of greater than 15 mph (24 km/h)	Diagnostic lamp turns 'on' for all speeds greater than 15 mph (24 km/h).	▶ GO to A4.1
	Diagnostic lamp does NOT turn 'on'.	▶ GO to D1
A4.1 VEHICLE SPEED SENSOR SWITCH CHECK (cont'd)		
• Reduce vehicle speed to below 10 mph (16 km/h)	Diagnostic lamp turns 'off' when vehicle speed drops below 10 mph (16 km/h)	▶ Electrical portion of the system is functioning; GO to A5
	Diagnostic lamp does NOT turn 'off'.	▶ GO to D1
A5 SERVICE POWER STEERING		
• Refer to Section x-xx • Perform PUMP FLOW and Pressure Tests, and REPLACE AS REQUIRED		

Figure 8-38 A portion of the quick-test used in diagnosing the Thunderbird LX/Cougar LS EVO steering system. (Ford Motor)

the Tech 1 and signal generator into the system to determine the actuator duty cycle under various conditions (Figure 8-39). The results of the system check will direct you to a diagnostic chart (Figure 8-40) which details the circuits to be checked with a digital multimeter.

The multifunction chime module controls operation of the EVO-3 system. The chime module energizes/de-energizes the TFE steering solenoid according to a vehicle speed signal from the powertrain control module. The simplicity of the control system makes diagnosis of the EVO-3 equally simple. A digital multimeter and fused jumper wire are used with a

ACTION	NORMAL RESULTS
• Disconnect VES Control Module. • Back-out terminal 'A2' (DK GRN wire) from the connector. • Connect Signal Generator Tool J 38522 to the Controller connector at cavity 'A2'. Use a jumper wire consisting of a 1 ft piece of 16 or 18 gage (1 or 0.8 mm) wire and a female Metri-Pack 630 Terminal #112015870, part of Terminal Repair Kit J 38125. Insert the female terminal into cavity 'A2' of the connector. Strip the other end of the jumper wire and clip the Red lead of the Signal Generator to it. Clip the Black lead from the Signal Generator to a good ground. • Reconnect VES Control Module. • Connect Tech 1 with ABS Cartridge and select VES Duty Cycle Test. • Signal Generator J 38522 NOT plugged in. • Start engine.	- No Duty Cycle present for all aplications.
• Engine idling. • Rotate steering wheel with half turns to left then right, quickly 2 or 3 times.	No change in Duty Cycle. Full power steering assist with no lag or decrease in assist.
• Plug in Signal Generator J 38522 and set for 5 V square wave at 30 Hz with a 50% Duty Cycle. Use the 'Y-splitter' (J 38522-92) from the 4T60-E Pin-Out Box (J 38791-20) to power the Tech 1 and Signal Generator J 38522.	Duty Cycle increases to approx. 42 to 52%.
• Increase frequency to 60 Hz.	Duty Cycle increases to approx. 57 to 77%.
• Rotate steering wheel with half turns to left then right, quickly 2 or 3 times.	Duty Cycle decreases and returns to previous Duty Cycle changing rapidly.

Figure 8-39 Part of the system test used to check GM EVO-1 and EVO-2 steering systems. (Oldsmobile Division, General Motors)

circuit diagram (Figure 8-41) and diagnostic chart (Figure 8-42) to determine TFE steering solenoid operation.

ELECTRO-HYDRAULIC 4-WHEEL STEERING

Electronic 4-wheel steering systems are just beginning to appear on production vehicles. The Mazda and Honda systems are representative of the systems available.

MAZDA 4-WHEEL STEERING SYSTEM

The control module can detect system malfunctions and will display trouble codes

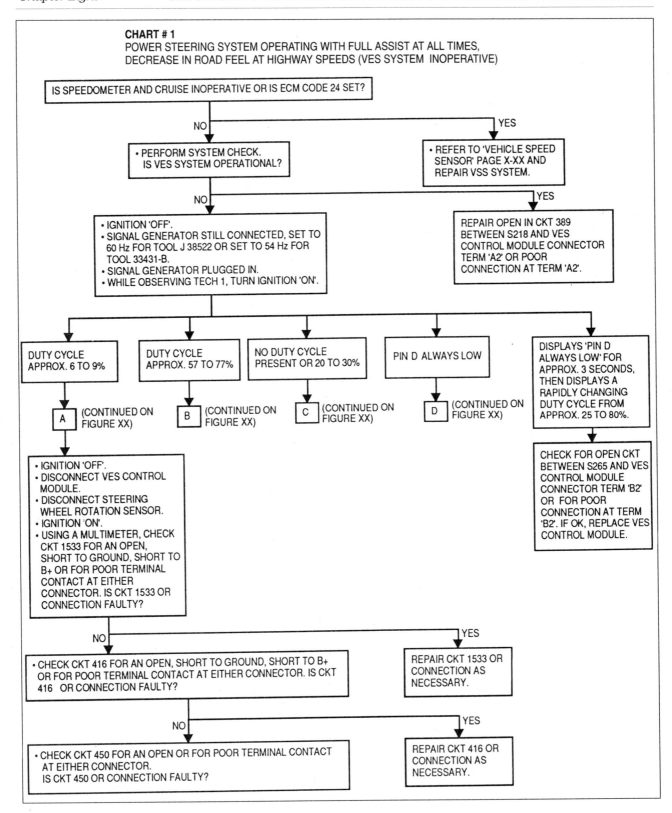

Figure 8-40 After performing the EVO system check, a diagnostic chart is used to check various circuits with a digital multimeter. (Oldsmobile Division, General Motors)

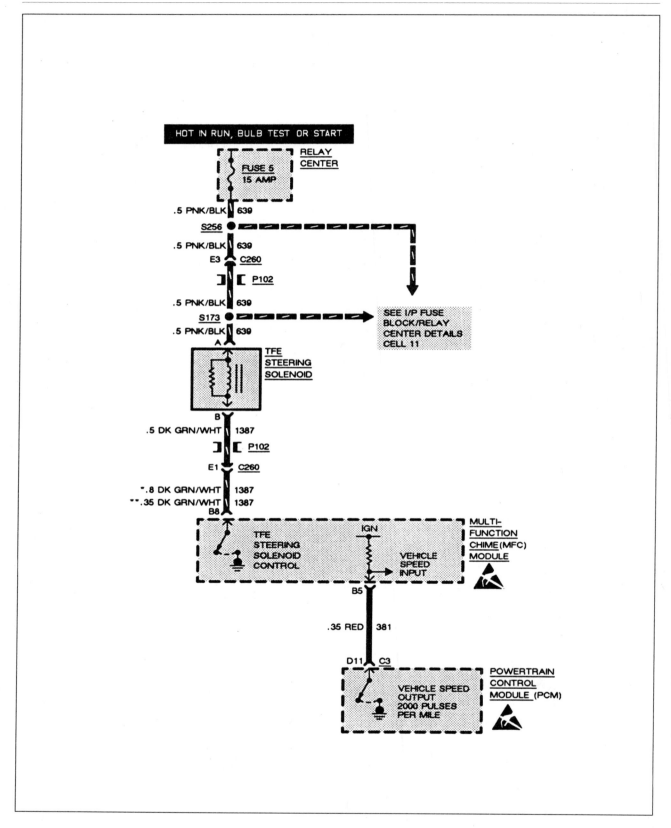

Figure 8-41 The GM EVO-3 steering system circuit diagram. (Oldsmobile Division, General Motors)

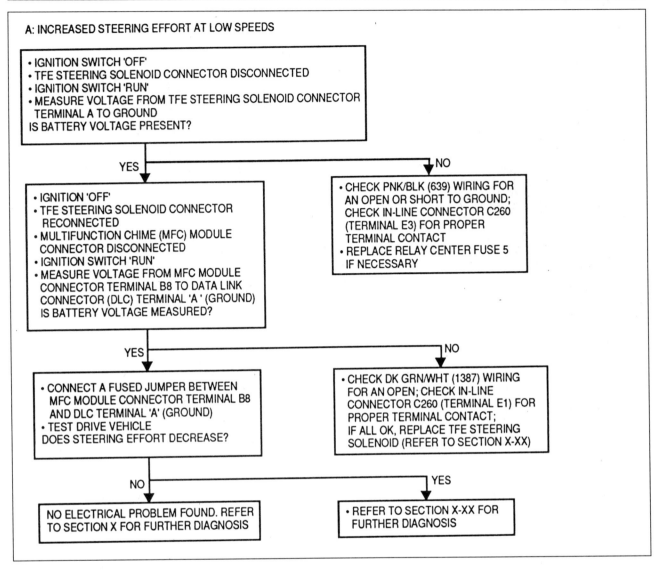

Figure 8-42 A typical diagnostic chart used in troubleshooting the GM EVO-3 steering system with a fused jumper wire and digital multimeter. (Oldsmobile Division, General Motors)

through its self-diagnostic program. If a malfunction is detected, an indicator lamp in the instrument cluster flashes a particular pattern for one minute, warning the driver of a need for system service. To diagnose the problem, the vehicle must be operated on a chassis dynamometer or similar device. Do NOT attempt to do this test with the vehicle on a hoist or stands. Vehicle speed must exceed 25 mph with the transaxle in gear. If a system problem exists, the indicator lamp flashes one of nine different single-digit codes. The code is used to select the appropriate diagnostic flow chart that outlines the necessary voltage and resistance checks to locate the cause of the problem.

HONDA ELECTRONICALLY CONTROLLED POWER-ASSISTED 4-WHEEL STEERING

When the control module detects a problem, it turns on a 4WS indicator lamp

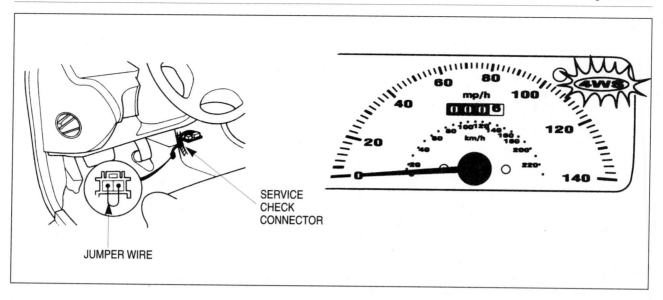

Figure 8-43 When the 4WS service check connector is grounded, trouble codes can be retrieved through the flashing of the 4WS indicator lamp in the cluster. (Honda)

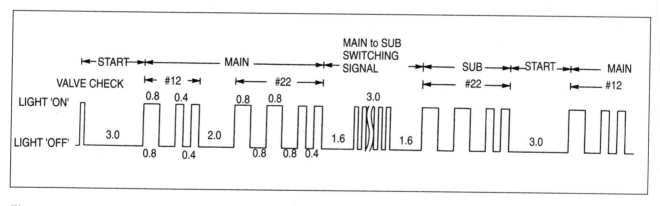

Figure 8-44 An example of the trouble code pattern flashed by the 4WS indicator lamp. Note that codes are read from the main CPU first, followed by a switching signal if codes are stored in the secondary (sub) CPU. (Honda)

in the instrument cluster and sets a trouble code in memory. The module consists of two CPUs (main and secondary), can detect 48 different problems, with each CPU retaining up to 10 separate codes in memory. Codes are retrieved by grounding the blue two-terminal service check connector (ignition 'on', engine 'off') located behind the center console (Figure 8-43) with a jumper wire and reading the series of long and short blinks of the indicator lamp (Figure 8-44). Once the codes are retrieved, they are used with a symptom-to-system chart to select the appropriate diagnostic flow chart (Figure 8-45). After correcting the problem, erase the codes from memory by disconnecting and reconnecting the battery cables.

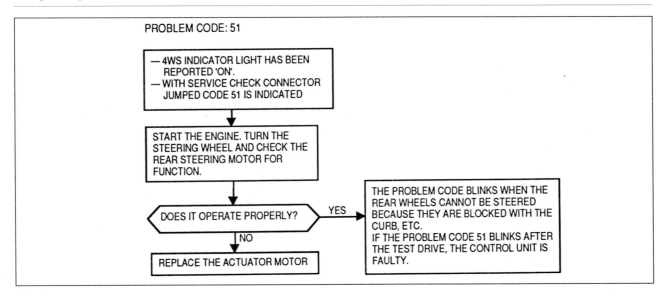

Figure 8-45 The pinpoint test for a code 51 in the Honda 4WS system. (Honda)

♔ REVIEW QUESTIONS

1. Technician A says that if an electronically controlled steering system fails totally, the electronics should be checked first. Technician B says that all electronic suspension and steering systems have an indicator lamp to alert the driver to a system problem. Who is right?
   (A) A only
   (B) B only
   (C) Both A and B
   (D) Neither A nor B

2. When troubleshooting an electronic control system problem, your first step should be to:
   (A) perform an area test.
   (B) perform a pinpoint test.
   (C) evaluate the driver's complaint.
   (D) road test the vehicle.

3. Checking the control module memory for stored trouble codes is the equivalent of:
   (A) an area test.
   (B) a pinpoint test.

   (C) a functional test.
   (D) an operational test.

4. A trouble code set in memory and present at the time of testing is called:
   (A) a hard or continuous code.
   (B) a soft or continuous code.
   (C) a hard or intermittent code.
   (D) a soft or intermittent code.

5. Technician A says that not all control systems set trouble codes. Technician B says that trouble codes in some systems are retrieved with a lamp sequence check. Who is right?
   (A) A only
   (B) B only
   (C) Both A and B
   (D) Neither A nor B

6. Technician A says that once you have retrieved a trouble code, you have located the problem. Technician B says that to locate the problem, you must use the troubleshooting chart indicated by the code. Who is right?
   (A) A only
   (B) B only

(C) Both A and B
(D) Neither A nor B

7. Technician A says that Chrysler trouble codes are retrieved with an analog voltmeter. Technician B says that GM trouble codes are retrieved with a Super STAR II tester. Who is right?
(A) A only
(B) B only
(C) Both A and B
(D) Neither A nor B

8. The weak point in any electronic control system is the:
(A) control module.
(B) wiring.
(C) connectors.
(D) solid state circuitry.

9. Technician A says that the control module should NOT be disconnected or connected with the ignition on. Technician B says that a control module located in the rear of a vehicle does not need to be disconnected when using an electric welding unit at the front of the vehicle. Who is right?
(A) A only
(B) B only
(C) Both A and B
(D) Neither A nor B

10. Technician A says that the on-off switch of a variable shock dampening system must be turned off before working on the system. Technician B says that disconnecting the battery negative cable is an effective way of disabling an electronic control system. Who is right?
(A) A only
(B) B only
(C) Both A and B
(D) Neither A nor B

11. Technician A says that the Ford Probe PRC control module does NOT store trouble codes in memory. Technician B says that Probe trouble codes are retrieved with a flashing indicator lamp. Who is right?
(A) A only
(B) B only
(C) Both A and B
(D) Neither A nor B

12. Technician A says that a special tool must be used to activate the self-test function in the Thunderbird Turbo Coupe PRC system. Technician B says that the Thunderbird ARC system is diagnosed with a Super STAR II tester. Who is right?
(A) A only
(B) B only
(C) Both A and B
(D) Neither A nor B

13. Technician A says that the control switch lamps are used as a diagnostic tool in the TEMS system. Technician B says that the GM CCR system does NOT store or display trouble codes. Who is right?
(A) A only
(B) B only
(C) Both A and B
(D) Neither A nor B

14. Technician A says that electronic leveling systems operate on ALL four wheels. Technician B says that they operate only on the rear wheels. Who is right?
(A) A only
(B) B only
(C) Both A and B
(D) Neither A nor B

15. Technician A says that the Chrysler EHC system uses a combined control module/height sensor. Technician B says that the EHC system is diagnosed by an operational check since the module stores NO codes. Who is right?
(A) A only
(B) B only

(C) Both A and B

(D) Neither A nor B

16. Technician A says that the GM Electronic Level Control system uses a combined height sensor/module that stores NO trouble codes. Technician B says that some of the Ford Air Suspension System diagnostic tests require technician input. Who is right?

(A) A only

(B) B only

(C) Both A and B

(D) Neither A nor B

17. Technician A says that the Chrysler Automatic Air Load Leveling System is diagnosed with the DRB II tester. Technician B says that the DRB II is used to diagnose the Chrysler Automatic Air Suspension System. Who is right?

(A) A only

(B) B only

(C) Both A and B

(D) Neither A nor B

18. Technician A says that diagnosis of variable assist or progressive power steering systems is relatively simple.

Technician B says that the Toyota PPS system is diagnosed by an indicator lamp and trouble codes. Who is right?

(A) A only

(B) B only

(C) Both A and B

(D) Neither A nor B

19. Technician A says that the Ford Probe VAPS control module does NOT store trouble codes in memory. Technician B says that the GM EVO-3 power steering system is controlled by the multifunction chime module. Who is right?

(A) A only

(B) B only

(C) Both A and B

(D) Neither A nor B

20. Technician A says that the Honda 4-wheel steering system control module contains two CPUs. Technician B says that the Honda system must be diagnosed on a dynamometer. Who is right?

(A) A only

(B) B only

(C) Both A and B

(D) Neither A nor B

Subject Index